FORTEAN TIMES 16–25
DIARY OF A MAD PLANET

FORTEAN TIMES 16-25
DIARY OF A MAD PLANET

Edited for volume Publication by
PAUL SIEVEKING

John Brown Publishing
London 1995

This edition was prepared by Fortean Times (PO Box 2409, London NW5 4NP) and published in August 1995 by John Brown Publishing Ltd.

Second printing August 1995

Fortean Times is published every two months by John Brown Publishing Ltd.
It is also available on subscription – inquiries to:
Fortean Times, 20 Paul Street, Frome, Somerset BA11 1DX, UK. 01373 451777
E-mail ft@johnbrown.co.uk
In the United States and Canada, direct inquiries to:
Fenner, Reed & Jackson, Box 754, Manhasset, NY 10030-0754. 516 627 3836
E-mail sgrudnick@aol.com
In Australia and dependent territories, direct inquiries to:
Fortean Times, 5 Eureka Court, 9 Palm Avenue, Bribie Island, QLD 4507
07 3408 9506

British Library Cataloguing in Publication data available.
Fortean Times 16-25: Diary of a Mad Planet
ISBN 1 870021 25 8

Printed in Great Britain by Redwood Books, Trowbridge, Wilts

Cover painting: The Baptism of Christ by Aert de Gelder (1645-1727) reproduced by permission of the Fitzwilliam Museum, Cambridge.

PREFACE

The ten issues of *Fortean Times* reprinted in this book have been out of print for over a decade. Published between Summer 1976 and Spring 1978, they are largely the work of Bob Rickard, who typed them himself with some help from Steve Moore.

The magazines are reproduced facsimile, except for new running heads, the improvement of some pictures and the correction of a few hundred minor errors. I have made the contents as detailed as possible, as compensation for the lack of an index. One day soon there'll be a Grand Index for the complete run of the magazine, just you wait !

Issue 16 in June 1976 was, strictly speaking, the first *Fortean Times*, as the previous 15 had been called, simply, *The News*. The new title emerged from correspondence between Bob Rickard and Paul Willis, one of the founders of the American Fortean group INFO and editor of its journal. In encouraging Bob's early efforts, Paul saw *The News* as the latest in an impressive line of influential British periodicals. What the world was waiting for, they imagined, was a Fortean version of *The Times*, full of weird and wonderful news and read by millions worldwide.

Fortean Times was gestated in these rough pages and began its struggle towards a kind of reality.

Paul Sieveking
March 1991

FORTEAN TIMES 16-25 (1976-1978)
CONTENTS

FORTEAN TIMES 16 – JUNE 1976

FORTEAN TIMES 17 – AUGUST 1976

FORTEAN TIMES 18 – OCTOBER 1976

FORTEAN TIMES 19 – DECEMBER 1976

FORTEAN TIMES 20 -- FEBRUARY 1977

FORTEAN TIMES 21 – SPRING 1977

FORTEAN TIMES 22 – SUMMER 1977

FORTEAN TIMES 23 -- AUTUMN 1977

FORTEAN TIMES 24 – WINTER 1977

FORTEAN TIMES 25 – SPRING 1978

THE SUBSCRIBERS TO THIS VOLUME

Richard Alexander, David Allen, Alan Lance Andersen, Gail-Nina Anderson, Jack Arnell, Jan Arter, Russell Ash, K C Austin, Greg Bale, John Ball, Lisa Barnes, William C Barwell, Ed Baxter, Peter Bayliss, K A Beer, Rodd Bench, Colin Bennett, Paul H Birch, Gordon Black, Johnny Black, Richard D Blacklaw-Jones, Claire Blamey, Mr C J Bond, Mr C M Bone, Janet & Colin Bord, Mr J Bosscher, Joanne Bourne, Jonathan Bowcott, Richard Bowden, P Braithwaite, George Bromley, Mrs E Brook, Peter Brookesmith, Mr Paul Brough, Mark Brown, Donald Buchanan, David J Burns, Kevin Busby, Kathleen L M Butterfield, Rosamund M Calverley, Ken Cambell, Diana L Hudson Carr, Rachel Carthy, Brian Chapman, Dag Christiansen, Peter Christie, D A Clark, Loren Coleman, Elaine Colvill, the Viscount Combermere, John Coombs, David T Cooper, Les Cornwell, Mat Coward, Kay Criddle, A S Crisp, S P Croucher, John A Cunningham, Jim Darroch, Mike Dash, John Degenhardt, Robert Dehon, Michael K Diamond, Stephen H Dickens, Joseph M DiGiacomo, Mrs E C Donkin, Serena Roney-Dougal, Michael Eaton, Mark Ellis, A S Evans, Bob Everett, Hal Faretto, David Farrance, Harry Fearnham, G R Featherston, Craig Fees, Jon Felix, Mr M Ferrier, Lucy Fisher, John Fleming, Folklore Society, Robert Friede, Jon Fry, Brian Funnell, Richard Furlong, Rob Gandy, Alan Gardiner, W Gaworzewski, Dr T J Gaynard, Mr G S Gildersleeve, Mr D J Godbear, Peter Godfrey, Henry C Goodrich, R R Gordon, Alan Grant, Paul Green, Mr A J Greenhalgh, Mark Kevin Griffiths, David Grimbleby, Michael R Haigh, Lucy Hall, Kim Möller Hansen, Brian Harder, Michael Harding, Mr P Harmson, Merrily Harpur, M K Harris, Jim Haslam, John Hawkshaw, I Hayes, Jeffrey Helfont, Mr A H Henshall, Stuart A Herkes, Jenny Hierons, Richard Holland, Mr M J Holman, Peter A Hough, Dean Howard, A J Howell, William Bradford Hutchins, Chris Hylton, Mr P M Imber, Graham Jacobs, Oli James, Mike Jay, Karl Jeffery, Fiona & Jerome & Nigel Fletcher, Jason John, I D Johns, I K Johnson, Terje Jonassen, Gordon Keast, Paul King, Gary Kingham, Jake Kirkwood, Daniel Kleinman, William A Knight, Andrew Knowles, Walter Krieger, Curt A Krumpe, C H Lambert, Jason Lane, Walter J Langbein, Stuart Leadbetter, Nick Lowe, Mr M Luke, Alexis Lykiard, Mick Lyons, Ulrich Magin, Chris Makepeace, Nick Maloret, K C Mann, Dr Vladimir Markotic, Jeff Marriott, Eileen Marshall, Jeremy Marston, Otto A Martinussen, Craig Y Matsuda, Marcus John Matthews, Colin McKay, Steve McKeogh, Gordon McLellan, Jim McLennan, Mike Merrington, John Michell, Hugo Miller, Russell Mills, Barbara Millspaw, Pat Missin, Robert Mitchell Jr, John Mollett, Edward Molloy, Steve Moore, Mark Moravec, Val Morgan, Mr J R Munns, Ron D Murrell, Ray Nelke, Dr D Norman, Ralph Noyes, John Vincent Omally, John S Oney, Michael Orson, Peter Overton, Chris Owen, G Palmer, R H Partridge, Elaine Paul, Gordon Perkins, Tom Perrott, Jennifer Petrie, Hugh Pincott, Andy Pitchforth, Ian Pollard, Colin Potter, Larry Potter, Steve Pratley, Linda Price, Michael Prime, Clive Prince, Mr K D Pugh, Carolyn Pyla, Terry Pyle, Simon A Queen, Robin & Luuc Pascoe van der Raaij, Mr F W G Rau, Kurt Reimel, Samuel Renshaw, Barry Reynolds, Frank Roberts, Perry Roberts, Brian Rogers, Alan J Rooke, Sven Rosén, David Rossiter, Steve Roud, John Rowe, Mike Rowe, the Earl of St Germans, Craig Saunders, Genya Savin, Jeff Saward, Ronnie Scott, Stephen Scott, Dr Keith Seddon, Robin Shelley, Michael T Shoemaker, Dr Karl P N Shuker, Caryl Sibbett, Ian Simmons, Bruce A S Skeer, Gordon Skinner, Ian Skinner, A C Moody-Smith, Norma Smith, Paul Smith, Paul D Smith, John Sproull, Margaret A Stacey, Mr P Stallard, Paul R Standing, Mark William Stephenson, Hugh Stiles, Peter Suchin, R D Summers, Henry Tenhovaara, Steve Thackery, Lars Thomas, R Thorburn, Mark Tinkler, Anthony Tocker, Mr W J Toombs, Andreas Trottmann, Mr G Turnbull, Chris Tyler, Jeffrey Vallance, Leen Verhoeff, John Viney, Wendell Wagner Jr, Mrs C Walker, David Wallechinsky, David G Walley, James Wallis, George E Wallwork, Geoffrey Wareing, Nigel Watson, Arthur Waugh, Theo de Weert, S P Whatley, Mr J C Wiesen, Terry Wilkin, Michael D Winkle, Gene Wolfe, Gerald L Wood, Jeane Worthington, Cliff Wren, Jon Wright, Chris Xenis, Terry Young. ∎

FORTEAN TIMES

strange phenomena - curiosities - prodigies - portents - mysteries

Stoke Tremors and other Quakes.... 6

50p : $1·00.

UK ISSN 0306-0764

FORTEAN TIMES

A Contemporary Record
of Strange Phenomena

FORTEAN TIMES is a non-profitmaking bimonthly miscellany of news, notes and references on current strange phenomena and related subjects. Formerly THE NEWS. Affiliated to the International Fortean Organisation (INFO) in continuing the work of CHARLES FORT (1874-1932). **FORTEAN TIMES** is edited and published by Robert JM Rickard: **Post Office Stores, Aldermaston, Reading RG7 4LJ, Berks, England.**

SUBSCRIPTIONS: 1 year (6 issues) £3.00/USA $1.00. Back issues (if available) 50p/USA $1.00. Airmail (overseas) add £1.50/USA $3.00 per year to sub. rate. Annual index free to current subscribers, otherwise 30p/USA 60¢. *Special joint subscription to Fortean Times and INFO Journal: 1 year (12 issues) £7.00/USA $14.00.* All overseas payments by cheque should *include* 10% to cover banking exchange commission.

CONTRIBUTIONS: of articles, notes and artwork on related subjects are always welcome and duly credited. *You can help by sending us a copy or clipping of any item you think will interest other readers — just add a note of the source, date, and your name for the credit.* Please don't assume our omniscience — there are very few duplications.

RIGHTS: All artwork and articles in *FORTEAN TIMES* are the copyright of the artists and authors; and the views expressed not necessarily those of *FORTEAN TIMES* or INFO. Uncredited material is by the author. All notes herein may be freely quoted in return for a *credit to FORTEAN TIMES with our address.* Heading artwork is by Hunt Emerson.

JUNE 1976

Fortean Times.

This is the first issue under the name Fortean Times - and nothing else has changed, and we pledge ourselves anew to serving Forteanism by working towards a quick, reliable and broad coverage of contemporary Fortean events and relevant subjects and information, to get cases into circulation, research and the record. As an information source, and a tool, we are only as good as our own sources. For this reason we can never guarantee truth, but regard the data as 'descriptions' and points at which to begin further research. We try to present the raw material, with minimal editorial interferance - ultimately the choice of interpretation is yours.

For that reason, also, our coverage is largely determined by the goodwill of readers in sending us notes, clippings or copies of any interesting items that come their way. We are always keen to receive such data from local papers, and are always seeking to extend our coverage. One day we might be able to do this more actively than our present limitation of passively collecting from journals and papers; but where possible we do encourage local correspondents and first-hand accounts.

Donations:

We are pleased to record donations from the following: James Chambers, Mrs PD Dixon, I Farrell, Chris Furse, Mrs V Lewis, R Shane Parkhill, Anthony Smith, David Sutton, and Mike Ward.

All donations are genuinely appreciated and will go towards the production of **FT**. As the pound sinks to new depths, there has never been a better time for a small amount of foreign money to achieve so much over here. Because of internal difficulties it is often less possible for UK readers to donate than for our foreign readers, who constitute about half the readership.

Introduce a Friend...

Donations ease our short-term problems, but there is no substitute for growing readership. Having booted around various schemes, we can announce that perhaps the most practical appreciation we can show , is to extend your sub. by a free issue for every new subscription brought in by you. Considering the size of the American potential Fortean readership, we would very much like to see more subs (and donations,) from the USA...in fact we'd go further, and say our survival depends on it. If you think we are doing good work - support us all you can. Think of what we could achieve with more readers scouring the world's papers, and with more subs we could afford more pages to print more data.

* * *   * * *   * * *

Hunt Emerson 'FT' Poster offer - see p13.

Fort didn't invent the notion of spontaneously combusting humans - it was a classic mania of the 17th and 18th centuries, and featured in lurid popular literature, tomes of medical jurisprudence (on the grounds that murderers would burn the evidence and appeal to SHC), temperance tracts and all manner of warnings against the ungodly. Dickens, Marryat, De Quincey, Zola, Melville and others all refer to SHC in their works. Scientists such as Baron Justus von Leibig have refuted the idea on the grounds that it makes a nonsense of the known behaviour of the universe. We Forteans are not   much interested in proving science wrong, or in proving the existance of SHC - both are secondary to studying what evidence we can gather. If we apply rigorous standards, SHC can be shown to have neither been proved nor disproved - to us it should only have the temporary function of serving as an aid to correlating our evidence. To hold fast to SHC may blind us to other more fundamental phenomena in the evidence because the 'obvious' patterns that we can recognise are those imposed on us by our culture and not those arising spontaneously in the world. What follows is data correlated around a theme suggestive of SHC. Some of it is shaky, some enigmatic and made easier to grasp by the SHC hypothesis. Caveat Emptor!
(For futher discussion - see 'Reviews' p24.)

Spontaneous Localised Fires.
In the latest issue of Pursuit (Jan 76) R Martin Wolf details a case that seems as classic as the burning of Mrs Reeser on 1 July 1951, perhaps the most famous SHC case of all. We refer you to p16 of Pursuit for the account of the strange death (unaccountable burns and injuries) of Mrs Esther Cooks on 12 Jan 75 in Miami, Florida.
    Can people spontaneously flame? It's a complicated issue, but one interesting piece of information recently appeared in an interview with Soviet parapsychologist Genady Sergeyev, in the Sunday People 14 March 76. Referring to the powerful telekinetic medium Nina Kulagina, he said: "She can draw energy somehow from all around her...On several occ-

asions the force rushing into her body left burn marks up to 4ins long on her arms and hands...I was with her once when her clothing caught fire from this energy flow - it literally flamed up. I helped put out the flames and saved some of the burned clothing as an exhibit." Shades of Fort's Lilly White!
    Now if something similar happens in SHC, fatally, you can imagine the consternation among the police, fire departments and coroners and doctors, who are obliged in law to fix the cause of death. According to the Daily Mirror 17 July 75, the number of fire-deaths had risen again (1973;758: 1974;827) and if the breakdown is anything like that of previous years, the largest single category is 'Cause-unknown', followed some way behind by the next largest cause:'Smoking materials'. We sympathise with the authorities when they have to resort to "supposed" causes of fire, but for our purposes we must remember this lack of positive evidence cuts both ways, leaving the matter open. From that point of view, we must omit here perhaps 20 cases of which nothing more can be said than someone died in a fire of unknown origin, and devote what little space we have for meatier stuff.

Some Fire-death Riddles.
    After being alerted by a neighbour, fire and police officials discovered Mrs Edith Thompson,75, dead in her Littlewood Rd, Cheslyn Hay, Staffs, flat. Although the officials said she had apparently been lighting a fire, we notice they also said they were trying to "locate the cause" of the fire. There was little damage, except to an armchair - one of the signatures of SHC. Birmingham Evening Mail 17 Feb 72.
    TV actor, Derek Boote, was dressed up in a space-monster costume ready to shoot a Welsh-language children's space comedy thriller, 'Maldwyn Aldwyn' at BBC's Cardiff TV studios ((can you accept that?)) when screams were heard from his dressing room. Rescuers rushed in to find him in flames, and attempted to beat them out. Boote was taken to hospital where he was said to be critically ill. The

cause of the fire was said to be unknown. Daily Express 14 Oct 74 - CR; Roger Randle.

A man was killed in a fire at his home in Walker, Newcastle-upon-Tyne, but not by the fire. It appears that Thomas Watt died when two aerosol cans exploded. The slow-fire that caused them to explode and start another fire is the mystery, for its origins could not be traced. Daily Mirror 24 Aug 74.

Mr William Cashmore, 82, died in a fire in his home at Autumn Close, High Heath, Walsall, along with his dog and budgie. Investigating officials found gas and electrical appliances in order and the only signs of fire were in Mr Cashmore's clothing, and a charred chair. One in the eye for the usual anti-SHC theory is that he was a non-smoker, and the origins of the fire remain unknown. Sunday Mercury 23 March 75. All the above happened the day before the report, except Mrs Thompson, who died the same day as the report.

Hot Beds of SHC?
Roland Davies was "rather poorly" in hospital - 26 Aug - after his bed caught fire in his flat in Corby, Northants. Cause unknown. Daily Express 27 Aug 74. Cr: Steev Moore.

Firemen rushed into a bedroom at the Air Terminal Hotel, Kensington, London - 12 Sept - to put out a fire in a bed. A doctor examined the bed's occupant, and staff changed the linen, while the man slept soundly throughout the entire proceedings. Either he was a Taoist of legendary imperturbability, or victim of the strange trance-like state which Fort was first to notice accompanying SHC, rendering the victim oblivious to what was happening until too late. The Sun 13 Sept 74. Cr: Phil Ledger.

Mrs Ellen Steers, 79, died, in the early hours of 29 Aug, during a fire, which started in her bed and spread to the rest of her room in her house in Stoney Lane, Shaw, Berks. She had a history of hypochondria and once overdosed, and regularly smoked in bed, despite warnings from friends of the danger. Her husband had been buried the day before, but she had not seemed "unduly stressed" by the event, said her doctor. Despite all these 'conventional' clues, the cause of the fire could not be ascertained - the burning of the bed had been so fierce as to leave virtually no evidence. Mrs Steers was found behind the closed bathroom door - asphyxiated. Whether or not it is applicable here, Fort was also the first to note the incidence of strange fires, sometimes fatal, on or in the vicinity of 'no-hopers'. Newbury Weekly News 19 Sept 74.

Terry Nelson, 33, of Digby St, Scunthorpe, Lincs, was treated in hospital for burns on his leg after his mattress burst into flames while he slept on the night of 18 Oct. No cause was found, or given, by the firement. Scunthorpe Evening Telegraph 19 Oct 74. Cr: Nigel Watson.

David Webb, 20, pleaded guilty at Maryle-bone Court to arson - so officialdom is satisfied, but we are not, for verily, this is a fishy one. The date isn't given but we assume from usual proceedures that the report and arraignment each followed very shortly. At a guess then, on the night of the 24/25th March, David was arrested for being drunk in a Paddington street. He was taken to Paddington Green police station, where, according to the later court testimony of Det.Sgt Hawkins, he was searched and put in a cell. 30 minutes later, according to David's statement, he was sitting quietly on the bed when flames began to rise around him. After attempting to beat them out with his jacket he passed out from the smoke, and was dragged out by alerted officers. In court it was said that David "had a drink problem" and was frequently in suicidal depressions, commiting acts he could not later recall. If the mattress had spon.combed, David was in no state to notice - in fact he would have been the first to agree that in the absence of any 'rational' explanation, he "must have started it" and said so, adding that he could not remember doing so. We wonder too, about that search, and whether we are right in assuming that all dangerous items are taken from prisoners, as a matter of course. If so, David had nothing to start the fire with. We wonder... Paddington Mercury 26 March 76. Cr Colin & Janet Bord.

Fire-prone.
Your editor has long been interested in the connexion suggested by Fort between poltergeist-type activity and outbreaks, even series, of strange fires. The connecting notion is one of unconscious human agency. Closely associated with this is another notion -that some people can be fire-prone, just as others are prone to runs of accidents, good luck, etc. I mention these as observable phenomena without, at this point at least, ascribing any process or meaning to them.

We have mentioned fire-proneness before - News 1/10; 3/10 - the case to hand is of Mrs Barbara Booley who, when questioned about 7 fires, told police: "Fires seem to follow me around. But I swear on any child's head that I didn't start them." Fire 1: at Berkeley Vale Hotel, Stone, Glos, in Aug 71. Mrs Booley worked as a cook, and had been given notice. The fire was the night before she left. Fire 2: at St Hilda's School, Bridgewater, Somerset, Nov 71. Two pupils smell smoke and raise the alarm - blaze in one of the dormitories. Fire 3: in Bath High School for girls, Easter 73. "Because I'd had a few words with a housemistress the previous day, police tried to pin the fire on me." Fire 4: Swan Hotel, Tewkesbury, Glos, Aug 73. A car caught fire in a yard, and police accuse Mrs Booley. Fire 5: same hotel, two days later. Fire found in a furniture storeroom & Mrs Booley questioned. Fire 6: same hotel. Mrs Booley had left, but was nevertheless questioned again. Fire 7:

Torbay Hotel, Sidmouth, Devon, early Oct 75. Mrs Booley had been sacked the day before, but when bedding caught fire on a stair, she helped put out the blaze. "One hell of a coincidence," she claims. And how! She says she wishes she had been charged, then she'd be able to clear her name. She admits she has a temper, and had rows with managements 24hrs before a blaze-up, but swears she had no hand in the fires. See Fort (again - but then he was the pioneer who blazed the trail - oops!) ch13 of Wild Talents, for stories suggestive of repressed hates and vengences that may have been expressed through spontaneous outbreaks of fire. The Booley story is from News of the World 19 Oct 75. Cr: Carl Grove.

Sometimes the poltergeist-analogy is more specific - see the National Enquirer 4 Nov 75 for a story of the van Reenan family (with 8 children) who have had to move from their 2nd home in Plettenberg Bay, South Africa,because of fiery persecutions. An estimated 100 fires had broken out in about 3 months from 5th May. Carpets, toys, curtains, chairs, beds would suddenly flame putting them in "continual terror". "Our two family Bibles began showing scorch marks," says Mrs van Reenan. "They got worse day by day, until one day both Bibles caught fire at the same time." This convinced them that they were under attack by something "evil", a view supported by Rev. Jacobus van Zyl, of the African Methodist Church, who has himself seen at least a dozen fires spring out

of nowhere in their home. Apparently local housing officials and policemen have also seen thing suddenly smolder and blaze, and a forensic examination of various items concludes that no chemicals were causing the phenomena.

The true value of Fort's pioneer work is the way some of his scenarios seem destined to be repeated again and again. This time we are referring to officials confronted with an enigma for which they lack a 'rational' explanation, and coerce the principle (usually, as in many polt cases, a pubescent, unhappy, youth or girl) into confessing they did it, however that jibes with the factual evidence. In Bath Juvenile Court, police alleged a boy went into a deserted house and lit a fire, and when it went out of control, shoved it down a hole in the floor in the hope it would stop burning. They suggest the boy panicked and called the fire-brigade - who, when they arrived found another fire going not far away. Police took the boy to be questioned, and he "admitted" causing both fires. The defending solicitor suggested the boy only admitted this because he was "under pressure". The boy's headmaster confirmed this, saying the boy was sub-normal. The magistrate reprimanded the police for interrogating the boy without waiting for the boy's parents or a solicitor to be present, and found the boy not guilty. Which leave two unexplained fires. Story from Bath & West Evening Chronicle 3 Oct 75. Cr: J Michell

Geophysical Curiosities

There's some damned weird things going on. This first quarter of 1976 has seen much geological activity. But first:

The Blood that Failed.
In the Santa Chiara basilica, Naples, are two phials of dark powder, said to be the blood of St Januarius, patron of that city. Twice a year, the first Saturday in May and 19th Sept the phials are held up to the congregation and if the powder turns to liquid the whole of Naples breathes a sigh of relief, for although Rome frowns on this miracle, it is popularly believed to be an assurance from

the saint of good luck for the city for the next six months. Records have been kept since the first recorded liquifaction in 1329, and naturally the event has attracted poohpooing scientists and philosophers over the years, who, pained at a mess on the floor of their tidy universe, cover it up with explanations. But it won't go away. If the priests really are working a con, why should the 'miracle' fail,eh? It increases its value as a miracle the scoffers would say, and in all fairness, I suppose any disaster that happens after it fails will be blamed on its failing. Ah well, swings and roundabouts. Well it failed in 1527 heralding a great plague; in 1835, it was cholera; and in 1944, the massacre of an uprising against the Germans. That's not overdoing it, is it? In writing up a section for the book with John Michell I had just finished mentioning that the Washington Post 8 May 1967 recorded that the blood failed to liquify on time, but did so after 24hrs strenuous prayer - I had just noticed, then, that the first Saturday in May this year was none other but that grand pagan feast kept by church-goer and communist alike - Mayday. The blood failed to liquify. See the Daily Express 3rd May, and Times 5th May, for the "great disappointment" of Naples and a growing expectation of doom among the superstitious.

Quake - Udine, N Italy.

As if to confirm the worst fears of the Napolese, at 10pm on the 7th, on the sixth day of the failed liquifaction, at Udine, the earth opened and gnashed with jagged jaws, rumbling its own prophecies of destruction, and fulfilling them. Hundreds died and thousands lost their homes.

According to the Daily Express 8 May it was 6.9 Richter - New Scientist 13 May gives 6.5 Richter - either way the severest in the region for 75 years. For full details see these sources (most national papers for the 8th & 9th). Tremors were still being felt on the 12th May.

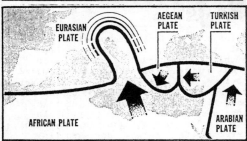

The blood of St Januarius has still refused to liquify, and many Italians, looking for an omen for the coming General Election in which the Communists are expected to sweep to power, have taken it as a sign of worse to come.

Rumbles from Jack Ashley and Stoke.

As a footnote to the Udine quake, Dr Patrick Willmore of the Global Seismology Unit, Edinburgh, warned that it could happen in Britain. He said there had already been "22 tremors within the last 3 years, and statistics show they are getting worse." - Daily Express 8 May 76.

We feel Dr Willmore has been over-cautious, for this figure has been exceeded in the trembling area of Stoke alone. For the beginings and background to the continuing saga of Trent Vale tremors, see the article on Leicestershire phenomena, in News 12, by Paul Devereux and Andy York. As far as our notes go, a tremor on the 9th April was announced as the 25th in just under a year (Daily Telegraph 10 April). Another came on the 13th. A conference at Stoke two days later of the Institute of Geological Sciences (IGS), the Coal Board, Keele and Edinburgh Universities teams investigating the problem, revealed the astonishing news (to everyone outside Trent Vale) that the tremors were coming at the rate of 12 per week, totalling 86 since investigations began in Sept 75 (Telegraph 17 April). According to the Sunday Telegraph, 18 April, residents of Flash Lane have noticed that of all the nights of the week, the rattlings seem to occur most frequently on Fridays, dubbed 'Tremor Night'.

Alluding to the frequency of the tremors, the Minister of State, Department of the Environment, Mr Denis Howell, said in the Commons, on 27 April, that of nearly 90 tremors recorded between Sept 75 and March 76, most were too small to be discerned by the inhabitants, but "Six were severe enough to be felt, particularly the two on 9th and 13th April." This was in reply to Mr Jack Ashley, MP of the affected area, asking the government for assurances that the research teams would be kept in the area until the cause was found. "While there is no cause for panic, there is cause for concern...People are entitled to know the causes...(and) who or what is responsible for them. They are entitled not only to peace of mind, but to the fullest possible information..." (Hansard 27 April. Cr: Ken Rogers.) Indeed it is estimated that there are about 125 claims for damages pending. One early theory was that mine-workings were collapsing, but this is not the case. Mr Ashley won his assurance - not only were the investigations going to be cut short, but when the latest wave of tremors began, the work was only going to be extended to October. In a statement (Hansard 5 May), Mr Shore gave a repeated assurance that the equipment and teams would stay in Stoke "until the cause of the tremors has been established."

The seismologists have been under pressure from all sides to come up with an 'explanation', poor sods. But they did not make matters any easier for themselves by announcing (Daily Express 12 April) their plans to set off a test explosion. "Just a small exploratory bang," Jeffry Rains, a Mines & Quarries Inspector, joked weakly. This we must see, and await news that Flash Lane has slid into the bowels of the earth. Our last intelligence is of tremors on 13th and 19th May (Daily Mail, 14 May; Times 20 May. Cr: S Moore, K Rogers; and for most items above, RE White.)

Other Recent Quakes.

4 Feb - San Martin, Guatemala.
6 Feb - San Martin, Guatemala; with many small tremors between the two. Estimated 10,000 dead. Details in most national papers between 5 & 8th Feb.
18 Feb - mystery tremor rattles Fife & Lothian. Global Seismology Unit (who know only what their instruments tell them, ie., what they are set up to look for) blames a plane breaking the sound-barrier. Come off it fellas

this is the 20th century! Why not admit it, if you don't know? Times 18 Feb 76. Cr: Tony Roberts.
20 Feb - mystery tremor shakes house in Faulkner St, Liverpool. Local rock adjustment blamed. Liverpool Echo 20 Feb 76. Cr: Peter Rogerson.
25 Mar - Hopkinsville, Kentucky. Audience reel out of cinema showing the film 'Earthquake' praising the special FX only to find a real ∧quake in progress outside. Synchronicity, eh? Daily Mail 26 March 76. Cr: Steve Moore.
17 May - Gazli, Tashkent, Samarkand & Bokhara in Soviet Uzbekistan. Measured 7.2 Richter, and claimed to be more destructive than Udine (see opp. page). London Evening News 17 May.
18 May - Same area of Uzbek Republic as above but less strong. Daily Mail 19 May. Same paper for 21 May, reports 10,-000 homeless. Soviet authorities claim to have predicted the quake & evacuated towns in time - but curious detail: "torrential rains & landslides also caused casualties on the same day." Cr: Steve Moore.

Bleeding Christ Cures Many.

There have been some strange 'coincidences' as John Michell and I have tackled various sections of our book. As we wrote about St Januarius (see 'Geophysical Curiosities' on p 5) the liquifaction failed and a quake struck northern Italy. Again, as we worked on a section on bleeding and weeping icons and statues, in January, two astonishing new cases came to hand that very month...one we present here because of the miracle healing associated with it; the other will be kept back for a future collection of stories of strange flows and seepings of liquid.

One night in Jan 1968, an altar boy was approaching the crucifix in the church in the small Brazilian town of Porto das Caixas, when he saw a bright red substance dripping onto the table below the cross, and shouted in amazement. The entire congregation saw blood seeping from the 300-yr-old painted

wood life-size statue of Christ on the Cross. The next day the story reached the ears of Archbishop Antonio de Almeida Moraes, who immediately instigated a commission.

The commission has ratified 8 miraculous cures to date, though the unofficial number is many times greater than that. The eight are: a 6-yr-old boy whose vision was restored after an eye was punctured by a sewing needle; a 29-yr-old wife who recovered from a crippling disease; 3 cancer victims whose symptoms just vanished; a 66-yr-old judge whose cateracts cleared over night, restoring his vision; a 20-yr-old man paralysed from the waist by a spinal injury who got up out of his wheelchair and walked; and a 35-yr-old woman whose internal hemorrages healed up. In each case the commission was presented with doctors' records, including the biopsies of the cancer sufferers,

cont on p13...

NOTES ON GREENWICH PHENOMENA

Part 3 of a

Taoist interpretation of

Fortean phenomenology

by Steve Moore.

The time has now come to attempt to intrepet Fortean phenomena in terms of yin and yang, and their relation to local geography. Let it be understood that I am not seeking to apply the doctrine of Feng Shui here, which, even if it had any particular relevance to the phenomena, would probably not be applicable outside its native Chinese context. The yin and yang are believed to be universal principles, though, so we may be on firmer ground. And while basically sticking to the Greenwich area, I hope to be forgiven for straying into other locales for additional evidence...

YIN, YANG & THE GEOGRAPHY OF GREENWICH.

A broad outline of the yin-yang balance in the area is shown in the sketch map, which should be compared with the map accompanying part 1 (NEWS 14). Shooters Hill is the highest hill in S.E. London, and the only major eminence for miles around. High ground, it will be remembered, is yang.

To the north, south and west of the area, the ground drops away, giving low-lying yin ground. The rest of the area is fairly level overall, but other factors give it a high yin:

Water: The River Quaggy (though little more than a large stream) runs through the SW corner of the area, and is joined from the north by Kid Brook and the Lower Kid Brook. Drainage streams, rising to the west of Shooters Hill, feed into the latter. There are also numerous ponds, natural and artificial, and reservoirs, especially to the west.

Tunnel, caverns & deneholes: these, being under the earth, are places of high yin. There is a denehole to the north, and another to south of Shooters Hill. Tunnels or conduits, seemingly from Tudor times, exist in the region of Eltham Palace, and also under various parts of Greenwich Park, which may be associated with the, since-disappeared, Greenwich Palace. These tunnels are traditionally supposed to link up, taking in a huge underground apartment near Eltham, but there is no evidence to back this up. There are three miles of ancient chalk tunnels north of the Hill, near Plumstead Marshes, in the NW of the area (Marshes, we need hardly point out, are further yin areas). There are also natural caverns under Blackheath, near Greenwich Park.

Tumuli: these can also be defined as yin, being associated with death and burial underground, and being constructed of earth. The greatest concentration of burial mounds is in Greenwich Park, about 30 in close proximity, ris-

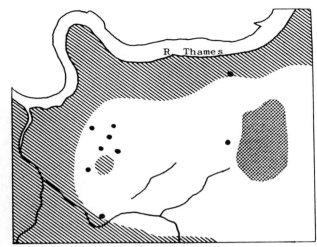

Yin & Yang areas in Greenwich.

Compare with map accompanying Part 1 for positions of phenomena.

Rivers, streams, ponds, etc, are shown in solid black.

High ground (major yang):

Low ground (major yin):

Level ground (medium yin):

ing no more than a foot or two above ground level. I am suggesting here that the yin is increased by the presence of the graves, not that they were placed there because it was yin. There is no suggestion that our ancestors knew anything of Feng-Shui (the graves are badly positioned anyway) and I am looking at conditions that might apply to phenomena currently taking place, regardless of when those conditions began to apply. are

There also three mounds extant on Shooters Hill, which may be seen as reducing the yang of the hill, but any effect they may have is more than compensated for by the presence of four radio masts, a Victorian Water Tower, and the single tower of 'Severndroog Castle', all of which can be taken as of high yang potential by reason of their shape; tall, thrusting toward heaven, pointed, even phallic...

Simply, we have a high yang area in Shooters Hill, while the rest of the area can be taken as highly yin. We now turn to the phenomena, listed in part 1 (NEWS 14).

MYSTERY ANIMALS

(See Part 1, cases 1 & 2). The one common factor in all sightings of the 'cheetah' is water. But in order to establish a geographical link between MAs and water, we must look at a wider range of reports than this. And there we run into the problem mentioned in Part 2: that such geographical details are frequently omitted from reports... so we are left with some cases where there is a positive link, and many where there may, or may not be. However,

Bob Rickard (1) finds enough evidence to suggest a possible link, although by no means enough to establish it positively...there are just not enough details in the reports.

If MAs, in their most usual, panther-like form, were simply ordinary animals, a relationship with water would not concern us. But the evidence seems to show that they are anything but ordinary. It has been suggested (1,2) that MAs and 'Black Dog' apparitions are closely connected. I would further suggest that they are differing forms of an identical phenomenon. To take an analogy from UFO studies: it now seems accepted that the 'airships' of the 19th century, and the 'flying saucers' of the 20th, are differing forms of the same phenomenon, 'shaped' to fit the world-view of the time. So, I believe our MAs appeared of old, and still do in country areas, as Black Dogs, while at present, perhaps as a result of increased knowledge of zoology, perhaps because the majority of city-dwellers would be too ignorant to notice anything strange about a large black dog, they appear as panthers and such like.

MAs seem to exhibit varying degrees of solidity, from little more than apparitions, to leaving behind physical traces such as paw-prints. Black Dogs seem to be more rarified, though there are accounts of physical remains. One I have to hand (3) mentions that after the 'creature' disappeared, there remained 'a large spot as if gunpowder had been exploded there'. It seems then, that MAs and Black Dogs 'condense' out of some invisible state, and, as they are never caught, 'evaporate' again after a certain time.

Whether MAs and Black Dogs are 'materialised psychisms' is open to question. I admit to having no idea to what state of the mass psyche they would synchronistically correspond. But an idle notion occurs to me while typing this: although the impending deadline prevents me following it up. This century has seen a massive increase in world population, which would presumably 'strengthen' our posited mass psyche. This might explain not only the upswing in UFO sightings, but also why modern MAs seem to be more material than their predecessors. But this of course is merely speculation.

Let us return to the subject of Black Dogs, which I think can be defined mainly as yin manifestations. Their colour, their associations with death and so on, their appearance mainly at night, all seem to indicate this. The name of the Welsh Dog is also interesting, the Cron Annwn: 'Annwn is an adaptation of Annwfn, a bottomless or immeasurable pit, voidless space' (4).

With Black Dogs we are on much firmer ground with our water associations. Dan Butcher (5) has pointed out several connections between the Dogs and water, and several cases in Notes & Queries connect them with pools and streams, and also valleys and churchyards...both yin areas.

The connection does not seem to require the actual physical presence of water, however. A dried up stream bed would retain the same characteristics. An interesting parallel comes from China, where influences carried by water are "called 'Shui Shen', 'aquatic spiritual agencies'. Rivers and rivulets, brooks and gullies, lakes, tanks, ponds and seas, being the bearers of the waters showered down from the heavens, are all bearers of these Shui Shen. Even when perfectly dry, they are still regarded as such..."(6). In China, these Shui Shen are positive influences; in the West it would seem that negative influences (Black Dogs) are connected with water (more notions on this reversal will be found in forthcoming articles (7)).

Finally, and because nothing is ever simple, it must be said that MAs/Black Dogs are not entirely yin. They have the power of movement, which is a yang characteristic, and several Black Dog accounts mention them having large, blazing red eyes, which would also indicate a certain yangness. We might say they are nine parts yin, one yang.

To summarise, we would expect MAs and Black Dogs to appear in connection with water, and perhaps more interestingly, moving along watercourses...non-straight lines of negative influence which might balance the positive influences carried by straight ley-lines.

GHOSTS.

(Part 1, cases 5-20) The Chinese believed that man had two souls, the Hun (yang) and the P'o (yin). After death, the Hun becomes a Shen (an immortal, ethereal soul) and goes to the otherworld, or is reborn. The P'o becomes a Kuei (the animal soul) which remains in or near the grave, and is variously thought either to fade away after a time, or to receive the ancestral sacrifices, and if it does not get these, it goes haunting (6), similar to our classic idea of the ghost. Thus to the Chinese, at least, ghosts are yin.

Some less abstruse pointers to the yin condition of ghosts can also be found: They general appear at night, when the yin is most powerful, they are associated with burial, and thus with earth, there is frequently an unnatural cold associated with their presence, and they generally stay in one place: by this I mean that, although they may perform repetitive local motions, they seem generally to be tied to one location. 'Phantom Armies' and the like, which move through an area once and are not seen again, I would imagine to be a completely different phenomenon; a vision, rather than a 'true' ghost.

From this, I would expect all the ghost cases to lie in the yin portion of the Greenwich area, and none on the yang heights of Shooters Hill; and this is exactly what does happen. Whether the correlation can be extended to other areas remains to be seen...

UFOs.

UFOlogy is such a complex field that I approach the subject with considerable trepidation. Because of this complexity, I hope to be forgiven for narrowing my sights, disregarding such controversial aspects as 'contact' cases, and concentrating on the simple 'lights-in-the-sky' and 'fireball' variety, which I intend to treat as strange 'natural' phenomena arising in the vicinity of the Earth. I realise that I leave myself open to criticism by doing this; but on the other hand, the complexity of the subject might suggest that there are several solutions, rather than just one, to the several aspects of the UFO phenomenon.

UFOs of this class, then, can be defined as Yang. They are bright lights, appear in the sky (and so are of Heaven) and are extremely active. Jung (8) likened them to "a volatile liquid which condenses out of an invisible state into the form of drops". We have, perhaps, a similarity to MAs...though here the phenomenon is yang. Also, we note that UFOs seem to appear with greater frequency in the summer months (9), when the yang is at its peak.

I have found only two UFO sightings in the area (Cases 3 & 4), so my notion here is distinctly theoretical. These sightings occured close to, but on either side of Shooters Hill. If UFOs arise from the yang, the most likely place of origin would be over or near a hill, where the high yang ground rises toward the greater yang Heaven. If, in the Organic Universe, everything seeks balance, the UFO would then be expected to move away from the yang hill toward yin, either to low ground or water.

Dan Butcher (5) has expounded on the connection between UFOs and water at some length, showing how many UFOs appear to seek water, and his recommendable work lists numerous examples.

Paul Devereux & Andrew York (10) list many UFO sightings in Leicestershire, and a great number of these occur in the vicinity of Croft Hill, as we might expect. Cradle Hill at Warminster is another UFO-active eminence which springs to mind. Devereux & York also point out that there was considerable UFO activity at the time of the Trent Vale tremors, and we also have numerous records of fireballs appearing in conjunction with quakes. One might almost speculate that imbalances in the yin Earth set up imbalances in the yang sky which result in UFOs; and if there should be anything in this notion, the case where UFOs appeared in conjunction with a waterspout (11) is especially interesting...

ICE FALLS.

Up to now, we have been looking at phenomena which arise in a predictable way, yang UFOs from the yang sky, etc. In this and the following section, events become more complex, as the process seems reversed: we might look upon them as, 'breakdowns' or 'short-circuits' in the system.

It will be recalled that the T'ai Chi diagram (part 2) shows the yang containing the 'seed' of the yin, and vice-versa. This is a pictorial representation of the idea of cyclical change, which will be familiar to any reader of the I Ching. At the moment of greatest growth, decay begins to set in; and so, as the yang reaches its greatest concentration, it begins to give way to the yin. The change can be gradual, or very sudden...

Let us begin with the Shooters Hill 'ice storms' (Case 21, and the almost identical event mentioned in the Tailpiece to this article). In both cases, the day was exceedingly hot and, toward the end of the afternoon when the temperature was at its highest, lightning started to flash, without a noticeable build-up of storm clouds, in the second case at least. We can say, in effect, that the sky was massively charged with yang. This electrical storm moving into contact with the yang height of Shooters Hill resulted in an overload of yang which, turning into its opposite, showered down chunks of yin ice (Of course, I am not entirely ignorant of the usual explanations of the weather: but a yin-yang interpretation can be made as well...).

Falls of single blocks of ice, in apparently normal weather conditions, present greater problems. But there do seem to be enough cases where ice has fallen out of a clear blue sky, and thus, presumably, on a hot day, to suggest that a similar interpretation might be placed on them.

Falls of other material, such as straw, blood, etc., would seem inexplicable in these terms, even if frogs, fish and toads are thought by the Chinese to be yin animals. But such as these can hardly be looked on as 'condensations from an invisible state', which is what most of our phenomena are. Ice can, although its materialness means that we are here pushing the notion to its limit...

SPONTANEOUS COMBUSTION.

Unfortunately (or perhaps fortunately) there seem to be no cases of spontaneous human combustion in my area. But this can also be seen as a 'breakdown' event.

I referred earlier to the Chinese notion that man has two souls. In the male (and we can deal only with the male, as Chinese philosophers seem to have disregarded the female entirely, and it seems uncertain if the same principles apply to both sexes) old age and death are believed to be caused by a build-up of yin in the body and the strengthening of the (yin) P'o soul. When the build up reaches a terminal imbalance, the result is death.

Although there are some cases of younger people combusting spontaneously, most of the 'classic cases' involve persons of middle or old age. Also, an attempted analysis of 50 cases that I carried out some time ago (12) showed (and it was just about the <u>only</u> conclusive result!) that 80% of these events occurred between December and May...winter and early spring, when, by the calendar, the yin may be considered at its peak. We have, then, an imbalance among the victims, caused by a build-up of yin, at very yin times of year. In combustion cases it seems the yin is overcharged, and produces its opposite: very yang flames from inside the body. In both this and the case of ice falls, balance is restored, though rather in an over-compensatory way...

CONCLUSION.

Although the Chinese believed in the reality of the yin and yang, I cannot expect the reader to do the same. They should, instead, be looked on as symbols relevant to the phenomena discussed. As in acupuncture, a meridian line seems to show no physical difference to any other part of the body, yet by using that meridian (a symbol, if you will), definite physical results can be obtained; so, by using the yin and yang as symbols, we can work out a general theory about some Fortean phenomena, and also, perhaps, predict those areas where they are most likely to occur.

At certain places, and times, there are concentrations of yang, at others of yin. But the tendency seems to be toward balance: toward an even distribution of yin and yang.

So yin ground thrusts up ghosts and Black Dogs/MAs (and it would be interesting to know if the latter moved toward yang ground, but data is lacking). The yang sky sends down UFOs and fireballs, usually moving toward yin. These phenomena could be regarded as part of the 'natural' balancing process. But occasionally the system overloads, and there is too great a concentration of one principle. As the system tries to balance itself, the overload is converted into its opposite, giving ice-falls and spontaneous combustion. These could be regarded as 'unnatural' processes, though the movement toward balance is still present. The accompanying diagram attempts to show this graphically.

Naturally, a great deal more information, from other areas, would be needed to confirm any of this, and turn these inadequate gropings into some sort of theory. Whether such a task is worth undertaking, I can only leave the reader to decide...

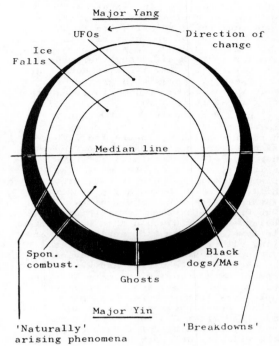

'Naturally' arising phenomena

*** *** *** *** *** ***

REFERENCES.

1) RJM Rickard: 'If you go down to the woods today...' INFO Journal 13, May 74.
2) J Bord: 'Some Fortean Ramblings' NEWS 7
3) Notes & Queries, Vol 1, No 29, p 468. 18 May 1850.
4) Notes & Queries, Vol 1, No 19, p 294. 9 Mar 1850
5) D Butcher: Water Symbolism in UFO Encounters. Surrey Investigation Group on Aerial Phenomena, 1971.
6) JJM De Groot: The Religious System of China. Rpt: Literature House, Taipei, 1964.
7) S Moore: 'Feng Shui & Ley Lines', 'Mirroring'. Ley Hunter 72, 73.
8) CG Jung: Flying Saucers. Collected Works, Vol 10. Routledge.
9) RJ Willis:'UFO Statistics' INFO Journal 4, Spring 69.
10) P Devereux & A York: 'Portrait of a Fault Area' NEWS 11, 12.
11) NEWS 6, p 17.
12) This work has not been published. Cases were drawn from Fort, Edwards, Russell, Willis, et al.

*** *** *** *** *** ***

TAILPIECE - NEW FALL OF LARGE HAIL.

8th May 1976. The day had been hot and sultry, the temperature being in the upper 70s, generally, and sometime before 6-00pm an electrical storm broke out to the west, moving closer to Shooters Hill up until 6-50, although without any noticeable build-up of storm clouds, almost negligible wind, and no particular indication that rain was imminent. I was at the top of Shooters Hill at 6-50, when the hail announced itself from the west with a noise like gravel being unloaded onto concrete. About 5 seconds later, hailstones over an inch across were falling, and continued to fall, unaccompanied by rain, for about two minutes, being followed by half an hour of torrential rain. Apart from Shooters Hill, the hail also seems to have struck Plumstead, Woolwich, Charlton and Eltham. Damage seems to have been generally slight, though I have come across one or two reports of damaged greenhouses and conservatories. And apart from bruises, there seem to have been no casualties.

One report from Shooters Hill mentions hailstones the 'size of golfballs'. A more measured estimate from Plumstead mentions a diameter of 1½ inches. The random examples I picked up hurriedly in the pouring rain measured, on average, 1 inch across, with the biggest 1⅛ inches. Most of the stones were of a somewhat flattened, irregular shape, though many were more nearly spherical. The outer layer of ice was clear, and the surface was covered in irregular, crystalline formations. Within was a thin opaque layer, a thicker clear one, the thickest opaque one, and the clear centre.

A fullish account can be found in the Kentish Independent, 13 May 76, and mentions in (Kentish) Mercury, same date, and Sunday Express, 9 May 76.

Steve Moore, May 76

■■

Fortean Times Poster.

To help publicise FT, especially in bookshops, and to establish the name-change, we commissioned a 4-colour silk-screened poster from Hunt Emerson...and a glance at our heading artwork will tell you what to expect. We had a few extra printed off to sell to readers as a way of raising some cash. They will cost £1.00 / $2.00 including surface post. Anyone donating more than this sum will receive one as a matter of course. Spread the word - it'll soon be a collector's item.

■■

MIRACLES, cont...

and the subsequent medical reports which showed the remarkable improvements or complete cures believed to have been affected by a prayer before the bleeding Christ. Other reports refer to a British diplomat cured of heart disease, and a cocaine addict relieved of his need. For details see the National Enquirer 3 Feb 76, and Sunday People 11 Jan 76. Cr: Ivan Bunn & Nigel Watson.

We have only these news reports to hand and they are vague on several points: eg we would be interested to know if the statue is bleeding from the stigmata, or just the knees as the photo below shows; and whether the blood is applied as a curative agent at all, or is the miracle by power of prayer alone without contact? The People mention an analsis of the blood ("Analysis No 4380/68" sic) but it is not said by which laboratory. Its conclusion reads: "The tests and research proved that the substance really was blood, the origin and species of which are beyond our technical knowledge." The Enquirer quotes a "respected Brazilian physician"-Dr Enias Heringer - that the substance was "undoubtedly pure blood." Archbishop Moraes, of Niterol, the capital of Rio state, whose commission presumably initiated these tests, told the Enquirer that a second doctor "confirmed that the 'liquid was human blood.'"

The miracle cures, it seems, date from the day following the appearance of the blood when a villager claimed to be cured of a heart complaint. There is no doubt in the minds of most of the doctors that something inexplicable is happening. The Archbishop is sure that these are miracles and due to the power of the "Blood of Christ", and is ready to recommend to Rome that Porto das Caixas be designated a holy site. But others cannot wait - see the People for an account of the increasing waves of pilgrims.

Two Tomb Cures.
Quoting a middle-eastern paper, L'Orient, the Express & Star,19 May 1967, reports the claim of a 30-yr-old woman cured of paralysis at the tomb of Father Cherbal in the mount- ain-top convent of Annaya, north of Beirut. Jeanette Howard said she was praying before the tomb, when the side of it opened and a thin trickle of blood appeared. Suddenly she felt the paralysis leave her left side, and she was cured. (cr: Anthony Smith.)

11-yr-old Lorella Colangelo was paralysed, in the grip of leukoencephalitis which att- acks the brain. On 23 June 75, her family took her on a pilgrimage to the shrine of St Gabriel, near Florence, against the advice of the head of the neurology dept. of Ancona Civil Hospital, where Lorella had been lan- quishing. Lorella's father said: "I carried her inside the sanctuary and laid her on the tomb of St Gabriel. Almost at once Lorella fell into a deep sleep. We prayed on our knees, watching her. Fifteen minutes went by like an eternity. Then, suddenly, I saw (her) get up on her feet, climb over the three-foot railing surrounding the tomb, and run toward us...it's a miracle!" Lorella says that the saint had appeared to her in dreams on seven consecutive nights, urging her to come to the sanctuary and be healed. Her mother said: "I was skeptical, even though we are relig- ious...but when she had the same dream seven nights in a row, that finally convinced us." Lorella continued: "I fell asleep on the tomb and St Gabriel appeared in a dream, and told me, 'Get up and walk'. And when I woke, I did." Her doctor affirms the cure with his records of brain scans before and after the miracle. The astonished Dr Primo Angeleri, of the Ancona Hospital, had to accept the evid- ence of his eyes: "Medical science did not heal her; something else did." National Enq- uirer 11 Nov 75; Reveille 21 Nov 75 (Cr: Anthony Smith).

Good Lourdes.
Mrs Josephine Hoare, 28, claimed that a trip to Lourdes cured her of chronic nephritis, a severe kidney disease - doctors only gave her two years to live. When she came back from Lourdes, the doctors admitted the disease had become dormant, and warned

her never to have a baby in case the disease was again activated ,almost certainly to claim her life. Nevertheless she did, and according to the Sunday Mercury 30 Dec 73, both mother and baby were doing well. Again Mrs Hoare claimed divine intercession - the doctors, just as certainly, were confounded.

Glove gets Big Hand.
Friends of Lady Armstrong, wife of the 3rd baron and insurance magnate, Lord Armstrong, have nothing but praise for a relic of the Italian-born Lady's ancestor, that has cured many of them. It is a red glove that once belonged to her great-great-uncle, Cardinal Guiseppe Dusmet Desmours, who died in Sicily 90 years ago, and whenever she hears of a friend's illness, Lady Armstrong snips off a piece of material to send to them. "I was terribly ill with cancer some years ago," she says, "and I recovered. A friend of mine - I wont give his name, but he was well-known 25 years ago - had a terrible accident and was com- pletely paralysed. I gave him a piece of the glove and two months later he began to walk. The stories I could tell are endless...I know of so many instances where the person has recovered." She admits she believes in mir- acles, and that her husband doesn't - he claims they all would have recovered anyway. She adds: "The cardinal was a very good man and had extraordinary powers. He has already been beatified, and I hope that soon he will be sanctified by the Vatican." Sunday Exp- ress 31 March 74.

A Miracle in Glasgow.
A few days ago as I type this, the Pope formally announced the canonisation of the Blessed John Ogilvie, who died on a scaffold in Glasgow in 1615, for preaching Catholicism in Scotland. Only two months before this, the papers were full of the miraculous cure of John Fagan who had prayed for the interces- sion of Blessed John, and this miracle, off- icially ratified by the Pope in February, was given as evidence for the canonisation pro- cess. The miracle actually happened 9 years earlier, when John Fagan was reduced to an emaciated skeleton by cancerous tumours in his stomach and colon. He was given last rites 3 times, and just when he thought his suffering was over "I felt that once again I had got the will to live." He called out to his wife for a boiled egg (the first food he had eaten for several weeks) and steadily improved from then - he even went back to work in the docks before he was made redun- dant there. Local priests, who were appointed 'Devil's Advocate' were charged to find any basis for a natural explanation - but when faced with the medical evidence from before and after the miraculous cure (which happened on 4 March 1967) they had to admit "there was no clinical or radiological evidence of res-

idual disease" and concluded "There was no natural explanation." Experts said it was nothing more than a spontaneous remission, of which there are many – but they would be the first to admit they are baffled by such cases and, as one specialist noted, had no record before of any spontaneous remission of colon or stomach cancer. See most national papers of 12-14 March 76. Cr: S Moore, P Rogerson & Tony Roberts.

...And Italy, again...
Two years ago, Elena Budelacci suffered from insipid diabetes and paralysis of her lower body – her muscles had atrophied after 20 bedridden years and her bones were decalcified so that she could not sit, let alone walk. On 2 May 1974 she was taken to the shrine of the Madonna at Lareto, on the Adriatic coast, and today 36-yr-old Elena can walk again, as her amazed doctor puts it: "as if she had never been sick a day...the spring in her step is that of a little girl." National Enquirer 6 April 76.

LIGHT WORK...
Everlasting lightbulbs are one of those dreams along with electric nose-pickers and something-for-nothing machines that galvanise inventors into perpetual motion. One can easily imagine how this might relate to tales in the classical mythologies of perpetually burning lamps as a recurring archetype. But the matter to hand is the announcement of the development of long-life bulbs, or rather two announcements within 2 months of each other.

Firstly, Donald Hollister of Lighting Technology Corp., released news of their new bulb that consumes 70% less electricity and could burn for up to 10 years; and the US Research and Development Administration plan to produce it as soon as possible. South China Morning Post 10 March 76 – Credit: Ion Will.

According to New Scientist 29 April 76, Philips Research Laboratories are developing fluorescent tubes filled with glass-fibre... which nearly doubles the light output and consumes about a third as much electricity as the ordinary incandescent equivalent.

Back in the good ole days, John Campbell (of Analog) used to rant against the giant monolopies that buy up neat ideas like the everlasting razorblade or longlife battery only to sit on them. It seems it's taken the great energy crisis to create enough of a commercial market for such things. Let's hope some good will come of it. (I meant, of course monopolies, but what the hell...)

However neither of these announcements cuts much cake with us Forteans. We remember the lightbulb in the Old Byer's Opera House in Fort Worth, Texas, which was put in on 21 Sept 1908, and was never switched off. INFO Journal 8 p9 prints a note from an unidentified newspaper dated 27 May 1969, to the effect that the bulb was still going. It's career was vouched for by OC Carlson, VP of Texas Electric Service, who had kept tabs on it for 40 years, and confessed to being mystified by the phenomenon. The last note we have on it is a sad one. It seems that in November 1974, the Opera House was closed, and concern over the bulb, understandably something of a celebrity around the old 'Cowtown USA', was noised publicly. Daily Mail 26 November 74 – Cr: Steev Moore. Perhaps one of our readers knows what happened next; we have a vague recollection of hearing a radio story that the bulb was finally switched off and auctioned, and the building demolished – a sad end to 66yrs 6mths as a shining example.

"When it's steamengine time..."
A mysterious inventor from Los Angeles, 61-yr-old Sam Leach, has sold "automotive" and "residential application" rights for a cool $million to two Californian companies, in his suitcase-sized device for producing combustible hydrogen from tap water "without any continuous outside energy source". Newsweek 19 April 76 says that if the device works it could be the answer to the dream of "an unlimited supply of clean energy for homes, autos and industry at practically no cost." If it doesn't, it could be the biggest bilking this century. When rumours of the purchase of

these rights began to circulate, stock in both companies shot up - in fact so high and fast the Securities and Exchange Commission stopped their trading and launched an investigation into the possibility of stock manipulation and other security-law violations. It is expected that the SEC investigation will also clear up doubt about the device.

Leach says the process is simple - an electric charge is passed through the water to split it, and an "unidentified reactant metal" absorbs the oxygen in such a way as to leave combustible hydrogen. Once started the process runs on its own heat - a statement that had a hydrogen expert at UCLA saying it was impossible because it violates two of the laws of thermodynamics. Needless to say developments are being awaited in more than one camp with baited breath. (Cr: Ion Will).

The steam-engine effect never ceases to amaze us - just a few days before the above story, the UK Ministry of Defence squashed another story of a mystery magic metal, this time in Wales. Arthur Adams, a retired ultrasonics engineer from Ipswich, said he had discovered a strange metal which could provide endless supplies of cheap electricity. He found a silver-grey nugget in a gold-bearing deposit on a mountain near the Mawddach Estuary, North Wales. A piece the size of a button, he claims, could power a car, and a slab the size of a shoe-box could supply all the power and light for a family for next to nothing. "You can connect pieces of the metal in series and get as much power as you like. Believe me, this is very big indeed. It can produce a limitless supply of power. It gives off huge voltages and amps, and is self-regenerating."

What is more, Mr Adams claims to have synthesised the metal himself, and it was through filing patents and a trade-name that the MOD came to hear of it. The Patents Office say it is standard practice to refer all patents of "defence interest" to the MOD. Mr Adams received a letter from the MOD warning him under Section 18 of the Official Secrets Act (ie publication of inventions likely to be prejudicial to the defence of the realm) not to release details of the components of the substance, nor its location.

Mr Adams, a prospecting specialist, had been out testing a detector of his own design in this mineral-rich region of Wales, when it went haywire. He dug and found the metal, which he sent to London for analysis. "The metal is self-regenerating," he said. "It shouldn't be, but then it does a lot of things it shouldn't according to known scientific laws...This substance is a combination of natural elements in a hitherto undiscovered form and which could have taken tens of thousands of years to discover scientifically... This energy source is like a huge natural battery in the earth - and it has nothing to do with the fusion of zinc and copper."

Naturally the protests of experts have provided some amusement. Officials of the Institute of Geological Scientists, who of course know every mineral in these isles, said: "We have not discovered any minerals with these properties. If it is a substance unknown to science it is extremely exciting - but we doubt it." We remember hearing on radio and TV quotes peppered with the word "impossible". But Arthur Adams knows - he had already had clocks, a radio, a portable TV, motor and lightbulb running off his metal.

How can any government justify keeping the people who elect it in energy-poverty if this is true? Surely the crisis, and the grave doubts over our future, demand a rethink of the very sort of bureaucratic madness that will damn us all? Mr Adams has doubts over this censure too: "I'm a bit worried that people with vested interests will try to prevent this potential from being exploited." Hmmm - I wonder if we can induce Mr Adams to market his special detector. Let's have a new California or Alaska in Wales! Story taken from Yorkshire Evening Post 7 & 8 April 76, & Daily Express 10 April 76 - Cr: Anthony Bell & Steev Moore.

Legacy of the Mad Scientist.
When the Daily Mirror published its Little Black Book (Wolfe, 1975) a correspondence ensued in the Mirror's letter column about Britain's classic mad scientist, Harry Grindell-Matthews, which in turn suggested a solution to one item of enigmatic data in our files. But first some background. Grindell-Matthews was born in 1880, and after fighting in the Boer War, withdrew to a laboratory in remote Welsh mountains where he experimented with the new science of radio telephony. His contribution to the First World War was a remote-controlled gun-boat that homed in on a light beam. In 1924 he was rumoured to have invented a death-ray that could "stop a motor, kill plant life, destroy vermin, explode gunpowder, fire cartridges and light lamps".(See also Port's comments on G-M's death-ray in The Books p956; Wild Talents ch17). In 1930 he demonstrated his "sky-projector", startling the inhabitants of Hampstead Heath with a vision of a voluptuous angel projected onto a cloud, dissolving into the words "A Happy Christmas". In New York he shone the Stars & Stripes onto clouds. In 1938 he married a Polish widow, reputedly worth £25 million, and began work on submarine detection.

The point of all this is that in 1935 he developed what he called "aerial torpedoes" or "aerial mines" which were clutches of bombs suspended on wires from parachutes, and fired as a sort of multiple warhead into the sky by rockets. The correspondence in the Daily Mirror (10, 24, & 25 Nov; 9, 13 & 15 Dec 75) was largely reminisences of the men who manned the rocket-firing stations (called Unrifled Projectors, or Parachute & Cables) in the latter days of the Second World War, and they tell of such disasters as the things blowing up in the launchers, or masses of these aerial mines drifting back inland (over Dover, for example) if the wind changed. But by all accounts they worked well: the wires could cause a sudden 1 ton drag on the planes, snapping off wings; or would catch and slide the bomb up to explode on contact. They were defeated only by the Germans putting blades on the leading wing edges.

Stick with me - I'm getting warmer. Brad Steiger never tires of mentioning one of his favourite data : "On Feb 7, 1958, an artillery shell fell from a clear sky over Naples, Italy, and clanged loudly as it struck the street. The shell casing bore the date 1942." (of <u>Mysteries of Time & Space</u>; Prentice Hall; 1974; p66). The suggestion is that it had been fired during the war, vanished into some space-time limbo, and dropped out again in 1958 - interesting, but contentious. Now, (he says with a grand flourish) I may have

something even more interesting. Grindell-Matthews' 'aerial mines' were in use (as far as I can tell) most frequently from 1940-42, and as far afield as Tobruk, Crete, Malta and perhaps even Italy. I had filed away in my 'Falls' box an item that appeared in the <u>Sunday People</u> and <u>Sunday Express</u> 11 March 1956 (Cr: Harold SW Chibett), to the effect that (presumably the day before) a man working in his garden in Athelstan Rd, Bitterne, near Southampton, looked up to see a 5ft cylinder on an unopened parachute, and trailing wires dropping out of the clear sky towards him. Edward Garnham said: "It exploded twice in mid-air, dived toward my house and hit the ground where it exploded in flames, wrecking my garden and greenhouse." Police investigation established that it was a wartime defence device, of the 'aerial mine' sort and made in 1942. "Where," they ask in all reasonableness, "had it come from?" Wherever, we reply in all helpfulness, it had been since it was fired into the air between 1942-5, and for nearly a year less than Steiger's shell.

UNIDENTIFIEDS

More Cornish Capers.

Our Cornish correspondent, Doc Shiels, The Wizard of the West, has been keeping us up to date with developments on the monster front down there, and credit for most of the following news items goes to him.

Prof. McCormick—and his skeleton of 'an imp.'

Falmouth Packet
2 April 1976.

At the end of March Doc was joined in his hunt for Morgawr, the dragon (see last issue p13ff) by Mike McCormick, a "professor of metaphysics" who lectures on monsters, owns a 'Matchbox Circus' and eats fire. McCormick was soon telling the press that Morgawr could change size at will, and the plan was to use Doc's telepathic powers to lure the monster from its lair, and capture it when it was about 30ins long -- see the <u>Falmouth Packet</u> for 2 April, and the <u>West Briton</u> 25 & 30 March, for further publicity (and for those interested, McCormick unveiled one of his collection of monsters, being the "skeleton of an imp" complete with horns and wings on its 18ins blackened smelly frame.)

Let me just add that through correspondence with Doc, I've found him to be well-read, aware and intelligent about monsters. He has a pretty good idea of what he is doing and clearly understands that the ballyhoo he has been involved in had a specific purpose: as a professional magician it was good PR,

and in the popular imagination created a role
for himself that led to him being approached
many times with information that was not
given to the press. Beneath the song-and-
dance, he has a genuine interest in strange
phenomena, and as he says, being a stage
magician is an acceptable vehicle for an
interest in the real thing. His other motive,
and one we as Forteans applaud was to provide a counterpoint to what he has described
to me as a tense and even frightening atmosphere there (with UFOs, monsters, alleged
photos of fairies which Doc has forwarded to
us and which we are having examined by Kodak,
and finally, a 'mothman' right out of one of
John Keel's nightmares).

However...as events approached April 1st,
the inevitable happened and a giant 3-humped
long-necked 20ft red and green monster came
out of the Penryn River, near Falmouth, at
9.30 on Fool's Day, suspiciously following
the trawler 'No No'. People waved from the
piers, ships hooted their welcome, and the
Falmouth Pilot's cutter nosed around suspiciously. It was believed the spectacle (photos
in the Packet 2 April) were laid on by the
editor of the Packet.

Another Photo...
The Packet for 9th April, contains a letter from Peter Costello, author of In Search
of Lake Monsters, who said: "There is no
doubt in my mind (sea and lake monsters)
exist". He calls Mary F's photos (see last
issue) the "first ones of a sea serpent..ever
published" and pleads with Mary F to get in
touch with him - not even the Packet editor
knew her address. But alas, Costello's plea
was too late - a letter from Mary F appeared
just 15 days earlier (26 March) in that paper
saying "My brother has just sold the negatives for me to an American gentleman." Doc
told me that he didn't know who that was;
McCormick didn't have them. In a letter dated
23 April, Doc told me he was at one of his
"observation posts" on the Helford River,
when he was approached by a schoolboy called
Andrew ("I don't know his address. He wouldn'
t give it - said his father would be angry!!")
who showed him a large photo-print of what
he claimed was Morgawr swimming between Toll-
point and The Gew, on the river. Doc sent me
the photo, but it was too blurred to print,
but contained suggestive shapes thus:

It didn't look very convincing to me, but who
knows? I had to send it back to Doc without
being able to copy it. It was, apparently,
shown on BBC 'Spotlight SW' on 22 April.

More Sightings...
The Packet for 9 April also contained a
strange letter from John J Bickenson of Horn-
sea: "In 1936 I was strolling along Castle
Beach, when to my utter amazement I saw thousands of limpets detach themselves from the
rocks and attach themselves to a huge piece
of floating sea-weed. I was astounded to see
that on the other end of the sea-weed were
thousands of winkles. There ensued a 'tug-of-
war' ending in the whole disappearing about
2 miles offshore. I did photograph this, but
had no film in my camera."-!!!- sounds like
the sort of joke-letter that is the bane of
Forteans who optimistically believe that any-
damned-thing is possible...limpets swim?...
anyway it hardly clears up the Morgawr mystery as JJB claims it does. Hmmm, Doc mentioned being plagued by MIB journalists...so why
not MIB letter-writers too?

The Packet for the 16th April, has a letter from Miss M Jenkins: "A friend of mine
confided to me some years ago that she had
seen a large snake-like creature swimming in
the sea at Mylor. In turn this reminded me of
a report in a national newspaper, about 1934,
concerning local fishermen seeing a monster
at sea. A gentleman who encountered the creature suggested it was 25 to 30ft long."

The latest sighting to hand suggests there
may even be more than one monster. In the
Packet, 14 May, is the story of two young
bankers from London, on holiday in Falmouth.
The men, Tony Rogers and John Chambers, were
fishing, at 10.15am, 4th May, from the rocks
at Parson's Beach at the mouth of the Helford
River (the scene of the schoolboy's photo)
and both "insisted they had no prior knowledge of its alleged existance." Rogers said:
"Suddenly, something rose out of the water,
about 150 or 200 yards away. It was greeny-
grey in colour and appeared to have humps.
Another, smaller one, also appeared. They
were visible for about ten seconds and looked
straight at us." Chambers said he didn't see
the smaller creature, and that had he been
on his own, would have thought he was going
mad. "Perhaps a bull and his cow, or a cow
and her calf," as Costello writes in his
book,of an old monster photo from elsewhere?

More Helford Hi-jinks...
Doc had told me sometime previously that
two, perhaps three,witches would be attempting to summon the beast by swimming nude in
the Helford estuary. The press too, keenly
awaited the event, not least because Psyche
(from Inverness), Vivienne (from London), and
Amanda (a Cornish lass) were all described
as young and beautiful. The whole Cornish
monster saga was in fact written up for
Reveille by Frank Durham, who insisted on
calling the monster 'Fessie' -- the splendidly archaic 'Morgawr' is Cornish for 'sea-
giant'. In Durham's piece, Doc is quoted as
having watched Psyche swim, then two days
later, both Psyche and Vivienne: "Both girls
said an incantation - Psyche, in Gaelic."
Later, Vivienne wrote to the Packet: "I swam,

sky-clad, in the name of Cernunnos. I called
up the creature and felt its presence." But
Doc saw nothing...or nothing materialised.

Precursors at Falmouth...
The West Briton 13 May, digs up a report
from its own pages, "100 years ago" -- "Mr
Botisto sends us the following from Port-
scatho: 'The sea serpent was caught alive in
Gerrans Bay. Two of our fishermen were
afloat overhauling their crab-pots, about 4-
500 yards from the shore when they discovered
the serpent coiled about their floating cork
(buoy). Upon their near approach it lifted
its head and showed signs of defiance, upon
which they struck it forcibly with an oar,
which so far disabled it as to allow them to
proceed with their work, after which they
observed the serpent floating about near the
boat. They pursued it, bringing it ashore yet
alive for exhibition, soon after which it was
killed on the rocks and most inconsiderately
cast again into the sea.'" Sounds to us
more like an ancestor of Miss Jenkins' snake-
like creature, than one of Morgawr's family.
Perhaps we can do slightly better -- the
following is a footnote to a mention of Irish
lake-monsters by Harold T Wilkins:

"Myself, and another man, saw, on Tuesday
5 July 1949, at 11.30am...two remarkable
saurians, 19-20 feet long, with bottle green
heads, one behind the other, their middle
parts under the water of the tidal creek of
East Looe, Cornwall, apparently chasing a
shoal of fish up the creek. What was amazing
were their dorsal parts: ridged, serrated,
and like the old Chinese pictures of dragons.
Gulls swooped down towards the one in the
rear, which had a large piece of orange peel
on his dorsal parts. These monsters - and
two of us saw them - resembled the plesiosaurus of Mesozoic times. Unfortunately I had
left my camera behind. It is futile to report
such phenomena to marine biological stations.
...A young news editor of the Daily Mail
promised to investigate this, but did not do
so." cf Strange Mysteries of Time & Space
(Ace pb; 1958; Ch 10; p196) - undelinings
mine.

...And at Barmouth.
Another interesting point made by Wilkins
is that "In that month of 1949, the Gulf
Stream showed an aberration from its normal
course; so that fishermen at Mevagissy, not
far away, were scared when they netted a 20ft
long tropical turtle." (ibid). Could the
creatures seen in the same area today be
giant turtles? Can anyone help us by checking on any purturbations of the Gulf Stream
over the last couple of years?
This brought to mind a passage in Colin
Palmer's letter to me about the Barmouth
Monster (see News 10/18f; 15/12f): "The un-
timely appearance of a large leathery backed
turtle (given national coverage) in Cardigan

Bay, and another one in the North-west of
England, seemed to be the answer to all "this
monster nonsense"." Hmmm...so we went digging in the files and found a note from the
Daily Mirror 16 Sept 75 - that a 7ft leather-
back turtle, weighing half a ton, was picked
up by a Scottish trawler; doesn't say where,
but the North Sea is implicated, which is a
strange place for the Gulf Stream to stream.
But no notes on the Cardigan Bay turtle.

                    cont on p21...

The 'Mothman' at Mawnan.
In Doc's letter, dated 27 April, he says:
"A very weird thing happened over the Easter
weekend. A holidaymaker from Preston, Lancs.,
told me about something his two young daughters had seen...a big feathered bird-man,
hovering over the church tower at Mawnan (a
village near the mouth of the Helford River).
The girls (June, 12, and Vicky, 9, daughters
of Mr Don Melling), were so scared that the
family cut their holiday short and went back
three days early. This really is a fantastic
thing, and I'm sure the man wasn't just
making it up because he'd been told I was on
a monster hunt. I couldn't get the kids to
talk about it (in fact, their father wouldn't
let me try), but he gave me a sketch of the
thing, drawn by June, a copy of which I enclose." (The copy was too large to fit here
so your editor has redrawn it, faithfully.)

- - -   - - -   - - -

Mawnan 'Bird-man' witnessed by June Melling
17 April (Easter Saturday) 76; (based on a
sketch made by her the same day: DS/RJMR).
- - -   - - -   - - -

Doc continues: "There have been no reports
so far as I know, of anyone else seeing the
bird-man...even if it turned out to be just
a fancy-dress hang-glider, you'd think someone else would have spotted him...But Mawnan
is not a place for hang-gliding! I really
don't know what to think... it's as if a
whole load of weirdness has been let loose
in the Falmouth area since last Autumn..."

LEYS, UFOs and CHANCE

A reply to FWHoliday by Robert Forrest

Mr Holiday seems to suggest, in the final paragraph of his article (1) that my chance UFO-ley study (2) argued why UFOs would not appear on his Pembrokeshire triangle. What my article did in fact show was that under certain conditions, a strikingly high correlation would appear to exist, completely by chance alone between UFO sightings and alignments of ancient sites. Or in short, why UFOs would appear to be associated with leys rather than why they would not,

The artical was based on a statistical study which showed that in many regions the 'ley line density' was so high that it would be possible to find at least one ley line passing through virtually any point on the map. This of course implies that chance effects could account for not only the UFO-ley link, but the puma-ley link as well, not to mention the curious phenomenon of 'subconscious siting' on leys of many entirely modern churches. (3)

* * *   * * *   * * *

Mr Holiday claims, quite rightly, that if leys do not exist then "the critics have an awful lot of aligned tumuli to get rid of".

In the first section of my booklet, from which my last article was extracted, I claim to have shown statistically that in fact chance alignments are extremely numerous - far more numerous than most ley hunters seem to believe.

Let me take an example from Mr Holiday's area of study. An analysis of the upper half (the lower half is largely sea) of sheet 158 of the new 1:50,000 OS map series, contains 130 tumuli, burial chambers, forts etc., and 135 churches. I did not count hill-peaks, as most are rather ill-defined and difficult to deal with mathematically. However it is clear that even more alignments can be expected if hill-peaks (plus other items such as coastal promontories) are counted, than can be expected if only churches and assorted ancient monuments are counted. Let us therefore consider simple church/ancient monument alignments, and bear in mind the fact that these can be 'filled out' with hill-peaks, etc.

Now supposing half the churches on our section of sheet 158 are non-valid as ley-points, and are therefore to be discounted. We are left with a total of about 200 valid ley-points on the map, and from 200 points in such an area we can expect (4):

144 alignments of 4 points
10   -"-   -"- 5   -"-
1   -"-   -"- 6   -"-

these being to an alignment limit of $\pm\frac{1}{3}$ mm on a 1:50,000 scale map (ie. a ley-point is to be counted as on a line if its centre lies within $\frac{1}{3}$ mm of that line).

This is certainly quite a number of chance alignments, and if the alignment limit be relaxed to $\pm \frac{1}{2}$ mm we can expect even more; thus:

284 alignments of 4 points
30   -"-   -"- 5   -"-
3   -"-   -"- 6   -"-

plus a chance of 1 in 4 of finding an alignment of 7 points.

Mr Holiday is therefore working in a relatively densely populated region, though by no means as dense as some regions of the British Isles, eg Salisbury Plain eastwards to the heart of the ley-following UFO country, Warminster, where 'leys' of order 8, 9 and above can be expected by chance on a single map, and where the number of chance alignments of 4, 5 or even 6 is so colossal as to render their evidential value to the ley hypothesis virtually nil.

Incidentally, for the upper half of sheet 158, calculation shows that on average one ley will pass through any given UFO, puma or elemental sighting, hospital, pub or post office.

* * *   * * *   * * *

My previous article concerned UFOs and their apparent association with what might be called non-specific ley systems - ie ley systems which delineate no specific geometric configuration. I simply showed in that article that under certain conditions there was a high likelihood of finding an alignment of ancient points passing through a given UFO

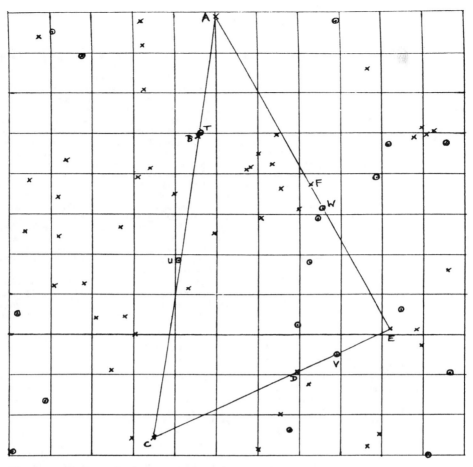

Fig 1   UFO-Ley Simulation Diagram (repeated from News 13).

All pseudo-leys have been erased except those which delineate a triangulation
with attendant UFOs.   Key: X = ley point.   O = UFO.

Barmouth Precursor, cont...

Steev Moore sent notes from the Daily
Mirror & Daily Express 30 July 75 - that a
crocodile was seen basking on a sandbank at
the mouth of the Stour, Sandwich Bay, Kent.
Again the value of coverage is shown - the
Express item adds that the croc was 6ft long,
and that a Dover council official said there
had been "no other reports." Another mal-
observed turtle, or 'dragon'? Further clippings from this period would be welcome.

But back to precursors...and this time we
find a snake-like thing, rather than a dragon,
in the area of the Barmouth Monster. Heuvelmans, in his In the Wake of the Sea-serpents

(1968; p116f) quotes an incident from George
Borrow's ramblings in Wild Wales (1862). Borrow heard some Welshmen arguing over the
existance of the sea-serpent in a tavern in
Port Dyn Norwig, and tells them a story that
he read in an old Welsh book, called The
Greal ((shades of Machen's The Great Return))
in which a large snake-like sea-serpent
chased a ship in the Menai Straits, in October 1805, and it crawled up the tiller-hole
and coiled itself (like the Gerran Bay serpent) around the mast. The sailors attacked it
and drove it overboard, and it followed them
until a wind sprang up and it was lost.

sighting, and frequently more than one such alignment. Mr Holiday has not explained how six random, non-existent UFOs in the Chilterns came to possess the same ley affinity as the soundless, translucent UFO he saw back in 1966. He has simply added a new element to the game - namely ley-triangulation.

Now it is possible to show that such ley-triangulation as that on News 14/9 is not an uncommon chance configuration, and I will forward a copy of my results on this to Mr Holiday as soon as it is ready. What has yet to be decided, given the expected number of chance ley-triangulations, is what proportion of UFOs (or fire-balls) would appear to have an affinity with such configurations. This is no easy task - certainly not as easy as it is with non-specific ley systems - but upon looking over my ley-UFO simulation diagram in News 13, I was gratified to find in the midst of it, a very telling chance configuration, comparable to the antics of my non-existent Chiltern UFOs.

The diagram is reproduced here (fig 1), but with the majority of the 'leys' erased to pick out the relevant details. The reader can see how this totally chance simulation reproduces closely the effect illustrated by Mr Holiday's diagram on News 14/9 - namely a 'ley triangulation with no less than 4 attendant 'UFOs'.

Let me emphasise again that this figure represents an imaginary (randomly simulated) ley-landscape, with imaginary UFOs on it. Yet it demonstrates the same phenomenon Mr Holiday claims to have found in South Wales. The reader must draw his own conclusions from this, but to my mind, if these effects can happen by chance on graph paper, they can just as easily happen on Mr Holiday's maps, or for that matter, over the actual landscape of South Wales.

* * *   * * *   * * *

Finally we come to the 8:15:17 triangle, which first appeared in Mr Holiday's book The Dragon and the Disc p147, though without the 8:15:17 stipulation. The fact that the triangle might be 8:15:17 was first suggested by myself in a letter to Mr Holiday (dated 3/9/1975), based on measurements from the diagram in his book, and was therefore suggested with extreme caution as to its limits of accuracy. Map inspection reveals that my stress on caution was well founded, for although the triangle might be 8:15:17 in proportion, it might equally be several other things, for example a chance effect which can all too easily be made to appear what it equally easily is not, by judicious jugglery of ruler and map. I am not accusing Mr Holiday of 'forgery' in any way - I am sure that he is sincere in his belief that this triangle is meant to be Pythagorean. But what I am saying is that the structure of this triangle is so

loosely defined as to reduce its evidential value to a rather low level, to one not already converted to Mr Holiday's theories.

To begin with, the raths which mark the Northerly and Westerly corners of the triangle are rather ill-defined on the map (1:50,000 OS sheet 157). Further, although Mr Holiday lables the Southerly corner "Kilpaison Tumuli", and though there are about ten of these tumuli, it is doubtful whether any one of them actually marks the southern vertex. In answer to my query "Which one?", he implied that it wasn't actually a particular barrow of the group, but a point on the periphery of the group (letter dated 11/9/75).

The result of this vagueness of location of the triangle's corners is that the angle claimed by Mr Holiday as a right angle, could be anything from 86 to 91 degrees. Such a five degree spread of error throws considerable doubt on the proceedings, since given the same allowable error, I could claim points C and E in fig.1 to be raths and thus make my 'ley-triangulation' into a perfectly respectable 3:4:5 Pythagorean Triangle!

However, suppose Mr Holiday's Pembrokeshire Triangle is a bona fide 8:15:17 triangle. Is it necessarily the design of some ancient architect, or could it still be simply a chance effect?

Strikingly similar effects can be seen to be delineated by alignments of ordinary buildings, pubs, farmhouses and natural landmarks etc., which have nothing to do with the conventional ley system (though I note Mr Holiday's comments in The Dragon and the Disc p153-4). One such example is shown here (fig 2), being a 3:4:5 triangle in the same area as Mr Holiday's 8:15:17.

Are we to believe then that some subconscious magical drive leads farmers to build their farmhouses, and breweries their pubs, so as to map out giant Pythagorean Triangles over the landscape; or are we to believe that the thing is a chance effect? Personally I believe the latter.

Mr Holiday claims the support of Professor Thom for the ancient use of at least three Pythagorean Triangles. But let us be quite clear about this. Professor Thom only claimed their use within individual stone circles of the egg-shaped (I & II) and elliptical types (5), whereas Mr Holiday's triangles concern juxtapositions of distinct monuments. These are two quite different concepts, as Mr Holiday has agreed (letter dated 22/8/75). The fact that Thom's work is valid, therefore, does not necessarily lend support to Mr Holiday's assertions.

By chance alone many elaborate patterns of juxtapositions are to be expected. A prime example of this is Major Tyler's concentric circular distributions of ancient monuments surrounding Stonehenge (6). Statistical analysis, backed by random simulation, reveals

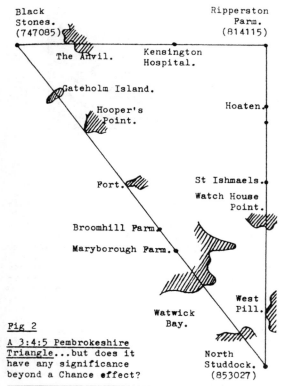

Black
Stones.
(747085)

The Anvil.

Gateholm Island.

Hooper's
Point.

Fort.

Broomhill Farm.

Maryborough Farm.

Watwick
Bay.

Ripperston
Farm.
(814115)

Kensington
Hospital.

Hoaten.

St Ishmaels.
Watch House
Point.

West
Pill.

North
Studdock.
(853027)

Fig 2

A 3:4:5 Pembrokeshire
Triangle...but does it
have any significance
beyond a Chance effect?

that chance can quite easily reproduce Major
Tyler's arrangements. Anyone who is inter-
ested can write to me at: 68 Chesham Rd, Bury,
Lancs, for further details.

*** Robert Forrest; February 1976***

Notes:

1) 'Leys and those Whatsits'- FW Holiday.
The News 14/9-10.
2) 'Leys, UFOs & Chance'- R Forrest.
The News 13/12-13.
3) See, for example Janet Bord's article
in The News 7, and Phil Grant's article in
The News 3; also FW Holiday's The Dragon &
the Disc pp153-4, and Phil Grant's article in
The Ley Hunter 50.
4) "The figures I originally gave were
calculated using the Furness Formula from
Paul Screeton's Quicksilver Heritage pp57-8,
or rather a suped up version of it. I now
have reason to believe that there is a flaw
in the Furness Formula - not in my suping-up,
I hasten to add, but in the original as in
Screeton...Chris Hutton Squire (of Undercurrents) still holds that the Furness F. is
correct, and would therefore defend the figures I give in the original version of (this)
reply to FWH. A battle of computers is in
progress at the moment over this formula -

computers, since the point at issue involves
literally millions of calculations to sort
out. If I am right and the Furness F. does
have a flaw, the figures (I originally gave)
are unfairly high...Now there is a formula
which predicts deliberately low results, and
in view of the possible error in Furness, I
would prefer to publish in (Fortean Times)
'low' rather than 'high' results for chance
alignments." Letter from RF to the Editor
dated 18 April 76. The 'low' figures have
been inserted into the article in place of
the 'high' Furness expectations as requested
-- Ed.
5) Megalithic Sites in Britain - Prof.A
Thom; pp29-31.
6) The Geometrical Arrangement of Ancient
Sites - Major FC Tyler; p36.

* * *   * * *   * * *

Ed's Note: Robert Forrest and FW Holiday
have between them raised some interesting
issues about leys. Many people, and your ed.
among them, feel, instinctively, that there
is some significance to ley alignment - but
vague feelings are clearly not enough for
serious study. Rob Forrest's work should not
be interpreted as an attack on the idea, but
rather a critical appraisal of methodology.
On that basis, it seems, one cannot substantiate the existance of leys by appealing to
alignments of points significantly higher
than can be accounted for by Chance alone. As
Rob shows, this is simply not the case, even
with low-yield formulas. So anyone wishing to
establish the existance of leys must invoke
other and more substantial arguments, and
for an exposition of these, I refer the reader to Paul Screeton's Quicksilver Heritage
(Thorsons; 1974; £4.50). However, paperwork
is no substitute for fieldwork. Single lines
of thought, or single facts, can always be
demolished - this is how the establishment
reacts. You can see it operating in UFO or
monster sightings - singly these things can
be discredited. But we are interested in
their cumulative effect, and whether these
phenomena, leys included, be merely natural
effects ordered and given meaning by the will-
to-believe, or whether they are demonstrable
facets of the physical world, in no way dim-
inishes their 'reality' as ideas. We hope to
continue with this debate from time to time;
but as the more practical arguments and evidence can be more properly presented by those
closer to the whole field of study than we
are here, they and the readers are referred
to the pages of our sister mag, The Ley Hunter
(see our review section). Readers wishing to
go deeper into the question of mathematical
probability of leys may be interested to know
of a postal folio on the subject being circulated privately - please apply to Paul Screeton, c/o TLH. Those wishing to tackle Rob
Forrest direct will find his address in his
article above -- Editor.

HARDBACKS

<u>Fire From Heaven</u> by Michael Harrison.
(Sidgwick & Jackson; £5.50; pp240; index,
bib, photos.) -- Some ideas inevitably
precipitate incomprehension, but mention the
subject of spontaneous combustion of humans
(SHC) and listen to the din of minds slamming
shut. It is a terrifying prospect - you can
almost feel the Lovecraftian horror of Charles
Dickens' conception: "Call the death by any
name Your Highness will, attribute it to whom
you will, or say it might have been prevented
how you will, it is the same death eternally
...inborn, inbred, engendered in the corrupt
humours of the viscous body itself, and that
only...Spontaneous Combustion, and none other
of all the deaths that can be died." (<u>Bleak
House</u>, 1853, ch32.) We are talking about a
process that burns quickly, intensely (leaving
only cinders and oily smoke), that seems to
use a different fuel from ordinary fire (water will not extinguish it), that lulls its
victims into trances (like a vampire, mused
Fort), that is selective (eg burning the body
and not the clothes encasing it), that is
peculiarly confined (eg a heat intense enough
to carbonise bones, yet leaving easily combustible materials nearby untouched), and so
on. It is a 'hell-fire', and one has the suspicion it is the real cause behind the fear
of fire. There are no SCs of animals that we
know of - man, it seems, has earned its fiery
vengence having enslaved it for millenia. Fire
is magically associated with final material
dissolution, and in SHC is, in microcosm, a
Ragnarok of the guts.

It is one of the many opportunities missed by this book, that apart from a curious
diversion into Roman law (lightning victims
are not to be picked up "above the knees")
there is so little discussion of the powerful
yet elusive undercurrent of the mythic in the
subject. If I seem harsh or overly critical
in my comments, it is because the appearance
of a book on one of the central Fortean mysteries is a rare event - and whilst this book
will undoubtedly take its place alongside
Vincent Gaddis' <u>Mysterious Fires & Lights</u> and
Eric Frank Russell's <u>Great World Mysteries</u> on

the Fortean reference shelf, I am sad that
the full potential of that opportunity has
not been realised.

Harrison's main claim is that he has gathered together most of the known cases of SHC
- drawing on and extending the work of Gaddis,
Russell, and even Fort (and though Fort is
credited with bringing fresh insights into
this macabre subject, Harrison tends to see
him as little more than a collector of strange
stories). Harrison's methodology is not systematic and the books main fault lies here: it
is annoying to find interesting cases without
proper or full mention of sources, and he will
often quote a case from, say, Gaddis (whilst
Gaddis quotes from Fort, and Fort from a contemporary source) without going to the source
directly, thereby compounding the likelihood
of error.(Indeed this does happen, as we'll
see). There was also the opportunity here for
a chronological or other listing of known
cases -- the only such list known to me is
in Ivan Sanderson's <u>Investigating the Unexpl-
ained</u>, and that contained the gross error of
fragmenting the case of the Countess Cornelia
Zangari and Bandi (1731) into <u>two</u>, ie Countess
Cornelia Bandi (1763) and Countess Cornelia
Zangari (1836)(Appendix A, in Sanderson's
book).

Harrison opens with several cases which
were in fact cited by Dickens as authorities
for <u>his</u> belief in the phenomenon, including
the Countess di Bandi case (Harrison quotes
the case from Sir David Brewster, and both
give no date; yet professing to have investigated Dickens' interest, Harrison seems unaware
that the case was often mentioned in <u>The Dick-
ensian</u>, eg., its March 1936 issue reproduces
the original testimony of the investigating
prebend of Verona.) Readers new to the idea
of SHC will be surprised to learn that belief
in it was widespread in the 17th,18th and 19th
centuries. Among the writers of those days
who incorporated it into their works are Zola,
Marryat, Melville, de Quincey and Charles
Brocken Brown - and of course, Dickens. The
idea was also a favourite whipping-boy of the
textbooks on medical jurisprudence, and forensic toxicology - but it was merely considered
as a ploy by murderers who've tried to burn

the evidence, or in terms of strange tissue disorders that give off methane or "phosphoretted hydrogen" gas. It is generally claimed that the pioneer chemist, Baron Justus von Liebig, settled the matter in his Familiar Letters on Chemistry (1851) by experiments in burning animal tissue (even soaked in alcohol) and an examination of some cases - but he, like the reviewer of this book in the Daily Mail 29 April: "refuse to believe that people can suddenly catch fire for no reason whatever." Liebig explained in terms of the known behaviour of fire under 'normal' conditions - today we could investigate on the basis of plasma or radiation physics, as in fact suggested by Cade and Davis in their Taming of the Thunderbolts, but not only does Harrison not know of their work on the strange effects of ball lightning, but does not take the possible connexion with SHC up beyond a speculation in passing. Liebig's demolition job on SHC virtually killed off any hope of serious research into it overnight. Cases still flared-up occasionally, and still do, and because the medical profession was only too glad to forget the subject collectively, each case would catch them unawares. Harrison has collected isolated reports on SHC victims, and sporadic correspondence on the subject from the pages of the medical journals. It is interesting to note that Dr Gavin Thurston, who personally doesn't believe in SHC but in 'Preternatural Combustion', wrote to the British Medical Journal (18 June 1932) pointing out that professional opinion on the matter had not progressed in over 100 years, since Marryat included a case in his Jacob Faithful (1834) taken from The Times in 1832. Harrison thinks the abhorrence of the subject comes from "the impossibility of presenting a true explanation". I don't think I'd go that far, but taking the book as a whole it becomes clear that much of the ballyhoo for and against centers on preconceptions of what SHC is; the very term, like 'Flying Saucer', strangles the discussion.

We need to redefine, and find a new approach; Harrison tries the latter but fails to get anywhere. Harrison's reference to "impossibility" (above) is because, he thinks, orthodox medical science will never accept some of the radical fringe-medicine concepts and researches going on today - to do so would be to completely alter our notions of disease and the physical and mental world, and that is even more abhorrent to them. Harrison's quest for an answer takes him down the byways of spiritualistic notions (auras, etheric bodies, mentally directed energy), psychic healing and Kirlian photography until he loses his way several times over, rescued by the bell heralding a new chapter. He hardly ventures into new territory at all. He could have profitably made a whole book about the poltergeist con- but seems to content himself with re-telling

(and he has an irritating habit of trying to dramatise stories with imagined dialogue) the classic tales easily found elsewhere. The blurb's claim, that this is a "puzzle-solving book" of "pioneering originality" that "provides an answer" is wrong on all counts. He also adds (in a manner that recalls the boasts of vonD) "It is not often that the reader is offered a completely unprecedented book: Fire From Heaven is such a work." Yet not 4 pages on he's quoting and acknowledging a "pioneer work", Jonas Dupont's De Incendiis Corporis Humani Spontaneis (Leyden, 1763) - indeed, a bibliography full of similar precedents lies in the back, and Harrison's "pioneering originality" does not extend beyond any of the ideas found in some of his sources (eg all the elements of his "answer" can be found in Gaddis). The book does not solve anything because his "answer" is hypothetical, and, strictly, posed as a question, for the last lines of the book breathlessly propose little more than an unsubstantiated guess: "Is it like this? When the control breaks down, a control which must superintend and ensure the perfect functioning of the two linked and interdependent bodies... is the sudden excess energy of Body II blown off through Body I, in a sudden, titanic burst of force which leaves Body I nothing more than 'a rag, a bone and a hank of hair'...and often not more than that?"

This rather pompous tone seems to have caused lots of errors in the book - eg he refers the reader to "the victim's screams which brought Dr BH Hartwell of Ayer, Mass.," to a woman burning in a wood in 1891, to show that Fort was exaggerating when he mused on the "notable absence of outcry or seeming unconsciousness of victims..". If Harrison had quoted the full case (or the little that is known), the reader would learn that Dr Hartwell was called from his car by another; the victim being in advance conflagration - if Harrison wanted to counter Fort's idea, he could have picked some beauties from Fort's own cases. In dealing with Russell's famous 3-in-1 burning of John Greeley on the ship, SS Ulrich, George Turner in a lorry at Upton-by-Chester, and Willem Ten Bruik in his car at Ubbergen, Holland within minutes of each other on 7 April 1938 (incidentally, Russell's own writings are not credited, nor listed in the bibliography, so I'd guess Harrison is quoting 2nd-hand from Gaddis), Harrison observes that the other two sites are both 340 miles from Upton - to his credit, an original discovery, but what does it mean? He also suggests the sights are linked by the sound/vibration of the initial 'U' - laughable when you realise it's two 'oo's and an 'uh'. If we're linking sounds, he's missed three of the principal cases whose victims were Wright, Knight and White - and what about Bertholi/Bertillon/Bartholin, though to be fair the last two are authorities (which in continuity may be being a victim of sorts). Another obvious link, usually overlooked, is the fact that as Greeley was at the helm when struck, each victim was driving or steering a vehicle - whatever that may mean. The danger of 2nd-hand quoting is illustrated by the way Harrison has obviously been influenced by the sensational aspects of cases as hammed up by Russell via Gaddis, for example. One such classic is the burning of Phyllis Newcombe in a ballroom in Chelmsford about midnight, 27 August 1938. Russell/Gaddis maintain the girl "suddenly burst into intense bluish flames and within minutes was a blackened mass of ash" (cf Gaddis p224). Now Harrison has tracked down the original report in the Daily Telegraph 20 Sept 1938 and summarises: the girl and boyfriend, Henry McAusland, stepped off the dancefloor having danced most of the night (Harrison finds something suggestive about "rhythmic, rotary movements") the girl screams as flames sprout from around her; Henry tries to beat them off with his hands and is burned; "within a minute or two" the girl dies. I have a copy of the key news report here as I write: no mention of bluish flames, charred heaps, or Henry flapping his hands. According to the report, an ambulance arrived about 35 minutes after the incident and took Phyllis to hospital, where she died, I'd guess, not less than an hour later. The mystery is how her dress became alight - it was inflammable, but the inquest ruled out the explanation by Henry himself of a casually flicked cigarette butt. Modern Fortean literature has generated and perpetuated similar distortions and sensationalisations to an unknown extent. You must be cautious, because Mr Harrison sometimes is not, and without the original sources you cannot tell where.

I am coming to the conclusion that to tackle the existance of this genuine and puzzling phenomenon from the classical notion of a spontaneous burning will get us nowhere - it has been argued against (equally hypothetically) so many times, and in my view successfully. We need a new approach; one based soundly on the best observational data - because the trouble with SHC is that both sides select cases to prove or disprove the point, as in all logic about hypotheses. It is automatic, and Harrison is not above it. Several times Harrison verges on an intuition that could be a break-through - but it passes, ungrasped, and even sometimes unnoticed. I've been rough with the book deliberately, and beyond what I've said, bearing in mind the caveat and the lack of a listing of cases, it is a valuable collection of data. The definitive sourcebook on SHC has yet to be written - but Fire From Heaven will do well enough in the meantime.

Brigantia by Guy Raglan Phillips (Routledge & Kegan Paul; £4.25; pp224; index, bib, drgs) -- If there is something comical about the question "Was Giggleswick a sanctuary of the goddess Brigantia?" it shows how much we are out of touch with our own past. Phillips, whose name will be familiar to readers of The Ley Hunter, sets out on a search for the almost unknown kingdom of Brigantia, which may have begun in the pre-Celtic Bronze Age more than 3000 years ago, and lasted, maybe, 1200 years, until the Romans found it straddling Britain (roughly from The Wirral to The Wash and northwards to the Scottish border.) The quest wanders through history, prehistory, topography, folklore and tangential subjects compounding what Phillips calls a "mysteriography".

The book is a fascinating web of complex themes: the worship of the eponymous goddess of the Brigantes (also known as Bride, Brid, Brigid and even St Brigit) "whose very name may be far older than the Celts"; the cult of stone and severed heads; the network of leys and ancient sites in the area (including a major datum, 4° West of Mag. North, he calls 'The Belinus Line' after that king (apx 500BC) who in legend established holy sites and the roads to them as sanctuaries; the links with the kingdom of Clinschor (Klingsor) of the Germanic Grail legends and other Arthurian relationships; witches, fairies (The Luck of Edenhall), magic ravens, stones and hills, the Green Man and the Horned God of the Witches, and Black Horses in legend and hillside figures; etc. This is a startling mine of exciting cross-connexions - a veritable springboard for new research - yet consolidating the known fragments of myth, fact and folktale.

A Guide to Occult Britain by John Wilcock. (Sidgwick & Jackson; £6.95; pp314; index, bib, photos; also paper, £3.95). -- When I attended the Fortfest in Chicago last year, much mirth was generated by the Ghost Tour, with Rich Crowe intoning seriously "..and up on that hill is a Haunted House, but we can't go in....and on your right a Haunted Churchyard, but it's closed for the night...and..". Mr Wilcock is the author of several guides for travellers and may well qualify for The Oldest Hippie Journalist In The Business, having fought in the Undergrounds on both sides of the Atlantic. I don't blame him for combining his talents with his interest in the 'Occult' - this is a grand way to get a paid holiday - but it has the casual triviality of a street-transaction - wham!bam!thank'ee mam! In introducing himself as your guide, Wilcock admits to being "somewhat glib, unusually articulate and a shade too dominating", and though he is entertaining (in short doses) you get the feeling he'd talk the pointed-hat off a pixie if he met one. Wilcock says that he had to learn "archeology and history. And comparative religions. And contemporary occult thought.." for the book, but he doesn't seem able to take it seriously - oh! he doesn't laugh at it all, but the slick verbiage tries unnecessarily hard to convince you of the good time he's having (and by implication you will too), and in pre-digesting his information speil for each place he has reduced it all to uniform banality.

It's a fat book - but does it work? Turning at random, I see on p56 "back to the A366 ...then...onto the A36 for Warminster." There then follows just over 2 pages on Warminster.. no wait..they're on Arthur Shuttlewood's vision of the town as UFO capital of the UK; but apart from a mention of "the telephone kiosk at Boreham Field" from which Shuttlewood received calls from outer space (sic), there's no mention of places to visit, things to see. Just keep your eyes peeled for a phonebox, folks, as you drive through reading my book. Not being a driver myself I can't vouch for his directions, but they seem a little terse, especially for the Foreign Visitor unaware of the mysteries of country signposting - but I did notice a distinct lack of milages between Places of Note (essential for planning I'd have thought); or whether you need permission before traipsing across a farmer's fields to see earthworks or tumps, or if some sites have 'opening times' or admission charges. If I were you, I'd take along a Michelin Guide, or the Readers Digest Folklore Myths & Legends of Britain, whatever, along too. The index, which might also have served as a gazetteer, seems arbitrary and inadequate - indeed the structure of the book leaves a lot to be desired, as though all these considerations were the last concern of Wilcock's wandering Gypsy soul. The book draws heavily on the work of Anthony and Jan Roberts, who it seems did all the hard work, mapping the routes and compiling the basic information about places of interest and whose works are frequently quoted but not listed in the bibliography. They are credited, of course for their help, which in a way exonerates them from what follows, when Wilcock and friend take that initial guide material and have fun touring, opining and writing - doing, so he's told us, what comes naturally to him. The result is band-wagon pap, as ultimately unsatisfying as the Chicago Ghost Tour, but by no means as edifying.

Fabulous Beasts & Demons by Heinze Mode. (Phaidon Press; £9.95; pp280; index/glossary, bib, notes, plates & drgs.) -- This is not just a large glossy coffee-table book, but a valuable reference on mythical & fabulous beasts and beings, beautifully produced, and copiously illustrated with drawings, engravings, architectural artwork, sculptures and ornaments and utensils and paintings, of curiosities ranging from the lascivious tritons and buxom mermaids of Arnold Bocklin, to the rampant Chinese and Babylonian dragons, to the demonic statuary of India and Tibet, and to the humanoid angels of Islamic and Christian illuminated manuscripts. However, Mode appears to have selected and categorised his bestiary arbitrarily into five divisions, divisions that become quite impractical both inthe text and the illustrations as he tries to accomodate monsters which are multiple composites of other animals, or in the quaint Victorian term, 'nondescript'. Here you have animals with human heads, and humans with animal heads; multiple-heads; and winged things, strangely mixed with winged-suns, boatmen and walking drums - and a final chapter on 'Journeys to Fabulous Countries' which surely could have included more than ancient geographical speculation and morbid visions of life (if that's the word) in Hell (what about Wonderland, for example, or Never-never land?). Nevertheless, the book is packed with information, even if he does neglect some areas of the fantastic (eg no fairies, or SF). Compared to Borges' Book of Imaginary Beings Mode is fairly dry, but one fancies thisbthe result of the translation from the German, because he is obviously caught up in his subject. The text, illustrations, extensive bibliography, and index/glossary ensure its usefulness. One pecadillo - though the layout of the pages is visually excellent, the price will cause many a rueful glance at the lavish use of blank paper.

Parapsychology & The Nature of Life by John L Randall. (Souvenir Press; £4.00; pp256; index, bib, photos.) -- A sound critique of the rise of mechanistic reductionism, the material philosophy that has, from Darwin on, sought to reduce all the highest qualities of life, creativity and thought to the random and automatic jugglings of basic materials and processes. Randall also takes a swipe at the prominence of Chance-theory, to which many materialists have recourse in their arguments against any theory of phenomena outside the norm or expected, and which does not mesh with their orthodoxy. In the final chapters, Randall sees this recourse as a last battle, heralding the emergence of a new synthetic science that will acknowledge the "non-physical components of man". Alas space prevents us treating the book in the depth it deserves - but since it discusses the clashes and shortcomings of "dogmatic religion and mechanistic science", no doubt we will be referring to it often in these pages.

The Method of Zen by Eugen Herrigel. (Routledge & Kegan Paul; £1.50; pp102.)
Tao: The Watercourse Way by Alan Watts. (Jonathan Cape; £3.50; pp134; bib of Chinese & Western sources, plus calligraphy.)- Herrigel's stark narrative distils the essence of his learning about Zen - his concise style cuts, like a sword-master, through superfluity and his words like arrows fly straight to their targets. The Watts book, similar in intention, is quite different, and rambles like a lazy stream through the peculiar Taoist concepts of yin-yang polarity, tzu-jan (the natu-

ral state of things), Te (the power of this natural state), and wu-wei (allowing natural movement without force or interferance). This was Watts's last book and finished off after his death by his friend and T'ai Chi master, Al'Chung-liang Huang. In our quest to understand phenomena, we need the mental tools here extolled. Both books contain clear and even original insights into Zen and Tao, and have direct relevance to the central issues of our studies. ((The Zen book is in paperback.))

PAPERBACKS

Very Special People by Frederick Drimmer. (Bantam; $1.95; pp357; bib, photos.) -- In 1898, members of circus sideshows met in London to object publicly to the hurtful lable 'Freaks', and asked to be referred to as 'Prodigies' if a word were needed. Largely their case has been forgotten or ignored as people could be parted from their money just to gawp at them. Drimmer's book is a compassionate biography of many of of these 'Very Special People' as he prefers to call them - tender but not sentimental, as he tells of the physical and emotional tragedies that inevitably prevented the VSP from leading normal lives; eg Julia Pastrana who died of heartbreak when her baby turned out to look as gorilla-like as she did; or Merrick, the Elephant Man, whose cauliflower-textured skin and facial deformities caused such revulsion in all who saw him that he was driven into fantasies about love he could never experience with a woman, and whose enlarged head prevented him sleeping like normal people, until one day he tried, and his neck dislocated, killing him.

Aliens From Space by Maj. Donald Keyhoe. (Panther; 75p; pp303; index).
The Great Beast by John Symonds. (Mayflower; 60p; pp464; index.)
Loch Ness Monster by Tim Dinsdale. (Routledge & Kegan Paul; £2.25; pp171; also hardcover at £3.95.) -- welcome reprints.

INFO's 4th Annual Convention.
Fortfest 76 will be held this year in Washington, at the Hospitality House Motor Inn, Arlington, Virginia, over August 6-8. Those interested in attending, or wishing to receive the progress bulletin, please write to Fortfest: INFO, Box 367, Arlington, VA22210.

The Complete Books of Charles Fort.
INFO has a stock of this long-awaited reprint, by Dover, of the old Fortean Society 1941 edition. This omnibus volume contains 'The Book of the Damned', 'New Lands', 'Lo!', and 'Wild Talents', keeping the same index & pagination as the 1941 edition. You could pay up to $30 for a disastrous hardcover set of the separate books - so the INFO price of

** ** We have kept some books received for review for the next issue as we're running out of space to deal with them adequately. ** **

To Any American Readers...
Our subscription to the National Enquirer has ended, and we cannot afford to renew it. Would any USA reader be willing to send us Nat.Enq. and even Midnight when they have finished with them? Not only does it help to keep us informed, but the data, for what it is worth, goes into our files. To avoid duplication of effort, and possibly even to arrange a deal, please write to the Editor, FT.

Binders -- we have two possibilities, and I'd like to hear from you before I commit any money, so I can judge the response. Choice A uses wires to hold the mags down the centrefold; and Choice B uses plastic strips. B is certainly neater, but also more expensive - A could be done within the guestimate of £2 all in (and made in USA). But B, made in this country, is subject to all sorts of additional costs and VATs so that it could not be offered for less than £2.50. Both will hold 12 issues (ie 2 years) plus their indexes - and both would be in black plastic with silver logos. If we go for A now; we could switch to B later when we can afford it. The other main problem is that minimum orders for A are 100, and B, 200, both of which mean laying out several hundred pounds in advance - this is why it is essential to raise the orders in advance - we just don't have the capital to tie up like that. Please help me decide... ED.

*** As we go to press, the TV news for 2 June tells of 2 severe quakes in China's western Yunan province; Rines is back at Loch Ness; and a Bigfoot has snatched a California Girl. We've run out of room - so we'll have notes on these and other monsters known and unknown next issue; even our usual review of journals will have to be held over. Apologies. ***

£7.50/$15.00 (to non-members), £6.25/$12.50 (to members) is superb value. UK orders can be paid to Fortean Times for convenience; all others apply direct to the INFO-USA address given above.

INFO Journals.
INFO Journal 16 should have arrived at most UK addresses by now. Due to inscrutable mysteries of international postal systems, and reorganisation of INFO administration system, there will be people who are entitled to issues of INFO who've not yet received them. Will anyone who thinks he/she should have had their copies by now, but haven't, please let the Ed of FT know, so he can check the system for errors. That applies to UK readers - all other countries apply direct to INFO-USA.

FORTEAN TIMES

strange phenomena - curiosities - prodigies - portents - mysteries

BIRDMEN of the APOCALYPSE !.. .. ..p14

50p : $1·00.

17

UK ISSN 0308-5899

AUGUST 1976

FORTEAN TIMES

A Contemporary Record of Strange Phenomena

FORTEAN TIMES is a non-profitmaking bimonthly miscellany of news, notes and references on current strange phenomena and related subjects. Formerly THE NEWS. Affiliated to the International Fortean Organisation (INFO) in continuing the work of CHARLES FORT (1874-1932). FORTEAN TIMES is edited and published by Robert JM Rickard: **Post Office Stores, Aldermaston, Reading RG7 4LJ, Berks, England.**

SUBSCRIPTIONS: 1 year (6 issues) £3.00/USA \$6.00. Back issues (if available) 50p/USA \$1.00. Airmail (overseas) add £1.50/USA \$3.00 per year to sub. rate. Annual index free to current subscribers, otherwise 30p/USA 60¢. *Special joint subscription to Fortean Times and INFO Journal: 1 year (12 issues) £7.00/USA \$14.00.* All overseas payments by cheque should *include* 10% to cover banking exchange commission.

CONTRIBUTIONS: of articles, notes and artwork on related subjects are always welcome and duly credited. *You can help by sending us a copy or clipping of any item you think will interest other readers — just add a note of the source, date, and your name for the credit.* Please don't assume our omniscience — there are very few duplications.

RIGHTS: All artwork and articles in *FORTEAN TIMES* are the copyright of the artists and authors; and the views expressed not necessarily those of *FORTEAN TIMES* or INFO. Uncredited material is by the editor. All notes herein may be freely quoted in return for a *credit to FORTEAN TIMES with our address.* Heading artwork is by Hunt Emerson.

These are Fortean times!

So much has happened in the last four months that we are not able to cram it all into our paltry 28 pages. Apart from the whacky weather, we have seen a whole menagerie of monsters down in Cornwall, a rise in the number and intensity of quakes all over the world, meteors, fireballs, huge swarms of normally innocuous insects, a massive drought in Europe and the UK, floods and dam-breaks in the US, more sightings of Nessie, the Surrey Puma and other MAs in England, not to mention Bigfeet and Birdmen. Nor does it end there! Some of these you'll find in this issue - the rest will be presented in the following issues. I wish we could afford the extra pages to give it to you as it happens (almost). We continue to need your support to survive and improve and do justice to these truly Fortean times.

Truss Fund

We are pleased to record the donations of: Don Bolin, Peter Hope-Evans, Dave Fideler, CS Kershaw, Mrs V Martin, PJ Williams, towards our survival fund. Financial support in this form is always welcome and put to good use. US readers are assured that the exchange rates in their favour mean there has never been a better time for a little financial gift to achieve so much over here.

Binders

There has been much interest in the idea of binders for FT, but not really enough to warrant us tying up a lump of money in a batch of 200. So we have decided to postpone the idea until we can better afford it; perhaps next year. Those who have paid in advance may have their money refunded, credited towards their next sub., or towards that future binder. Advance orders can still be placed as these will hasten the day.

The Ley Hunter...Excelsior!

The first issue of TLH under the new editorship of our own Paul Devereux, earns our praise and congratulations. From next issue (FT 18) we will be offering a joint subscription rate with TLH to cater for that combination of interests. We will also be printing a joint blurb - please help us by sending for as many as you like and try distributing them in your area (eg to libraries, colleges, shops, clubs etc).

Next Issue: Robert Forrest will inaugurate our own postal folio on the Great Pyramid and its mysteries; and we begin a new series, Corrigenda Forteana, on corrections of errors in the literature, for which we welcome contributions. This spot is not intended as a pillory, but a vital research tool to counter some of the more gross misconceptions previously thrust upon an increasingly bewildered public..and researchers.

BEHAVIOURAL CURIOSITIES

BIRD ATTACKS ON PEOPLE

Since our last run-down on people being attacked by our feathered fiends (News 6/4) we have gagged through 'Jaws' and its sequals - but in real life the Game War continues to be slugged out in all departments. Here's an accumulation of reports from the Feathered Front on the Beaked Brigades.

Kevin Graham, of Tweedmouth, Northumberland, was crossing Tweed Bridge, Berwick, when he was attacked by screaming dive-bombing seagulls. Shouting and waving his arms, he made his way to a couple on the other side, also under attack, and the three ran for cover. They were shaken up but unpecked. Sevral other people said they had been flapped at while crossing the bridge. Local authorities put it down to birds nesting in the structure who feel threatened - but normally seagulls are quite harmless. Weekly News 10 August 1974. (Cr: Nigel Watson.)

Terry Hauf took to the fields south of Yoder, Wyoming to hunt for game birds. He stopped to look at the sky, and the next thing he knew he was lying dazed and wounded on the ground - and 15ft away sat an eagle also a bit dazed. The bird came out of the sky to strike him, cutting his head and seriously injuring his right eye. When he got up to go for aid, the bird "took off at a kind of trot". An official from the Wyo. Game & Fish Dept said that it was "extremely abnormal behavior" for an eagle to attack a human. Denver (Colorado) Post 22 Nov 1974. (Cr: Mark Hall.)

On 14 Jan 1975 a Jackdaw hailed a group of school-children at Leighton Buzzard (yeah!) Beds, with a friendly: "Hello Jack, my name's Mary." But no one was deceived. In the previous two weeks it had swooped on five children at Beaudessert Infants' School, cutting them about the face and hands. Mothers were also attacked as they collected their kids - and teachers armed with sticks were needed to escort children to the outside toilets in the playground. A police marksman was called, but missed. The next day (16th) the gunman had another go, that this time successfully blasted the pest out of his tree. As an exercise in public relations, however, the triumph was immediately soured. The gunman went

to pick up the bird, and found its wings still fluttering as he held it up for all to see. Mothers screamed and children began crying. As the police drove off, one mother shouted: "You rotten lot, why didn't you catch it?" Daily Express, The Sun, Daily Mail 15 & 16 Jan 1975. (Cr: Steve Moore & Nigel Watson.)

Another jackdaw terrorised children on the playground at Cogan, near Penarth, Glamorgan, where at least two children ran home in terror bleeding from holes pecked in their heads. Attacks by a bird on children fishing off Penarth pier were also blamed on this jackdaw. Sunday Mirror 14 Dec 1975. A postscript to this report mentions that a seagull had attacked a young girl, her dog and a horse at Llanon, Cardigan, also in Wales. As no date is given for either event, we can assume they took place sometime in the preceeding week.

Approximately concurrent with the previous two events, a magpie was accused of stealing £11 worth of golfballs on a course at Aldershot, Hants. It swoops on any ball it sees on the thirteenth green and drops them over the fence of a nearby top-security aircraft establishment. Daily Mirror 15 Dec 1975. Earlier in the year, the News of the World 5 Jan 1975, mentioned a crow who similarly swooped to swipe the balls from Windmill Hill Golf Course, Milton Keynes, Bucks. (Cr: Nigel Watson.)

Two mistle thrushes nesting in Philip Clarkson's new carport, at Fairfield Gardens, Ossett, near Leeds, Yorks, have made his life a misery; and that of his wife, the postman and the milkman. The birds have swooped on all who approach the carport, and have even attacked a child. The birds drop from a height aiming for the head, and sometimes come straight at the windows. The Clarksons' nerves were rapidly disintegrating and they were clearly thinking of some horror-film type conspiracy against them. "Look," Philip told the reporter, "there's one now. Just waiting to pounce on us!" The RSPCA, as expected, is more worried about the birds, and warned the Cooksons that the nest, with its six babies, was protected by the 1954 Birds Act. Sunday Express 30 May 1976. (CR: S Moore)

A loose note in the file has surfaced

and may as well be included here for the record. At Hugglescote, Leics, on 21 May 1960, several magpies attacked a crowd of school-children, injuring four of them. New York Times 22 May 1960. (Cr: INFO/Willis.)

BIRD ATTACKS ON HOUSES

The above stories deal with mere skirmishes - the following are of full-scale assaults.

We open with a couple of old but unrecorded notes. At Peterborough, Derek Reegan was woken up in the early hours of the morning by the noise of "thousands" of starlings battering against the doors and windows of his house. Atlanta Journal 13 Jan 1969. Cr: INFO/Greenfield.

On the evening of 30 May 1970, the Bensons of Westwood, California, sat down to dinner. On hearing a strange rustling noise from their living room, they rushed in to find it filled with small writhing black shapes flying around, bumping at the window and clinging to the drapes. Larry Benson gathered his two young daughters and rushed them outside, where he found a crowd gaping at his roof - there were hundreds of birds waiting and struggling around his chimney, trying to get down it. Benson and his wife ran inside and tried to stop the avalanche of birds from the fireplace with a bearskin rug, but there were too many birds already in the room throwing themselves at ceiling, floors and walls and filling the air with soot from their flappings. Neighbours responded to cries for help; they eventually blocked the chimney and opened all the doors and windows, and began the long job of clearing all the birds out. It was a night the Bensons wish they could forget. National Enquirer 2 April 1970. Cr: INFO/Dobbins. Oh yes...the birds were identified as northward migrating swifts, but no explanation could be given for why they should all want to go down a particular chimney at the same time!

According to the Weekly News 30 Nov 1974, houses in a road called The Weavers are under siege from hordes of blue tits, who perch in great numbers just waiting for the slightest opening through which they stream into rooms and rip the wallpaper from the walls in Biddenden, Kent. For the month prior to this report the birds have been stripping walls and pecking the putty out of the windows. A spokesman for the RSPCA waffled vaguely about deficiencies in their diet, but it does seem that the wall paper gets shredded in the frenzied effort to get at its paste. (Cr: Nigel Watson.)

About the begining of June last year, John Payne and his wife were woken up at 5am by two large crows battering their bedroom window. As they watched, more crows joined them and soon every window on that side of their house at Broad Oak, near Heathfield,

Sussex, was under similar attack. There were about 20 birds. Mr Payne managed to go out and drive them off with a stick. But the next morning they were back with an extra ten for support - and at the same time of 5am. Again Payne drove them off, but they stared menacingly from nearby trees and even on his lawn. The third morning, at 5am, 40 turned up attacking the house - and again they were driven off. Mrs Payne's nerves began to suffer: like nearly all our victims they had seen Hitchcock's film The Birds, and the eerie nature of the event, their raucous cawing, and the sound of beaks and claws against glass were too much for her. The Paynes went on a short holiday. They returned on the 13th and at 5am that night the attacks began again ((though we have no idea if they ceased in the Payne's absence)). As a postscript to the report in the Sunday Express 15 June 1975 (Cr: John Michell) is the opinion of Mr Guy Mountfort, president of the British Ornithologists' Union, that the birds are attacking their own images in the glass, seeing them as invaders of their territory, and because the first incident happened at 5am, the birds remember and come back to repulse the punctual trespassers. Sounds far too glib to me! I'm intrigued by the vague suggestion of a closer link between the events and the family - that the phenomenon ends when they go away, and begins when they return - but there is no further information on this in the report in Sunday People (same date. Cr: BR Bates) either. What is brought to mind are numerous tales perused by John Michell and myself, for our book, of birds associated with families as recurring omens of death. For more on this you'll have to wait for the book - but in the meantime here is a curious note from the Daily Mirror 2 Jan 1976: Mrs Dorothy Jones had a disease commonly called 'Bird Fancier's Lung' (psittacosis), and her husband and neighbours did their best to frighten birds away from her house, near Gatwick, Sussex, to protect her from their droppings and the dust of their feathers. Sometime at the end of last year Mrs Jones was critically ill with the disease and a flock of pigeons landed on the roof of the house. The birds didn't stay long - but long enough for Mrs Jones to be affected by their presence, causing her death. Her husband describes it as a "terrible coincidence" that the birds should arrive in a great number just when her allergy made her weakest. It was a similar case that alerted Jung to the possibilities of acausal connexions between events - see his Synchronicity (RKP 1972) pp 31f,37.

The Daily Telegraph (Cr: John Michell) and Daily Mail (Cr: Peter Hope-Evans) of 14 June 1976 announced that the dream home of Mrs Margot Swatton, at Paul Hill, Newlyn, Cornwall was under attack by a kamikaze rook division. For a week the birds had been dive-
cont on p8

There are many different approaches to our studies, and as Forteans it behoves us to be open to them all. They are after all only different kinds of tools contributing to the greater understanding of the world's mysteries. Anthony Bell has by turns, startled, amused, intrigued and stimulated your editor by his unorthodox approaches and theories. They remind us that study without insight can be a dry and often empty exercise, and there is much to be learned from inspirational views of the same problems. Up to now Anthony has confined himself to letters to your editor, who thinks the world is now ready for...

LEXI~LINKS

NATURE'S PLAY ON WORDS

by AJ Bell

While reading the Bible I have been struck by the frequency of certain words which have no obvious religious significance. Also I am impressed by the fact that these same words are often used in pairs or in larger groups; a usage I take as suggesting that they are in some way complementary. Take the admonishings and sayings of Christ as an example. We are told not to sift a mote and let a camel pass through, to cast the motes out of our own eyes first, and the divine capability of getting a camel through a needle's eye. In this case the words mote, camel and eye are used in pairs, and in one case the words needle and eye are juxtaposed. Remember the 'Interrupted Journey' of the Hills, and how hands were allegedly rubbed in front of Betty's eyes (symbolic washing in water?) as a needle was thrust in her abdomen, and the account of a contactee who said his eyes watered when he looked upon a 'space needle' (1). The mythmakers have not overlooked the

association of eyes and piercing things - hence the pin, stake and arrow into the eyes of Oedipus, Samson and Harold. Note also that the MIB are said to sometimes wear lapel pins bearing an eye symbol (2).

I feel that the words mote, camel, eye and needle are related, possibly by being important components of the supposed ley system. In such a system the needle would refer to the obelisk or menhir (as in Cleopatra's Needle); the camel with its water-storing hump would imply a tumulus; and mote would signify the phonetically identical moat where water and clay come into contact. What about the eye? I suggest that the eye is the Eye of Horus, the pattern of 'geodetic' lines of influence associated with a blind spring (3). (Incidentally notice that the shape of a watch spring has the same spiral form as the alleged geodetic spiral of a blind spring). Perhaps certain aspects of the Bible should be seen in this light; eg, when Christ said the light of the soul is the eye, did this identify the soul-energy with geodetic lines of influence? In a similar vein, the winking eyes of the whore of Babylon may refer to fluctuations in the Eye of Whore-us - the expanding and contracting geodetic lines noted by dowsers and said to be related to the moon's phases (4). If there is nothing new in Christianity except Christ, then perhaps it is not surprising that words attributed to Christ are references to the artifacts of cultures of an earlier season. Beneath the conventional exterior of the Bible, old ideas are expressed, and because of the cyclic nature of civilisation we may now be able to assimilate these ideas, some of which may soon be recognised as 'scientific' such as Christ's designation of John as the "Son of Thunder", explained when you consider that John was derived from Ion (5).

Whatever the significance of the key-words mote, camel and eye, they appear to act as a link between various concepts, and I feel that the phenomenon of link-words in the Bible is mirrored by the link-words of events in the physical world. Personal experience tends to support this idea, but for examples I'll draw mainly from news items in the press in recent months, and reports in recent issues of The News, so that Fortean Times readers will be in familiar surroundings. These data are of various violent events and no doubt have some sort of sociological significance. Last summer there was a spate of coaching accidents and one of the first fatal crashes occured at Devil's Bridge (6): key words, coach, devil, death. According to a recent FSR article, strange coach-tracks were found years ago on a frozen lake but not in the snow on either side, and attributed to a black phantom vehicle called the 'Devil's Coach' (7): key-words coach, devil, ice. In News 13 is the story of a lightning observer in Manchester who saw a flash followed by an icefall (8): key-words ice, bolt. Recently IRA operatives in Britain have used coach-bolts as shrapnel in their bombs: key-words coach, bolt, death. In the Moorgate underground crash, the driver seemed (according to witnesses) to stare glassy-eyed as if in a trance (9): key-words Tunnel, death, staring-eyes. The heiress Leslie Whittle was killed in a tunnel by Donald Neilson, the 'Black Panther', described by his victims and witnesses in his PO robberies as having "staring eyes": key-words tunnel, death, staring-eyes (NB: one witness saw him buying binoculars!) ((At the time of typing this up there has been a third attack on a woman, with a long piercing knife, by a female assailant with "staring eyes" outside Reading coach station.

Also, a letter from Doc Shiels (19 June 1976) wonders if there is any connexion between the current wave of 'Birdmen' sightings in Cornwall (see p17 this issue) and the legendary Springheel Jack. The thought is stimulated by a series of attacks on young girls in the Camborne area of Cornwall "a few months ago" by a mysterious man with 'strange staring eyes' - we are attempting to find out more on this -- Ed.))

These violent events are linked to one another by various combinations of the key-words, a process of connecting unrelated events by a descriptive lexicon that I call a 'lexilink'. Events can be joined by lexilinks to form acausal chains of events. In the above examples, notice that i) Lesley Whittle was heiress to the proceeds of a coach firm; ii) the Moorgate disaster is lexilinked with the Devil's Coach as both run on or make two parallel tracks; iii) the train was electric, and the lightning observer worked for the Electrical Research Association; iv) the train and staring driver crashed into a blind tunnel; v) the IRA had previously bombed a coach in Manchester (where the ice fell)((but not on the exact same site - Ed.)); vi) the IRA recently shot a tube-train driver.

Like the seven daughters of Nefertiti - one of whom died young - and the sevenfold geodetic spiral of a blind spring (the smallest terminating in the spring), so the seven key-words of our examples (coach, bolt, devil, death, ice, tunnel, eyes) seem to go together. An eye or bolt symbol, for example, is said to be displayed on the MIB motorcars (10). Touching on the MIB autos, I notice John Keel gives the impression that they tend to use Cadillacs and Lincolns often (11). These makes were founded by Leland, a name suggesting 'ley' to me. The Lorenzens (12) mention a tan-coloured Dodge used by a couple of "witness intimidators". The juxtaposed colour and make seem connected with leys, as tan describes the beacon fires (eg: Tan Hill,

Beltane, etc), while dodge suggests the movement of the dod-man's alignment gear (13). Keel describes a strange "air force officer" who drove a white Mustang, suggestive of the megalithic hill design of a white horse, and hence leys again (14). This strange "officer" visited a UFO percipient's house and tried to eat jelly without a spoon. Are his peculiar table manners lexilinked to the feats of Uri Geller who turns parts of spoons to jelly? (15).

For the present, the notion of lexilinks may throw some light on strange events repeated in UFO literature - for an example I'll draw on two articles in FSR 15:4 (16) - but first a little digression. I mentioned earlier John, Ion and the Son of Thunder. Taking the 'N' out of Ion and extending the verticals one obtains the classic lightning bolt symbol ($\frac{1}{7}$); and by placing the 'O' above the 'I' we get a 'keyhole' shape ($\frac{1}{7}$). Solidify this keyhole shape and you arrive at a cylinder surmounted by a sphere, a bolt-like symbol I call a 'rodball' (17). Note that bolts and keyholes are features of doors, and doors are mythologically connected with the thundergods. Interestingly one of Matthew Manning's automatic drawings shows a rodball with St John's Head on it, and one of Vallee's books has a painting showing many rodballs in the doorways of a wall of cubbyholes (18). It has even been said that a rodball once stood on Silbury Hill (19).

Some years ago, strange unopenable spheres were found in Australia ((Apx 1963; others were found in New Zealand in 1972 -Ed)) and in the first FSR article under consideration a strange cylinder was found in Caconde, Brazil, near the door of a house. Like a bolted door, the Aussie spheres and this cylinder couldn't be opened. On each end of the cylinder were two "dials", the faces of which were covered by transparent material and had grooves on them. Pointers on the dials pointed to a zero-symbol suggesting inactivity. I feel the separation of pointer and symbol suggests separation of rod and ball - as St John lost his head, so the mystery cylinder had lost its sphere, hence its inactivity. Incidentally, each pointer was tipped with a small ball! Perhaps the cylinder represents ions of the carbon or nitrogen cycle that have been left underground - like the rest of St John's body in the dungeon. Caconde's radioactive springs may be to blame and I wonder if the kelly green fireballs sometimes seen may also be a sign of ionic trouble as a kelly and a fireball have a distorted rodball shape...rodball lightning?! Like the cylinders of a UFO-stalled car, our mystery cylinder eventually automatically sparked into life, and with a sound of thunder disappeared leaving a hole in the roof above where it was kept! Did the ions finally make it back to the sky? Ivan Sanderson (20) once examined a 'mystery cylinder'. There were four holes in one face and six in the other, and carbon came out. Did this cylinder represent the carbon ion with a valency four and atomic number six?

In the second FSR case, an entity in a "diver's suit" was seen in New Zealand. "His" head-piece was cylindrical and his face was covered by transparent material. John Keel, in Operation Trojan Horse, notes a cylindrical "flying roll" mentioned in the Bible where it is said to be the curse that goes forth over the face of the whole earth. In the third FSR case, also in NZ, a man stumbles on an amazing scene. A woman in white, looking dead, lies across a ditch. Two Men-in-Brown sit gazing at her. Is the white woman a representation of the whole earth, and is she cursed by the Biblical flying roll? Now the Caconde cylinder had grooves on its face, and the woman lies across a groove on the face of the whole earth. The witness tried to get face to face with the two men, but they turned their heads away, and an invisible barrier stopped the witness coming closer. As the above cases repeat combinations of words that describe them, I feel we have a lexilink situation. Note that the witness of the 'groovy lady' case chewed rolled tobacco after his encounter. Later he revisited the scene with a friend and they noticed a long neat flattened strip in the grass but saw no people. It looked like it had been rolled...and the witness was employed as a ... groundsman!

Anthony J Bell: June 1976.

Notes & References

1) 'Appendix to the preliminary report on Carl Higdon' (quoting National Star reporter Frank Bourke), FSR 21:3/4, 1975.
2) John A Keel, UFOs: Operation Trojan Horse 1970 (Abacus 1973). ((Also note the occult usage of the Egyptian 'Eye of Horus' pattern in a pyramid or triangle - see Illuminatus, in this issue's reviews, for extrapolations of this symbol - Ed.)) The 'tooth' is in the category of piercing things, thus eye-tooth, and "eye for an eye and tooth for a tooth".

3) ((a pierced eye? - Ed.)) The similarity in shape of the subterrantean eye of spiral lines and the human eye can be improved by extending a line back from the outer part of the human eye and around the face parallel to the eye's major axis. This was done by the ancient Egyptians on sarcophagi, etc. MIB sunglasses have a similar 'wraparound' line. See G Underwood's Patterns of the Past for diagrams of the 'geodetic eye'; and Elizabeth Taylor in make-up as Cleopatra.
4) Guy Underwood, Patterns of the Past, 1969 (Abacus 1972).

5) WR Drake, Gods & Spacemen (Amherst 1964).
6) The News 11/20.
7) Janet Bord, 'UFOs in Folklore', FSR 20:1, 1974.
8) The News 13/9.
9) The News 11/20
10) John A Keel, Our Haunted Planet, 1971 (Futura 1975).
11) John A Keel, Op.Trojan Horse; FSR Special Issue 2, 'Beyond Condon', notes p38.
12) Jim & Coral Lorenzen, UFOs Over the Americas (Signet 1968).
13) ...and of course the MIB are oft described as having good sun-tans. Using wrap-around sunglasses, however, the MIB keep the sun out of their eyes - but then isn't the subterraneam Eye of Horus out of the sunlight, and didn't the lady passengers in the 'mystery airships' of 1897 use sunshades and keep in the dark? This symbolic segregation of the male sun from the female (earth) element is the stuff myths are made of ((see Steve Moore's articles on yin-yang symbolism in phenomena in the previous three issues - Ed.)) whether we deal with contactee material about the dense wraparound clouds of Venus protecting its inhabitants from solar rays (see Drake's Gods & Spacemen, or Richard Shaver's 'Elders' taking to the caves to escape those harmful solar rays. The black colour associated with MIB may be a reference to black's power to absorb some radiation, or to the 'Blackmen' said to have built the ley system (see Alfred Watkins' The Old Straight Track, 1925 (Garnstone 1970, Abacus 1974))
14) John A Keel, Op Trojan Horse.
15) ((Anthony Bell has expounded to me in a letter the lexilinks from Uri Geller to to subterranean tell-uri-an forces -Ed.))
16) Dr Walter Buhler, 'The Mysterious Caconde Case', and Anthony J Brent, 'Two Creature Reports from New Zealand', FSR 15:4,1969.
17) When we hear descriptions like "an aircraft with its tailplane removed" or "an Egyptian glider with slots where the tail plane was attatched" etc, I think we are dealing with a solidification of the tau shape. You see,"they" are religious fanatics, and have got tired only of chopping trees into tau shapes! Similarly the "Flying Trumpet" UFO shapes are solidifications of the Eye of Horus shape. Talking of trumpets, note the similarity between Horus and horn.
18) Matthew Manning, The Link, 1974 (Corgi 1975); & Jacques Vallee, Anatomy of a Phenomenon, 1965 (Tandem 1974). ((At this point your Ed began to see rodballs all over the place. Flicking through FSR Case Histories August 1973, I found drawing of an entity with rodball eyes

Cont on p16...

bombing the house from trees and nearby power-lines, hurling themselves against the windows - then, dazed and bleeding, fly back to their posts to begin again. A fuller report in the West Briton 17 June 1976 (Cr: Doc Shiels) said that Mrs Swatton tried cutting out large black birds from cardboard and other suggestions from neighbours - but the trouble only stopped when a friend shot one bird and hung it over the balcony. Curiously , Mrs Swatton said the birds never attacked her or her daughters, even when they beat them off with sticks. Another ornithologist is quoted about birds attacking their own reflections during breeding seasons - the standard offering these days on the altars of explanation. But Mrs Swatton doubts it, and her reasons apply equally to our other cases. She says: "People have suggested the birds were attacking their own reflections in the glass, but could the birds have seen anything at night? " In the Payne case (above) the ornithologist expert suggested covering the windows with paper

to minimise reflections -- the Telegraph quotes Mrs Swatton: "I hung up sheets and newspapers on the windows and laid blankets over the carpets. Even then there was no stopping them." In the West Briton, she adds: "It has also been suggested the house is in the bird's flight path. But the house was here last year as well, and they never came then!" We might add that the reflection-attack theory sounds like a classic mystery-defusing placebo of an explanation to us - just plausible enough to sooth any anxiety in the public, but not compatible with reality under a close examination. Most experts really do think their laity are mindless morons. If birds attack their reflections on the scale of these events, even granted the ritual hostilities of the breeding season, why the hell doesn't it happen en masse up and down the county?

There's just so much stuff coming in on swarms of all kinds, we will have to leave it to the next issue.

MARS.
At the time of typing, Viking is making mudpies and cooking them on the surface of Mars and we await any signs of life. In commoration of the event here are a few Mars-items of interest.

Earlier this year, the controllers of Viking's flight at Pasadena lost contact with one of the soil experiments - this was about 24/25 January. The Daily Mirror 26 Jan 1976, quotes John Casani, of JPL, that this curious failure (which presumably rectified itself in time for the landing) happened in a volume of space known to the NASA bullpen as 'The Great Galactic Ghoul', a sort of interplanetary Bermuda Triangle where mysterious things go wrong with equipment. Casani amplifies this allusion in National Enquirer 16 March 1976: "Mariner Six was launched first in 1969, and Mariner Seven followed a week later. The Six flight went okay, but Seven ran into trouble about 35 million miles from Earth - a battery got dented, pressure built up and circuits

began to arc. A lot of batteries and antennas ((sic))were wrecked. We began to check out the area - no meteoric activity, no cosmic dust, no solar winds and no radiation - nothing, just clean empty space. Then somebody remembered that this area of space was the same place the Russian Mars probes, Zond Two and Mars One, got fouled up. Further checks showed that two more US space vehicles had suffered damage in the Ghoul's lair...and Mariner Nine, in 1971, had radio failure there. It could be a coincidence..." On the other hand it could be something familiar to every Kurt Vonnegut fan, his deus ex machina, a hiccup in Spacetime called 'The Chronosynclastic Infundibulum'!

Later, as Viking One neared its destination, its on-board cameras started to send back strange pictures of the Martian surface. Harold Masursky at Pasadena was quoted in the Daily Mirror 26 June 1976, on some features visible from 940 miles up: "We often see

things in these pictures that remind us of
things on earth. This looks like features
that we see in aerial photographs on earth,
but they all turn out to be roads." Masursky
thought the idea of roads on Mars "a little
extreme". Fortunately the scientists were
never pressed by events for long, for as the
craft neared the surface,all trace of the
lines, like the famous canals before them,
vanished. It seems to us they knew we were
coming. (Cr: also to A Bell for item in the
Yorkshire Post, same date.)

Perhaps the best summary to date of the
findings and interpretations of Mars data is
in New Scientist 29 July 1976. However, one
photo you won't find in it is the following,
published in the Daily Mail 27 July 1976 (Cr:
Ken Rogers), apparently showing the Roman
letter 'B' inscribed on one of the central
rocks in Viking's view...

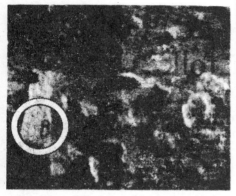

...The official explanation (there's
always one, Virginia) is the peculiar Martian
light playing tricks with chance erosion.
With a bit of luck the rest of the message
will appear on other rocks in the weeks to
come. ((I'm taking bets on "ugger Off!")). Post
Script: Having said you wont find this in
New Scientist, it inevitably turned up - see
the 12 Aug 1976 issue for confirmation of the
mark on the rock, but for once, no explanation.

As we go to press, the Viking Mission
Control, at Pasadena, announce that some of
the orbital photos reveal a peculiar ground
feature they liken to "a ploughed field". Dr
Michael Carr, jested about them being artifacts, but confessed that they were not dunes,
being regularly spaced and "changing direction". He could give no explanation - Daily
Telegraph 19 Aug 1976 (Cr: Ken Rogers).

CHINESE METEORITES.
On 8th March a large fireball exploded
over Kirin city in the province of Kirin, and
according to the official Chinese news agency
Hsinhua, it yeilded more than a 100 meteor-

ites of 200lbs each, the largest weighing
nearly 1½tons, believed to be a record for
recovered stoney meteorites. The smallest
weighed less than a ½lb. The fall occured in
an area of 260 sq miles on the outskirts of
Kirin, in north-eastern China, and despite
a population of more than 100,000 in the area,
no one was hurt. It began nearly 2 minutes
after 3pm and lasted just half a minute
before the largest chunk buried itself 18ft
in the ground,having smashed through 5½ft of
frozen soil. The final crater was about 10ft
deep. Its atmosphere entry speed was reckoned
at 7.5 miles per second. Newcastle Journal
(Cr: Paul Screeton), Royal Gazette (Bermuda)
(Cr: Phil Ledger), Los Angeles Times (Cr: MA
Hall), Daily Telegraph (Cr: Mrs V Martin.)
all dated 22 April 1976. See also an extensive
report in Peking Review (19:18) 30 April 1976,
and China Reconstructs (25:8) August 1976.

RUSSIAN METEORITES.
The Academy of Sciences seems to be
very busy these days, intensifying its interest in meteorites. It seems to be mounting
quite a few expeditions to search them out -
both geologically ancient falls and those
preserved in folk memory - and to judge from
recent reports they are having much success.
We have the following notes on file:

A 2276 gram meteorite was found in
Chukotka, north-east Siberia, during the
clearing of a brook. It is 90% iron with
nickel and cobalt traces, has a lamellar
structure of large crystals. Its age has not
been ascertained yet. Novosti Bulletin 15916.

According to the Soviet Weekly 11 Oct
1975 (Cr: Bryan Hartley) two meteorites, each
about half a ton, are being excavated in the
Soviet far-east (place unidentified). A rain
of 'meteors' was reported from the district
on 12 Feb 1947, falling over a wide area,
shattering rocks and leaving 24 craters of
30-90ft diameter and nearly a 100 smaller
ones.

An iron meteorite weighing an estimated
25 tons before it fragmented as it fell in
the Sihote-Alin mountains about 30 years ago
has finally been dated as 450 million years
old. Novosti Bulletin 36589.

Searches for a meteorite that fell near
Omsk in 1922, have, since that time, repeatedly failed to locate it. The puzzle was
finally solved by Prof Dravert of the Omsk
Mineralogical Institute...it was being used
by a local farmer as a weight on the lid of
a barrel in which he ferments his sauerkraut!
Sunday Express 20 June 1976, Reveille 16 July
1976 (Cr: Steve Moore.)

SUDANESE METEORITE.
A 5 kg stone meteorite that fell in the
Malakal region of the Sudan 3 years ago, has
been dated by Soviet scientists at 570 million years old, from fragments sent to the

Academy of Sciences by Khartoum University. The apparent youth of the object (most meteorites are thousands of millions of years old) suggested it had undergone several collisions with other bodies as it fell through space, gaining some traces of other elements and losing some radiogenic gases, Novosti Bulletin 14430.

NEAR MISS FOR NORTH AMERICA.

According to Time 4 March 1974 (Cr: Ion Will), a meteor streaked across the sky above Salt Lake City to pass over Idaho and Montana before disappearing north of Calgary, Canada, on 10 Aug 1972. The event was observed by a US Air Force satellite but the details were not released until the end of February 1974 - perhaps just as well. The 1000 ton meteor was hurtling along at 33,000 mph and just missed our planet by a heart-stopping 36 miles. It was about 13ft across and could have caused devastation on a scale not seen since Nagasaki and Hiroshima.

A GIFT FROM THE GODS.

So-called primitive societies have been scorned because they believe curious or powerful natural phenomena had or generated magical powers and properties. Ground struck by lighting is held sacred the world over, a sign of a god's passing, and never used for burial. Similarly meteorites acquired magical reputations, as talismans (the Kaaba, eg) or (being virtually a steel) being forged into swords whose potency was clear to all. Well here we are in the 20th century and must apply the word primitive to ourselves for the same reason. According to the Sunday People 11 January 1976 (Cr: many) Lady Eve Stuart Knill found this meteorite five years ago at Edingworth, near Bristol - lying on a road!

The meteorite . . . "like a cannon-ball.".

It doesn't say if its meteoric origin has been confirmed, but at least Lady Eve insists on calling the orange-sized thing by that name. She says that on impulse one day, she rubbed the stone on her shoulders where she had long suffered arthritis "and the pain stopped." She did the same for her feet and ganglion sores on her hands with equal success. News of the curative powers of the stone reached the ears of Dr Jack Fowler, a cancer research specialist at Mount Vernon Hospital, Northwood, Middlesex, who was intrigued enough to borrow it from Lady Eve to experiment with it on mice. His idea is that it is radioactive in a begnign ((yes Virginia, that is a typewriter word)) mode. We wrote to Dr Fowler some time ago, and needless to say we have no reply to date. It is interesting to note an archetypal structure to this story - as in the accounts of so many discoveries we have a chance (almost unbelievable) finding of an item and the impulse of intuition in putting it to use, almost as though it was the logical and natural thing to do!

BUFORA Conference 1976, Friday 5 Nov - Sunday 7 Nov, at Centre Hotel, Birmingham. Fee: £5 to members. Contact Jenny Randles, 23 Sunningdale Drive, Irlam, Gt Manchester.

The Northern UFO Network (NUFON) will be holding a meeting with W Raymond Drake, in Manchester on 23 October, to which those interested are invited. Inquiries to Jenny Randles: 23 Sunningdale Drive, Irlam, Greater Manchester M30 6NT. ((Illuminatus-spotters won't have missed those 23s - Ed)).

A lavish conference organised by the Institute of Parascience, will be held at the City University, Northampton Sq, London EC1V 4PB, Friday 27 August to Sunday 29 August. Apart from discussing latest developments in the parascience field, some of the planned talks link the subject with UFOs. Non-members £3; members £2,per day. Last minute bookings and info, contact: Peter Maddock, Parascience Conference 1976 c/o City University (tel: 01 253 4399).

*** <u>Tim Church</u> is interested in obtaining
material on UK mystery animals - will swap
for similar USA material or any other subject. Contact Tim: Box 932, Missoula, Mont
59801, USA.

*** <u>Frank Adey</u> has a Kirlian photography kit
(<u>Edscorp</u>, USA) for sale (£45). 130 Victoria
st, Willenhall, West Midlands WV13 1DW.

*** Your Editor wishes to move to London, for
various obscure reasons - so if anyone there
knows of a vacant flat that could house two
and a roomfull of books, please let him know
ASAP...(ideally, unfurnished & s/c...).

*** <u>Dr EC Krupp</u> writes that he is to lecture
on '<u>Fads & Myths in the Name of Science</u>' at
the University of California, Los Angeles,
throughout this Fall. Topics include UFOs,
Bermuda Triangle, Phantom Zoo (ABSM, Bigfoot,
Nessie, etc), Pyramid Power, the Earth Spirit,
Velikovsky, Continents Lost & Found, Ancient
Astronauts, etc. Those interested contact
UCLA.

*** <u>Fortean Times Poster</u>, silk-screened in
four colours by Hunt Emerson - £1.00/$2.00
(inc. slo-post); <u>free</u> if you donate this
sum or more to our survival fund.

UNIDENTIFIEDS

OLIVER...WHO?

"Why haven't we heard about Oliver?" an
irate reader wrote to me. Truth is I didn't
know much about him myself - nobody had sent
us any data. But we opened an Oliver file and
magically the data appeared, not much, but
some info and a story.

Sometime in the second week of January
this year, we heard a radio news item that a
man was hiding out on the west coast of the
USA with a baby Bigfoot he had aquired. We
didn't think much of this until CW Murray
sent us a page from <u>Time</u> 12 Jan 1976, which
named man and beast - a New York lawer,
Michael Miller, and a creature resembling a
"bald chimpanzee with an ear job and a sour
disposition." Miller was said to have bought
Oliver from an animal show for $10,000.

This stirred our normally sieve-like
memory, and sure enough, we found in <u>Pursuit</u>
(Oct 1975) a description by Robert E Jones,
of a visit he made with another SITU member
to a South African owner of an animal act,
Frank Burger. This act featured a peculiar
chimp called Oliver. Berger claimed that in
his seven years of life Oliver had never gone
on all fours, preferring to walk on two legs.
He has very little hair on his chest and
head, which is domed and has a squared-off
jawline. His eyes and ears are not like those
of normal chimps. His intelligence is exceptional: give him a quarter and he'll go off to
a soft-drink dispensing machine and bring
back a bottle. Apparently he even uses the

human's toilet, flushing it afterwards. Jones
said that specialists at a NY university
thought Oliver was a mongoloid chimp, which
is hard to accept in view of the claims that
he is much brighter than ordinary chimps.
Jones and his colleague thought Oliver a
cross-breed between chimp and a "Sehite or
Agogwe, the pygmy ABSM reported for many years
in Central Africa."

CHIMPLIKE CREATURE CALLED OLIVER
A peculiar fascination for humans.

Two items in the <u>Sun</u> for 4 March 1976:
that Miller was claiming Oliver to be an important discovery and may be the "missing link"
between apes and men (Cr: Ivan Bunn); and
cont on p20...

BLACK DOGS and WATER

BOB RICKARD (?) APOLOGIES TO MARVEL PREVIEW #5.

by Ivan Bunn

I was very interested in Steev Moore's articles on Greenwich Phenomena, and in particular his suggestion of a link between 'Black Dog' apparitions and water.

Over the past twelve months I have been collecting Black Dog stories from all over East Anglia (Norfolk, Suffolk, Essex and Cambridgeshire). This region is steeped in Black Dog lore, with the most famous (or infamous?) being 'Black Shuck'. Initially I was only concerned with the collection and collation of Black Dog legends, some of which are many generations old. Then it occured to me that if the creature had been so prolific in years gone by it would be interesting to see if I could obtain any recent first-hand accounts of it.

To this end I wrote to local newspapers throughout the region and I was astounded at the response. I have now collected over forty first-hand accounts of East Anglian Black Dogs spanning the last fifty years or so.

These stories all exhibit many common factors, but there is definitely one common denominator: almost without exception the location in which the dog has been seen is very close to, or on, a river or the coast, as a cursory glance at the accompanying map shows.

Perhaps at this juncture I should point out that the rivers marked on this map are the principal rivers of the area and do not include lesser tributaries or streams. The Black Dog locations marked on the map include every single one that I have reference to (both from local legend and first-hand accounts), and I have not just plotted those that occur on or near water. This map only covers a portion of the area from which I have obtained Black Dog stories, but the pattern is the same all over. As a matter of interest I did a breakdown of all the stories and legends (62 in all) to find the Black Dog/water relationship, if any. The results are quite startling, as the table shows... ((see foot of next page -Ed))

In a number of cases details were too scanty to plot exactly where the Black Dog was seen. In these cases I have taken the measurement to the furthest point possible from the river/sea within the bounds of the area stated in the legend.

Further evidence of this predeliction that Black Dogs seem to have for water can be found in an article written by Ethel Rudkin in 1938 (1). Miss Rudkin did an intensive survey of the Black Dog legends and stories of Lincolnshire. In her article she also comments on the fact that the majority of the stories of the Dog occur near rivers, streams and ponds.

In part three of his article, Steev comments on the fact that Black Dogs seem to occur mostly on level or low-lying ground. This is also true of over 95% of stories that I have collected. Steev also says that "Black Dogs are not entirely yin. They have the power of movement, which is a yang characteristic, and several Black Dog accounts mention them having large, blazing red eyes, which would indicate a certain yangness."

His first statement is unquestionably true, but I have reservations about the second. A large proportion of the legendary accounts of East Anglian Black Dogs do indeed mention 'large blazing eyes'. However, I have not yet received one first-hand account which mentions this characteristic. Almost without exception, eye witnesses talk of a large (sometimes huge) black dog which is often likened to a Great Dane. The dog is usually silent and appears and disappears very suddenly. In about 50% of these accounts the witnesses state that shortly after their encounter with the Black Dog a close relative has died suddenly. In fact the creature is generally regarded as a portent of death. I would venture to suggest that the 'large blazing eyes' are a feature which has been added to older stories and legends to add a bit of weight and colour.

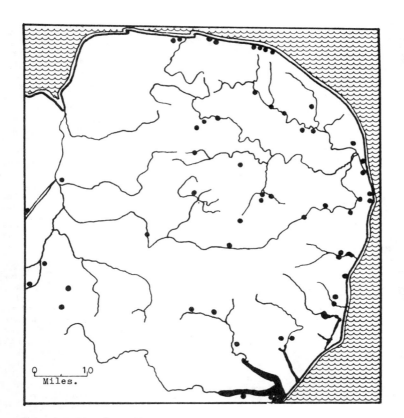

NORFOLK and SUFFOLK

with county boundaries
omitted, and showing
PRINCIPAL RIVERS and
sites of some
BLACK DOG LEGENDS.

Miles.

0   10

    East Anglia (and Norfolk and Suffolk
in particular) is still predominantly a
rural area, and it is interesting to
note that reports of MAs (except Black
Dogs) are very few and far between. So
it seems that Steev's suggestion that
MAs are just modern versions of Black
Dog apparitions, seen by more ignorant/
knowledgeable city-dwellers, stands up
well.
    Most readers will no doubt have not-
iced that I have made very little reference to yin and yang. This is simply
because my knowledge of the subject is

almost nil, to say the least. However,
I found Steev's arguments and hypothesis very interesting and thought provo-
king, and they have given me plenty of
ideas for further research in the East
Anglian 'Black Dog' apparitions. Thanks
Steev.
    Naturally, if any readers can supply
me with more details of Black Dogs,
either East Anglian or from further
afield, I would certainly be very
pleased to hear of them.

                        Ivan Bunn, 1976.

LOCATION TABLE

A.	Apparition	seen	on or very near a main river:		15 cases
B.	"	"	on or very near the sea/coast:		15 cases
C.	"	"	within a mile of the river/sea:		16 cases
D.	"	"	"	two miles of the river/sea:	9 cases
E.	"	"	"	three miles of the river/sea:	4 cases
F.	"	"	"	four miles of the river/sea:	1 case
G.	"	"	"	five miles or more of the river/sea:	2 cases

REFERENCE
1) Ethel Rudkin: The Black Dog.
       Folklore, Vol 49, 1938.

((Ivan edits the BSIG journal, Lantern, and
readers wishing to contact him about Black
Dogs can write to him at: 3 Dunwich Way,
Oulton Broad, Lowestoft, Suffolk -. Ed.))

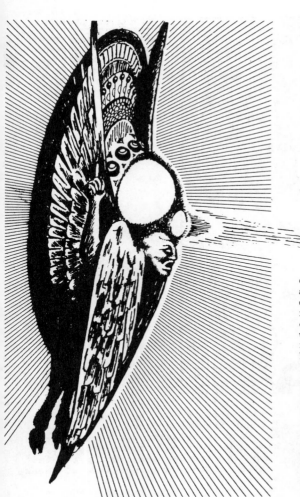

"..it is not enough to distinguish supernatural imaginative visions from the
natural products of the imagination; we
must also distinguish them from <u>diabolical
visions</u>...images which the devil is able
to produce in us never go beyond our
previous knowledge or the natural scope of
our mind. Even if he should provoke
heavenly images of our Lord, the Blessed
Virgin, or the saints and heavenly joys,
or else infernal images of spectres,
devils, infinite despair, or again, the
most seductive pictures of human passion,
there will be no new revelation, no
prophecy, nothing transcendental...the
transcendence of imaginative visions ▶

of nearly every scientific discipline, the
assimilation of just a few of which could
change the face of science as we have known
it. Bold explorers have been opening up our
conception of reality itself by recognising
whole new fields of phenomena not previously
included in the scientific world-view. We
have so few ways of guiding ourselves into
the Unknown that we could do much worse than
rely on Farges' distillation of the wisdom
of Sts Teresa and Thomas Aquinas (above)
reserving, of course, our interpretation of
the religious jargon. Another way of summarising it would be that only the truly
mad or the truly sane have any claim to
certainty, the rest of us as shades inbet-
ween have only degrees of doubt - doubt
first and foremost about whether our world-
view (or 'description' to use Castaneda's
term) corresponds at all, if it ever did,
with what is really going on in the universe.
For one thing we know the universe is reflexive (I prefer this term to Keel's use of
'imitative' or 'mimicing' - see <u>The Mothman
Prophecies</u>, 1975), and this reflexion involves the human mind and perception in ways
we scarcely dare to accept let alone understand.

    John Keel was probably the first of
the new breed of explorers to extend the
phenomenon of enigmatic entities in UFO cases
beyond the confines of the extraterrestrial
(ET) concept, recognising the continuity
with their counterparts in the mythology of
religion and folklore. More recently Jerome
Clark and Loren Coleman established this
legitimate insight, in their <u>The Unidentified</u>,
by showing that beneath the form of the
myth lay complex patterns of archetypal processes. This puts a different complexion on
previous interpretations of strange entities.

    If the last two centuries have seen
the rise of materialism and its handmaiden,
Science, it has also seen the parallel rise
in the unexplained, much to the former's
discomfort. Never before has interest in
mysticism, spiritualism, cult religion, the
occult, and indeed anything else which actually or apparently contradicts the edicts
of scientists, been so great or open. And
almost as if the universe has obliged us,
never before has there been such frequency
and variety in mystics, visions, miracles,
ghosts and poltergeists, monsters, UFOs and
their attendant menagerie, or the whole
range of Fortean phenomena. This year alone
must have topped any previous record, as <u>FT</u>
readers will have grasped, if not by now
then by the time we have published all our
bulging files. There are radical new discoveries and theories waiting in the wings

will always be a
characteristic of the
divine, which it is
impossible for the devil to
imitate or falsify. This is
the first test."

Mgr. Albert Farges,
Mystical Phenomena
(1926) p335f.

BIRDMEN OF THE APOCALYPSE!

by RJM Rickard.

BLIMEY!

BOB RICKARD: AUG. 76
(WITH APOLOGIES TO -
OZ 31 & THE FANATIC 3).

There are now two modes of interpretation in
the ultraterrestrial (UT) school, of reports
of weird entities in UFO contact cases or
associated phenomena, and it is likely that
both have a role to play in the drama. The
first view assumes that the contact experience was a 'private' affair and that some
sort of personal relationship exists primarily between the percipient and the phenomena
(which   may not have been entirely subjective) EG. in the case of the images that appeared on Stella Lansing's films (FSR 20:4-6,
21:1) Dr Berthold Schwarz suggests generally
that psychoanalysis of contactees may help
expose subconscious veins of experience,
expectation, psychoses etc being mined for
the imagery of the experience. (Further,
that the UFO may be in a strong psychodynamic relationship with the percipient, acting
in effect as a catalyst ((or psychoanalyst))
in drawing the material out into the consciousness to be experienced -- FSR 20:5 p22 &
24).   But although this could account for
personal details of the experience (NB: the
many references to personal relationships
with entities, telepathy etc, and the entities knowing personal details about the percipient, and indeed some of the phenomena
having a direct dream-like relationship to
events in the percipients life), it is very
weak in accounting for the form of the experience as related by many people all round
the world, and as Keel, Clark & Coleman, and
Vallee (Passport to Magonia) have shown, in
previous centuries too. The morphology of the
contact experience is remarkably consistent
for all times and places, whether these

entities be angels, fairies, elementals, demons, BHMs, the 'eternals' or 'Secret Chiefs'
who initiate mortals, MAs, BVMs, the pilots
of craft from other realities, or the winged
weirdos called variously 'mothmen', 'batmen'
or 'birdmen'. Even more significant is that
this morphology shows a continuity between
mythology, subjective visionary experience,
and apparently objective reality. ((This has
tremendous implications for Fortean data,
and your editor's book with John Michell sets
out to explore these.)) Thus the second view
of the UT hypothesis, that the psychodynamic
drama being played out, draws on deeper

levels of the psyche, the archetypes of unconscious symbolism. On this level there is
little that relates to the percipient that
does not also relate to every human mind on
the planet. I venture to suggest the experience may even be deeper than that, and that
what we are seeing is participation in the
unconscious life process of this planet, considering the planet as a living complex sym-
biotic whole, just as a man's dreams may be
related in a distant and impersonal way to
the individual cells of his body. Both views
are valid since each refers to a different
level of the experience.

Most of you know of Keel's special
interest in the 'mothmen' of West Virginia
(from 1966), and some of you may know that
Keel summarised most of the known similar
reports from earlier days in a chapter in
Strange Creatures from Time & Space - these
range from Brooklyn (1877), through Nebraska
(1922),to the 1946 'Ghost Rocket' scare in
Scandinavia. ((I can recommend readers, interested in the subject,   Loren E Gross' booklet The Mystery of the Ghost Rockets (1974) -
see our review section under his Fort/UFO
booklet, for details.)) Last issue we gave a
report from Doc Shiels (FT 16/19) on a 'bird-
man' (or 'owlman' as Doc prefers) seen at
Mawnan, Cornwall, during the sea-monster
scare - well we have had several more communications from Doc on further sightings. So
we decided to dig around to present a few
of the cases not included in Keel's books, or
that have happened since. Firstly, though, we
make the following portentous announcement:

THE KING OF CELESTIAL BEINGS
is coming! The 16th of April 1976 was
the first day of the year 1338 in the Burm-
ese calendar - and according to a note in
the Bangkok Post, 17 April 1976 (Cr: Ion Will)
astrologers have pointed out that this is
the appointed time in which the king of celestial beings will come down to earth with
a sickle in one hand and a scimitar in the
other to fight the galon, a gigantic bird

with supernatural powers. As if on cue, the
'owlman' of Mawnan was first seen on the
17th April. Before that though, we have the
'birdman' in Texas, seen in January. This
may indeed turn out to be the Year of the
Galon! But before we get onto these 1976
reports, let's stay in the far East, not far
from Burma, where a marine in Vietnam saw a
winged crittur in 1969.

THE WINGED LADY IN BLACK.
One night in July or August 1969, at
about 1 or 1.30am, Pfc Earl Morrison was on
guard duty, casually talking with two colleagues, when suddenly all three looked into
the sky and saw a glowing figure coming towards them "real slowly. All of a sudden we
saw what looked like wings, like a bat's,
only it was gigantic compared to what a regular bat would be. (As it got closer, they
could see) it looked like a woman. A naked
woman. She was black. Her skin was black...
the wings were black, everything was black.
But it glowed. It glowed in the night - kind
of a greenish cast to it...she glowed and
threw off a radiance." The creature's flapping wings were noiseless, and appeared to be
supported by normal arms "each with a hand
and fingers and everything, but they had
skin from the wings going over them...It
looked like (they) didn't have any bones in
them, because they were limber just like a
bat." The vision lasted about 3-4 minutes
and all the while the men were frozen, stunned by what they saw. "..about 10 feet or so
away from us, we started hearing her wings
flap. And it sounded...like regular wings
flapping." As a passing observation, I have
noted that a flapping sound or vibration is
a frequent detail, not only in contact experiences, but in many poltergeist cases,
often described as "like an invisible bird".
This winged lady was reported to FSR Case
Histories (June 1972, p14f) by Don Worley,
who transcribed the story from a taped interview, and who vouches for the veracity of
the main witness.

cont on next page...

Lexilinks (refs) cont...

19) ((I seem to remember this was suggested
in an article in The Ley Hunter by Mollie
Carey, but I cannot find the issue after
searching the heaps on my shelves. Her
drawing of a beacon on the flat top of
the mound was distinctly suggestive of a
rodball. A   coincidental discovery
while I searched for that TLH may shed
further light (literally) on the subject.
In Andrew Tomas' Atlantis (Sphere 1973)

he mentions that a delegate to a conference on streetlighting, in Pretoria 1963,
spoke of the accomplishments of a tribe
of Amazons located in the jungles of New
Guinea, near Mount Wilhelmina. Traders
reported they had 12ft diameter stone
spheres mounted on columns and radiating
an actinic light (p88)!!- Ed.))
20) Ivan T Sanderson, Uninvited Visitors
1969 (Tandem 1974).

MORE SEE MAWNAN'S OWLMAN.

The drawings on this page were sent to us by Doc Shiels in a letter dated 10 July 1976 - but in an earlier letter, he had hinted that the Owlman was back: "He's been seen again, I'm told, about a week ago ((as of 11 May)) over the village of Lamorna." Doc thought this might be a rumour because Lamorna is "quite a few miles outside Morgawr ((the local sea serpent)) territory. Maybe McCormick's talk about the Texan 'Big Bird' created Cornwall's version ...I know he mentioned it to several newsmen." (For data on McCormick, Morgawr and the Owlman's first appearance see FT 16). But just in case our overseas readers think any of these subjects got a coverage that could be noticed let me say that the press as a whole has been singularly silent; the only items being tiny generalised sarcasms tucked away in the back pages, and a couple of larger stories -but all on Morgawr, nothing on the Owlman, and minimal stuff on the Texan 'Big Bird'...in both cases our data comes from local papers (though the Big Bird got quite a lot of coverage in US papers).

Back to the latest on the Owlman. On 10 July, Doc wrote, saying: "The Owlman has been seen by two 14-year-old girls, Sally Chapman from Plymouth, staying with her friend Barbara Perry (who would only say that she lived 'quite near the river'). I met them last Sunday morning (the 4th) on Grebe Beach. They simply came up to me and said: 'Are you Doc Shiels? We've seen the bird monster.' We chatted, and they both drew pictures of the thing in my sketchbook. Now...it's a fact that the girlS had read the Morgawr booklet (*) and seen me interviewed on the telly, so they both knew, in advance, about the 'thing' and had a fair idea of what he

* *

* MORGAWR: The Monster of Falmouth Bay, by A Mawnan-Peller; a neat summary of the ancient & modern history of the Cornish sea serpent, plus its friends. Available from: 'Puck Fare', Ponsanooth, Truro, Cornwall, at 25p by post.

I saw this monster bird last night. It stood like a man then it flew up though the trees. It is as big as a man. Its eyes are red and shine brightly. Sally Chapman 4./7/'76.

Birdman monster. Seen on 3rd July, quite late at night but not quite dark. Red eyes. Black mouth. It was very big with great big wings and black claws. Feathers grey.

B. Perry 4th July 1976.

was supposed to look like...so it's quite possible that they invented the whole story to play a joke on this eccentric monster hunter. BUT...in various ways, they convinced me they could have seen it."

"They were camping out for the night among the trees not far from Mawnan Church ((site of the 17 April sighting)) . These trees cover the banks of the river for a great part of its length, above the rocky beaches. They were brewing-up around 10pm when they both heard a peculiar 'hissing' noise close by. Then they saw it, about 20 yards away (no more, they both assured me), standing among the pine trees. Sally said: 'It was like a big owl with pointed ears, as big as a man. The eyes were red and glowing. At first, I thought it was someone dressed up, playing a joke, trying to scare us. I laughed at it, we both did, then it went up in the air and we both screamed. When it went up, you could see its feet were like pincers.'"

"Barbara said: 'It's true. It was horrible, a nasty owl-face with big ears and big red eyes. It was covered in grey feathers. The claws on its feet were black. It just flew straight up and disappeared in the treetops.'"

"It seems they only saw the thing for a matter of seconds. The main things they noticed were its owl-like appearance, its size, the red glowing eyes and the 'claw-like pincers'. After they'd talked to me for awhile, I asked them to draw the pictures, separately, without either seeing the other's until they'd both finished. They agreed on most points, though Sally thought Barbara had 'done the wings wrong'".

Doc also sent a clipping from the Fal Mouth Packet, 9 July 1976, on an almost identical sighting by another young girl, on the same Sunday morning that Sally and Barbara were telling Doc about their experience the night before. The letter to the Packet is from Jane Greenwood, of Southport, and reads: "I am on holiday in Cornwall with my sister and our mother. I too have seen a big bird-thing like that pictured in the Morgawr booklet. It was Sunday (4th) morning and the place was in the trees near Mawnan Church, above the rocky beach. It was in the trees standing like a full-grown man, but the legs bent backwards like a bird's. It saw us and quickly jumped up and rose straight up through the trees. My sister and I saw it very clearly before it rose up. It has red slanting eyes and a very large mouth. The feathers are silver grey and so are his body and legs. the feet are like big black crabs claws. We were frightened at the time. It was so strange, like something out of a horror film. After the thing went up there were crackling sounds in the treetops for ages. Our mother thinks we made it all up just because we

read about these things, but that is not true. We really saw the bird man, though it could have been somebody playing a trick in very good costume and make-up. But how could it rise up like that? If we imagined it, then we both imagined the same thing at the same time."

And we might add, how did two pairs of young girls see almost identical things (one on the 3rd, one on the 4th), in the same place, apparently without collusion? The Morgawr booklet makes no mention of red eyes, black claws or the silver colour of the feathers, and its mention of "flapping wings" is absent from these girls' stories which both agree the thing was on the ground first then "rose" into the air in an unfamiliar way which startled them very much. We are very struck by the detail of the claw-like feet, which remind us of the entities who kidnapped Hickson and Parker at Pascagoula, in 1973 (see Ralph Blum's Beyond Earth, 1974) who had claws instead of hands.

We have discovered only two English bird-men cases before these modern ones, though according to Frank Hamel's Human Animals (1915 &1973) when English witches flew to their Sabbat, they frequently took the form of an owl, more so than any other bird. The oldest case is mentioned in the Morgawr booklet: that according to the Cornish Echo for 4 June 1926, two young boys were attacked by a peculiar, very large and aggressive "feathered thing", between Mount Hawke ((a suitable name, that)) and Porthtowan. Apparently it was hunted and eventually killed, and the body defied identification by all who saw it. If this was simply an attack by a bird alien to Britain, then note too the house at Newlyn, Cornwall, under attack by birds about the same time, but 50 years later (14 June 1976) in our bird-attack section, earlier. ((Also on this tack, Doc, in a letter of 19 June, mentions: "Birds have been acting strangely, in a Hitchcockian manner, down here, recently...Is it a coincidence that Daphne du Maurier (who wrote 'The Birds') and Frank Baker (who wrote 'Our Feathered Friends' - a nice horror story on which 'The Birds' was based) both live in Cornwall..? A fellow called Paul Francis, a fisherman, was telling me how oddly the gulls were behaving these days, attacking fishing boats, stealing bait from mackerel lines, etc. It all ties in. of course."))

The other UK birdman case happened in 1963, at Sandling Park, Hythe,Kent, and is definitely linked to UFOs. A group of young people were walking along a country road when they realised that a light in the sky was descending towards them. They "felt cold all over" and ran, but the light kept pace with them, 80yds away and 10ft above a field, until it disappeared behind some trees. Then they felt they were being watched.

"..the next thing (they) knew was that a dark figure was shambling across the field towards them. It seemed to be completely black, human-sized, but with no head. One strange feature was that it appeared to have wings of the kind associated with bats... with webbed feet.." (cf The Humanoids by Charles Bowen; Futura 1974 p20). The kids didn't wait, but ran. In the days that followed there were more sightings of lights, and discovery of flattened bracken, and large footprints. As a matter of interest we note that in the last week of June 1976 there were several UFO sightings in Cornwall (ie a few days prior to the two Owlman sightings). The first by a group of boys camping near Rock, near Wadebridge,of a light in the sky they thought was a UFO, and accompanied by a "spine-chilling sound" (The West Briton 1 July 1976 -- their schoolmaster later tried to debunk this as an aircraft and the calls of a peacock (!); his name was given as Mr Fernley Furze). The second was by a housewife of The Beacon, Falmouth, who saw three "fireballs" at 12.30 am on 1st July, over St Mawes and Flushing. This lady, who wished to remain anonymous, felt it was a "personal experience..it may be some intelligence contacting me as an individual." ((The nature of telepathic surveillance, as I mentioned earlier, seems to be interpreted as a personal contact, or a feeling of being watched.)) This story is from the Falmouth Packet 9 July 1976. (Cr: on both to Doc Shiels).

THE TEXAS BIG BIRD.

The collection of reports we have are a bit jumbled - so we venture this chronological reconstruction. Sometime in November 1975 rumours of a giant bird-like creature, the size of a car, which glided silently

in the night sky, were born during a sighting over a childrens' playground in Robstown, near Corpus Christi, Texas. Since then there have been a steady trickle of reports from places located along the Rio Grande valley, on the Mexican border. San Benito police chief Ted Cortez said that in December 1975, a terrified man rushed into the department saying he'd seen it, and later "two kids came over and said they saw it. It had a kind of bald head like a monkey."

During the first days of January 1976, the reports increased. A TV station at Harlingen showed a photograph of giant bird-like prints in a freshly-ploughed field. They had three toes, and were 9" wide by 12" long. That same day, two San Benito policemen, in separate cars, reported seeing a huge bird with a 15ft wingspan gliding over the city. Arturo Padilla said: "It more or less looked like a stork or pelican type of bird, with a wing-span like a pretty good sized car. It was white. I've done a lot of hunting but

I've never seen anything like it." Experts (who never saw the thing) later dismissed it as a blue heron. That same week Alverico Guajardo reported to the police that something hit his mobile-home with a sound like a sandbag. He ushered his wife and child into the home, grabbed a knife, and drove to the trailer's back in his car. There he saw a terrifying creature "4ft tall, with eyes like silver dollars, wings like a bird, and a face like a bat."

At Rio Grande City, 75 miles west of San Benito, the Sheriff spoke of rumours for the last 45 days of a giant bird in the area, and that there were reports that a half-man half-bird thing perched on top of the courthouse - but he emphasised he had no evidence to believe the stories were anything but rumours. By mid-January station KRIO in McAllen was offering a reward of $1000 to anyone who captures the monster alive and brings it to the station's studio. Despite this,nothing seems to have been seen of the BigBird until 24 Feb, when three teachers described two giant birds that swooped on their cars. Patricia Bryant, in one car, said they were "as big as a Piper Cub plane, with a wingspan of 15-20ft or more". She later identified it as similar to a picture of a pteranodon in an encyclopedia. "It was the biggest thing I've seen alive, particularly flying. My Lord, it lived 160 million years ago. It's just unreal. Where did it come from? How could it have survived all those millions of years and still be flying around here? It's enough of a shock to see one. Then to discover two is really frightening. It happened so fast and was such a shock. It was enormous and frightening." The other two teachers, David Rendon and Marsha Dahlberg, said one of the birds flew low over their cars, and cast a shadow over the entire road, and when they stopped they saw another one circling like a buzzard over a herd of cattle. Bryant added: "I could see the skeleton of this bird through the skin or feathers or whatever and it stood out black against the background of the grey feathers." School officials urged the teachers not to discuss the matter on campus for fear of frightening the children, and the school is identified only as a "rural district school". There is a brief statement of what "scientists believe", which demystified adds up to (and get this): it can't have been a pteranodon because they didn't have feathers. I bet they think that clears up the mystery too! Fontana Herald-News (CA), 12 Jan; Vancouver Sun (BC), Chicago Tribune (IL), 13 Jan; Houston Chronicle (TX), 14 Jan; Pretoria News (South Africa), 15 Jan; Thunder Bay Chronicle (Ont), 17 Jan; Houston Chronicle (TX), 26 Feb; Toronto Sun (Ont), 27 Feb 1976. (Cr: Crawford, MX, Mark A Hall, Chris Holtzhausen.)

A recent letter from Jerome Clark told us of his personal investigations into the Big Bird reports (to be published in the October 1976 issue of Oui). Jerry warns that some of the reports must be approached with some caution: that the "much-cited sighting at San Benito by two policemen was almost certainly of a conventional bird. The famous 'attack' at Eagle Pass appears to have been nothing more than a clumsy hoax. Still, there were authentic encounters with a shape-changer, as there have been in the San Benito area particularly for the past 3 decades."

###...LASTLY, BUT NOT THE END...

A few loosely connected comments. Doc rightly reminds us of the creatures relatives, the Harpies (which incidentally are suggested by Jungians as a symbol of the negative anima), the Garuda (a divine solar eagle used as a steed by Hindu gods), and the Tengu. The Tengu? I had to look that one up - but I should have known. The Tengus are supernatural birds who can turn themselves into men, and in Japanese folklore are often associated with deceit, but towards true heroes they use their powers of illusion constructively. (They taught Yoshitsune the art of swordsmanship.) Lafcadio Hearn translates a charming tale of a monk who rescues a Tengu from being beaten to death. By way of a reward the Tengu recreates the Buddha's sermon on Mount Gridhrakuta, which the monk had always regretted missing by living many decades after the Great Teaching. The Tengu produces the illusuion of going back in time so well the monk breaks his vow not to worship the image of the Buddha, and is catapulted to the present to confront the severely wounded Tengu - In Ghostly Japan, 1899. Now this vision, instigated by the Tengu, takes place in a pine grove, and glancing back over these pages I see that the site of the three Mawnan experiences were pine woods, and that brought to mind another story - one which may be a vital link in the continuity of the archetype between the phenomenal reality and the collective unconscious.

Geoffrey Hodson was a Theosophist who wrote several books on his experiences of seeing, psychicly, other realms of being and their denizens. In the penultimate chapter of Fairies at Work & at Play (1925) he describes the role of the 'Devas' (shining ones) in nature, most of them being associated with fir or pine trees, but 'overseeing', say, a wood, as a single living unit. One of his entries for June 1922 tells of encountering a deva in an open space on a hill in the Lake District. "My first impression was of a huge, brilliant crimson, bat-like thing, which fixed a pair of burning eyes upon me. The form was not concentrated into the true human shape, but was somehow spread out like a bat with a human face and eyes, and with wings outstretched over the mountainside. As soon as it felt itself to be observed it flashed into its proper shape, as if to confront us, fixed its piercing eyes upon us, and then sank into the hillside and disappeared." Hodson estimated the spread of its 'wings' and 'aura' to be "several hundred feet" sweeping back behind the body in "wing-like sheets", and its final form was about 10-12ft high. It radiated virility and a powerful, raw natural force that profoundly affected Hodson. "My physical body thrilled for hours afterwards with the force of the contact and the rapport established between us." Later Hodson describes some tree-Devas, who rise up to, and move about "at the height of the topmost branches of the trees, and though they occasionally rise further into the air they do not appear to descend to the ground."

RJM Rickard - July 1976

■■

Oliver, cont...

that John Blashford-Snell was flying to NY to examine a captured "missing link" from Zaire, described as an"intelligent hairy pygmy" (Cr: Nigel Watson). These two items are uncorrelated in the paper, but seem to refer to the same case, ie Oliver. Blashford-Snell, some of you may remember, is the man who "solved" the Yeti question as a family of snow-squatting holy-men with big feet (see News 15/11).

The final item we have is from Reveille 2 July 1976 (Cr: Graham Crowley), and refers to Oliver's country of origin less specific ally - "the Congo River basin of West Africa" - but it does allude to legends of "hairy men" in that region. Other new information about Oliver is that he has four teeth (no one knows what happened to the rest), and emits a pungent smell most of the time. He also seems to generate "excessive aggression" in other animals towards him, a familiar detail in most stories of mutants (see 'The Malton Mutant' in News 15/6). As to what he is - this item suggests that he is being examined by the "world's top zoologists" who so far have discovered the missing teeth and that Oliver is 7yrs old. Wonderful! they can read newspapers! Actually my sarcasm is directed not at the experts but the fatuous standard of modern reporting which insists on patronising its public by being deliberately facile about scientific details its thought they 'are not interested in'. Reveille says that in tests, scientists have discovered Oliver has "abnormal chromosome levels" whatever the hell they mean by that! No details of any kind, or even a name, are given. Doubtless we haven't heard the last of Oliver...but meantime here's a comment from Hunt Emerson:

THATS **ANOTHER** FINE MESS HE'S GOTTEN ME INTO!

HUNT EMERSON

A YETI HOAX?

On 24 May 1975, Sri R Das, Superintendent of Police for Dibrugarh district, Assam, announced that tribesmen in the Khamti forest in Arunachal Pradesh had captured a pair of "wildmen", a male and a female, with an estimated height of 10ft. He said that arrangements were being made to ship the creatures to the Tirap district headquarters at Tezu for investigation.

The next day reporters discovered that Das's information had come from a report by the officer-in-charge of the Doom Dooma police station. This officer said his information, in turn, came from widespread talk that the creatures had been captured alive in the Chowkhani part of the forest, about 50 miles from Doom Dooma. He had not been able to find any eye-witnesses or official sources to confirm this. Another unconfirmed report alleged that the creatures were seen in the company (or custody, no one is sure) of personnel of the Military Engineering Service, and a squad of policemen led by an Army captain set out from Doom Dooma to check on this lead.

On the 26th, the officer-in-charge at Doom Dooma said that this squad had been unable to discover any thing at all, and that it looked like the original reports were a hoax. Experts from Gauhati University, as is the wont of experts everywhere, theorised in terms of gibbons and bears. Meanwhile, back at Dibrugarh, Superintendent Das had egg on his face, and rather weakly joked about being amazed how the press could pick up a casual comment made by him on a provincial rumour and blow it up into a full-scale mystery.

Perhaps he's right - but we are intrigued by a footnote saving the "experts ruled out the possibility of them being Yeti as they were not to be found at such low altitude." Sounds like some things are taken quite seriously. This story is compiled from reports in the Assam Tribune (Gauhati, India) 25, 26 & 27 May 1975 (Cr: Mark A Hall).

...AND A BIGFOOT KIDNAP HOAX?

Four witnesses said they saw "a large hairy ape-like animal" carry off a 23-yr-old blonde girl, called variously in reports, Sherie Darvell, Cherie Darvell and Sherry Nelson (!), on 22 May this year, in rugged country outside Eureka, California. The beast was described as "smelly" which reminds me that when Archimedes leapt out of his bath yelling "Eureka!" someone said to him, "You don't smella so good yourself!", which just about sums this case up. Not only was it the first time anyone is alleged to have been attacked by a Bigfoot, but the girl was part of a television crew hoping to film the crittur. Despite the huge likelihood of a hoax police took the claim that a girl was missing seriously and began a ground and air search. Two days later she turned up outside the Bluff Creek resort, about 5 miles from where she was allegedly abducted. According to statements by the sheriff and his assistants "She was in good shape" with a few minor scratches and bruises on her arms, one of her shoes was missing, and more cynically, "She certainly smelled pretty sweet for having been snatched by a smelly old beast." Sheriff Gene Cox, who is quite unamused, said that attempts to question the girl about what happened in the two days, brought only screams from her and a refusal to answer any more questions. Daily Mirror, (Reading) Evening Post 25 May 1976; (Bermuda) Royal Gazette, (NY) Herald Tribune, 26 May 1976; (NY) Herald Tribune, 27 May 1976 (Cr: Robert Forrest, John Michell, Phil Ledger, Ken Rogers, Steve Moore.)

YETI ATTACK.

The dubious case above put me in mind of the reports of an attack by a yeti last year which has a higher probability of truth, and which, though widely mentioned in the press, I've not seen recorded in any Fortean magazine. We'll remedy that here.

The attack was a few days before 18 July 1974, at a place called Marche, not far from the village of Pheriche, Nepal. A 19-yr-old girl, Lakpa Sherpani, was looking after a herd of yaks, when she says she was knocked unconscious by a yeti which slaughtered her cow and four of the yaks. She described it as: "..about 4 or 5 feet, covered with thick black hair below the waist and brown hair above. It had thick stout fingers with long nails and its heel was turned forward." It killed the yaks, according to some reports, "by twisting their horns around their necks."(!!) San Francisco Chronicle 18 & 26 July 1974; St Louis Post-Dispatch 18 July 1974; Sunday Times 28 July 1974; Atlanta Journal & Constitution (GA) 9 March 1975, which mentioned that police photos of the footprints did not turn out, that the girl was "still hospitalised", and that her description was remarkably like that given by Sherpa Tenzing in his autobiography , of beasts seen by his father in the Barun glacier, eastern Nepal, of a large pointy-headed monkey, with sunken eyes, walking on its feet about 4ft tall, with its hair growing upward above the waist, and downward below it. (Cr: for these sources: Mark A Hall, Loren Coleman, Phil Ledger, Leslie Shepard.)

Nigel Watson sent us a piece from the Reveille 2 May 1975, which seems to be under the impression the event had only just happened - in fact they were nearly a year late. However they do have some additional quotes from Lhakpa Sherpani on the monster, now said to be "over 7ft". She saw it as it ripped the throat out of her cow and "smashed the yaks' heads with his huge fists. He had a white stripe running down his chest to his stomach and another white stripe from the centre of his forehead to the top of his head. His eyebrows were grey and thick and he had round eyes like an ox. His lips were black and his mouth was large and he had big white teeth like human teeth. His feet looked human except they were covered with hair." There is also a quote from a police Inspector Chatra Nan Ral, who is convinced it was a yeti because "no beast I know of could have mutilated her animals that way. One yak had been ripped apart and savagely gnawed by a beast with phenomenal strength. I found prints at the scene which were not human. Four footprints were about 14" long and 6" wide, and deep indicating the yeti was extremely heavy. There were two handprints." By all accounts it seems as if Lhakpa had a very lucky escape.

MORE BIGFEET TALES.
Under the classic Fortean heading of 'Zoo, Police solve Bigfoot mystery' comes the news that in recent months there were numerous reports of a "large hairy creature" roaming in the countryside near Cincinnati, Ohio. After a sighting "last week", police rushed to the scene and made a mould of what they supposed was one of the prints, later identified by the director of Cincinnati Zoo, as "a large dog." And that, as far as officials are concerned, is that - for them the problem has been 'solved', which in the Fortean dictionary means grasping at the most acceptable solution. By acceptable, we mean safe. It's an easy guess for us the matter is far from ended. Houston Chronicle (TX) 2 March 1976 (Cr: Mark A Hall).

Something is leaving giant footprints, 15" long by 6½" wide, in the hills of Alcorn County, Mississippi, near Corinth. They were first spotted on 14 March near Smith Bridge road, north of US 72; since then other huge tracks have been found within 5 miles of Hatchie Chapel. Joe McKewen, a local naturalist, reckons the tracks indicate a creature 8ft tall weighing 450-500lbs. He said a "big hairy creature" was seen by two boys about 2 years ago, knocking down the door of their cabin and scaring them before they ran away - and a farmer saw a BHM ((for convenience we'll use this for big hairy monster, since ABSM seems out of place, not all BHMs being Abominable Snowmen, nor identified as Bigfoot)) in one of his fields. Richmond News Leader (VA) 24 March 1976 (Cr: Mark Hall); Victoria Colonist (BC, Canada) 25 March 1976 (Cr: MX).

A BHM that screeched horribly & walked upright, left a disembowelled and mangled deer carcass at Mill Valley, California, on the north side of San Francisco Bay, where there is a legend of a Bigfoot on Mount Tamalpais. Just after midnight on 23 March this year, Caroline Morris, 26, reported to the police a frightening "screaming, screeching and growling" in a ravine below her hillside home. Two patrolmen also heard the noise when they arrived. They searched the wooded slopes by flashlight and heard something moving through the underbrush, breathing heavily. One of them thought he glimpsed a "large dark coloured thing climbing over an 8ft retaining wall." In the morning they returned to the scene to follow a trail of blood to the deer. Experts thought the deer had been killed by a mountain lion. Los Angeles Times (CA) 26 April 1976 (Cr: Dr EC Krupp).

A foul-smelling BHM that haunts the Florida Everglades, nicknamed the 'Skunk Ape', has once more eluded capture. Two brothers were driving along a dirt road, near North Fort Myers, when they saw an ape-like creature in a clump of pine trees about 10yds from the road, "about 6ft tall with long black hair." The area was searched, and samples of lice-ridden hair, thought to be from the BHM, were found on a barbed wire fence. They were sent to Dr J Manson Valentine, anthropologist and Atlantis-hunter, of University of Miami, for identification. Atlanta Constitution (GA) 11 June 1976. (Cr: Mark Hall).

■■

SURVIVAL REPORT -- very slowly the number of readers is creeping up. There have been no increases in prices beyond the expected in the last months so we have on paper at last passed our breakeven point on costs. But because not everybody renews at the same time, not all the money is here at one time. We still need more subscribers to iron out the fluctuations and allow us to grow. I hope you will all continue your appreciated help.

NEWS

This year has seen some exciting changes in the little but far-reaching field of our interests. We changed our name without too much disagreement, and MUFOB, The Ley Hunter and Pursuit have new editors (John Rimmer, Paul Devereux & John A Keel, respectively). Here in the UK the small mag world is particularly precarious and TLH, MUFOB and ourselves have discussed working together in mutual support, and between us three we cover the major fields of current interest. Your editor is also highly chuffed that MUFOB and TLH both consulted him on production matters before finally deciding to switch to very similar formats to ours - the result reinforces our unity of intent, I think. FT also bridges the Atlantic into another triumvirate - forming the 'Big Three' of Forteana - ourselves, INFO Journal and Pursuit. Here too, all the editors involved have expressed their desire to work towards closer cooperation and mutual aid, all of which bodes well for our joint future. The most predictable benefit will be the fast exchange of up-to-date info, etc - from there on there is no limit to joint projects. Stay tuned for developments.

In one of the early issues of The News we gave the address of Tom Miller's Assassin's Information Bureau. Reader Wilfried Pardon wrote saying the address was incorrect or changed. The AIB's new address is: 63 Inman St, Cambridge, Mass 02138, USA. This is not a set-up for would-be assassins, but to disseminate info and investigation reports and theories on assassination mysteries.

According to a news announcement we saw back in May, Mr Spock, aka Leonard Nimoy, is to introduce a new series of TV films, called In Search of ---. The blank will be filled in by 'UFOs', 'Atlantis', 'Bigfoot', etc. Whether these are documentaries or not we can't say. Does any reader know more?

Anthony and Jan Roberts' Zodiac House Publications have scheduled for release at the winter solstice a compendium of articles on the traditions and mysteries of Glastonbury, from John Michell, Mary Caine, Kenneth Knight, and many others, to be called Glastonbury: Ancient Avalon: New Jerusalem. This will be followed in due course by a book on dragons by Paul Screeton; 'Chinese Fox-Faries' by Steve Moore; a gazeteer of major British leys; and a booklet on megalithic 'egg-stones'. Their publication in 1972 of Richard Holder's poems Songs of Mu & Atlantis has a grand follow-up. Canterbury University have commisioned the whole suite to be set to music and performed at the Gulbenkian Theatre, Canterbury, on Sunday 8th November. Holder has been given full electronic facilities. For details of ZH material, write to: Zodiac House, 7 Hugon Rd, Fulham, London SW6 3EL.

Arthur Shuttlewood and friends have set up an information centre at Warminster as a clearing house for UFO and other local data, accommodation for sky-watchers, and general informed hospitality for questing visitors. The Fountain Centre, Star House, 78 Portway, Warminster, Wiltshire.

Ken Campbell tells us that he has written a cycle of 5 plays, called The Eye in the Pyramid, based on the Illuminatus novels (see book reviews, this issue). From 23rd November (naturally) there will be a different (5 x 23min acts) play each night, from Tuesday to Saturday; and on the Sunday, the entire cycle will be performed in a bum-numbing marathon. The venue is the Liverpool School of Language, Music, Dream & Pun (no kidding), 18 Mathew St, Liverpool 2. Ken assures me that the plays will make brains boggle, and will be the biggest thing in the theatre for some years. If you can, read the novels before you go, so you won't miss any of the intricacies or paranoia.

Peruvian Ground Drawings -- the last scheduled UK stop of this exhibition of Maria Reiche's astonishing photos of the now famous and enigmatic lines on the Nazca plains, Peru, in the Mappin Art Gallery, in Sheffield, 28 August to 19 Sept. A catalogue of the photos is on sale, or otherwise available from the ICA gallery, London, or the Arts Council, 105 Picadilly, London.

HARDBACKS

The Sirius Mystery; Was Earth visited
by intelligent beings from a planet in
the system of the star Sirius? by Robert KG
Temple (Sidgwick & Jackson; £6.95; pp290;
index, bib, appendices, plates, diagrams)--
I have been harshly critical in the past of
the von Daniken school, not for any flaw in
the basic concept, but because their breathless advocation of the concept was spiritually bankrupt, 'explaining-away' any evidence
(sometimes not even puzzling evidence) of
human ingenuity and creativity as the result
of alien intervention, as though those
qualities never spontaneously arise, or
count for nothing. Temple admits the temp-
tation to write another catalogue of wonders
was very great, but thank heavens he manag-
to restrict himself to one fascinating problem. How did the Dogon tribe of Mali in
West Africa know of the companion star of
Sirius, invisible to the eye, and only
photographed in 1970? As the detective work
unfolds the question is answered (they learned it from the ancient Egyptians who enshrined their knowledge of Sirius in a wealth
of legend, and in the network of oracle-
centres that ring the Mediterranean) and replaced by the more complex and far-reaching
question of the title.

The conclusion is inescapable - the
facts of the Sirius mystery are incontrovertible - and Temple seems a little embar-
assed by having to voice an emphatic "Yes!"
For once the blurb is right: where others
have offered only weakly supported conjecture, Temple provides a singular and specific
proof of extraterrestrial contact. I for one
hope this will reverse the distressing trend
away from scholarship in the field, for
The Sirius Mystery is a model of reasoning
and research in a difficult subject. Like
Velikovsky, Temple had to aquire new skills
and one hopes that unlike Velikovsky, Temple
will be spared the childish chauvinism of
scientists outraged at the intrusion of an
'outsider' into what many of them regard as
their own private preserves of knowledge.
Like Velikovsky's work too, the spinoff implications for the social history and origins
of man are of incalculable consequence. That
is the essence of this book and there is
nothing I can add further, other than to
urge you all to read and buy a copy. As a
bonus you will get here not only rare documentation on the problem, but for the first
time in translation, rare fragments on the
strange beings from other worlds recorded in
the writings of the Neo-Platonist philosophers, and others of the early centuries of
our era who bothered enough to record this
ancient (even then) knowledge. You will also
learn much about Greek and Roman mythology

that is not included on any academic curri-
culum. At last an authoritative reference
on the subject of ET contact, and one I
would feel confident in recommending to even
the most dedicated anti-ET skeptic.

Gifts of Unknown Things by Lyall Watson (Hodder & Stoughton; £3.95; pp240;
brief bib) -- The story of a period Watson
was marooned among a small moslem community
on a pseudonymous island, Nus Tarian, in
Indonesia. Taking off on the various events
of an unusual (to him) nature that happen in
that community, Watson contrasts the unity,
simplicity and harmony of their lives with
how we live (if that's the term) in the West.
The book is very thin on material, and largely follows the annual ritual dance dramas,
and a young girl, Tiamat, who (Watson claims)
can raise the dead, bring down fire from
heaven, heal at a touch and induce visions
in those who watch her dance.

Watson's intention is to show the basic
differences in the approach to the great
universe as a whole between 'us' and 'them',
and to invoke our sense of wonder (and indeed
worship) at the "suchness" of it all (to
borrow the Zen term). Unfortunately he fails,
because his heavily impressionistic style
very suitable for the natural magic of the
events themselves is spread over the entire
book creating a monotonous chant. One can
also detect a sad pessimism behind the brave
smile, as though Watson realised that despite
his fine words, 'the West' will continue on
its blind, uncaring, materialistic path. This
makes it a very personal book — one man's
meander around the age-old problems of ont-
ology and eschatology - and completes his
slide from the objectivity of Supernature
into a romantic subjective and disillusioned
retreat from the world most of us live in.
For example he is scathing about the "cult of
extraterrestrial intelligence" which has
already become a "fashionable creed" with its
own dogmas - and he finds more inspiration

in the life-cycle of the liver fluke, which
at one point gangs-up and hijacks an ant by
overriding its brain, ordering it up to the
top of a grass stem to await a browsing
sheep, the host for the colony's next transformation. The book is peppered with little
drawings of ants, and I guess Watson is implying that for all our vaunted intelligence
we have no more control over our affairs, en
masse, than a fluke-ridden ant - that we are
all subject to a greater pattern of events.

Watson is clearly in a transition
phase between his scientific and his natural
mystical views of the world. If he can hold
it together until the two fuse his next book
could really be something - this one should
have remained in the pages of his diary until
then.

The Power of the Pendulum by TC Lethbridge (Routledge & Kegan Paul; £3.25;
pp138; appendix) -- This is Lethbridge's
last book and develops his earlier ideas on
the nature of time, higher dimensions, and
the 'fields' around things that can be detected with the pendulum technique. From his
observation that most objects appear to have
two distinct pendulum rates, and that the
fields around them can be 'charged' with
thoughts, images or impressions, Lethbridge
postulates a higher existance which can be
practically explored through dreams, the
pendulum and other methods of uncovering the
layers of information in these fields. The
exposition, as always, is intriguing, with
the honest humility of a genuine pioneer, and
we can only wonder with Colin Wilson (in his
introduction) to what new insights and discoveries Lethbridge would have worked had he
lived. The record of his thoughts is with us
here, waiting to picked up on, and together
his books seem to hint at pieces of our cosmic jigsaw. There is a long appendix on
different types of dreams, drawn from his own
experience and those of friends.

The Mystery of Atlantis by Charles Berlitz (Souvenir Press; £3.50; pp212;
bib) -- Not a sequel to his incredibly successful The Bermuda Triangle, but in fact a
book written in 1969, now released in England
for the first time. It is an attempt to con-
solidate the evidence for Atlantis drawn
from material and literary sources, myth and
lore - and an interesting collection it is
too, especially the sections and photographs
of the discoveries at Bimini, the Azores and
the Aegean sea. Though Berlitz devotes much
space to the numerous fascinating remains of
cities now below the sea, the links to Atlantis remain contentious - the name (like biro,
cellotape or hoover etc,)now applies generally, in this case to any sunken land. There is
minimal reference to the obligatory UFOs and
Berlitz is more restrained in his speculations, a factor by which the book benefits.
If only he had continued this approach into
the Triangle book.

Strange Artifacts compiled and published by William R Corliss (The Sourcebook Project, Glen Arm, Maryland 21057, USA;
$7.95; pp287; fully indexed) -- This is vol-
ume M2 in the laudable Sourcebook project
which is endevouring to collect and reprint
key and rare reference material on the whole
gamut of the odd - the M series being on
'Ancient Man'. This volume contains material
on the origins of the American Indians; fossil footprints and curious petrified human
remains; ancient technological artifacts and
evidences; hill figures, and other graphic
'macroforms'; petroglyphs and marked stones;
undeciphered inscriptions; collossi; Chinese
contacts with America; legends of giants,

dwarfs and relics of same; legends of cosmology and the origin of technology; celtic
flints; megalithic structures (buildings,
canals, dolmens, forts, mounds, henges, pyramids, roads, tunnels and walls). The series
is constructed so that sections can be assembled to suit the researcher's predilictions.
The indexes are divided into sources, places
and subject, and are cumulative (ie. they
include the material in vol M1). This is a
reference series no researcher or library
should be without - more details on the
other volumes and subjects can be had from
Corliss at the above address.

Speak, Shining Stranger (from AUM: Box
5310, Austin, Texas 78763, USA; $8.95;
pp239) -- The Association for the Understanding of Man (AUM) is involved in projects
ranging from what they call "psychical archeology" to UFO monitoring to research into
the psychic components of pregnancy, birth
and child rearing. Many of these activities
seem to centre on Ray Stanford who appears
to have picked up where Edgar Cayce left off.
Regular sessions are held in which he goes
into trance and delivers sermons or readings
on all manner of topics. Some of these are
collected into this book, and deal with
healing, prayer, dreams, drugs, the 'occult',
the meaning of suffering, death and after,
the 'White Brotherhood', the life of Jesus,
and so on. Although the readings are given
a variety of voices and personalities, Stanford confesses that he does not know if they
exist "outside my own unconscious mind", and
if not then we have an indication of the
extraordinary capacities of this unknown
region. Your editor knows no way to evaluate
this kind of material except to judge it on
its 'spirit', and these writings seem honest,
clear and inspired. Whatever you make of them
will depend on your inclinations - I found
them interesting and worthy of my time. Who
knows what they are? In the presence of this
kind of material I usually feel quite insignificant, like standing on an unknown shore
and staring out at some vast and infinite
sea. I have my reservations, but I'll not
deny any path to knowledge on the grounds
that it is absurd, or for the faithful or
the gullible.

PAPERBACKS

Charles Fort, The Fortean Society &
UFOs by Loren E Gross: 38675 Paseo
Padre #305, Fremont, CA 94536, USA; 113pp;
$2.00. -- At last someone has seriously
examined and recognised, in a study, Fort's
important contribution to the problem we
now call UFOs. Although Fort broached the
idea of visitors to this earth from elsewhere many times since The Book of the Dam-

<u>ned</u> first came out in 1919, we are only just beginning to understand the breadth of his vision. Not only was he a serious advocate of spaceflight at that time ((several let-including this subject appeared in New York papers)) but saw the overlap with many other areas of his data. Consider his shocking suggestion: "I think we're property...That once upon a time, this earth was No-man's Land, that other worlds explored and colonized here, and fought among themselves for possession, but that now it's owned by something...all others warned off." (<u>The Books</u> p163). Here, long before the von Däniken school, are the suggestions that perhaps giants from space built the huge megalithic monuments, and that the lights in the sky were "super-constructions", the ships of voyagers from other worlds. Fort even anticipated the parapsychological link of the UTH, now proving to be a fruitful field of study: "Some day I shall publish data that lead me to suspect that many appearances on this earth that were once upon a time interpreted by theologians and demonologists, but are now supposed to be the subject-matter of psychic research, were beings from and objects that visited this earth, not from a spiritual existence, but from outer space." (<u>The Books</u> p419f). It is important to stress that contrary to the opinion of many authors who show a fundamental misunderstanding of Fort's singular technique by insisting he believed these theories, Fort regarded them merely as possibilities, like many other possibilities as subjects for discussion, patterns around which information could be organised. Belief, which implies a degree of intellectual allegiace, was furthest from Fort's mind.

Gross, refreshingly, avoids this error in a direct way; his interest is primarily as a historian of the UFO phenomenon itself, and Fort as probably the first in modern times to collect accounts of sightings. Gross is far less interested in Fort's speculations on the subject than in this data gathered by Fort, and later the Fortean Society under Thayer. Nevertheless his picture of Fort seems to be accurate and well researched, even if this picture is limited (at one point Gross calls Fort's UFO data, his "only really significant contribution to history" This pecadillo aside, we have here a rare & valuable work of scholarship in the history of the study of UFOs, covering the period of mysterious aerial lights between August 1895 and August 1947 - a period which also saw the airship flap of 1896, and the 'Ghost Rockets' of 1946, both detailed in two earlier booklets by Gross ((copies now only obtainable from Centre for UFO Studies, 924 Chicago Avenue, Evanston, IL 60202, USA)). One fascinating aspect that Gross mentions

(and I wish he could have devoted more space to - but hell! it's a whole subject in itself) is the relationship of reported sightings to the rising genre of science-fiction in the pulp mags of the first half of this century. He does mention, though, a story in <u>Amazing Stories</u> of October 1946, which anticipated the now classic contactee elements as the invisible ray that stops the car, the telepathic contact with the entities, and the statements by the entities that they have come to save mankind from the errors of his technological path.

This is a booklet no serious UFOlogist should be without. Only 500 were printed, so you'd better hurry and send your $2.00 to Gross at the address above.

<u>Dowsing for Metals</u> by Michael Wild; 24pp; 60p (postage: 15p UK, 20p overseas) -- being a concise and practical guide to the methods and theories of dowsing for metals, based on a review of the contributions of the key innovators in the field (eg. De France, Mermet, Trinder, Lethbridge, etc). All you need to know to get those good vibrations on your own...

From Fenris Wolf/ Institute of Geomancy -- <u>Central European Geomancy</u> (75p) being translations by P Jones & M Behrend of selected studies by Kurt Gerlach and Josef Heinsch on traces of the prehistoric geomancy of Central Europe, medieval Bohemia, and the Holy Roman Empire. Classic material of the National Socialists' search for their pagan roots - valuable material in English translation for the first time -- <u>WH Black:</u> <u>Pioneer Geomantic Researcher</u> (IGR occasional paper 4) being selected writings of a pioneer who preceeded Watkins in the 1820s -- <u>Stan-ton Drew</u> (IGR occasional paper 5) a reprint of the 1876 study of this famous megalithic complex by CW Dymond -- <u>Geomancy of Glaston-bury Abbey</u>, being a geomantic analysis of the legend, site and architecture by Nigel Pennick. All inquiries to <u>FW/IGR</u>: 142 Pheasant Rise, Bar Hill, Cambridge CB3 8SD, UK.

<u>Illuminatus!</u> by Robert Shea & Robert Anton Wilson; Dell; 3 volumes; $1.50 each -- a rambling story that trips through the Kennedy assassinations; a plot to release a heinous Anthrax-Leprosy virus; the notorious Chicago convention; how Hagbard Celine, the last of the freebooters, bought the Mafia with gold looted from an Atlantean temple; how 'they' shot a fake John Dillinger, leaving five clones on the loose; a revolution on the small island of Fernando Poo inspired by the minions of Chthulu; a whole regiment of Nazi stormtroopers in suspended animation on the bed of a Swiss lake awaiting activation by a rockgroup bent on world domination. Meet talking dolphins; Adam Weishaupt, who founded the Illuminati in

1776 (yeah! on 1st May, too) then fled to America when the sect got busted, changing his name to George Washington, and tending his huge marijuana plantations (why d'you think he looks so stoned on the dollar bill?) Padre Pederasty who recruits for numerous anarchist movements all using each other as cover; Atlanta Hope who uses her frightful anti-porn female militia, God's Lightning, as one of the outlets for her operations as an Illuminatus; and many other cranks, fanatics, schemers, dreamers, liberators and their victims. This is a compendium of madness culled from all the key books of the (what used to be underground) culture on everything you can milk for laughs or shudders - drugs, sex, black magic, sex, comix, sex, horror & fantasy, sex, secret societies and even sex - written into a gut-busting, brain-withering riot guaranteed to become a cult novel (Tolkein will be spinning in his grave) and packed with enough paranoia to keep you glancing furtively over your shoulder for weeks. The authors prove the penis mightier than the sword on a philosophical battleground that draws on Lovecraft, Leary, Hassan-i-Sabah, Kesey & Ginsberg, the Tzu brothers (Lao & Chuang), the Zen masters, Crowley & Levi, and other apostles, true and false, in the ancient conflicts between orthodoxy and unorthodoxy, the state and the individual, establishments and iconoclasts, us and them. Is the world really run by the Illuminati, and are a confused bunch of dope freaks really our last chance? Who is the lama who lives below Dealy Plaza and juggles with space-time? Why do our heroes stand by while a giant leviathan makes love to their computor? Is there any truth to the significance of the numbers 5, 23 and 33, upon which the entire novel is structured? Is the novel structured? (Be prepared for streams of consciousness in which not only identity, but time and space no longer confine the narrative, which zips up and down time-lines and flashes into other minds with consummate ease).

A damned good read. Has to be read to be believed (and even then I'm not sure - it really is preposterous in parts). See if you can spot all the allusions. Though Fort has only one fleeting mention that I can remember, the authors are fully aware of the Fortean philosophy, and indeed, the scope of the book is a brilliant exercise in Fortean flexibility, and an outrageous mirror of modern folly.

Experiment in Depth by PW Martin (Rouledge & Kegan Paul; £1.95; index) -- Martin extracts from the works of Jung, TS Eliot and AJ Toynbee, three approaches to the human unconscious, the psychological, the poetic and the historical. If these three could be combined - the experiment of the title - we would see, says Martin, the flow-

ering of the full creative spirit of man in a unique blend of science and religion. An important book I wish I could devote more space to. Much insight on phenomenal reality.

...re-issues...Colony Earth by Richard Mooney (Panther; 75p)...The End of Atlantis by JV Luce (Paladin; 95p)...The Occult by Colin Wilson (Mayflower; £1.75)

These and other books are available from Dark They Were & Golden Eyed in Berwick St, London W1 - tell'em FT sent you.

JOURNALS

** Due to our omission of journal reviews last issue we are a bit behind - we've had to squeeze a lot in this issue to catch up, and some have had to be held over to next issue...but keep sending us info. We print on a need-to-know priority and urgent or more relevant material jumps the queue **

The Ley Hunter -- 70: GR Phillips on Sir Montagu Sharpe's network of rectangles (proposed 6yrs before Watkin's leys); the mystery 'Walls of Feizor' in Yorkshire; & 'French & Belgian Literature on Sacred Geography'; & 'A Computer Study of the Megalithic Alignments of Land's End' by Chris Hutton Squire & Pat Gadsby -- 71: prior to the change in editor, some retrospective views on TLH; extract of Paul Screeton's forthcoming book The Living Stones; the maths of 'Ley Plotting' -- 72: the eagerly-awaited debut of Paul Devereux as editor and a dramatic change to litho & FT-style format.. it allows the welcome feature of photos, something Paul has promised more of in the future, begining with a photo-feature series of views of leys, stones & topographic curiosities. Also this issue: GL Phillips on 'The Black Horse of Busha' (a hillside figure); Avebury considered as 'The Home of the Holy Grail'; a summary of Maria Reiche's ICA lecture on Nazca; Steve Moore straightening out some current misconceptions of Leys & Feng Shui'; & how to compute Leys from grid co-ordinates. TLH: 1yr £2/$4.00 ** new address: TLH, PO Box 152, London N10 1EB. NB: TLH & FT will be working closer together in future, and from our respective next issues will be offering a joint subscription at a small discount. Things are looking up!

Pursuit -- Jan 76: Sanderson on UFOs; report on NJ Bigfoot expedition; Roy Pinney on spontaneous image on series of photos; notes on survival of extinct (?) peccaries in Argentina, African neo-dinosaurs, petrified human remains & a MA at Sheep's Hill, Penn.; Wayne Meshejian on 'Erratic Satellites over the Bermuda Triangle' & Ron Dobbins exposing Meshejian's errors; UFOs linked to human behaviour patterns by TE Bearden; a grim SHC case in Florida, 1975; & a curious mutilation of a mouse -- April 76: John Keel bows in as new editor with comments on the rising tide of Fortean awareness; articles on 'Fort's Books', 'Bias in Perception of Fortean Events', 'The Dodecated Globe'; & notes on an entombed turtle, Bermuda mysteries de-mystified, giant pterosaur remains in Texas, & the Allende Letters. Pursuit is the journal of the Society for the Investigation of the Unexplained (SITU): inquiries to SITU, Columbia, NJ 07832, USA. Membership is $10/yr - Pursuit is quarterly.

INFO Journal -- 17: pt 1 of Gary Mangiacopra's account of the giant octopus carcase, Florida 1896 "still considered by science as a joke"; Ryan Drum on the rocks found in Peru by Dr Cabrera which appear to be engraved with details of complex surgical operations; Dave Drake on the wild talents of St Severinus (5th C); HL Mencken's 'Bathtub Hoax' still going strong nearly 60 yrs later -- 18: pt 2 of the Florida giant octopus article; Dick Hall's notes on the classic "Flying Saucer"; DN Peck's 'Guide to Detecting Paranormal Voices' on tape etc, with circuit diagram; John Holden on the taxonomy of Bigfoot, ABSMs, and notes on the Giant Tortoise mystery. INFO: Box 367, Arlington, VA 22210, USA. £5/$10.00. For a special joint sub rate to INFO & FT see details in the colophon (inside front, this issue).

MUFOB - now that FSR has become the UFOlogical establishment, MUFOB is fast gaining a reputation as a radical voice - worthy of your support -- Summer 76 (ns3): Jenny Randles summarises 'The Strange Affair of Apen', a sort of UFOlogical guerilla group, reputed to be allied to the far right 'Column 88', disrupting the sanity of its selected victims with an Ummo-type conspiracy here in the UK; Roger Sandell spotlights the avatars of the UFO vehicle-stopping effect in folklore; and Peter Rogerson gives a nice literary impressionistic view of the mythological complexity of UFOlogy. MUFOB: 1yr £1/$2.50: (John Rimmer, ed.): 11 Beverley Rd, New Malden, Surrey KT3 4AW.

Lantern -- Spring 76 (13): Nigel Pennick on the 'Puddingstone Track' from Berks to Norfolk; The Southend Sea-serpent (1930s); E. Anglian ghosts; Biorhythms & Psi; 'The Phantom Hedge', etc -- Summer 76 (14): hauntings of Kessingland churchyard; unusual stones of E Anglia; report on diamond-shaped UFO (Rugby, 1951); WC Chambers on 'Bealings Bells' etc. Lantern is the journal of the Borderline Science Investigation Group (BSIG) - consistently interesting and worthy of your support. Only 75p/yr. Lantern: (Ivan Bunn, ed.): 3 Dunwich Way, Lowestoft, Suffolk NR32 4RZ.

New Scientist -- 27 March: item on a naturally-formed fossil nuclear reactor in sandstone strata, found at Oklo, Gambon in 1972, dating back to 1780 million yrs ago -- 15 April: 'Healing by Electromagnetism', Dr R Benthal reviews the fact & fiction; 'Was the parting of the Red Sea a Mirage?', yes, says AB Frazer, no, say others. (Soon NSci will discuss the number of angels on a pinhead!) -- 20 April: more discoveries of magnetic monopoles; letter on nematodes that hitchhike in passing flies -- 13 May: two articles (for and against) the emergence of yet another field of specialism, 'Sociobiology' (its detractors see it being used to prop up racial facism - !) -- 27 May: Dr A Locket on Coelacanth reproduction methods & anatomy; photo of Comet West breaking into 4 parts (more on this in FT 18); another "extinct" critter found living, this time a crustacean (glyphid) in the Philippines supposedly dead 60-70 million yrs; Dr Donald Gould rails at faith healing -- 10 June: metal artifacts indicate an indigenous technology in northern Thailand 3000 to 3600 yrs BC, who or what they were remains a mystery; and so soon after all the fanfares for the new statistical tool, the 'Catastrophe Theory', comes warnings of dangers of its use with wrong data -- 24 June: Dr R Wallace on the discovery of 3 stable superheavy new elements beyond Uranium in Madagascan rock; discovery of 2 new "galaxy-like objects" (!) in our stellar vicinity.

Analog -- June 76: G Harry Stine on experiments with the 'Dean Drive' (a paradoxical engine which appears to generate thrust without reaction) and why the tests had to stop on the verge of a radical breakthrough . (pp60-80).

Flying Saucer Review -- 21:6: Aime Michel on the robots of Hephaestus from the Iliad; SE Priest on 'UFOnauts as Timetravellers'; some curious reversed TV images during a USA TV UFO documentary -- 22:1: image of 'entity' on photograph; a water-sucking globe in Japan; more occupants, cases & photos. FSR : West Malling, Maidstone, Kent.

SOBEPS News -- 2: Bermuda Triangle bibliography; UFO reports; article on the 'Physiological Effects of UFO Contacts' -- 3: summary of Bermuda Triangle events; summary of man's achievements in space; pt 2 of 'Physiological Effects of UFO Contacts'. SOBEPS News is a highly recommended supplement giving the English translation of Inforespace, the journal of the Belgian UFO research group, SOBEPS. They also put out a catalogue (in English) of an analysis of 130 'Solid Light Cases', by Claude Bourtembourg and Alice Ashton. Inquiries to: SOBEPS: Boulevard Aristide Briand 26, 1070 Brussels, Belgium.

FORTEAN TIMES

strange phenomena - curiosities - prodigies - portents - mysteries

DIARY OF A MAD PLANET, p8

50p : $1·00.

18

UK ISSN 0308-5899

FORTEAN TIMES

A Contemporary Record of Strange Phenomena

FORTEAN TIMES is a non-profitmaking bimonthly miscellany of news, notes and references on current strange phenomena and related subjects. Formerly THE NEWS. Affiliated to the International Fortean Organisation (INFO) in continuing the work of CHARLES FORT (1874-1932). **FORTEAN TIMES** is edited and published by Robert JM Rickard:

PO Box 152, London N1O 1EP, England.

SUBSCRIPTIONS: 1 year (6 issues) £3.00/USA $6.00. Back issues (if available) 50p/USA $1.00. Airmail (overseas) add £1.50/USA $3.00 per year to sub. rate. Annual index free to current subscribers, otherwise 30p/USA 60¢. *Special joint subscription to Fortean Times and INFO Journal: 1 year (12 issues) £7.00/USA $14.00.* All overseas payments by cheque should *include* 10% to cover banking exchange commission.

CONTRIBUTIONS: of articles, notes and artwork on related subjects are always welcome and duly credited. *You can help by sending us a copy or clipping of any item you think will interest other readers — just add a note of the source, date, and your name for the credit.* Please don't assume our omniscience — there are very few duplications.

RIGHTS: All artwork and articles in *FORTEAN TIMES* are the copyright of the artists and authors; and the views expressed not necessarily those of *FORTEAN TIMES* or INFO. Uncredited material is by the editor. All notes herein may be freely quoted in return for a *credit to FORTEAN TIMES with our address.* Heading artwork is by Hunt Emerson.

OCTOBER 1976

NEW ADDRESS

We are pleased to announce we finally have a permanent address for FT (see the colophon opposite), to be used from this issue onward. It has come just in time as your editor is about to begin a year of flat-hopping. I was having nightmares over the address confusion this could have involved. Those in personal communication with me can continue to use the Aldermaston address (as mail will be forwarded) until I can give you another one. If in doubt use the PO Box.

DELAY DEPT.

Many apologies for the lateness of this issue — due to my commitments to my book (see below) and to finding a place to live, this latter having thrown my routines, files etc, into utter chaos. At this time the problem is not sorted out yet, so please excpect the December issue to be delayed also. Similarly my grand plans for the 1975 index are postponed once again. I hope to be back on schedule with the first issue next year.

JOINT DEPT

We share our new address with The Ley Hunter, and as announced, from this issue on, we offer a joint sub to both TLH and FT at a 10% reduction. This will bring you 6 issues of each for £4.50/$9.00. Payments may be made to either magazine - we have the same address. We are also continuing our joint sub with the INFO Journal - so please indicate (on the address-lable when renewing) which you want.

TRUSS FUND

- in which we appeal for support! Many thanks to the following for their kind donations to our survival fund: Frank Adey, Nick Cohn, David Dunthorn, Bill Figorski, John Glover, Chris Holtzhausen, Phil Ledger, Udo Schlegel, Aaron Sussman, Nigel Watson. Our special thanks go to Gary L Abbott for his parcels of US weeklies and gift sub to the National Enquirer; and to Bram Stokes of Dark They Were & Golden Eyed, the famous London weird bookshop, who gave us a boxfull of old US editions of Fate (very timely too, see p7 If you have piles of old mags (relevant ones) you don't want - send them to us. Our long-term plan is to build a central Fortean reference facility.

NEWS DEPT

INFO has undergone a considerable change of staff at its Arlington, VA, headquarters, in the last few months. They wish to assure their members of their survival, continuity, and intentions to improve their services.

...cont on p5

CHRIST IN A HEN HOUSE

On 19 Sept this year the Sunday People published a large photo of a stained asbestos wall on the inside of a hen house. They told that the owners and workers of Billsdown Poultry Farm, St Ives, near Bournemouth, Hants, can plainly see the head and shoulders of a crucified Christ in the stains. We thought about reproducing the photo but its large white area and faint grey stains would not have come out at all. The image, says Jack Griffin, a partner in the farm, appeared sometime in mid-August, when one of the workers spotted it. The asbestos is 15-years old, and usually goes black, said Griffin. They kept quiet about it because 'we didn't want people to think we were religious nut cases'. It seems that far from fading, the picture is developing details 'like a photo-graph', the eyes, nose and hair, particular-ly becoming more clearly defined. If Fort was reporting this, he'd probably have fast-ened onto a notion that at first a vague patch of stains is interpreted as a meaning-ful image, and then, perhaps because of the magical feelings associated with the image, it fleshes out in response to the interpret-ation. We note that the hen house stands in the shadow of All Saints' parish church, for whatever significance that may hold. The farm owners say they tried to brush it off but the stains are in the material itself. 'This is certainly not a hoax or a con trick,' said Griffin.

The People asked their readers what they saw in the photo, and in their 26 Sept issue they publish a selection of replies, and three quite different drawings of where they saw the head and shoulders, etc. People sent in drawings of images ranging from 4 angels; Boris Karloff; a jug, candle, river and trees; 5 separate heads; and Christ reclining on a sofa, among the more convent-ional interpretations. It was even likened to the Holy Shroud of Turin which bears the body-image of Christ. (Cr: both items - Ion A Will).

This reminds me of a documentary earlier in the year on the work of the sculptor Rodin. When he died in 1917, a few drawings were found and claimed as the only landscapes he ever drew. They showed 'wooded valleys, curving hills and waving fields of grass'. Just before they were due to be exhibited, it was found that each bore a woman's name, and were, in fact, close-ups of their (cough) private parts! Just goes to show, eh? But let's get more explicit.

BEHIND THE SCREEN DOOR

About the 10th June 1969, the image of a face 'resembling a painting of Christ' was first noticed on the screen door at the back of the Bass' home, 816 Avenue C, Port Neches, Texas. The image was attracting large crowds and could be clearly seen and photo-graphed. The story appears in the Port Neches Chronicle 18 June 1969, along with a good photo, but alas, we only have a thin grey xerox useless for reproduction here. It is said that the face is life-size and can be more easily seen in the afternoon when direct sunlight falls on the back of the house. (Cr: INFO/Gaulding). An interesting detail is that some people have reported that they can see it in colour.

CHRIST STUCCO ON THE WALL

On 18 May 1975, the 'face and chest of Christ' appeared on a pink stucco wall, facing the Immaculate Heart of Mary Church in the small village of Holman, north central New Mexico. Since then, according to Rev. Leonard Bayer, whose church it is, it app-ears, 'without fail', about 9pm each night. 'It's quite distinct with long hair, beard and all. Sometimes a cross is visible and other times the Virgin Mary or an angel app-ears alongside Christ,' he said. It fades before dawn each day, and according to the National Enquirer, 19 Aug 1975, it is no hoax or trick of street lighting. It was even filmed successfully for TV.

THIS IMAGE of Christ, with long hair and beard, glows on pink stucco wall at 9 o'clock every night.

The image appears to glow, and measures 4ft by 2ft, and is 7ft up the wall. The chancellor of the archdiocese of Santa Fe came over to see it but said it would be some time before any decision would be made on the image's authenticity. Meantime Rev Bayer seems to be relishing the fame that has come to his small church in a small village. With the neighbours saying things like 'I went there and saw the image of Jesus holding a cross in his arms', the Rev was grinning at the prospect of full pews in the months ahead. Does anyone know how the story developed?

A FACE AT THE WINDOW

Sometime last summer the image of a face appeared on a window pane of a schoolroom of an Episcopal church (presumably) in Denver, Colorado, and it was believed by parishioners to be the face of Christ. ((Why must every bearded long-tressed face be that of Christ when we have no evidence of what the Man looked like? Or is it another case of strange but natural phenomena mimicking art?)) The rector, Rev H David Wilson, called in a glass expert to examine the 16" by 14" pane.

According to the Milwaukee Journal 24 April 76 (Cr: Mark A Hall), the expert came to the conclusion the face had been painted on the glass 'some time ago', and scrubbed it off with steel-wool. This however failed to remove the image and left faint traces. Rev

Wilson had another view: 'It's sort of an impression in the window but it's not an optical illusion. It is very much in the window. We feel it is a sign that what we're doing in the church is right.'

FACE-GAWPERS ANGER BISHOP

The Catholic bishop of Nimes, Msgr Pierre Rouge, has closed the church in the French village of Suave after the image of a face appeared on a wall of the nave sometime early in April. He said that crowds 'came to see a spurious miracle rather than to worship.' The parish priest, Augustin Rieusset, was equally pragmatic, saying the apparition was 'created by the imagination of overly zealous persons. The effect of daylight on the plaster wall creates the impression of a face at certain moments, but it is nothing but an optical illusion.' Ah, but sight too is an optical illusion, n'est ce pas?

Just how much the priest was saying on orders from above we don't know, but the reaction in Suave was opposite to the credulity of the clergy in the cases above. The priest went on to add that if you looked closely '...it could also be a flower or any other object, which disappears as soon as the sun goes down.' Interestingly, we note that the AP story of the Suave face is dated 24 April, the same as the Denver story above; so that a face was developing in France at the same time as an expert was demolishing one in the USA. St Louis (MO) Post-Dispatch 25 April 76 (Cr: Mark A Hall.) Also in this period a BVM was sighted in Beirut (see p24) and the case below developed...

BAFFLEMENT IN BENONI

On Good Friday this year (16 April) Stratus Voustas saw a collection of religious symbols in a windowpane of the Greek Orthodox Church at Benoni, in South Africa. He is the son of the architect who built the church, Paul Voustas, only two years previously. Voustas senior said: 'The image is formed by bluish watermarks in the amber frosted glass...if watermarks appear in glass they are usually noticeable in the first couple of months.' A spokesman for the firm that supplied the glass says the symbols are definitely there but doesn't think they could be watermarks, as the odds against the formation of such a complex meaningful set of designs must be quite fantastic. 'They could have arisen in the manufacturing process or through weathering, but it's strange they should manifest themselves in this particular manner.' Later other scientists said it was caused by 'a chemical reaction attacking the soda of the glass, and the alkaline solution reacted with the surface.' The Pretoria News, from whom we take the drawing below, points out that the scientists fail completely to account for the strong design of the discolouration.

The image of the crucifixion of Christ which appeared in a glass window of the St Athanasios Greek Orthodox Church in Benoni.

The head of the Greek Church in the Transvaal, Archbishop Paul Langris, made the trip and was suitably impressed. It was, he said, a message to South Africa from God. The faithful responded by identifying the following images in the see-through icon:

'The sign of a cross; the Holy Trinity; two pelicans, symbols of the soul of Christ ((ref to the legend that they pierce their own breasts to feed their young on their blood during a food shortage)); the flame of life; the lance used to pierce Christ's side; a letter 'B' ((alleged to stand for Balileus, Greek for King)); the forms of two women kneeling in prayer at the foot of the cross; a halo behind the head of Christ on the cross.'

Interestingly it is said the image is visible only at certain times of the day, from noon to sunset, and can only be viewed in natural light from the outside of the church. A similar detail is mentioned in several of our stories above.

Could it have been a portent of the latest troubles in South Africa? Pains reflected in a pane. Or... No! Oh very well. In April this year Viking 1 was begining its final approach to Mars for its landing on 20 July. Pictures released by NASA have shown several interesting images; one taken of Mars during the approach is said to show a face in the Martian features ((We would like to see this - can anyone supply the reference or a copy?)), and one taken of the surface after landing shows the letter 'B' (see FT 17/9). Story compiled from South African Sunday Times, 23 May 76, Pretoria News, 16 Oct 76 (Cr both: Chris Holtzhausen).

■■■■■■■■■■■■■■■■■■■■■■■■■■■■■■■■■■■■■■■

Editorial/ cont from p2...

By the time you read this, Dark They were & Golden Eyed, will have moved to their spacious new premises, 9-12 St Anne's Court, London W1. This is just off Wardour St. and near their old shop in Berwick St. It has to be seen to be believed, and must make Dark the largest comix, SF, and all-round wierd-book shop in Europe! Stan says that there will be more room to display small mags like TLH and FT. Go and see - tell'em FT sent you!

PLUG DEPT

The final details of my book on Fortean phenomena with John Michell are now known. Its title is Phenomena: A Book of Wonders, and will be published by Thames & Hudson this Spring in a large paperback format at £4.50. It contains 58 categories of illustrated phenomena, and (in all modesty) will become a front-line reference work. We've certainly put a lot of effort into it, and we hope you will think it's been worth it.

Privately many researchers in these fields have expressed their grave concern over the amount of misinformation currently in circulation. It multiplies the numbers of deadends and red herrings in the way of any piece of research, and there is nothing more tedious than to spend much valuable time on a project, checking your information back to its original sources, only to find the whole thing is based on a lie, a hoax or an error of scholarship. I don't exclude myself from errors in scholarship - hell! we've all blithely quoted writers we thought were authorities, without checking or qualifying the information. But it must not be allowed to pass unchallenged. As Forteans, we must question all authoritative statements - and if we cannot check it out ourselves, the only truly scholarly and scientific thing to do is to treat it as a hypothesis, one possibility or interpretation. We must find our own balance between caution, enthusiasm, belief and scepticism.

As our own small contribution to putting matters right, we conceived this column, which is open to anyone who has investigated any piece of Fortean data and found that the popular accounts jibe with the facts (as far as they can be established). The only proviso is that the information must help clear away doubts and misconceptions and errors in the field, and should be as accurate as possible. It is not intended as a pillory to villify the perpetrators of the error, however much some of them may need it. None of us are free enough to cast such stones. Let's have arguments and debate, and differences of opinions by all means, but let's all uphold the quest. (Cynics will be mildly amused at our new toast: 'To the truth, wherever it may lie!')

****** ****** ****** ******

THE DISAPPEARANCE OF DAVID LANG

The best known account appears in Frank Edwards' Stranger than Science (1959), in which it is the first item. Briefly, Edwards tells that Lang, who had a farm a few miles from Gallatin, Tennessee, stepped from the porch and crossed a field in front of the house on 23 September 1880, and vanished in full view of his wife and children. Two other witnesses were Judge August Peck and a companion driving a buggy up the adjacent lane towards the house. Lang had seen the Judge and waved to him, turned back to the house and promptly disappeared. Subsequent searches failed to find Lang, a hole or any clue to where or how he might have vanished.

What made this story particularly interesting to Forteans was its sequel, when Lang's two children were crossing the same field, as Edwards tells it, 'one still warm evening in April 1881, about seven months after he had vanished. The children noticed that at the spot where he had last been seen, there was a circle of stunted yellow grass some fifteen feet in diameter. On that evening as they stood beside the circle, 11-year-old Sarah called to their father; and to their astonishment, the youngsters heard his voice...calling faintly for help...over and over...until it faded away, for ever.'

Edwards gives no references or indications as to where he might have picked up this evocative story. The only previous mention of the story known to me (your Ed.) is in Strange Mysteries of Time and Space by Harold T Wilkins, published, not without significance, the year before STS, in 1958. Wilkins' story, though, does not name the judge, and identifies the judge's companion as Lang's brother-in-law. Other differences appear in Wilkins' version of the sequel, here (pp180-2 in my Ace paperback edition) dated August 1881, ie nearly a year later.

The peculiar circle of grass is said to be 20ft wide and 'high and rank' and that 'All around the circle had been cropped by sheep, or grazed by cattle; but no cow, or sheep, or horse would venture into the circle, not even a cricket or grasshopper. They would approach it, but shied away in fear...'

According to Wilkins the girl called to Lang four times, and as they were about to walk away, heard a faraway voice calling for help. 'The startled mother was told. She went to the spot in the field and called, and her husband answered. They went back for several days; but each day the voice grew fainter, and at last was heard no more.'

Wilkins claims to have summarised the account from various contemporary newspapers but does not name them.

Robert Forrest had the bright idea of checking with the public records of the local libraries in that region of Tennessee and had the following reply (dated 3 June 1976) from Herschel G Payne of the Public Library of Nashville and Davidson County, who was familiar with the story and had even investigated it. Our thanks to them both for permission to quote directly from this correspondence.

'Fortunately...I do have quite a bit of background research on it. The story is supposedly only a fabrication which was told by one Joe Mulhatten, a travelling salesman who was in these parts during the 1880s. There were, at that time, lying contests in which men vied for the title of "biggest liar" and Joe Mulhatten was a champion. The story of David Lang was his best. Throughout my research I have talked and corresponded with the top newspaper men and literary people in this area who have written on this subject and they guarantee me there is no such thing as documentation to be found."

"I personally have checked census records and other material in our collection and there is nothing to indicate that David Lang or Judge Peck were ever in this vicinity. I have talked with the Librarian of the Gallatin Public Library and she in turn has contacted knowledgeable persons there who also attest to the story's fictitiousness. The Sumner County historian, whom I also contacted, says there is absolutely no verification and no pictures of the farm to be found. Even with all the above information from the most reliable sources I did not "accept or believe" that the story was not possible and even drove up to Sumner County to check it out for myself. The farm was supposedly located on what is now called "The Old Cottontown Road". I had a beautiful drive - nothing more!'

So there you have it - on available evidence both Wilkins and Edwards embroider-ed a story that won a lying contest, and by omission of sources and lack of investigation and the proper qualifications it passed into popular acceptance as a factual event. One remaining mystery for purists to clear up is just how the Lang story was picked up again so long after the early 1880s?

My only observations come from the folklorists' approach of disregarding the impossibility or not of the elements of the story to note its continuity with tradition. I note with interest the association of the peculiar circle with the vanishing, the return to the same spot on something like an anniversary of the event, and the hearing of a faint calling as if from far away in some other dimension - these are the classic elements of stories of kidnappings from fairy circles. Perhaps the story passed so easily into popular acceptance because it was hauntingly familiar, either of childhood fairytales, or of some real or archetypal event in the collective unconscious, or even perhaps all of these. Fictional or not, the event does have what I like to call 'phenomenal reality' (intermediary between the soft, psychological realities, and the hard, factual realities), and thus may be an ingredient in the shaping of the world since its 'invention'.

Postscript -- Those irreverent creatures the library angels seem to be overworking on my behalf lately. A few days after I had typed the above section I finally collected from Steve Moore a number of backcopies of the US edition of Fate, donated to FT by Bram Stokes, of Dark They Were & Golden Eyed. In one of these, dated December 1956, was an article in an occasional series on 'Mind over Space' by the great psychic scholar Nandor Fodor, on the subject of human teleportation - and the first case he mentions is that of David Lang. Some details differ from those given above: the girl is called Emma; the field was for horses; and the faint voice was heard 'the following Spring', and Lang's wife admitted hearing her husband's calling before the children came to tell her on this occasion.

As another link in the chain, we note that Fodor himself is quoting from an article several years earlier in the same magazine; 'How lost was my father' by Stuart Palmer, in Fate, July 1953. As this is unavailable to us we can add nothing more. Perhaps one of you might like to take this up and work back from Stuart Palmer? If so, please let us know how you get on.

*** Next time - the famous case in 1897 of an airship that kidnapped a calf from Alexander Hamilton's farm at LeRoy, Kansas - with new material unearthed by Jerome Clark and Robert J Schadewald.

DIARY OF A MAD PLANET

What follows is an experiment in correlating the Fortean data accumulated here
this year. It is incomplete and inconclusive
because I don't have the time or the facilities, or of course anything like the full
information, for a full analysis.
                    Several commentators in
this calamitous period refered to the work
of Gilbert White, who recorded much strange
phenomena during the extreme weather of the
late 18th C. In the Fall of 1781 he chronicled the progress of a severe drought in
southern England; and during another spell
of hot dry weather in 1783, he told of huge
swarms of flies that maddened livestock; of
meat rotting within a day, and expensive
dairy products. A volcanic mountain grew out
of the sea off Norway; there were quakes in
Calabria; and "strange meteors" - in fact
the year was "full of horrible phenomena."

The same could be said of 1976. Data
kept coming of quakes, volcanoes, monsters,
monsoons, strange deaths, sudden swarms of
insects that disappeared as suddenly. The
reports seemed full of superlatives: 'worst',
'hottest', 'strongest', 'driest', 'wettest',

'longest', etc. Fortean times indeed!

I thought of simply doing a listing of
quakes - then someone pointed out the torrential rain that seemed to follow each one,
and someone else mentioned lunar periodic-
ities. Gradually the listing absorbed other
data in an attempt to reconstruct the different kinds of phenomena that happened on
particular days, or other relationships. I
have listed the events under the date they
happened as reconstructed from news reports
varying from the evening of the same day to
some weeks afterward. Those events marked
with (*) will be given in full in a future
issue.

WHAT ON EARTH IS GOING ON?

This question was shrieked by more than
one journalist as daily the papers reported
more quakes from more countries around the
globe this hectic August. After the grave
damage to northern Italy by a quake on the
6th May had begun to slip from people's
minds, a huge quake hit Tangshan on 28 July,
to be followed by so much geological and
meteorological violence that when Biblical

prophecies of the end of the world appeared in the papers no one blinked or laughed them off. Experts were thrown into confusion. There was talk of a new Ice Age, of the planet's tilt having altered, of shrinking ice caps, of sunspots and solar winds, of UFOs firing rays at earth from space, anything. Some experts said the series of events was explained by coincidence.

In the Fortean view nothing happens in isolation, and all these events form an interconnected pattern in universal continuity. William Golding, writing in a book review in the Guardian, 30 Sept, brilliantly caught the Fortean vision (in a style reminiscent of Fort's):'Those who think of the world as a lifeless lump would do well to watch out. Only the other day something irritated her and with a moue, it may be, she wrecked cities from China to the Philippines and blew out the side of a mountain in Ecuador.' I guess we've pretty much taken her for granted of late and her 'See if I care,' pouts have shown us firmly just who needs who.

Before plunging into the list, I'd like to offer the following summaries and notes.

We are told that there are something like 30,000 tremors each year throughout the world, of which only 5-6000 are ever felt by people living in the vicinity; again, of which only 25 or so are severe enough to cause destruction and death on the large scale. Perhaps the toll this year is not geologically unusual, but it certainly seems so, and not just because the press spotlight was focussed on it. The Tangshan quake of 28 July was the strongest recorded in the 12yrs since the destruction of Anchorage, Alaska, was followed by an unusual number of quakes greater than 6 Richter.(It was a 6.5 Richter quake that did so much damage in the Udine area of N Italy, occuring under a heavily populated region). We learn from the US Severe Storm Forecast Center that the first six months of this year saw a record number of tornadoes (773 against the 26-yr average of 440 for the same period) - Los Angeles Times, 4 July 76 (Cr: W Grimstad). Just look at our list for the other superlatives.

THE DROUGHT

At the time of this writing it seems hard to believe that only a few months ago most parts of Britain were having the worst drought for 200 years, and some parts for 250 years. Parliament was granting powers to local water authorities to cut off public supplies; and in south Wales, the worst hit area (with only 5 days supply in the reservoirs, at 22 Aug) the shut-off was for 17 hours a day. Remote and elevated villages and towns had to fetch water from standpipes

or wait for a mobile water tanker; car washing and water wasting became heinous crimes; and there was a huge exodus of livestock to the relatively greener pastures of north Wales and Scotland. Brown became the predominant colour of the English countryside as all kinds of plants and trees died of thirst. The watertable was so low that rivers and streams dried up, stood still and even flow-backwards because of leakage by millions of gallons a day into the surrounding land. In many estuaries the flow of freshwater was too weak to keep back the tides and salt water wiped out river-life and bankside vegetation for huge stretches as it flowed far inland.

Britain was on the verge of having a water police when, on 27 August, a light rain fell over parts of the South. It's some measure of the national thirst that this normally innocuous event became headline news. The change was as dramatic as it was sudden, for the September that followed went on record as the wettest for 50 years.

Full effects of the drought will not be known for some time, as, for example, the death from thirst and fire of large areas of woodlands, heaths and moors, will upset the complex ecology of various regions. In many cases rare plants, insects and birds, residents of these areas, were killed off in the disaster or made homeless at precisely the wrong time of their life-cycles. The drought will undoubtedly have repercussions too in the supply of dairy products and various crops this winter and next year.

THE RAIN-MAKERS

The drought brought out a good selection of rainmakers in August. The one who most seemed to know what he was doing was Guru Jagat Singh Ji, hired by the Sikh community in Southall, London, who arrived on the 27th with a 20-man orchestra to begin a week's prayer for rain. How the press laughed at his confident promise of rain within 4 days. Yet the very next day, in the peak dry period, it rained. In some parts of southern England it rained for 3 days. Pity the Guru couldn't stop rain - like the Malaysian witchdoctor who kept a golfcourse dry while parts of the city around it were deluged (see 27 March) - for back in his Punjab great rains caused extensive misery (see 10, 12, 20 & 24 Aug).

On 9th Aug a man did a nude rain-dance and was prosecuted for indecent exposure - but at his trial it was said it rained within 24 hours. On the 26th, the Archbishop of Canterbury turned down appeals for a national day of prayer for rain - so the Guru got the credit.

But the unintentional rain-making prize must go to Denis Howell, Minister of Sport, appointed to organize the drought effort. For an account of the   rains that began 3 days after his appointment, and which fell during his tours to various parts of the country on at least 12 occasions see <u>Daily Mirror</u> for 30 Sept.

EXPERTS, THEORIES & PROPHETS

I cannot recall a period in recent years to rival this one for sheer bullshit and bamboozlement from the so-called experts. I was going to list the errors in predictions, the contradictory opinions of different specialists, and the facile explaining-away of both errors and events, but what the hell! We've better things to do with the space. It could be considered great fun really - just don't let them tell me I'm not being scientific about the Unknown. Hail Eris!

We note that several scales were used to guage the strength of quakes (Richter, the lesser known Rossi-Forel, and Mercali, and several quite meaningless to us laymen, like the obscure Soviet scale). So, in the absence of comparative information, we include only the Richter measurements where known. As early as the Yunnan quakes (see 29 May) reports began to mention a belief among the Chinese populace of a change of dynasty -the mood having been set by the huge Kirin meteorite on 8 March, the same day the head of Comet West began its split into 4 parts. The belief was revived in the huge series of quakes in central and NE China after 28 July. Mao was dying, of course, but he outlasted that series of portents, finally dying on 9 Sept, one of the few relatively peaceful days in the 2 devastating months that followed the Tangshan quake (28th July).

There is much we could add on the subject of quake prediction, and the behaviour of animals prior to a quake, but we'll have to leave this to a future article.

We cannot allow, however, the frightening pronouncements (on 16 Aug) of the French vulcanologist, Pierre Brousse, to pass. He said (from his observation post at <u>Fort St Charles</u> !) that the volcano, La Soufriere, on Guadeloupe, would explode within a few hours with the force of (2 to 17 - in various reports) atom bombs. It never did! This build up was said to be 'inexorable' and 'past the point of no return'. Brousse later revised his time for the explosion; and admitted that he had tried to instill a sense of urgency into the lazy island. Nearly 2 weeks later, farmers were pleading to be allowed back to evacuated areas; and on 30 Aug a sudden but minor eruption took a party of scientists camped near the summit completely by surprise.

In contrast to Brousse's exaggeration, we have a statement from a London Weather Center official (<u>Sunday Times</u>, 4 Jan) that: 'We don't want to over emphasize in case nothing happens.' This was the basis of a row

over whether the weathermen could have given better warnings, sooner, of the 100mph plus gales that caused considerable damage to much of western Europe on the 3rd January.

Complaints against the weathermen were world-wide. In England they consistantly failed to anticipate each change in the situation in their forecasts for the month ahead. See the <u>Daily Mirror</u>, 16 June & 12 July, for red-faced apologies for rain that never came as they said it would; and London <u>Evening News</u>, 29 Sept, in which they again apologise for saying the drought would continue to get worse through that month, when in fact, in a dramatic reversal, it turned out to be the wettest, in parts, for 50 yrs. I kept expecting someone to prosecute the Met. Office under the Trades Descriptions Act!

COINCIDENCES

We also have several fine coincidences in this period. Many involved the accident-prone 'Operation Teamwork', the first large-scale NATO exercise for some years.

On 6 Sept, a Russian pilot defected to Japan in a top-secret jet-fighter, the MiG-25 'Foxbat'. The big grin on faces at the Pentagon soon dropped, when, only a few days later (17th), a USAF jet-fighter, the F-14 'Tomcat', packed with secret surveillance equipment, rolled off the deck of a carrier off the north coast of Scotland and sank to the seabed. Similar names, similar planes, similar top-level embarassment!

This double-loss of secret aircraft was preceeded by two other accidents. On 4 Aug, a Soviet long-range surveillance plane, the TU-95 'Bear', crashed into the sea off Nova Scotia -- and on 28 Aug, 2 USAF cargo planes, the C141 'Starlifter', crashed within 4 hrs of each other, one at an airport in Greenland, and the other close to Thorney, Cambs, near Peterborough. A spokesman at their base, Maguire, NJ, said part failure and sabotage were ruled out. He said that it was the first time they'd ever lost a C141, and to lose 2 together was an 'unbelievable coincidence' - <u>Daily Telegraph</u> 30 Aug.

For a listing of some of the other NATO calamities, including the loss of 'HMS Fittleton' after a collision at sea on 20 Sept, see <u>Daily Mirror</u> 21 & 22 Sept.

Air accidents seemed to increase. On the same day that Yugoslavia suffered a quake (10 Sept), a Yugoslav DC-9 collided with a British Airways Trident, near Zagreb, killing 177 in the 'worst air collision in history.' And a few weeks later, on 25 Sept, there were 6 separate plane crashes in the USA, 4 of them within 4 hours.

There were two mysterious fire-deaths in Bath, Somerset (17 & 20 Aug); the name Herne cropped up several times (5 June & 22 Sept); and a mystery kangeroo was sighted at Golden, Colorado (17 Aug), a place named frequently in the reports of quakes as the base of the US Geological Survey where they measured the effects of quakes in all parts of the globe. Some quakes seemed synchronous too, not just the series (see eg 16 & 21 Aug). On 1 Sept, one rocked the Kanto plain in Japan. It happened on 'Disaster Prevention Day' which commemorates a devastating quake in the same place in 1923 which killed 100,000. There were even days (eg 17 Aug) when it seemed as if the whole range of Fortean phenomena were being played out.

There's no doubt about it, from March to September, we've had a hell of a Fortean time.

THE LISTING

1 Jan
2 children at Harlingen, Texas, see 'horrible-looking' black 'bird' with red eyes, this morning. Tracks found layer. Four days earlier (28 Dec 75) Big Bird is seen by two San Benito policeman; and another San Benito encountered what he thinks is the creature the night before (31 Dec 75).

Dr Berthold Schwarz, driving near Great Notch, New Jersey, sees an enormous long-necked 'luminous' white bird gliding in the night sky. *< resident*

3 Jan
'Worst storms & gales in UK for 30 yrs'. Flooding on both UK coasts; 23 dead; 100s injured; est £100 million damages. Also felt on European coast from Holland to France. Its severity caught weathermen by surprise.

7 Jan
A red-eyed 'something from another planet' attacks a trailer in Brownsville, Texas, at 8.30pm.

14 Jan
A 'massive shock' rattles the Kermadec Islands, apx 600 miles NNW of New Zealand.

Man in Raymondsville, Texas, attacked by man-sized red-eyed bat-like creature; 10.30pm.

19 Jan
105 mph cyclone batters coast of Queensland, Australia.

21 Jan
Man attacked by large red-eyed bat-like creature in backyard at Eagle Pass, Texas; 12.45am (poss. hoax).

26 Jan
Huge quantities of Brown-tailed moth cocoons at Havering, E London. Large scale attempt by Council to destroy (see 3 June).

3 Feb
Violent quake at San Martin, Guatemala (over 8 Richter).

4 Feb
Another strong quake at San Martin, Guatemala.

Approximate time of 'Mary F's sighting and photos of Morgawr in Helford estuary, Cornwall (see FT 15/15-17;16/17-19,21).

5 Feb
Minor tremors continue at San Martin.

6 Feb
Another strong quake at San Martin. Dead toll of last few days put at about 10,000.

7 Feb
'Millions' of seaweed flies invade naval base at Portland, Dorset.(✳).

18 Feb
Tremor in the early hours in Fife and Midlothian, Scotland. Global Seismology Unit blame a sound-barrier breaking plane.

19 Feb
Quake in Cuba.

15-yr-old Philip Watts vanishes from Colwyn Bay, N Wales, to turn up in a London underpass a few hours later and 220 miles away, with fatal head injuries. Curious case; will be reported in detail in future FT.(✳)

20 Feb
Tremor shakes house in Faulkner St, Liverpool. Rock adjustment blamed.

24 Feb
3 teachers see giant bird in sky SW of San Antonio, Texas (poss. hoax).

25 Feb
a 'yellow rain' in Hongkong; during 5th warmest Feb on HK records (*).

27 Feb
Apx dating of Bigfoot sighting at Cincinnati, Ohio (see FT 17/22).

5 March
Plague of millions of rats in Senegal, 'displacing or affecting 150,000 people'; thriving despite poisons and flamethrowers.

8 March
Massive stone meteorite breaks into over 100 fragments to fall in region of Kirin City (Chi-lin), China; 3.02pm (see FT 17/9).

Comet West begins to split, first into 2, then 4 parts by 12 March (photos & details in Sky & Telescope June 76).

14 March
Big-footprints found in Alcorn County, Mississippi, over next few weeks (see FT17/22)

Vast numbers of cockroaches invade office building of Sutton Community Health

Office, S London.(✳).

Many girls in South African TV company in Natal, convulse, dance, stare, make weird noises over last week. Believed possessed by devils. (✳).

(Apx date) A wild boar, supposedly extinct in Scotland since 18th C, is killed by vehicle on estate of Earl of Cawdor, near Nairn.(*).

19 March
Chimps in Tarzana, California, pelt 24 policemen with sticks and cabbage stalks (*).

21 March
Fall of 'contents of airliner's toilet' over Bridgwater, Somerset (see FT 15/17).

24 March
Bigfoot makes noises & leaves carcase in early hours, in Mill Valley, California (see FT 17/22).

25 March
Quake at Hopkinsville, Kentucky (during showing of film 'Earthquake'.
Mysterious fire death of man at Paddington police station; early am (see FT 16/4).

27 March
A witchdoctor hired to keep rain off the Malaysian Open golf tournament in Kuala Lumpur. He is successful as other parts of the city are deluged with 'torrential rain' (*).

3 April
Glowing green light seen from Bentwaters near Ipswich, Suffolk; supposed meteor burn-up. (✳).

7 April
Mystery kangaroo sighted in Rock Island, Illinois (*).

9 April
Severe tremor at Stoke on Trent (see FT 16/6-7).
Quake; Ecuador; 18 dead.
15 girls at school at Sand Flat, near Memphis, Mississippi, taken to hospital after writhing and collapsing over last few days; voodoo, food poisoning & drugs suggested, but no evidence found. (✳).
Bluefish in frenzy attack bathers at Pompano Beach, Florida (*).

13 April
Severe tremor at Stoke - now coming at 12 per week.

14 April
2 policemen see large 'unidentified object' with 2 fins rushing through waters of Loch Ness.(✳).

16 April
A woman refugee from Beirut tells that on this day, Easter Friday, 'the clouds came down low and turned red and stayed that colour well into the night. She later learned that a vision of the Virgin Mary had been seen.' (SEE P 24 THIS ISSUE).

Image of crucifix and other Christian symbols discovered in a church window at Benoni, South Africa. (Detailed on p 4 this issue).

17 April
2 girls see the Owlman at Mawnan, Cornwall.

21 April
Vast numbers of caterpillars swarm over courthouse at Bentong, Malaya, interupting proceedings. (✳).

24 April
Bishop closes church in French village of Suave because crowds coming only to gawp at a 'miraculous apparition' of a face on one of its walls over last 2 weeks. (SEE P 4 THIS ISSUE).

26 April
15 red-haired giants attack a hunters' camp in Peruvian jungle, killing several men & abducting 3 women (*).

29 April
Tremor in Riverside Rd, Trent Vale, two days after Jack Ashley promises Government aid in investigating '90 tremors in the last 10 months' at Stoke. Recent activity began 3 weeks ago after a lull of 6 months - Express & Star 30 April 76.
Annular eclipse of sun - account in N.Scientist 6 May 76.

1 May
Blood of St Januarius fails to liquify over next six days (see FT 16/5ff).
3 witches swim nude in Helford estuary to summon Morgawr, but it didn't turn up (see FT 16/18-19).
Sometime between 1 and 7 May a 'big blue dome-shaped object with a revolving red light on top' hovers above rooftops at Braunstone, Leics. The object was described as 'disturbing' and was first see over an army camp at Woodhouse moving towards Leicester - (Radio Leicester 8 May).
2 farming brothers in Heloup, Normandy, see a TV film about rural witchcraft and imagine someone is bewitching them in the same way. They went out and murdered Jean Camus whom they said was responsible for their misfortunes. (✳).

2 May
Last in a series of mysterious 'arson' attacks in village of Winnersh, Berks, kills an old lady. (✳).

4 May

2 men claim to have seen two monsters in the Helford estuary; 10.15am (see FT 16/18).

Apx date of sighting of an Owlman-type creature at Lamorna, Cornwall (see FT 17/17).

6 May

Destructive quake at Udine, N Italy, at 9.02pm - (6.5 Richter). NB: this happened on 6th May, not 7th May as stated on FT16/6. Over 1000 dead, 7500 injured, 150,000 homeless in 24 villages.

Warmest UK May for five years - begining of exceptionally long hot summer.

Grey snow fell in Oestland district of South Norway, 'recently' - Weekly News 6 May 76.(*).

7 May

Multiple fall of chunks of ice near Timberville, Virginia (see full report by Paul Willis in INFO Journal 19 & 20.)(*).

8 May

Severe hailstorm over S London (Eltham, Shooters Hill, Plumstead, Woolich & Charlton) at 6.50pm. Some hail over 1½"dia (see FT 16/13).

9 May

High temperatures (and some violent thunder and lightning storms) over central England.

Sunday Mirror tells of 'phantom sniper' attacks over last few weeks in which 'unknown madman' hurls bricks and stones through windscreens of cars on road between Yarnton and Cassington, Oxon. (*).

11 May

Undersea tremor hurls a tidal wave onto villages on W coast of Columbia.

12 May

Small tremors have been intermittent at Udine since major quake on 6th May.

13 May

'Biggest yet' tremor at Trent Vale, Stoke, in early morning, 'preceeded by a loud bang' - Daily Telegraph 20 May 76.

Partial eclipse of moon.

14 May

In Udine region, N Italy, 'torrential rain, light snow, rock and land slips' make refugees' and rescuers' lives more miserable. 12hrs continucus rain. 69 tremors since 6th May.

Fall of large lumps of ice - one size of football - hit two houses in Reading, Berks, early morning (*)

15 May

Quake; Peru.

Deer kills son of Sultan of Perak (*).

16 May

Quake: Vancouver region of BC and Washington states (5-5.3 Richter) at 1.37am. No casualties - minor damage.

Tremors in N Italy/Yugoslav border continue.

Dr Frazer Tripplett, of Mississippi Allergy Clinic, warns of millions of fireants marching across several southern US states - animal attacked, crops ruined, 1200 cases of treatment for bites and at least two deaths. (*).

Wolf bites boy at Edinburgh Zoo (*).

17 May

Quake in Soviet Uzbekistan (Gazli, Tashkent, Samarkand and Boknara), 7.2 Richter.

Landslide kills 5 in Totos, Peru.

Underground train driver attacked by rabbit at Blake Hall, outer London (*).

18 May

Weak tremors in Uzbekistan - 10000 homeless.

3 tremors in N Italy - '76 since 6 May'.

Volcano on Sakurajima Island,Kyushu, Japan, erupts.

19 May

More tremors at Stoke - major one'preceeded by loud bang'(D Telegraph 20 May).

'Strong quake' on Burma/China border.

20 May

Weird storms over southern England - 'thick blanket of hail' over Sproughton, Suffolk - lightning blacks out villages S of Leicester.

'Typhoon Olga' hits Manila, Philippines; 19 dead, 19 missing, 20,000 flee to shelters. NE provinces of Philippines also badly hit.

21 May

Typhoon Olga continues to batter Philippines.

Typhoon Pamela hits Guam, 1300 miles SE of Philippines.

22 May

Bigfoot kidnap hoax, Bluff Creek, California (see FT 17/21).

More sightings of Morgawr in Helford estuary, Cornwall (*).

23 May

Mistle thrushes attack people in Ossett, near Leeds, Yorks (see FT 17/3).

29 May

2 'severe' quakes in Yunnan province, South China.

Day after Dr Robert Rines announces a new expedition to Loch Ness, sonar on the research ship Cornwall today picks up 2 moving objects 46 and 20 ft long. (*).

CONTINUED ON PAGE 16

This article was conceived partly in answer to statements in previous issues of FT/The News, and partly as a "light hearted interest arouser" to introduce those interested in Robert Forrest's plan to circulate a dossier on the numerous Great Pyramid theories. We hope this will succeed in stimulating much discussion and comment.

That Damned Pyramid by R Forrest

There is a theory about UFOs which says that, whatever they are, they have a curious habit of being moulded according to the contemporary psychology of their observers. In the nineteenth century they were 'dirigibles' (with or without propellors). Here in the twentieth century they are atomic powered saucers.

As a collector of curious ideas about the Great Pyramid, I have come to formulate a similar theory regarding that monument: viz that theories about its origin and significance are somehow a function of contemporary psychology.

In the nineteenth century pyramidology had an intensely Biblical flavour. The pyramid was the Bible in stone. Here in the twentieth century the Great Pyramid has been adopted by the 'Megalithic Mystery' schools as well as by Space Age theorists.

What prompted me to write this little piece was Stuart Greenwood's article in The News 15 (1), where the idea was tentatively put forward that Stonehenge and the Great Pyramid have an approximate great circle relationship (OMITTED - SEE REF). One of my reactions to this piece was that if the Megalithic Builders had intended to indicate such a reciprocal relationship, they would have made a rather better job of it.

But it was the illustration which Mr Greenwood's observations gave to my idea of psychological pyramidology which struck me most of all, because it bears a strong resemblance, in principle at least, to John and Morton Edgar's 'Bethlehem Indicator'(2).

The passages of the Great Pyramid are inclined at $26^{\circ}18'$ to the horizontal. According to the Edgars, a rhumb line (a line of constant bearing) from the Great Pyramid on a bearing of E $26^{\circ}18'$ N (see fig.2.) passes directly through Bethlehem.

In the Bible-in-stone era, this result was welcomed by devout Christian and Pyramidological minds as another miracle incorporated prophetically into the Great Pyramid by the divinely inspired Ancient Architects.

But Pyramid fashions change.

Mr Greenwood, using the great circle instead of a rhumb line, and a face slope angle ($51^{\circ}51'$) instead of the passage angle, finds an admittedly hazy suggestion for the Megalithic Mystery school.

Elsewhere (3) Mr MW Saunders is performing his own brand of numerical acrobatics to link the same face slope angle with an ExtraTerrestrial theory...

It's an odd old world, of course, but the picture of a band of ExtraTerrestrials rigging up the pyramid with one eye on Mars, another eye on Bethlehem and a third eye (no problem for ETs) on Stonehenge is, well, a bit strained.

In any case, in 1923 appeared Conar MacDari's book, Irish Wisdom, with evidence that the Great Pyramid was really built by a band of Irish priests. A fascinating book that one...

* *   * *   * *

A few weeks after the appearance of The News 15, I had a letter from Anthony Bell pointing out that a great circle through the Great Pyramid and oriented towards W 51°51' N (see fig.3.) passed through London and (nearly) Dublin. It was in checking out this claim that I did an experiment which had an amusing and not altogether un-symbolic outcome.

I decided to follow that W 51°51' N great circle, and reasoned that a point on it, strongly indicated by the Pyramid, was where the circle crossed the 51°51' latitude parallel (4). Assuming a spherical earth, I calculated the longitude co-ordinate of the point in question - it was 1°10' W of Greenwich.

To discover what choice secret of Megalithic/ET wisdom I had uncovered, I transferred the co-ordinates (latitude 51° 51' and longitude 1°10') on a 1:50,000 OS map. It turned out to be the Oxfordshire village of Merton with its most prominent architectural structure - a sewage works!

Whether the Cosmic Joker manufactured this coincidence as a comment upon pyramid speculation in general, or my own hypothesis in particular, I have no idea.

Robert Forrest. July 1976.

Notes:

1) Greenwood, Stuart W - 'The Giza-Stonehenge Connection'; The News 15/14-15.

2) Edgar, J&M - The Great Pyramid Passages and Chambers (2nd edn) vol 1, p236. See also Adam Rutherford's Pyramidology, vol 2, p343. For a debunk of the 'Bethlehem Indicator', see W Kingsland's Great Pyramid in Fact & Theory, vol 1, pp47-9.

3) Saunders, MW - Destiny Mars (2nd edn), available from Downs Books, Caterham, Surrey. I have put together some critical notes on this interesting case of Pyramid speculation; copies free on request from me at 68 Chesham Rd, Bury, Lancs...but please enclose postage.

4) A feasible assumption in view of Mr Greenwood's article 'Pyramid Slope and Northern Latitudes' in The News 9/12-13.

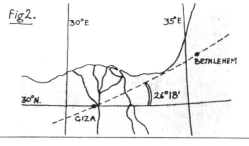

Fig2.

30°E 35°E

BETHLEHEM

30°N. 26°18'

GIZA

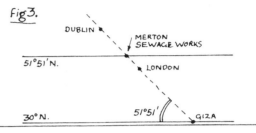

Fig3.

DUBLIN

MERTON SEWAGE WORKS

51°51'N.

LONDON

30°N. 51°51' GIZA

-- Robert Forrest - July 1976 --

GREAT PYRAMID - POSTAL FOLIO

Pyramidologists, like the buffs of many other Fortean topics, tend to work in isolation, breaking cover only occasionally to wrestle others over some obscure point. It is a complex field, full of individual interpretations, some conflicting and others complementary, and based on a wide range of systems (numerology, mythology, anthropology, ET-ology, occultism, cultural diffusionism, etc). Our aim in supporting Robert Forrest's plan for a 'postal folio' is to provide a specific forum in which the serious students can discuss, compare notes, share knowledge and comment on the various theories of the origin and purpose of the GP.

Rob writes: "Anyone who would like to be in on it should write to me (68 Chesham Rd, Bury, Lancs) and I will put them on the mailing list. Obviously we are after people who will actively participate, rather than 'sightseers'. The folio will centre on the GP, though contributors may wish to raise other points.It does not matter how bizarre or orthodox the theory presented - contributors will not necessarily be expected to spout new theories or even learned tomes on existing theories - the main purpose is to contribute to the discussion." Whether this contribution is an article, theory, critique, criticism, notes or any other observations is up to you, but they should be relevant.

3 June
Tremor at Stoke; wardrobe falls on girl; '17th in latest series' of shocks.
'Strong quake' in Soloman Islands, S Pacific; (6.5 Richter).
'Worst cyclone in 40 years' hits Bombay coast at 125mph. Fishing community complains they were not warned by weathermen.
Huge numbers of Brown-tail moth caterpillars hatching around Thamesmead, Kent, causing rashes on all who handle them. This plague seems separate from one at Havering, on northern bank of Thames (see 26 Jan).(*).

4 June
Bombay cyclone moves NE to Gujarat coast.
Monsoon rains in Bangladesh bring heavy floods.

5 June
Glowing orange object in sky over Herne Bay, Kent. One witness (apx 12pm) insisted it was not a flying object, but 'like a big balloon coming down...' No trace of it - Hearne Bay Press 11 June 76).(*).

6 June
Minor quake in Japan.
Many reports of a large fireball seen in England from W Yorks to E Anglia and Kent, moving in a straight line NW to SE to finally explode over the sea off Anglia & Kent. (See report in Essex UFO Group journal Sept 76.(*)

7 June
Quake at Acapulco, Mexico (6 Richter).
Rooks attack house at Newlyn, Cornwall over next 1½ weeks (see FT 17/4,8).
Heavy rains cause extensive floods in Serbia - some dead - towns cut off.

8 June
3 tremors in Udine area.
Heat wave continues in W Europe. London has hottest June day for 6 years (84F) and 88F was recorded at Heathrow Airport.

9 June
Team studying Trent Vale tremors set off own control explosion 'within 330ft of centre of natural tremors' at Clayton.
Hiker claims to see band of 'gypsies' emerge from UFO near Echo Lake, Colorado; gone next morning. Mentioned in letter from Jerry Clark to yr Ed. Case under investigation by Len Stringfield.

11 June
Strong tremor in Friuli area of N Italy, followed by 3 lesser ones.
Huge swarms of ladybirds reported on Somerset coast, near Watchet.
100 children and 6 teachers from primary school at Gravesend, Kent, admitted to hospital; suspected food poisoning; nothing discovered. (*).

15 June
New series of tremors begins at Stoke, to continue over next few days. One was 'severe'.

16 June
'Phantom sniper' fires dart at woman in Hartsdale, NY, at 12.30am. First of several attacks (*).

17 June
'Strong' tremors in N Italy; late night.

18 June
'4th tremor in 4 days' at Stoke, to the surprise of geophysicists who 'thought the pressure had eased.' (D Express 19 June 76).

20 June
'Brilliant pink' light came down near Melton Mowbray, Leics, at 11pm. It was about the 'size of a football' and trailing 'smoke' (*).

21 June
Quake at Medan, Indonesia.

22 June
Axeman runs amok in central Johannesburg hacking 4 down before shot by police.

23 June
'Phantom sniper' fires dart at woman in Greenburgh, NY.
Man who helped traditional Midsummer's Eve bonfire on top of St Agnes Beacon, Cornwall, collapses and dies during lighting ceremony (West Briton 1 July 76).

24 June
'White/green' UFO speeds at 'Mach 1' at North Bay, Canada, near NORAD base.

25 June
Heatwave continues in UK; 91F in London (fraction under hottest ever in 1940); 100F recorded at AA station, Romford, Essex.

26 June
Quake in Indonesian province of Irian Jaya (formerly New Guinea) in remote mountain region (7.1 Richter).
While Britain swelters, torrential rains in Japan. One place had 33½ inches in 3 days causing landslips & floods.
Cook on cruise ship 'Ellinis' docked at Southampton found to be carrier of Paratyphoid B, after mystery illnesses on board.

28 June
Complications in Irian Jaya as huge landslips follow the quake, cutting off and burying whole villages. Est. over 9000 dead; and in Bali, 70,000 homeless.

30 June
Letter to Daily Mirror today tells of huge swarms of ladybirds in West Country recently. (*).

1 July
Quake; Orange Free State.

2 July
2 mile long carpet of ladybirds at Westward Ho!, Devon. (*).

3 July
Mawnan Owlman seen by 2 girls (see FT 17/17), late tonight.

Shellfish bites woman in Weymouth (*).

4 July
Two more girls see Owlman at Mawnan (see FT 17/19).

Doc Shiels, wife & kids see Morgawr from Grebe Beach (*).

5 July
Woman sees 'puma' on Surrey/Hants border
(*).

6 July
Ogopogo sighted on (presumably) Lake Okanagan, Canada. (*).

7 July
50 wild horses dead and an 'unknown number' dying on Cedar Mountain, near Dugway, Utah. Nerve gas blamed, but later verdict was death from shock (!) (*).

Black bear attacks girl in Yukon (*).

Begining of series of sightings of large 'sea-horse-like' monster, chasing boats near Cape Sable Island, Nova Scotia (throughout July - *).

8 July
Luminous UFO changing 'red to bright green' seen in Fly Hills, BC, Canada.

2 Fishermen sight Morgawr 25 miles off The Lizard, Cornwall; and a youth says he saw three small monsters off Grebe Beach (*).

9 July
Schoolchildren and teachers at Redruth, Cornwall see a white spinning 'flying saucer' cross the sky emitting flashes (*).

After weeks of cold & rain, Iceland has a freak heatwave.

11 July
Mines at Stoke reopen after a 2 week holiday in which there were no tremors. This is proof, scientists say, the tremors are linked to mining operations.

Many thousands of starving emus marching across drought-stricken Western Australia 'like a moving sea' in search of water and food.

13 July
2 mechanics testing a boat on Loch Ness say they were surrounded by 5 monsters for 15 minutes (*).

14 July
'3rd quake in 3 weeks' at Bali (5.6-6 Richter); over 250 dead, 2300 injured and 70,000 homeless.

Fall of 'hot ash' and 'white stuff' from strange 'black cloud' accompanied by sulphorous fumes, at St Catherines, Ontario.(*).

'Greenish' UFO reported at CFB Portage La Prairie, Canada.

15 July
Thousands of rabbits invade Atomic Weapons Research Establishment at Aldermaston - yes folks! just up the road from here.

16 July
Quake at Tashkent.

17 July
Millions of ladybirds disrupt life in Scunthorpe, Cleethorpes and Humberside coast. Huge clouds of ladybirds also drive holidaymakers from beaches at Deal, Kent.

Sighting of 'eel-like' creature on Lake Okanagan, Canada.(*).

18 July
Quake at Santiago, Chile.

Ladybird plague along E Anglian coast. (These ladybird swarms will be detailed in a future FT).

20 July
Viking 1 lands on Mars.

The worst drought in 200 years begins to bite in UK - however sudden brief storms happen over SE England; floods in S London; 1½" rain in 90 minutes at Eastleigh, Hants, (see p 9. this issue).

21 July
'Hundreds of thousands' of moth caterpillars swarm over a factory in Hartlepool, Co Durham, blocking out light on many windows. Earlier they had completely stripped a privet hedge in 2 hrs and demolished a rose garden. (*).

(Apx date) Woman sees 'puma' in backgarden in Odiham, Hants (*).

Bigfoot seen near Rainbow Dam, Montana, by 4 men (*).

22 July
Scientists in Canary Islands see giant transparent sphere above road at 10.30pm. 2 humanoid figures inside, with glowing eyes (*).

Bats have been attacking a flat near Wimbledon Common, S London (*).

Swarms of ladybirds cause a mass walkout by steel-men at Hessle, near Hull.(*).

Fleas drive out policemen from station-house at Pewsey, Wilts. (*).

Rain of straw over city of Lincoln.

'Phantom sniper' fires dart at woman in Yonkers, NY, at 10.30pm. Police say 17 women have been hit by darts since Feb. (*).

Sighting of 'large reptile' in Lake Okanagan, Canada.

24 July

American Legion Convention (21-24 July) at Bellvue Stratford Hotel, Philadelphia - later 28 die and 138 hospitalized from a mystery illness (✳).

Aetherian group, lead by Dr George King, charge a prayer-battery on top Holdstone Down, Devon. King warns of quakes, war and pestilence to come on 23 Oct (D Mirror 19 Jly)

25 July

6 'shiny blobs' fly across sky at Garforth, near Leeds. Witness also saw meteorites, but these were 'different' (✳).

27 July

Swarms of ladybirds attack bathers on beaches on S coast of England. (✳).

Swarms of Midges biting women in Lochgoilhead, Argyll. (✳).

Rain of straw over Scunthorpe, Lincs (to be detailed in future FT).(✳).

'Rustlers' kill and skin 13 sheep near Newcastle upon Tyne (✳).

'Violent cloudburst' douses Olympic flame in Montreal, 11 days after opening.

28 July

2 major quakes at Tangshan, 100 miles E of Peking in Hopei province of China, at 4am. The 2 shocks within 2 minutes registered 8.2 Richter, the strongest anywhere since the destruction of Anchorage, Alaska, in 1964. Later est of dead: 100,000. Observers spoke of explosions on the skyline and electrical discharges from the ground (!). Followed by torrential rain - air 'hot and humid'. British Embassy staff in Peking were woken by barking of staff pet retriever seconds before the tremor.

Major shock in Montana (7.9 Richter).

Woman sees Bigfoot near Great Falls, Montana (*).

29 July

Tremors in South Fiji.

Tremors on Panama/Columbia border.

'Strong' tremors in the Caucasus.

Official alert in Peking of a 'heavy quake due within hours'.

Ladybirds invade factory at Killingholme, Lincs, driving out the workers. Other swarms of ladybirds attack bathers at Mablethorpe, Lincs. (✳).

20 wild boars swim river and rampage in small East German village of Calvoerde (*).

2 milkmen sight a lion at Tollerton, Notts, at 6am (see p 25 this issue).

30 July

Series of 'aftershocks' in Tangshan.

Swarms of ladybirds in Derbyshire...and the Derbyshire village of Ashton-on-Trent suffers a plague of crickets. (✳).

31 July

More tremors in Tangshan..

In Big Thompson Canyon area of Colorado, a freak torrential rain (10" in 4 hrs) causes sudden flood - 15ft wall of water. 129 dead, 84 missing (extensive report in National Enquirer 21 Sept 76).

Huge plague of scorpions in Kashan, Persia.(✳).

Huge jellyfish invade beaches on S & W coast of England.(✳).

1 Aug.

Tremor at East Barstow, California .

More tremors in Tangshan (15 in 3 days) and another 'official' alert in Peking for an imminent quake.

Sunday Times today tells of outbreaks of Bubonic Plague in California, Arizona, New Mexico & Colorado.

Doctor sees lion near his home in Normanton, Notts (see p 25 this issue).

2 Aug

Tremor in New Hebrides (6.9 Richter).

Tremor in Nevada.

'Official' warnings in Peking region of 'imminent' quake. Refs to '125 aftershocks' since 28 July of between 4 and 6 Richter.

Huge plague of crickets continues at Ashton-on-Trent, Derbys.

Woman arriving at Toronto International Airport, from London, collapses. Rare Lassa fever suspected. (✳).

4 Aug

Celebration of Pakistan's 29th anniversary cancelled due to continuous rain over last 2 weeks; severe floods; 50,000 homes destroyed.

Complaint in Scunthorpe Evening Telegraph today of swarms of warble flies attacking cattle around Louth & Alford in East Lincs.(✳).

5 Aug

Tremor in Nicaragua.

6 Aug

Tremor E of Honshu, Japan (4.8 Richter).

High hysteria in Logan, Ohio; fear of animal mutilators; increased gun sales; police warn against vigilantes and breaches of the peace.

7 Aug

NE coast of China (Gulf of Po Hai) lashed by torrential rainstorms and floods. This is the recent quake zone and homeless in Tangshan region forced to abandon their tents and take shelter in the city.

Bats continue to attack home near Wimbledon Common, London (see 22 July). (✳).

Twin kills his brother in a 'rage' after curious masquerade attempt; Dieppe, France(✳).

A rare white elephant, a Hindu 'good omen' sighted near Katmandu (*).

8 Aug
6 'aftershocks' around Tangshan, of more than 5 Richter (2 were over 6 Richter).

Tremor in Guatemala.

'Phantom sniper' hunted by police in Milton Keynes, Bucks, after firing at people in a car park. (*).

9 Aug
A 'powerful aftershock' rattles Peking for about an hour.

Tremor in Tungus region, Siberia (5.5 R).

Tremor E of Galapagos Islands off Ecuador (5 Richter); also fell in Nicaragua.

Typhoon Billie hits Japan; torrential rains, floods; 41 dead, 16 missing, 1333 homes damaged.

Hurricane Belle hits Virginia & NY.

Keith Davies does a 'witchdoctor dance' at Kidderminster, Worcs, to end the drought. He was later fined £10 for indecent exposure. Prosecuting police Inspector admitted it had rained within 24 hrs.

Swordfish attacks boat off Massachusetts.

Man encounters lion in Thorganby, Yorks (see p 26 this issue).

Baby dies in fire of unknown origin, in Middlesborough (*).

10 Aug
'Official' alert in Peking for another 'imminent' quake. Fresh tremors in Tangshan.

Tremors in Columbia and Ecuador (5.5 R).

2 Tremors SW of Zagreb, Yugoslavia.

Hurricane Belle spreads out to New York, and Connecticut and New Jersey; 110mph winds drop to 50mph in Connecticut River Valley after blacking out Bridgeport area; 1000s abandon homes.

Week-long deluge of rain affect 5281 villages in 19 districts of Lahore, Pakistan, as Indus and tributaries overflow.

Typhoon Billie hits Taiwan at 115mph; floods; Keelong port blackedout.

Police in Barking, London, hunt a phantom marksman who has hit 5 women (in single shots) over last few weeks, wounding them. No readily apparent connexion with similar phantom sniper MC 45 miles away on the 8th Aug.(*).

Announcement of discovery of 2 'perfect preserved bodies' interred before the eruption at Pompeii in 79 AD.

11 Aug
Tremor in Riverside/San Diego area of California; 8.30am; (4.3 Richter).

Volcano of Mt Sangay, in Ecuador's Andes erupts. 6 man scientific team only few feet from top (later rescued; 2 dead).

Lone sailor, 30 miles NNW of Scilly Islands, sees Morgawr for 20 minutes (*).

A monkey discovered wild in fields near Gainsborough, Lincs (*).

12 Aug
Tremors in Galapagos ridge.

Tremors in Soloman Islands.

Tremor in California.

Torrential rain in 3 Korean provinces over next three days.

Floods in Jammu province, Kashmir; 67 dead, 3000 homes damaged.

13 Aug
An 'air-quake' at Radstock, Midsomer Norton, Chilcompton and Chewton Mendip in Somerset; 10am; 'crackling in the sky'(*).

Tornado hits Largo, Florida; 1 dead, 7 injured, much damage.

30,000 evacuated from area around 5000ft volcano, La Soufriere, on Basse Terre Island Guadeloupe; lava moving down slopes; clouds of hot ash; 'activity growing'.

UFO like large ball of fire seen over London, Ontario, for 20 mins at 10.30pm.

14 Aug
Vast floods follow deluges in Korea; 16" rain in 3 days; 34 dead, 32 missing.

Gulls attack woman in Berwick.

Apx 100 teenage bandsman marching in Walden, NY, collapse with mystery nausea and cramp.(*).

Police take away a rapidly-growing mystery plant found in garden in Reading, Berks(*).

15 Aug
Peking lifts 'quake alert'...'no strong quake will occur in near future'.

'Swarm of mild quakes' SE of Berkeley, California.

16 Aug
Massive quake near Mienyang, 250 miles N of Chunking (Ssu-ch'uan province), 800 miles from Tangshan; 7.2 Richter; 2.07pm.

2 hrs later, quake in Moro Gulf, 550 miles S of Manila; 7.8 Richter; followed by 24ft tidal wave which smashes island of Mindanao. Followed by 6 'aftershocks'.

Another quake in the Moluccas, between New Guinea and Halmahera Island, 600 miles SE of Philippines (8.1 Richter).

Gouts of hot ash & sulphorous fumes with quake-like tremors from La Soufriere. Experts say full-scale A-bomb-like explosion will happen 'within 12 hrs'; 70,000 evacuated. (See p 10 this issue).

Image of 'Christ crucified' found on asbestos wall of henhouse in Hampshire (see p 3 this issue). APX DATE.

'Noiseless silver' UFO with white lights seen over New Hamburg, Ontario.

Ken Rogers writes to yr Ed: 'Where have all the ladybirds gone?' Where indeed! (✳).

17 Aug

Philippine damage put at over 3000 dead, 2000 missing, 30,000 homeless. Later figures estimate 6000 dead & missing.

Quake in Central Japan, 60 miles SW of Tokyo.

La Soufriere, on Guadeloupe, giving '1000 tremors in 24 hrs'; ash 'completely covered' abandoned town of St Claude; geyser of fire lights night sky from 500yd gash in its flank.

'Giant wave' sweeps over Mayaro Beach, near Port of Spain, Trinidad; 5 dead.

Bats invade house at Corsham, Wilts.(✳).

Giant plant discovered at Shalford, Surrey (✳).

Old man dies of burns in Bath, Somerset, after found in blazing armchair; cause of fire unknown. (✳).

A kangaroo evades police at Golden, Colorado (*).

18 Aug

Tremors in Izu peninsula, Japan.

Tremors in Brisbane, Australia.

Tremor in N Italy.

19 Aug

2 quakes within seconds at Denizli, Turkey; 4.6 Richter.

Severe storms on Adriatic coast causing floods and landslides.

Horde of wild cats invade waste ground near Heathrow Airport.(✳).

20 Aug

'Minor' quake at Tocopilla, Chile.

'2 aftershocks' at Denizli, Turkey.

'Scores' of tremors on La Soufriere.

'2 mild' tremors in Manila.

Severe floods in Pakistan after further 2 weeks of torrential rain; 200,000 homeless in Punjab; and in Sind province, Indus over-flows damaging 85,000 homes.

Death of girl in mystery fire in base-ment, Bath, Somerset; apx 6-7am (✳).

21 Aug

Quake; N of Cheng-tu City (Ssu-ch'uan province); 6.5 Richter; late night.

2 quakes;at Urfa on N Turkey border with Syria; and at Siirt, also N Turkey.

2 'strong' tremors at Cotabato, S Philip-pines; 7am; followed by 'aftershocks'.

Tremors in Alaska.

Strong tremor near Iquique city, Chile.

22 Aug

Farmers ask to go back to La Soufriere to harvest threatened fields; request denied despite failure of predicted eruption. Other warnings given for Cyclone Emmy about to hit the island.

Man sets fire to himself (fatally) at police station, Pontefract, Yorks.

Official figs on drought; UK rainfall down 25-33%.

Anglican clergy at Exeter Cathedral resort to 17th C prayer for rain.

23 Aug

'Major quake' between Ssu-ch'uan and Kansu provinces in W China; 6.7 Richter; 3.30am; 'aftershocks' in Cheng-tu region.

Shortly after that a quake rocks Philip-pines; '6th since 16th Aug'; 6 Richter.

'Strong tremor' in Guadeloupe.

7 'minor' tremors in Turkey.

Tremor in Yokohama region, Japan.

'Mild' tremor in Athens, Greece.

'Aftershock' in Alaska.

Casting of petrified woman from Pompeii landed in London for exhibition at Royal Academy on 20 Nov.

24 Aug

Tremor in Florence, Italy.

Anniversary of destruction of Pompeii in AD 79.

Typhoon Ellen gives Hongkong 'worst deluge in 50 yrs'; 19" in just over a day; floods, landslips, black-outs, traffic chaos.

'Worst monsoon in 20 yrs' hits Punjab; 180 dead; floods affect 2,500 villages, & 170,000 homes damaged; crops wiped out.

Bigfoot seen near Whitehall, NY (*).

25 Aug

2 red & blue flickering UFOs seen at Walkerton, Ontario.

2 policemen sight Bigfoot near Whitehall, NY (*).

26 Aug

Sikh community in Southall, London, hire a guru (Jagat Singh Ji) to end the drought. No rain mentioned in official forecasts.

Thames Water Authority announce that 15 million gallons per day is leaking from the Thames near Oxford, because of low water-table. 'To all intents the great river has now stopped flowing.' Millions of gallons being pumped from Teddington lock to rep-lenish reservoirs at Thames head.

'Clusters' of multicoloured UFOs near Sioux Falls, S Dakota. 'In recent weeks' a woman driver is followed by glowing 'saucer'; and 2 boys see 'tall figure in shiny blue uniform' (✳).

'More than 30' ducks dead from unknown causes in several S London parks. (✳).

27 Aug

First rain in some parts of England for at least 2 parched months. A light drizzle at Heathrow Airport causes round of applause and 'great excitement'.

A sailor sights Morgawr in Carrick Roads off Restronguet Point, Cornwall, '3 times in 10 minutes' (✳).

Mystery animal (later identified from tracks as puma) kills geese at Eaglesham, Renfrewshire, near Glasgow (*).

28 Aug

Hailstorm of 'hurricane force' in Mexico City; 12 dead, dozens injured, 10,000 evacuated; black-outs. In some districts so much ice fell it was '4ft deep in the streets' and caused flooding when melted.

Body of nude man found in empty house on fire in Rotherhithe, London; clothes neatly folded beside body (✳).

Number of sparrows drop dead in Bath, Somerset; cause unknown (✳).

Woman in Glenfarg, Perthshire, discovers a 'lynx' in her garden (*).

2 USAF C141 cargo planes crash within 4 hrs; one in Greenland, one near Peterborough, in Cambs. 'Unbelievable coincidence' (see p 10 this issue).

29 Aug

Small Bigfoot seen near Kelly AF Base, San Antonio, Texas. Refs to sightings of larger creatures, & animals killed, in previous week (*).

30 Aug

'Sharp' quake in Cotobato, Philippines.

La Soufriere erupts after 2 explosions slightly injuring 12 scientists on summit. 'Scientists do not expect it to erupt again'.

Pheasant attacks postmen in Devon (*).

31 Aug

Quake at Simitli-Berovo area of Yugoslav/ Bulgarian border.

Incredible proliferation of duckweed on UK canals and rivers throughout August; described as an 'explosion'.

1 Sept

On 'Disaster Prevention Day' in Japan, the Central Meteorological Agency detects two minor tremors, one on the Kanto Plain, and the other off-shore near Tokyo.

For the first time this century there was no rainfall throughout August, in Brisbane, Australia.

Milkman at East Grinstead, Sussex, sees a bright white and yellow light speeding across the sky (✳).

Millions of maggots in Rosebank Rd, Hanwell, Middlesex; and a plague of fleas at Thanet and E Kent coast.(✳)

2 Sept

Taal, a volcano 60 miles S of Manila, begins a series of eruptions that continue for next three days.

For 2nd time in 2 days, a mystery illness hits the employees of Robertshaw Control Co in Grove City, Ohio. (✳).

3 Sept

Colony of Colorado beetles found in a potato field at Minster-in-Thanet, Kent.

4 Sept

Hurricane Francis hits the Azores at 75mph - the '2nd hurricane in several days'.

Viking 2 lands on Mars (appx).

'Puma' sighted near Nuneaton, Warks (*).

5 Sept

Taal, in Philippines, erupts again with molten rock.

Sunday Times warns of huge increase in feral mink population of Britain, from Devon to Cumbria - urges introduction of a trapping programme and a mink bounty.

Weird gourd-like plant thriving at Canterbury baffles gardners (✳).

6 Sept

Taal again hurls rocks into the sky.

Soviet pilot defects to Japan with top-secret MiG-25 'Foxbat' (see p 10 this issue).

8 Sept

Swarms of poisonous adders invade The Humps, a beauty spot near Canterbury. (✳).

A sceptic sights Morgawr for 3 mins off Gyllyngvase Beach, Cornwall, now 'believes'(✳)

9 Sept

Mao tse-tung dies.

10 Sept

Quake at Skopje, S Yugoslavia, late pm.

Taal rumbles and lights the night sky with incandescent gas.

SW Japan flooded by 24" rain in 2 days.

Numerous reports of Sasquatch over this last week at Kimberly, BC, Canada.(✳).

'Worst air collision in history' near Zagreb kills 177, as British Airways Trident hits Yugoslav DC-9.

11 Sept

2 Quakes in Friuli region, near Udine, N Italy, 4 mins apart; 5.1 & 5.4 Richter.

100mph typhoon nears SW Japan, already flooded with 12" rain in parts.

Appx date of Italian groups sighting and photo of a monkey-like being, 4ft high, in leather overall and white helmet descending from a landed Flying Saucer. Italian police say they are taking it seriously. (✳).

5000-gallon petrol tanker overturns & explodes destroying center of Bedfordshire village of Westoning; despite extensive damage only 3 slightly injured.

12 Sept
A freak 5ft wave floods through Yorks market town of Stokesley, as River Leven swells from 24 continuous hours of rain. River Ouse at York rises 10ft; floods. The long severe drought comes to an end with heavy rain all over Britain.

2 holidaymakers see Morgawr on Grebe Beach, Cornwall, at 8.30am. First land sighting (✻).

13 Sept
Heavy UK rainfall continues creating bizarre anomaly as during extensive flooding some areas are still under water restriction and the use of standpipes.

15 Sept
'21 tremors between early morning and lunchtime in 5th successive day of tremors' in Friuli region, N Italy - 2 were greater than the 6 May quake. Fortunately most people were still in 119 tent cities.

Coldest night in Paris for 103 years.

'New genus' of giant sponge found off Californian coast. Despite being found growing on barrels of Plutonium waste, Robert Dyer, of Radiation Dept of US Environmental Protection Agency, does not blame radiation leaks. (✻).

17 Sept
Cardinal Ursi, of Naples, urges people to pray that the blood of St Januarius will liquify on his feast day (19th) and avert disaster for another six months.

Huge swarm of wasps attack crowd at community festival in Florence, Italy.

USAF F-14 'Tomcat' lost in sea off north Scottish coast in NATO exercise (see p 10).

19 Sept
St Januarius's blood liquifies on schedule in Naples.

20 Sept
RN minesweeper 'Fittleton' sunk after collision during NATO exercise; 12 dead (see p 10 this issue).

21 Oct
'Puma' bounds across the Glasgow road at Blantyre, Lanarkshire (*).

22 Sept
Manila rocked by quake 90 miles SW under South China Sea.

Despite rain in other parts of England, drought continues in central & S Wales. The Severn flows at a fifth of normal rate, and losing water into surrounding land at 15 million gallons/day.

Soldier on night duty at Windsor Castle collapses after seeing statue 'move' (see p 24 this issue).

2 separate haystack fires near Manassa, Texas - 8th & 9th in series of fires of mystery origins in Conejos County throughout Sept (✻).

24 Sept
'Freak wave' during night swamps Cornish village of Polperro.

In hotel at Penmaenmawr, N Wales, a man shoots 5 people, sets fire to building and shoots himself. 2 other cases of suspected multiple murder and arson reported in the previous week (✻).

25 Sept
6 air crashes in US; 4 of them in 4 hrs. (USAF KC135 tanker at Alpena, Mich.; 'Gulf- stream' jet at Hot Springs, VA; a Cessna at Peoria, IL; 2 engined at Kent, Wash.; 2 engined at Steamboat Springs, Colo.; 2 single trainers at Beatrice, Nebraska.)

1 Oct
The 'wettest Sept for 50 years' in parts of England - so soon after the worst drought for 200 years.

A mystery contagion caused over 80 deaths near Juba, in Maridi area of Sudan in Sept. It appeared & vanished; that's all we know (✻).

3 Oct
Block of flats in Southwark, London, invaded by millions of maggots from refuse chute.(✻).

4 Oct
In Japan, trains unable to make a steep gradient because of plague of worms.(✻)

A series of quakes begins in central Ecuador.

6 Oct
Major quake in Cotopaxi province of Ecuador; 10 killed, 100s homes destroyed over last 3 days.

8 Oct
'Strong' quake in N Japan & Tokyo area.

A strong and 2 weak tremors shake Valanduvo, 75 miles S of Skopje, Yugoslavia.

15 Oct
15,000 ton cargo ship, 'Slylia L. Ossa', reported missing, feared sunk, in Bermuda Triangle area (✻).

23 Oct
'Lioness' spotted wandering around Upton district of Chester; none missing and police search finds nothing (*).

28 Oct
Soviet ship is circled by a mysterious 'white spot' in Arabian Sea. The 'Unknown mass, 60ft below the ship's keel' disappeared suddenly after half an hour. (✻).

PARTIAL ANALYSIS OF 1976 & LUNAR PHASES

Date	1	2	3	4	5	6	7	8	9	10	11	12	13	14	15	16	17	18	19	20	21	22	23	24	25	26	27	28	29	30	31
JAN	i		p		noo	o o	i								io		FULL MOON		p		i	3/4				q					NEW MOON
FEB			o		q																			i	j		f				
MAR			c m				b	c	dl o				o			s l		o	o goo		j			ko		p		co			
APR	g m	k		in		hj o		p	e	o	o		o	n		s i			d		q	p n d		f	f			no		q	
MAY	o		opp q			c mp			e				co jl op		o l		o	o to	o o	p l	egm k		h	m h	opi					
JUNE	o		di in			n	gl n	m n	imo o	lq				jmq o	e l	e o	nq oq	o	cm o	o	o g	g	egm k					no		q	
JULY	bo oq			pqo	o		bde gp	bde kq pi	bde kq pi	afai opop	bn ot	pr l r	dp pr l r	dp om r	o pm os t	bdo ko pr t	opko qt	opko qt		r a	chbf p	de ijn q		egm h	l m	fm m n p	jg i qp	fo oq	bd oq	op q l	op op q l
AUG	m oq	lt q		bc pp	o		o	nq						ar			ad q		r a		hk os		gk a			ab f gk p				do t	o o t
SEPT	l		q	qo			o	oi												b		b						r			
OCT																															

KEY : UNDERLINED LETTERS = MULTIPLE EVENTS.

Accidents (major & series)........a
Animals (mystery & out-of-place).b
Astronomical events...............c
Attacks by animals................d
Attacks ('phantom snipers; etc)..e
Bigfoot & other 'manimals'........f
Deaths (strange, & murders).......g
Drought (heat, etc)..............h
Entities (inc Owlman, Bigbird)...i
Falls.............................j
Fires (inc possible SHCs).........k
Illness (mystery).................l
Lights (inc UFOs).................m
Monsters (lake & sea critters)..n
Quakes & tremors..................o
Rain, winds & waves & floods....p
Swarms, migrations & plagues....q
Various others....................r
Visions (inc mystery images, etc)s
Volcanoes.........................t

I'd like to thank the following from whose clippings the list was compiled: GL Abbott, TR Adams, Jeremy Beadle, Anthony Bell, Mollie Cairncross, Tim Church, Jerry Clark, Richard Cotton, Robert Forrest, Mark Hall, Chris Holtzhausen, P Hope-Evans, Phil Ledger, Mrs V Martin, DO Mayes, John Michell, Steve Moore, P Rogerson, Roger Sandell, Paul Screeton, Doc Shiels, Anthony Smith, Nigel Watson, Ion Will, I, Andy York. Special thanks to X from whose Res Bureaux Bulletin I've taken all the Canadian data; to Jerry Clark from whose article 'Unidentified Flapping Objects' in Oui, Oct 76, I've updated our info on the Texas Big Bird; to Doc Shiels for the constant flow of Cornish clippings; and to Ken Rogers and Ion Will who bombarded me with welcome bundles of clippings on the geo-meteorological chaos. Keep it up fellas!

** RJM Rickard - Oct 1976 **

BVM AT BEIRUT

The Scunthorpe Star, 14 May 76 (Cr: Nigel Watson) tells of the homecoming of a local girl who fled back to Britain with her two children from the civil war in the Lebanon; her husband remained there looking after their interests. Tucked away in the story of Janice Mekhdjian's eventful flight was this interesting paragraph:

'The most unusual thing she saw, apart from the fighting, was on Easter Friday ((16 April - Ed)). The clouds came down low and turned red and stayed that colour well into the night. She later learned that a vision of the Virgin Mary had been seen.' Does anyone know any more about this event?

BVM IN SICILY

The only other BVM sighting on file and untold says that about 30 people in the small village of Cefala Diana ((Oh those classical allusions)) claimed the Madonna had appeared to them every afternoon for a week in the window of a ruined castle nearby. The local priest refused to see the apparition with them. Daily Mirror, 2 June 1967 (Cr: Anthony Smith).

A MOVING EXPERIENCE AT WINDSOR

It appears that on the night of 22nd Sept a 19-year-old Coldstream Guardsman on duty overlooking a sunken garden in the grounds of Windsor Castle   saw something which frightened him so much he collapsed. After he was discovered and recovered in hospital he 'swore to hospital doctors that a statue of a horned man in chains suddenly came alive before his eyes.' Despite several mentions of the story in the press very few details are known because the Army have refused to make any more information available. The unnamed Guardsman was sent away for several days rest and attempts to get statements from the barracks near the castle have met with silence.

We wrote to the Guardsman via his commanding officer and received a reply from a Major EBL Armitage (1st Battalion CGs) who kindly informed us that he had passed the letter to the soldier who in turn asked the Major to reply for him. The soldier said 'that he wished to be allowed to forget this rather frightening incident.' The Major added that he hoped we 'will understand his feelings and will wish to respect his desire to say no more of the matter.' It is clear that despite the police dismissal of the occasional reports of ghosts in the Castle grounds as 'the imagination, lonliness and fear' of young Guardsmen', the Army at least was taking the man's frightened state seriously.

Much comment in the press centred on the famous Berkshire legends about a horned character called Herne the Hunter, a curious and complex blend of fact, fiction, myth and folklore (see Herne the Hunter by MJ Petry (William Smith, London St, Reading; 1972).

The press seemed to regard Herne as a strange
ghost with phantom footsteps and phantom
horses, and some of the subsequent correspondence in the Sunday Express told of other
Guardsmen being frightened by phenomena of
this kind in the past. The more ancient folk
lore links Herne with Cernunnos, the Celtic
god associated nowadays with witchcraft; and
to the horned leader of the Wild Hunt. These
references should be easily available in any
good book on English folklore and are too
complex to go into here.

What interested me more was that I had
just finished writing a section for the book
with Michell on 'Images which come to life',
covering the whole subject of statues and
icons seen by many to come alive. Obviously
the notion of the poor soldier being frightened by a ghost was less preposterous to many
people than any literal interpretation of his
statement that he had seen a statue become
unexpectedly animated. You will have to wait
for the book to see some of the precedents
for the soldier's story because we've no room

here. Naturally I respect the man's wishes,
and share the Army's concern for his recovery, but I can't help regret that this rare
opportunity to learn of a phenomenon that has
repeated throughout history should so suddenly be withdrawn.

As a footnote it's worth mentioning that
Windsor is not far from the barracks at
Aldershot where Springheel Jack first played
his pranks on lonely sentries in 1877. Also
Fort mentions (Books p647; cf Daily Mail 6
March 1906) that on the 3rd March 1906 a
sentry on night duty in the ornamental garden
at Windsor Castle shot at something that
frightened him. The man's account is not
given but it was said to have been one of the
stone elephants which had 'looked ghostly in
the moonlight.'

(Cr on the modern accounts go to Steve
Moore, Ian Thompson, Peter Roberts, Peter
Rogerson & Chris Castle, for clippings from
Sunday Express 22 Sept & 10 Oct 76; Daily
Mirror & the Guardian 27 Sept 76.)

OUT OF PLACE

THE NOTTINGHAM LION SAGA

A story to rival the 'Surrey Puma' began
shortly after 6am, 29 July 76, when two
milkmen were delivering to a bungalow opposite the entrance to Nottingham Airport on
Tollerton Lane between Nottingham and Tollerton. Different accounts put it at 15 or
50 yards away from the men; they were in no
doubt: 'We both saw together what certainly
to us was a lion...its head down and its
long tail had a bushy end. It was walking
slowly away from us.' They watched it walk
around the edge of a field, then called the
police from the bungalow. By nightfall the
police mounted a huge search, with dogs,
guns, loud hailers, and a helicopter, in
the Tollerton and West Bridgford areas. The
police also said they had calls from people
telling of the mysterious restlessness of
their pets on the night of the 28/29th; and
a local farmer, at Clipston, near Cotgrave,

reported 'strange pawprints' on his land.
Nottingham Evening Post, 29 July 76 (Cr:
Mollie N Cairncross, DO Mayes); Leicester
Mercury (Cr: R Cotton), Yorks Post (Cr: AJ
Bell), London Evening News (Cr: K Rogers) all
of the same date.

They found nothing. They checked zoos
and private lion-owners within 100 miles but
'no one appears to have lost a lion.' They
said they were taking at least 15 sightings
seriously. The hunt hit a turning point in
its second day when a sighting at Radcliffe-
on-Trent turned out to be somebody's Great
Dane. At the same time a sighting came in
from Basingfield. One of the reports was
from as far away as Norfolk by a couple who
said they saw a lion in a lay-by at Lowdham
but did not report it because they didn't
think they'd be believed. Yet despite these
sightings, the police were getting disappoint-

ed by the lack of anything positive. As in the 'Surrey Puma' cases (see INFO Journal 13 and The News 14) one of the puzzling elements was the lack of any sign of killed livestock, no pets missing etc, as there would be if a lion were conventionally on the loose. The milkmen were re-checked and both (David Crowther and David Bentley) were unshaken in their belief they had actually seen a lion. Nottingham Evening Post (Cr: Mollie N Cairncross, Janet & Colin Bord), Leicester Mercury (Cr: R Cotton, Ken Rogers), Derby Evening Telegraph (Cr: Ken Rogers), and the national dailies (Cr: Steve Moore, Ion Will, Ivan Bunn, Peter Hope-Evans, Judith Gee) all of 30 July 76.

On the third day of the hunt reports of sightings were still coming into West Bridgford police station, the nerve-centre of the operations. Eg: one caller heard something large crashing through Bunny Woods, and another heard something in a copse near Trent Lane church at East Bridgford. In fact the police were obliged to maintain the alert. Nottingham Evening Post 31 July 76 (Cr: Mollie Cairncross, DO Mayes).

Martin Lacey, a former Nottingham Zoo owner, enters the fray, saying all the noisy activity has driven the lion into hiding, and offers the use of his lion-hunting Rhodesian ridgeback hounds. Sunday Express 1 Aug 76 (Cr: Steve Moore, Mrs V Martin).

Just as the press were losing interest in the 'Nottingham Lion' the story receives a shot in the rump. John Chisholm, a doctor of Normanton-on-the-Wolds, near Tollerton, saw a large animal trying to break through some undergrowth to get to a stream on the evening of the 1st Aug while he was walking near his home. When he returned home he and his wife watched it leave the area from their upstairs window. Police said they were following up several other sightings in the same area. Nottingham Evening Post (Cr: Mollie Cairncross, DO Mayes), Leicester Mercury (Cr: R Cotton), London Evening News (Cr: Ken Rogers, Steve Moore) all of the 2nd Aug 76. Oh yes...it may be nothing, but we note with interest in the Evening Post account that police searching the A610 at Temple Lake, near Kimberley, found a large tortoise on the embankment. They were unable to trace any owner and so they adopted it.

The dailies for the next day (3rd) run the story of Dr Chisholm's sighting. Naturally in everybody's eyes the fact that he is a deputy coroner makes the sighting more impressive and believable. (Cr: Ken Rogers, Ion Will). The Nottingham Evening Post for the 3rd deals mainly with an intensification of police searches, and contains the official statement that they were 'now 98% certain

there was an animal in the area! (Cr: Mollie Cairncross).

The Nottingham and Leicester papers continue to mention the police searches, but already Chief Inspector John Smith is publicly wishing 'it had been seen by any of my men.' He also asked farmers to make regular checks on their livestock. It's the sixth day and still no reports of any depredations. (Cr: Mollie Cairncross, R Cotton, DO Mayes).

By the 6th Aug the lack of results was telling on the police. They issued a statement saying they 'no longer believed there was a lion at large despite 65 reported sightings in the last 8 days.' They said they they proved to be mistakes, large dogs, and even a large brown paper bag. Oh how ole Charlie would have roared at that! It seems that no Fortean phenomena can continue without incurring efforts to kill off the mystery. Any one looking for a thesis theme could attempt to plot critical kill-off periods - I'd say between 1 and 2 weeks. Nottingham Eve. Post (Cr: Mollie Caincross) Scunthorpe Eve. Telegraph (Cr: Nigel Watson), London Eve. Standard (Cr: Ken Rogers), all of 6 Aug 76; and most of the dailies the next day (who really went wild over the paper bag theory) (Cr: Steve Moore, Ivan Bunn, Peter Hope-Evans); Sunday Times, 8 Aug 76 (Cr: Steve Moore, Ken Rogers).

So...it was never there and people were mistaken! A paper bag with a lion's tail and which walks around fields imitating our feline friends would be a marvel in its own right. So...despite officially non-existing, the police announce three more reports of it in the Plumtree and Normanton areas - Nottingham Eve. Post, 9 Aug 76 (Cr: M Cairncross). This is the last we heard of the 10-day illusion, to date - but doubtless the story will not end there just yet.

A YORKSHIRE LION
No sooner had the Nottingham mystery been killed off, it turns up over 70 miles away just south of York. On the night of the 9th Aug, Alan Pestall was on the way to his local, walking down the moonlight main street of the village of Thorganby, when a black shadow crossed in front of him, by the church. He thought it was a dog and spoke to it. 'Then I realised it had a cat's face and a long tail. It was about 3 to 4ft long and nearly 3ft high. Before I had a chance to run, it leapt over a fence and was away over the fields.' He kept walking slowly to the pub, believing if he hurried or turned it would attack him. Police took his story seriously and mounted a search on the 10th, but found no sign of a lion. A police spokesman said: 'We have no reason to connect this report with the recent sightings of a lion in Nott-

inghamshire.' If they had,they'd have to explain how it could move so quickly over 70 miles of industrial landscape without being seen. Teleporting phantoms are plainly inconceivable. Yorkshire Eve. Post, 10 Aug 76 (Cr: Anthony Bell); Dail Mail, 11 Aug 76 (Cr: R Cotton). Where will it pop up next, I wonder?

*** This has been an astonishing time for the Fortean menagerie, not just in England, but some correspondents have mentioned the return of phantom kangaroos in Indiana and Illinois. More of this soon, hopefully next issue, when we'll also tell of the latest puma, lynx, wild boar, exotic snakes and other animals on the loose in the UK. We'll also have a very interesting article by Peter Roberts on the alien insect life in this country. There's so much to squeeze in.

The Secret Country by Janet & Colin Bord. (Paul Elek; £5.95; pp238; bib & 3 indexes; copiuosly illustrated; hardback, 1976). The secret country is, of course, in plain view all around us if we'd open our eyes. It is veiled by the mental and cultural barriers instilled in us by the world-view we were taught at school. In the Victorian apotheosis our ancestors were primitive savages from whose deplorable condition we raised ourselves smoothly, inexorably, by wit and natural selection. That view founders as more evidence comes to light that cultures rose and fell, and that we are just one of many peaks - as were the megalithic builders. It is so easy to judge on the basis of cities and amenities - they were no worse or worse-off than ourselves - just different! The studies of Michell, MacKie, Borst, Hawkins and Thom, et al,have shown they had a high degree of mathematical skill, all the more impressive for the lack of notational records. It is reasonable to suppose that they developed quite different mental abilities from those we have today, so that the things the archeologists look for (written records, pots, tools and trinkets, roads and cities, money, etc) are the very things they thought least of. With a shift in our own mentality the signs of that ancient culture become a little clearer. All around us are the eloquent stones and the fragmented traditions of folklore, myth and symbolic order, not to mention the unexplored reaches of racial memory.

Slowly, and in the face of hostility from an orthodoxy that should know better, some patient scholars are bringing the fragments together, inching their way toward a vision of the living megalithic culture before the long dissolution and degeneration of its science, beliefs and traditions. In this welcome book the Bords continue the journey through the secret country, down folk-memory lane, that they begun in their Mysterious Britain.

The central theme in SC are the sites and stones in the ancient British landscape - but this is not just another of those books on old stones that seem to be springing up like overnight mushrooms. They form the linkage in this essential collection of folklore and anecdote (a surprising amount of it modern) about these stones and sites. It's certainly a book I've felt was needed for some time. I'm glad to say it's a damned good read; packed with interesting information quoted from rare and varied sources, richly illustrated with Colin's beautiful new photos of most of these locations; plus 3 indexes (general, geographical, and sites named in the text), and a bibliography. I enthusiastically recommend it.

As a Fortean I'm in search of continuity, and SC has plenty of it. The correspondence between folk tradition, the landscape with its strange monuments, and the world of unconscious imagery is striking - particularly as most of these links describe or hint at what we would today call Fortean phenomena.

For example, one of the most intriguing, and baffling, traditions of British folklore is the amazing wealth of stories about the founding of early churches which are later said to have been moved to the present site by the devil, fairies or magic, even teleportation; the original site being sacred to the earlier religions who used supernatural beings to frustrate the Christian invaders. This accords well with the ancient belief that the stones were alive, and were quite able to move by themselves thank you , if they were driven to it.

The living stones naturally were products of, and could control, the currents of terrestrial energy, and although this force was normally associated with fertility, its negative aspect was terrible. We hear of stones that heal and destroy; that warn and guard as well as any dog; that get revenge on their desecrators; that grow in size and multiply themselves; that occasionally get up and dance, or wander about, or fly through the air; or that could become immovable during any sacrilegious attempt to shift them. It is testimony to the power of these beliefs that they have survived into this cynical age through uncaring and hostile centuries.

The Bords give these subjects room, and in some cases a chapter, and their love of folklore shows in the fascinating stories that illustrate them, many of which have been hidden away too long. Nor do they forget our other friends from the Fortean menagerie; fairies and ghosts, UFOs and lake monsters, and their time-lost cousins, the dragons that traditionally guarded the treasures in the earth, and slept under stones, coiled around the terrestrial pulse.

They correctly identify a curious anomaly presented by the notion of leys and their energy. The only (relatively) clear tradition of geomantic technology , the feng-shui of China, abhors straight lines, and indeed provides a few cosmetic measures to counter the evil 'winds' or 'arrows' generated by them (eg. spirit-walls, bends in paths, mirrors placed opposite windows, etc). So why the proliferation of straight alignments here in the West? Steve Moore (TLH 72 & 73) has suggested the idea of 'mirrored' forces, so that what was negative and destructive in the East becomes benign and constructive in the West. Perhaps it was just as negative in the West, muse the Bords, and that megalithic man, typically Western, sought a material solution in the technological control and manipulation of this energy using stone devices (basically a large-scale transistor circuit without wires!). Naturally this contained the seeds of its own destruction, and although it could have worked well initially, soon milked the land of vitality. It is a matter of record that fertility, ecology and climate over areas of western Europe declined and brought to an end the Bronze Age.

This book would make a nice Christmas gift to those interested in the past, or the strange. Again I urge it upon you, and thank the Bords for a valuable compendium of obscure and wonderful data.

Visitors from Space by John A Keel. (Panther; 75p; pp237; paperback). At long last John Keel's The Mothman Prophecies has been published in England, and at a price which puts it within easy reach. But why in Bog's name did Panther have to go and change its name? It's as inexplicable as the stuff in John's book.

VFS (I suppose I'll have to call it) is the account of the UFO-centered phenomena that led up to the collapse of the Silver Bridge that crosses the Ohio river between Ohio and West Virginia, at 5.04pm, 15 December 1967. It is a personal story because Keel was not only intimately involved in the events, but had many friends who were too, and frequently visited the area. The narrative is woven around factual events and filled in with the complex events experienced by Keel's many confidants, most of whom never told their stories to the media. The old journalist Keel comes powerfully to the fore; in style and fantastic events it reads like one hell of a novel.

But it's all true, says Keel, the strange, winged, almost headless giant with red eyes, that would observe people in lonely woods and through the windows of their homes, or drift through the sky without flapping its wings, and which was in some way connected with the UFOs; the CIA, FBI, mysterious phone-tappers, MIBs and the enigmatic Mr Apol (the book froths with conspiracies - it seems a miracle that John kept his head); the weird events, clues and prophecies in a non-sensical game that led to a grim conclusion on Silver Bridge. At one point Keel flashes 'descend' to a UFO in Morse with a flashlight, not thinking why it should ever understand; but it does! The UFO phenomenon, in its entirety, whatever it is, seems to deliberately mimic 'real-life' situations, and some of the stories are quite hair-raising. I wish I had more room to mention some of the many insights Keel brings to the UFO problem, but his greatest is his flexibility of thought and long experience of facing the terrors and paranoia in obsessive UFOlogy.

He broke out of this dark borderland of inexplicable reality and fantastically explicable surreality. This book is essential reading for all interested in strange phenomena (and, more cautiously, for those who dare to investigate them.)

*** Most regrettably we have to keep back many book and magazine reviews to next issue, which will have a large review section. Also flows, monsters, MAs, & mystery illnesses.***

FORTEAN TIMES

strange phenomena - curiosities - prodigies - portents - mysteries

MORE PHOTOS OF MORGAWR, p15

50p : $1·00.

19

UK ISSN 0308-5899

DECEMBER 1976

FORTEAN TIMES

A Contemporary Record of Strange Phenomena

FORTEAN TIMES is a non-profitmaking bimonthly miscellany of news, notes and references on current strange phenomena and related subjects. Formerly THE NEWS. Affiliated to the International Fortean Organisation (INFO) in continuing the work of CHARLES FORT (1874-1932). Edited and published by Robert JM Rickard. Assistant Editor: Steve Moore. PO BOX 152, LONDON N10 1EP, ENGLAND.

SUBSCRIPTIONS. 1 year (6 issues) £3.00/USA $6.00. 2 years (12 issues) £5.40/USA $10.80. Airmail: add £1.50/USA $3.00 per year to sub. rate. Annual index issued free to subscriptions current at the time — otherwise 30p/USA 60¢. For details of availability of back-issues and other deals, including joint subscription rates to INFO JOURNAL, and THE LEY HUNTER, see our address label. NB: OVERSEAS SUBSCRIBERS should add 10% to their cheques to cover bank exchange commission. Payments payable to FORTEAN TIMES.

CONTRIBUTIONS of articles, artwork and notes on related subjects are always welcome and duly credited. YOU CAN HELP BY SENDING US A COPY OR CLIPPING OF ANY ITEM YOU THINK WILL INTEREST FT READERS — just add a note of the date, source and your name (for the credit) — all clippings go on file and will be published in due course. Please don't assume we know about the item — there are very few duplications.

Over Christmas, your editor finally made a foothold in London. Now comes the hard task of getting back on schedule both with FT and the indexes for 1975 and 1976. This December 1976 issue appears in January 1977, for which I offer apologies, but it couldn't be helped. There may be a slight delay to the Feb.77 (20) issue but by April (21) we should be on the rails again.

PLANS

1977 will be the turning point in our career. I want to double our circulation (at least) by the end of the year, as a step to ultimately getting FT published as a professional job. The Ley Hunter has similar ambitions. Indeed if Paul Devereux and myself are to give you the services you need and deserve we need to be free to devote our full time and resources to the task. Our aim is to have FT and TLH published to a professional standard and distributed both nationally and internationally without sacrificing our involvement with the subject or the reader for sheer commercialism. We are convinced that there is enough popular interest in strange phenomena and earth mysteries to support the enterprise...but ultimately it is you, the hard core who've supported us to date, who are the key, and to whom we'll always listen. Without you the venture would be a meaningless exercise in commercialism. The money is secondary to the genuine interest in disseminating facts and research as honestly, independently, and as quickly as possible to all interested parties. I hope you'll back us further.

In order to cost and plan for the best we find ourselves in need of specialist advice, preferably from someone who is familiar with our approaches and subjects. Do we have an accountant and a solicitor out there among our readers, or anyone who can advise on the business side of magazine production? We're serious enough to be thinking in terms of formal (but flexible) structures. If you could play a part in our development, let's hear from you.

LETTERS

While we encourage letters on all matters related to FT and its coverage, it is not physically possible for your editor to reply to all of them, or even promptly, except in cases of immediate business or editorial concern. Sometimes, to save (punitive) postage, we send replies with the FT mailing. I apologise in advance for their terseness. Be patient with us, please. Thanks.

Cont on p28...

ASTEROID MISSES EARTH

An asteroid estimated to be several hundred yards in diameter, named Adonis, grazed by this earth a mere three-quarters of a million miles away on 20 October, last year. Dr Brian Marsden, director of the Central Bureau for Astronomical Telegrams, at Cambridge, Massachusetts, said: 'In space distances that was close indeed.' The AP reports said that the only minor asteroid to have come closer in recent times was Hermes, in 1937, which passed by only 500,000 miles away.

Officially listed as '1976 UA', it was discovered by accident on the night of 24/25 Oct by a student at Mt Palomar Observatory, William Sebok, who called it to the attention of a researcher, Eleanor Helin, who managed to photograph it. But she was not the first — a colleague, Charles Kowal, had photographed the object, said to be the smallest astronomical object ever observed, on 22nd Oct, and did not find out until the excitement sent him scurrying for his old photos. Adonis is reckoned to orbit the sun every .775 years, the shortest period of an asteroid on record, and apparently won't be giving us another close shave for hundreds of years. Minneapolis Star, 2 November 1976; Times, Daily Mirror, Daily Telegraph, South China Morning Post, 3 November 1976; St Louis (Mo) Post-Dispatch, 7 November 1976; New Scientist, 11 November 1976. Cr: Mark A Hall, Ion A Will, Mrs V Martin, John Hitchens.

This accidental discovery is all the more interesting because the previous December Dr Marsden's Bureau issued a statement that Adonis would make its 1976 approach in February! South China Morning Post, 8 December 1975, giving an AP dispatch, quotes Dr Marsden that Adonis will 'pass as close as 1.3 million miles or as far as 40 million miles, a close call by astronomical standards.' When it turned up in October it was only three-quarters of a million miles off - an astronomical error by any standards. What went wrong, fellas? (Cr: Ion A Will).

NEW STARS

Fort had some choice things to say about the number of astronomical discoveries, many of them important ones, by amateurs with more limited equipment than the professionals -- read New Lands. He was also quite vitriolic about the predictions that fail and the accidental discoveries (vide the story above) that also feature in modern astronomy, despite its practitioners' pride in their mathematical precision, updated theories, and computer-controlled scanning. Anyway - here are two quite recent discoveries of stars by amateurs.

Amateur astronomer George Alcock, who has previous discoveries to his credit, was in his back garden in Peterborough, on the night of 21 October 1976, scanning the sky with his binoculars. His knowledge of the sky is famed and respected; Alcock says he noticed the star, heading for nova, instantly - beating the professionals with their giant telescopes. He contacted others in the British Astronomical Association, who confirmed his sighting, and cabled the news to the Smithsonian, and later that same night the nova was confirmed by spectrograms of the new star by Lick Observatory. For other details see New Scientist 28 October 1976.

The other amateur is a postman, Graham Hosty, of Crossland Moor, Yorks, who located a new star (to be called Nova Sagitta 1977) with his backyard telescope. These are the only details to hand at the time of going to press - from the Sun, 14 January 1977 - which adds that Graham is only the second Briton in 15 years to find a nova. It seems they don't know about George's nova (above), which incidentally was in the constellation Vulpecula.) According to the London Eve. News 13 Jan, the discovery has been confirmed by the International Astronomical Union. For Astronomy professors with one eye on next years' equipment budget we can add that according to the Daily Mail 14 Jan, the telescope Graham used was in fact half of an old pair of binoculars he had bought for £10 and was on the verge of throwing away because 'one of the prisms was loose.'

While we're on the subject, the Novosti Bulletin No.16363, reported that on 30-31 August 1975, astronomers in the Crimea located a new star in the constellation of Cygnus as it flared-up more than 10 million times its usual brightness.

LOST PLANET FOUND

Professor Elena Guskova, of Leningrad, has worked out the dimensions and mass of the hypothetical planet Phaeton, which once occupied the orbit between Mars and Jupiter. She bases her study on the magnetic properties of meteorites that reach earth from that region now occupied by a vast belt of innumerable asteroids. Phaeton, which suffered a stupendous cataclysm, possibly due to a collision in space, may have been smaller than this earth but hundreds of times larger than the moon, said Prof. Guskova, who studied over a thousand meteorites from all over the world and found that many had a small magnetic field of the same magnitude and direction, and may have been fragments from the same source. Novosti Bulletin No.16178. Would any Velikovskyan care to comment on how that squares with the master's teachings?

NEW PLANET VANISHES

Professor Richard Hodgson, of Dordt Colledge, Sioux Center, Iowa, took a leaf out of the amateur astronomers' notebook, and began stargazing from his backyard. Close to midnight on 28th October 1976, he was studying an asteroid in the constellation of Pisces when 'a fast-moving object' suddenly came into view, 'like a star, but about 1,600 times fainter than what can be seen with the naked eye.' Convinced he had sighted a minor planet or asteroid, Prof Hodgson contacted Dr Marsden's Bureau for Astronomical Telegrams, who alerted other astronomers to the object - no one else has been able to confirm it.

Hodgson said there were about 2000 known minor planets in the solar system, and to see a new one was fairly rare 'because there are not many people looking.' This object appeared about halfway between the earth and the moon, Hodgson said, and he suggested it might be one of the Apollo planets that orbit the sun. Minneapolis Star, 30 October 1976. Cr: Mark A Hall.

FACING UP TO MARS...

In response to our request last issue for any clipping of the Face on Mars, our thanks go to David Dunthorn, who sent the detail below from Science News 7 August 1976.

It was taken by Viking 1 during its approach to Mars as the sunlight shone at a $20°$ angle to the curious domed mesa 1,162 miles below.

Thanks also to Dave Fideler, who sent the larger scene (taken from Ancient Astronauts January 1977). This shows the relationship between the face and the curious complex of apparently pyramidal formations on the left. For scale, the face is over a mile wide. Are we looking at an alien Sphinx and pyramids? Lets hope we learn more!

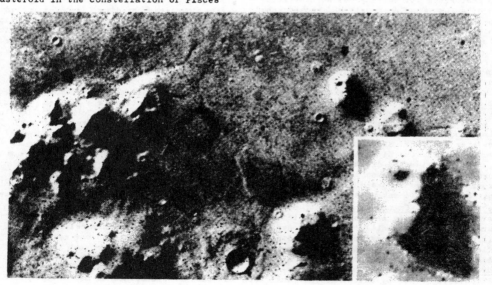

THE TENTH PLANET, etc.,

According to the Novosti Bulletin No. 16237, Professor Gleb Chebotaryov, of the Institute of Theoretical Astronomy in Leningrad, has calculated that there should be a tenth planet to our system, out beyond Pluto at about 54 times the radius of earth's orbit. Its volume and mass should be about the same as earth's, with a diameter of between 8000 and 12,000 km. His calculations were based on an analysis of the perturbations in the orbit of a comet known as '1862-3' which appears to be drawn towards 'a planetary body' which has so far remained 'invisible'. Prof Chebotaryov also thinks there may be an eleventh planet, 100 times earth-radius out from the sun and twice as big as earth. It appears that the Prof's theory cannot be tested until 1992, when '1862-3' is due for a reappearance.

I discovered, in the file here, a clip-ping from the Daily Mail, 1 May 1972 (Cr: Nigel Watson), that astronomers of the Livermore Radiation Laboratory, California, believed they had evidence of the existence of the tenth planet. A team led by Joseph L Brady worked on perturbations in the orbits of Halley's comet and two other (unspecified) 'celestial bodies' with a computer. It suggested a body three times the size of Saturn against the constellation of Cassiopeia - this is near the center of the Milky Way which is quite bright, making it almost impossible to locate 'Planet X' visibly or by radio-telescopes.

The same piece wryly comments that this 'Planet X' was calculated by a schoolboy, Graham Conroy of Stockton-on-Tees, whose thesis was sent to the British Astronomical Society three months earlier (ie in February 1972). Graham, of course, had the advantage of not having a computer.

PERSISTENT PUDDLES

A puddle outside the Underground station at Leicester Square, London, defied experts for two years up to the time of a report (which appears in the London Evening News 31 January 1975.) This report says that waterboard gangs and experts had followed up every clue and sign, dug a veritable lunar landscape of holes (which emerged in cellars and occasionally put the phones out of action) but were unable to find the source of the leak. On the surface the puddle was plain to see, regularly blocking the exit on the corner of Charing Cross Road and Newport Street, and causing London Transport to have at least one man on permanent mopping duty.

Intrigued, I went to the corner of Newport and Charing Cross and was mildly astonished to see evidence of the puddle still there. I asked the newspaper-seller, who was mentioned in the report as losing business, if they ever found the cause. 'No,' he said. 'They say they have, but they haven't. It's still pouring in down there - go and have a look! They don't even try anymore. Once, they put a dye in the water-pipes to see if it leaked out anywhere, but the water that comes up here is crystal clear, like spring water.' I took his advice and went down into the Tube station and found the tunnel to the Newport Rd exit, lined with phone-booths, barricaded with a 'No entry!' sign. I pushed past and saw that it was dug up at the end with a puddle across the whole floor.

On the whole this is a pretty innocuous story. A Water Board official said that the mains pipes were put down during the war and tended to get porous in parts and the leak could be anywhere. But it isn't anywhere; it consistently floods the same spot, and has done for over three years now. If it was a spring why haven't they located it yet? Perhaps any London-based dowsers might like to try their hands on this. Let us know. Now for a different tack, but one which extends the notion of persistent puddles into the possible teleportation of water...

From 5th to 10th July 1975 mysterious puddles kept appearing in unlikely places in the house of Clyde Frederick, of Ayersville, Ohio - on floors, a piano-top and even inside drawers. Mrs Frederick said: 'The ceilings and walls were never wet. The water seemed to be coming from nowhere.'

At 10pm on 5th July the Fredericks left their house for an hour and returned to find the kitchen floor flooded. Thinking a pipe had burst, Clyde shut off the main supply tap and they began to mop up. Then they found water on the bathroom floor and on the piano and the living-room rug. By the time they had mopped up these too and returned to the kitchen, big puddles had formed there. They called a plumber who spent the next day searching but found no sign of any leak, yet the Fredericks repeatedly found pools on their floors, the piano and inside cabinet drawers, and a few other places that were nowhere near any pipes (even if you assume a spontaneous leakage from points all over the house). This happened everyday until the 10th when the phenomenon stopped as mysteriously as it had begun.

The plumber, George Voigt, said he'd never encountered anything like it in his 40 years experience. He checked all the pipes and possible sources of condensation and is confident there were 'no leaks of any kind.' Yet, he continues, 'I'd open a wooden kitchen cabinet drawer and there'd be half a gallon of water in it. I picked up a rug with an 18-inch wet spot...but the floor underneath was dry. It was really eerie!' Harold Root, manager of the Defiance water department, also came to check the house,   declared the absence of leaks, and added: 'Right before my eyes, little puddles formed all over the bathroom floor! It's a mystery to me!' National Enquirer 2 September 1975.

This phenomenon is no stranger to us, and a primer, with references, appears in my forthcoming book, Phenomena, with John Michell. For the moment we must refer you to the ubiquitous Fort for two of several spectacular cases. One took place in a house in Eccleston, Lancs, in February 1873, and was reported in the Chorley Standard on the 15th of that month. The elderly inhabitants were driven from their home by 'torrents' of water while the ceiling remained dry throughout this indoor rain.(Books p570f). The other is the famous incident at Swanton Novers rectory in Norfolk, where during August and September 1919 (see national papers during this period) there were constant flows of oil, water, methylated spirits and Sandalwood oil from the walls and ceilings which always remained dry upon examination. (Books p577ff).

Fort was interested in the question of

'human agency' in the sense that very often an unhappy or ill or dying or pubertal person seemed to be the focus of the phenomena, in the same manner as has been suggested for cases of poltergeistery. This connexion still needs exploring and it's my guess will yield many exciting and fruitful discoveries.

BLEEDING STATUE

In Phenomena, Michell and I follow Fort in suggesting that the puzzling puddles, indoor showers and miscellaneous seepings are part of the same phenomena as their religious counterparts, the weeping and bleeding icons and statues. As we were gathering material for that section the following case came synchronously into our hands.

In St Luke's Episcopalean Church, in Eddystone, near Philadelphia, is a 28-inch-high plaster statue of Christ which bleeds from its upraised hands. The bleeding was first noticed the Friday after Easter 1975, and like the classical stigmatics, bleeds on Fridays and Holy days. The first occasion took place during a fervent prayer in the home of Mrs Ann Poore, of Philadelphia, who had received the ordinary commercial statue as a gift the previous year. As hundreds of people began turning up to see the figurine, she decided to donate it to the church. Father Olszewski, of St Luke's, says that since it went on display in November 1975 many hundreds have witnessed the flows of blood. He said: 'It stands on a shelf 10 feet above the altar, where nobody can touch it. It has bled as long as 4 hours. I know there can be no trickery. Several times I've seen the palms dry, then, minutes later, observed droplets of blood welling from the wounds.'

Father Olszewski called in Dr Joseph Rovito, a respected Philadelphian physician, to conduct tests on the blood. He said that the blood is 'obviously fresh' when it oozes from the palms, but laboratory analysis shows it to be 'of apparent great age!' 'Fresh blood,' said Dr Rovito,'contains millions of red cells. The older it gets the fewer red cells - but even after a few weeks there are usually millions of cells left - yet this blood has only an occasional red cell. It is so old we can't even determine the blood type.' Dr Rovito even X-rayed the statue in an attempt to locate hidden reservoirs and the like, but found nothing to account for the appearance of blood on the hands.

Also called in was a Father Lovett, from Corbin City, NJ, who studies religious phenomena. He told the National Enquirer 20 January 1976, that at first he was 'very skeptical' but now 'totally convinced' the phenomenon was genuine. 'I've personally taken the hands off the statue - they are held in place by wooden dowels - and examined them.

They're solid chalk, nothing else...and (they) bled profusely even as I watched in astonishment.'

Father Olszewski said: 'Sometimes it bleeds more profusely than others - the blood will flow down the plaster robes of the statue in a stream. Incredibly, the blood seldom runs off the statue. Its robes are now encrusted with dried blood.' This detail reminds us of of an observation of tears on some weeping icons, that the tears vanish at the foot of the picture; and of the stigmatic, Domenica Lazzari, d.1848, (whose case we give in Phenomena - sorry if the plugs are getting boring) from whose skin the dried discharges would vanish, some of these flows of blood having been observed to have flowed uphill!

Needless to say, the clergy involved in the Philadelphia stigmatic statue case believe that somehow the blood of Christ is being transported through time to the statue's palms 'to call attention to religion again.' In a way it's disturbing to think that there is no evidence to the contrary!

WEEPING CROSS

The Pretoria (South Africa) News 17 July 1976 (Cr: Chris Holtzhausen) reported on the annual weeping of the 'miraculous' cross, made in 1919 to commemorate those killed in the battle of Delville Wood on 20 July 1916. The cross stood in the Carbineers Garden by the Maritzburg City Hall until 1950 when it was moved to a niche under a concrete dome in the Garden of Rememberance in Maritzburg. According to one official, the cross has wept resin from its knots in each of the 56 years since its making - usually, fittingly, and with wonderful timing, during the annual commemoration service for the fallen men. The seepage has noticeably increased during the last five years and it was seriously doubted that such a small piece of wood could go on producing resin for over half a century.

Maritzburg's director of parks, Mr FN Smith, was quoted, saying: 'The concrete dome above the niche acts as a heat trap and this naturally affects the resin flow.' He is conveniently forgetting that for 31 years the cross weeped annually at its former site without the benefit of a 'heat trap'. The enigma persists!

Next issue: the recent spate of mysterious explosions and fires; attacks on animals; mystery illnesses; and last summer's ladybird (and other) swarms.

OUT OF PLACE

The saga of Britain's new wildlife continues unabated. Celia Haddon, writing in the Sunday Times Colour Magazine, 26 September 1976, briefly mentions a few species that have established breeding colonies: mink, coypus, the rabbit, the grey squirrel, 'edible dormice', Bennet's wallabies, 'racoon dogs' - not to mention numerous kinds of insects (see Peter Roberts' article elsewhere this issue), reptiles and birds, or alien invaders from the plant kingdom. We collect stories of these invasions because we delight in keeping track of the changes in our environment - even if naturalists get rather stuffy about 'naturalising' the new immigrants.

Another aspect is the importance of keeping some kind of record of the escapes from captivity of exotic animals - naturally we are more interested in those which are not recaptured. Ms Haddon mentions that the minks escaped from a farm a few years ago and have now spread rapidly from Devon to Cumbria. She says of our old friends, the Indian porcupines of Devon (see News 8/17): 'A pair of crested porcupines escaped from a Devon wildlife park and began to breed. Though the Ministry of Agriculture claims to have trapped all of them, unconfirmed reports of porcupine at large still continue.' (Cr: Peter Roberts, Steve Moore).

We have notes on escapes, captures, and the turning-up of animals of which there has been no record of escape. In the latter case it is usually assumed that some private animal-lover has illegally imported the creatures which managed to escape, the lackless owner being too frightened of the legal consequences to notify the authorities. We have no way of knowing, especially as there seems to be no control or registration of the ownership of exotic and dangerous animals, the only hurdle being the quarantine regulations.

Our interest is in exotic animals at large in our countryside, and the flurry of panic among the authorities when they poke their heads out of the undergrowth. I've warned of the inadequate responses of the press and authorities, but a definite scenario repeats itself each time - the press treats the subject facilely and is ready to drop it if the mystery shows signs of becoming 'serious'; the zoo authorities are quick to say they have had no escapes; and the poor police are forced into often futile searches, which when (or because) they are unsuccessful, force the police spokesmen into dismissing the original sightings as either hoaxes or mistaken observations. They each forget the previous sightings, and will forget the current one too - until the beast turns up again. It seems to be left to the likes of ourselves to correlate these events into patterns. Anyway, here is the current collection of animals where they — officially - shouldn't be:

WILD HOGS

On the 6th July 1975, drivers on the M6 near Sandbach, Cheshire, were startled to find themselves overtaking a pig heading North, apparently unworried by the roaring traffic. By the time a police patrol crew was alerted, it had vanished - there was no sign of it on the road. A police spokesman said that it was a mystery, especially as no one had reported losing a pig. Daily Express 7 July 1975. Cr: Nigel Watson.

A domesticated pig at large doesn't seem like an exciting enigma, but a wild boar would be. One was hit and killed by a vehicle on a forestry road on the estate of the Earl of Cawdor, near Nairn in Scotland. The wild boar has not been seen outside captivity in Scotland since the 19th century - this one was a year old. The Highland Wildlife Park, near Aviemore, about 40 miles from Nairn, has a breeding pair, but they and their offspring are all accounted for. The Park's director of information, Willie Newlands, said no others are known to be in private collections and that it was apparently impossible for the dead boar to have come from 'original Scottish stock.' All concerned remained baffled, and that's the last we heard. Daily Telegraph 16 March 1976. (Cr: John Michell).

This would be a good place to record the sudden appearance of at least 3 wild boars in Hampshire (yes, 'Surrey Puma' country) in the Autumn of 1972. (I have included these events in my Southern England mystery animal sighting lists in INFO Journal 13 and News 14). Throughout the summer of 1972 there had been vague reports of a strange animal in the Hook, Odiham, Hartley Wintney area of Hampshire but we don't have any information on these sightings.

About 9.30pm, 5 August 1972, a man knocked on the door of Det. Constable Bernard Startup's house, in Linden Ave, Odiham, to tell him there was a wild boar in his front garden, eating his young fir trees. As they watched, it over-reached itself and fell into a fishpond. Bernard quickly blocked his driveway with his car, turned on the headlights, and dashed inside to phone for help. Some of his colleagues arrived and they tried to lassoo the beast, but it escaped into the road. The policemen trapped it in another garden with their cars and successfully roped it - then a vet tranquilized it. The 200lb boar, with 2" tusks, was eventually taken in by Marwell Zoological Park, where an expert said that,officially, boars have been extinct in England for at least 400 years. The police phoned around and no zoo or private collectors in the South had any boars missing. Aldershot (Midweek) News 8 August 1972.

A few days later, on the 10th, a woman living at Up Nately, near Odiham, saw 'a big black animal' which looked like a boar, dash into woods near her home. She phoned the police who arrived with tracker dogs. All they found were some tracks, and the dogs followed the spoor into the woods and along the banks of a canal - but didn't find the animal. Aldershot (Midweek) News 15 August 1972.

On 16 August, a man cycling to work past the Lord Derby pub, in North Wanborough, near Odiham, saw 'a funny looking pig' in a field running with some horses. 'It had a long tail with a sort of tassle on the end and it was dark grey with a kind of pointed head. I reckon it weighed about a hundredweight.' It ran off into nearby woods - and a police search later found no sign of it. Aldershot (Weekend) News 18 August 1972.

It is interesting to note that there were many sightings of the mysterious cat-like creature known as the 'Surrey Puma' (neither limited in location to Surrey, nor

in form to puma) during this period - but the next we hear of a wild boar was on the 2nd September when Frederick Ratky spotted a strange animal feeding on one of his barley fields, at Moor Place Farm, Bramshill, north of Hartley Wintney. Ratky was out hunting a fallow-deer buck which was causing damage to his crops. He shot the beast, and as it began to run away, shot again killing it. It was a wild sow weighing 2½ hundredweight. Daily Echo 4 September 1972 (Cr: Loren Coleman); Aldershot (Weekend) News 5 Sept.

Police and zoo spokesmen again confirmed that there are no known wild boars living in the wild in this country - Dr Maurice Burton, the naturalist with an opinion on most mysteries from the 'Surrey Puma' to the Loch Ness Monster, said they had not existed in the wild for the last 100 years (which clashes somewhat with the figures of 200 and 400 years we have previously been given.) Even so - the mystery is how, if these animals have not been let loose by or escaped from surrepitious collectors, they could have existed, breeding in the wilds, all this time without being detected before now. The same problem exists in relation to explanations of the aquatic monsters in terms of physical creatures. Recent 'wild' notions that do account for the anomalies have been proposed, ranging from Fort's idea of teleporting animals, to FW Holiday's revival of the ancient idea of a genius loci, a spirit associated with a geographical location which materializes and dematerializes according to laws we have yet to discover.

Farmer Ratky promptly came under fire himself from naturalists and animal lovers - a spokesman for Marwell Park said: 'It is absolutely disgusting that this farmer should shoot the animal.' Mr Ratky countered by pointing out that it was a danger to smaller animals and children, and would be almost impossible to find in the high bracken and 2000 acres of forestry on his land. 'Besides,' he said,'who would pay for the damage to my barley?' With almost commendable defiance, Ratky seemed to relish telling the authorities that he had the carcase cut up, stuck in his freezer, and had eaten the liver already. Aldershot News 8 Sept 72.

In the same report the Marwell Park spokesman hinted at the existence of a third wild boar - but were not telling in case some nasty farmer pots their pig.

HYENA IN SUSSEX
After I had published my listings of 'Surrey Puma' sightings (referred to above) both Nigel Watson and Loren Coleman wrote telling me of a few I had missed. These will be included in my next listing (whenever!)- but one bears mention here. The story was

picked up from the Times 23 July 1971, by FSR Sept 1971, to the effect that police were hunting a wild animal in the Ashdown Forest, Sussex, which attacked a dog belonging to a farmer on the forest's edge. The report continues: 'People who have seen the animal in the forest, including two policemen, describe it as like a puma, black and tan coloured with streaks of yellow, and pointed ears.' (My underlining.)

I wrote to the farmer, Mr Alistair Whitley, of Outback Farm, Nutley, on the south side of the forest, whose eyeopening reply came six months later when I'd forgotten all about it. He said the animal haunted his farm from the Spring to the Autumn 1971.

'Our first signs were over-large "dog" pawprints on the woodland paths, and portions of half-eaten wild rabbits in the cattle drinking troughs in the fields. Our first clear sighting was when it seized our little pet dog (a Tibetan spaniel, about 10lbs in weight) at a distance of about 12ft. I managed to throw a shovel and hit it causing it to drop the dog and make off. Subsequent and many sightings could be condensed thus: very heavy strong dog with fierce eyes and round pricked ears, yellowish in colour splotched with darker marks. It spent much time lying in whatever field our sheep-flock was in, which frightened us, but in fact it never attacked them. (Mind you, it was not with us at lambing - March - or it might have been a different story. It didn't arrive til early May.) It appeared to "camoflage" itself with the sheep to catch rabbits. It urinated in all the water troughs, and was excited by our little dogs - (we kept them shut in the garden after it came into the farmyard to catch one).'

'We were very lucky in being helped by Dr John Lisgoe, a marine biologist who lived locally, and a Professor at Sussex University, who helped us collect pawprints both in plastercasts and digging up the actual earth, which he took up to the Curator of the British Natural History Museum, who positively identified (the beast) as an African Spotted Hyena, from hairs and prints. We were warned that it was a very formidable animal which couldn't be doubted if you'd met it as closely as we had. I had a good shot at it in late October as it stood by the wood-side, but whether I killed it or just terrified it away I cannot say. It crawled into the dense undergrowth and we didn't dare follow in case it was wounded. Neither our family, nor neighbours, have seen or heard it since.' This shows how press reports must be taken carefully - in this case the 'puma' turned out to be almost certainly a hyena - but where in God's name did the hyena come from - and where did it go?

WALLABIES AND KANGAROOS

In my letter to Farmer Whitley I asked if he had ever encountered any of the wallabies said to be breeding in the forest. He thought there weren't any there at all. He said he knew some foresters, and his family often ride in the forest, and none of them, to his knowledge, had ever encountered an unidentified leaping object - but he did know that wallabies and kangaroos 'are always escaping' from a private park between East Grinstead and Tunbridge Wells. Hmmm, I thought. The Ashdown Forest colony of Bennett's wallabies was formally recognised in a study by PJ Taylor-Page in the Sussex Mammal Report 1969. It is conceivable that they were severely depleted by the severe winter of 1962/3, as was the Peak District breeding colony, but unlike the latter never fully recovered and died out. Some recent wallaby sightings and escapes in the Sussex/ Hampshire/Kent region are given in News 9/18 - here are some that have accumulated since.

But I think the colony in the Ashdown Forest continues - there have been several references to it recently. A letter to the Daily Mirror 17 December 1975, begged to be assured of the existance of the Derbyshire colony. A brief article by Joe Steeples in the Daily Mail 5 August 1975, on exotic UK wildlife, quoted Dr Gordon Corbet, deputy keeper of zoology at the Natural History Museum, on the survival problems of the two colonies, both from harsh winters and curious tourists. Celia Haddon also refers to both colonies (see our opening reference) - and a photo of a Derbyshire wallaby appears in the Daily Mirror 16 September 1976, again appealing for tourists to keep from trampling all over the wallabies' food, and this also refers to the Ashdown group.

This latter datum says that 3 wallabies had been killed by day-trippers' cars in 1976 alone. We have no notes of these, but we do know that one was killed by a car at Garboldisham, in Suffolk. According to the Daily Mirror 26 June 1975 (the collision happened the day before), the wallaby was one supposed to have escaped from Barnham Zoo, Suffolk, eight miles away, about three months before. Another wallaby turned up in a road near Whipsnade Zoo, in Bedfordshire, in early August 1975. The lady who nearly ran over it, stopped off at the zoo to inquire if one of theirs had escaped. Apparently it was not one of theirs. Daily Mail 4 August 1975.

There was a rash of kangaroo-sightings in Indiana and Illinois towards the end of 1974 (see News 9/18f for a brief resume). We have had only two notes since then, both from last year. On 7 April, Harry Masterson, out walking his dog, at Rock Island, north-western Illinois, reported seeing a kangaroo hopping through his neighbour's yard. Montreal Star (Quebec) 8 April 1976. Cr: X. The other kangaroo was spotted near Clear Creek Canyon, west of Golden, Colorado, on 17 August, by a citizens' band radio operator. He called a policeman who tried to trap the beast near the city limits, but the 'full-grown' animal hopped away through some clay pits. Denver Zoo said they had none missing. Tulsa World (Oklahoma) 18 August 1976. Cr: Tom Adams, Tim Church.

RACOON, POLECAT & PORCUPINE...
Police are said to be baffled by the discovery of a North American racoon near Daventry, Northants. Sunday Mirror 21 November 1976. Back in News 9/16, we noted that during a hunt for a bear on Skipwith Common, Yorks, the Flamingo Park Zoo, near Pickering, had to admit that one of their racoons had escaped. Neither bear nor racoon was found despite the convenient layer of snow for tracking. I suppose it's possible that in a year it could have moved south to Daventry.

Here's a little tale that ties up quite conveniently - but we're supposed to be suspicious of such convenience. Anyway, I'm quite proud of having put two separate clippings sent by different readers, a year apart, together so neatly. From the Darlington & Stookton Times (Co. Durham) 7 August 1976 (Cr: Paul Screeton), we learn that what experts believe to be a polecat turned up 'some weeks ago' under a garden shed in Ashville Ave, Norton, Co Durham. It seemed quite tame so two families looked after it. The story came out because the animal was daft enough to get bitten on the stomach by a rat. Experts are quoted saying that there are no known polecats in the wild south of Scotland, and the only captive one belonged to a family in Whitby. George Iceton, who looked after the animal,doesn't think a polecat could be this tame - 'It's probably a ferret,' he said. Well - we just happened to have in our polecat file two notes from the Scunthorpe Star (Lincs) - the first, of 25 April 1975, announcing the escape of a polecat ('the animal resembles a ferret...') from a house in Burringham Rd, Scunthorpe - the second note, dated 2nd May, merely said it had not been seen or recaptured. Cr: Nigel Watson. I guess if racoons can go south, polecats can go north!

It's a long way from Devon to the Salisbury Plain - at least for porcupines. The Scunthorpe Eve. Telegraph 21 April 1975, told of the sighting of a 35lb porcupine in (unspecified) woods on the Plain, and of experts attempting to track it down. They say it is a porcupine of the North American variety, which may be an error in reporting or an indication that we now have two species of immigrant porcupines at large. The Devon animals are identified as Indian crested porcupines. Cr: Nigel Watson.

MONKEY BUSINESS
The Daily Express, 12 August 1976, reported that a monkey had been seen in fields near Gainsborough, Lincs. (Cr: Ion A Will).

Nigel Watson sent us clippings from the Gainsborough News 13 & 20 August 1976. It seems there were three sightings of a monkey in the Blyton - Northorpe area. The first was on the 9th August by a woman hanging out her washing who saw the animal among some plants before it scampered across a field. It was about 2ft tall, dark brown and timid. Another lady, who saw it run across a road on the 7th (this is the first sighting, but she didn't come forward until news broke of the other sightings - sorry about that) described it having 'bright eyes, pointed ears and a square face.' The later news report is mainly about a woman who lost her seal-point Siamese cat a few weeks before the monkey-sightings and wondered if the people weren't seeing her cat. One would have thought that the gaits of a cat and a monkey were immediately distinguishable, even if one somehow overlooked the fact that the cat had a collar and is a creamy white with dark-brown 'socks', ears and tail! Ole Charlie Fort would have said that our datum is one of transmogrification (sorry!). That a cat vanishes, and a monkey appears in its place. Continuity. It could just as easily become a racoon or a hyena. Do we have any data on vanishings of cats in areas where other animals mysteriously appear?

Who knows? But a baboon dashed past a string of policemen chasing it through gardens in the Clewer Hill district of Windsor, Berks - and vanished. The item in the London Eve. News 30 September 1976 says 'It is thought to have escaped from Windsor Safari Park.' Don't they know? Couldn't they check? I'd guess they were guessing, just as I could guess that it was one of the four still at large in Worcestershire after a mass escape of 80 from a safari park in the Wyre Forest on 8 July 1974, (see News 9/15 for stories of this, and the escape of a large number from another park in Co Durham the following month).

Next issue we shall have some stories of lions, leopards and pumas, wolves, and snakes and things.

UNIDENTIFIEDS

MORGAWR UPDATE

It's been a few issues now since we last had any data on Morgawr, the Cornish sea-serpent (see issues 15 & 16). Some of the latest developments have been quite exciting - a couple of dramatic sightings at sea; and two sightings by Doc Shiels, our man in Cornwall, on the second occasion of which he managed to take photographs. But first let's get up to date with the known sightings since Chambers and Rogers saw two monsters, one large and one small, off Parsons Beach (FT16/18).

DOC SHIELS - FIRST SIGHTING

As you may know Doc Shiels was busying himself collecting all the information and accounts (published and private) on Morgawr. He established a coast-patrol hoping to spot the beast himself, but to his disappointment it seemed he was always in the wrong place as the sightings occured literally all around him.

This was the time of the long hot summer (see FT18/8ff), and Doc took his wife and four of his kids down to Grebe Beach, about 9.30 for a   morning swim, after which they lazed on the beach in the sun. Doc had brought his binoculars just in case and took to glancing out into the Helford river estuary with them. Three times he saw 'something which immediately disappeared by the time he could locate it through the glasses. It was 'a dark shape of a head and long neck...about 500 yards away'. A few minutes later he saw two humps appear, moving through the water - and again it vanished. Then a head on a long neck rose up and he shouted to his family.

Christine, Doc's wife, wrote an account to the Falmouth Packet 9 July 1976: 'We missed it that time, but within a few short minutes the kids started pointing and yelling, "there it is...the monster!" Finally I saw it (or them) for myself. It was at the edge of my vision, and when I tried to focus on the image it simply and suddenly wasn't there.

After two or three attempts to get a clear picture of the thing by staring at it, failing each time, I decided to allow it to be coy, to stay in the "corner of my eye" so to speak. This worked.'

'For several seconds I saw a large, dark, long-necked, hump-backed beast moving slowly through the water, then sinking beneath the surface.'

Christine says she was writing because Doc was unwilling, firstly because he felt no one would believe him, having had his name linked with Morgawr almost since the business began in the Autumn of 1975, some people might think this sighting 'convenient' or otherwise dismiss it because Doc is a professional entertainer (ie stage-magic and puppetry); and secondly, because Doc was full of doubt himself. Christine wrote: 'Now, my husband, of all people, suggests that we were all hallucinating because of the unusual heat and strong sunlight. In short, he seems rather thrown by his own family and himself actually seeing Morgawr!' Doc told me he hoped for another encounter to confirm the matter, if not convincingly for others, then at least to himself for his own peace of mind.

THREE LITTLE DRAGONS...

The same issue of the Packet had a letter from Roy Peters, 17, a hotel worker from Helston. It seems he was skin-diving off Grebe Beach (a few days before the 9th) when he startled three 'serpent-like things' about five feet long, swimming along quietly just beneath the surface. 'They had skin like seals, but because of their ugly heads and necks were definitely not seals,' he said. They escaped into some weed-beds.

TWO SEA SIGHTINGS

Again, a few days before the 9th July, two Cornish fishermen, John Cock, 40, of Redruth, and George Vinnicombe, 55, of Falmouth, were 25 miles south of Lizard Point (now there's a good correlation for lexilinkers). The sea was flat with visibility of several miles, when they saw something appear ahead. 'If we had not reversed engines we would have been right on top of it,' said Mr Vinnicombe. 'It looked like an enormous tyre about 4ft up in the water with a back like corrugated iron. We must have woken it up because a great head like an enormous seal came out of the water. It just turned its long neck and looked at us and very slowly submerged. The body was black and the head was grey. It had a big rounded back with lumps on the top like prehistoric monsters have. I've been fishing for 40 years and have seen nothing like it.' Mr Vinnicombe estimated its length at the waterline was about 22 feet, and its weight at about several tons. Western Morning News 9 July 1976. Cr: Jeremy Beadle. This was one of the few sightings in the whole Morgawr saga which made the national press - see the tiny paragraph in the Daily Mirror also 9 July.

The other sea-view was made by Patrick Dolan, of Cardiff, an art historian and enthusiast for single-handed sailing. Mr Dolan set out from Falmouth in his sloop, Daisy, en route to Kinsale, Ireland, via the Scilly Isles. On 11th August he was about 30 miles NNW of the Scillies when he saw a peculiar disturbance in the water near sunset. 'I could see quite distinctly a kind of worm-like shape in the water and the neck was about 8ft out of the water. It was about 40ft long and propelled itself with an undulating movement. It was moving at 10-12 knots and overtook me. I must have had it in my vision for about 20 minutes.' Mr Dolan said he had had plenty of experience sailing but this sight made him 'extremely nervous' and was like nothing he had ever seen before. Falmouth Packet 24 September 1976. Cr: Doc Shiels.

THREE MORE FALMOUTH SIGHTINGS

On the evening of 27 August, Bramwell Holmes, director of a Penryn furniture firm, returning through Carrick Roads with his wife and son from a trip to St Mawes in their motor-boat, saw two humps rise up, off Restronguet Point. 'The water seemed to boil before they broke surface.' They were a dark greyish mottled colour, and were each about 2ft high and 5ft across in the water. 'The sun was just setting, and there was hardly a ripple...then the water boiled before it appeared. We saw it three times in ten minutes. It was very interesting but also a little frightening. Whatever it was submerged but came up again briefly after we had turned our boat around to get a better look at it.' This time they caught a glimpse of a 'snake-shaped head.' West Briton 2 September 1976 (Cr: Doc Shiels); Falmouth Packet 3 September 1976 (Cr: Doc Shiels, Peter Hope-Evans).

Twelve days later, on 8 September, Donald Ferris thought he saw an upturned boat drifting towards Gyllyngvase Beach from the direction of Swanpool, on the south side of Falmouth. Mr Ferris was walking his dog on the beach, at 7.10am, and the first thing he noticed was that the diving raft was at a 'funny angle', and then saw the 'boat' between the raft and the beach. 'It was a massive thing, 50 to 60ft long. When it got closer, I realised it was a creature like a giant eel, at least 60ft long and dark grey. As it submerged, its back reared out of the water in a hump formation, within 40 yards of the shore.' Falmouth Packet 10 September 1976 (Cr: Doc Shiels, Peter Hope-Evans); West Briton 16 September 1976 (Cr: Doc Shiels).

A few days later, on the 12th Sept, Morgawr, or something at least, was seen again on Grebe Beach. Brother and sister, Allan and Sally White, on holiday from Gloucestershire, were walking near Durgan at 8.30am, when they became aware that something strange had happened. 'We didn't really see it all that clearly but something long and brown definitely slid off the beach into the water. I suppose it was about 15 to 20ft long. Neither of us was frightened. It was more surprise than anything else. I've certainly never seen anything like it before,' Allan told the Falmouth Packet 17 September 1976 (Cr: Doc Shiels). Interestingly, we note a degree of perceptual confusion in the sighting, for Allan said: 'At first we thought it was a dog, but it was obviously too big for that. I can't really describe it...except for the brown colouring. One minute it was on the beach and the next it had gone.'

A MONSTER IN 1926

We have alluded to previous monsters in the Falmouth area (FT15/16, & FT16/19) - another old sighting has surfaced, this time in pages of the West Briton '50 years ago' - alas they don't give a precise date.

'A strange catch was effected by Messrs. B Rees and B Gilbert while trawling in an auxiliary motor boat about three miles south of Falmouth harbour. After hauling their trawl for an hour, rather longer than it usually takes, they discovered that their net contained a strange monster about 20ft in length. The animal had a tail quite 8ft long and a beak about 2ft long and 6ins wide. It had four legs, connected to the body with armour-like joints and covered in thick scales. The creature had a wide flat back covered with matted brown hair, some of which the men brought ashore. The animal was brought up from the sea bed. The monster managed to escape, ruining the net and leaving behind a big splat of blood. Plymouth Marine Biological Observatory authorities were unable to offer any opinion on the nature of the beast.' West Briton 19 May 1976. Cr: Doc Shiels.

DOC SHIELS - SECOND SIGHTING

In mid-September, Doc told me he was
going to intensify his searches for Morgawr -
he had retreated for a while after his previous (and ambiguous) encounter, to let his
subconscious dwell on the matter, and to give
a chance to natural divinatory processes..to
see if the Powers that Be could arrange for
him and Morgawr to meet. Sometimes you can
try too hard, on your own.

On 17 November 1976, between 9.30 and
10.00am, Doc was with David Clarke, editor of
Cornish Life, walking near Parsons Beach,
below Mawnan Old Church. David was taking
photos of Doc for a projected feature; 'It
was cold...and I was all for leaving when
(Doc) started shouting that there was something in mid-river,' he later told the Packet
3 December 1976 (Cr: Doc Shiels). 'I saw a
small dot moving towards us, which I presumed
to be a seal. It came across the river to
within 60-70 feet. It started to zigzag backwards and forwards, and I could see movement
in the water behind the head which suggested
it was a great deal longer than a seal.'
David Clarke took some photos through his
telephoto lens but (Oh cosmic Trickster!) the
camera jammed, giving double and triple exposures. The Packet reproduced one of Doc's
photos, which David agreed showed what he had
seen. It seems that David, like Doc earlier,
began to doubt the evidence of his own eyes,
and was 'reluctant to confirm the existence'
of Morgawr. (More on this below. David Clarke
's own story will appear in an imminent issue
of Cornish Life. See also Dinsdale's letter
for a comment on Clarke's double exposures,
below.)

Here is Doc's description: 'The animal
we saw was small by monster standards...no
more than fifteen feet in length. The head,
very small in relation to the thickness of
the long neck, was about 6 to 8 inches long,
like a coconut. It had horns, stumpy little
things, which Dave saw clearly through his
viewfinder. One of my three pictures shows
a profile very similar to that of Nessie in
the famous Wilson picture. We saw a double-
humped back when it first appeared...though
most of our pictures show just the head and
part of the neck...the head was extremely
ugly, like a big snail's head with those odd
little stalks.'

((On this point I've discovered we have
not yet recorded the first sighting of Morgawr, made one evening in September 1975 off
Pendennis Point, by Mrs Scott and Mr Riley,
of Falmouth. They saw a hideous, hump-backed
creature 'with stumpy horns' and bristles
down the back of its long neck, dive and re-
surface with a live conger eel in its jaws,
(Details from Morgawr by A. Mawnan-Peller,

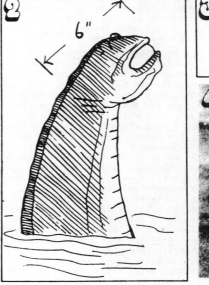

6"

CONT.on P.16...

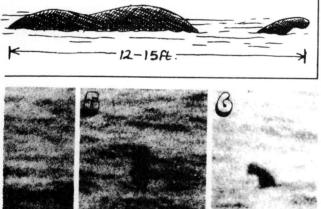

12-15ft.

17 November 1976 - apx 9.30am.
1) We've matched the background landscape features on two of Doc's photos
to show the movement of the object
(from right to left - notice the wake
in the right photo), which eliminates
the possibility (mentioned by Dinsdale,
p17 this issue) of a stationary object,
like a tree-branch, in a tidal flow.
2) Doc's drawing of the 'ugly' head,
which opened and closed its mouth.
3) The appearance of the monster most
of the time. It submerged as Shiels
and Clarke took their photos from apx.
100 yards away.
4-6) Details, taken from Doc's photos ,
of the head and neck of the creature.
They bear many similarities with Mary
F's photos (see p17 this issue) and
the classic Wilson, and O'Connor photos
of Nessie (see In Search of Lake Monsters by Peter Costello (1974).

Drawings and photos copyright Anthony
Shiels - November 1976.

** ** ** ** ** ** ** ** ** ** ** ** ** **
Our cover is an engraving taken from
PH Gosse's Romance of Natural History
(1859).

from Puck Fare, Ponsanooth, Truro, Cornwall.-
25p.) This is all the more interesting because this was at least two months before Dr
Rines was to release his now celebrated
photo showing a 'gargoyle' head, with stumpy
horns, taken in Loch Ness (see News 14/13).))

Doc told me: 'I've done exactly what I
said I'd do...I've captured the beastie...on
film!...and all good sympathetic-magicians
should know what that means...now I have its
image on film, that should give me a certain
amount of power according to standard magical
practice...if my theatrical dragon-invoking
antics really caused the monster to appear,
then it should be possible to repeat the experiment.' But Doc has little enthusiasm or
motive for another encounter. He at least is
certain Morgawr exists: 'I know that the
thing we saw and photographed was not a seal,
a skin-diver, a dolphin, shark or boat...or
radio-controlled rubber model. It was, and is
a very unusual creature...we saw a bloody
sea-serpent!' Nor is Doc convinced that even
a herd (or is it shoal?) of monsters materialized before the massed lenses of every
reporter in the whole Southwest would convince them.

THE LOCAL PRESS REACTION
The whole Morgawr saga has been scandal-
ously neglected and ignored by the national
press (except for a few feeble, cynical lines)
and by the scientific establishment, who
don't seem to care a hoot about the possible
existence of a new unidentified animal within
a day's journey of the British Museum.

The local press reaction was a little
different, and we recognize that since the
days of Fort's investigations very little has
changed in the way the press becomes party
to the putting down of a mystery. It seems
to be a sort of antibody reaction, if we see
society as an organism and the damned data
as the irritant. At first it is a novelty,
then as preposterous pseudo-explanations fail
to account for the mystery, it becomes by
turns something boring, or hoaxed, and then
frightening. We are dealing with events that
are nothing less than confrontations between
natural (if rare and unexpected) processes
of the universe and our own blinkered cozy
world-view conditioned by the mass-concensus
of what that ought to be. Naturally the
strange phenomena win tentacles down because
they, in Fort's phrase, are 'more nearly real'.
But sometimes the resistance against new or
threatening information or events takes bizarre forms. It is easy to see conspiracies
or the shadowy MIB behind things. Perhaps
man is a more organic unit than its parts
like to think and we all react in some grand
strategy on the orders of the Whole to close
ranks against Change.

Here is Doc's view of what happened:
'During the last few days (written on 26 November), the local press boys have expressed
the opinion that the whole thing must be a
fake, simply because I was on the spot, and
I'm known as a magician. David was warned by
a fellow reporter (Mike Truscott of the West
Briton)'not to underestimate the powers of
the Doc'...implying that I was not to be
trusted. The editor of the West Briton will
now only print reports of Morgawr sightings
if my name is never mentioned in connection
with the beast! The editor of the Falmouth
Packet avoids me carefully these days. The
BBC showed an interest in the fact that David
had seen and photographed Morgawr...but lost
it when my name was mentioned. Dave, himself,
has recently asked me if I'd rigged up some
cunningly controlled rubber model monster,
programmed to act like the real thing on that
fateful Wednesday morning!!! He's worried and
puzzled by the whole episode...including the
chicken-livered reactions of his fellow journalists, whispering like nervous old women
about Doc Shiels and his nasty monster...Dave,
although he was there and saw the thing, is
not totally convinced...he thinks I may have
been responsible for the appearance of the
animal although he has no ideas as to how I
could have possibly done such a thing (unless
as mentioned, I used a 15ft rubber monster,
beautifully made and expertly controlled...I
wish I knew how that sort of thing could be
achieved without tons of money and the services of a Hollywood special-effects man! Maybe I'm becoming paranoid about press men -
they certainly seem disturbed by the fact that
one of their number (the respectable editor
of a glossy county magazine, no less!) actually happened to be unlucky enough to find
himself on the spot, in the company of the
dastardly Doc, when our Morgawr decided to
lift his head above the waves.'

If anyone wanted to do a thesis on the
reactions of everyday people to encounters
with the unknown; or to the press 'kill-off'
time as the critical period the press will
tolerate a mystery before they kill it off,
then FT would co-operate with the stories on
file here. Weird, isn't it? However, I'm mind-
ful that Doc too was sceptical of his own
first encounter with Morgawr, as were some
of the other witnesses, according to their
own admissions. It will be interesting to see
David Clarke's story when it comes out. We'll
keep you posted.

TIM DINSDALE ON THE SHIELS PICTURES.
Doc wrote to us saying that Tim Dinsdale,
the famed investigator of Loch Ness and auth-
or of three mandatory books on the subject,
had examined his evidence and been very imp-

ressed. I asked Tim if he would care to give FT a statement of his opinion. His letter, dated 12 January 1977, contains some very interesting information:

'Dear Bob - As you have asked for my opinions on the Cornish sea-serpent 'Morgawr' appearances off Falmouth this last year (1976) particularly in relation to the sighting recorded by Dave Clarke, editor of Cornish Life, and Doc Shiels, on November 17th in the mouth of the Helford River - I will be glad to make comment.'

'I visited Falmouth in May after talking to Bill Cane and Tony Shaw at Penelewey, two interested local researchers, and had the good fortune to meet Doc Shiels, and several other local witnesses, including a lady who had seen the beast in the sea, but quite close up off Fendennis Castle Point ((see p 14 this issue for our own belated mention)). She described a large, hump-backed, long-necked animal with a strange head with 'horns' on top of it - which she and another, male, adult witness watched, as it dipped below the surface to come up with a live-and-kicking conger eel in its mouth. Her sincerity, and obvious amazement, came over on the tape, also the fact that she was familiar with the usual sea animals - like seals.'

'As you probably know there had been some photographs published in the Falmouth Packet ((5 March 1976; News 15/16; and below -Editor)) purporting to show the beastie - taken by an anonymous person, a certain 'Mary F', and perhaps a dozen or so other eyewitness accounts, some from local mackerel fishermen.'

'I left Falmouth feeling the trip had not been wasted. Later I had a note from Doc indicating that he and members of his family had seen something strange off-shore ((see Doc's wife's account on p 12 this issue)), then later he was kind enough to send me some blow-ups of the more recent Nov 17th surfacing.'

'I wrote back asking for more info and perhaps a tape recording, which he and Dave Clarke kindly put together - the latter sending me pictures from his own film-strip taken with a Pentax and telephoto lens, which mysteriously double exposed, showing the head and neck. Actually they are not too bad, and show an object which is hard to identify, producing a very distinctive wake. Fixed objects like poles and tree-branches can produce such a wake in a tidal river mouth or estuary, (I saw a magnificent sea-serpent 'head and neck' doing this in the Solway Firth last summer, with the tidal rip providing 'movement'.), but this does not explain what Doc and Dave saw, which they said was clearly animate - flesh and blood alive, with features clear to them at about 100ft. I believe them.'

'Looking for a rational explanation, bearing in mind the dimension of 12-15ft, we can rule out otters - and no seal has a head like that. The only possible alternative is a giant leathery turtle which had been swept off course by the Gulf Stream. ((We mentioned some notes in this connection on FT16/19. See also the curious Falmouth monster of 1926 above, and our reportage of the Barmouth monster in issues 10, 11, 15 and 16 -ED.))

'Unlikely though it may seem, this happens occasionally, and in 1971 I actually saw a gigantic turtle ashore in Mallaig (N. Highlands W. coast) which had been killed by a trawler's prop. It weighed about "13 hundredweight" according to the fishermen - an immense reptile, a marvellous specimen about 3 times bigger than the one in the Natural History Museum ((London)) - but it was shipped south for "soup" I believe, and nothing more was seen of it. The head of such a turtle bears some resemblance to the photos, but it has no 'horns' and no ridge, and the back of a leathery turtle is unmistakeable, being ridged with knobbly lumps. This does not fit the description either.'

'Altogether the 'Morgawr' sightings are a puzzle, but seem real, notwithstanding the odd events which appear to coincide with them. Perhaps, with luck, 1977 will produce some more and better photographs - maybe another 'jaws' incident with bathers vacating the briney at speed!

Regards: (signed) Tim Dinsdale.'

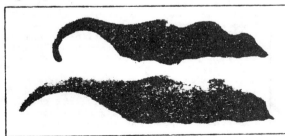

The two photos taken by Mary F from Rosemullion Head just south of Falmouth sometime in the first 2 weeks of February 1976, against the sun (hence the bleaching out of the sea). The negs are unobtainable, Mary F having sold them to an anonymous American and remaining untraceable herself. Despite this note of dubiety the photos show a credible form and movement.

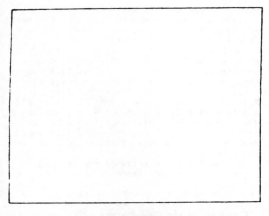

ALIENS AMONG US

by Peter Roberts

Recent issues of The _Fortean Times_ have devoted considerable space to 'Mystery Animals' (MAs) sighted in Britain. Basically these have been headline-makers: large creatures or occasionally swarms of lesser ones that have attracted the attention of the average passer-by and have found their way into the local newspapers. But what else is crawling around in the undergrowth, unnoticed except by the few? For that matter, what about the undergrowth itself?

On the basis that for every large exotic creature in Britain there should be hundreds of smaller strangers, I've been looking through a few of the periodicals and books in the British Library's massive natural history collection. The result? The United Kingdom is packed with small aliens of every kind. I've just peeped at the tip of an iceberg - the subject is vast and complex. All I can do at the moment is present some patchy notes which I hope may offer a glimpse of the field and an indication of some of the problems in investigating it.

These notes, on various creatures and plants, are roughly grouped in families. I've ignored mammals since they've already been comparatively well-covered - the larger ones. at least (if Britain is infested with invading voles and strange shrews, that's just too bad).

BIZARRE BIRDS.

Surprisingly, this has proved to be the most difficult area to research, largely because bird-watchers in the UK are numerous and well-organised. This means that there is an ornithological establishment, conservative and dogmatic, which imposes, or at least encourages, an impressive and oppressive self-censorship in the reporting of strange birds. A Rare Birds Committee vets all reports, giving only its approval to those birds that can be shown to have arrived in Britain on the wing; the aim of most local societies seems to be to pander to this committee for which they show a remarkable respect. As a result, few exotic birds are ever mentioned - only borderline cases (which are usually bracketed in the bird lists, awaiting the committee's ruling). Look, I myself have seen at least two feral budgies and, recently, a gaudy little red-beaked bird (Java sparrow?); but the British ornithologists ignore these 'obvious escapes' and introductions.

Perhaps some rogue group is keeping track of these avian oddities – if so, I haven't traced them. In the meantime, here's some sparse notes from the conventional journals.

A flamingo at Benacre Ponds; this is a borderline bird, a 'rare vagrant', hence it made the list; but a later note gives it the chop in typical fashion: "It proved to be of the Chilean race and was therefore obviously classed as an escape" (Lowestoft Field Club – 24th Ann. Rep., 1969). 'Obviously' – though nobody bothered to check... Three white pelicans at Breydon Water (Ibid: 26th, 1971) attracted some attention, if only as a mass break-out (and it's another borderline bird for the committee's attention). I've other scattered notes, all of them hopefuls for the rare vagrants section of the British Birds lists – even the following rarity: Two Sudan Crowned Cranes (a European record, if confirmed) sighted in the fenlands from June 1958 to at least February 1959, with two newly-fledged young as well. Inquiries failed to reveal any known escapes (Nature in Cambridgeshire, No 2, 1959).

Before leaving the birds, I should note that the official lists are prepared to accept vagrants from as far afield as East Asia, North Africa, and Western North America. I should also mention bird-ringing, where records should be unequivocal and straightforward; the trouble is, I haven't been able to find the annual Ringing Reports issued by the B.T.O. They'd be worth checking for anomalies, like the following: a knot, ringed on The Wash and recovered in Liberia eight days later – that's a quick 3500 miles or so! (BTO News, No 1, 1964). Finally, here's a quotation from R Whitlock's 'Rare and Extinct Birds of Britain': "Obviously if we were to count all introductions we should have a truly formidable list". 'Obviously' again – but just where is this formidable list?

ROGUE REPTILES.

This is better documented, thanks to JFD Frazer's "Introduced Species of Amphibians & Reptiles in Mainland Britain" (Brit. Jour. of Herpetology. Vol. 3 No 6, 1964). This includes notes on some twenty-eight foreign species, many of them in breeding colonies and a few in several localities throughout the UK. Most are said to be 'known introductions'

and a few have pedigrees and histories; that's fine – all data on foreign species in Britain is worth having if we're trying to sort out the known from the unknown.

Frazer mentions a few reptiles found in Britain that are unaccounted for and classed as 'escapes'; they include Viperine Snakes in Kent, a Tessellated Snake in London, and many instances of Salamanders and Tortoises – he doesn't include reports of ultra-exotic species, largely because he's interested in potential breeding colonies of naturalised animals that can survive in this climate. Beyond this I've only a few reports, for example: two Italian Grass Snakes in Lowestoft (Low. Field Club – Ann. Rep., 1961).

MYSTERIOUS MOLLUSKS:

This may seem a ludicrous area of investigation, but amazingly AE Ellis's 'British Snails' lists a remarkable number of slimy foreigners in Britain and even more that we've exported abroad (here's a typical entry – Oxychilus alliarius: "Introduced into St Helena, Greenland, USA, Cape Colony, Australia & New Zealand"). A preliminary checklist (Jour. of Conchology, Vol 23) lists 38 alien species in the UK and Ellis's book (revised Ed., 1969) gives details and additions. It's too arcane a subject for most natural history clubs and the only other note I have is of a Japanese Sea Squirt (I think that's a mollusk!) in the Helford estuary (Jour. of the Camborne-Redruth N.H. Soc., Vol 2, pt 4, 1972). Otherwise, Ellis's handbook gives ample details of non-marine gastropods, and there's a special tit-bit for Forteans: "Whirlwinds can disperse molluscs and other animals" (p.37) – I thought you'd like that!

CURIOUS CRUSTACEANS:

There's just a single oddment here: Talitroides dorrieni – a land sandhopper from New Zealand which has established itself in the Scilly Isles and Cornwall: it has a curious preference for the plant Helxine. another alien but one from the Mediterranean coast! (Jour. of the Camborne-Redruth N.H. Soc, Vol 2, pt 5, 1973).

BARBARIAN BUTTERFLIES:

This is the area I first thought of when researching this article, since I'd already come across two butterfly mysteries. The first is the presence in Britain of the Milkweed or Monarch butterfly, an American species which is infrequently but repeatedly found over here. Nobody knows how it arrives - different writers put forward different explanations: it may fly across the Atlantic (possibly resting on the water!) or it may be released from the holds of banana boats (though I have a reference to Milkweed sightings correlating with reports of American birds). Who knows? The things just keep on returning. The other mystery is possibly my favourite contender for a genuine Fortean oddity. It's the case of Albin's Hampstead Eye, a distinctive butterfly mentioned in J Petiver's 'Papilionum Britanniae' (1717) as being taken on Hampstead Heath; for many years this was the only known specimen and it was variously considered as a freak hybrid or the last of an extinct species. It was finally found to be alive and well - in East Asia and Australia. As one commentator says, "It is interesting to speculate on how it came to be recorded from such an unlikely locality and at that period of leisurely travel".

Most butterfly books ignore aliens; the exception is TG Howarth's 'South's British Butterflies' (1973) which gives details of over thirty 'introduced' species from Asia, Africa and America found at one time or another in the UK. Unusually, he even includes oddities found in greengrocer's shops and so on - an area, important to us, which is continually ignored in reference books and periodicals on the British flora and fauna.

INTRUSIVE INSECTS:

Butterflies are a comparatively easy subject to deal with; but there are just too many other insects (80% of all known animals are insects and there are over 20.000 species on the British list alone) All I have are a few notes on obvious aliens, namely New Zealand Stick Insects, two species of which (the 'smooth' and the 'prickly') are naturalised in Cornwall (Jour. of the Camborne-Redruth N.H. Soc., Vol 3, pt 1, 1974, and Chinery's 'Field Guide to the Insects of Britain & N. Europe, 1973).

PERTURBED PLANTS:

A glance at any garden will indicate the extent of the problem here. There are vast numbers of exotic plants in Britain, many of which are now classed as naturalised or appear on the lists as 'casuals'. Clapham, Tutin & Warburg's 'Flora of the British Isles' (2nd Ed.,

1962) includes a fair number. I've also come across monographs such as "Alien plants in SE England" (Trans. of the Kent Field Club, vol 3, No 1, 1965) and "Alien Plants of Cornwall" (Jour. of the Camborne-Redruth N.H. Soc., Vol 2, pt 2, 1970). Trees are hopeless: there are thirty-five native species in Britain, out of roughly 1700 now found here! (Mitchell's 'Field Guide to the Trees of Britain & N. Europe' is useful). Fungi are also awkward, since their distribution is little known and they grow quickly and furtively; only the weirdest are likely to attract attention. Ramsbottom's 'Mushrooms & Toadstools' mentions a few of these, possibly Australasian but found in Britain on one or two occasions.

CONFUSED CONCLUSION:

The above notes are sketchy, to put it mildly; but they should at least indicate something of the vast wealth of our exotic plant and animal species. Where did they all come from? Many are documented introductions (most of those 1700 alien tree species seem to have a firm pedigree for example); others are likely to be escapes (like my favourite record of a feral yak which lived for many years in the Derbyshire moors); many are accidental introductions (I've several reports of things scuttling out of banana crates).

But there's still a residue of inexplicable oddities, less flamboyant than a puma in Surrey perhaps, but worth a moment's thought.

There are plenty of local and specialist journals to provide sources of information. Those quoted above don't actually do my reading justice; most of the newsletters and transactions are conservative, almost as bad as the ornithologists', and only print notes on the acceptable wildlife of Britain. An exception, like that of the good people of Camborne & Redruth, is a welcome relief to the monotonous catalogues of thoroughly native species. From now on, I'll try to specialize - examine a few notable cases perhaps. But anyone can join in - how about discomforting the bird watchers with an open-minded examination of the bird-ringing reports? Be my guest, please...

Peter Roberts, 1976

((Editor's note -- we have accumulated quite a few notes on some of the aliens mentioned by Peter; some animals appear in this issue, but the birds and snakes will be kept for another time when we have more space.))

THINGS THAT GO BUMP IN THE EVENING

Few can have failed to notice the rash of newspaper stories concerning the mysterious 'booms' afflicting the west of Britain throughout November 76 ...events which received considerable but largely uncoordinated and contradictory coverage.

The first thing to notice about the reporting is its relative exclusiveness ...nowhere is there any mention of similar past cases, although this sort of event seems to happen all the time (See Fort: Books: Index-'Explosions', including the classic 'Barisal Guns' case, and the News 3/15-16). The mystery was finally 'solved' by attributing the noises to Concorde, but as we shall see this leaves many pieces of the puzzle unexplained...and consequently forgotten.

First though, in order to keep the chronological record straight, we must move north to Bangor and Anglesey, where on Saturday 15 Feb 76, at an unnamed time in the afternoon,'a tremendous mystery bang' shook property, rattled windows and swayed light-fittings. This obviously came as a surprise to the staff of the marine science station at Menai Bridge, who seemingly don't allow for earthquakes outside office hours... their seismograph was switched off for the weekend. However, tremors have been recorded in the Menai Straits before, and this was the conclusion again. A microbaragraph was switched on, and this recorded no disturbance in the atmosphere...which seems curious, considering the apparent volume of the noise. (North Wales Chronicle, 19 Feb 76. Cr: Phil Ledger)

The Somerset epic began at around 10-00am, 13 Aug 76 (Bath Evening Chronicle; Cr: John Michell). There was a noise described as a kind of juddering and a series of loud bangs or crackling. The noise lasted several seconds and the air seemed to shake, according to witnesses. A vapour trail was seen overhead, and Concorde was immediately blamed. However, British Airways and BAC swiftly informed the public that none of their Concordes had been out of the hangar for three weeks, and tried to shift the blame onto military aircraft...even so, all aircraft are banned from flying supersonic over populated areas. These questions only have any relevance if we assume that the noise and the vapour trail were connected; and as Forteans we know that the obvious ain't necessarily so. Interestingly, the same report mentions an earthquake in the Radstock/Bath area, one week short of 50 years previously, in the morning of 20 Aug 1926... and also that there was an unexplained 'mini-storm' in nearby Frome the preceding day (12 Aug 76) which threw a 4cwt fibre-glass boat-shell over a hedge and broke fences and trees.

We have no more data on the Somerset noises until November, although it is obvious from the reports that they had been occurring for some months previously. Basically, the story is of a vibrating double-bang, sometimes followed by a second double-noise, occurring most nights of the week just after 9-00pm. maintaining the same clock-time despite the change from British Summer Time to GMT. Much of the attention seems to have focussed on Mr George Lawrence of North Petherton, Somerset, and various experts descended on his home throughout late November to make tests and recordings. The noises were first described as 'vibrations and underground thunder'. and were thought to be subterranean explosions. They had been going on throughout the summer, and were heard in 3 counties: Somerset, Devon and Cornwall. By 16 Nov 76, the Civil Aviation Authority and scientists from Bristol University had joined the Police in the investigation, and the possibility of Air France Concordes being responsible was mentioned, though they were thought to be too far away.

On the 17th, UFO activity is mentioned with a bright orange ball being seen in the sky at 9-03pm, to be followed by the bump at 9-05. There were also references to considerable UFO activity in the west country, including more orange glows, an alleged landing at Winchester, humming noises, and pink-eyed men running round the countryside. Certain parallels were drawn with the noises heard at Warminster some years ago (See A Shuttlewood: 'The Warminster Mystery', Tandem Pb, 73)

At the same time, Concorde and military aircraft were supposedly cleared of blame, as the bumps had occurred when they were not flying. Also, an unnamed aero-dynamicist said that the bangs sounded nothing like sonic booms.

By the 19th, bangs, rattles and groans were being reported from various other parts of the country, including Reading and Chelsea, London. Dr Robert Adams of Bristol University stated about the bangs: "I have no theories at all except that it was not caused by an aircraft." Two days later, Dr Adams began to change his opinion, describing the noises as "airborne and man-made". Bangs were also reported at 6-30 & 8-00pm, but these were rapidly and conveniently forgotten, as was the extra bang at 10-20pm on the 22nd. Birds were said to be disturbed by low-frequency vibrations some 15 seconds before the bangs were heard.

22 Nov also brought a newcomer to the explanation field. He was Dr HK Zienkiewicz of Exeter University. He attributed noises to the decaying sonic booms of Concorde, still carried through the air after the 'plane had slowed to sub-sonic speed. He made his statement 'to set the fears of the public in the West Country at rest'. Whether that calmed down the inhabitants of Horsham, Sussex, some hundred miles to the east, we don't know ...but they were apparently having bangs every Saturday at 6-30pm.

By 27 Nov 76, the national papers were writing the story's epitaph. It was now 'definitely' Concorde, the sonic booms carried an unexpected distance by a combination of temperature, humidity and wind. Incredibly, it was stated that the booms arrived every night except Tuesday ...the only night Concorde did not fly in from Washington. And every boom fitted in with the British or French timetable for the supersonic plane. Considering all that has been said above, this understandably caused your editors to boggle somewhat. The good Dr Adams proved more flexible, however, and completed an admirable about-face by stating his certainty that Concorde was to blame. (Story compiled from: Daily Mail, 15 Nov 76, Bristol Evening Post, 16 Nov, Guardian, 17 Nov, 18 Nov, Western Daily Press, 18 Nov, Guardian, Western Morning News, Western D. Press, 19 Nov, Guardian, 20 Nov, Observer, 21 Nov, Guardian, Western D. Press, Sun, D. Mirror, 22 Nov, Scunthorpe Evening Telegraph, 23 Nov, D. Mirror, 24 Nov, Sun, 27 Nov, Sunday Times, 28 Nov, Guardian, 2 Dec, Aerial, 7 Dec 76. Cr: R Sandell, J Michell, K Rogers, N Watson).

That effectively put an end to the story, at least as far as the national dailies were concerned, and the only other reference we have is from the Cornish & Devon Post, 11 Dec 76 (Cr: N Watson): the inhabitants of North Cornwall were getting together a petition to present to their MP, to have the noises reduced. Whether they succeeded or not, we don't know. The papers, at least, have been quiet ever since.

Concorde wasn't quite out of trouble though. An AFP bulletin for 1 Dec 76 (Cr: K Rogers) reported that earth tremors in NW Spain, measuring 3 on the Richter scale, were being blamed on the plane by experts in Vigo, Galicia. They were all felt early in the morning. The story was already dead as far as British papers were concerned, and the only newspaper that seems to have picked up the story is the South China Morning Post (H.K.), 2 Dec 76 (Cr: Ion Will). How much else have we missed because the editors got bored with the story?

We interrupt the end of this section to include some last minute information sent by Ken Rogers. Ken was listening to John Dunne's news progamme on Radio 2 (5pm, 19 Nov 76) and managed to note the story of a man who phoned from Porlock, Somerset: 'All my friends and family began hearing these strange bangs which happened about 9pm each evening, 20 years ago. As children we were very frightened and taught to call it the 'Big Bang' or 'Big Gun'. I'm now married and still living in Porlock, and still hear this odd noise, and the sound hasn't changed in all those years...' (**Whaaat! 20 years ago!**)

HUMMING AN UNHAPPY TUNE

Much more persistent, and still unsolved, mystery noises have received less coverage: extremely faint but distressing hums and buzzes which have plagued numerous householders throughout Britain. The earliest story we have is from autumn 1975, when Mr Donald Wood, of Dorstone, Herefordshire, first became aware of a faint, high-pitched buzz during a power-cut caused by a storm. At first he thought it was distant machinery, but then discovered that none had been working during the power-cut. He soon found he could hear it all the time, not only at home, but in the car and at work...and his wife could hear it too. A couple of months passed, and Mr Wood, an amateur pianist, identified 3 notes in the sound: fifth octave A flat, A natural, and B flat. Eventually, a blind piano tuner, Mr Berris, came to the house, heard the noise and, without prompting, picked out the same notes. Then, as if he had caught some infectious disease, he found he could still hear the noise when he left the house and returned to London; and other callers at the house '**took it with them**' as well.

August 76 brought Mr Paul Wallace of Poole, Dorset on the scene, although he had apparently been campaigning for four years to have a scientific investigation into the noises, having collected letters from sufferers in various parts of the country, including reports of four suic-

ide notes complaining of noises that no one else could hear. He described the noise as like a diesel engine, fluctuating in volume and sometimes inflicting intense pressure on the eardrums. There seem to be two different types of noise: in one case the sufferer carries the sound with him wherever he goes, in the other it is localised in one place, for there is also a mention of a man in Berkshire, in 1975, who slept in a hotel to escape a similar noise.

Adding to Mr Wallace's campaign was Miss Lydia Gilbert of Bognor Regis, who recorded the mystery hum on cassette during June 76, apparently the same noises as Mr Wallace was hearing. It was estimated that one person in 10,000 hears the sounds.

With Mr Wallace attempting to get the matter raised in parliament, the investigations started. Numerous theories were put forward, and mostly rejected, including: the sufferer hearing the sound of his own blood circulation, tooth-filling radio-receivers, vibrating gas mains, street-lamps, or even <u>echoes from the hollow core</u> (sic) <u>of the Earth</u>.

Prof Brian Clarkson of the Institute of Sound and Vibration Research acknowledged that the problem exists, and that 'quite a lot of research' was being carried out on the sound. But so far we have heard nothing in the way of results. (<u>Sunday Express</u>, 30 Nov 75; <u>D</u>. <u>Express</u>. 5 Aug 76; <u>S</u>. <u>Express</u>, 8 Aug 76; <u>D</u>. <u>Express</u>, 10 Aug 76; <u>Evening Standard</u>, 10 Aug 76: Cr: I Thompson, J&C Bord, V Martin, K Rogers, RG Twine, S Nicholls).

ℜⓒⓌⓈ

INFO have begun to restructure themselves beginning with a Washington DC phone listing under 'Charles Hoy Fort', and a new address: 7317 Baltimore Ave, College Park, MD 20740, USA. Mail to the old Box No. will still reach them - but not so quickly.

There will be an exhibition of original paintings, prints and sculpture on the 'Earth Mysteries' theme at the Acme Gallery, 43 Shelton St, London WC2, for 3 weeks from 22 March 77. Material by Thom, Michell and Critchlow will also be on display. At the same time the Research into Lost Knowledge Organization (RILKO) will issue their third book in the '<u>Studies in Patterns</u>' series, to include original articles by Devereux, the Bords, Raine, Michell, Graves, Thom, Critchlow, and Glover. This will be published as a limited edition at £2.35 (inc p&p) initially. You can reserve a copy by sending a cheque to The Ley Hunter: Box 152, London N10 1EP.

Linda Johnson of Fairfax, Virginia has designed and made a few 'Charles Fort' medallions. They are 1½" diameter, with a profile of Charlie, and the quote, 'One measures a circle begining anywhere' on opposite faces, complete with chain. Send £2.00/$3.00 to Fortean Times: Box 152, London N10 1EP, and we'll forward the order. Includes p&p.

As we go to print, David Watson, head of religious education at Rickmansworth Comprehensive School, Herts, has been dismissed for refusing to teach Darwinian evolution in place of a factual belief in Adam and Eve. He appealed to the council against his dismissal and lost - next he plans to take the matter before an industrial tribunal under the 1944 Education Act which says no teacher may be 'deprived of an advantage' because of his religious opinions. You might be amused to note how the matter is specified in the Herts. Council syllabus, drawn up in 1954: 'The Genesis stories of creation, read as their writers intended them to be and not as literalist interpreters have read them, do not conflict with evolutionary theories... They are, of course, only part of the collection of the myths and legends - Hebrew religious folklore - which make up the first 11 chapters of Genesis and they should be seen in that setting.' (My underlining. I wonder just what they think myths and folklore are! - Ed.) To his credit Mr Watson says he knows evolution theory is an alternative view, but 'cannot accept that it is the only view permissable.' This is an issue of fundamental importance and should be interesting to watch - academia may go all out to squash Mr Watson, but could be stopped, not by the triumph of a better cosmology, but by modern employment legislation. Incidentally, as the Sunday Telegraph 23 January 1977, points out, this case is almost a reversal of the trial of John Scopes in Dayton, Tennessee (a mere 52 years ago!) for crossing the education authorities by teaching evolution not Biblical creation. Genes vs Genesis, you might say!

Forteana in the media. Some recent films have had some interesting sidelights. The vastly overestimated The Omen portrayed the devil as our old pal the Black Dog, albeit a tame looking one. Apart from the basically facile interpretation of the portents of the coming of the Antichrist given in Revel-

ations, was the interpretation of his birthdate from the 'Number 666' - ie 6th day of 6th month. They conveniently forgot the other 6! You might like to know that 6th June 1976 saw a huge fireball come down NW to SE, to hit the sea somewhere between E Anglia and Kent in the Thames estuary. We're waiting now for Ivan Bunn to tell us that that evening a huge Black Dog revisited the churches at Blythburgh and Bungay.

One film we can wholeheartedly recommend for sheer excellence and beauty in all departments is Picnic at Hanging Rock, an Australian film about the disappearance on St Valentine's Day, 1900, of 3 girls - a 4th came back from their mountaintop date with destiny but could not remember what had occured. No bodies were found, nor was the mystery solved. The blurb says it actually happened - we'd like to know more as it's not in Fort. The direction steers strongly & unerringly between providing answers and empty mystery-mongering to revel in a brooding, haunted suggestion of something beyond our comprehension. A truly Fortean film (I don't often say that!) and I urge you to see it.

There is still time to catch the multimedia exhibition 'Pompeii AD 79' at the Royal Academy of Arts, London - it closes on February 27.

HARDBACKS

Velikovsky Reconsidered by the Editors of Pensee. (Sidgwick & Jackson 1976; £5.50; pp260; index) -- It is rather frustrating that if one wished to quote this book in a scientific paper the reference would include "edited by the Editors of Pensee". Confidence is not increased by the note which states that Pensee was an organ of the Student Academic Freedom Forum which discontinued publication in 1975. Still no names and addresses, and the brief information about the status and qualifications of the 19 or so authors is hidden in the text. Unfortunately the casual scientific reader may be unaware that Pensee was an excellent and responsible journal with lively and informative articles on all aspects of the Velikovsky affair, including much criticism and background material.

There is a brief summary of the theme of Worlds in Collision (1950) and Earth in Upheaval (1955), and then six sections covering the enormous range of Velikovsky's work in history, geology, astronomy, mythology and controversy. Part 1 - the appalling record of the response of nearly all the established scientists to Velikovsky's views and, what was far more offensive to them, his pungent, racy, and somewhat arrogant style. Part 2 - evidence for earlier "unlikely" solar system body alignments and absences. Part 3 - attempts to explain the remarkable orbital changes necessary to support such catastrophic happenings as the ejection of Venus from Jupiter. Part 4 - the problems of the high temperature, retrograde rotation and atmospheric composition of Venus. Part 5 - the problems of the magnetism, origin and history of the Moon, and the age of its craters. Part 6 - the debate about Velikovsky and the continuing struggle for serious consideration and study of his researches into many branches of science.

On the whole this is a splendid book, particularly for those who have actually read Velikovsky in the original. A list of contributors and their status details would been a useful addition to the adequate index and lists of references. Some of the comments about electricity in the solar system should be read with caution in the absence of the criticisms which were published in Pensee. For instance, evidence quoted for a charge on the earth is equally valid for a charge between the ground and the upper atmosphere, a totally separate characteristic. The fascinating subject of Venus crops up in many places as well as in Part 4. Robert Treash (who are you? Please contact.) quotes Varro of ancient Rome, writing about earlier times: "To the brilliant star Venus...there occurred so strange a prodigy, that it changed its size, color, form, course, which never happened before nor since". Of course it did, as many others have testified! Read the book and see for yourselves!
-- Eric Crew. January 1977.
((For further material on the Velikovsky Affair and catastrophic themes, see our review of Kronos, under 'Journals'. Eric Crew has agreed to write us an article on the Venus problem - Ed.))

The Indefinite Boundary by Guy Lyon Playfair. (Sounevir Press 1976; £4.25; pp320; index, references & photos) -- Continuing GLP's solo voyage into South American psychic phenomena, and detailing the mediums, investigators, healers, theorists and victims of polts, reincarnation, spiritism, etc. I cannot do justice to the book's wealth of new information in so short a space, but as it goes into circulation it (and GLP) will be quoted frequently, as will his earlier The Flying Cow. Not only is this one of the first records in English of the phenomena of Brazil, it will remain one of the best and most readable.

Many books are being held back til next issue to review them more fully.

PAPERBACKS

Strange Minds compiled and published by William R Corliss (Sourcebook Project, Glen Arm, MD 21057, USA. 1976; $7.95; pp285; subject, author, source indexes.) The Unexplained by William R Corliss. (Bantam paperback,1976; $1.95/75p; pp 338; subject, date, place, author, & source indexes.) -- Strange Minds is volume P1 in the Sourcebook series and covers reprinted reference material from rare and out-of-print sources on the following aspects of mental phenomena: automatic writing; delusions, possession, hypnogogic and other hallucinations; scrying; dowsing; deja vu; sleep and dream phenomena; telepathy; calculating prodigies, memory feats and eidetic images; out-of-the-body experiences; fire-walking; stigmata and skin writing; oddities of perception; and poltergeist noises. The selection is mind-watering and this volume is up to the standard set by the previous ones. We fully endorse this project as a set of references no serious researcher or library can afford to be without. These volumes will be listed next issue, and you'll be able to order via FT (to ease the transfer of money). Meanwhile, if you'd like a sampler of the more physical data in the 2 Strange Phenomena volumes, try The Unexplained. I'm sure you'll find it worth it. This book covers archeological, astronomical, geophysical, and geological enigmas.

Glastonbury - Ancient Avalon: New Jerusalem edited by Anthony Roberts. (Zodiac House Publications, 7 Hugon Rd, Fulham, London SW6 3EL; £2.70; pp106; bibliographies, illos.) -- Tony declares that this anthology of esoteric and exoteric views about the ancient sacred site of Glastonbury is his personal tribute. The list of contributors is impressive: Mary Caine, the Pennicks, John Michael, Jess Foster, Kenneth Knight, John Michell, John Nicholson, Donald Cyr, and the Roberts themselves (who also produced the book). The articles cover a wide range from the factual approaches of topography and gematria to personal speculation on the mystique and meaning of Glastonbury as a multilevel symbol. Other sections deal with the zodiacs, the Holy Grail, the maze, the hidden treasures, the underground tunnels and the geomantic structure of the Glastonbury complex. A baroque metaphysical synthesis by John Michell makes a fine flourish to top off the book. Many text and decorative illustrations. (When ordering from Anthony Roberts - address above - please include 40p postage.)

Recent reprintings in paperback:

The Magic of Findhorn by Paul Hawken
(Bantam 1976; £2.25; pp343; illos.) in which
our rather glib hero spends a year at this
miraculous garden in Scotland and sees many
wondrous things, like giant cabbages growing
in sand, and hears of the gardeners' pacts
with elemental beings to make the garden grow.
Very Special People by Frederick Drimmer
(Bantam 1976; £1.95/95p; pp357; biblio, many
photos.) Compassionate and informative bio-
graphies of many famous human curiosities
like 3-legged, rubber-skinned, gorilla-look-
ing people that supersedes chunks of Edwards'
Strange People. There are Giants in the Earth
by Michael Grumley (Panther 1976; 60p; pp155;
index, biblio, photos.) The best British Yeti
and Bigfoot book, well written with insight.

JOURNALS

INFO Journal now published from: 7317
Baltimore Ave, College Park, MD 20740, USA.
No19: Steve Moore with a pioneering article
on gravity-defying feats in the Chinese
martial and meditational arts; Paul Willis
on the falls of ice at Timberville, Virginia.
No20: (with Richard Hall as the new editor)
FW Holiday on the 'Great Serpent Mystery';
Stuart Greenwood on the Meydum-Avebury con-
nection; A Moraru on a UFO landing in Rom-
ania; plus notes on historial Forteana.
$10.00/£5.00/year -- or as a joint sub with
FT, $14.00/£7.00/year. Payments to either
INFO or FT.

Pursuit, the journal of SITU: Columbia,
NJ 07832, USA. Summer 76: John Keel in another editorial on Fortean news problems; a
symposium on land and water monsters; & Keel
again in a concise summary of modern para-
UFOlogy ((a big step for SITU!!!)). Membership
$10.00/year.

Shadows, a newsletter from Tim Church
covering (mainly but not exclusively) American monster material and sightings. Issue 2
includes a note on the possible sighting of
the supposedly extinct Tasmanian Wolf. To
receive Shadows just keep Tim supplied in
stamps. Tim Church: PO Box 932, Missoula,
MT 59807, USA.

Anomaly Research Bulletin, published
monthly by the newly formed Michigan Anomaly
Research, edited by David Fideler, covering
(mainly but not exclusively) UFO and Fortean
data on Michigan state. Write to Dave for a
free sample of ARB (if you're in the USA,
please send two 13¢ stamps): 7098 Edinburgh,
Lambertville, Michigan 48144, USA.

Ness Information Service. All interested
in the antics of monsters and men in and
around (mainly but not exclusively) Loch
Ness will be interested to learn of the NIS
Nessletter which gives up-to-date info on
all aspects of the subject in a stencilled
format, edited by Rip Hepple: Huntshieldford,
St Johns Chapel, Bishops Auckland, Co Durham.
£1.50/year (USA/Canada: $7.00/year/airmail).

The Braheian Debater, a free newspaper
debating and defending the notion of a geo-
centric universe, with many notable contributors. PO Box 254, Sunnymead, CA 92388, USA.

Clypeus, and **Gli Arcani**, two high quality
magazines of interest to Italian-reading
Forteans from a stable of fine writers and
researchers. Clypeus is (mainly but not
exclusively) devoted to the folklore, mysteries and antiquities of Piedmont. Inquiries
to Clypeus:Casella Postale 604, 10100 Torino
Centro, Italy. Gli Arcani is a monthly covering the whole spectrum of the occult & the
mysterious. Gli Arcani: 20162 Milano, V.le
Ca Granada 2, Italy.

Kronos, modestly subtitled 'A Journal of
Interdisciplinary Synthesis', taking up the
banner of the defunct Pensee (with many of
the same contributors) in promoting discussion, examination, criticism and development
of Velikovsky's catastrophism. Recent issues
have contained many original contributions
from Velikovsky himself; a revised chronology of Egypt and Isr 1; the correspondences
between the gods and goddesses of various
cultures and the major planets with references to events of astronomical violence; the
problems of tektites, frozen mammoths, and
the vanished dinosaurs; ancient records of
astronomical dramas; and many articles of
loving and impressive scholarship embracing
astronomy, cosmology, astro-physics, history,
psychology, anthropology, geology, archeology, and contemporary reaction. Quarterly:
USA $10.00/ Overseas $18.00/year. Kronos: %
Warner Sizemore, Glassboro State College,
Glassboro, NJ 08028, USA. (Singles, $3.00).

New Horizons, the journal of the New
Horizons Research Foundation, in Toronto.
Much valuable and original research into
poltergeists, psychokinesis, metal-bending,
sound-phenomena, telepathy, healing, hypnotic regression, etc. For details write to:
New Horizons Research Foundation: PO Box
427, Station F, Toronto, Ontario, Canada
M4Y 2L8.

**Journal of the Society for Psychic Res-
earch** June 1976 — 'DD Home and the Physical
World' by Guy Lambert, suggesting that DDH
chose sites of underground disturbances to
hold his sittings. Interesting implications
to be explored in a future FT article. SPR:
1 Adam & Eve Mews, London W8 6UQ.

The Christian Parapsychologist, an excellent little journal. June 1976: St Columba & psychic phenomena; Biblical condemnation of pagan occultism; biography of the late great Father Herbert Thurston, SJ; one of the foremost historians of psychic and mystical phenomena. $3.00/£1.00/year. The Christian Parapsychologist: 284 Earls Court Road, London SW5 9AS, UK.

Lantern: Autumn 1976: A "Fearefull and Terrible Noife in the Ayre...with a Stone that fell from the Sky..." in 1642; Cambridgeshire ghosts; and a zodiac at Bury. Winter 1976: More on the Puddingstone Track; a UFO at Hainford, Norfolk; a 'batmobile' at North Walsham; Norfolk's mystery flares. Easch issue has usual features of local curiosities and other data (mainly but not exclusively) on East Anglian mysteries. The Borderline Science Investigation Group have just published their Proceedings (on investigating Borley Church); and a booklet on Haunted Lowestoft (35p). Lantern: Edited by Ivan Bunn: 3 Dunwich Way, Oulton Broad, Lowestoft NR32 4RZ, UK.

The Ley Hunter (continues in excellence and relevance, particularly the innovation of photographic exploration of leys etc. Our sister mag.) No73: the Bords on 'Ancient Sites and Folk Traditions'; photos of Maeshowe and Castlerigg; Steve Moore on the apparent 'Mirroring' in East/West Cosmotopography. No74 (a special 'Earth Energies' issue): Tom Graves on 'Earth Acupuncture'; photo of the 'Ring of Brogar'; speculations by Jimmy Goddard and M de Styrcea on 'Ley Power'; John Michell refuting the recent attacks by the school of statistical leyhunters; instructions for making a 'Ley Energy Detector'; Richard Elen on the synthesis of the 'New Magic'. £2.00/year/$4.00 (USA $7.00/airmail); or available as a joint sub with FT, $9.00/£4.50, payable to either TLH or FT at: Box 152, London N10 1EP, UK.

Institute of Geomantic Research. Nigel Pennick continues his valuable publishing and reprinting venture with the IGR's 6th paper, 'The Round Church of Ophir, Orkney' by Ian Worden. The IGR now issues a journal. No1: E Anglian round towers; an eclipse in 2983BC; Forrest on the math-case against leys; ley metrology; the geomancy of Ely Cathedral; Glastonbury's tunnels. No2: artificial mounds and mark stones; ancient sun alignments; dowsing to locate leys; the Stanley zodiac; an appreciation of the Spanish architect Antoine Gaudi's geomantic work (yay!!!); a fold-out of Stukeley's 1724 engraving of Avebury. IGR: £3.00/year. IGR: 142 Pheasant Rise, Bar Hill, Cambridge CB3 8SD, UK.

Essex Dowser, a newsletter edited by Frank Dineen and privately circulated to members and friends of the Essex Dowsing Group. Often contains a log of Frank's own experiences and experiments. Donations welcomed. ED: 4 Brentwood Rd, Ingrave, Essex CM13 3QH.

Fate. May 76: sorcery in ancient Peru; a girl at the epicentre of some poltergeist fires in Washington. June 76: a lady's experiments in thoughtography; Curtis Fuller interviews Hynek; Arthur Guirdham on a woman who projects her double. July 76: the feats of ancient manpower (as opposed to hypothetical spaceships); experiences with a kahuna; Mangiacopra on the Florida giant octopus. August 76: UFOs like biological organisms; Maiden Castle hillfort. Sept 76: the Cabrera rocks, which suggest some dinosaurs coexisted with men; Louis E Navia 'In Defence of Ancient Astronauts'. Oct 76: 2 Alabama women chased by a UFO; the medium Katie King's performances in America; some Japanese kids who can Gellerize cutlery. Nov 76 (and the UK edition is superseded by importing the USA original): phantom aircraft; the old chestnut of the vanished Eskimo village; the return of Patience Worth. Dec 76 (with our friends Jerome Clark and J Gordon Melton installed respectively as Assistant Editor and Book Review Editor. Our congratulations to you both): Curtis Fuller on the weird thought pictures of Willi Schwanholz (the psychic photos with the biggest tits in the world, yet!); radio before Marconi; and Jerry Clark on pairs of Oklahoma monsters. Available on newsstands.

UFO Abduction in N. Dakota. A long and valuable account of the bizarre Sandy Larson incident (26 Aug 1975) - and hypnotic reconstruction by Dr Leo Sprinkle - investigated and written by Jerome Clark in UFO-Report Aug 1976.

MUFOB. No4: Rogerson and Rimmer on an important case of 'Bedroom Visitors' and dream (!) UFOs; Nigel Watson on winged entities. No5: Dr Ron Westrum on the sociology of UFO sighting and reporting; Roger Sandell on the current fetish for 'Monster as Metaphor.' MUFOB is an independant UFO-oriented mag which consistently researches parts other UFO mags can't or wont reach. 1 year a bargain at £1.80 (USA £2.50/airmail). John Rimmer (ed): 11 Beverley Rd, New Malden, Surrey KT3 4AW, UK.

SOBEPS News, the English abstract of Inforespace, the Journal of the Belgian Society for the Study of Spatial Phenomena (SOBEPS): No4: pt 3 of a study of Bermuda Triangle claims; analysis & history of the

'Warminster UFO photo' taken by Faulkner; analysis of a UFO-sound on tape. No5: analysis of Marjorie Fish's 'Star Map' from the Hill abduction; analysis of a Belgian UFO photo. Sobeps News: Boulevard Aristide Briand 26, 1070 Brussels, Belgium.

WATSUP Journal of the Wessex Association for the Study of Unexplained Phenomena. Local sightings and investigations, articles and notes. Edited by Nick Maloret: 180 Locksway Rd, Milton, Portsmouth. £1.50/year.

UFONIC News Data Sheet by Martin Shift & Martin Moffatt: 142 Frobisher Drive, Walcot, Swindon SN3 3HF. Don't know much about this but their Sept/Oct 76 issue consists of an interesting article by Terence Amey on 'Strange Clouds in Antiquity.'

EUFOSG Journal, being sightings, investigations and data on local UFOs, etc. Edited for the Essex UFO Study Group by DJ Goring Jr: 5 Carlton Terrace, Gt Cambridge Rd, London N18 1LB. Singles 25p plus postage. A recent scoop was a new case from 1944 of a spherical UFO inspecting four V1 rocket-bombs over London (EUFOSGJ Nov 76.)

Flying Saucer Review. 22:2: a light-emitting UFO hovers over a French car; three studies of an astonishing and important UFO abduction of 2 youths in Maine, USA, and their visions; a critique of 'The Sirius Mystery'. 22:3: incidents at Stonehenge apartments, N Bergen, NJ; UFOs and '4th dimension'; ambiguities in hypnotic regression of abductees; an entity in W Yorkshire. 22:4: UFOs seen from a 'Trident' in Spain; more Stonehenge, NJ, incidents; philosophical reflection on current status of UFOlogy; UFO meets helicopter in Ohio, 1973; another Brazilian teleportation; and another Brazilian abduction; UFOs on an astronomer's films. Each issue carries the usual round-up of world sightings and letters. £3.35/$9.00/yr. FSR Publications Ltd: West Malling, Maidstone, Kent, UK.

Journal of Meteorology. For a professional but independent assessment and record of (mainly but not exclusively) British weather, we recommend the J. Met., edited by Dr GT Meaden from : Cockhill House, Trowbridge, Wiltshire BA14 9BG. Dr Meaden has an awareness of Fortean phenomena, and notes on contemporary and historical Fortean meteorological events frequently appear in the journal. Recent issues have valuable data on 'falls'; a pillar of light; the outstanding freaks and changes of 1976 weather; tornados in E Anglia, fireballs, and the 'inadequacy

of broadcast weather reports.' £5.50/$16.00 ($24.00/airmail) 1year/12 issues.

New Scientist, 1976. 1 July: a new chronology of human evolution incorporating latest findings, 'The First 33 Million Years' by Stuart Fleming. 8 July: part 2 of the revised chronology of evolution. 29 July: the Viking discoveries on Mars. 5 Aug: biologists manage to fuse plant and animal cells together. 19 Aug: 'Mysteries at the centre of the galaxy.' 2 Sept: 'Hydrogen is a metal'!; N.Sci begins an investigation into cheating among scientists; human suggestibility and hypnosis; a new kind of lunar meteorite. 9 Sept: report on the 1976 NATO symposium on biofeedback & behaviour. 16 Sept: a critique of megalithic observatories. 28 Oct: report on a 15-year test of Einstein's general theory. 18 Nov: ring-shaped collisions between galaxies. 25 Nov: results of N.Sci's questionnaire on 'Cheating in Science' (some do - is anyone surprised?). 2 Dec: the current status of the 'Big Bang' theory of cosmology.

cont from p2/

TRUSS FUND...
...in which we acknowledge the kind support of: Connie Bell, Alex Ashcroft, Livingston Gearhart, JW Scaife, and Mike Ward. Thanks - your Hunt Emerson posters will be mailed when we get a gap in time.

CORRECTIONS TO FT18
Several errors last time:
p5 - according to the Thames and Hudson catalogue for 1977, the book by John Michell and myself, Phenomena, will cost £2.95, not £4.50 as we originally thought. Production of the book is in its final stages - we'll keep you informed.
p11 - the item listed under 24 Feb, the sighting by 3 teachers of a giant bird near San Antonio, Texas, has no suggestion of hoax attached to it. I was in error, confusing it with the item listed under 21 Jan. Apologies - and thanks to Jerry Clark for pointing this out.
p14 - the passage angle mentioned in para 2, column 2, should read 26°18', not 28°18'.
    I also wish to apologise to Ken Rogers for not crediting him more fully for the huge amount of material on quakes and weather anomalies he sent us, used in 'Dairy of a Mad Planet'(p8). I was attempting to save space (Ken's name would have come up on the majority of items) but even so could have phrased my/our appreciation better.

FORTEAN TIMES

A Contemporary Record
of Strange Phenomena

FORTEAN TIMES

strange phenomena - curiosities - prodigies - portents - mysteries

BIG~CATS AT LARGE in the UK, p18

X ISSN 0308-5899

FORTEAN TIMES

A Contemporary Record of Strange Phenomena

FORTEAN TIMES is a non-profitmaking bimonthly miscellany of news, notes and references on current strange phenomena and related subjects. Formerly THE NEWS. Affiliated to the International Fortean Organisation (INFO) in continuing the work of CHARLES FORT (1874-1932). Edited and published by Robert JM Rickard. Asst Editor: Steve Moore. **PO BOX 152, LONDON N10 1EP, ENGLAND.**

SUBSCRIPTIONS. 1 year (6 issues) £3.00/USA $6.00. 2 years (12 issues) £5.40/USA $10.80. Airmail: add £1.50/USA $3.00 per year to sub. rate. Annual index issued free to subscriptions current at the time — otherwise 30p/USA 60¢. For details of availability of back-issues and other deals, including joint subscriptions to INFO JOURNAL, and THE LEY HUNTER, see our address label. NB: **OVERSEAS SUBSCRIBERS** should add 10% to their cheques to cover bank exchange commission. Payments payable to FORTEAN TIMES.

CONTRIBUTIONS of articles, artwork and notes on related subjects are always welcome and duly credited. **YOU CAN HELP BY SENDING US A COPY OR CLIPPING OF ANY ITEM YOU THINK WILL INTEREST FT READERS** — just add a note of the date, source and your name (for the credit) — all clippings go on file and will be published in due course. Please don't assume we know about the item — there are very few duplications.

FEBRUARY 1977

We must apologise for the standard of some copies of the last issue - badly printed, collated and stapled. If you'd like your copy replaced please let us know.

With this issue we hope you'll note a lot of improvement - some of the thanks must go to Kay Thompson for her offer of typing part of each issue.

Truss Fund

In which we gratefully acknowledge the donations to our survival and growth fund, from: Kurt Lothmann, George Gati, SN Morgan, Peter Roberts, Roger Randall, Frank Satterthwaite, Anthony Smith, Stephen M Ward, and CA Worth.

Plans...

It may sound like a platitude but you really are important to us. TLH and FT exist for your information and participation - so we'll keep you informed of our planned partnership and growth.

Our own status has been one of small but steady growth - the annual intake of new subscriptions just keeping ahead of the lapsed. This has meant that we are operating at breakeven with no capital for growth. Hence our Truss Fund (see above) which provides this support - and we really must thank its supporters for their gifts (some of which have been very generous) - for without it we couldn't have got this far. If you can afford it, and think we deserve it, please send something to help us grow.

TLH and FT have prepared new blurbs and have taken a part share of a stand in the forthcoming Festival of Mind and Body (Olympia, 19-24 April) in the hope that we can attract more readers.

We hope this new intake will finance our next step - improved production and distribution. But events have a way of sneaking up and mugging the best of plans and in the wake of the recent increase in printing costs there is the spectre of a postal cost rise (after printing, our biggest single cost).

Our dilemma is that though FT is at a bargain price in the USA, an increase in the UK price would be counter-productive. The only other solution is for more readers to buffer us and amortise the costs better. Everyone can help. With this issue you'll receive a blurb - please use it to encourage a friend. If each of you brought in one new sub, we'd double overnight (almost).

Please give it a try.

/cont on p13.

January this year saw an astonishing series of mystery explosions in Britain. I say 'mystery' explosions because despite the attempts of investigating authorities, rightly outraged and inconvenienced public, parties with vested interests, the police and the firemen to pin the blame on our natural gas supply, the series seems to have been way beyond any normal expectation or reason. Faulty gas mains or gas appliances doubtless figured in some cases but as we shall see they can not account for them all.

I'll briefly list the salient details; the material is drawn from the daily and evening papers of the day or day after, being widely covered and easily available. I apologise for the imprecise dating of the early events but we were not collecting data then - the full realization of the series per se only becoming clear in the first days of the new year, whereas we can see some kind of run-up from the preceeding November.

November 1976 -- Sometime at the begining of Nov there were two explosions on the same day, one demolished a house in Leeds, and the other damaged an old folks home in Keighley, both in Yorks. On the 15th a blast damaged a house in Hackney, London. Gas leaks blamed in each case, but no real evidence.

December 1976 -- Houses were damaged on the 16th at Ealing, London, and on the 18th at Chadsmore, Staffs; both blamed on gas mains leaks. On Christmas Day a gas heater exploded in a home in Kentish Town, London. In the following week, on the 29th, there was a huge explosion in a shopping-center in Bristol and in a house in Bradford, Yorks, on the same day; gas leaks blamed. On 30th shops in Brentford, Middlesex, blew up, again leaks were blamed. That night there was a gas-leak alert in the Regent's Park area of London, but nothing was found.

3 January 1977 -- shops exploded at Beckenham, Kent, and there were alerts in Odsal, Yorks, and Knightsbridge, London, after people thought they smelled gas. As gas-men were searching for a leak in a house at Sutton-in-Ashfield, Notts, it blew up (as if to confirm their suspicion).

4 January 1977 -- houses in Liverpool and Huddersfield, Lancs, were blasted, supposedly by mains leaks. Gas smelled in a street put Nottingham on an alert; and hundreds of gallons of whiskey blew sky high at a distillery in Renfrew, Clyde-side.

5 January 1977 -- a gas cooker exploded in a home in Leytonstone, London; and in a curious coincidence two liquid gas cylinders blew up in separate incidents in Roberton, Lanarkshire, and in a fruit warehouse in Huddersfield.

6 January 1977 -- a leak alert in Boston, Lincs; and a house blows up in Islington, London, after gas-men call to fix a leak and install a new meter.

7 January 1977 -- a cafe at Newark, Notts, damaged by exploding gas cylinder only three days after gas-men fix a leak there. Two explosions in Edinburgh within an hour: one in the bakehouse of the Royal Infirmary when an oven pilot-light went out; and the other in the sugar-mill of Burton's biscuit factory at Sighthill, on the city's outskirts.

8 January 1977 -- the Bristol shopping center, scene of the blast in late December, closed down again because someone thought they smelled gas - nothing found.

9 January 1977 -- gas cylinder blows up at Kettering, Northants.

14 January 1977 -- explosion ruins house at Leeds, Yorks, as road-works team outside manage to break the mains. Bungalow in Tonbridge, Kent, damaged in blast supposedly caused by a mains leak. In Glasgow a gas cylinder rolls off a lorry and explodes in a street.

The rest of January 1977 -- another blast in Newark, Notts, this time in a block of flats as an old man fell and grabbed at a cooker which came away from the wall, on the 15th. On the 16th, another house in Leeds is explosively demolished. On the 17th, shops in Rotherhithe, London, evacuated after gas is smelled. On the 22nd, four houses in Seaton Delaval, Northumberland, are damaged in an explosion, as was a house at Walsall, Staffs, on the 25th.

February 1977 -- the series of blasts is slowing down. The only ones we have a note of are an explosion in the center of Manchester on the 5th, thought to be the work of an incendiary; and a major evacuation of houses in Plaistow, London, after gas was smelled in a street.

Vaporings

The theory that raised most tempers was that the gas mains were at fault, having been baked during the drought in Summer of 1976 and now cracked during some of the bitterest nights for many years, and to make matters worse, Britain had shut down for a long Christmas holiday (over a week in some parts) which allowed the gas to accumulate. Like all plausible-sounding theories it looks impressive until you examine it. But some people were impressed and by the 6th Jan, Wedgewood Benn, the Energy Secretary, announced an inquiry. It was welcomed by the chairman of British Gas who was sure it would vindicate both his industry and product from "ill-informed and irresponsible" criticism. The in-fighting between all the public bodies involved is of no real concern to us here except that it is a familiar Fortean scenario - the Establishment falling into panic when confronted by the Unknown. The matter was summed up nicely by our inestimable friend John Rimmer (editor of MUFOB) in a letter of 6th January:

"It is interesting to watch the public reaction - there is an obvious fear of unstructured, random events, so all the explosions have to be put down to a single cause - the long Christmas holiday - a particularly good scapegoat, as it has itself turned into a 'moral-panic' with a great deal of guilt and self-flagellation about 'idle' British and 'industrious' Europeans...The Gas Board is catching the flak, and will probably fulfil the role of the USAF in the UFO mystery. An interesting confrontation on TV today between a Gas spokesman and someone from the National Safety Council who was amazingly irrational. It looked as though he would be satisfied with nothing less than an admission from the Gas Board that they were totally, personally responsible for all the bangs. The Gas Man, like the Blue Book people, tried to emphasise that each event had an individual cause, that there was no one explanation that would wrap the lot up - but he was practically shouted down by this Donald Keyhoe of the Safety Council. All

the elements are there; we must now wait for the Condon...sorry, Benn Report."

We're still waiting! Meanwhile it may be worth noting some of the causes of explosions other than mains leaks. We've had explosions involving cylinders of both liquid petroleum and methane/butane, some standing still (powering commercial space heaters or domestic central heating) and one dropping off a lorry, and no one has yet explained how they managed to explode. We've had a tank of whiskey explode, and to date no cause has been officially given. We've had workmen bashing their diggers into the mains pipes; and falling old folk pulling cookers away from the wall. In the Brentford event (3 Jan) the manager of the exploding laundromat said he could not smell any gas when he closed the shop the night before, or when he reopened that fateful morning. My favourite is the explanation of the Edinburgh biscuit factory explosion (7 Jan) as the "spontaneous combustion of dust and air." You takes your pick! The fact is that we have had a curious series of explosions, many of unknown origin, far beyond any usual average!

Before moving to an allied phenomenon, we'd like to acknowledge the Ken Rogers information network for providing most of the source material on the blasts mentioned above. Credit is also due to the Bords, Mrs V Martin and Peter Rogerson.

Fires and other Disasters

Concurrent with the extraordinary series of explosions were a number of major public disasters, most of them involving fires usually of unknown origin. We include them here partly because they may have some close relationship to the blasts (both being violent expressions of some collective explosive spirit), and partly because it doesn't really matter where we use them since our overall thesis is that our categories are merely conveniences and that in reality all events must merge away into all other things.

We notice that Christmas Day seemed particularly disastrous: fire sunk an Egyptian ship carrying pilgrims back from Mecca; fire destroyed 30 homes in Bartlesville, Oklahoma; fire killed 13 people in Chicago; and fire damaged a club at Henley, Oxon, to the tune of £20,000. ((We also note that it was a bad day for Egyptians, apart from the pilgrim-ship disaster, an Egyptian 707 crashed in Thailand killing over 72 people. Sometimes the link between coincidences can be a country, as here. This reminds us of 10 September 1976 when a quake at Skopje in Jugoslavia was followed by 'the worst air collision in history' over Zagreb, killing

'77. The next day the news reported that President Tito was seriously ill; a group of Serbo-Croats hijacked a plane and left a bomb in New York to draw attention to the plight of Croatians in Jugoslavia; and the international guerrilla, Carlos the Jackal, was reported to be planning nasty things to do in that country.))

On Boxing Day, 26 December 1976, a fire destroyed an old folks home at St John, Newfoundland, killing 20 inmates; and 6 died in a hotel blaze at Hamilton, Ontario.

On the 1st January 1977, 3 children died in a fire at Rochdale, Greater Manchester; and a school at Gravesend, Kent was extensively damaged by fire which appears to have begun in two separate parts of the afflicted building (a neat Fortean datum that), which makes the police suspect arson.

On the 2nd January, 3 girls died in a mystery fire at Wimbledon, London. Gas was thought to have leaked and ignited (shades of the concurrent mystery explosions) but no leak could be found. A girl died in a

fire at her home in Hull, Yorks; and an elderly brother and sister died in a fire at Berrynarbor, near Ilfracombe, Devon.

On the 3rd January, a mystery fire gutted a home at Wellingborough, Northants (at noon!) killing a boy.

On the 5th January a bus crash injured 70 children at Rainworth, Notts; and a mystery fire destroyed a launderette (another one) and the flats above (another £20,000's worth). They arrested a young girl for this on suspected arson (another Fortean datum).

On the 9th January, 5 die in a housefire at Newton Aycliffe, Co Durham; and at West Bridgeford, Notts, 27 physically handicapped people were evacuated from a center for the handicapped because of a serious fire.

(Credit once more to Ken Rogers, Mrs Valerie Martin and the Bords.)

We note that most of these dates fill in gaps in our explosion list, or coincide with blasts; and seem to have mainly afflicted children and old folks.

HAMILTON'S AIRSHIP HOAX - KANSAS 1897

One of the most important stories in the UFO catechism is that of the airship that hovered over the Kansas farm of Alexander Hamilton, at 10.30 pm 19 April 1897, and dragged off one of his heifers. A neighbour later discovered the hide, legs and head of the calf (identified by Hamilton's brand) with no tracks on the soft ground or any clue to what could have happened to it (1). The story was profoundly valuable to the study of the airship-mode of UFO phenomena for two things: firstly Hamilton's apparently impeccable and detailed description of the incident and 'six of the strangest beings I ever saw' who manned (if you'll excuse the chauvinism) the craft; and secondly, the unequivocal link between the airship/UFO and the kidnapped and butchered calf preceeded (or initiated) a new category of UFO phenomena - those

linked with mystery livestock mutilations, still going on today - and, because of our first point, lent this UFO connection great credibility. It is probably true to say that every writer in the field, from cautious sceptic to breathless uncritical advocate, has been impressed by the details of the story, the affidavit and other evidence of Hamilton's respected position in the community (2), and by the fact that the story has apparently been investigated and reported on many times without anyone finding any cracks. Oh, there have been those who've had their doubts alright, but there's been no evidence until now that the story was anything but true.

The person who unravelled the core of the hoax is Jerome Clark, now Associate Editor of _Fate_, and he has his own summary of what happened in the February 1977 issue. The incident was frequently revived in Kansas papers as a wonderful relic of the old days, and Jerry, who had long been fascinated by the case, was prompted to trace any of Alexander Hamilton's relatives. Hamilton himself died in 1912, but Jerry located his granddaughter, Mrs Elizabeth Hamilton Linde (daughter of Hamilton's son Wallace who was with his father that day, according to the reports), who still lived in Yates Center, Kansas. Mrs Linde, 72, told Jerry that the family like to believe the story was true – they were familiar with the published accounts and credited Alex with a 'darn good imagination'. Although they had never heard Alex or Wall discuss the 'family legend' they had been told that the story was concocted by Alex and the editor of the Yates Center _Farmers Advocate_ by several of Alex's contemporaries, a number of decades back when many of them were still alive.

The next piece of the jigsaw arrived fortuitously (3) – a clipping from the _Buffalo Enterprise_, 28 January 1943, an obscure Kansas weekly. The previous week the _Yates Center News_ had re-run the calfnapping story and received a letter from Ben S Hudson, editor of the _Fredonia Daily Herald_, son of Ed. F Hudson, Alex's crony, the unnamed editor of the _Farmer's Advocate_. Ben said: 'Hamilton and father concocted that story following a Saturday afternoon pow-wow,' and included a statement from his father who had been amused by the story's persistence. The statement reads:

'I had just bought and installed a little gasoline engine, the first I believe to come to Yates Center, using it to run my machinery, replacing the hand-power on the old Country Campbell press and kicking the job presses. I invited many of my friends into the back shop to see the engine work. Hamilton was one of them. He exclaimed: "Now they can fly," hence the airship story that we made up. After we had published it, the story was copied in many of the largest newspapers in this country, England, France and Germany, some illustrating it with pen-drawn imaginations of their staff artists. There were also hundreds of inquiries from every part of the globe. Soon afterward there came the various experiments in flight. I have always maintained that Alex Hamilton was the real inventor of human flight. (Signed: Ed. F. Hudson)'

This claim to the scope of Hamilton's originality should perhaps be taken cautiously; Mr Hudson Senior's memory is probably dimmed by time, and by Ben's admission

the Alexander Hamilton affair 'has been a great topic of conversation in our family since the event occurred.' The incident date puts it past the peak of the great airship flap of 1896/7, so the notion of airship encounters had certainly passed into the popular vocabulary.

I passed the above clipping onto Jerry, who admitted that he was very fond of the calfnapping story and would be sorry if it could be definitely proved a hoax. We still needed a piece of airtight evidence to link the testimony of Mrs Linde and Mr Hudson Senior. Jerry placed a letter in the _Yates Center News_ (16 September 1976), asking for any further information on Hudson's claims – a simple step that paid off handsomely. He received a letter from Mrs Donna Steeby, of Wichita, Kansas, saying that her 93-year-old mother, Ethel L Shaw, heard the story from Alexander Hamilton himself (she was then Ethel Howard and a close friend of Alex's daughter Nell, Wallace's sister. There had been no social contact between Mrs Shaw and Mrs Linde.) In a second letter Mrs Steeby sent along her mother's statement:

'How well I remember that beautiful afternoon almost as though it were yesterday. I, as a young girl about 14 years old, was visiting in the Hamilton home with Mrs Hamilton and their daughter Nell, when Mr Hamilton came home from town, put up his team and came into the sitting room where we were visiting. He pulled up a chair and almost immediately began relating this story by saying: "Ma, I fixed up quite a story and told the boys in town and it will come out in the _Advocate_ this weekend." He seemed quite elated over what he had done but Mrs Hamilton was rather shocked at what he told them and and at times would remark: "Oh, Alex," or "Why, Alex!" But it didn't disturb us girls as we felt it was just a fabricated story, yet I pondered a little over it as I walked along on my way home that evening. I told my parents about it but they gave it no concern, saying: "Pay no attention to it as it's just another of his stories." It seems there were a few men round about who had formed a club which they called 'Ananias' (Liar's Club). They would get together once in a while to see which one could tell the biggest story they'd concocted since their last meeting. Well, to my knowledge, the club soon broke up after the 'airship and cow' story. I guess that one topped them all and the Hamilton family went down in history.'(4)

Jerry asked Mrs Linde if she believed Mrs Shaw's statement. She seemed reluctant to give up belief in the entertaining family legend, but said: 'If she says that's the way it was, that must be the way it was.'(5). Jerry, who has had some suggestions from other UFOlogists that this exposé is itself a hoax, summarises the position: 'It is extraordinarily improbable that Mrs Shaw and Mr Hudson should have lied about the matter. What could their possible motives be? One correspondent suggests it was to "clear the family name". As my wife comments: "Isn't it kind of late to do that now?" If that were the case, why should it be Mrs Shaw (with whom Mrs Linde has no social contact) and the late Mr Hudson who tried to do this - and not a direct descendant such as Mrs Linde, who apparently wants to believe in the "incident"? Moreover, what kind of attempt is it to "clear the family name" when its patriarch is revealed as a liar?'(5) To which we might add that there are too many individuals, too far apart, involved in this unmasking for there to be a hoax on our part (unless you're over the top and see conspiracies behind everything). We could also observe that Mr Hudson's statement has been on record since 1943, before some of us

Hamilton's airship calf-napping has passed into the modern folk-lore of UFOlogy, and is believed to be true because of the pseudo-factual style of presentation in literature aimed at the mass-market. This panel appeared in USA newspapers (week of 26 Feb 1968) which ran Otto Binder's widely syndicated feature 'Our Space Age'. ((Our thanks to Page Research Library Newsletter for bringing this to our attention.))

were born, and that there is no sign of any collusion between Hudson and the two ladies (Linde and Shaw), or that they even knew of Hudson's statement that 'the airship story was made up.'

As Jerry has found out, the reactions of some, who have a personal unshakeable faith in the story, have been predictably scornful - they feel they have something to lose when this airship is deflated. Perhaps they have - their faith would have been better placed, and less sorely tried, if they had believed in the quest for truth. In a letter to me (6) Jerry said he had told John Keel of this confirmation that the calfnapping was a hoax. John told him that now 'we are in real trouble. It always seemed to be the best of the 1897 incidents. If it collapses we can seriously question all the other cases.' We should be doing this anyway - but I guess that to make any progress at all we have to judge approximations to truth. This story fell at the first point - Hamilton, with impeccable credentials, loved a joke, and managed to get 10 of his friends, all officials of Le Roy and Yates Center, to sign the affidavit attesting to his veracity. The joke was on all of us who believed it (me included).

I personally feel that the case is still important because of the second of our points: whether the original incident actually happened or not, it was published as a true account and possibly thousands of people worldwide have since believed it actually took place. This invests it with a phenomenal reality, and, hoax or not, it conforms to a classical scenario, both ancient and modern, in myth and in fact, for animal kidnaps and mutilations. If you have been following developments in UFO studies in the last few years, you will realise that we are just beginning to appreciate that hoaxes are as much a part of the phenomenon as the actual cases. We must be on our guard - nor, in our zeal, must we throw the baby out with the bathwater.

References:

1) The main account, with an affidavit signed by 10 citizens, was in the Yates Center Farmer's Advocate 23 April 1897. Since then it has been quoted in virtually every major UFO book, the key ones being Jacques Vallee's Anatomy of a Phenomenon, 1965 (Spearman 1966, Tandem 1974) which quotes the entire clipping; John Keel's Operation Trojan Horse, 1970 (Abacus, 1973) Frank Edwards' Flying Saucers - Serious Business; Lore & Deneault's Mysteries of the Skies. Leading journal sources include Lucius Farish's article in Fate April 1966;

and Flying Saucer Review 12:4/12. The
Leroy Reporter (Kansas) was reviving the
story as late as 14 August 1970. Many
thanks to Peter Rogerson, of MUFOB, for
this potted bibliography.

2)For information on Hamilton's history
and standing (he had been a member of the
House of Representatives) see Lore and
Deneault's Mysteries of the Skies.

3)Fortean Researcher Robert J Schadewald
had written to the Kansas State Historical Society about the Hamilton story, and
received by prompt return from the Assistant Librarian, Mrs V P Allbert, the
clipping from the Buffalo Enterprise –
'so someone there was apparently familiar
with the hoax,' wrote Bob, who sent it to
me, and I forwarded it to Jerry. This
clipping is reporting on the story as it
developed in the Yates Center News.

4)Letters from Mrs Donna Steeby to Jerome
Clark, 18 and 24 September 1976.

5)'Some Clarifications of the LeRoy,
Kansas, Calfnapping Hoax.' - A privately
circulated summary of the matter from
Jerome Clark, 19 November 1976.

6)Letter to me from Jerome Clark, 2 October 1976.

Robert J M Rickard - February 1977

Next time in Forteana Corrigenda we review further developments in the unravelling of the disappearance of David Lang
(see FT 18/6.)

■■■■■■■■■■■■■■■■■■■■■■■■■■■■■■■■■■■■■■■

Precession/Bell:
...cont from p17.
7) Flying Saucer Review 21: 6/14 (1976)
8) The Mothman Prophecies John A Keel 1975
(Visitors from Space Panther, 1976)
9) Fortean Times 17/20
10)UFOs: Operation Trojan Horse, John A
Keel, 1970 (Abacus, 1973)
11)Beyond Earth Ralph & Judy Blum
(Corgi 1974)
12)Fortean Times 16/19; 17/17
13)Our Haunted Planet John A Keel 1971
(Futura, 1975)
14)Gods or Spacemen? W R Drake (Amherst 1964)
15)The Coming of the Saucers? Kenneth
Arnold & Raymond Palmer (Amherst 1952)
16)Invisible Horizons, V Gaddis (Ace 1965)
17)Destiny Mars & ET Databank on Phobos,
M W Saunders (Downs, 1975/76)
18)The News 9/7
19)The News 4/7
20)G H Williamson, The Road in the Sky,
1959 (Futura 1975) & Secret Places of
the Lion, 1958 (Futura 1974)
21)Gods and Spacemen in the Ancient East
W R Drake 1968 (Sphere, 1973)

ZEBRADIA

THE
WONDERHORSE
OF
HIBALDSTOW.

by NIGEL WATSON

On the 10th June 1976 a rather remarkable foal was born in Hibaldstow, South
Humberside - remarkable because his
appearance is more like a zebra than a
horse.
  Mr Bill Sargent, the owner of the
foal, christened him 'Zebradia' for
obvious reasons. "It's only once in a
lifetime ought like this happens, I
reckon. I've been breeding horses for
years and I've never seen one like it.
I've had coloured ones, black and white,
blue and white, and lemon and white, but
never one like that with stripes on," he
said.
  Zebradia's parents were a mare called
'Spotty', and a five-year-old stallion
called 'Wheelgates Bill', a pure-bred
Cleveland Bay, both owned by Mr Sargent.
  Although one newspaper report (Scunthorpe Evening Telegraph 12 July 1976)
claims that Zebradia's markings "have
astonished veterinary experts," no
thorough veterinary examination or report
has yet been carried out.
  Roger Hebb and myself visited Mr
Sargent on 4 October 1976 and were able
to see the foal for ourselves. Mr Sargent
is the owner of an icecream business and
an icecream parlour is situated next to
his house and the stables. The combined
attraction of icecream and the unusual
horse meant the area was inundated with
children, particularly at weekends. For
the foal's sake (it developed a predil-
ection for icecream) and for peace of

mind the foal is kept with his mother in a secluded field a few miles from Hibaldstow. We found Zebradia to be a particularly frisky varmint as we tried to photograph him in the failing light. The session was like sparring with Mohammed Ali! Surprisingly, the shots came out quite well.

Zebradia is still something of a celebrity in the area. In July the children of Class 10, Kirton Lindsey County Primary School, presented Mr Sargent with a book of paintings, stories and poems celebrating the wonder horse. We excerpt one here, by Jennifer Ashley.

It should be noted that Zebradia is only remarkable for his markings - he does not possess any other strange features (eg the deformations of the 'Malton Mutant' - see The News 15/6). Zebradia will probably grow into a 16.2hh stallion.

Nigel Watson - January 1977.

((Photo: Copyright N Watson & R Hebb.
Poem: Copyright Jennifer Ashley.))

Zebradia

At the icecream parlour
There's a new little foal.
His mother and father
Have reached a great goal;
For the new little foal
Has a very nice coat.
Oh! So bright!
The colours are...guess!
Yes! Black and white.
He's just like a zebra
Come in from the wild!
But really he came into
                    this world
In a normal way,
With the vet's calm hand
Helping him through
          to a world of delight,
At the icecream parlour,
In Hibaldstow.

LEGION FEVER - PHILADELPHIA 1976

Since our last listing of mystery illnesses (News 8/9) we have accumulated quite a heap of clippings. By far the biggest story was that of the unidentified illness that killed 28 (we think!) and hospitalized nearly 180 in Philadelphia, Pennsylvania, in the last half of last year, before it vanished as mysteriously as it arrived. This period saw an extraordinary number of strange and exotic diseases - typhoid, paratyphoid and polio outbreaks in the UK; Lassa fever and Marburg (or Green Monkey) fever (both from Africa) pop up in Britain, and scare health authorities in Canada and USA, both of which were in the midst of hysteria about a new form of Swine flu and controversy over the innoculations; an 'impotence' panic breaks out in Thailand; the 'Black Death' turns up in California; and US papers in 1976 announce a new strain of gonorrhea, and that 9 million inhabitants of Michigan face the possibility of being poisoned by an industrial pollutant called PBB which can cause brain damage - which will be detailed in the next and future issues of FT along with mystery illnesses of the "mass hysteria" kind, and their equivalents among animals.

But for now we detail the 'Legion Fever' as the press called it, that broke out in Philadelphia after the annual convention there of the state's American Legion at the Bellevue-Stratford Hotel on the weekend July 21-24. It is a classical scenario of clashing experts, contradictory theories, inefficiency, bungling, scaremongering and general ineffectiveness of the various kinds of establishments (commercial, political, medical, scientific etc) caught with their collective pants down by the Unknown.

Reconstructing the story from the first news reports, it seems that the first sufferers came down with flu-like symptoms within 2-4 days of the last day of the convention (ie, 24 July) - chills, headache and high fever temperature with congestion and chest pains. Later autopsies revealed a foamy bloody fluid that filled up the spaces between the air-sacs in the lungs, preventing oxygen reaching the bloodstream - a condition easily identifiable, even in its early stages, by X-ray. By 4 Aug, there were 120 hospitalized and 20 dead in various hospitals in Pennsylvania and New York states. No one realized the scale of the danger until perhaps the 2nd Aug - and one of the first to alert the authorities was Edward Hoak, an official of the American Legion, who suddenly noticed the high number of deaths and illnesses among his friends and friends' friends, all of whom had attended the convention a few weeks before at the Bellevue. Formal recognition of Legion Fever (hereinafter LF) as an epidemic of unknown origin came on 3 Aug with the rapid mobilization of a team of investigators from the Center for Disease Control (CDC) with a backup of 1000 federal and state medical researchers.

Several important statements were issued the next day (4th). State Health Secretary, Leonard Bachmann, was rash enough to say to the press that the symptoms were consistent with swine flu and viral pneumonia - that touched off another swine-flu panic and his office was pressurized into identifying if it was indeed this disease - a course of action that later suffered heavy criticism. Dr Walter Dowdle, CDC's virology director said: "It could be anything from an infectious disease to a toxin." If it was an infectious disease we were now well into the period when secondary cases (ie those who had come into contact with the initial victims) should be showing themselves. Indeed, six were suspected but found to have a readily identified form of flu. What made the authorities hold their breath even more was another much bigger convention now going on in the Bellevue, the 41st International Eucharistic Congress, with an expected 1 million attendees. Curiously, we only learn much later that 2 of these developed LF when they died (27 Aug), and the only connexion it was possible to identify was that they had stayed at the Bellevue. Other than that, we know that a man who delivered food to the hotel, a woman who attended an auxilliary meeting only, a busdriver who took passengers to the convention and 4 passengers from his and another bus, but as all these were directly associated with the Bellevue site they were considered to be primary cases.

On the 5th Aug a UK professor calms us by warning that if it's a new type of flu it could become pandemic worldwide. The toll is now 23 dead, 138 hospitalized; and Gov. Milton Shapp announces that the disease remains unidentified but it "does not appear to be swine flu" nor bubonic plague, lassa fever, Marburg disease or lymphatic memengitis - nor does it seem to be bacterially based. The first of the survivors recovers.

By 7 Aug 25 were dead, 152 in hospital. Papers carry a quiet announcement that the FBI will probe the theory of a "biological attack" with an airborne poison since the disease has behaved more like a toxin than a virus, both in treatment and in confinement. This marks a fundamental change in the whole investigation. The major questions being asked are: if it was a viral flu, why has it shown in early summer instead of the usual autumn-winter season; why, given the short incubation period (3 days apx) was there no secondary spread; why are there no runny noses and coughs in what was "clearly" a respiratory illness; was the disease latent in Philadelphia, or was it brought by a carrier; if the latter, then from where; why did it seem to kill men aged 40-50 (on average) in their prime when it had missed the more vulnerable young and elderly ((the victims' ages ranged from 39-82)); and the key question of all, why had the hotel staff escaped when LF struck at incidental bus drivers and delivery-men (see 4 Aug)? So the search switched from an organism, to hunt a chemical poison, and daily, as the dreaded secondary wave failed to materialize, more experts switched to the new opinion. However, one top toxicologist, Dr Richard Cohn admitted their searches had found nothing so far in this line. On the 9th Aug, with 27 dead, Bachmann said the disease seemed

to have a 3-day incubation period and that at least 9 of the sick had only attended on one day, the 23rd July (now there's one for the 23-spotters!) - whatever happened must have happened then, he said.

The papers on the 15th Aug now drop the toll back to 25 dead & 152 hospitalized - no reasons are given, but in retrospect we'd guess that some deaths could now be attributed to identifyable sources. The 2 attendees at the Eucharistic Congress (also held at the Bellevue, but 1-8 Aug) come down with LF. Two men at a candlemakers' convention held in the city earlier that July also develop a suspect condition. Then matters are made worse by the collapse of 100 young bandsmen in Walden, NY, but we'll give you this one in the next issue. By now the investigation had switched "almost wholly" to chemical poisons - 17 metal toxins had been ruled out and the hot favourite was nickel carbonyl. On the 19th Aug a leading toxicologist, Dr F William Sunderman Jr, said that some symptoms of LF and the degenerate state of victims' lungs was consistent with nickel carbonyl poisoning - but other symptoms (like the high fever) were not! It is also revealed that the research team found 19 plumbing violations in the Bellevue, the most relevant being that a hose taking cold water to the hotel's air-conditioner lacked a valve to prevent any "backflow", thus putting the whole drinking supply at risk from nasty things like ammonia compounds. Since most of the investigators agree that not all of the afflicted ate or drank at the Bellevue, it seems we can discount this theory. 27 Aug - the 2 Eucharistic Congress attendees die. 29 Aug - a 12-man team is appointed by the CDC to continue searching for possible causes of LF. The toll finally stabilizes at 29 dead, 180 hospitalized.

That same day some scientists at MIT and Harvard weigh-in with their idea that if a toxic metal was involved, it could have accumulated in the victims' hair within a few millimeters of the root. Nothing more is heard from them. Toward the end of September a pathologist, Dr Jerrold Abraham, says at least 4 of the deceased showed traces of "metal fumes" in their lungs, but he doesn't say how that squared with any other fact in the case. Around Sept 1st the Soviet weekly Literaturnaya Gazeta speculated that a secret Pentagon chemical warfare experiment had gone wrong.

Then came another bright theory. Dr Edward Schantz (in National Enquirer 12 Oct 76) said "all the indications point to a poison...it could well have been ricin," (a deadly toxin extracted from castor beans.) Then this famous bio-chemist suggested it could only have got to the legionnaires by a wilful act. Ricin, it seems, can be extracted fairly simply, and the castor bean grows plentifully all over the southern USA; it could produce the raging fever and deteriorated lungs of LF. But wait! that only accounts for 2 of the symptoms, and the hot favourite, nickel carbonyl, was doubtful for the same reason. It's no use; the experts have fallen upon each other. The CDC say they considered ricin and dismissed it because there was no sign of its usual effect, intestinal damage - LF damaged only lung tissue.

Ah, said Dr Schantz, that's because the legionnaires sniffed it, not ate it. A toxicology professor from the Vanderbilt University Medical School, Dr Wayland Hayes Jr, agreed that airborne ricin might produce effects like LF - CDC toxicologist Dr Renate Kimbrough dis-agreed, saying we don't know because it's not been studied in tests before. But Dr Schantz now has the bit between his teeth and, with imagination straining, steps out into the realm of artistic creation. "I wouldn't put it past the saboteurs to have put the ricin into an ordinary air-freshener spray and sprayed it around the rooms," he said. What a splendid effort, sir! and we guess that if it's as toxic as you say they all went about spraying wearing gas masks! Perhaps we have missed something, but why were only a few affected - "Every-one at the convention could have ingest-ed this toxin...but some were more sus-ceptible than others, and died." Ah, then ricin can't really be "one of the most toxic substances known to man" as you said earlier. It is? Oh, excuse us for being dim, but if it is a powerful poison that can pass through the body in less than 24 hours leaving behind very serious damage to internal organs, how come it was as long as 3 days before there were any symptoms?

Perhaps Dr Schantz can be forgiven for being a bit vague, as a colleague, Dr Sunderman Jr, is back having quite forgotten his own reservations about the nickel carbonyl hypothesis, now getting breathless about villains mixing the stuff with dry-ice and dumping it all over the Bellevue (!). What seems to have changed his mind is an "anonymous, ominous" letter he received ranting about the substance and how it could be used to kill "authority and military-type figures". Dr Sunderman sprung this on the Congressional committee on 29th October, and was supported by the chief forensic psychiatrist at Walter Reed Army Medical Center, who said the writ-ing was characteristic of "an envious para-noid, full of hatred." Curiously, the letter was dated 28 July, before the public became aware of epidemic. Just how significant this is, we never learn.

On the 10th November the Bellevue-Stratford announces that it will close in 10 days. The adverse publicity caused huge business losses as custom stayed away, other conventions switched their bookings elsewhere. Yet Gerald Ford came there after his first TV encounter with Jimmy Carter; Gov. Shapp spent a night there, and the Pennsyl-vania Medical Society deliberately held their convention there, each an attempt to reassure the public and reestablish confidence in the city's tourist bus-iness...but none of it helped. In its last few days the Bellevue bravely hosted a meeting of over 170 medical scientists who met to discuss the latest theories and findings. There are virtually no new leads or conclusions - and ricin seems to have gone the way of the swine-flu theory. The only new lead developed as recently as 10 Jan 1977; Dr Leslie Page, a microbiologist at the Animal Disease Center, said that recent tests showed that chlamydiae bacteria, spread by pigeons, could cause pneu-monia-like symptons similar to those of LF. This backed the claim (18 Nov 76) of Dr Gary Latimer, at Sacred Heart hospital, Allentown, Pa, who said he had cured 8 sufferers by treating them for chlamydia infections. But wait a minute! - weren't we told in the early days of the panic that bacterial infect-ions were the first to be ruled out? (see 5 Aug).

This surprising series of turnabouts (bacterial/viral/metal toxin/plant toxin/metal toxin/ and back to bacteria) could only arise from inconclusive and ambiguous evidence feeding the pet theories of various experts - so it seems inevitable there would sooner or later be allegations of blunders and inefficiency. Dr Carl Wecht, Allegheny county coroner and spokesman for the CDC team of medical vigilantes, told National Enquirer (12 Oct 76) that such was the initial headlong rush to estab-lish the cause was swine-flu that likelyhood of it being a toxin was not considered, despite some experts' opin-ions, until it was "probably too late to find anything." He alleges that vital samples were never collected, samples were wasted in swine-flu tests, samples had been taken from "inappropriate areas of the lung", and that blood and urine samples were made useless from the toxicologists point of view by not being frozen immediately "because toxic chemicals break down very quickly in the body." On top of that, investigating experts were not given full autopsy reports, and that "even now" only reports on 10 of the 29 deaths were available.

Well - we don't know what the findings of the committee were - perhaps they're still sitting - but to the public (especially the American public) this bickering is a poor substitute for hard facts, and we know from many a Fortean scenario that in the absence of concrete graspables and the persistance of mystery the public and the media can conjure up their own explanations to our mind if not equally valid then doubly fascinating. On 25 Nov we are told that previous speculations about ruthless, mad (but scientifically adept) assassins received another boost as a legionnaire, George Chiavetta, told the committee that on at least 3 occasions (and once in the company of four others) he had noticed a strange "glassy-eyed man in a royal blue suit". ((Hmmm - for comments on 'staring-eyes' linked with strange phenomena see Anthony Bell's article FT 17/6)) Chiavetta said he overheard this man muttering: "It's too late. You won't be saved. The legionaires are doomed." Chiavetta had told the police who reported it to Leonard Bachmann, the Health Secretary, who handed it back to the police because his department, he said, was not equipped for police-work and was fully employed in the virus-hunt at that time. The police, it seems, thought it was Bachmann's worry and did nothing about it. We wonder if this portends a schism among the Men In Black, or whether some among them are becoming more sartorially conscious? Nothing is said about how this figure relates to Dr Schantz's ricin-sprayers or Dr Sunderman Jr's hate-filled paranoid dry-ice dumper. A thought occurs to us of a grim parody of a scene in Shea & Wilson's Illuminatus! - that perhaps all three (and maybe some other unnoticed weirdos) seeded their own brands of death there, oblivious of each other and the Pentagon and Russian agents doing the same thing!

That's no more bizarre (or unlikely) than the latest theory - according to a hysterical (rabid and laughable) article by P.R. Wilshire in the January 1977 edition of Ancient Astronauts, UFOs and their occupants and contactees are resposible by (deliberately or not) omitting any decontamination procedure! In passing, Wilshire suggests that many previous plagues, mystery epidemics and (of course) the recent wave of USA animal mutilations all have similar ET origins. As a matter of interest, the earliest mention of an ET connexion for LF appears in a letter in Midnight 16 August 1976, in which an Alabama reader counters a previous suggestion in that paper that secret Russian germ warfare was responsible with the idea that the UFOs were firing germs at America "to make us think it's the Russians and start a war."

The mind boggles!

((The story was reconstructed from extensive coverage clipped from the (Newport News, Va) Daily Press, and Times-Herald; (Virginia Beach, Va) Pilot; and the Washington Post of the mentioned dates, for which a huge debt is owed to Gary L Abbott. Many thanks also to Ken Rogers, John Michell and Ion Will for clippings of the UK coverage, and to Dave Reissig for the copy of Ancient Astronauts.))

Robert JM Rickard - February 1977.

■■■■■■■■■■■■■■■■■■■■■■■■■■■■■■■■■■

Plans /cont from p2...

Plans /cont from p2...

Another possibility is for some of you to place blurbs in the Fortean books in your local library. Write if you want any.

Beyond that we want to build up the mag to be the best of its kind in the field. We'd like more articles, more research, more letters, more speculation and actual discussion of Fortean themes. We want our book reviews respected by publishers so that our recommendation will mean something. We may at a later stage take in advertising from the book companies. After all, most people interested in Fortean matters are, automatically, book-oriented people. There's a great awareness generally today of our topics - all those latent readers. It's only a matter of reaching them!

Phenomena: A Book of Wonders by John Michell and myself has been subject to the vaguaries of the publishing world recently, with several changes in its detail and schedule. Last issue we said that the price will be an agreeable £2.95 - now we learn that the planned Spring release has been put back to the Autumn or late Summer. The American publisher will be Pantheon Books.

Anthony Bell continues his exposition of 'lexilinks' as a research tool, and contemplates some of the associations that can be found in a case we reported in <u>The News</u> 15/17, that of the silver notecase that fell out of the sky to tangle in the hair of Lynne Connolly, a Hull housewife.

Tony also discovers, evocatively, that Mrs Connolly has a history of strange phenomena, as does her family, which suggests that we Forteans should perhaps begin to consider the <u>witness</u> as well as the phenomena just as the new UFOlogists are doing, and profitably - Ed.

AN' MILL'ENCH TOO, & REMEMBER CAPT. MILLER OF THE JOYITA

EEE BY GUM! ONCE THERE 'AS TROUBLE DOWN AT MILL BUT NOW MILLER'S GOIN' DOWN IN TROUBLE ALL REET!

Precession of the Gracious: Fallout of the Damned

by A J BELL

DRAWING BY ANTHONY BELL

In 'Lexilinks' (1) I noted words repeated in Bible sayings, such as 'cast' in 'Do not cast pearls before swine' and 'Cast the motes from your own eyes first'. Though doubtless of earlier origin, Caesar said: 'The die is cast' before committing his army to crossing the Rubicon. The image of an army plunging into water reminds me of Christ's saying that it would be better for a man to be cast into water with a millstone around his neck than for him to continue sinning. The word mill suggests rotation, and lexically we have an idea of rotation preceeding a dunking into water, a theme I will pursue.

Perhaps the dunking of Ronald Milhench and the supposed dunking of Glen Miller is Nature's expression of lexical rotation followed by a plunge - if THEY can't drop

a man with a millstone round his neck into water, someone with an appropriate name will do! There is an East Anglian legend of a lady in white, sometimes seen near a Mill Road, who throws herself into a river. (2) Another East Anglian legend also concerns a white lady, one who seeks a partner for a dance on a castle-top. If the partner displeases her he is <u>cast</u> into the dried-up <u>moat</u> below (3) - he dies after falling from grace and then falls away from the graceful lady. I note that Glen Miller was a dance band leader.

Lynn Connolly, who also loves dancing, found a strange little notecase in her hair as she was hanging out her washing. Her hairstyle being a lexically rotational whirligig. She felt a tap on her head and felt something in her hair. She shook her head and the notecase fell to the ground – rotation followed by a fall. Interestingly, the notecase seems to be the kind a lady would use at a dance to keep a record of partners' names. Perhaps it belongs to that white lady on the castle top! Phyllis Newcombe burst into SHC after dancing.(4) – another hazard of rotation. In the Allende letters we are told of a man 'taking fire' after handling a ship's compass (5) and there is the case of three men blazing after holding a vehicle's wheel (4). The similar names of SHC victims and authorities suggest the idea of holding or contacting a rotating thing: eg Lilly White (describing hands), Wright (a maker of wheels), and Knight (suggesting Round Table)(4). Also Bertholdi, Bartholin etc are similar to 'berth', a fixture about which ships pivot. Note that we dial 999 in case of fire, and London's Great Fire was in 1666 – I feel 6 and 9 are associated with fire. Inverted commas have a 6 or 9 shape and 'coma' is Greek for hair – the hair Mrs Connolly rotated. Note the 'com' in Newcombe, compass and combustion. In News 7/3 there's the story of Pat Cummins who SHC'd while jailed. Cummins is a make of compression-ignition engine – Perhaps Pat pressed the round supper-plate causing ignition! The inventor associated with this type of engine was Deisel, thought to have fallen overboard and drowned in the Channel. The first 3 letters of 'fire' are the 6th, 9th and (2x9)th in the alphabet – the blazing man in the Allende Letters who held the compass burned for 2x9 days.

The idea of rotation involving dials is illustrated by the action of Agar, as described in The Silver Bridge (6), when he examined a TV set's dials minutely before rotating the set; and the reversed pictures taken from a TV by August Roberts where the dial and screen section were separately rotated about the vertical axis (7). In the Allende Letters reference is made to a 'reverse snap neutralizer' – just what August Roberts needed! – and the remark is made that such a device in a magnetic net could catch a UFO and that if the Russians had one they would have cornered the world's diamond market as a dead giveaway. Well, a dead giveaway is a die castoff! I note Agar is similar to Agartha, derived from Argha, meaning a long ship, and thus similar in turn to Ark and Argo.

The Silver Bridge on the Ohio was the scene of a mass auto-dunking when it fell from grace, and the area around it had seen visits by a mysterious mothman entity (8). Our editor's view that mothmen/birdmen type entities are associated with softwood trees (9) is indicated by the fact that the Silver Bridge fell when LBJ switched on the lights of the White House softwood Christmas tree (8,10). It's interesting that the author of Silver Bridge is Gray Barker, for 'gray' is similar to 'grace', and silver-grey is the typical mothman colour. Mrs Connolly who found the silver notecase (or was it the other way round?) had the maiden name Gray.

Pincer-like eclipsing dial sweeps are reflected in the pincer-like claws of the silver-grey Pascagoula entities seen by Hickson and Parker (11) and the Cornish Owlmen of 1976 (12). Hickson and Parker were fishing near a bridge when their experience began. I associate mothmen/birdmen with bird attacks and I note that the bird attack reported in FT 17/3 on Kevin Graham (gray-ham) occurred as he crossed a bridge. Pont is French for bridge and the grey-suited visitors of George Adamski rode in a 1946 Pontiac, a division noted for its silver streak ornament. One of these visitors was called Fir Kon, which perhaps equals conifer (or fir-cone – Ed.)

In Silver Bridge there is the story of Woody Derenberger's contact with an entity called Indrid Cold and his (com)panions. Perhaps Woody = trees = silva = arbor, so that Woody Derenberger + Indrid Cold = Coldharbor? I notice that one of the 1897 airshipnauts tried to purchase a cold chisel, bluestone and oil (shades of Coldharbor, Stonehenge and Beltane.) Speaking of airships, I'm reminded that THEY tried to get a lawyer called Collins to front for them in the airship project, and an airship dropped a parcel into Lincoln Park (10) – Collins is almost an anagram of Lincoln. The Pascagoula case involved a lawyer called Colingo, and Doc Shiels has written to me mentioning a mothman type entity at Lincoln's Inn, Cornwall. Lincoln's Inn is also the name of one of the four 'Inns of Court' in which British lawyers are called to the Bar – one of the others is Gray's Inn. On the same Thursday night as Hickson and Parker's contact, three UFOs were sighted in the area and reported to a Sheriff Diamonds. One involved a man in the Pinecrest subdivision, and another concerned three men on their way to a place called The Home of Grace. Diamonds, pines and Grace – THEY're laying it on thick! (Incidentally JFK was killed in the company of Texas Governor Connolly in a make of car named for the lawyer and statesman Lincoln.) The similarity between Collins, Colingo, Lynn Connolly and Lincoln suggests Linn, a Gælic word associated with a fall. One entity, Linn Erri, made initial contact by radio and her name suggests to me 'fall into error', in other words a fall from grace.

Another radio-entity, Nacoma, once gave a lecture on the dangers of atomic explosions - THEY don't like the fall-out (13). Yet another radio-entity was called Ankar-22, which suggests an airship anchor that got caught thereby berthing the vessel (14). In a letter to the San Francisco Bee, 24 November 1896, it is said that the Lord Commissioner of Mars' airships can anchor themselves in space and wait for the rotation of the earth to bring them near their destination, very suggestive of holding and rotation (11). The letter also mentioned aluminium (a common silver-grey element found in combination), and diamonds.

Continuing the theme of rotation preceeding a fall I notice that in the Tacoma affair a rotating group of saucers touched another and then a 'slag' fell partly onto a harbour patrol boat, and witness Dahl compared the saucers to dials on a Buick dash. Later the owner of the boat saw a similar saucer emerge from a cumulus cloud. There were 6 saucers over the boat, and Ken Arnold (a man partly concerned with fighting softwood forest fires) and Capt. Smith of United Airlines investigated the affair. Both had previous sightings - Arnold's being the famous 24 June 1947 incident when he saw 9 discs while he was searching for the wreck of a Commando aircraft; Smith's was also of 9 discs (15). Incidentally, Arnold's book contains photos of a strange fire on a wooden (arbor/silva) bridge over a river in softwood country.

Pascagoula UFOs and Sheriff Diamond - the diamond is a jewel associated with the god Mars (14), who with his brother Vulcan formed a mythical military-industrial complex. Vulcan is also symbolized in the industrial processes of milling, casting and die-making, words I've previously drawn attention to. Incidentally, the Rubicon, which Caesar crossed after the die was cast by a phantom reed (red-Mars?) player, is suggestive of the jewel ruby. The name of that strange derelict of Capt. Miller's, Joyita, means 'little jewel'(16). Imagine the scene at Vulcan's Forge when a red hot ingot is taken from the fiery furnace with pincer-like tongs, hammered violently and then plunged into water. Perhaps Vulcan drops the slag from UFOs à la Maurey Island!

I note that about the same time that the Viking spacecraft was studying Mars there were a number of mishaps - especially fires and dunkings - concerning military inventory. A fire on a RN ship in dock, and a man fell to his death from her sister ship. Two US cargo planes of the same type had 'accidents' on the same day, and a NATO exercise had more losses than usual including a plane dunked from a ship. This plane in turn lost a 'phoenix' missile - the phoenix being a mythical creature (associated with fire) related to the Sphinx and the Garuda and hence to mothmen/birdmen. The Sphinx is near the Great Pyramid and I see that the numerical equivalent of lexilinks found by M W Saunders between Mars and Earth's pyramids involve volcanos (17), a word associated with Vulcan. The Sphinx is a man-lion, and along with the Cornish Owlman, the Viking mission and military mishaps there was a spate of UK lion sightings in that 1976 summer, including at least one sighting in my own county of Yorkshire.(See also the cases given elsewhere in this issue)

When visiting Woody Derenberger, Gray Barker saw people sitting in cars near Derenberger's house and as Barker drove near, the people 'huddled low' in their vehicles - ie they fell. In one vehicle, however - a station-wagon, a 'woody' - a man twiddled an illuminated dial and Barker thought he could hear the Danse Macabre music (6). Dials and dancing. Often strange vehicles appear in UFO flaps with violet illuminated dials. Violet, a blue-red colour, reminds me that the first pictures from the Viking-lander on Mars showed a blue sky; later it was said to be a deep pink after instruments had been properly calibrated. Helene Smith claimed contact with Martians and once saw a vision of a bridge over a blue-pink lake (presumably a reflection of a Martian sky). A man flew off this bridge, touched the water below and returned - luckier than some! (13) The page edges of the notepad in Mrs Connolly's silver notecase are red with a slight bluish tinge - perhaps dye instability, and suggestive of Mars.

Mrs Connolly was hanging out her wash at about 10.30 am on (about) 21 October 1975 when she felt a tap on her head and something in her hair which turned out to be the notecase. The case measures approximately 36.5 mm in width and 63 mm long. Strangely, I was told the case measured exactly 1½"x2½", an erroneous datum that is highly significant as the ratio 1½:2½ was a characteristic of Noah's Ark and the Ark of the Covenant - someone fell into error! Essentially, the case is made from two old-type silver rectangular plates hinged together containing a notepad - could a bird have been attracted by the silver flash, picked it up and dropped it on Mrs Connolly's head? Alternatively it may have been thrown from a neighbour's upper window - or materialized at a spot

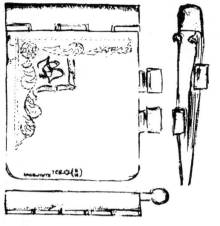

A sketch (by Anthony Bell) of the silver notecase that fell from 'no where', landing in Mrs Connolly's hair. It measures 63x36.5mm.

near Mrs Connolly's head! Mrs Connolly finds it difficult to accept that a bird was responsible and the origin remains a puzzle. Her maiden-name was Lynne Victoria Gray - reminiscent of Victor Grayson, an MP who vanished on his way to Hull in 1920 (18), where Mrs Connolly lives. I wonder if there is a connection between the notecase and Grayson or perhaps the Hull fishing vessel, Gaul, which vanished (19).

As I associate the Fall from Grace with boats, ships and fishing, I find it interesting that the word 'Klaipeda' is found on the notecase, oddly, upside down. Klaipeda is a Baltic port, and I note that Tacoma, San Francisco (where the US airship started out), and Falmouth (haunt of the Cornish Owlman)   like Hull and Klaipeda share similar industries like docking, boat building, flour milling and fishing. Pascagoula is also a ship-building centre. The case bears the legend 'SE' and 'C8' near a six-pointed star on the front together with a scroll design of the letters 'JB' or 'TB'. Only 13 pages remain on the notepad with the stubs of the rest still in the clip.

Mrs Connolly finds the 13 remaining pages rather ominous as she has had a lot of 'bad luck' and illness since moving to her present address, culminating in her husband's near-death a few years ago. During this crisis Mrs Connolly and her sister saw Mr Connolly's face appear in profile on a wall while he was gravely ill in hospital. Electrical equipment in the

house often gives trouble, and Mrs Connolly claims to hear a breathing sound in her room whenever she is alone, but not in the company of her husband. About Christmas 1964, Mrs Connolly, her brother, sister and parents lived for a time in a flat in which the family dog refused to enter certain rooms, including the attic shared by Mrs Connolly and her sister. Doors would open on their own, and occasionally a Little Green Man could be seen seated crosslegged on a wall, repeatedly turning pages in a book and doffing his Trilby hat. Most of the family witnessed strange events in the flat and were glad to leave. Being no stranger to unusual phenomena myself, I told Mrs Connolly and her sister of my own experience with this type of phenomenon - if I hadn't I doubt whether they would have mentioned the LGM episode. I feel many people have seen strange events - eg UFOs - and feel embarrassed to relate them unless prompted.

Interesting that Mrs Connolly's 'vision' was on a wall. When she was young she told her father that a certain neighbour had died and been taken away at 7 o'clock. She said this at 6 o'clock, accurately predicting the event. 6, 7 and death. Sometimes one reads of seven things, one of which is later destroyed or taken away, leaving six. Eg G H Williamson writes of the 'Unholy Six', a group of six planets where originally there were seven. The unwhole theme is echoed in the myth of the spotted sun Akhenaton and his spotless wife Nefertiti who had seven daughters; one died early (20). Doubtless things were at sixes and sevens when this occurred and the legend of the Pleiades, Snow White and the seven (green?) dwarfs, and the story of Moses and Ziporah (21) also highlight the number seven.

I am still investigating the Silver Notecase affair. I went to see the notecase because I felt Mrs Connolly had a significant name, and because I wonder if people with mystically significant names have a specially close contact with the world of the strange - an idea that also occurred to Fort.

Anthony J Bell - November 1976

References:

1) Fortean Times 17/5
2) Lantern 15/20
3) Lantern 14/3
4) Fortean Times 16/26
5) Uninvited Visitors, Ivan Sanderson, 1969 (Tandem, 1974)
6) The Silver Bridge Gray Barker (Saucerian 1970)

Cont on p8...

OUT OF PLACE

Since our last listing of 'Surrey Puma' stories (The News 14/3ff.) we have accumulated a few more, old and new.

The first case is from a letter to me from John Michell (dated 8 May 1976): "Here's a good story to fill a gap in your puma record told me today by my friend Mark Palmer. On Xmas Eve 1968 he and his friend, Maldwyn Thomas, were taking horses across Devon and camped on Know Stone Moor, near Tiverton. In the late evening a local policeman roused them to ask if they had seen a puma. One had been reported there that day."

Next, another anecdote, from Auberon Waugh's column in the New Statesman, 26 December 1975: "...a few years ago... I was standing at an upstairs window (of a house in West Somerset) in the late afternoon with about 4 cricketers and their wives or girlfriends - one of whom was a teetotaller - when we distinctly saw a black panther run across the fields in front of the house." Waugh suggested writing a letter to the press to record the event but "several of the witnesses started to back down... they thought it might have been an extremely large black cat." Then Waugh says wryly: "The modern mind isn't interested in ghosts; it rejects them as unwelcome reminders of some discredited past." (Cr. John Michell John Rimmer, Roger Sandell). The letter from John Rimmer (dated 23 February 1976) also contained notices of two books to be released in the summer that year: one called Man-eater by Ted Willis, and the other The Surrey Cat by Andrew Sinclair - the former about two tigers that roam and kill on the Yorkshire moors and the latter about a black puma which terrifies a Surrey village. Little did we realise that that summer would see fiction become a pseudo-fact - see 'The Nottingham Lion' drama, FT 18/25 - 'pseudo-fact' because despite some authentic sightings of a lion, no lion was ever caught (see items below) and it was explained-away as a paper-bag!

Our most modern sightings of the 'Surrey Puma' begin with an infuriatingly brief note in the Daily Mirror 6 July 1976, that a journalist, Sally Rose, claimed to have seen the beast, it says not where or when. That same month, the Basingstoke Gazette 23 July 1976 reported that just a few days earlier a young housewife, Anne Barnes, was hanging out washed nappies in the large garden behind her house in Odiham, Hants, when she turned to call her child and froze in her tracks. "At first I thought it was just a well-fed cat, but when I looked closer I could see the animal had huge shoulders like a bear ... a real live puma in my own English country garden - I just can't believe it." She said it stood very still for a few seconds and then in one bound leapt on to a 10ft wall and disappeared into some dense trees beyond. (Cr.: Mike Rickard)

That latest note we have is from the (London) Evening Standard 31 January '77 -- that in the early morning of the 29th (that's my guess - I wish reporters would give us a few facts, like dates) a motorist reported seeing 'the puma' in Nutfield Mid Street, near Redhill, Surrey, about the size of a retriever, loping along like a cat. (Our reporter clearly doesn't want to bore us with details!). The police said the man seemed sincere enough for them to switch all their patrol cars to search the area. Nothing was found.

SCOTTISH MYSTERY CAT UPDATE

The last news we had of the 'Ayrshire Puma' was a double sighting on 14 June 1974, which we recorded in News 7/2. About 26 August last year Ballagioch Hill, near Eaglesham, Renfrew, a 'shadowy cat-like creature' left tracks at the scene of a killing of five geese. Large chunks had been ripped from a 6 ft fence, and an alsatian in a nearby kennel, 'normally vicious', was found cowering in terror. Richard O'Grady, director of Calderpark Zoo, Glasgow, was brought to the scene by police and admits he was prepared to dismiss the killings as the work of dogs as he says he had done 'many times in the past with similar incidents.' 'Now,' he says, 'I have very little doubt it was a puma.' 'Each goose had puncture marks on its body 1½" deep and 4-5" apart. That's how a puma kills,' said O'Grady. Deep tracks were found in a stream nearby, and in O'Grady's opinion these too point to puma: 'They went in a straight line, some of them overlapping the way a cat moves.' Bath Chronicle 28 August 1976 (Cr: John Michell); Sunday Times 29 August 1976 (Cr: A J Bell). There are interesting aspects to this incident. Firstly, the report mentions that the geese bore no other sign of injury. By the tone of surprise at the killings we might guess that these were the first for some time or at all, which would make it very strange indeed in a landscape with no evidence of any other puma kills that these geese were killed and not eaten, or partly eaten as the large cats are in-clined to do. Instead we are reminded of some of the cases in Fort of the mystery killings of animals 'in a vampirish way'. We might also ask of the Scottish puma, as of its Surrey cousin, why there are no remains of kills - pumas are alleged to be hungry or mean most of the time - des-pite the fact that it has, according to the police, been in the Renfrew/Ayrshire area 'for the last three years'? The police say they have sightings from 'hun-dreds of people including at least a score of policemen over this period.'

The latest note we have is that late on the night of 21 October 1976 a driver says a large 'cat-like animal' bounded across the Glasgow road in front of his car near a housing estate on the outskirts of Blantyre, Lanarkshire. (Glasgow) Sunday Post 24 October 1976 (Cr. John Rimmer).

The 'Ayrshire puma' also seems to be developing another characteristic of its Surrey cousin - that is, we can say of it that it is no longer limited to a puma or to Ayrshire. We have commented before on the way the Phenomenon seems to shift the form of its manifestation just when it seems to have been labelled or 'explained-away' - a feature of all our categories of pseudo-facts in the Phenomenal Reality. Anyway, this particular were-puma showed itself in another form about a week before the Glenfarg sighting (above). On the night of 10 August 1976, a woman in Glenfarg, Perthshire (apx. 60 miles from the Ayrshire sighting near Beith), was washing her supper dishes when her dog whined and scratched at the door. The lady let it out, and on hearing its bark-

ing change to a whimper, she looked out to see it on the lawn shivering with fright. Sitting on its haunches on top of the garden wall was a huge cat, 'the size of a fully grown Labrador,' its eyes glowing orange in the dark. When she went out (brave woman!) the creature got up and began to spit and howl. She noted its long pointed and tufted ears and that it stood at least 3 ft high. Quickly, she scooped up the dog and dashed inside. The cat leapt into fields and vanished. Police claim there have been other sight-ings, including one in the main street of Glenfarg, and that chickens have gone missing. The description, though, is of a lynx, not a puma. (Glasgow) Sunday Post 15 August 1976 (Cr: Ion Will).

THE CENTRAL ENGLAND CAT

No area can consider itself respectable these days if it doesn't have its own large-cat myth. In FT 18/25f we summar-ized the story of the Nottingham 'lion' of July last year. In less than a week after the unfinished story died out in an embarrassed silence from the press and the authorities, another 'lion' popped up at Thorganby, Yorks, about 70 miles away. In this case, police thought it had no connection other than coincidence with the Nottingham scare (see FT 18/26f). JW Scaife sent us a clipping from the Yorkshire Evening Press 11 August 1976, which is worth giving here as it adds a few more details to the story of Alan Pestill (NB: Pestall, in earlier accounts). He says: 'I left home at 9.55 (on night of Monday, 9 August 1976). The evening was dark but the centre of the road was well lit by the moon. Out of the shadows came what I first thought was a dog, but as it got close I froze. It stared at me as it padded past and I stepped into the light to look at it. I was amazed - it was a large lioness!' The rest of the clipping testifies to Alan unliklihood of making the story up. The police took him seriously but a search the next day pre-dictably failed to turn up a trail or a clue. I have speculated before about the apparent continuity between the old folk-lore tradition of 'Black Dogs' - well, if you're at all familiar with any of these tales you'll recognise the modus operandi of the BD here - the encounter in a lone-ly lane, and the creature's stare (if creature it is) as it pads by the witness. Make of that what you will. (Incidentally, BDs are still seen. Ivan Bunn has sent us a recent clipping, which we regret will have to be kept till later; and just last year a BD hit the headlines as haunting Princess Anne's new house.)

The next month, September, gave us two cases. The <u>Leicester Mercury</u> 5 September 1976 reported a large-scale police search in the Bermuda Village area of Nuneaton the day before, after a puma-like animal was reported seen. Police checked the zoos in the area but no large cats were missing. (Cr: Richard Cotton). A 'cougar' was reported seen on the 20th in the grounds of a seafront convalescent home at <u>Skegness!</u> Police gave the story a high credibility because the witness was the town's police surgeon, Dr Alec Jamieson. He said: 'It was a large sandy coloured cat about 5 ft long; definitely a cougar.' He called in PC Jock Gartshore, who also saw the beast. Staff at the home said they had seen the thing several times over the previous few weeks and dismissed it as just a large unusual dog! A search in the grounds found tracks measuring 2½x3" across - and later an RSPCA inspector and a naturalist hid in the grounds with cameras, but, again, predictably, nothing materialised. Dr Jamieson remains convinced he saw a cougar, and thinks it may have been the 'Nottingham lion' on a walkabout. <u>Scunthorpe Evening Telegraph</u> 21 September 1976 (Cr: Nigel Watson).

On 23 October 1976, a lioness was found wandering around the Upton district of Chester. Advocates of the 'elemental' or '<u>genius loci</u>' hypothesis (see <u>FT</u> 19/9) will be tickled by the fact that it was first spotted in <u>Deva</u> Lane (devas, of course, being ethereal beings taken over from Hindu beliefs by the Theosophists, and applied to 'shining beings' who supervise plant and animal life from a different plane or existence from ours. Hmm!) As the news and alarm calls spread, nearby Chester Zoo was quick to point out that all theirs were accounted for. Police mobilized foot and car patrols but the damned thing suddenly became unfindable (the 'teleportation' advocates will be chuckling at <u>that</u>!) To our knowledge no trace of it was ever found and the story evaporated as quickly as the creature. <u>Liverpool Echo</u> 23/10/76 (Cr John Rimmer).

TWO HANGOVERS FROM 1975

We were recently sent two cases from 1975 that we have not related before. On the night of 4 August, Ken Pearce left the door of his Fallowfield, Manchester, home open while he watched TV - it was very hot and he wanted a breeze. Much to his surprise the wind blew in a female leopard cub, which he later handed to the police. It's fairly certain the cub had been a pet (it was wearing a blue collar) and had been let loose. It was underfed

and doubtless the thoughtless owner was contemplating the foodbills which would keep pace with the animal's growth. Needless to say, the police have failed to trace any owner and its origin remains a mystery. <u>Daily Mirror</u> and <u>Scunthorpe Evening Telegraph</u> 5 August 1975 (Cr: Nigel Watson).

Earlier that year, the <u>Wolverhampton Express & Star</u> 29 April 1975, told of a huge police search in the Park Road and Rose Hill area of Willenhall for a creature resembling a panther. Willenhall seems a most unlikely place for such a panther-hunt being in the heart of the Wolverhampton/Walsall/West Bromwich industrial connurbation NW of Birmingham - but there it is! It was described by some residents of the area as about 3'6" long, 1'6" to 2' tall at the shoulder, black, and having 'very bright, red eyes. Police said no such beast had escaped from any zoos - and as far as we know they never saw or caught it.(Cr: Frank Adey).

THE END OF A CAPER

In our experience, most <u>escaped</u> animals, certainly the larger ones, are caught or killed within a short period. Recently, a case of a clouded leopard which had survived 9 months in the fields of Kent surprised experts by surviving at all. It was shot by a farmer whose lambs it killed, having escaped from Howletts Park in August 1975. <u>Daily Express</u> 10 April 1976. Here are some other cases:

On 4 May 1975, a puma kept by a man in the Hampshire village of Medstead, broke away, terrifying neighbours who thought it was the infamous 'Surrey puma'. It was recaptured by police, using drugged darts, after only 4 hours freedom. <u>Daily Mirror</u> 5 May 1975. Police and dogs managed to recapture an escaped pet cougar at Blackley, Manchester - it too had only a 4hr taste of freedom. <u>Bath Chronicle</u> 27 Oct; <u>Daily Mirror</u> 28 October 1976. (Cr: John Michell).

3 lions escaped from a circus at Epsom, Surrey, but were captured after one savaged a horse. <u>Daily Mirror</u> 16 September 1976.(The previous year a lion attacked a boy at this circus - see <u>News</u> 14/8.) 3 lion cubs were recaptured at Stevenage, Herts. <u>Sunday Express</u> 26 September 1976. 6 lions escaped from a zoo at Ringgold, Georgia, 25 Oct -within a few hours 4 were shot (by police with machine guns), the other 2 on the 26th & 27th. (Newport News, Va) <u>Daily Press</u> 28 October 1976. (Cr: Gary Abbott.) A lion tasted 2 hours of freedom in Belfast on 13 Jan, hunted by dart firing police. <u>The Sun</u> 14 January 1977.

SWARMS and MIGRATIONS

The summer of 1976 was a period abuzz with swarms; a bumper crop comparable to the vintage year of 1869, chronicled by Fort (<u>Books</u>, 741ff). A mild winter followed by a hot summer brought insect hordes to most of NW Europe as well as Britain, where the majority of our reports come from. Greatest of all the plagues were those of ladybirds, though many other insects also featured...including a wave of anonymous 'bugs' which invaded a rest room at Heathrow Airport: <u>D.Mirror</u>, 29 Sept 76 (Cr: K Rogers). We have a vast pile of clippings to contend with, so we hope to be forgiven if we run through them fairly briefly:

LADYBIRDS.

Westward Ho!, Devon: Ladybirds carpetted a two-mile beach in a thick, crawling mass. <u>D.Mirror</u> 3 July 76.

Deal, Kent: Millions of ladybirds invaded the beach, and then the town centre, shutting shops for half an hour. They were thought to have made a 20-mile channel crossing. <u>S.Mirror</u> 18 July 76.

Humberside & Lincolnshire: the same days as the above, millions of ladybirds swarmed over both counties. However, experts here thought the bugs indigenous rather than foreign; positing that the ladybirds swarmed together near the coast, flew out to sea, and then flew back across the coast elsewhere. The logic of this escapes me: but then I can't come to grips with the idea of even big tough ladybirds flying a 100 miles or more from the Continent to Humberside either. The swarms were blamed on a super-abundance of aphids, the ladybirds' food, although there seem to have been no reports of aphid swarms prior to the ladybird invasion. (Scunthorpe) <u>Evening Telegraph</u> 19 July 76. The same source also states that the

East of England has a long history of ladybird invasions, going back to the 18th century. One of the most recent invasions was in 1952, when 40 miles of S.Lincolnshire coastline turned red under the little bugs.

3 days later, at Hessle, nr Hull, ladybirds stopped construction work on the new Humber bridge. Workers complained that ladybirds were getting inside their clothes and biting them, so they walked off the site. (Hartlepool) <u>Mail</u>, 23 July 76, BBC <u>Radio Humberside</u>, 22 July 76.

West Somerset: Ladybirds carpetting beaches, biting people, and apparently drowning themselves by the million in the Bristol Channel. <u>Evening Standard</u> 26 July 76.

South Coast: Millions of ladybirds descend on beaches at Brighton & Worthing. <u>D.Mirror</u> 28 July 76. Same source: a swarm of bloodsucking midges attacking women in Lochgoilhead, Argyll.

Mablethorpe, Lincs: the beach there got the red carpet treatment too. <u>Leicester Mercury</u>, 30 July 76.

Killingholme, Lincs: Ending of a strike by men at Refinery & General Engineers, which started after a plague of ladybirds made working conditions difficult. (Scunthorpe) <u>Evening Telegraph</u> 30 July 76.

More plagues at Hove, Sussex, and Bridgwater, Somerset. <u>Evening Standard</u>, 30 July 76. And at Hunstanton, and Great Yarmouth, Norfolk. <u>Anglia ITV</u> aprox 18 July 76.

<u>D.Express</u>, 7 Aug 76, ran a long article on the subject, noting also an increase in butterflies and other insect life at the same period. The majority of swarms consisted of the large 7-spot variety, and further swarms were reported from Chester-le-Street, Durham; Cheltenham, Glos; and all parts of East Anglia. In the biggest year for ladybirds since 1920, the little runts had by now eaten all the aphids, and were looking for new sources of food and

water...which included people, it seems.

The ladybirds were back at Hunstanton, Norfolk: D. Express 9 Aug 76. They were causing chaos on the beaches and in the streets of Skegness, too. Skegness Standard 11 Aug 76.

After this, apart from a late report in the D.Mirror 7 Nov 76, of a ladybird plague in Ainsdale, Lancs, 'during the summer', there are no further reports. Instead, a controversy broke out as to whether ladybirds literally bite, or sting by exuding an irritant from their knees. Observer 8 Aug 76, S.Times 15 Aug 76 New Scientist 28 Oct 76. The net result seems to have been that they do both...perhaps.

For a detailed study of ladybird populations, breeding cycles, the 'opportunism' that led to a preponderance of the 7-spot variety, etc, see Denis Owen's article in New Scientist 30 Sept 76, and correspondence in the 14 & 28 Oct 76 issues. (Crs: Paul Devereux, Judith Gee, Nigel Pennick, Ken Rogers, Paul Screeton, Nigel Watson, Ion Will).

ANTS.

Specialists had to be called to handle an invasion of ants at Mount Vernon Hospital, Northwood, Middx. D. Mirror 10 Oct 75.

Fire-ants stung their way across the southern states of the U.S.A in 75-76, causing at least one death in both Texas and Mississippi. In the year ending May 76, more than 12000 people needed treatment for stings. Animals were attacked, crops ruined, and fields neglected because workers refused to go near them. S. Express 16 May 76, Weekly News 29 May 76 (Cr. Nigel Watson).

BEETLES & COCKROACHES.

With a nice sense of irony, thousands of cockroaches invaded the Sutton Community Health Office (S. London). Eggs were believed to have lain dormant in the building for months, which then hatched when the health staff moved in and switched on the heating. Public health inspectors exterminated the little beasts. Evening News 15 March 76.

A breeding colony of 130 adult Colorado beetles were discovered at Ebbsfleet Farm, nr Minster, Thanet, Kent on 3 Sept 76; the first outbreak in Britain since 1952. The area was chemically treated, but most of the beetles were taken to the Plant Pathology lab at Harpenden Hertfordshire, where they were encouraged to breed...in order that new poisons could be tried out on them. Except for specimens destroyed at the docks, the beetle is almost unknown in this country. Times, 7 Sept 76, S. Times, 12 Sept 76. (Cr. Ken Rogers).

Cockroaches plagued St Catherine's Hospital, Birkenhead. Nurses threatened to boycott the 115-year-old former workhouse unless they were cleared. D. Mail 10 Feb 77. (Cr: P. Rogerson)

CATERPILLARS.

Havering, E. London, was plagued with Brown-Tail moth caterpillars in 1975, it seems. In order to stop a repetition of the same event, the local council were intending to wipe out the cocoons before they hatched. Evening News 26 Jan 76. Apparently they succeeded, for we have no further news...

Bentong, Malaysia: Hundreds of caterpillars swarmed over the walls, roofs and floors of the local court house, interrupting hearings until the place could be sprayed. Bangkok World 22 April 76 (Cr: Ion Will)

Originating from a 4-acre disused site, millions of furry caterpillars plagued people in Birchington, Kent. D.Express 29 May 76.

Thamesmead, Kent, suffered from hundreds of furry Brown-tail moth caterpillars (a separate outbreak to the nearby Havering case). Innumerable kids, unable to resist picking up the cute little devils, found themselves with skin irritations, swellings and rashes. Kentish Independent 3 June 76.

Hundreds of thousands of caterpillars of the 'common British moth' hatched at once in Powlett Road, Hartlepool. Within 2 hours, they had completely stripped a privet hedge, demolished a rose garden, and 'attacked' a nearby factory. Then they ran into a batch of insecticide. The hot weather was blamed for the outbreak; in normal summers, most of the eggs stay unhatched. The Mail (Hartlepool) 22 July 76 (Cr: Paul Screeton)

FLEAS.

Pewsey, Wilts: An invasion of cat fleas forced the town's three policemen to vacate their station and work from a mobile HQ. The plague apparently originated when one of the policemen moved into a new house...which had formerly been occupied by a cat-lover. The Wilts Police Authority agreed to pay £860 compensation to the man for ruined furniture and fittings. D.Express 23 July 76, Reveille 13 Aug 76, D.Mirror 3 Sept 76.

The hot weather also brought a plague of fleas to Thanet, on the E. Kent coast. D.Mirror 2 Sept 76.

FLIES.

Plans to combat 1975's U.S. fruit-fly invasion, the most serious ever known in that country, ran into a slight hitch. The idea was to breed 4 million sterile flies, introduce them among the invaders, and then sit back and watch them die out. Unfortunately, someone packed the sterile flies in a container that had just been fitted with chemical fly-killer strips. Ooops! D.Mail 5 Nov 75.

Mild February weather brought millions of seaweed flies to the Portland naval base in Dorset. S.Express 8 Feb 76.

Hot weather and the importation of untreated cattle brought an infestation of warble flies to East Lincolnshire, causing ill-health, boils and ruined hides: to cows, that is, of course. (Scunthorpe) Evening Telegraph 4 Aug 76. (Cr: N Watson).

LOCUSTS & CRICKETS.

Aston-on-Trent, Derbyshire: swarms of crickets, originating on a rubbish tip outside the village, invaded homes and shops. The plague seems to have gone on for several days, before council workmen counterattacked with sprays and repellants (Derby) Evening Telegraph 30 July 77. (Cr: K Rogers). D.Mirror 3 Aug 77.

Abundant rain in winter and spring 76 brought predictions of new locust plagues, in the 'locust belt' from Africa to Pakistan and India, after a decline in the insects for 15 yrs. New Scientist 12 Aug 76, Evening Standard, 8 Sept 76.

As Forteans, we're not surprised to find that our files contain no reports whatsoever from these areas. Instead, the locusts turned up in Australia, carried south on the wind from the desert area of the continent. Attacking on a 50-mile front, they ravaged the grain-producing Riverina area, and then descended on the city of Adelaide. Damage ran to millions of pounds as the malevolent munchers ate everything down to ground level. Troops, radar and helicopters were brought into fight the swarms, which were described as worse than the great locust plagues of the 1920s. S.Express 12 Dec 76, South China Morning Post 31 Dec 76, S.Express 6 Feb 77.(Cr: Ion Will, Peter Rogerson).

SCORPIONS.

A plague of scorpions drove people from their homes in a village near Kashan, Iran, making it too risky to sleep there at night. S.Express 1 Aug 76.

MARINE SWARMS.

Huge jellyfish, rhizotoma or 'Rootmouth' swarmed along the south and west coasts of Britain during the summer, apparently attracted by the warm weather. S.Express 1 Aug 76

And in Woolacombe and Ilfracombe, N Devon, scores of people were stung on beaches by common jellyfish. (Scunthorpe) Evening Telegraph 27 Aug 76 (Cr: N Watson)

A new genus of sponge, 3-4 feet tall and shaped like vases, are thriving in the pacific, just outside San Francisco's Golden Gate Bridge. 47,500 barrels of radioactive waste were dumped in the area 25 years ago, and the plutonium content of the seabed is 25 times what was predicted. Robert S Dyer, discoverer of the sponges and an oceanographer, said he would 'have a hard time justifying' the idea of giant mutant sponges caused by the radioactivity. He must be the only one who would..! Houston Chronicle (Texas) 16 Sept 76 (Cr: Mark Hall).

Tiny shrimp-like creatures, Asellus Aquaticus, invaded the mains water supply of Newquay, Cornwall. They were 'harmless but undesirable', and were removed with pyrethin when the mains were flushed Press Association bulletin, 17 Nov 77 (Cr: Ken Rogers).

Steve Moore - February 1977.

■■■■■■■■■■■■■■■■■■■■■■■■■■■■■■■■■■■

Next issue we hope to have some strange deaths of people and animals; the results of the recent worldwide psychic monster hunt; mystery holes; and some poltergeists; and more if we have room.

news

Ken Campbell's play <u>Illuminatus</u>! is
currently playing at the Cottesloe
Theatre, in the National Theatre's London South Bank complex. By the time you
get this (alas!) it will be in its last
week there. Because the cycle of 5 sub-
plays will be performed in sequence the
whole performance lasts a bum-numbing
8½hrs with 3 intermissions, and can
only be performed over the weekends. If
the reviews are anything to go by you
could witness an astounding and entertaining piece of innovative theatre. It
begins at 2pm on 25/26/27 March, and
tickets cost from £2.50 (that's for the
whole cycle, remember.) The play was a
hit in Liverpool and Amsterdam, and if
we learn where it'll pop up next we'll
let you know. To catch all its nuances
I recommend you read the <u>Illuminatus</u>!
trilogy by Robert Wilson and Robert Shea
(available in paperback from Sphere (UK)
and Dell (USA) - though Sphere haven't
yet put out the 3rd volume and deserve
a visit from the men from Swift Kick Inc.

<u>Sourcebooks</u> -- FT has made an arr-
angement with William Corliss for FT
readers to order volumes of this essential reference series on Fortean sources
and phenomena through us (also saves
the fiddle of foreign money problems).
The volumes published so far are:
A1 - <u>Strange Universe</u>; B1 - <u>Strange Life</u>
E1 - <u>Strange Planet</u>; G1, G2 - <u>Strange
Phenomena</u>; M1, M2 - <u>Strange Artifacts</u>;
P1 - <u>Strange Mind</u> -- each at £4.78. (inc
surface postage from USA). Please make
cheques payable to FT. For reviews of
these volumes please refer to earlier
issues of <u>News/FT</u>.

Dave Fideler, editor of <u>ARB</u> (see
journal reviews), wrote saying how much
he liked our 'Diary of a Mad Planet'
feature (<u>FT</u> 18/8ff), and   how much it
echoed his own attempts at compiling an
across-the-board chronology of Michigan
phenomena. Extending the idea, he thinks
that if Forteans on both sides of the

Pond could cooperate we could compile
a pretty meaty chronology each year.
There is no doubt that if this could be
accomplished, and published (as a supplement to <u>FT</u>?), it would an invaluable
research tool. We're not short of ideas
or data, but man-hours. If you think
such a project worth taking seriously,
and are willing to put your energy where
your brain is (!), please contact me at
the FT address, or Dave, at 7098 Edinburgh, Lambertville, Michigan 48144,USA.

<u>Reincarnation</u> - a weekend confer-
ence is to be held on the subject by the
College of Psychic Studies, from 1-3
April. For details of speakers, prices
and accomodation write the College at
16 Queensberry Place, London SW7. It will
be held at King Alfred's College, in
Winchester.

We have heard from various sources
that the long awaited UFO movie <u>Close
Encounters of the Third Kind</u> may be
released soon. The film stars Richard
(Jaws) Dreyfuss and Francois Truffaut,
is directed by Stephen Spielberg, and
centres on contactee-problem in a small
USA town. Being a big budget production
we can certainly look forward to some
good special effects. Its title suggests
its writers are versed in the new UFO-
logy - dare we hope for a thoughful and
thoughtprovoking treatment? I hope so.

Also, the previously announced
RILKO exhibition, <u>Earth Mysteries</u>, will
be showing at the Acme Gallery, 43
Shelton St, London WC2, in the old Cov-
ent Garden area. It is an interesting
blend of   'Lost Knowledge' - the
stones, sacred geometry, etc   of the
Neolithic era - and modern skills in art
and photography. This exciting synthesis
works well, and I feel it significant
that so many of the top researchers into
the Earth Mysteries today should be quite
accomplished artists as well. The whole
subject lends itself to synthesis and

inspiration, and after all, who better to show us that there <u>are</u> other legitimate methods of interpreting the mysterious universe than those bounded by the confines of material science? For details of a book accompanying the exhibition please see the 'News' section last issue.

HARDBACKS

<u>The Silbury Treasure</u> by Michael Dames (Thames & Hudson 1976; £5.50; pp192; notes, bib, index, illos throughout) -- Dames maintains that after the rather simplistic view of Silbury Hill (in Wiltshire; the largest man-made mound in Europe) as merely a tomb-cover failed to be established by successive excavations the archeological establishment regarded it (if they had to regard it at all) with "total incomprehension".

Dames' own approach profits, in contrast, by being based on the techniques of modern comparative religion. His net is spread wide, gathering in to his central narrative of the history and effect of the site on men of curiosity, from the earliest writings down to the BBC 'Chronicle' dig of 1969, gems of information from the geography and antiquities of the surrounding area (beautifully illustrated with photos of the different 'moods' of Silbury); metrology; astronomical correlations; folklore and surviving customs (like corn dollies and harvest hills); and some etymology (eg an interesting derivation of the nearby river Kennet, supposed to rise up under the Hill, from the local name of River Cunnit (in use in Stukeley's day), almost certainly sharing the same root as 'cunt' (considered obscene since 1700 but arguably "a true language word of the oldest stock") punned into the name of another spring at Silbury's foot, the Swallowhead. The eye-vulva-mouth of hell are recognized attributes of the Great Mother.)

Dames patiently, and with insight, reconstructs the different roles of the monument in the Neolithic cosmology. It synthesizes the pregnant squatting/sitting goddess; the half-buried goddess; the eye goddess of supreme intelligence; the mountain/axis mundi emerging from the primordial waters; the cosmic egg; the sickle, grain and cornstook; the throne; the stag; umbilical snakes; mother and child; the androgynous woman with phallus - all of spinning and weaving goddess - all of

which have been enshrined throughout Europe, but which appear together at Silbury in a unique symbol of "awesome comprehensiveness."

We are left in little doubt that the spiritual and mythological value of this total symbol to the Neolithic world is the real Silbury treasure.

<u>Earth Magic</u> by Francis Hitching (Cassell 1976; £4.50; pp196; bib, index, illos throughout) -- Whereas Paul Screeton's <u>Quicksilver Heritage</u> argued for the existence of leys and 'ley energy', the wisdom of the ancient engineers, the megalithic monuments and their mysterious purposes and effects, from the stance of a believer, Hitching attempts here to examine <u>both</u> sides of the argument - and does it fairly, finding extremists on both sides relying on an untenable dogmatic faith in their own exclusive view - the other side being the orthodox teachings of the archeological establishment.

Hitching glides smoothly and clearly through some of the latest relevant controversies in modern archeology, still reeling from the double impact of radiocarbon dating methods (which demanded a radical reappraisal of the old dominant 'diffusionist' overview that culture spread out from Mesopotamia) and of the modern verifications of astronomical alignments embodied in megalithic monuments, which shows that our Neolithic ancestors were (as Prof Glyn Daniel has been forced reluctantly to admit) "not only skilled architects and builders, but had considerable mathematical and astronomical knowledge as well."

The first half of <u>Earth Magic</u> considers the many different kinds of old stones, tracks (straight & winding), hedges, ditches, moats, mounds and barrows; holed and rocking stones; petroglyphs and other markings; who were the British aborigines, and the Druids?; the astro-geometry of sites and the ley network which links them. The second half of the book looks at some of the more unconventional approaches to the past but which seem to promise considerable contributions, like dowsing and related theories of subtle energies; psychic and spiritual experiences in the vicinity of stones; the folklore of moving, growing and healing stones and the fairy-connexion (this tack is a bit thin, but admirably dealt with by Janet & Colin Bord in their recent <u>The Secret Country</u>); terrestrial zodiacs; and finally, Glastonbury and the link with the Arthurian tradition. In most of these subjects Hitching finds more than enough food for serious thought, but the crucial question of the motivation of the ancients in erecting these artistic, functional, powerful, meaningful, magical monuments in the Neolithic landscape is only tasted in passing in the closing chapters; for a more satisfying meal try Dames' Silbury Treasure.

All in all, Earth Magic is one of the soundest introductions to and summaries of one of today's most exciting, vital, important and growing areas of study.

PAPERBACKS

Arigo: Surgeon of the Rusty Knife by John G Fuller (Panther 1977; 75p; pp253; bib, index,photos) - 'It is an established fact that Ze Arigo, the peasant Brazilian surgeon-healer, could cut through the flesh and viscera with an unclean kitchen- or pocket-knife and there would be no pain, no hemostasis - the tying off of blood vessels - and no need for stitches. It is a fact that he could stop the flow of blood with a sharp verbal command. It is a fact that there would be no ensuing infection, even though no antisepsis was used.'

So Fuller introduces his biography of the man, his healings and the legend that already surrounded him before he was killed in an automobile accident in 1971. Before this, his skills at psychic surgery and 'trance' diagnosis were thoroughly tested time and again by doctors and scientists, all of whom saw things with their own eyes and cameras that baffled them. There was no doubt that trickery was not involved in Arigo's case, nor that the cures were effective. Fuller also tells of Dr Henry K (Andrija) Puharich, who during his investigations submitted himself to Arigo's crude surgery, and shows photographic proof of the efficacy of the 'rusty knife'. Many case histories are given (as narrative) and we see the development of Arigo's clinic against the background of a fast rising Kardecist spiritualist movement and a crisis in the Catholic church.

Effective psychic surgery, like fire-walking, is one of the few non-ordinary types of phenomena that deal directly with physiological and physical realities, and suggests that at the interface (a la JC Pearce) the very structure of reality in being altered. Just what this metamorphic power is, and its method of intervention, remains one of the (perhaps the) greatest challenges to the inquiring spirit our universe has to offer.

Ghost Hunting by Andrew Green (Mayflower 1976; 60p; pp159) - Green gives us the benefit of his 25years experience as a ghost hunter in a comprehensive guide to techniques, experiments, equipment, site proceedure, interviewing witnesses, and the sorts of phenomena you might encounter. He also summarizes some theories, and gives a good list of useful addresses of societies and associations. The book will serve to introduce many new young minds to the subject and hopefully fire them enough to inquire for themselves.

Europe's Inner Demons by Norman Cohn (Paladin 1976; £1.75; pp302; bib-notes, index) - Prof Cohn continues his unique style of sociological history that brought us The Pursuit of the Millennium. Demons is concerned with society's persecution of minority religious groups, in particular the persecution of the witches and Knights-Templar drawing many surprising lessons from earlier history (eg the Roman persecution of embryo Christianity). It matters not to Cohn (indeed not to us) if there really were witches and magicians, night-hags, demons and devils - it was enough for the societies at the time to believe in them and that they thought they could see the devil's pointy tail dangling out from under the most innocent cloak of secrecy generated by any closed group. The early Christians were accused of precisely the same crimes (baby eating, sex orgies, incest, blood-drinking, etc) alleged against the witches, the Cathars, the Jews, and the new and immigrant religious groups in America. Although Cohn makes no judgements about the magical and mystical phenomena that were an integral part of the mythology of these pogroms, his book is essential reading for Forteans providing essential background to much of our historical data.

Apparition Phenomenon manifest at Zeitun, Egypt edited and published by Page Research Library: 6708 Colgate Ave, Cleveland, Ohio 44102, USA. (PRL 1975; pp44; $3.00 (inc postage)(I make that £1.74) - The PRL had done us all a great service by collecting the crucial data on the apparitions at Zeitun (1968-70), widely noised as a visitation of the Virgin Mary, angels and UFO-like 'doves' of light. Here is the testimony of the major witnesses (including some Muslims); the report of the patriarchs of the Coptic Church; miracles of healing; a summary of contemporary news reports; a list of key publications and promulgating organizations; plus 32 photos, many of them collected together for the first time. PRL have let the enigma speak for itself without making it fit any pet theories - the only interpretations are obviously coloured by the religious views of the witnesses, but behind them the phenomenon can be clearly discerned, even if we ourselves don't know what to make of it. My only pecadillo (quite minor in an otherwise excellent and well illustrated booklet) is that it lacks an index.

Mysterious Britain by Janet & Colin Bord (Paladin reprint 1977; £1.50; pp287; bib, index) - brief essays on a whole range of British mysteries (from hill figures, wells, mazes, leys, zodiax to King Arthur and UFOs) copiously illustrated with photos and engravings. A good introduction to earth mysteries.

The Natural History of the Vampire by Anthony Masters (Mayflower 1975; 60p; pp258; bib, index) - an excellent historical and pan-cultural compendium of vampire lore, tales, true cases and mythology.

Gods of Air & Darkness by Raymond Mooney (Panther 1977; 75p;pp190) - The same old Ancient Astronaut drum banged with just a little more style and consistancy than vonD himself.

Mysteries of the Ancients: Early Spacemen & the Mayas by E&C Umland (Panther 1976; 50p; pp175; bib, index) - quite possibly the most preposterous crap in the whole AA genre. 'Earth's most sinister secret' (as it says on the cover) is why anyone bothered to publish it in the first place.

Also received: The Meaning of the Loch Ness Monster by R Grimshaw & P Lester; and a new magazine The Zetetic -- both to be reviewed fully next issue.

𝕵𝕺𝖀𝕽𝕹𝕬𝕷𝕾

Anomaly Research Bulletin (ARB) No4-Michigan phenomena; report on Vestigia's New Jersey spook-light investigation; mystery animals; mutilations; a look at Arthur Clarke's ET contact concepts. $3.00/£1.50 (6 issues/year) to David Fideler: 7098 Edinburgh, Lambertville, Michigan 48144, USA.

Pursuit 36, Fall 1976 - The burning of Dr Bentley (abridged from Larry E Arnold's forthcoming definitive study of SHC); fossil tracks; prescription for the 'New Science'; vampire cats?; mutilations; notes. $10.00 in USA (outside USA sub increased to $12.50 - I make

that apx £7.25). Society for the Investigation of the Unexplained (SITU): Columbia, NJ 07832, USA. (4 issues/year).

INFO Journal 21, Jan 1977 - Golden models of ancient spacecraft?; pyramid power & mummification; phantom butchers in Sweden; the Timberville ice-fall pt2; notes. International Fortean Organization (INFO): 7317 Baltimore Ave, College Park, MD 20740, USA. (6 issues/year) $10.00/£5.00. Joint sub with FT = $14.00 £7.00 (12 issues). Payable to FT or INFO

Fate - getting meatier each issue - Jan 77 - UFO car-napping in Rhodesia; phantom hitchhiker; a new reincarnation case; ancient stone fort in Georgia. Feb 77 - the 'Solar miracle' at Gibeon; do UFOs jinx satellites?; life after death?; Hamilton's great airship hoax; the vanishing of Col. Fawcett. Mar 77 - who wrote the Book of Mormon?; ghosts; a car teleported in time; psychic surgery; disappearance of a cargo ship and its subsequent sightings as a phantom derelict. Fate is now available on UK newsstands.

'Why I'm disturbed by astrology' by Prof. Hans Eysenck - a brave public statement by a scientist who (like many other eminent men before him) bothered to investigate for himself and came away with questions the orthodox view could not answer . (London) Evening Standard 2 March 1977.

Christian Parapsychologist Sept 1976 - psi & UFOlogy; difficulties of evidence for miracles at Lourdes; a parapsychology reading list by John Beloff; 2 early 'charismatic' movements; PK in eastern Europe;etc. CP (subs): 284 Earl's Court Rd, London SW5 9AS. $3.00/£1.00/year.

Argosy Dec 1976 - 'Bigfoot: man, beast or myth' by T Jeff Williams.

Science Aug 1976 - USAF hands Project Bluebook files of 12,618 UFO cases over to the National Archives. March 76-solar variability & its effects.

Scientific American Jan 76 - the volcanoes of Mars; 'Paleoneurology and the evolution of mind'; killer bees. Feb 76 - is gravity getting weaker? June 76 - historical records of supernovas. March 77 - the moons of Mars.

Institute of Geomantic Research, & Fenris-Wolf -- 2 new papers in the 'Megalithic Visions' series: no13 Regent's Park: Town-planning or geomancy?(30p); no14 Sacred Geometry - an introduction (35p). IGR Occasional Paper no7 Ludovic McLellan Mann: a forgotten researcher (who seems to have discovered that certain groups of barrows on Salisbury Plain reflect stellar patterns). IGR have also published a fundamental book on the Nuthampstead and Pendle zodiacs, Terrestrial Zodiacs in Britain by Nigel Pennick & Robert Lord. There is no particular reason why neolithic British zodiacs should conform to the graphic designs familiar today; even so,one wonders, looking at some of the tortuous and obscure shapes illustrated in this study, if things (roads, edges of fields & woods etc) have not been imaginatively stretched a little to make something halfway recognisable. The authors of this professionally printed booklet, however, have an argument that should be listened to, backed with quite detailed data. Inquiries to IGR. Fenris-Wolf & IGR: both at: 142 Pheasant Rise,

Bar Hill, Cambridge CB3 8SD, UK.

SOBEPS News - the valuable English summary of the Belgian Inforespace - pt4 of a study of Bermuda Triangle cases & books; history of ET communication attempts, like Project Ozma; possible UFO propulsion systems implied by latest magnetohydrodynamics (MHD) research; Poitiers conference; study of 10 Sept 74 when 10 UFOs appeared at Charleroi. Inquiries to : SOBEPS, Blvd Aristied Briand 26, 1070 Brussels, Belgium.

Awareness Winter 76 - orthoteny; Poitiers conference; new interviews in Apadoca, Mexico, contact case; UFO occupants - enquiries Contact (UK): 11 Cumnor Rd, Wooton, Boar's Hill, Oxford.

((Cr: Roger Waddington, D Baxter. If you see notes of possible interest to us and other readers please let us know.))

FORTEAN TIMES

strange phenomena - curiosities - prodigies - portents - mysteries

WALKERS ON AIR «levitations», p16

G Doré   H PISAN

75p : $1·50

FORTEAN TIMES

A Contemporary Record of Strange Phenomena

FORTEAN TIMES is a non-profitmaking bimonthly miscellany of news, notes and references on current strange phenomena and related subjects. Formerly THE NEWS. Affiliated to the International Fortean Organisation (INFO) in continuing the work of CHARLES FORT (1874-1932). Edited and published by Robert JM Rickard. Asst Editor: Steve Moore. **PO BOX 152, LONDON N10 1EP, ENGLAND.**

SUBSCRIPTIONS. 1 year (4 issues) £3.00/USA $6.00. 2 years (8 issues) £5.40/USA $10.80. Airmail: add £1.50/USA $3.00 per year to sub. rate. Annual index issued free to subscriptions current at the time — otherwise 30p/USA 60¢. For details of availability of back-issues and other deals, including joint subscriptions to INFO JOURNAL, and THE LEY HUNTER, see our address label. NB: OVERSEAS SUBSCRIBERS should add 10% to their cheques to cover bank exchange commission. Payments payable to FORTEAN TIMES.

CONTRIBUTIONS of articles, artwork and notes on related subjects are always welcome and duly credited. **YOU CAN HELP BY SENDING US A COPY OR CLIPPING OF ANY ITEM YOU THINK WILL INTEREST FT READERS** — just add a note of the date, source and your name (for the credit) — all clippings go on file and will be published in due course. Please don't assume we know about the item — there are very few duplications.

UK ISSN 0308-5899

SPRING 1977

CHANGES

As you hold this in your hands you'll know we've expanded to <u>fourty</u> pages. The reason is that **FT**, from this issue, will be published quarterly (Feb, May, Aug & Nov.) - and by putting out four 40 pagers (instead of six 28 pagers) we can maintain the same number of pages over the year. The annual rates therefore stay the same, but the individual price must go up to 75p/$1.50 (from this issue on). We emphasise that this is <u>not</u> an increase in the annual rates. The reasons behind this alteration is not economical, but personal (ie the work-load on your ed.) and explained in an accompanying letter to current subscribers. However it is not without some economical advantages, and these little savings have allowed us to use a thicker paper on the cover. As we get larger we shall be able to afford proper typesetting, and a more professional addressing system. It is also possible that our quarterly schedule may be temporary - when it's possible, I'd like us to go back to bimonthly, which was a very useful periodicity, but <u>keep</u> 40 pages.

We've also been inquiring about an airfreight deal, which for a small increase on our USA rate would allow air speed delivery. But to qualify we need 300 or more US readers. We have about half that now, so please help us obtain more US readers. It's in your own interest - ie we'd be able to offer a standard US airfreight rate and you'd get **FT** within a week of publishing.

So the message - as usual - is that our survival depends on expanding, and so does our growth and improvement.

TRUSS FUND

...in which we acknowledge, gratefully, kind donations from the following: Janet and Colin Bord, RJ Howes, JP Kain, Martin Lorber. I must ask those to whom **FT** posters are due to be patient. Unfortunately matters of some urgency took precedence - but they <u>will</u> be posted as soon as possible.

■■■■■■■■■■■■■■■■■■■■■■■■■■■■■■■■■

<u>Marseilles murder mystery</u> (Cont from p14)

(Cont from p14)

... by the wise - I delight in a detail in this story -- that the shooting happened in a house in the Rue **Flammarion**, named for a man who had an abiding and scientific interest in the phenomena of coincidences! <u>Sunday Express</u> 16 May 1976.

Polter-Ghosts

JUMPING APPLES & HANGING CLOCKS

Fort never accepted fully that by the term 'poltergeist' we automatically mean we are dealing with 'spirits', despite the etymology of the word. We are talking about telekinetic movement of objects and other associated phenomena of which the most complete, extreme and dramatic form can be seen in classic poltergeist phenomena. Whether or not spirits are involved we will use the term 'poltergeist' as the most apt appellation of this particular syndrome or set of effects. It is convenient, just as using the term 'Fortean' is convenient. After all, what's in a name? - they are all noms-de-plume for some inexpressible but unique secret.

So - when apples, by all accounts looking like 'normal' apples, start leaping out of their dish with such force that they fly across a room to hit and bounce off a pantry door, the family concerned, and indeed ourselves, can be forgiven for filing the story under 'poltergeist'.

This story is given in a reader's letter in the Daily Mirror 6 October 1967 (Cr: Anthony Smith). The lady, whose name and address were unfortunately not noted) wrote: "This happened in our house (last) weekend, starting about 2pm on Saturday and finishing about 11am on Sunday. The first time it happened we didn't believe it, but when the second apple jumped we knew we weren't seeing things. In all, eight apples jumped and one just missed a neighbour standing in our hall. We noticed that before they took off there was a slight rustling or hissing sound. My son Trevor, aged 7, ate two of the apples without any ill effect, but the apples which hit the pantry door were too badly bruised to be

eaten. At first I was very frightened but it happened so many times that I became used to it. I wonder if there could be a poltergeist haunting the house?"

This phenomenon immediately calls to mind Fort's documentation of epidemics of jumping coal, leaping with force out of scuttles, in France, Belgium, Switzerland and London in the years 1921-3 (see The Books p947f.). One of these was during a distinctive poltergeist 'haunting'.

Mrs Irene Slaymaker, of Oakes Rd, Bury St Edmunds, Suffolk, was given a clock, as an anniversary present, in 1971. All was well until she (recently) began keeping it on a window sill instead of the sideboard. Mrs Slaymaker says she repeatedly finds it suspended by its winding handle among the lace curtains at the window. She remains quite puzzled, indicating that there are no pets, or draughts, or other apparent causes to account for this. However, she seems content to disentangle the clock each time rather than move it to another location, as neighbours have suggested she do. No harm has come to it yet, and she fears that by moving it she may provoke a more violent effect. Reveille ? June 1975 (Cr: Anthony Smith)

ALL BY THEMSELVES!

Now for a few more obvious poltergeists - the sort of effects I fondly imagine would predominate if 'The Exorcist' had been animated by Disney studios.

Maureen O'Connor, 17, screamed, bringing her mother running. Together, in fear and amazement, they watched a younger daughter's skipping rope stand on end, then spiral through the air above the kitchen floor, coming gently

to rest on the other side of the room.
This was just one of many strange effects in their house, in Beechings Way,
Gillingham, Kent, since, Mrs O'Connor
said, her husband died 2 years previously. Vases, flowers, pictures and
furniture moved around the house; there
were slow plodding muffled footsteps,
and frightening waves of "cold damp air".
She complained to the Kent County Council Children's Dept because her children
were exceedingly frightened, and they
took the brave step of contacting Canon
Pearce-Higgins - who in turn sent along
a husband-and-wife exorcism team. The
phenomena stopped! News of the World
10 March 1974.

A similar appeal was made by Mrs
Janet Greene to the St Albans' Diocesan
Authorities, landlords of the 3-storey
Victorian house in Ashburnham Rd, Bedford,
in which she has a small flat. She says
that since she moved in the previous May
her children often begin crying and screaming in one particular room. The
matter came to a head when she heard
them screaming and went to investigate.
A few moments before, she had left their
door ajar, but now it was shut firmly
and she could not get to her children.
She called the firebrigade who rescued
the two children (aged 2 & 3) through a
window. The firemen found a large heavy
sideboard had moved in the room, completely blocking the door. Mrs Greene is
convinced that it must have moved on its
own, or by a ghost - the Bishop of Bedford, on the other hand, was resisting
strongly the notion that his church's
property was haunted: "There may well be
a rational   explanation but I
don't know enough about the case at the
moment." Sunday People 12 October 1975.

A science technician and his wife,
described as "sensible and level-headed",
both complained that they were deeply
disturbed by the "strange atmosphere" in
their Handsworth, Birmingham, house.
Furniture and objects would move of
their own accord, and lights would go on
and off by themselves. Though not religious, they sought the help of the Bishop
of Aston, who sent along the precentor
of Birmingham Cathedral to comfort them.
The priest, Rev David MacInnes, saw "a
number of remarkable events" in the
house, including a bedspread that suddenly got up off the bed, walked downstairs "as if on legs" and threw itself
angrily against the front door. The previous night a heavy sideboard, as in the
case above, moved itself across the
((almost aptly named)) living-room to
block the door. The couple had to get in

via a window. Both the Bishop and Mac-
Innes confirmed these reports, but refused to name the family or discuss them
further. They simply said that over a
period of several weeks they both said
prayers there and the phenomena seem to
have subsided. Sunday Express 20 Feb 1977.

A GHOSTLY BUSYBODY
Most families afflicted with poltergeist phenomena do not regard them with
much enthusiasm or amusement- they are
pests in the most ancient meaning of the
word - so a tale of a helpful poltergeist seems quite remarkable to me. The
Reveille 19 September 1975, shows a
photo of the particularly haggard-look-
ing Usher family, of Bow Rd, Bow, London.
They claim their 1st-floor council flat
is haunted by the ghost of a bad-temper-
ed woman in a white dress and blue slip-
pers who makes the beds, tidies the cup-
boards and cleans the bathroom! Despite
this eerie boon various members of the
family are at their wits' and nerve's end,
knocking back tranquilizers and sleeping
pills. The lavatory door opens by itself
the same time each day (12.50pm), and
the ghost has been seen with a bottle of
brandy, and once with another ghost: "A
man (wearing) corduroy trousers, a sweat-
er and glasses. I ran for my life," said
Peter Usher, 33. A psychic investigator
said the ghost was "very abusive" to him
and resented the attempts of himself,
and a visiting priest, to remove her.
It's not said whether they were successful and this was the last we heard. If
any enterprising reader feels like following this case up (the family live in
Barton House flats) we'd be interested
to hear from them. (Cr: John Michell &
Nigel Watson.)

PICKED BONE CRACKS CASE
We give the following story here
because it seems to have similarities
with tales of exploding crockery etc.
It seems there was a showcase in the
War Memorial Museum, in Aukland, New
Zealand, which kept cracking in the
same place, repeatedly, for no readily
apparent reason. The case housed a number of Austrailian aboriginal artifacts,
including a yellowed 6" bone used in
witchcraft rites. It is a 'pointing bone'
and used for cursing etc. The museum
officials found that the bone pointed
to the exact site of the cracks, so,
just playing safe you understand, they
moved it to point at a concrete wall.
The glass has not cracked since, but
neither, says the report, has the wall.
Ah, one day... Weekend 24 April/1 May
1970 (Cr: Anthony Smith).

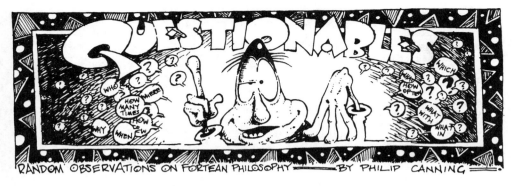

RANDOM OBSERVATIONS ON FORTEAN PHILOSOPHY ———— BY PHILIP CANNING

It is hard to imagine a breathing, walking-around human being who has not heard the remark: 'I'll believe in UFOs when one lands on the White House lawn,' or whatever the appropriate National Site might be in one's country. This is considered an event that would constitute evidence of the corporeality of UFOs, with the assumption that UFOs would then be 'proven' to be extraterrestrial space craft. (Though why any ETIs would want to try to communicate with beings on the intelligence level of politicians would be harder to explain than the operation of the vehicle itself.)

Philosophically this is quite naive. As naive as was Dr Johnson's 'refutation' of Berkeley's denial of the existence of the external world. He accomplished this one day when, in conversation with Boswell, he kicked a stone. A comment on the impractical vagaries of philosophy perhaps, but neither a proof nor a disproof of anything.

It's easy to see what reactions would most likely be forthcoming. 'Mass hallucination' would be dragged out. 'Swamp gas' would flit by. Esoteric ones would mumble of the 'collective unconscious.' 'Salvation' from the saucers would be trumpeted by the cultists. And the opposition party would accuse the government of absurdly expensive chicanery to win votes. Not to mention the conspiratorialists, who would find a tangled web of deviousness designed to distract attention from something really important but hushed up.

Evidence is in the eye of the beholder. To use Fort's words, such an event '...which seems so final and authoritative to some minds, is no more nearly absolute than is identification by a child or description by an imbecile.' Have you ever compared the descriptions of an automobile accident given by the witnesses thereto? Sometimes one can hardly accept that they were all watching the same event.

All reasoning is circular. Sometimes it takes more exotic shapes though. A recent book on the ancient astronaut business -- and it is quite a business, isn't it? -- contains these expressions: 'The evidence for the existence of UFOs in the present also suffers from the problem of inconclusiveness.' Two pages later, we read: 'But often the real world makes no sense at all, at least none that we can discern within the limits of our information and intellectual abilities.' The author, having dipped his toe into inconclusiveness, apologises for not getting wetter.

The issue is not merely UFOs, or any oddities, freaks or damned facts. It's also catsup bottles, the stock market and you name it, as Fort pointed out. It is possible to be critical, and inconclusive, and still realize '...that there is one integrating organism and that we have heard its pulse.'

Perhaps Sam Johnson's rock kicking was a witticism. Whether or not, we needn't go around kicking rocks in the hope of demonstrating truth.

****   ****   ****

Now for an entertaining heresy, or: American Indians in 16th century Wales; but first a quote from Lewis Spence's The Fairy Tradition in Britain (Rider, 1948; Ch iv, pp78f):

'A tradition survives in Merionethshire respecting a certain race of folk known as the Cochion, or "Red Ones", who were noted for their strength and pugnacity, and who, in the middle of the 16th century, inhabited the afforested tract known as Coed y Dugoed Mawr, or "The Great Dark Wood". They were regarded with fear by their neighbours, and are said to have survived until about a century ago. "In some old cottages in Cemaes there are scythes put in the chimneys to prevent their entrance." But we get a clearer view of the actual character of these dubious folk when we learn that they were known as Y Gwyllied Cochion, that is "the Red Fairies". "They built no houses and practised few of the arts of civilised life. They possessed great powers over the arrow and the stone and never missed their mark." At last a certain John Wynn ap Meredydd, along with a local dignitary, Baron Owen, feeling that their tyranny over the surrounding countryside should receive its due chastisement, fell upon them on Christmas Night 1534, and hanged upwards of a hundred of them. The remnant vowed a terrible vengence against Baron Owen, and on a later day, while that noble was on his way to the Montgomery Sessions, they set an ambush for him and slew him. Some of their descendants were said to be living in Llangarig so recently as the year 1852 ((Ethnology in Folklore, GL Gomme, pp186-8.)) The likelyhood is that the legend of this band of outlaws was transformed into a tale of evilly disposed fairies through the alchemy of popular tradition. But the historicity of the account seems to be feeble, and it may well be that the folk in question were

actually of Faerie as the name appears to indicate.'

This may be a far-fetched idea, but suppose that the Cochion were descended from Amerinds who floated across the Atlantic. Accounts of Red Men turning up on the coasts of northern Europe occur from Roman times down through the 17th century. If this case is one of a tale of banditry converted into a fairy tradition, it seems to be unique. Anyway, if Prince Madoc could 'discover' America, why couldn't folks from America 'discover' Wales?

The business of the scythes in the chimneys, I gather, is typical of Merionethshire lore (see Evans-Wentz, The Fairy-faith in Celtic Countries, 1911, p144) but may not be specifically connected with the Cochion. I haven't been able to look up Gomme's work, so I don't know what light he throws on the matter.

It would be interesting to check the historicity of the alleged Cochion massacre in 1534 - a curious allegation - as I have yet to encounter any other story from Wales or elsewhere that deals with a mass execution by hanging of fairies!

Philip Canning - April 1977.

MINES - LOST AND FOUND

The legendary 'King Soloman's Mines', placed by Rider Haggard in Central Africa, have been 'found' in Saudi Arabia, according to the claims of Dr Robert W Luce, a US Geological Survey geologist, who was part of a Saudi-American research team working on a region between Mecca and Medina known as Mahd adh Dhahab, the 'Cradle of Gold'.

According to I Kings chs 4-10, the mines of Ophir delivered 1,086 talents (apx 34 tons) of gold to Soloman in Jerusalem - which is an awful lot, and thought to have constituted about half the known gold holding in the ancient world. Although Ophir is mentioned in several Biblical books it has never been pinpointed - some have ventured to

place it northward in the Urals, and even southward in India. Dr Luce says there are huge quantities of waste rock on the site - still with a gold content of six tenths of an ounce to a ton - indicating that the ore used for refining was undoubtedly richer, and probably nearer the surface. Much of the early gold could have been had by simple panning, augmented later by mining, as evidenced by the litter of old tools on the site. The mine was near one of the oldest trade-routes, and certainly within the reach of Judea at that time. Dr Luce says the teams findings confirm the 'reasonable guess' of KS Twitchell, a mining engineer who visited the site in the 1930s,

that this was the most like source of
King Soloman's gold. New York Times 24
May 1976 (Cr: Mark Hall.)

The Sunday People 8 August 1976
has a brief story on the legend of the
Lost Dutchman Mine, hunted by dreamers
and fanatics for nearly a 100 years in
the canyons of Superstition Mountain,
Arizona. It was apparently originally
located on sacred Apache ground by a
Mexican cattle-baron called Miguel Per-
elta. He sent a force of 400 miners and
guards - all massacred by the Apaches
for desecration of the land where their
Thunder God dwelt. About 30 years later
the 'Dutchman', Jake Walz, staggered
into Apache Junction, 35 miles east of
Phoenix, with a sackful of gold and a
tale of a gold-vein 18" wide. It's said
that an Indian girl had her tongue cut
out for leading him there. The Dutchman
himself shot several men who tried to
follow him into the mountains. He died
in 1891, taking his secret with him.
Today Apache Junction still plays a
humouring host to the steady trickle of
gold hunters. But the old-timers suggest there is something "weird up in the
hills," and are content to let the
Thunder God keep his well-guarded secret.
(Cr: Ion Will.)

Apache gold also figures in another
story. The gold, stolen from Mexican and
American wagon trains by Geronimo and
his fellow chief Victorio, was allegedly
buried on a mountain in the San Andres
range, in southern New Mexico, now called Victorio Peak. The known details
date back 270 years when a French Jesuit,
Father Philippe La Rue, reputadly found
a mine full of fabulous riches. The then
government in Mexico City sent an army -
but La Rue had reburied the mine. He
died under torture and never revealed
its location. The Lost Padre Mine, as
it's sometimes known, was next found in
1937 by an itinerant doctor, Milton E
'Doc' Noss, who said he stumbled into a
narrow shaft to find a room stacked with
thousands of gold bars guarded by 27
human skeletons. He dynamited the shaft
to widen it - but overdid it and the
whole lot caved in. In 1945 the area
was closed to the public as the White
Sands missle range (where the first atom
bomb was about to be exploded) was only
50 miles away. In 1949 Doc Noss died;
shot by an irate backer after spending
a small fortune helping Noss'unsuccessful attempts to relocate the mine.

The first note we have is from the
Daily Mail 22 June 1976, in which it's
said the US Army at White Sands, fed up
at being continually nagged by treasure-
hunters, finally agreed to let a group,
known as Explorations Unlimited, into
the restricted area in July. It's not
until earlier this year that we learn
that EU, who specialise in 'electronic
searches' and who had been hired by a
group of six 'old-timers' all claiming
the fortune, estimated in various reports as worth between £500 million, and
$250 billion, had to postpone their ex-
pedition.

On 19 March this year, the Army again
granted permission for a 10-day search.
All they found,up to the time of a note
in the Daily Telegraph 21 March 1977,
was a few bloody hand-prints left by
 Indians. If there had been more, I'm
sure we'd have heard by now. Other
sources - Jacksonville, Florida, Times-
Union 29 January, 19 March 1977 (Cr:
Gary Abbott.)

BONES OF LOST ARMY
When Cambyses II, of Persia, sent an
army of several thousand into Egypt,
2,500 years ago, it vanished,becoming
one of the great mysteries of the past.
Now Egyptian archeologists say they have
found what they believe to be their
remains - thousands of bones, weapons,
and amphorae (identifiably Persian) -
near Mount About Ballassa. Officials
say the army was probably on its way
across the 'Sea of Sand'- an area as
big as Switzerland, in the Western Desert - to the Amon temple at the Siwa
oasis, when they were engulfed and lost
in a tremendous sandstorm. Sunday Express 6 March 1977; and Stampa 19 February 1977, for the translation of which
thanks to Edoardo Russo of Clypeus.

ON THE DOORSTEP
You don't have to travel far to
exotic places these days to make exciting archeological finds. Since most of
these places have undoubtedly been loot-
ed for museums, it stands to reason that
the richest picking now lie in museum
basements, waiting to be rediscovered by
some intrepid individual who dares venture where no higher-up has been before.
The latest find in the 'New Archeology'
is the discovery of six chests full of
rare Chinese pottery, worth "tens of
thousands of pounds", in a storeroom in
the museum at Taunton, Somerset. The
collection had been bequeathed by a
local businessman in 1946, at which time
they were "loosely" catalogued and packed away, to be forgotten until Mr John
White, a local enthusiast of Chinese
ceramics, asked some awkward questions
about the long-ignored catalogue entry.
Daily Mail 28 January 1977.

THE EDALJI CASE
...AGAIN!

by X.

In view of the increased attention given to animal mutilations in the USA and elsewhere in recent years, Fort's reference to the Edalji case should be consulted by those interested in investigating animal slashers - see <u>Wild Talents</u> (Kendall, 1932, pp67-70; Ace, p41f), <u>Books of Charles Fort</u> (Holt, 1941; Dover, 1974; both pp878-880). George Edalji was the victim of a most unusual crime perpetrated by a madman and perpetuated by a legal system incapable of correcting its errors.

One can only imagine the horror with which police read an anonymous letter stating: 'There will be merry times at Wryley in November when they start on little girls, for they will do twenty wenches like the horses before next March.' From February to August of 1903, a person or persons unknown had been attacking horses, cattle and sheep, ripping them.

Captain George A Anson of the Staffordshire Constabulary already had grave suspicions as to who had committed the atrocities at Wryley. After inspecting a pony which had its stomach slit open on the morning of 18 August 1903, Inspector Campbell proceeded to arrest George Edalji.

The evidence against Edalji was overwhelming. The police were well aware of previous trouble at the Edalji household. The community had not yet fully accepted the arrival of the Rev. Shapurji Edalji, a Church of England clergyman and originally a Parsee from India married to an Englishwoman. Between 1892 and 1895, while their eldest son George was attending Rugeley School, the family fell victim to a series of persecutions; garbage was dumped at the vicarage, false advertisements were made and answered in the reverend's name, malicious letters and postcards circulated, and a large key, stolen from Walsall Grammar School, was slipped under the vicarage door. Capt. Anson accused young George of this mischief and openly suggested he be given a stiff prison sentence once he was caught. Later in December 1903, the last false advertisement appeared in a Blackpool newspaper, and George Edalji continued his education hoping to become a solicitor.

Then the outrages began. Sixteen animals were slashed in a peculiar manner wherein the shallow wound did not penetrate the gut but let the animal bleed to death. Letters were received alleging that a gang of slashers was being led by George Edalji, and were signed 'Greatorex'. Police were assigned to watch the vicarage where George still lived with his parents while working in Birmingham. At 6.20am 18 August, a pony was found lying in a pool of blood. By 8am the police arrived at the vicarage and took away several bloodstained razors, a damp coat and trousers covered with horsehair and stained with blood, and a pair of damp muddy boots belonging to George. It was a clear case against him when prints from his boots appeared to match some found by the slashed pony. No wonder they could not understand why he did not confess when they confronted him in his office that afternoon and arrested him.

It did not seem to matter to the court that the razor stains proved only to be rust, nor that Insp. Campbell had placed the clothes in the same box with some of the pony's hide, nor that the scene of the crime had been trampled by local colliery workers and sightseers who probably bought their boots nearby, nor that the police insisted the slashing took place around 8 to 8.30pm the previous evening despite the veterinary surgeon's testimony that it had happened about 2.30am. Tried by a county justice who was nearly as incompetent as the police, George Edalji was sentenced to seven years in prison. When asked to explain Edalji's guilt after another attack took place while he was in custody, the police said it was the work of his gang, and showed no further interest.

In 1906, for reasons unknown, George Edalji was released after serving only three years of his sentence. He was to remain under police supervision as a discharged convict, but the circumstances were puzzling. Why had he been released prematurely? Had he been pardoned? Had the petition signed by ten thousand people, including hundreds of lawyers protesting at the weakness of the evidence against him, anything to do with it? It was a mystery worthy of Sherlock Holmes.

Although Holmes was not available, Sir Arthur Conan Doyle was, and decided to pursue the case. From their first meeting, Doyle knew Edalji was innocent. In the foyer of the Grand Hotel, Charing Cross, Doyle diagnosed from the manner Edalji read a newspaper that he had a severe case of astigmatic myopia. It was clear he could not have found his way to the pony slashing in the dark, let alone evade the police patrolling the area.

On 11 January 1907, the first installment of Doyle's 'The Case of Mr George Edalji' appeared in the London Daily Telegraph. While a shocked nation learned of the scandalous nature by which Edalji had been convicted, Doyle pursued the identification of the real culprit. Soon he began to receive letters from the slasher.

Doyle deduced the slasher was familiar with George Edalji and his family, had been a resident (of Wryley) from 1892 to 1895, probably had attended Walsall School where the stolen key came from, knew a student there by the name of 'Greatorex', and apparently was absent from the area up to 1903. Also, it appeared the slasher was familiar with animals, all too handy with a knife, and foul-mouthed. An inspection of the school rolls at Walsall soon revealed the identity of the slasher.

Royden Sharp had been expelled from Walsall and had been apprenticed to a butcher before joining the merchant marine in 1895. Prior to his return in 1903 he had served aboard a cattle boat for ten months and had taken with him a large horse-lancet, which has but one cutting edge which would not penetrate deeply into the animal. Doyle compiled his list of evidence in a report entitled 'The Case against Royden Sharp for the committing of those outrages upon cattle from February to August 1903, for which George Edalji was condemned to seven years' penal servitude at Stafford Assizes, November, 1903.'

Unfortunately, a mystery remains in the case, for instead of concerning itself with the innocence of Edalji and the possible guilt of Sharp, the Gladstone Commission spent most of its energies shielding Capt. Anson's incompetance and interference in the initial letter-writing between 1892 and 1895. Undoubtedly Royden Sharp was involved, but how much of an accomplice was Royden's brother? Royden appeared to feel secure from prosecution in his letters to Doyle, for in one he states: 'I know from a detective of Scotland Yard that if you write to Gladstone and say you find Edalji is guilty after all, they will make you a lord next year. Is it not better to be a lord than to run the risk of losing kidneys and liver.' It is curious that Royden escaped prosecution, that the Home Secretary announced no new evidence had come up, and that a second cousin of Capt. Anson (Sir Alfred de Rutzen) was one of the three members of the Gladstone Commission. The fate of Royden Sharp after 1907 seems as elusive as that of his predecessor, Jack-the-Ripper.

Modern techniques in ink-analysis and handwriting pressures may yet yield clues for Doyle's scrapbook, entitled 'The Edalji Case', contains the original letters sent to him. Inquiries may yet be made as to Royden Sharp's fate.

The complicity of official investigating agencies is equally suspect in the recent cattle mutilations in the United States. Attacks have taken place in 24 states, starting in 1974 in Colorado and Kansas. Though there have been notable animal mutilations previously (such as 'Snippy', a horse whose death in Alamosa, Colorado, in September 1967 was not satisfactorily explained), the modern series are almost systematic and identical in their execution. Two veterinarians, employed by the US Department of Agriculture in Utah and Colorado, were apparently told not to pursue their investigations of mutilated cattle. It has been suggested by some that aliens in flying saucers, or Satanists in unmarked helicopters, are responsible, but with the exception of local town and county police, those responsible for these outrages are not being actively persued by the law enforcement agencies on state and federal levels of government. Meanwhile the atrocities continue on ranches and at least one zoo (at Lufkin, Texas, where, in December 1976, otters, foxes and racoons were slaughtered.)

Another case study is needed, and all that is wanting is another Sherlock Holmes, Sir Arthur Conan Doyle, or other reputable investigator, to apply the principles of deduction in solving the case - if officialdom will allow!

X - May 1977.

HOLE IN THE HEAD

Some of you may have seen the recent movie, Network, in which the late Peter Finch gave an Oscar-winning performance as a batty newscaster called Howard Beale who threatens to commit suicide on TV before millions of viewers. As in all things, there are fashions in exits and occasionally we hear of a real stylist. Knowing of a factual event which preceded this fiction we could hardly give a tip of the hat to the scriptwriters for novelty.

The suicide which may have given the writers of Network the idea happened back in 1974 when 30-year-old Chris Chubbock shot herself in the head while reading a news item - another first for Women's Lib! She was the presenter of a local news programme, Sarasota Digest, on Florida's Channel 40, which had just switched to a new format involving her reading the news and interviewing local personalities. Soon after the programme began, technical trouble ruined a film clip of a shooting in a Sarasota bar. Ms Chubbock continued saying: "In keeping with Channel 40's policy of bringing the latest news in living colour, you are going to see another first - attempted suicide." Then pulling a .38 revolver from her lap, beneath the desk, she held it to the back of her head and fired. As she slumped forward thousands of viewers saw the screen blacked out. A spokesman for the TV company later said she must have planned the attempt because they found on her desk an "unscheduled script" outlining a special news bulletin on her own suicide. She was taken to hospital - and that was the last we heard. She was not expected to live. The Sun 16 July 1974.

Oddly, a similar incident happened only last month (as I write this) when American TV viewers, watching an Easter service from a Baptist church in Biloxi, Mississippi, saw an armed man order the preacher from the pulpit. The gunman then delivered a sermon on death, put a pistol to his head and killed himself. TV technicians blanked out the fatal drama, but the 600-strong congregation had to witness it all. The suicide was named as retired USAF Major Ford Dawson. The pastor commented that the man kept mumbling about resurrection and death. "I'm convinced he came specifically to commit suicide on television." Let's sincerely hope this is not a trend. The Sun 12 April 1977.

When we fished the sad tale of Ms Chubbock from our files a few other notes fell out too and this is as good a place to deliver them as any. Some holes in the head, it seems, can go wrong - you can't even rely on it as an effective form of suicide. Consider the case of Henri Schuster, of Troyes in France, who had a row with his wife and in a fit of pique shot two small-calibre bullets into his head. Nothing happened! The only signs were two small drops of blood near his right ear - and for two days the poor man couldn't even get any sympathy from his wife who refused to believe his story. The next day he got a headache and went to the hospital in Troyes, where an X-ray showed the two bullets clearly penetrating his brain. The report in the Sunday Mirror 6 March 1977, ends: "Last night, Henri, 47, was seriously ill." (Cr: Peter Hope-Evans.)

Something similar was told of another Frenchman, Rene Bouchard, who was so depressed when doctor after doctor told him there was no cure for his progressive deafness that he shot himself in the head. When he regained consciousness, after doctors in a Paris hospital had removed the bullet from his brain, he found he could hear again! Reveille 10 Dec 1976 (Cr: Nigel Watson); News of the World 9 January 1977.

The best laid plans - not just of the would-be suicide - often go astray in a fatal way. That his gun would go wrong was certainly not in the mind of Finnish circus star, Aimd Leikas, who for 20 years had been performing a Russian roulette trick in which a spectator mixes 10 blank and 10 live rounds and then picks out six, and loads the performer's pistol. The gun was built so it would only fire the blanks. Before an audience in Helsinki, he put the gun to his head and pulled the trigger. A real bullet killed him instantly. Reveille 1 October 1976 (Cr: P Hope-Evans).

As a comedy set piece you've seen and laughed at it many times - a gun is cocked and fired but nothing happens, it's picked up again by someone who thinks it's not loaded...and bang! At a recent trial at Exeter Crown Court this happened for real. A barrister picked up an exhibit, an air pistol, and it went off in his hands, the pellet whistling between the court clerk and the shorthand recorder to hit the bench just two feet from the judge. The Chief Clerk said: "I can't understand why it was still loaded. It has been in police hands some time." A police spokesman said that a pellet had "obviously" become jammed in the automatic feed channel and was dislodged when the pistol received a severe jolt. The judge said he was satisfied with the explanation and rebuked the barrister for carelessness. Not really a 'Strange Death' story but I thought you'd like it. The Daily Telegraph, & Guardian 10 March 1977 (Cr: Peter Hope-Evans.)

ODD WAYS TO GO

According to the Daily Mirror 6 Apr 1974, a baby died in a West German hospital from a combination of meningitis, blood-poisoning and a lung disease. This lung disease was caused by a germ, called Erwinia, which normally lives on and only attacks plants. Doctors found it had been brought into the labour ward on a bunch of flowers.

A Nottingham inquest determined that Joseph Harrod, 81, died from natural causes. He contracted pneumonia four days after making five separate suicide bids, including electrocution. Daily Express 23 January 1974. We have a positively ghoulish file on curious suicides that is just dying to be released. Some day when we have room...

I don't know if a British comedy TV series, The Goodies, has ever been shown in the USA, but their surreal antics regularly attracted a large audience in the UK. One of their devoted fans was Alexander Mitchell, 50, a bricklayer of King's Lynn, Norfolk. I say 'was' because like the true fan he was, he died laugh-ing, watching a fight between bagpipes and a black pudding. His widow, Nessie, said: ' After 25 minutes of laughing he slumped and died. The doctor said his heart failed after a meal; with his stomach full the laughter was too much. He literally died laughing.' Sounds like the ideal way Forteans should go out! Nessie added: 'I can still hear him laughing and it's a lovely remembrance. I shall write to The Goodies to thank them for making his last minutes so happy. The Times 29 March 1975.

SOME CULTISH DEATHS

Over the last year or so there have been quite a few deaths in connexion with cultish practices: murders by folks who believed they were possessed, and by other folks who were trying to exorcise demons from the unfortunate victim - but these cases we shall have to leave to another time. For now we'll just mention:

That on 28 Oct 1976 a 30-year-old man was found without identification on him, sitting in a car without number plates, near Las Vegas airport, in a dazed condition. He was taken to hospital where he died on 13 November without regaining consciousness. He was identified at the inquest (in Las Vegas) as Geoffrey Hubbard, son of L Ron Hubbard, founder of Scientology. Scunthorpe Evening Telegraph 23 November 1976 (Cr: Nigel Watson.)

Two members of the Children of God sect were found dead in Belgium last year - both bodies were found at abandoned fortresses, and the internal organs of both men had been crushed 'by an amazing force', police said. Jean-Paul Meurice's body, 20, was found beneath the walls of the Dinant citadel in December 1975, and he is assumed to have died of natural causes. In February 1976, the body of Michel Piersotte, 21, was found near Namur Castle - an examination showing that he had been crushed to death only a few hours before. When police established that both men had been friends and members of the sect, (which both had expressed their desire to leave), the police exhumed Meurice and discovered he had died in the same way as Piersotte. According to the report in the Guardian 17 March 1976, the Belgian police were studying files sent over from Scotland Yard - the Children of God were founded in California in 1968, and their recent activities in Britain had led to police investigations and questions in the House of Commons - to establish further links between the two deaths. That is the last we ever heard - perhaps some of our

Belgian readers could tell us if anything transpired.(Cr: P Roberts & J Michell).

See back to The News 13/14f for the mysterious death of Frank Merry in June 1975. Merry had a few days before joined a secretive sect called The Emin, or 'Faithful One'. Maybe there is nothing behind these cultish deaths. Maybe... but the mind raceth all the same. Perhaps the Old Ones are returning...Cthulhu no longer lies dreaming...Nyarlathotep sits down on two neophytes...Aieee! Shub Niggurath! Yet another scenario from Shea & Wilson's Illuminatus!

SUDDEN DEATH & DEAD DUDES

We have often noted a datum - that death has overtaken someone during a normal act, freezing them, as it were, in a life-like pose. We have some historical accounts of cosmic 3D 'photography', where, say, a man was frozen in the act of mounting his horse by the flash of a lightning bolt, but more of that another time. In the following 2 cases there was no hint of lightning.

Robert Antosczyk, 29, a yoga-instructor and university student of Ann Arbor, Michigan, apparently died while meditating in a yoga posture. He was found, 2 days dead, still in the position. Doctors are mentioned as thinking that his heart slowed down sufficiently to starve his brain of oxygen, finally stopping forever. Death by yoga? Daily Express, Daily Mirror 30 June 1975.

On 26 July 1976, Dennis P Graham, 46, left on a short drive to a grocery store in nearby West Point, Virginia - he never returned. In the first week of October, following a sighting of a car in woods 2 miles north of Shacklefords, his brother and brother-in-law found him sitting on the ground near the car, quite dead. There was no evidence of 'foul play' and we don't know the autopsy results, but it looks like a mystery. Interestingly, the Newport News, Virginia, Daily Press 8 October 1976, says this was the third disappearance that year from the West Point area - the body of one turned up in the Mattaponi River, and the other is still missing. (Cr: Gary L Abbott.)

Another datum we notice is that many bodies seem particularly well dressed - like the skeleton in an immaculate business suit complete with rolled umberella found several years ago (I can't lay my hands on the ref. at this moment) half way up a Cornish (I think) cliff! We are also accumulating notes on bodies (some are suicides) with a pile of neatly folded clothes nearby. But back to natty corpses we note a 38-year-old mystery

retold in the Sunday Post 18 July 1976. On 19 September 1938 a highlander came across the body of a man by a stream on the south face of Ben Avon, near Braemar in Scotland. The next day a police party of six set out to find the spot. They found a man in a dark suit with a light check pattern face down at the edge of the stream. Nearby was a plain walking stick, a bowler hat, and a brown attache-case containing pyjama trousers, 2 collars, a toilet roll, scissors and matches. On a rock ledge was set out some shaving gear, and it seemed to the party that the man had been about to shave when whatever happened happened. He'd been dead for two months - there had been no reports of missing persons, and he had nothing on him that led to identification. The Grampian police, who have kept the file open, were most baffled by the man's dress, completely out of place for camping out halfway up a Caingorm mountain. (Cr: Nigel Watson.)

THE SCREAMING DEATH

Janet Bord sent us a note of a weird death from The Times 23 October 1969, after a coroner at Pangbourne, Berks, the previous day said there was no physical explanation of the sudden death of Mrs Sheila Shearer, a healthy mother aged 30 - it seemed likely, he added, that a bad dream caused her to die of fright. Her husband, Hugh, said that on the morning of Monday, 20 Oct, his wife did not get up when the alarm-clock went off, but began breathing heavily and shouting. "Her eyes were wide open and fixed. She was shouting loudly, so I gave her a good shaking, but this had no effect whatever." Then suddenly she was dead.

Shades of Illuminatus! again...but it seemed familiar. Sure enough, a rummage in the wonderful files unearthed the following unearthly story:

At about 6am, Sgt Robert Rush, of Santa Maria, California, who had just returned from Vietnam 3 days previously, was roused from sleep. His wife Patricia was shaking him. Then she gave a short scream and collapsed dead. Resuscitation attempts by Rush and a policeman failed to revive her; and there were no clues to her death. Patricia was - and get this Illuminati-spotters - 23-years-old. It's not quite true that there were no clues - there was one which was both tantalising and useless. The girl's parents revealed that Patricia's sister, Beverley, died in a similar manner in 1963, aged 17. She had been swimming, in Porterville, California, when she emer-

ged from the pool, looked around wildly
with a horrified expression on her face,
gave a 10-second scream, stopped breathing and fell dead. An autopsy then failed to identify any cause of death. The
parents, who have two surviving daughters, say they are worried in case the
same happens to them, and felt that in
Patricia's case too, the cause of death
would remain a mystery. This was so -
Dr John P Blanchard, Santa Barbara
County's autopsy surgeon, could only
find that the girl died of 'natural but
undetermined causes.' Newport News, Va,
Times-Herald; Reno, Nevada, Evening
Gazette both 18 Jan 1968; & unidentified paper 19 Jan 1968. (Cr:INFO/Brooks).

TRAIN DRIVER DEATH MYSTERY
The national papers for 14 January
1977 contained only a brief note - eg.
The Sun, that a 100 passengers escaped
disaster when the driver of a train to
London was killed, apparently by a
projectile as he looked out of a window,
and two sleeping-coaches derailed as
the automatic safety breaks brought the
train to a halt. (Cr: Sam.)
Frank Adey sent us coverage from
the local paper, Wolverhampton Express
& Star 13 Jan 1977. The train from
Stranraer to London was travelling at
60mph or more when it shuddered to a
halt near Warrington, Cheshire, waking
most of the sleeping passengers, at
about 6am. No one was hurt except the
driver, who was found dead in his cab
with a 'large slit' in his head. The
police then said: 'He must have had his
head out of the window for some reason.'
They think this because: 'He had definitely been hit by something, but the cab
windows were not broken.' The same paper
the next day reported that an inquest
had been opened and adjourned, and it
was suggested that the driver, named as
Frederick Dale, 46, may have been hit
by an icicle!
I don't know how that strikes you,
but I smell puzzlement. If he was looking out of the window and was killed
suddenly by a falling projectile,the
windows would still be open - and surely
if the windows were open there would be
no need to add-that they were not brok-
en? You'd only comment on the unbroken
windows if there was some doubt about
whether he had been looking out - like
if the windows were still up! Frank
Adey notes that that day was one of the
worst of last winter's blizzards, and
thinks the driver may have had his head
out because of this. On the other hand
I see that as a very good reason to keep

the windows shut! One wonders also
about the choice of an icicle - is it,
my Fortean mind prods, because the man
was found with a slit in his head, the
windows closed, and no sign of the offending instrument? Frank says that to
him 'the icicle sounds like a relative
of the "ice dagger" favoured by Agatha
Christie & Co in their "locked-room"
whodunnits.' Frank, like a good Fortean,
also realized that we may have a fatal
example of one of our 'phantom marksman'
stories. We know too of many instances
of projectiles materializing in motion
inside rooms...but I don't know of one
where anyone was killed. There's always
a first time I suppose...hmmmm!

THE CASE OF THE SUPERCLEAN BOY
Sometime shortly after 3.30pm, on
the afternoon of Sunday 18 January 1976,
Peter Watts, 15, left a note for his
parents, in their home at Colwyn Bay,
North Wales, saying he had gone round to
a friend's house to help him revise for
examinations. About 9½ hours later he
was found dying in an underpass near
Euston Station, London. The father had
reported the boy's disappearance almost
immediately, and said Peter knew noone
in London. The British Rail ticket
clerk at Colwyn Bay said he recollected
a youth handing him a £10 note for a
return ticket to Chester, that evening
at about 4.20pm, but could not be certain it was Peter. The next train was
a through-service to London, via Chester. An inquest in London found, on 20
May 1976, that the boy must have been
abducted and murdered by person or persons unknown - mainly because the wounds
were not at all consistant with self-
injury.
The boy was found lying on his back
in the Euston Rd underpass about 1.33am
Monday 19 Jan, by a taxi-driver, John
Morgans. Morgans rushed to the boy's
side and found him barely alive, with a
sluggish pulse and not responding to
verbal or physical stimulation. He had
some injury to the left side of his head
and there was a pool of blood beside him.
He was taken to nearby University College Hospital where he was found to be
deeply unconscious from a depressed
fracture at the back of the head, and
died about half an hour later.
Now it starts to get curious. The
police said that 3 drivers using the
underpass between 1 and 1.30am had not
seen the body - it must have arrived,
or fallen, between 1.30-1.33am. When
Peter's clothing was searched they had
no road dirt in them, and nothing in

the pockets - nor was there any road dirt or grit in the head wound consistent with a fall into the underpass, even though the wound itself was compatible with such a fall. When the clothing was removed the boy's body was found to be 'impeccably clean' as though he had just been bathed. Further injuries were revealed by X-ray: fractures of the head, several ribs, and the left shoulder - all more consistent, in the opinion of Dr Hugh Johnson, a pathologist, with a fall 'from a great height than a direct assault'. The death was due to these multiple injuries.

What further complicates matters is that there is some doubt about whether the boy came by train at all. Det.Chief Insp.John Harris said: 'To date we have not found anyone at all who positively saw Peter at Colwyn Bay, Chester, or London,' although one paper mentions an under-butler at Buckingham Palace who is 'convinced' that Peter was the boy who helped get his luggage to a taxi at Euston at 10.50 that night. Euston is infamous for homosexual 'punters' on the lookout for young boys arriving alone and homeless in the capital. On the other hand police were also considering the possibility that someone gave the boy a lift in a car all the way. Either way, the boy's father believes the boy was abducted and killed resisting or after an assault, and dumped in the underpass...

...but those unnaturally clean injuries and clothes confound the theories and the case remains a mystery. Compiled from: Liverpool Echo 27 Jan & 8 April 1976; Liverpool Daily Press, The Guardian, Daily Mail, Daily Express all of 21 May 1976 (Cr: Peter Rogerson.)

MURDER MYSTERIES
When police found 73-yr-old writer, Joseph Lewi, dead, his wrists slashed, sitting in a pool of his own blood (see back to our other 'sitting' deaths!) it seemed obviously suicide. Examination later found several stab-wounds in his chest and _was thought_ Lewi, husband of mystery writer Charlotte Armstrong, both of Glendale, California, to have been murdered, then dressed and slashed! But by whom - and why - nothing appeared stolen. Scunthorpe Evening Telegraph 13 November 1976 (Cr: Nigel Watson.)

Somewhat similarly, I note that in the trial of Mrs Hamida Rahman for the murder of her butler Ibrahim El Shubini, the police originally thought the man died of natural causes - so did a doctor who visited the scene at their Chelsea flat in London - yet the man had been

shot five times in the head! (see back to our hole-in-the-head cases). Insp. John Bond, of Chelsea police, spoke of blood on the man's face, around the mouth, nose & forehead, and on a chair, but saw no sign of a struggle or weapon. 'I had no reason to suspect that death was in any way suspicious.' Dr Michael Harding said: 'There was some congealed blood (on)the left side of the chin, but I did not see any gun, knife or empty bottles of tablets ((!)). I...detected no obvious cause of death.' Mr Justice Lawson, hearing the case, was heard to say: 'It's just like the Pink Panther to me!' Yorkshire Post 13 July 1976. (Cr: Anthony Bell).

Finally a drama from Marseilles. M. Emile Herve, 47, was taken ill at home, and police inspector Jean Darian drove Dr Joseph Cambassedes to the house in the Rue Camille Flammarion (a name familiar to most Forteans). As a power failure plunged the Herve house into darkness (an odd omen that!) they were taken upstairs to the sickroom by a member of the family with candles. They left the door open for more light as the doctor bent over his patient. The doctor said:'We are too late, he has just died!' Immediately the door slammed shut, blowing out the candles, and a gunshot rang out. Almost immediately the door was opened as the family rushed in to find out what happened, their candles revealing an astonishing scene. The doctor was face down over his dead patient, dead with blood oozing from a gunshot-wound in his back- and on the floor by the inspector was a .22 rifle. Immediately detectives were called, and an examining magistrate who ordered an immediate reconstruction of the scene. The two dead men were left on the bed, the same candles were lit, the door was opened, the rifle (which had been fingerprinted) was stood back against the wall. All the circumstantial evidence pointed to the inspector, after a search failed to find an intruder, and the windows were found closed from the inside. They went through the reconstruction several times, the inspector still protesting his innocence - but it was only near dawn that he was cleared - as he was implicated - by an accident. A gust of wind slammed the door shut, blowing out the candles and knocking the rifle down with its muzzle pointing to the bed. The inspector, I'm sure breathed a huge sigh of relief. Pausing only to raise an interested eyebrow at the omens of the death - traditionally respected by

Cont on p2 /

Black Dust Riddles

I've just noticed that a number of notes we have on rains of black dust cluster around London. On the night of 27 August 1967 a huge quantity of soot-like black dust rained on the Isle of Dogs area of London's dockland. House-holders, angry that their lawns, cars, curtains and washing had turned black overnight complained en masse to their council and to Greenwich gas works, blaming the latter for cleaning out their chimneys in a wind. A spokesman for the works said it was a mystery to him as a check on the whole plant showed everything was in order - and there the problem lay, unsolved! Daily Mirror 29 Aug 1967 (Cr: Anthony Smith).

Council health officials at Bexley, Kent, tried unsuccessfully to locate the origin of a fall of "corrosive soot" which descended on nearly a hundred cars parked outside a factory there, about 19 July 1970. The men were given time off to wash the cars, but the "soot" had already burned matchhead-sized areas on the bodywork. The National Council For Clean Air issues the obligatory: "There must be a fault in the boiler of some factory." But it could not be found. Daily Mirror 21 July 1970 (Cr: A Smith).

Later the same year, we learn of a mystery fall of "soot" in 1969, that layed a fine blanket over a Cranford park, on the eastern edge of Heathrow airport. Park-keepers, annoyed at the clouds raised by their attempts to mow, called in Greater London Council experts. In their report to the GLC (for 1969) Dr Basil Brown said the "soot" was spores of a fungus called Pithomyces chartarum, a black fungus parasitic on grasses and to be found only in New Zealand! But this doesn't stump our imaginative GLC friends - it "must have" come on the wheels of planes from New Zealand and "shaken loose" during landing at Heathrow. That's brilliant! This ingenious solution requires tiny spores to cling to planes lightly enough to be dislodged in the same place on landing in England, but not lightly enough to be dislodged en route or on landing in other countries! Another thing - come 1970, the park was searched for them again and not a trace was found, there, or anywhere in the UK (including airports receiving flights from NZ.) Soot-like dust, so a soot source is searched for. Spores from alien planes that by all logic must repeat again and again. Looked for and not found! Daily Mirror 25 November 1970 (Cr: Anthony Smith).

The Times 11 January 1973 - that a fine black dust blanketed Dartford, and the Sidcup, Crayford and Bexleyheath areas of Bexley, in Kent, the previous day. I can find no note of its origin being traced.

Other Coloured Rains and Snows

In the 3rd week of Sept 1975, residents of the maritime Alpine regions of South France found their houses, yards, cars etc covered with layers of grey sandy mud. Meteorologists said this was caused by storms in the Sahara sucking up sand which is then swept across the Mediterranean. Tulsa, Okla., Daily World 18 September 1975 (Cr: Mark A Hall.) This event was not picked up by the UK papers until December - or perhaps it's a separate event. At any rate the Daily Mail 19 Dec 1975 tells us that a 100mph blizzard dumped "thousands of tons" of "Sahara sand" over the ski slopes of the French resort of Isola - causing a pink snow as far as the eye could see! (Cr: Ken Rogers, Richard Cotton.)

February 1976 was the 5th warmest on record at the Royal Observatory, Hong-kong - and although it was drier than usual, a "yellow rain" occurred on the 25/26th. The Observatory said: "It was probably due to pollen being washed down from the pine trees." It's the "probably" that nags at me - didn't they investigate? And if it was that explicable had it happened before? Hongkong Star 13 March 1976 (Cr: Ion Will.)

According to the Weekly News 6 March 1976, the Oestland district of South

Cont on p24/

WALKING sitting & lying ON AIR

or the ups and downs of some non-christian levitations

by RJM Rickard.

While researching for Phenomena (1)
I came across several interesting accounts (mainly Hindu) of levitation, and
I welcome this opportunity to rescue
them from obscurity.

Levitation discloses itself as a
most complex phenomenon the more you investigate it. Like firewalking, there is
no one theory or strongly common factor
that can be seized upon to account for
the wide variety of methods, states of
mind, and effects achieved. The phenomenon is known to most cultures across
the world, and seems to function within
each   cosmology equally well. For every
ecstatic levitation there are simple
trance-states, and even non-trance spontaneous liftings (2). Christian and
Moslem saints jostle for take-off with
meditating fakirs, only to find the airways jammed with mystics (3), shamans
(4) and spiritualists (5). I ground for
the time being some Fortean cases while
I check them out further.

Traditionally and symbolically powers of levitation (real or imagined)
were allocated to divine rulers (6); but
in practice the power falls to saint and
shaman (7). Although I could write at
length on the extensively-documented

elevations of Christian saints - a phenomenon that continues to this day - I
must confine myself here to some equally
interesting, but rather neglected, non-
Christian examples. Although they are
performed in a religious context (ie by
'holymen') they are paradoxically trans-
religious (eg the accounts that follow
contain both Hindu and Moslem elements,
etc.) Even if this mixture were allowed
to be 'typically' Indian, we must point
out the ambiguous explanations of the
powers, some by appeal to spirits, and
others to the adept's trained ability
(8). This is underlined by the fact that
levitation has been equally attributed,
in various ages, to witchcraft, fairies,
poltergeists, and recently to UFOs (9).

Many accounts of the Hindu feats
follow the same format. Unfortunately
most of these date from the British Raj
in India when it was acceptable for the
shocked observers to rationalize in
terms of wily fakirs, greedy for bak-
sheesh, who were undoubtedly connivers
in a subtle conspiracy to undermine
Western Science, then on the ascendant.
Here is a typical account from that time,
concerning the feat of an old Cuddapah
Brahmin, called Sheshah, in 1828:

"He exhibited before me to examine a stool about 18" high, on the seat of which were two brass stars, inlaid, somewhat larger than a dollar. Then he displayed a hollow bamboo, 2' long and 2½" in diameter. The next item was a roll of antelope skin, 4" in circumference and 2' long. The man then concealed himself in a large shawl with these three articles and a large bag. After a delay of five minutes, during which he appeared very busy under the shawl, he ordered the covering to be taken off him, and he was discovered actually sitting cross-legged in the air, but leaning his right arm on the end of the antelope skin, which communicated horizontally with the hollow bamboo, which again was connected perpendicularly with the stool immediately over one of the brass stars." (See Fig 1 for my interpretation of this based on several contemporary engravings.) "He sat for more than half an hour, counting his beads with his right hand as calmly as if this new mode of sitting was no exertion to him." (10)

The witnesses offered the old man a large bribe to learn his secret, but he declined. Disappointed, our narrator turns to speculation: "...The brass stars conceal a receptacle for a steel bar passing through the bamboo; the antelope skin conceals another steel rod which is screwed into the one in the bamboo; other machinery of the same kind passes through the man's sleeves and down his body, and supports a ring on which he sits." (10)

A similar description appeared in the Calcutta Government Gazette of the following year (11) - indeed it may even be of the same Brahmin. The writer says: "He performs this feat at any gentleman's house, not for money, but as an act of courtesy." This doesn't sound like a very profitable trick to me! Prof. Harry Kellar, in an article on high caste Indian magic, seems to concur. He divides the "jugglers of India" into two kinds; the low-caste fakirs who travel in small groups with "an air of pitiable poverty and misery," contenting themselves with simple jugglery, feats of strength and sleight of hand, and who are "willing to explain any one of their tricks in private for one or two rupees,"; and the high-caste fakirs, "dignified men of patriarchal appearance, with ascetic faces and long beards, often quite advanced in years," who unlike their lowly cousins so common in every bazaar and hotel courtyard, are "to the contrary seen only at public fetes, such as the coronation of a Prince, the festival of

a Maharajah, the coming of age of a Nizam, the grand feast of the Mohorrum, and such special occasions as the visit of the Prince of Wales to India." Price added that he had seen levitations at all of these "...and confess that after thirty years as a professional magician ...I am still unable to arrive at a satisfactory explanation of the performances I witnessed." (12)

Our Brahmin from 1829 seems to have been such a 'high-caste magician' - he was old, dignified, dressed well, did not ask for money, and had even performed before the Governor of Madras, at which time he "continued on his baseless seat for fourty minutes." He carried a small bag with his stool, bamboo and hide, and worked his magic behind a blanket held up by "the servants of the house" - ie they were not his trained accomplices. When the blanket was held up again, all heard from behind it a strange gurgling sound, like "wind escaping from a bladder"; then the man was standing again. Our anonymous explainer again has recourse to metal rods concealed in the fakir's clothes - the gurgling sound, he claims, made by slipping a rod down the hollow bamboo. But he isn't sure about this - the fakir might have imitated the noise "as part of the hocus pocus." (11)

If I'm to be a sceptic, that must include apparently rational explanations. Now because I don't have the ability, I'd like to invite any reader who cares to, to consider the situation portrayed in Fig 1 as a standard force diagram,

Fig 1.

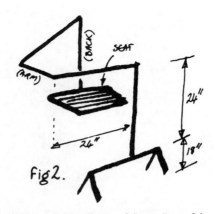

Fig 2.

and tell me if such "machinery" would
work (without the use of modern alloys
and manufacturing processes) by com-
puting how strong the various joints
and rods would have to be to support
an average man's weight, with some degree of stability, some distance away
from the ground contact point? (See my
crude diagram in Fig 2.) I may be wrong
but not only does the center-of-gravity
look 'impossible' (without a heavily
loaded stool!), but such a system would
have had to have been very heavy if not
very bulky. One would imagine that the
natural suspicions of the sahibs would
have noticed immediately any extaordin-
ary weight in the articles offered for
his inspection - and that to suggest the
fakir switched the inspected articles
for the working model would require him
to have two sets concealed in his effects. I note also there is no mention of
metallic sounds - and no precarious mid-
air wobblings!

No matter what we think of this
mechanical explanation of a few feats
of levitation (and I really would like
to hear any views on the above) it soon
passed into popular European acceptance
as how the Hindus accomplished their
'trick' of levitation.

Harry Kellar, on the other hand,
who was familiar with every trick in
the (Western) magician's repertoire,
said he saw no reason to doubt that the
high-caste fakirs had indeed acquired
powers through lives of asceticism and
meditation (13), which was the belief
favoured by the Indians themselves. He
says his first experience of levitation
was in a seance given by the famous
spiritualist William Eglinton, who visited Calcutta in January 1882. Kellar,
holding Eglinton's hand, was surprised
to find himself forcibly pulled to his
feet, and thence onto a chair and a

table to keep his grip on the medium.
Kellar then describes a remarkable
feat he saw in the Maidam, or Great
Plaza, of Calcutta, during the visit of
the Prince of Wales in the winter of
1875-6, before some 50,000 spectators
(14):

"After a salaam to the Prince, the
old fakir took three swords with straight crossbarred hilts, and buried them
hilt downwards about 6" in the ground.
The points of these swords were very
sharp as I afterwards informed myself.
A younger fakir stretched himself upon
the ground at full length...and after a
pass or two (by) the hands of the old
man, appeared to become rigid and lifeless." An assistant came forward, and
both taking hold of the head and feet
of the young man "laid the stiffened
body upon the points of the swords,
which appeared to support it without
penetrating the flesh. The point of one
sword was immediately under the nape of
the neck, that of the second rested midway between his shoulders, and that of
the third (at) the base of the spine;
there was nothing under his legs...The
body tipped neither to the right nor the
left, but seemed to be balanced with
mathematical accuracy."

After the third man retired to the
side, the master took out a dagger and
dug away the soil from the hilt of the
first sword, and removed it - the body
remained motionless. "The second and
third swords were likewise taken from
under the body, which, there in broad
daylight and under the eyes of all the
spectators, preserved its horizontal
position without visible support, about
2' from the ground." (12) After a while
the fakir summoned his assistant and
holding each end of   his stiff body,
gently lowered their companion to the
ground, where, after a few more passes,
he was animated once more. Kellar says
he could devise an illusion of this
feat (given a closed room, devices and
an audience facing one direction) - but
not in broad daylight on unprepared
ground and surrounded in the open by
witnesses. Naturally this does not mean
it definitely was not an illusion, but
if it was then it deserves study in itself as a remarkable phenomenon.

Kellar goes on to describe another
experience - this time on Dunn's reser-
vation, 200 miles north of Durban, South
Africa, during the Zulu war. He had put
on an evening of conjuring and it seems
that many of the Zulus thought his
tricks were authentic magic. Some stole
away to fetch a particular witchdoctor

who confronted Kellar later that night.
This man was obviously reluctant, but
under pressure from his 'parishioners'
agreed to demonstrate his power as Kellar had apparently done his.

   He took a club and fastened it at
the end of a tnong of rawhide about 2'
long and indicated to a fine athletic
native to do the same. "The two men then
stood about 6' apart in the full glare
of the fire and (in silence) began to
whirl the knobkerrys about their heads.
I noticed that when the two clubs seemed
in their swift flight, almost to come
in contact, a spark or flame passed or
appeared to pass from one of them to the
other. The third time this happened
there was an explosion; the spark appeared to burst, the young man's knob-
kerry was shattered to pieces, and he
fell to the ground apparently lifeless."

   "The witchdoctor turned to the high
grass a few feet behind us and gathered
a handful of stalks about 3' long. Standing in the shadow and away from the
fire he waved, with a swift motion
(similar to that of the clubs), the
bunch around the head of the young Zulu
who lay as one dead in the firelight. In
a moment or two the grass seemed to ignite in its flight (the fire was about
20' away) and burned slowly, crackling
audibly...To my amazement the recumbent
body slowly rose from the ground and
floated upward in the air to a height of
about 3', remaining in suspension and
moving up or down according (to the
speed of) the passes of the burning
grass. As the grass burned out...the
body returned to its position on the
ground, and after a few passes from the
witchdoctor's hands the young Zulu leaped to his feet, apparently none the
worse for his wonderful experience."(12)

   This African feat seems to accord
with the abilities traditionally attributed to shamans the world over, including power over fire, and the control of
the flight of other and inanimate objects (4). This ancient association establishes a pedigree for both seance-room
phenomena (15) and its associated cultus
of spiritualism.

   Personally, I'm inclined to accept
for now that levitations do occur, and
that we are very likely dealing with a
natural process which can be affected
spontaneously, or through an act of will,
which is independent of, though often
inhibited by, the local belief systems.
If anyone is looking for a thesis subject, I suggest they try to identify the
elements common to these various belief
systems.

   For my small part, I note that one
common motif, especially among the
stories I give here, is the maintain-
ance of at least a symbolic contact with
the earth - eg the grass, the bamboo-
and-stool contraption, the buried swords
and the sticks in two stories I give
below - hinted at by John Michell's
allusion (6) to the Druid's practice of
riding on levitated stones(16). Cynics'll
immediately claim this is a proof and
a necessity of the clever-trick hypothesis. Apart from maintaining that I'm
speaking here about 'phenomenal reality'
(ie reality as she is experienced and
not intellectualized about), I have a suspicion that the trick-hypothesis is a
self-contained answer anyway. We know
from experience that tricks are usually
in imitation of situations that were
originally real or believed to be real,
and there are ample cases of genuine
paranormal abilities that were supple-
mented by tricks when these powers waned
or were erratic (17)

   But to continue - our next case is
from Southern India in the first half of
1936, witnessed by PT Plunkett, who managed to take a splendid series of photographs (18). John Michell and I have
referred to this case in Phenomena (1)
but I take the opportunity here to give
the account and photos in full.(see pp20/1)

   Plunkett, who had seen the feat
twice before, was invited by a friend,
Pat Dove, to attend a performance on
the friend's plantation, and to bring
his camera to make a record. Plunkett
writes: "The time was about 12.30pm and
the sun directly above us so that shadows played no part in the performance.
The compound was about(80'sq.) in the
middle of which four poles had been
stuck into the ground to support a skeleton roof of branches...Standing quietly by was Subbayah Pullavar, the performer, with long hair, a drooping mous-
tache and a wild look in his eye. He
salaamed to us and stood chatting for a
while. He told us he came from Tinnivelly
and had been practising this particular
branch of yoga for nearly 20 years (as
had past generations of his family). We
asked permission to take photographs of
the performance and he gave it willingly,
thus dispelling any doubt as to whether
the whole thing was merely a hypnotic
illusion...With several gentlemen from
a neighbouring village (and the coolies)
we mustered about 150 witnesses."

   "Everything was now ready. Subbayah
Pullavar marked out a circle close around
the tent, under which he was going to
levitate, by pouring water onto the floor

CONTINUED ON PAGE 22

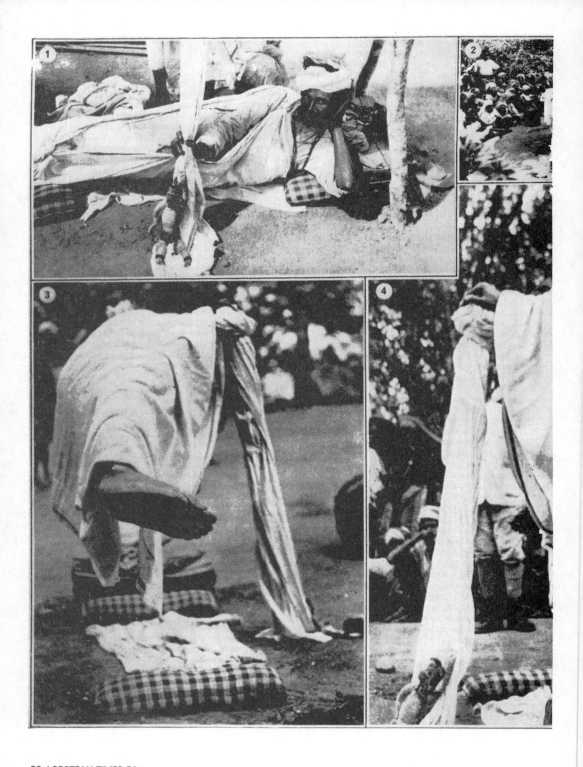

SUBBAYAH PULLAVAR - 1936 (see p19f)

1 Pullavar before levitation - note the queer doll at the foot of the stick!
2 The 'tent' covered in during the ascent and descent - but in the bright sunlight Plunkett saw through the thin material the <u>horizontal</u> was maintained throughout.
3, 4 & p16 Views of the levitation.
5 The stick was wrapped and unwrapped before the spectators, and pushed (not very far) into the hard earth.
6 Pullavar after the levitation - so rigid five men could not bend his limbs - still holding the stick.

of the hot and dusty compound (and instructed) that nobody with leather-soled shoes was to go inside it. When Subbayah's assistant told us it was time for the tent to be removed we took up our positions(on opposite sides) just outside the ring and photographed every position from every angle." Plunkett even prodded the space around the aerial fakir and had to conclude that the man had "no support whatsoever except for resting one hand lightly on top of the cloth-wrapped stick. (There seems to be something traditional about the cloth and hide wrapped accessory.)

The fakir remained horizontal in the air for about 4 minutes (see pictures on pp20-1). The tent was put back and the sides let down. "Pat and I could see through the thin wall Subbayah still suspended in the air. After about a minute he appeared to sway and then very slowly began to descend still in a horizontal position ((my emphasis - RJMR)). He took about five minutes to move from the top of the stick to the ground, a distance of about 3 feet. Evidently we were not meant to see this part of the performance or it would have been done in the open...When Subbayah was back on the ground his assistants carried him over to where we were sitting and asked if we would try to bend his limbs. Even with (their) assistance we were unable to do so. It was only after (he) had been massaged for 5 minutes and had cold water poured over his head and down his throat that he returned to normal." Plunkett ends by declaring that "as I have witnessed this performance with several of my fellow planters (on) several occasions, I am quite convinced of the total absence of tricking."

But there is an even more remarkable account by Louis Jacolliot (19) from the first decade of this century, who gave shelter to another fakir from southern India, for the time that man needed to be in Benares to attend some funeral services. He repaid his host by performing voluntarily and unpremeditated feats which we might liken to a 'controlled poltergeist'. His name was Covindasamy, and he said that his yoga enabled him to call on and direct ancestral spirits. He agreed to a demonstration of the spirits' levitating power and (mentally) prepared himself right then and there before Jacolliot.

"Leaning heavily on an ironwood cane he kept his eyes on the ground and uttered incantations...(then) the fakir rose gradually about 2ft from the ground. His legs were crossed beneath him and he made no changes in his position...for more than 20 minutes I tried to see how Covindasamy could thus fly in the face and eyes of all the known laws of gravity." The stick was Jacolliot's own and could not have been tampered with, and the fakir had no contact with the ground save through his right hand resting on the top of the cane.

The next night, Covindasamy sat cross-legged on one of Jacolliot's stools and with no discernable body movements traversed the length of the verandah by making the stool 'gallop' in jumps of 3-4 feet (20). He also calmly demonstrated how he could affect Jacolliot's furniture,levitating some items and making others immovable.

The next day, as he was taking his final leave, Covindasamy turned in the doorway to face his host, crossed his arms and slowly rose up. He remained at the highest position (apx 12") for about 5 minutes. Some goodbye!

Now before I bore you all off your own feet, let me close on the allied feat of "walking in the air"(21). One of the earliest accounts of the anti-gravity feats of the Brahmins can be found in Philostratus' life of Apollonius of Tyana - on his study-trip to India Apollonius met and studied with a group of Brahmins, who demonstrated their powers by levitating 2 cubits upward and walking in or on the air(22). Kellar had also heard of this feat, but always, to his great regret, second or third hand. For this the fakir would lie face down on the earth for a short time. Getting up and keeping his arms tightly against his sides, the fakir could step "forwards and upwards as if upon an aerial stairway, walking up into the air to an altitude of several hundred feet." (12)

Kellar's friend, who claimed to have seen this, also had a theory which should be of some interest to Earth Mysteries buffs. He thought: "This might be done through an occult knowledge of electrical currents, as if these fakirs changed at will the nature of the electrical current with which their body was charged...inhaling an electrical influence from the earth ((my emphasis - RJMR)) which had the effect of destroying gravity." (12) Not bad for 1878!

There you have it -- paradoxically all the **scoffers** are up in the air, and the levitators the only ones with their feet on the ground!

Robert JM Rickard - May 1977.

References

1 *Phenomena: A Book of Wonders* by John Michell & Robert JM Rickard (Thames & Hudson, London; Pantheon, NY – to be published in October 1977).
2 Amongst several examples we refer to in *Phenomena* is the following given in John Aubrey's *Miscellanies* (1784) who in turn is quoting from a letter dated 1671. An unfortunate Scotsman was carried "in the air several times in view of several persons, his fellow soldiers. Major Henton hath seen him carried away from the guard in Scotland, sometimes a mile or two. Sundry persons are living now that can attest this story."
3 eg see the NeoPlatonist Iamblichus' *De mysteriis* (III-iv) for a pagan mystic who was "lifted up".
4 eg Mircea Elidae's *Shamanism: Archaic Techniques of Ecstasy* (Princetown Univ., 1972) – see index under 'levitation'.
5 eg Eglinton, DD Home, Eusapia Palladino, Henry Gordon, Stainton Moses etc.
6 For a general discussion of magical flight as a universal myth see ch3 of John Michell's *Flying Saucer Vision* (Sidgwick & Jackson, 1967; Abacus, 1974.)
7 The curious Pentecostal Holiness Church (of Kentucky, Tennessee, Virginia and N. Carolina) have adopted shamanistic practices – taking literally Biblical sanction to test their faith by snake-handling, drinking poisons (like strychnine), and fire-ordeals. Dr Berthold E Schwarz published a record of his own (regretably brief) investigation in the *Psychiatric Quarterly* July 1960 (vol 34, pp405-429), in which we find the following tantalizing note in passing: "Other intermittent phenomena claimed by various members of Holiness have been the power of prophecy, clairvoyance, prolonged fasting and, in the knowledge of one saint, the levitation of 'a bearded (backwoods) patriarch.'" (My emphasis – RJMR.)
8 In our penultimate account, the yogi Covindasamy unifies these two approaches by claiming that although 'spirits' did the work, he had the power to apply their energy. The same claim was made by DD Home, but his control was at times quite erratic compared with accounts of the powers of true mystics.
9 For levitation phenomena associated with: witchcraft – see Joseph Glanvill's *Saducismus triumphatus* (1681); fairies – see Wirt Sikes' *British Goblins* (1880); poltergeists – see Harry Price's *Poltergeist over England* (1945); UFOs – see many issues of *Flying Saucer Review*, but a good general discussion can be found in *The Unidentified* (Warner pb, 1975) by Jerome Clark & Loren Coleman. In *Phenomena* we extract a few cases from these (considerably overlapping) sources.
10 The narrative is quoted in *The World of Wonders* (Cassel, sometime twixt 1865-1883 – records lost in wartime bombing!) without reference to the original source.
11 1829. I've not been able to locate this yet, but I quote the verbatim extract in the *Asiatic Journal & Monthly Register* (1st series) March 1829. This latter is the story referred to in E Cobham Brewer's *Dictionary of Miracles* (1884).
12 'High Caste Indian Magic' by Prof. Harry Kellar – *North American Review* January 1897, pp75-86.
13 Bodily levitation is classed as one of the *siddhis*, or 'marvellous powers' in Hindu and Buddhist yoga – see specifically Patanjali's *Yogasutra* (III-35ff); and generally Mircea Eliade's *Yoga, Immortality & Freedom* (1958).
14 The more astute among you will have noticed that the previous date, with Eglinton, was said by Kellar to be his 'first', whereas the event here is about to relate predates it by about 7 years. This paradox, probably due to a writing or typo error, is in the article itself.
15 In the accounts of the levitations of DD Home (basic references can be picked up in *Heyday of a Wizard* (1948) by Jean Burton) there were frequently additional phenomena; loose items in the room would also rise, and small green lights would appear and disappear. For your interest there are two good photos of levitations readily accessible – one of Colin Evans in 1938 appears in von Daniken's *Miracles of the Gods* (1975); and one of the Brazilian, Mirabelli, appears in Guy Playfair's *The Flying Cow* (1975); both published by Souvenir Press, who for reasons known only to themselves, would not allow their reproduction in *Phenomena*.
16 There is a rare reference to Taoist priests levitating on mats, in Rev John L Nevius' *Demon Possession & Allied Themes* (Redway, London, 1897)

which deals with the experiences of missionaries in China on the subject. Quoting a letter from a colleague in a far-flung province, Nevius says that these priests could rise up to 20-50ft and travel 4-5 li (say 1½ miles). Whether this tradition antedates the Middle Eastern one of 'flying carpets' I cannot yet say, but influences between that region and China are ancient and have flowed in each direction.

17 eg Eusapia Palladino; Lulu Hurst, the 'Georgia Wonder'; and, dare I venture, Uri Geller.

18 Illustrated London News 6 June 1936. Some ILN records, including the Plunkett correspondence, were lost in wartime bombing.

19 Occult Science in India & Among the Ancients by Louis Jacolliot (Rider, London, 1919).

20 Similar 'leaping' phenomena are described by Madame Alexandra David-Neel in her With Mystics & Magicians in Tibet (retitled Magic & Mystery in Tibet for the paperback edition) in the section on the lungompa rites. When Aleister Crowley's friend, Allan Bennett, went to Ceylon to study yoga, Crowley once discovered him "resting on his head and right shoulder (still in his yoga posture but) exactly like an image overturned...He was quite unconscious that anything unusual had happened...(&) had evidently been thrown (10-12ft) by the mysterious forces generated by Pranayama." (cf The Confessions of Aleister Crowley eds Symonds & Grant (Cape, London, 1969) p246. The Indian pranayama and Tibetan lung-gom seem similar in this effect, as Crowley describes it, of: "causing the body, while still absolutely rigid, to take little hops in various directions...(as if one were) raised, possibly an inch from the ground, and deposited very gently a short distance away."

21 Our cover illustration is one of Gustave Dore's Bible engravings depicting Christ walking on the water. The engraving I wanted for this cover was proving difficult and expensive to get in time, so I opted for this one - in Continuity 'walking on water' seems to be of the same order, and certainly merges, with 'walking in/on the air' - so I hope you'll accept the illustration's relevance.

22 Apollonius of Tyana worked his wonders about the middle of the 1st century AD. With reference to rare group levitations, I note that Col. Henry Yule's The Book of Marco Polo refers to the claim of a 14th century Moor, Ibn Batuta, to have seen a group of 7 "indian jugglers" rise into the air in a sitting position. With splendid timing I received a clipping from the London Evening News 16 May 1977, as I was typing out these last references (Cr: Cathy). It refers to the claims of a group of disciples of the Maharishi Mahesh Yogi that all 12 of them have been taught to levitate at will during meditation. We'll give this in full in a future FT.

Finally...powers of levitation and wilfully varying the gravity of objects are alluded to in Steve Moore's fine article on gravity-defying feats in the Oriental martial arts - 'Who needs you, Isaac Newton?' in INFO Journal Sept 1976 (19).

■■■■■■■■■■■■■■■■■■■■■■■■■■■■■■■■■■■■

Coloured Rains (cont from p15.)

Norway experienced a grey snowfall "recently". This time, not 'Sahara sand' but "industrial pollution" from Britain, W Germany and the Netherlands. I'd be interested to learn if this happens frequently - and if not, why not?(A.Smith)

On 22 and 23 November 1976, housewives in Northfleet (Kent, again!) protested to their council that they keep finding red spots on washing hung out to dry. They blame a local power station - who, naturally enough, deny responsibility. London Evening News 23 Nov 1976 (Cr: Ken Rogers.)

The problem of red rains is ancient. There do seem to have been rains of blood (as the oldtimers thought all red rains were) - but they also have been found to be coloured by micro-organisms, or dust, or pollen. There have been widespread reports of a red rain this March, over Western Scotland. The 'Sahara sand' notion seems reasonable (but not proven) with the anticyclone over Europe just then. Daily Telegraph 8 March 77 (Mrs V Martin), J.Meteorology Apr 77. The Yorks Evening Post 7 March, said "brown dust" fell on the Isle of Skye (Cr: Anthony J Bell). About 2 weeks after this, the Dauphine region of France experience a rain of mud and red snow. One man at Grenoble saw the "fine browny-red deposit" falling and accumulating quickly. The Japanese Met Office reported falls of fine yellow dust on 29 March. Gobi sand? Journal of Meteorology May 1977.

LINCOLNSHIRE PHENOMENA : 3

by NIGEL WATSON

(The first two parts of this article appeared in The News nos 6 & 8. We offer our apologies to Nigel Watson for the delay in publishing this third part - Ed)

In part one of this study (The News 6), I quoted extensively from the letters written to me by Mr Sidney Benton of Horncastle, Lincs. Now included with this article are a photograph of Mr Benton and a sketch map by him of the spot where he saw two bright shining eyes.

In no way has this series been a comprehensive survey of phenomena in the South Humberside and Lincolnshire regions. My intention has been merely to record incidents and rumours which I have had on file but were otherwise unpublished.

RIDDINGS SCHOOL (map ref: SE 881 077)
Built in the late 1950s, this is a modern and bright school - in the 1960s and early 1970s new wings were built when it changed from a Secondary Modern to a Comprehensive school.

During the 1967-1968 term, the school ghost manifested itself.

The event happened, I believe, in the classroom used for French language. Several girl students were present at the time and they claimed to have seen a face moving across the blackboard.

I was a pupil at the time, and most of the girls were in the same form as myself. The main witness had lost her father not long before the incident, and I think she thought it looked like her father's face. She was particularly distressed by the incident, displaying attendant bouts of sobbing and crying.

Photo of Sidney Benton (Copyright: S.Benton). See The News 6/18.

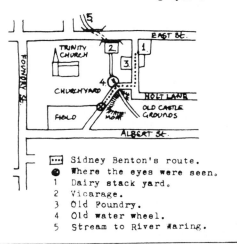

Map of Horncastle, Lincs, showing site of the 'Great shining eyes'.

···· Sidney Benton's route.
● Where the eyes were seen.
1 Dairy stack yard.
2 Vicarage.
3 Old Foundry.
4 Old water wheel.
5 Stream to River Waring.

The teacher present at the time had his back to the blackboard and so did not see the alleged phenomenon - but I remember him claiming that it was most probably a reflection of the sun!

The windows of the classroom - at the rear of the school - all faced West. The time of the incident was about 2 - 2.30pm, so the sun would conceivably have been in a position to cause a reflexion. But even schoolchildren know what a reflexion of the sun looks like!

This sighting can be regarded as highly subjective, with the recent death of the main witness's father, and the other 4 or 5 girls never really indicating precisely what they had seen. Another consideration must be their ages, between 13 and 14. It might also be noted that around this period, we had a music teacher who was interested in ghosts and ghoulies. I can still remember him relating to us his tale of seeing the ghost of a hooded monk at his old teacher training college, along with dating 3 girls at the same time - a real hero!

Although fairly young, after about a year at Riddings, he died of a heart attack...

BUCKINGHAM St (map ref: 888 119)
Back in 1959 my informant - who lived next door but one to the girl witness - heard a scream pierce the air at about 2am in the morning. Puzzled, he went to his bedroom window and looked outside. Besides a clear sky, he saw nothing to indicate the cause, although he did hear a few muffled moans.

However, next morning, he did find out what had happened. A young girl, aged about 14, had seen an evil face at her bedroom window, which caused her to scream and become hysterical.

The police were called, but there was not much they could do in the circumstances.

This case must be regarded as highly subjective - unless a peeping Tom was involved, which is unlikely but possible. Her bedroom was on the first floor, with a shed not far away beneath the window, which looked out to the East.

The same informant told me of a similar case involving a girl relative, aged 13-14, who lived in the house between his own and that of the girl in the first case. The incident happened in 1954, in the early hours of one morning, when the girl, sleeping in the attic room, saw among the attic rafters the face of her recently deceased grandfather. She had been quite fond of him, and

as she only saw the face floating above her bed for a few seconds, she was not really frightened by it. Again we must note the subjective element.

The names of my informant and the witnesses are known, but I feel it is not fair to publish them.

THORNE
Although Thorne is not in the area specified in my introduction to part two of this series (The News 8), I include this case because of its similarity to the above cases.

This report was given to me when I was interviewing Keith Todd, a friend of mine, about a UFO he had seen. Until I asked him if he had any other encounters with the unknown, I had not heard before of his 'ghost' sighting.

The incident happened in the late 1950s, when he was about 4 or 5 years old. At that time his family lived in Thorne, only later moving to Scunthorpe, oasis of the North.

In bed with his sister, about a year younger than himself, they saw a skeleton's head appear on the bedroom ceiling. The glowing head was seen for a few seconds and then disappeared.

Only after preparing this series for Fortean Times, from my battered old memo book filing system, did I finally discover this cluster of 'head' reports. I had known of Keith's case, for instance, for four years, and only now that I have compared Keith's "skeleton's head" with the Riddings school 'face' have I realised that in fact Keith was, at the time of his experience, a pupil of Riddings. However I doubt whether he had heard of the (much earlier) school 'head'.

SOME COMPARISONS

1) Further to Sidney Benton's "Great Shining Eyes" - compare the "Eye-witnesses account" of a similar phenomenon in a letter in the 'Reader's Reports' section of FSR Casehistories Supplement 18, Feb 1974.

2) With reference to the Riddings and Buckingham Street 'heads', see the first paragraph of 'Visions' in The News 7/11.

Nigel Watson - 1975 (May 1977).

** Nigel has raised a very interesting topic. Psychologists and researchers into perception know there is a class of visual hallucinations called 'hypnagogic images' - strictly images seen prior to falling asleep, but generally applied also to those in the somnolent state just after sleep. These are powerful, bright and often frightening images of anything from abstract patterns to spatial designs, to everyday objects, but are more usually of faces. The arch-sceptic DH Rawcliffe allies the phenomenon to the ancient art of 'scrying' or crystal-gazing, and to the long-lasting retinal images called 'eidetic images' (one of the truly neglected areas of perceptual study), and speculates that this could be the origin of sightings of demons, fairies etc. (See Illusions & Delusions of the Occult by Dover, a re-titling of his Psychology of the Occult (1952)).

However, Rawcliffe fails to account for the origin and genesis of this visual material, and the fairly frequent cases where more than one person sees the same thing, or an image of their own at the same time as the main witness. To call such communal effects 'hysteria' - as Rawcliffe and his school of self-professed 'rationalists' frequently do - is merely an evasion, not an explanation. This is an abiding mystery. Ed **

UNIDENTIFIEDS

Some of the following may seem old hat to a few of you, but as some of our future value lies in documentation, we'd like to update our monster record. Right now we concentrate on Nessie and good old Morgawr, and leave some other stuff till next time.

THE MONSTER-MIND EXPERIMENT

When last we met Doc Shiels (FT19), he had just seen Morgawr for the second time, and photographed her. Our photos didn't come out too well, and I'm hoping that a short history of Morgawr - the Cornish seaserpent - I have done for Fate, will, when published, have much better reproductions. Doc then expressed a not unnatural wish to have nothing more to do with Morgawr. As it's usually 'her' who chooses the time and place I don't take Doc's wish for retirement too seriously.

Early this year, Doc wrote to me saying that with six other psychic showmen they were going to have a concerted effort to raise monsters from the deeps in various parts of the world - by telepathic summoning! As the cannibal said: 'You can't keep a good man down!'

The Psychic Seven International (PSI), as they call themselves, was to occur over the three days leading to the Feast of Brigid (Candlemas) - ie 31 Jan to 2 Feb. Doc himself was going to concentrate on Lochs Ness, Morar, and his namesake, Shiel; Bascom Jones, in California, was to raise the 'Old Man of Monterey' (see 1, p478); and Max Maven, in Massachusetts, was to revive the Gloucester Harbour sea-serpent (see 1, p165); for starters.

In a letter to me, dated 7 Feb 1977, Doc outlines their successes. PSI Calcutta agent, Jadoo Chandra Rao, claimed he raised the giant snake-like creature seen in a Russian lake a few days before the Monstermind experiment while "practicing". David Hoy, in Kentucky, joined in at GMT midnight on 31st Jan; and Major Leslie May, in Edinburgh, joined in on Loch Morar. Well, to date I've heard nothing on the American monsters, if they appeared, but things certainly stirred in the UK.

According to Pat Scott-Innes, PSI member living at Loch Ness, four people saw Nessie on the first day; Helen Fleming and her father, and Mr & Mrs Alex McCleod, all of Inverness. There was an unconfirmed sighting at Loch Shiel on 2 Feb, by a man calling himself 'John Smith': that at 11.30am, he was on the footpath near Guesachan when he saw the creature enter the water from a small island called Eilean Dubh. Doc has his doubts about this claim. However there are better things -- a Miss Lindsay, of

Musselburgh took two photos of Morag, on the 31st Jan, and they show, she says, the head of a 40ft monster -- and in Cornwall, Gerry Bennett, took three colour pictures of what he thought was Morgawr that day too! I say 'thought' because the form they show is not like that described by Mary F, Doc, and other witnesses (see FTs 15,16 & 19) - this apparently looks like a giant greeny-black crustacean, ie with a hard seg-mented shell! If true, this confuses the matter even more - yay!

Rest assured that FT will try to locate the Bennett, and Lindsay photos, and various other witness statements for future issues. They need to be on record somewhere. We'll also have a few other pre-Monstermind lake-monster sightings and other goodies that surface from the murky depths of the filing cabinet.

Meanwhile, Monstermind phase 2 is in progress, this time begining on May Eve and lasting through to Lammas - a period of 3 months. However things have not gone happily in the wake of phase 1. Several psychic replacements refused to join the experiment after Max Maven had to drop out, and Dave Hoy suffered two coronaries!

Meanwhile...in his latest letter to me, Doc tells of Mr & Mrs Arthur Wood, of Plymstock, Plymouth, who both saw a bright orange and green "ball of fire" off Pendennis Point, near Falmouth, at about 9am on Friday 13 May 1977 - and just half an hour later, as Mr Wood told Doc over the phone, they both saw Morgawr in the water below the Point heading out to sea. A fairly explicit link that between strange lights and monsters. Doc sent along with this a clipping from the previous day's West Briton in which is a letter from a Mrs P Skentelbery, who saw a pulsing orange light over St Mawes at the begining of April; and an editorial ref to a similar light seen by a Penryn man late April. A letter in the same paper for 5 May 77, from a Mrs PR Packer, tells of a bright aerial light near Truro, early May. Doc wonders if the lights are announcing a new series of Morgawr appearances, as they did on her arrival in late 1975 (see FT (The News) 15/13.)

Reference:

1) In the Wake of the Sea-serpents by Bernard Heuvelmans (Hill & Wang, USA: Rupert Hart-Davies, UK; 1968).

DAVID CLARKE'S MORGAWR SIGHTING
Back in FT19 we showed Doc's photos of Morgawr as she appeared when he and David Clarke met at Parson's Beach on the Helford estuary. Mr Clarke, editor of the glossy 'County mag' Cornish Life, eventually published an account of the sighting from his side, in his Feb 1977 (vol4, no1) issue, interwoven with a brief history of Morgawr based in parts on the information in our own pages here. Mr Clarke took photos through a telephoto lens - but his camera jammed! I append the following summary from the Cornish Life article, and a letter to me (from Clarke) dated 14 Feb 1977:

'...Doc drew my attention to an ob-ject halfway across the river - a small dark head poking out of the water. We both stood on large rocks for a better view and I attached a telephoto lens to my camera. The object slowly moved near-er and I could see that it was definite-ly a head, probably a seal. It came to within 70 or 80ft (and moved) slowly up and down river in a zig-zag pattern. It was only when I saw it side-on that I observed that the greenish-black head was supported on a long arched neck, more slender than that of a seal. In the the wave-troughs at least 4 or 5ft of the neck were visible. There was a slow movement of water stretching back beh-ind the head and neck for about 10ft, and at one point a gently-rounded shiny black body broke the surface. The head was rounded with a 'blunt' nose and on the top of the head were two small rounded 'buds'. Doc and I were both busily shouting to one another as we took photos and I must admit to feeling rather afraid as the creature surged slowly back and forth. It had obviously seen us. I was also rather suspicious. After all, I had once seen Doc saw a lady in half and on another occasion bend spoons with a stroking touch. The first I knew to be a trick; the second I suspected to be. The appearance of Morgawr 'to order' as it were ((they had been talking about her and Doc's claim to have 'summoned' her appearances around Falmouth - ed)) seemed just too coincidental. Yet he was pulling no strings, operating no mechanism, and the head of the beast was certainly animate with no sign of air bubbles, snorkel, aerial or strings. If this WAS a hoax - HOW was it done? I moved to his side and found him as surprised as I was. The head of the creature turned to us and its mouth opened as it slowly sank in a swirl of water. We stood for another half an hour...but nothing else appeared."

David Clarke says he was halfway through writing the article on Morgawr – "not really 'County Mag' material, but we try not to be too stuffy – when in the course of research, he met Doc and together they saw the damned thing. Mr Clarke admits that "it took quite a bit of courage" to include his experience, and in spite of , or perhaps because of, his personal doubts, he thought "the only attitude to take seemed to be one of scepticism – at being wary of believing my own eyes. Not a very honest view I admit, but the only one that didn't sound either hysterical or downright stupid to the average reader." As it was, he says, subsequent reaction from women has been almost wholly sceptical, while most men showed a distinct interest. When he discovered the camera malfunction, he decided to "err on the side of journalistic caution."

However, "Perhaps I should say my reservations are not quite as strong as they may appear...I can vouch for the fact that (Doc's photos) show the same creature that I had seen...that the thing was alive, and certainly no seal or dolphin – the 'blunt-shaped' head and arched neck were animate and turned about to look around several times – dark in colour, black or dark green. It moved through the water making a wake and appeared to move in slow surges, rather like a 'slowed-down' seal."

Mr Clarke's photos of the incident, on 17 November 1976, are not in the article, but as I believe the head is fairly discernable among the double and triple exposures, we'll try to get a look at them.

TEAPOTS, BOATS & STONES
And what of Dr Robert Rines' intrepid team who will be back at Loch Ness this summer – the 7th year of their dedicated search? Doc Shiels, who says 7s figure well this year, thinks there will be some kind of breakthrough.

An interview with Prof Roy P Mackal, author of The Monsters of Loch Ness, in London for the annual meeting of the Loch Ness Investigation Bureau, appeared in the Guardian 1 February 1977 (Cr: P Rogerson.) Mackal said he was to advise other members of the LNIB to tone down the circus-approach to their investigations, and that the results of the 1976 searches were "damn meagre". Overselling for the benefit of an awed or derisive public, he warned, puts off the real experts who could help with the expeditions. Hmmm...with all due respect, there can be no 'experts' in the unknown, but I get his gist.

Mackal's despondency aside, a full report of the 1976 progress appears in the December 1976 issue of MIT Technology Review. It's worth summarising some of what they did find – not a monster, but in testing out the various sonars, all kinds of weird things turned up. The summer expedition by teams led by Rines and Martin Klein tested out navigation systems, and began mapping the Loch walls and floor. At Lochend, the northeast end, they found submerged stone-circles, 15 to 150ft diameter. According to the Ness Information Service Bulletin Feb 1977 (20) these apparently megalithic monuments were of two different types and at two different depths, probably built when the water-level was much lower. Let's hope we hear more about these.

They found a few ship wrecks, one of which had been discovered earlier in 1970; also coal residue from the early era of powered boats, and artifacts like teapots. Dr Robert Ballard, of the National Geographic Society expedition there said: "There seems to be more teapots in Loch Ness than anything else!" (UPI: 7 December 1976). They also found the wreck of an American-built PBY flying-boat, lost by the RAF. They followed a complex of ridges and undercuts that ran for huge distances along both walls of the Loch, and in which there was a squareish hole, near Invermoriston...and near the man-made Cherry Island they found what seemed to be "a three-sided square structure" ((A pyramid!?!)) I note that automatic cameras took a total of 108,000 pictures, none of which showed monsters. This could only be expected, if the monsters are rarer than other Loch-life, because only 33 out of that lot showed fish or eels, even. Just as the teams were ending their programs they found a "carcase-like" shape in 100 meters of water in Borlum Bay, near Fort Augustus. It was about 10 meters long and had a "neck-like projection", but could not be identified at the time. Doubtless when searches resume this summer many of these things will be re-examined -- but it's equally possible they will not when top men, like Mackal, seem to be thinking only of the monster and nothing else!

Reports on all these discoveries appeared in most national papers around 7 November and 7 December (Cr: Ion Will, Mrs V Martin, Gary Abbott, Mark Hall, Paul Screeton, TR Adams, AJ Bell & Ken Rogers.) – but for the full details see the MIT journal above.

The sonar experiments, though, have given at least three tantalizing glimpses of possible-Nessies. Dr Harold Edgerton reported traces of "large objects moving underwater" on 30 June and 1 July which came within 250ft of the cameras (not close enough!) and departed very quickly - South China Morning Post 11

Dec 1976 (Cr: Ion Will). And earlier in May the monitor ship Cornwall picked up signs of two 'monster' shapes -- one 46ft and the other 20ft - which they tracked for 80 minutes - Sunday Mirror 30 May 1976 (Cr: Robert Forrest.)

** Next issue, more monsters **

'Strange Tales' is a slot for some of the more weirdly uncategorizable (?) of our stories.

MAGICIAN & DWARVES RIDDLE

A Ghanaian magician, known as Prof. De-Ago, shocked a South African audience packed into a cinema hall. Before their disbelieving eyes they imagined they saw him cut open his wife's abdomen and begin to eat her intestines. Women in the audience hid their faces, cried and fainted. A doubter rushed onto the stage to stop the magician, but only succeeded in angering him. The magician forced him to the floor and pushed some of the intestines down his throat. Then he announced that he would revive his wife. The count lasted 30 minutes, with incantations between each count. When the wife's legs began to move the relieved audience burst into a thunderous ovation.

A clever and novel piece of stagemanship, you might think - but these days I wonder! Sometime I might write a piece on similar grisly events, and how they accord with creditable shamanistic experience, drawing on some fascinating notes. In itself the magical regeneration of grievous wounds is not unusual, as the vast body of authentic data on stigmata testifies.

But our story gets curiouser. De-Ago says he is aided by Komfo (Priest) Atia, a 75cm high dwarf, who works alone in a backstage room, providing the power for De-Ago's acts, and warding off the neutralizing spells of other magicians trying to sabotage the partnership. According to De-Ago, Atia is 125 years old,

drinks heavily, chain smokes, never gets sick, and works with 37 other dwarves. In true shamanistic manner, Atia claims that at an early age he was "taken mirculously" (often a euphemism for levitation - see back to my article - or teleportation) and that he is the greatest conjuror since "Okomfo Anokye", whom the newspaper calls: "An Ashanti fetishist...reputed to have conjured a golden stool out of the sky in 1687." Interesting! Its crazy enough to be perfectly true! Pretoria, SA, News 7 October 1975 (Cr: Chris Holtzhausen.)

SIGNS OF LIFE

According to Reveille 9 April 1976 Dr Adrian Upton, a Canadian neurologist, attatched the electrodes of a machine, used to confirm death, onto a lemon pudding. He got a positive reading, which by medical definition, means the pud was

alive! Roll over Frankenstein! Dr Upton seems naturally cautious about his wonderful discovery (which undoubtedly has shocking implications for all vegetarians), suggesting that maybe the machine picked up "brainwaves of nurses standing nearby" (as the paper naïvely puts it) or some kind of interference.

The timing of this note suggests it could have been picked up from some medical journal shortly after April 1st - but I doubt if this will dismay any Fortean. (Cr: Anthony Smith.)

THE ZAP-GUN MYSTERY

The following letter, signed simply 'A Wiltshire Teacher' appeared in The Guardian 30 November 1976, prompted by

readers accounts of "peculiar events".
It is worth quoting in near entirity:

"...in East Anglia a few years ago
...I was teaching in a small village
school and the caretaker's husband declared that he had seen strange orange
lights in the school field as he walked
the dog home at about 10.30pm. Cynics
suggested that he had seen more light
ale than anything else. I thought little
of it."

"Next day a little lad brought me a
small plastic toy pistol which he had
found near the school. I popped it into
my drawer until such time as someone
claimed it. Near the end of the afternoon of hectic pre-Christmas activities
I felt I could not tolerate the comp-
ulsive and ceaseless chatter of one
Sandra, and on impulse I pointed the
pistol at her, saying mentally 'Gotya!'"

"To my astonishment she immediately
vanished. The other children, conditioned to ignore her perpetual trivial-
ities, didn't even notice."

"At the end of the session I dismissed the class and sat down in the
ill-lit room to ponder over the unprecedented situation. I was suddenly aware
of the figure of a man standing by me
dressed in some kind of boiler-suit
protective clothing (*). I assumed he
was a parent on his way home from work.
He extended his hand, lying in the palm

of which was another toy pistol. Word-
lessly I passed the first one over to
him. He examined it briefly, clicked a
small ratchet at the side, pointed it
towards the corner of the room and pulled the trigger."

"To my utter amazement Sandra reappeared immediately in full spate, breaking off only to observe that it was time
to go home. And as I sat there, Sandra
and the stranger independently disappeared into the evening gloom."

The date of this letter, and the
mention (*) of boiler-suit clothing
make it fairly certain that the "peculiar events" referred to at the begining
were at least two UFO/humanoid encounters in England's West Country earlier
that month - particularly the case of
Mrs Bowles, at Winchester, on the 14th -
currently receiving attention in FSR,
MUFOB and other UFO mags.

It is also apparent to any folklorist that the letter encapsulates the
classical scenario of the finding and
misuse of a fairy artifact or gift. The
mysterious stranger will not be lost,
either, on those who are interested in
the theories of MK Jessup and his successors in the camp of UT UFOlogy. All
we need to discover now is whether the
damned story is a true one! I believe
Roger Sandall (to whom credit for this)
was trying to find out but getting nowhere.

₦ɛⱲ₷

All the signs are that the last
quarter of this year and the months
thereafter could be quite remarkable for
UFOlogy. A carefully-leaked news report
(US News & World Report 18 April 1977 -
Cr: Page Res.Library, Dave Fideler) says
that President Carter intends to reverse the official policy of the White
House on UFOs later this year by making
"unsettling disclosures" based on CIA
files on the subject. The expected
scramble to identify the source of this
leak has been unable to - but this note

appears in a dry, respected political
journal and cannot be dismissed without
doubt. This focussed attention again on
Carter's own sighting of a luminous,
multicoloured aerial light in 1969. He
was governor of Georgia at the time, and
filed reports with APRO and IUFOB.

Another factor will be the release,
around Christmas, of the film 'Close Encounters of the Third Kind'. Dave Fideler writes that this coincides roughly
with a computer-prediction of the next
big UFO-flap. It has been well observed
that the "Phenomenon feeds on itself",
and we wonder what sort of effect all
this will have on the public.

All this is preceeded by firstly the grand International Congress on UFO Phenomena, held in Mexico City, at the end of last April. Although well reported across the Atlantic, we only saw a small notice in the Sunday Times 1 May 1977, which gave a memorably succinct quote from one of the brightest stars of UFOlogy, South America's answer to John Keel, a renegade Jesuit called Salvador Freixedo: "Astronomy has little to do with UFOs. The relevant disciplines are psychology, psychiatry, quantum physics and parapsychology." The second event will take place 24-26 June at the Pick-Congress Hotel, Chicago, billed as 'International UFO Congress' and organized by the staff of Fate to celebrate the 30th anniversary of Kenneth Arnold's sighting (and coinage of the term "flying saucers")   on 24 June 1947. The speaker list includes most of the top authors and researchers in the field and deals with the key evidences, theories and controversies. Registrations cost $30. to the Congress, c/o Fate at Highland Park, Illinois 60035.

This latter event stimulated Page Research Library to pay a timely tribute to Fate which has served the UFOlogical and Fortean communities since its first issue in Spring 1948 - 29 years ago. We'd like to add our own congratulations and sincerely appreciative thanks to Curtis Fuller and all at Fate. May they thrive! Details of the Page Research Library's (PRL) extensive Fortean and UFO mailorder lists and informative Newsletter can be had for $4.50 (6 issues) from PRL, 6708 Colgate Ave, Cleveland, Ohio 44102, USA.

Finally on the subject of UFOs, we note that there continue to be reports of landings and encounters in the area of Broad Haven, South Wales - known now as 'The Pembroke Triangle'! Similarly the saga of Mrs Joyce Bowles lurches on. She had at least two more encounters beyond the one reported in FSR 25:5 (for the better ley study of the site, see TLH 75), including a partial abduction! The investigations of this series will preoccupy UK UFO mags for some time, being the most interesting cases here for some while. Where relevant, we might run notes on some Fortean overlap - but for now we note that back in 1973 the Bowles family was the focus of a widely-reported poltergeist case (see The News 3/12). We learned recently that Mrs Bowles has been sacked from her job as lavatory attendant at Winchester railway station. British Rail say it's because

she is "redundant", but Mrs Bowles, quite naturally, sees it as part of "a nasty campaign" to get rid of her. Her union branch said they would investigate the matter - but I suppose in some minds it'll always be blamed on the MIBs. Certainly she has had threatening phone calls, her car sabotaged, etc etc. News of the World 1 May 1977.

The Ley Hunter has arranged its 'Moot' for Saturday 2 July 1977 - the first meeting of like minds since the legendary 'Mystics Picnic' in 1971. It begins with a lecture period between 10.15 to 2pm at   'Ye Olde Gatehouse', the original high gate of London at Hampstead. This is at Highway Hall, where Hampstead Lane, Highgate West Hill, Highgate High St and North Rd meet. A snack will be served during this and editor Paul Devereux would like you to let him know if you wish to attend & require the snacks. Otherwise eats and drinks are your own problem - TLH have paid for the hall and are not charging. Afterwards, if weather permits the whole scene will walk across the heath to Jack Straw's Castle for farewell drinks. TLH: Box 152 London N10 1EP, or ring 01 883 3949.

It was with a flush of good memories that I learned recently of an appreciation society for Patrick McGoohan's brilliant TV series 'The Prisoner'. Called Six of One, they operate from 39 Union St, Cheltenham, Gloucestershire - and £2/year gets you membership, a journal called Alert. Write for more details, including their meetings (some at the hotel at 'Prisoner' location of Portmeirion, Wales.) Tell em FT sent you!

We recently heard from Peter Juhl Svendsen, in Denmark, that a group of Scandinavian Forteans have formed Scanfo - the Scandinavian Fortean Organization. Membership will cost Danish kr10 (£1.00) and their journal, Forteana will cost 15kr for 4 issues. Forteana has a newspaper format which fills me with envy; but it's all in Danish or Swedish of course, and will be of more interest to the European Forteans - a longed-for development that fills areal need in that area and hopefully will flourish and stimulate the study of Fortean phenomena. Scanfo also intend to open a bookshop, and publish books with help from Sphinx & Nihil. Scanfo: Classensgade 17 A 4 th, DK-2100 Copenhagen Ø, Denmark.

In February this year, Milan and other cities in Northern Italy were abuzz with rumours after several motorists said they had given a lift to an old lady who prophesied that Milan would be destroyed on the 27th Feb by quake. They all said she vanished, then, leaving evidence that established that she had died 10 years ago! According to our correspondent, Edoardo Russo, the city convened a group of mediums, astrologers etc, who assured them that this doom would not happen. Although the witnesses could not be traced,   the day came and went, with Italy gripped in morbid fascination. (Even Turin, Milan's "ancient rival", says Edoardo, looked on with grim expectation.) Now it's said that the Antichrist was born that day! Dallas Morning News (TX) 25 Feb (Cr: TR Adams); La Stampa 25, 26 Feb, 1 Mar; Stampa Sera 28 Feb 1977 (Cr: E Russo). The panic was not surprising remembering the calamities that afflicted north Italy last year following the failure of the blood of St Januarius, in Naples, to liquify (see FT 16/5 & 18/12f). A Reuter note this year, for 1 May, claimed that the liquification once more occurred on schedule – a perfectly timed piece of panic stopping (Cr Tim Jones). But will it work?

HARDBACKS

We welcome to our fold Stan Nicholls of Dark They Were & Golden-Eyed, the biggest collection of imports and paperbacks on Forteana in central London (9-12 St Anne's Court, off Wardour St, London W1). Stan will be keeping us up-to-date on book news. Books marked below with a (*) in the margin should be available at the shop as imports.

Because of a review backlog, numerous releases and a shortage of space we could not include the following – they will be reviewed next time:

Rhythms of Vision (L Blair); Unfinished Animal (T Roszak); The Uses of Enchantment (B Bettelheim); Space Time Transients (Persinger & Lafreniere); PSI/Consciousness Explosion (S Holroyd); Peoples of the Sea (I Velikovsky); The Paradise Papers (M Stone); The Virgin (G Ashe); More Lives than One (J Iverson) Handbook of Unusual Natural Phenomena (WR Corliss); and some others.

Ancient Mysteries by Peter Haining (Sidgwick & Jackson 1977; £5.50; pp178; index, bib; illustrated) – Ancient Mysteries Reader by Peter Haining (Gollancz 1976; £4.50; pp 321) -- Popularisation of a subject can be praised or criticised, depending on its motives and the care with which it is done. Some popularisers are out to cash in on others' success; some aim to introduce an important subject to a wider audience; and sometimes the two motives can be combined, I believe, as here. It is good that people should read serious writing on subjects which the Establishment will not take seriously; but it is not so good when the author's superficial knowledge of his subject shows through, as it sometimes does in Ancient Mysteries.

Haining devotes a chapter to each of ten 'mysteries' - the hollow earth, lost worlds, the discovery of America, stone computers (ie British megaliths), submerged continents, phantom islands, a second race, Sasquatch/Yeti, Loch Ness monster, UFOs. He gives a potted history of each, and an extract from a relevant published book - eg Hawkins' Beyond Stonehenge in the case of stone computers and Plato's Timaeus for submerged continents. The book is nicely produced with many black and white illustrations throughout.

But looking beyond the production to what Haining actually says, we learn, for eaxmple, that it was archeologist TC Lethbridge who discovered leys! (p61f). Not a mention of Alfred Watkins, John Michell, or other ley pioneers - apart from the fact, of course, that Lethbridge had nothing whatever to do with leys! Neither does Haining seem to be aware that Lethbridge, and Ivan Sanderson, are both dead. Nor is he apparently overfamiliar with AC Oudemans (author of The Great Sea Serpent 1892) for he appears here always as 'Dudemans'!

Readers of FT will recall discussion of the notorious 'hole in the pole' photograph. Haining states: "Enthusiasts have greeted this picture as a confirmation of their belief in the Hollow Earth theory; scientists are more inclined to the view that it is a vortex formation created by the spinning earth." (p22.) Also, the caption to the picture is careful not to destroy the mystery by giving the prosaic explanations, which can be found set out by Colin Bord in FT 8/22. ((The US Environmental Science Service Admin. later confirmed these explanations to me - Ed.))

But despite these flaws the book has its merits. Beside the work of von Daniken and his imitators, it is sane and level-headed, and potential readers of 'ancient mysteries' will be better served by it.

** Janet Bord **

It seems as if Haining, gripped by an 'ancient mystery' bug, has got double milage out of a simple idea. He adds very little himself to the discussion of his selected themes, preferring to 'pot' history and quote a long passage from a key work. At first I though AM was the factual approach, and AM Reader was the fictional half of the idea - but not only does Haining use works of fiction in the main quotes in AM, but whole parts seem interchangeable between the two books; ie the same phrasing, same quotes and even sharing some diagrams.

That said, AM Reader, the earlier of the two, is far more challenging than its 'factual' counterpart, since the fictional exploration of (virtually) the same themes (as those listed by Janet above) is invariably more powerful, exciting and evocative than the usual dry source-quoting method. Haining's choice of short stories is representative of the great attraction that strange phenomena had for the early mystery, fantasy and horror writers, and still has for their successors today. But the biggest mystery of all, of which Haining seems only half aware and regrettably neglects in both books, is that the key writers he anthologises - Lovecraft, Poe, Machen, Conan Doyle, Wells, Bulwer-Lytton, etc - have not only encapsulated the dynamics of these themes, but presaged the modern interest in them. They were often indeed ahead of their times. Since each story in AM Reader is prefaced by one of Haining's potted histories, you may be better counselled to chose this anthology - you'd lose the pictures in the other (nice one of the Caspar mummy) but you'd get the better read, and probably learn more too!
** RJM Rickard **

Terror: A History of Horror Illustration from Pulp Magazines by Peter Haining (Souvenir Press 1976; £4.95; pp176) - An Illustrated History of Witchcraft by Peter Haining (NEL 1975; £5.25; pp128) -- Following on from the successful formula he tried in Ghosts: An Illustrated History, Haining has produced yet another pair of books. I can gladly forget the paucity of text in Terror in view of the splendid and representative selection of B&W illustrations and colour covers from Horror and Fantasy magazines, from the days of the 'Penny Bloods' to the F&SF of today. Witchcraft, on the other hand, demands a concise if not substantial text, and here Haining glides shallowly and quickly through centuries of complexities. Of

the illustrations, many are familiar from other books of a similar nature, while others are both new and interesting. It's also good to see a hint of the work of new artists continuing the ancient association between art and the occult (eg a few frames of a strip by Richard Corben, the 'underground comic' genius, seem to link across the ages to graphic reportage of Goya).

Both books are well produced and will serve as stimulating samplers and introductions to the two subjects.
** RJM Rickard **

A Dictionary of Philosophy by AR Lacey (Routledge & Kegan Paul 1976; £4.75; pp239) -- Lately I've been doing some essential reading in philosophy and metaphysics - a grind at the best of times - but often a hard slog due to the excesses and necessity of jargon and obscure 'isms. I was grateful to have this dictionary with listings under key names, words, phrases and titles. These entries are crossreferenced, with critical bibliographies for further reading. Informative too - under 'Scepticism' I learned that "Descartes tried unsuccessfully to doubt his own existence."
** RJM Rickard **

Exorcising Devils by Dom Robert Petitpierre, OSB. (Hale 1976; £3.95; pp172) -- Dom Petitpierre is one of the leading, and probably most well-known of the Church of England exorcists, and has had considerable experience of psychic matters since the early 1920s. His view of ghosts and the 'atmosphere' of sites is similar to the 'psychic-fields' theory of TC Lethbridge, in that places can be 'imprinted' with coded or coherent energy, that, when 'read' back by sensitives, can deliver vivid shocks to the emotional and perceptual system triggering visual, auditory, tactile and emotional images, usually frightening.

The book is anecdotal, rather than a study or manual; a fascinating conversational ramble on many aspects of exorcism (of places, things and people) drawing on his direct and often quite bizarre experiences. Interestingly, he believes the modern 'occult explosion' has resulted from the failure of the Church to respond to the need for more profound beliefs by the young today, who are no longer satisfied by the extremes of dogmatic materialism in science and dogmatic faith in religion, and his comments on the Barnsley killing (when an exorcism 'failed' and the man killed his wife) and similar dramas going on today, often in the wake of the current trend for occultism in the cinema, are most interesting to students of individual and mass human behaviour.

His stories carry an implicit belief in the existence of ghosts (as departed souls or as place-memories), fallen angels and "little devils", the concrete manifestations of evil - although he clearly does not exclude Fodor's notion of "projected repressions" as the basis of some poltergeist effects. There are others too - eg his maddingly brief hint at a group of telekinetic drug-smugglers. Naturally, and to the relief of many, Dom Petitpierre rationalises in terms of Christian theology (eg he gives his views on the history of Occultism and its dangers) and ends the book with advice and prayers, both for the afflicted and for would-be exorcists.

Apart from his descriptions of the strange phenomena involved in his cases, most of our readers will be interested to learn that Dom Petitpierre has, on a number of occasions, had to exorcise churches - and he traces this necessity to disturbances of the 'place-memory' type. He is very interested in 'Leys' and does not doubt that these disturbances are more common, or more active, where churches are sited on ley lines, and devotes a chapter to the subject. He even identifies the source of these imprints: the Bull of Pope Gregory the Great, which authorised the early missionaries to integrate pagan feasts into the Christian calend r, and to build churches on already holy sites. Gregory seemed ready to allow even animal sacrifices on church ground, if this would bring the peasants within the reach of his priests. The present disturbances, argues Dom Petitpierre, are merely the unpleasant residue of some of these heathen rites. This leads him onto random comments about several very interesting pagan survivals.

The book is easy to read and carries Dom Petitpierre's character - but on the one hand the book is almost useless evidentially with very little corroboration given in the way of dates, names etc; and on the other, this witty, learned and experienced churchman, who has no motive for spinning you tales, has given us one of the most humane books on exorcism in a field which runs from obscure scholarship to sheer sensation-mongering.

** RJM Rickard **

PAPERBACKS

Castaneda's Journey: The Power and the Allegory by Richard De Mille (Capra Press, 631 State St, Santa Barbara, CA 93101, USA, 1976; $4.95; pp205; index, notes, refs) -- Carlos Castaneda's four books (Teachings of Don Juan, A Separate Reality, Journey to Ixtlan, Tales of Power) chronicling his apprenticeship to a Yaqui Indian sorcerer, Don Juan Mattus, have enjoyed a phenomenal success, all the more remarkable because the books claim to be based on field notes of Castaneda's anthropological study of the sorcerer's place, vocabulary, methods and pharmacopoeia, and not a work of fiction. At least this was the claim made by Castaneda, his host of supporters, and his millions of devoted readers across the world. Don Juan's drastic methods, sometimes by drugs and sometimes by his will, form an onslaught on Castaneda's (and thereby our own) sense of 'reality', recreating an attractively powerful vision of a universe of shifting forms stabilized only by magical powers, group 'belief' and mysterious entities - a vision that has appealed to yearnings in the 'underground' culture. (One sign of De Mille's thoroughness is that he includes in his appreciation of Castaneda's influence such minutae as, say, the character 'Don Long Juan' in Sheldon's 'Fabulous Furry Freak Brothers' comicstrip.) I have found much in these books of Fortean value, from the philosophies of life, phenomena and perception, down to the (subjective - or were they?) encounters with alternative realities in which Don Juan & colleague, Don Gennaro, could swim in the air, or teleport, or cause 'visions', or generate poltergeists and shadowy beings, and generally upset every notion we have of stability in the natural world.

Castaneda was a national hero before doubts began surfacing about his work. He kept himself a public enigma, and his mentor's whereabouts a secret; and yet many were impressed by the knowledge he was awarded his PhD on these field notes. The books almost screamed a huge paradox - they were fantastic, no doubt about it, and seemed like fiction; yet the details of shamanistic life and methods was impressively authentic. We know that the world hides surprises and so Don Juan's giggly nature, Don Gennaro's lavatory humour (these two loom in the books like the Laurel & Hardy of shamanism!), and Castaneda's portrayal of himself as a dull-witted and often reluctant pupil who frequently annoyed and amused his masters with ceaseless questioning and automatic note-taking, all this seems quite acceptable. Castaneda writes using the tricks of fiction to convey facts - my God! we are left thinking, if any of this is true, the world is completely different from all we have ever been taught! If it were true!

Some time ago Colin Wilson asked me why I thought Don Juan existed. I argued something along the lines that all his teachings seemed to conform to the description I had read of authentic shamanism; and that in another sense his real existence mattered as little as the historical Jesus, or the authorship of the Bible, say, because the problem in no way diminished the true value of their spirituality, or in this case, worldview. Now along comes De Mille with a beautiful book that should settle the question once and for all.

He talked to many of Castaneda's friends and colleagues and students from his UCLA days, including his wife; tracked down all the records on Castaneda; pieced together his amazingly enigmatic life; and performed a Herculean feat of analysis of the books. Castaneda emerges as a trickster-figure; a psychic visionary, a dissenting anthropologist, an original philosopher, a literary genius and perpetrator of a devastating hoax. It seems certain that the 'field notes' were written up in the UCLA library, and the professors who awarded him his degree on their brilliance and innovation (Castaneda had been hailed as the new model for anthropologists who try to 'get inside the head' of their victims) are now smarting under the knowledge that they had been played at their own game (ie impressing others with 'learning' - as De Mille says Castaneda took a gamble that they had not read all the books in their own libraries!) De Mille even identifies most of the sources of Don Juan's philosophy lectures - one of the major clues is that Don Juan (whom De Mille points out manifests two personalities, the shaman or 'Don Indian', and the university lecturer or 'Indian Don') nowhere hints at an exclusively Yaqui Indian teaching on sorcery despite the first book's subtitle of 'A Yaqui Way of Knowledge'. It is in the synthesis of the essence of these sources, gleaned from the mystical traditions of many cultures, that the true value of Castaneda's work lies.

But he has done more than merely write an interesting narrative of some anthropological studies and conclusions, he has, in De Mille's words, created a "modern myth, impervious to the puny assaults of sophisticated parodists, flying much too high to be brought to earth by proofs of fictioneering," and both Don Juan and Carlos are "destined to join the ranks of memorable teachers and tricksters, metamorphs and allegorists." De Mille's book is sheer delight, ranging from a perceptive understanding of Castaneda's need for allegory in his own life, to little gems like a reconstruction in Yaqui symbols of what their own account would be of a visiting hopheaded note-taker. De Mille has an eye for the bon mot and can match his subject for getting you giggling at his cleverness - and oh so well done too! This book will put a knowing smirk on your face. Get it somehow; by nagging your bookshop or sending to the address above. But is it all fact or fiction? The answer is an emphatic yes! If Don Juan never lived before, he lives now!
** RJM Rickard **

Atlantean Traditions in Ancient Britain by Anthony Roberts (Rider 1977; £2.95; pp120; index, bib, illustrated) -- Hopefully this reappearance of the 1975 Unicorn edition, under the imprint of a major publisher, will introduce Tony's writings and thought to the larger public he has long deserved. The is part of Tony's life-time project to recover the 'old traditions' of these isles, and traces the themes of fairies, the megaliths, and the mythology of archaic Wales, Ireland and Scotland. Tony's approach, which is quite different from the bankrupt von Daniken view of the origins of culture and which therefore may be a refreshing change to many readers, is firmly rooted in his passionate beliefs in the dynamic and poetic vision of William Blake's mystical Albion. * RJMR *

The Meaning of the Loch Ness Monster by Roger Grimshaw & Paul Lester (Contemporary Cultural Studies Center, Birmingham University, 1976; 25p; pp42; notes, bib) -- Basically a short study of the cultural roots of the Scottish (Celtic) monster phenomenon, society's need for 'monsters', and the age-old struggle of the 'entrepreneur' versus the scientific establishment. Where the authors stick to their (obvious) sociology backgrounds their observations seem well-founded, but their views of the subtle operations of the individualist and his motivations often seem quite naive - eg they see UFO "devotees" etc as trying to convince a "sceptical science of its errors and limitations," when fundamentally we are all trying to convince ourselves in the first place, with the function of one's colleagues being moral support. They also confuse the true meaning of 'sceptic' (as one who reserves belief for more convincing evidence) by using it in the sense of one who denies a phenomenon dogmatically if it conflicts with his worldview. However I'm sure they have a point when they say the monster mirrors in its elusiveness, its alienness, its animal nature yet with a supernatural element, its timelessness, and in its threat to the Establishment or Authority (as Science is popularly conceived) the psychic forces active in the minds of society's strata. This little paper is well-worth reading and reflecting upon, but lacks any real conclusion.

If their paper tells us (and them) anything it is that despite the grand social "superstructure", the monster is very much a living symbol of all the qualities that make us individuals. The typed booklet has a cover by Hunt Emerson. * RJMR *

Ancient Engineers by L Sprague de Camp (Tandem; £1.95; pp408; illos) - The Jupiter Effect by J Gribbin & S Plagemann (Fontana; 70p; pp156; illos) - The Curse of the Pharaohs by Philipp Vandenberg (Coronet; 70p; pp235) -- The most surprising aspect of De Camp's Ancient Engineers is that for a writer best known for imaginative fiction, the book should be so lacking in creative speculation. From the first line he clearly sees all the achievements of past civilisations as wholly or largely the direct result of engineering acumen. Practically no attempt is made to define the motivation behind the construction of those mysterious monuments. He dismisses inconvenient facts - eg the incredible precision invested in the Egyptian pyramids - implying that the mammoth enterprises were little more than passing diversions of their romantically caricatured originators. This, then, is a conventional assessment, using the time-honoured practice of viewing anomalous artifacts as ancient forerunners of contemporary objects (eg "4th century BC alarm clocks"). The book has some use as a historical reference.

The Jupiter Effect, on the other hand is much more stimulating and constructive - a truly scientific extrapolation of the possible causes of earthquakes. The authors have investigated solar 'explosions' (as distinct from sun-spots), 'tides' of energy that ripple through the body of the Sun, and even more interesting, the effect the positions of the planets seem to have on tectonic plates (jigsaw-like pieces of the continental masses). This results in the partial vindication of astrology, and even begins to confirm the age-old concept of universal 'oneness'. They contend that the gravity of the planets can and does exert an influence over the Sun, which in turn alters the magnetic field governing Earth's internal stability. These forces reach their height every 179 years when a major alignment, or conjunction, occurs. We are due for such an event in 1982 - heralding the house of Aquarius. If their theory concerning the amount of accumulated pressure under the San Andreas fault is correct, then the new age will come in with one hell of a fuss.

I found Curse of the Pharaohs a surprisingly informative and clearly expressed study, well researched and not reluctant to venture into seemingly unconnected fields to make a point. Since 1900, 30 people concerned with excavating the tombs of the Pharaohs have died in unsatisfactory, if not mysterious, circumstances. Indeed it seems that some kind of "Pharaoh's curse" can be seen operating over the last 150 years at least; its victims all involved in Egyptian funereal archeology. The main theories put forward include poison boobytraps, virulent germ 'time-capsules' (the tombs were found sealed airtight), and even the possibility that the Egyptians had discovered a uranium-type radioactive material (the undiagnosed fever that carried off most of the victims was in many ways consistent with radiation sickness.) There is a neat assessment of the synchronistic aspects, and a competent sketch of the (mathematical & archeological) "secrets of the pyramids. Vandenberg does not push any particular theory but leaves a lot to think on. An absorbing read. ** Stan Nicholls **

The Cult of the Fact by Liam Hudson (Cape 1976; £1.25; pp189; index, notes) - Unended Quest by Karl Popper (Fontana 1976; £1.00; pp255; index, bib, notes) -- Hudson, an Oxford philosopher, irreverently attacks the post-war trend of the 'Cult of the Fact' and reopens the Berkleyan enigma of what we can ever know of the world outside the limits of our own senses. He ends with a plea for the reexamination of the neglected Edwardian philosopher, FH Bradley - a man, we are just begining to appreciate, who paralleled Fort's vision

of an essentially unknowable universal
Continuity and Oneness. But whereas Fort
argued from phenomenal events, and Bradley from phenomenal experiences, Hudson
uses art and mysticism. The book is all
too short and left me wishing for more.
The limitations of sense-knowledge in
the 'Body-Mind Problem' are also discussed in Popper's book, but from his point
of view rooted in the 'world of facts'.
Popper is an objectivist and is so obviously at his best in analysis of 'things'.
This book is a retitled autobiography and
contains a representative collection of
essays on such themes, omniscience and
fallibility, music, knowledge, realism,
the Jewish problem, emigration, problems,
logic methods, time, and other exposit-
ions of his objective epistemology. A
good book to cut and sharpen your critical and philosophical teeth upon. *RJMR*

* Sasquatch by Don Hunter with Rene
  Dahinden (Signet 1975; $1.25) -
* The Search for Bigfoot: Monster,
  Myth or Man? by Peter Byrne & foreword by Robert Rines (Pocket Books
* 1976, $1.75) - Bigfoot by B Ann Slate
  & Alan Berry (Bantam Books 1976, 60p/
  $1.50) -- Bigfoot is America's Loch
Ness Monster, or so it seems from the
upsurge of interest in him/her/it over
the last few years. A number of books
have been published, of which these three
highlight different approaches to the
phenomenon.
      Sasquatch by Hunter and Dahinden -
the latter a Canadian adventurer who has
tracked Bigfoot for many years - details
sightings, including the best known cases
such as the capture of Jacko in 1884,
the Ostman kidnap of 1924, and the Patterson movie film of 1967. Dahinden describes his own search - he intends to
continue 'until one of these creatures is
collected dead or alive".
      Peter Byrne takes a more humanistic
approach. His The Search for Bigfoot details the founding of the Bigfoot Information Center in Oregon (Bigfoot territory), whose aim, as well as finding out
more about the creature, is to ensure
that it is not harmed in any way. The
arguments for and against 1) leaving it
alone, 2) shooting it, and 3) temporary
or permanent capture, are clearly set
out, together with sighting reports, with
special attention paid to the Patterson
film.
      Bigfoot by Slate and Berry reinfor-
ces the comparison between Bigfoot and
Nessie, for it seems the enigma has wider
dimensions than Byrne and Hunter/Dahind-
en indicate. Slate and Berry concentrate

on the more esoteric aspects of Bigfoot
encounters and quote some extraordinary
cases involving telepathy, hypnosis,
UFOs and attempted communication. Whatever Bigfoot might be, it is increasingly clear that he is not a mere apeman,
but yet another part of the massive
Fortean jigsaw.
** Janet Bord **

* The Ufonauts by Hans Holzer (Fawcett
  $1.75; pp304) - Project Blue Book
  Brad Steiger ed. (Ballantine/Futura;
  £1.00; pp423; photos) -- Personally,
the possibility of a 'non-material' solution to the UFO mystery is more plausible to me - but a strong argument can
still be made in favour of 'nuts-and-
bolts' origins for some sightings. Holzer's book, arguably, does the extraterrestrial lobby a disservice. Starting
from a strongly biased point of view,
and employing the gosh-wow brand of 'in-
vestigative' journalism beloved of sensational writers in the field, this is
basically the usual ragbag of semi-apo-
cryphal anecdotes. One for the "What
planet do you think they come from?"
crowd.
      It's difficult to know what to say
about Project Blue Book , the published
findings of years of "exhaustive" research into UFOs by US Airforce agencies;
it doesn't resolve anything either way.
It's a nice reference to have around,
and what a relief to have Steiger's
comments scattered in an otherwise pretty
indigestible lump of data. * S Nicholls *

* Is God Supernatural? by RL Dione
  (Bantam 1976; $1.50/50p; pp162; in-
* dex) - UFOs: What On Earth is Happening? by J Weldon & Z Levitt (Bantam 1976; $1.50; pp175; notes) -- After
all the heavily materialist, reduction-
ist, and 'salvation-from-the-stars' approaches to UFOs, the religious backlash
was inevitable. Dione examines Biblical
'miracles' in the rather fanciful light
of UFOs, taking a swipe at conventional
physics and evolution on the way. By
thus providing a rationale for the more
absurd miracles (eg parting the Red Sea)
which in his view are the traditional
obstacles preventing widespread acceptance of the Bible, Dione is convinced he
has refuted the last-ditch criticism of
vain scepticism. An interesting appendix
contains two short papers on anomalous
gravity effects on spinning objects.
      Dione, and the authors of What on
Earth is Happening? suffer from the same
'fault' - their zeal and faith . The
latter book covers the greater ground -

the antichrist, UFOs, demons, the occult renaissance, parapsychology, prophets, etc etc are all seen as part of a vast plot by Satan leading to the final stage before the Second Coming of Christ. Weldon & Levitt believe this implicitly; yet despite their marshalling and interpretation of evidence, each reader must make his own final leap of faith. The Bible must rank as one of the greatest of revealed books - but I'm worried when the criteria for rejecting such 'revealed' classics as Oahaspe, and Urantia (received in 'trance' & allegedly authored by 'non-humans') is that they contradict certain interpretations of the Bible, which are accepted as orthodox. Not a word is said about, say, the Book of Mormon or the Koran, also revealed by angels and upon which great religions have been founded. Nearly every point in these books is argued in exclusion - as though no thought, writing, act or art anywhere else in the world had any meaning whatsoever except in that it agrees or disagrees with the opinions of these rather extreme Fundamentalists. Time is running out, they say, for you to turn to Christ! Doubtless this will comfort many who are confused about today's occult chaos - but my karma is a doubting and inquiring mind; I do not reject science or religion, but I do have a right to question it and make up my own mind. As far as these books are concerned they are telling you what to think - and I question that as I do any self-proclaimed authority. This book also has interesting appendices: on the Biblical view of UFO occupants and on life on other worlds. * RJMR *

Satan and Swastika by Francis King (Mayflower 1976; 75p; pp288; index) Occult Reich by JH Brennan (Futura; 60p; pp188; bib) - An Occult History of the World vol 1 by JH Brennan (Futura 1976; 90p; pp320; index, bib)- The fascinating subject of occultism in modern warfare is complex and confusing and the casual reader is in dire need of guidance. Occult Reich is an adequate introduction for those who do not wish to take the subject any further - but King's book covers the same ground in more detail and is a good begining for the more critical reader. Both books, in the wake of Pauwels & Bergier's Dawn of Magic, outline the relationship of Nazi occultism to such diverse movements as

the Golden Dawn, the Thule group, the Theosophists etc; though, as I said, only King, of the two, can be said to have explored the subject. Brennan's Occult History of the World is also regrettably shallow - volume 1 dealing with planetary evolution up to "prehistory" in the light of the teachings of various occult cosmologies. He presents a summary of the scientific view, then some of the mysteries they fail to satisfactorily account for, and then launches into his notion of "Occult Prehistory". Anyone expecting the intricacies, scholarship and insight of, say, Trevor Ravenscroft, will be disappointed. But for all its glibness and tendancy to generalisation, it's a reasonable introduction to a neglected subject. * RJMR *

Also received:
The Dragon Malcolm Smith ed (Wild wood House; £2.50; pp104) - welcome large format reprint of chapters from Charles Gould's Mythical Monsters (1886). Illos.
Pyramid Energy Handbook by SV King (Warner/Wyndahm (UK); 85p; pp192; photos)
Pyramid Power by M Toth & G Neilson (Warner/Wyndham (UK); 75p; pp257; index bib, illos) - more "use the pyramid power to sharpen your razorblades" than archeological books.
The Tungus Event by Rupert Furneaux Panther; 60p; pp128; photos)
Tunguska: Cauldron of Hell by Jack Stoneley. (Star Books; 75p; pp198; bib, photos) - both originals about the June 1908 mystery explosion presenting the usual variety of explanations; the latter concentrating on the 'space visitor' hypothesis.
The Pursuit of Destiny by MB Hasbrouck (Warner/Wyndham (UK); 75p; pp302) - reprint of a work from 1941 on a sophisticated divination method using both astrology and the Tarot. Para-astrology?
My Story by Uri Geller (Corgi 1977; 85p; pp285; index, photos) - nothing that has not been covered by the other books on Geller, except this time it's in his own words, with more emphasis on his personal life than his 'powers'.
The Piltdown Man by Ronald Millar (Paladin; 75p; pp271; index, bib, illos) For such a modest price you get a ringside seat at the 'Evolution Circus' featuring the most far-reaching scientific scandal in modern times, starring really big-names in archæology & palaeontology who have been profoundly embarrassed by a fraud that passed among them for 41 years without detection, polarising prematurely opinions on the 'Missing Link'.

Now in paperback:

The Bermuda Triangle, & The Mystery of Atlantis both by Charles Berlitz (Panther; 75p; bib, illos).

Parapsychology & the Nature of Life by John L Randall (Abacus; £1.75; pp256; index, refs, photos).

Beyond Stonehenge by Gerald S Hawkins (Arrow; £2.50; pp319; photos, index, bib)

The Black Arts by Richard Cavendish (Picador; £1.25; pp414; index, bib)

Laser Beams from Star Cities? by Robin Collyns (Sphere; 75p; pp144; bib, photos)

The Unknown Power by Guy Lyon Playfair (Panther; 95p; pp332; index, bib, photos) Retitle of The Flying Cow.

JOURNALS

INFO Journal 22 (Mar 77) - study of an Irish lake monster; recent poltergeists; archeo-oddities; the McCarthy pond mystery and Bigfoot notes - the best balanced issue under the new team. INFO: 7317 Baltimore Ave, College Park, MD 20740, USA -- 6 issues/year $10.00/ £5.00. Joint sub with FT: $14.00/£7.00/ year. Payable to FT or INFO.

Fate April 77 - life after death; who wrote Book of Mormon?; psychic surgery update; Larry Arnold's SHC of Dr Bentley; psychometry; & more.

Pursuit Winter 77 - the Ohio Airship story (1897); prehistoric megalithic engineering; cattle mutilations; vile vortices continued. SITU: Columbia, NJ 07832 USA. Write for details.

Anomaly Research Bulletin (ARB) 5 - tracking bigfoot; profile of a UFOlogist; Fortean chronology project; Forteana. ARB: $3.00/£1.50 (6 issue/year) to Dave Fideler: 7098 Edinburgh, Lambertville, Michigan 48144, USA.

Lantern Spring 77 - the Bury zodiac; a 1913 mystery airship; a Fakenham haunting; a water-walking death-omen ghost; E Anglian Forteana; the luminous owl of Hellesdon; voice in the night; & more. BSIG: 3 Dunwich Way, Oulton Broad, Lowestoft NR32 4RZ.

The Ley Hunter 75 - earth currents; magic mounds & fairies; photo study of the leys that cross on the site of Mrs Bowles' Winchester CE-III (see FSR); the Avebury cycle; ghost lights; Firle Down. 76 - the Bimini road; magic mounds & fairies; a Lough Gur, Co Limerick, alignment, images in stone; standing stones in Japan. £2.00/$4.00/year; or available as a joint sub with FT, £4.50/$9.00, payable to FT or TLH: Box 152, London N10 1EP.

Journal of Meteorology March, April, May 77 (V2, nos 17-19) - continuing discussions, papers and reports on ice-falls, St Elmo's fire, coloured rains, weather anomalies, lightnings, whirlwinds, hail, etc etc. Its scientific approach makes the going hard, but worthwhile, for the Fortean interested in meteorological freaks etc. £6.50/$16.00. J Met: Cockhill House, Trowbridge, Wiltshire BA14 9BG.

MUFOB (Metempirical UFO Bulletin) Spring 77 - case for humanoids; sociology of UFO reporting; schematic chart of UFOlogy. MUFOB: £1.25/$3.00 (4/yr): 11 Beverley Rd, New Malden, Surrey KT3 4AW.

Flying Saucer Review 22-5 (1976) - published in Feb 77 - see, we're not the only one who have schedule problems! -- 3 articles on Mrs Bowles' encounter with a silver-suited entity near Winchester (see also TLH) UFOs & animal mystery deaths; UFO physics; Italian close-encounter; UFOlogist as counsellor & healer; UFO in Australia; etc. FSR goes up to 70p an issue, £4.20/$9.00/year. FSR: West Malling, Maidstone, Kent.

Because of lack of space, reviews of some magazines (including The Zetetic) are held over to next issue.

*** NEXT ISSUE -- mystery deaths of animals; holes; randy wraiths; mystery illnesses; and articles on the Gt Pyramid, and strange clouds; and hopefully a real scoop with some monster pix ***

FORTEAN TIMES

strange phenomena - curiosities - prodigies - portents - mysteries

MORGAWR, MORAG; photos, p18/23

best NESSIE photos yet! – p24/5

75p : $1·50

22

UK ISSN 0308 5899

FORTEAN TIMES

A Contemporary Record
of Strange Phenomena

BOX 152, LONDON N10 1EP, ENGLAND.

FORTEAN TIMES is a non profitmaking quarterly miscellany
of news, notes and references on current and historical strange
phenomena, related subjects and philosophies. Formerly 'The
News'. Affiliated to the International Fortean Organisation
(INFO), and the Society for the Investigation of The Unknown
(SITU), and other Fortean journals in continuing the work of
Charles Fort (1874-1932).

Edited and published by Robert JM Rickard.
Contributing editors: Phil Ledger, Steve Moore, Stan Nichols,
Paul J Willis. Heading art by Hunt Emerson.

SUBSCRIPTION information and details of other deals can be
found on the back page.

CONTRIBUTIONS of articles, artwork, notes and letters-of-
comment on related subjects are always welcome. **YOU CAN
HELP** by sending us a copy or clipping of any item you think
will interest FT readers — just add a note of the DATE, the
SOURCE and your NAME (for the credit). All clippings go on
file to be published in due course. Please don't assume we
must know about it already — there are surprisingly few
duplications.
The editor regrets that it is not always possible to reply to all
correspondence. Acknowledgements of money received will
be sent via the following issue of FT.

RIGHTS: All articles and artwork in FORTEAN TIMES are
the copyright of the authors and artists. The views of contributors are not necessarily those of FT, and vice versa.
Uncredited material is by the editors.

SUMMER 1977

MONSTERS IN THE BUSH!
A few weeks ago my phone rang...it
was Ken Campbell with some crazy scheme
to meet Doc Shiels (our Cornish monster
maniac) and have him star as Orson Welles
in a dramatization of Keel's Mothman
Prophecies...something like that! Well
Ken went to Cornwall to meet Doc, and
together they hatched a burlesque which
will boggle your brains. To be called
evocatively, Distant Humps, it chronicles
Doc's encounters with UFOs, witches,
fairies, Morgawr & Nessie (see p18),
the ominous Owlman of Mawnan, and Norman,
who bequeathed Doc the entire universe
(except this Earth, which is owned by
the Americans, Norman said). If you
can't imagine that, you'll have difficulty with the fact that Doc's talented
family (including the dogs) also appear
in it - as does Illuminatus! veteran,
Chris Fairbank. The evening's song, dance and stories will warp space/time around
the Shepherd's Bush Theatre, London, from
6 September 1977. Watch your papers for
programme details. Who said Fortean
music-hall was dead...

TRUSS FUND...
We gratefully acknowledge kind don-
ations from the following: Larry Arnold,
Lionel Beer, DI Baxter, Curtis Carlson,
Mrs Phyllis Dixon, Mrs V Martin, Olive
Oltcher.

TLH ANNIVERSARY
Our congratulations go to editor
Paul Devereux and his small but devoted
team on our sister mag, The Ley Hunter,
which is a year old in its new format,
and which has nearly doubled its circulation in that time. Keep it up, lads!
TLH prices have gone up recently, so
check our journal review section, and
our own panel (on p40) for latest rates.

UFOs & MUFOB & FT
Even with 40 pages at our disposal
we are finding problems fitting what we
would like to have each issue. UFO data
presents particular problems for us in
that modern ufology has become a whole
new field with its own complexities. We
have long admired and supported the excellent work of John Rimmer, Peter Rogerson and Roger Sandell, the main core
of the Metempiric UFO Bulletin, and
publicly proclaim it to be a worthy
sister mag to FT. Since we get more than
we can immediately print in all categories of Forteana, we will from now on
pass on all our UFO and related material
to the team at MUFOB, and urge you to
take out a subscription to it (see our
journal reviews for details). Naturally
Fortean implications of UFO data will
continue to be discussed in these pages
and we still welcome clippings on the
subject - we'll copy and pass them on.

Polter-Ghosts

It is some time since our last round up of sexy spectres (NEWS 12/22). The following have appeared in our files since then: we select only those stories having either acknowledged sexual overtones, and those in which the percipient actually _felt_ the ghost's touch. The more 'mundane' bedroom phantoms, whose intentions remain unproved, have been exorcised from this listing, and will appear at a later date.

Among the stories in our file it is noticeable that the great majority feature female percipients and male ghosts. There may be some social and metaphysical significance to this, which may also apply to all forms of sexual encounter with the 'supernatural', but this notion will have to await further research. For the moment, we merely present the data...

UNCANNY UNION

Tales in which the percipient actually achieves union with a ghostly partner, i.e., in which the ghost has an apparent physical reality, though very common in folklore and tradition, rarely figure in modern accounts. We have but one to hand currently, and that is somewhat apocryphal. _The Sun_, 18 Apr 74, reporting an appeal by the Institute of Psychophysical Research, Oxford, for personal ghost stories, has the following, without names or details: A young man met a girl who moved in with him, "was the perfect partner" for a few days, and then disappeared. When he searched for her, he found she had died the day before he met her. No further details.

GHOSTLY BED-PARTNERS

Normanton, Notts: The Hallam family, Peter, Mary and their daughters Rebecca,21, and Frances, 16, and son Tom,13, living in a 16th century farmhouse, appear to share the premises with a family of ghosts. The men of the family have seen the ghosts of an elderly couple. Another ghost, unseen except as a light in the shape of a person (but presumably male) reserves his attention for the ladies. After merely sitting on their mother's bed, he turned a more passionate attention to the daughters of the house. Frances, just going to sleep, heard heavy breathing; then the sheets were lifted off, and 'someone' got into bed beside her and put his arm round her waist. This then slithered down the bed and left at the foot. After that, she was regularly followed upstairs to bed. Rebecca also heard heavy breathing and sighing, but in her case the ghost remained outside the bed: bumping at the foot and then pressing on her feet and thighs, feeling like an animal crawling up the bed. She has also had her bottom slapped by the ghost in broad daylight. The occurrences began in June 1975, and we have no record of their ending, although Peter Hallam was calling in a team of psychic investigators. Interestingly, the phenomena peak at the full moon. (D.Mirror, 7th Sept, 76, _Sun_, 25 Feb, 77).

Newcastle, Staffs is the current address of Mrs S Fernyhough, though it is unclear where she was living at the time of the incident about which she wrote to the _Sun_, 22 Dec 76 (Cr:V Martin). When she was 14, she slept in the same room as her sister, and one night felt someone get into her bed and cuddle close. When she realised it was not her sister, she went cold and her hair stood on end. Whereupon she jumped out of bed and got in with her sister. The incident was not, apparently, repeated.

PHANTOM FONDLERS

Newtown Burgoland, Leics: The Belper Arms public house has a ghost known as Fred (presumably a nickname), who is most active when alterations are being made to the building. He first appeared some years ago, when the previous landlord was pulling down an ancient staircase in the 12th century inn, and is believed to be buried at the site of an old well close by. Young ladies, both bar-staff and customers, have their bottoms pinched or patted by Fred; a seemingly not unpleasant experience, as they frequently return for more. More mature ladies find themselves tapped on the shoulder, the notion being that Fred wants them to turn round so he can size them up. Men, on the other hand, feel a phantom hand over their nose and mouth, can't breathe, and have to rush out into the open air, sometimes having to get beyond the old well before they can breathe freely once more. Fred doesn't seem to like men much...but he did take a special liking to Janet Owen, of Ward End, Birmingham, 30 miles away. He followed her home one night after she left the pub, and appeared at the foot of her bed for a few seconds, before fading away in a misty haze. He was described as pale, with dark hair, wearing a high-collared jacket, and having glazed eyes. There's got to be a joke in that somewhere...(News of the World, 21 Dec 75, The Sun, 25 Feb, 77).

Austin, Texas: Miss A Guerrero writes to Fate (No 322, Jan 77) requesting advice. She and her sister bought a house in 1965, and made several alterations. At about 10pm, June 24, 1972, she was in the kitchen when her buttocks were slapped, first on the right side, then on the left. Since then she has frequently felt a 'presence' in the kitchen, and avoids it after 10pm. Her sister is not affected by the phenomenon.

Roldanillo, Colombia: we end this section with a curiosity that is tantalisingly short of detail. 16-year-old Maria Elena Vazquez was apparently the object of attention of something which ripped a crucifix from her bedroom wall, attacked her, tore her pajamas to shreds, mysteriously marked her school books and left behind a knife, vase, and shoe. A Roman Catholic priest blessed her room, but it's uncertain whether he carried out the full Catholic rite. A local newspaper, 'El Occidente' carried out a 2-day investigation, and blamed the attacks on a lesbian maid...which has originality, if nothing else...(Atlanta Journal & Constitution, 8 Feb 76. Cr:M Hall)

SPECTRAL SPOILSPORTS

The other side of the coin naturally turns up too: ghosts which seem to take exception to normal human sex. Rather than being impartial guardians of morality, however, they tend to have a close personal connection with either the percipient or the place, as the following examples show...

London (?): We note briefly another anonymous case, from an article on Spiritualism (D. Mirror 24 Mar 77). A 21-year-old girl had rented a flat in a Victorian mansion, and experienced almost nightly hauntings for 6 months, especially when she was alone in the flat with a man. Men were tipped out of bed in the middle of the night, and suggestive meter-readers had their record-books hurled downstairs. A seance was held, at which the medium identified the ghost as a former serving girl in the house, who did not want sex performed before the young baby she had before she was murdered. The medium's Guide was said to have led the ghost to the 'other side'.

Kensington, London: Frank Scott-Elliot's ghost was regular, if nothing else, calling on him every Tuesday and Friday at 3.48am. Named Helen, she was supposed to have been a servant in the house containing Frank's flat, 100 years previously, who killed herself over a love affair. As a ghost, she was jealous of other women in the place, and would knock on the door at her usual time. If Frank had company and didn't get up to let her in, tape-recorders and television sets would begin to fly round the room. Frank finally decided to have the flat exorcised, which was duly done in 1968. Although the disturbances stopped, Frank then got into a run of bad luck: he lost the flat, his private investigation business, boat and car, and is now homeless and on the dole; his girl-friend died from an accidental overdose of sleeping pills, and when he eventually married, he parted from his wife after 3 months. He blames it on Helen being jealous that he's no longer around, and he may be right..,but if she's no longer around either..? (News of the World, 14 Nov 76).

London: Tonia Campbell, widow of speed-record breaker Donald Campbell, claims that her late husband is still around to give her advice, particularly, it seems, in partnership matters. He has been known to appear at the foot of the bed and give a 'thumbs down' signal to her current partner. One can only wonder if any man, or ghost, in such a position would give a thumbs up...(Unidentified news cutting; & Sun, 25 Feb 77)

Pluckley, Kent has a reputation as Britain's most haunted village, and has 13 ghosts to prove it...it also has at least 13 broken marriages from the last few years. Locals blame it on spectral interference, though there seems to be no direct evidence of a connection. But in a village that numbers the Screaming Man amongst its spectral inhabitants, perhaps its not surprising there's a little tension in the air...

FOLLOW-UPS

Worksop, Notts: Readers concerned for the honour of Beryl Gladwin (See News 12/22 for encounter with an amorous, booted ghost) may relax, for a while, at least. The latest news we have (Sun, 25 Feb, 77) is that the aggressively caressive spectre has been driven off by the willpower of clairvoyant Simon Alexander. He is, however, expected to return..!

Charlton, London: The story of Sir William Langhorne, another supposed astral rapist, and the questionable foundations of the tale, have been discussed before (NEWS 12/22, 14/20). A couple of things have come up since then. In 1973 (at about the time when the

Langhorne tale seems to have been taking its current shape) a movie was made called "...And now the Screaming Starts!", in which the ghost of a nobleman rapes the wife of his descendant. The movie was based on the novel 'Fengriffen' by David Case. While we can find no evidence of a connection, the juxtaposition in time is interesting.

Even ghosts, alas, are subject to exploitation, and old Will Langhorne is no exception. In an obvious publicity stunt, the local council's entertainments officer, Dennis White, organising the annual Greenwich Festival, arranged a midnight ghost hunt at Charlton House, and took out a £3-million insurance policy against any visitor dying of fright at the appearance of Langhorne...a fairly certain way of making the papers. (Evening News (London) 27 Apr,77; Kentish Independent 5 May 77) As nothing more has been heard, we can only assume that old Will showed a proper disdain for the proceedings.

letters-letters-letters-letters

AIRSHIP HOAX

From Lucius Farrish, Arkansas:
Having finally had a chance to read your article on the 1897 airship hoax in FT20, I thought I would drop you a few lines to add a comment or two.

First, although all of us hate to 'lose' what appeared to be one of the more reliable airship accounts from the 1896-97 period, I, for one, am glad to have the case cleared up. As you know, I have been rather closely involved with it over the years, so I feel a responsibility for having given it a measure of publicity in various articles. Although I obviously did not know the true nature of the incident until Jerry Clark's recent investigations, I would like to offer my apology for inadvertantly misleading the readers of my articles in Fate, FSR and other publications.

Cont on p33...

We begin the first of 3 extracts from ABLAZE! The Case for, and Cases of, Spontaneous Human Combustion, a forthcoming book by Larry E Arnold. This part examines a correlation between pyrophenomena and Ley Lines; part 2 looks closer at these fire 'leynes'; & pt 3 will focus on the 'Binbrook Triangle' in East Anglia...

FIRE LEYNES

by LARRY E ARNOLD

HUNT EMERSON

Charles Fort postulated that our data relates "not to 'spontaneous combustion of human bodies', but to things or beings, that, with a flaming process, consume men and women." (1)

Research for ABLAZE! has revealed some curious incidents of beings (human or otherwise)and the fires to which they subject others. In this highly abridged article, however, we shall examine the other category mentioned by the avatar of the Unwelcomed - the nature and effect of "things" on weird combustions.

A BEVY OF BAFFLING BLAZES AROUND BIRMINGHAM.

Unknown to its residents, England's Midlands was preparing to engage in a series of sinister searings in the early 1970s. Things were about to get pretty 'hot' in the bustling city of Birmingham for firemen (who are trained to determine the origin of fires), for coroners (who are employed to ascertain the precise cause of a person's death), and for some of the people living there.

8 April 1973: John McRory is the victim of "accidental death" from a fire for which "no definite cause" can be found (3).

20 October 1973: Octogenarian William McLeod is found in a fire-damaged room in Nechells, Birmingham; no mention of how much--or how little--damage is done to the death chamber itself (3). On 26 October we learn that an 18-year-old patient at Birmingham's All Saints hospital is shrouded in flames, her bed found smouldering. She was taken to the Burns Unit. Matches are suspected, but no one wants to go on record as to why the victim became a "flaming torch"(3). On 28 October one is told about 23-year-old Diane Mold running across her yard in flames; she too goes to the Burns Unit. It is "believed" she fell on hot coals, revived in time to rip off the burning clothing and don a coat before making a dash for help; it is not stated whether Miss Mold agrees with this scenario (3).

In a corner of the Kaur living room sits 7-month old Parvinder in his pram; both are ablaze. The child is rushed to the Burns Unit while the fire officials concern themselves with the origin of this disaster. They come up with nothing, save that "kids could have been playing with matches". The matches, if there were any, are either magical or the victims of another phenomenon (teleportation): they disappear so the investigators can't find them! (4).

One week later the same Burns Unit is treating the fire-damaged legs and feet of Mark Bradbury, who slept through much of the destruction to his own body. "No specific cause was found and identified" for the blaze(4).

One begins to think that a physician or aide, interested in cyclical events, might have made a mental notation to be on the lookout for more baffling burns come October (six months away). What he would have found next was not a half-year interim, but a six-month old victim!

The Birmingham Evening Mail (26 Aug, 1974) notes that Lisa Tipton died in a fire limited to one room of her parents' house in Highfields, Staffordshire. Despite a strained attempt, no cause for the fire that singled out the young child for its havoc was identified.(3).

The next seasonal cycle of Birmingham's baffling blazes burst forth a month ahead of schedule, just barely making the advent of Spring...

Sunday Mercury: 23 March 1975: William Cashmore, 82, dies the previous day in his home at Autumn Close, High Heath, Walsall, just north of Birmingham. (One muses at the paradox of Fate, where the beginning of Spring brought combustion to Autumn Close!) All appliances were in working order, said the investigators. What they couldn't say was how the fire began, and why it limited itself to burning Cashmore's clothing and one chair. To those who might yet reject SHC as being real (a dubious word to Forteans, but we don't know what else to substitute), choosing to claim an external fire from cigarettes or matches is first necessary, put this in your mental pipe and smoke it: "he was a non-smoker"(5).

We look for the unconventional.

Unless our data is incomplete, and well it might be (though we have neither selected nor solicited evidence to fit a pattern), we find a roughly semi-annual periodicity of inexplicable (at the least, unusual) fires around Birm-

ingham, England, during the last few years.

This observation leads one to speculate that the weird outbreaks of flames are related. If so, how? What force would focus on this city to unite 8 people in a personal yet strangely shared holocaust?

LINES OF FORCE AND POINTS OF POWER.

A few years ago, while experiencing contact with a higher level of awareness, we encountered the phrase "lines of force". In that moment so many things that had heretofore eluded our grasp now came together. As with a briefly lit room, it would take years, maybe decades, to explore that unexpected revelation. That night was the beginning of a new journey for us; we'd like to share part of that trip's results here...

We began looking for support... or non-support, if the other wasn't forthcoming...for the concept that lines of force traverse the universe and, consequently, the Earth, to create zones of particular energy patterns conducive to various groups of manifestations and phenomena. An original idea, we thought.

Alas, our thinking was wrong (Whose is always correct?)

In the American Southwest 'footpaths' extended for miles in straight lines over hills and across valleys, and seem to have lead nowhere. The Nazca Plain in Peru hosts lines so straight that a modern-day surveyor emeritus with laser beams would be hard-pressed to duplicate them. Great Britain as every reader of FT must know, is blanketed with alignments noted by Watkins (6) and Michell (7) and others.

(We suggest that 30 June 1921, the day when Watkins sensed the ley system from the Bredwardine Hills, will become an international holiday when its significance is more fully appreciated. But we digress into a New Age science...)

Despite opposition and denials from the Establishment, belief in and evidence for a grid of unseen energy transmission continues to grow. But to some, the 'invisible' is removed from a mathematical exercise with cartography and, instead, is witnessed during clairvoyant transcendance. Alice Cooke speaks of seeing the luminous "Trackway" at several megalithic sites(8). Mrs Paul Screeton 'saw' a "streak of white light" later identified with a ley alignment(9). This ability for remote viewing, discomforting though it may be to some, is an ability now scientifically documented (10).

Ah, the progress since the days of Charles Fort...

Charges that Britain is subjected to some kind of mass hysteria that causes people to see lines through everything, are weakened when one encounters the same reports from cultures and geographies far removed. For instance, Carlos Castaneda, studying for years with the Mexican sorcerer Don Juan, was told to "stop the world" on 14 April 1962 and look across a valley at a mountain range. It was the typical desert landscape of Northern Mexico, thought Castaneda, until "flourescent white lines flashed into his vision and across the terrain. Said Castaneda, profoundly moved, "I could see the whole range of mountains as an intricate array of light fibers."(11).

Differing only in its location and arrangement, this was otherwise the same revelation of the radiant web of the world that Watkins had grasped more than 3 decades earlier.

On less clear-cut similarities, intra- and interdisciplinary studies (like Comparative Religion, for example) have become scholastically respectable...

Apart from seeing linear luminosity upon the landscape, there is evidence of a different sort found in the literature. That ley lines are not determined by mere architectural happenchance but chart transmissions of some energy is confirmed both indirectly... else, why should geometrical alignments pulse with flourescent radiance seen by Watkins and others? ...and directly.

John G Williams (7), Desmond Leslie (12), the author, and others have reported inexplicable columns of light appearing on film exposed at certain megalithic sites. The noted explorer Dr David D Zink told us about a diver's photograph taken off Bimini Island that shows "a column from whose base a beam of energy flares 15 degrees each side of the vertical. This energy was...invisible to the naked eye". Afterwards the diver experienced abnormal ailments (13).

Screeton goes so far as to propose, not without foundation, that certain stones "acted as boosters' in some way"(9) Boosters for what? Energy, it would seem. Our only disagreement with Screeton here is his use of the past tense, for it seems several sites still channel and discharge unexpected forces. We will dispense with enumerating support for this statement, on the belief that the reader has already encountered the necessary facts (Cf. 2,14,27).

Surely the immense undertaking of establishing straight lines over hill-and-dale, of siting buildings and indefensible earthworks upon or within angles formed by 'invisible' trackways, and the repeated discovery of altered streams, man-made ponds and holy wells in alignment, not to mention the logistics of constructing artificial islands having minimal military value, would lead one to conclude....even were there no substantiation from individuals' transcendant awareness...that much more than mere faith was at work here. Our ancestors must have been dealing with forces and principles as real to them as electricity and gasoline are to a Londoner today.

Additionally, since people are still seeing the luminous grid and being shocked by its discharge through standing stones (16), one concludes that, not withstanding Science's ignorance, leys (or something similarly mysterious) must yet be affecting life on the surface of the Earth.

How?

One can postulate four theories about the nature of ley energy: 1) there is none; 2) it is a known force, such as electromagnetism or aqueous currents, designated and manipulated by natural objects; 3) it is etheric in form, exceeding the boundaries of current physics; 4) it is a combination of the last two. Again without going into several columns of published comment, we assert the first theory can be discounted, and permit the reader to select his preference among the remainder (Cf.17).

Each of those postulates

prompts another question: How far out does their influence extend? Again, there is disagreement (perhaps, instead, only various aspects of an ungrasped truth). We note by use of an analogy, though, that if one stands beneath the current-carrying cables of high-voltage electrical lines and holds a flourescent lamp, the electric field radiating from 30 meters overhead is quite capable of lighting the lamp. Says one American scientist about the dangers of close proximity to high-voltage cables: "The point at which a light bulb in your hand is turned on is the point at which you are too close". We wonder what sort of manifestations provide a warning about ley proximity: "The point at which a living organism is combusted is the point at which you are too close"? Hmm...

One must also ask whether leys are planar, and relegated to the surface of the Earth. Might not a blind spring, for example, have a third dimension...penetration... that allows it to enter deep into the planet or, indeed, into the heavens to withdraw or impart and mix with the energies beyond the first few feet of the terrestrial surface? That is, blind springs and other ley-like phenomena can become, in essence, zones of vortex energy.

Vortices are known to produce weird and unexpected effects on humans (18); a regularised magnetic field flows toward a centre(7); gravity can possibly be focused at such points (Cf 19). Physiological processes are altered in these regions. One's emotions will change as well in such a field and as we show in ABLAZE!, one's mental attitude is linked both to the performance of one's physiology and the geographic environment in which one resides, and to one's physical transition...of which SHC is one mode.

Thus while many have seen or felt these lines of force, their points of power and the accompanying "zone phenomena" (as Fort called it), we believe we are the first to propose...though our limited awareness may be misleading ...that lines of force are a contributing factor in the production of another little-understood force: SHC. Let us proceed...

GRASPING FOR THE SECRETS OF THE UNTOUCHABLE.

Was Mr Cashmore's death by localised fire in Birmingham in late March 1975 an early prelude to another semi-annual cycle of mysterious fires, as indicated by the 2 previous years? Or is the information incomplete, thereby leading one to postulate a periodicity when in fact abnormal fires occur all year long in this Midlands city of 1,115,000 people?

Arguments could defend either view at this moment. As all honorable scientists do, however, we shall limit ourselves to theories based on the available data, subject of course to alteration when additional facts indicate such is necessary. The conclusion at this stage of research indicates a 6-month periodicity for bizarre blazes in Birmingham.

This regularity, though, would result from what?

Possibly it is due to variations in the relationships between the heavenly bodies and Earth's biosphere. After all, it's known that the strength and direction of this planet's magnetic current "varies according to certain phases of the Sun and Moon"(7). Severe perturbations in the geomagnetic flux have a correlation with Fortean phenomena in general (22), and SHC specifically (23). Additional unpublished work with astrology (or, if one must remain respectable, astrogeobiodynamics) supports an interaction between the planets of this solar system and fiery combustions on Earth.

Woe to those who insist that everything is isolated unto itself. (Fort's Organic Universe of Oneness shall one day triumph in the minds of men...for it already Is.)

Dowsers also find a plethora of fluctuations in energies of the Earth Spirit that elude Orthodoxy (24), with Underwood cataloguing a horde of "water line spirals", "geospirals", etc., that varied with astronomical positions (17).

Amid all this jargon, we hesitate to complicate matters or offend personal preferences by lumping all this into the Ley concept. Watkins' use of "ley" has been generally adopted to refer to the Earth's surface energy grid. As hinted earlier, however, we see a network not limited to one level but functioning on innumerable planes both above and below so-called Terra Firma.

To facilitate matters and to differentiate between the various aspects in the line-of-force concept, we digress to propose the following etymology: that telleynes (telluric ley lines of force) define surface and subterranean energy flows, while aerleynes (aerial ley lines of force) define atmospheric energy transmission paths.

Armed with a new vocabulary, we return to our examination of fluctuation in the Earth Spirit and learn that telleynes vary in polarity as well as strength (17, 9); geography is again involved (17). Folklore and clairvoyance (20) also support the assertion that the global energy grid and particularly power points fluctuate, in response not only to cosmic influences but cycles within the planet itself.

Therefore, an interconnection is found between astronomy, celestial mechanics, geography, and telleynes and aerleynes. It would seem the lines of force, or the angles formed by the ley grid around Birmingham, are activated...as far as pyrophenomena are concerned ...by forces focused upon telluric powers within, during the planet's revolution about the Sun.

The skeptic at this point would argue, "Well if this is so, then Birmingham should have been having weird fires every six months for decades, even centuries. Surely this would have been noted! Since I've seen nothing in print about it, therefore it can't exist and the whole contention is without foundation!"

Let us assure the reader, as the (New York) Sun did with Virginia when she asked about a Santa Claus, that just because denial is stated by someone doesn't establish the non-existence of the phenomenon. SHC itself is a pertinent case in point: we could fill an issue of FT with quotes denying its occurrence...but they won't explain away the many photographs we have that speak differently. Many things go unnoticed, as Forteans already know; a collective ignorance, if you will. Apples fell for

millenia, but until Newton postulated the force behind the event, gravity was unknown. A city's fire department, responding to calls every day of the year, might easily miss the significance associated with a small number of scattered blazes. It wouldn't be the first time that important discoveries have been obscured by a deluge of data...

Yet in the attempt to locate the causative force(s) behind pyrophenomena in a ley-like system, our hypothetical skeptic raises a valid point. Maybe Birmingham shouldn't be expected to have a semi-annual outbreak of enigmatic blazes stretching back into the mists of remembrance. The relocation of megalithic sites occured when the "magic had gone out of the place", say legends; Michell quotes no less (or more) a sage than Plutarch on the "cyclical" alterations of "the powers that are associated with the earth"(25). Therefore, the city of Birmingham may have been largely free of mysterious fires until the 7th decade of the 20th century, when a telluric point of a combustible nature either changed its geographic domain or increased the power of its flow to plague the industrial centre with an unsuspected and previously unencountered assemblage of unusual and inexplicable blazes.

A telluric point of a combustible nature, did he say?

INSIGHTS INTO TELLEYNE COMBUSTIONS

Alfred Watkins' son, Allen, believed the 4 Classic Elements played a role in the planet's life -flow: earth, air, water, and fire The ley system is filled with documented accounts of healings, trascendant awareness, levitation, uncanny phenomena, ominous sensations, fires...

Fires?

Yes. There are hints, curious ones (14); observations, fortunately recorded, about melted stones at megalithic sites (26) (we recall the vitrified stones at Castle Urquhart at Loch Ness, where the curator told us that archaeologists said camp fires fused the rocks together, but then were unable to duplicate the feat!); symbology, occult but decipherable facts (9), apparently ignored.

We reflect on Watkins' interest in Beacon points and beacon fires: he saw them as a means for surveying the megalithic alignments (6). Is this the only possibility, though? In the New English Dictionary one finds an archaic meaning leye: to be "flame or fire". Watkins, noting the abundance of "Brent" place-names, remarked that this was an old form of the word 'burnt'. But instead of accepting Watkins' conclusion(6) that all these references to burns and fires meant simply that beacon fires were "reflected in water", we propose the obvious: that many if not all such places were (or are) capable of generating etheric flames which, under certain conditions, become visible to the normal ocular range and a source for kindling whatever combustible matial is upon the site (8). Maybe this is why the ancient Celts conducted fire festivals on major alignments (like the one through Stonehenge)...

One example outside of Great Britain might be of interest. Mystery Hill, in New Hampshire, resembles many Old World megalithic sites. It's said by the NEARA to be an astronomical observatory similar to Stonehenge (27). But there are problems with this theory. During a recent visit we learned that the Jonathan Pattee family once lived within the site, but their house burned down in 1855. We asked how it ignited. Carelessness? Lightning? Something less conventional? No one at NEARA could tell us. Then we chanced upon a retired Air Force colonel... a materialised library angel, we suspect...who 'just' happened to decide to show us a Sectional Aeronautical Chart of New England, upon which he had marked a series of ancient sites and connected them with straight lines. Before our eyes lay linear patterns of Neolithic stoneworks, much as Watkins had seen so many years before ...only this time they stretched across eastern New England! It's a sensation we suspect few ley hunters have experienced...

I and my research assistant tuned into the same thought simultaneously: did this stone-ringed complex attract etheric flames, just as metal rods attract lightning, and did physical objects sometimes get burned in the process?

Bizarre? Then read the passage in Screeton (9) that tells of the fires that haunted a farmer who had the audacity to deface an ancient rath! Like so many individuals who debased the sanctity of Tutankhamun's burial chambers and died shortly afterwards, it seems that powerful megalithic sites carry a curse all their own, still intact and ready to unleash its fiery vengeance upon one whose reverence is amiss (21).

The evidence, some presented above and much that has been held in abeyance (for sake of brevity), strongly suggests a connection between combustion and ley centres. It is not merely an allegorical or spiritual fire, as many writers have correctly stated before, but a literal kindling of the objects mankind relegates to the physical world.

Upon this background we have proposed that Birmingham was exposed in the early 1970s to an anomalous concentration or discharge of telluric energy, whose 6-month wave length resulted in a series of perplexing and unsolved human combustions.

But the mysteries that haunt Birmingham are far from unique, and Birmingham likewise is not alone in its terror...

Larry E Arnold, 1977

Continued Next Issue.

References

1   Fort, Charles. Lo! Ace Books n.d. N.Y.
2   NEWS 7, Nov, 74.
3   NEWS 2, Jan, 74, p6-7
4   NEWS 6, Sep, 74, p16-7
5   FT 16, June, 76, p3-5
6   Watkins, Alfred. The Old Straight Track. Ballantyne Bks, N.Y., 1973.
7   Michell, John. The View Over Atlantis. Ballantyne Bks, NY, 1973.
8   Cook, Grace & Ivan, The Light In Britain, The White Eagle Publishing Trust, New Lands, Liss, Hants, Eng. 1971.
9. Screeton, Paul. Quicksilver Heritage. Thorsons Publishers Ltd, Northants, Eng., 1974.
10 Puthoff, H E & Russell Targ,

"A Perceptual Channel for Information Transfer over Kilometer Distances: Historical Perspective and Recent Research", Proceedings of the IEEE, vol 64, no 3, Mar 76, p329-54.

11 Castaneda, Carlos. Journey to Ixtlan. Simon & Schuster, NY, 1972.

12 Leslie, Desmond, and George Adamski. Flying Saucers Have Landed, Neville Spearman, 1970

13 Zink, David D. "Atlantis Research", The Road to Awareness Symposium of the Creative Living Institute of the Shenandoah Valley, Harrisburg, Va., personal interchange, 23 Aug, 1975.

14. Bord, Janet & Colin. Mysterious Britain, Doubleday, NY, 1973.

15 Wilson, Colin. Enigmas and Mysteries, Danbury Press, Conn. 1976.

16 "Tingling Stones of Abergavenny, Wales". Stonehenge Viewpoint, vol 7, no 4, 1974.

17 Underwood, Guy. The Pattern of the Past, Abacus, London, 1972.

18 Edwards, Frank. Stranger than Science, Ace Bks, NY, nd.

19 Sykes, Egerton. "Gravitic Anomalies", New World Antiquity, vol 18, no 7-8, 1971.

20 Roberts, Jane, Seth Speaks, Prentice Hall, NJ, 1972.

21 Forbes, John Foster, Giants of Britain, Thomas's Publications Ltd, Birmingham, Eng., 1945.

22 Gearhart, Livingston, personal communication, 11 Feb 1976.

23 Arnold, Larry E, "The Flaming Fate of Dr John Irving Bentley", Pursuit, vol 9, no 4, Fall, 1976, p75-82.

24 'Circumlibra', "The Earth Breathes", The Ley Hunter, no 7, 1970.

25 Michell, John. The Earth Spirit, Avon Bks, NY, 1975.

26 Craddock, Marjorie. "Unravelling the Great Stone Mysteries", Hereford Times, 4 Nov, 1966.

27 "Mystery Hill Tour Guide Map 'America's Stonehenge', 2000 BC". The New England Antiquities Research Association, North Salem, NH, 1976.

THE FLYING NUN

It was with great interest that we read the story, in the <u>Sunday People</u> 15 May 1977, about the invisible assailants, phantom persecutors and demonic doings that surround the tormented nun, identified only as 'Sister Rosa'. In her presence objects in the room rise up and fly around her - at other times it is she herself who is levitated. This, it is claimed, happened at least once witnessed by her terrified sisters, who saw her float slowly toward the ceiling and then <u>pass through it</u>! The Auxiliary Bishop of Rome, Monsignor Remigio Ragonese, told Paul House (the <u>People</u> reporter): 'It's amazing but true. The Sisters are highly educated and not the sort to imagine things. They told me about Sister Rosa floating through the ceiling. They found her standing on the floor above.'

The Mother Superior, of the Can esian convent in Rome, where Sister Rosa first became afflicted, called in Rome's top exorcist, Padre Candido, but, said Bishop Ragonese: 'The evil still prevailed.' She was sent to 3 different exorcists in different parts of Italy, and returned apparently healed. But some time later the persecution took up again - this time she was sent to 2 'powerful exorcists' in Padova, near Venice. One of them, German-born Padre Leone Haberstroch, later vowed never to perform another because he had become so frightened that next time the Devil might kill him.

The other priest, Don Franco Bartolomiello, told House of some of the phenomena that occurred while Sister Rosa stayed in the convent next to his church. The nuns themselves began to be plagued by mysterious happenings. Once, on hearing screams from Sister Rosa's cell, they rushed in to find her tearing at her cowl. When they removed it they found thorns from a cactus plant in their garden firmly embedded in her scalp. They resisted all attempts to removed them until they were washed with Holy water, we are told. An iron bar, from the back of a door, detatched itself and

travelled through walls to materialize in Sister Rosa's cell, and began beating her while she slept. On another occasion kitchen knives flew off a table, appearing in her room, trying to stab her in the chest. Don Franco said that while he was performing the exorcism, a piece of string rose out of his pocket and twisted itself round her neck as if to strangle her.

The tone of the piece, and the attitude of the Church, is geared to interpreting the phenomena as Diabolic. Although it is not apparent in the brief descriptions of the phenomena above, we are told the nun is 'possessed by the devil.' Describing other occasions, Don Franco said she had to be restrained by 5 nuns from attacking the cross and the altar, spoke obscenities and used a gutteral 'animal-like' voice.

It is in cases like this that we see possible relationships between poltergeist phenomena and chronic hysteria. We note that the thorns could have been a literal attempt to recreate Christ's 'Crown of Thorns', and the knife-attack Christ's 'ferita' or chest-wound. In this case the use of physical objects to reproduce the Stigmata is quite novel, and, in our knowledge, unique - usually some kind of psychosomatic process forms Christ's wounds directly in the stigmatic's body tissues. The beatings and persecutions, like the Stigmata, are often stimulated by an obsessive meditation on the sufferings of Christ, and it is the vowed intention of many Religious to personally identify with the Christ-image, to <u>share</u> the pain and lighten Christ's <u>burden</u> a little. Let me also say that in using the term 'hysteria' I am not explaining-away the condition. True clinical chronic hysteria is a very real state in which the psychosomatic processes take a real, if almost magical, part, and is still largely mysterious.

Levitations, apports of objects, and even demonic persecutions, have taken place in the lives of saints, as well as the lives of many who were not so pious.

but more clearly seriously disturbed people. That is why the Church deliberately, and wisely, makes the beatification process long, complex and thorough. Only if the phenomenon has as its object the bringing of people to Christ, will they acknowledge its authenticity - everything else is the devil's duplicity. This op- is their priviledge, and underlies a sound observation on the distinction between divine and demonic phenomena (we can't go into that here). But what interests us, is that a very similar case in 1661 occured in the witchcraft context, and another in 1850 was seen as the product of a poltergeist - both involved levitations and teleportations of the main 'victim' and other phenomena, but outside of any Roman Catholic imagery or connotations. The common denominator seems to us to be spontaneous manifestations of forces that under other, and more trivial,circumstances can even be deliberately controlled (eg spoon-bending).

We are trying to get more information on Sister Rosa, and would appreciate any help in the matter. (Cr: P Screeton).

HIGH RISE MEDITATORS

In my article on some non-Christian levitations (last issue) I briefly mentioned a case brought to me, even as I was typing up the piece, by a library angel (FT21/24 ref22). It was an announcement in the London Evening News 16 May 1977, to the effect that 12 fairly ordinary people had just graduated from the Maharishi Mahesh Yogi's first six-month course in levitation, at his university at Lucerne, Switzerland. One woman, Mrs Albertine Haupt said: 'I suddenly found myself 6ft above the floor and thought "Heavens, I've done it."' She had difficulty landing. 'Fortunately the floor was covered with foam rubber. But we all have bruises. It is just a matter of learning to control the power.'

These 12 have trained to teach the technique to others, they say, and declined to publicly demonstrate their talent. The announcement brought the expected challenge from the professional 'magicians'. Illusionist David Berglas offered £2,000 to any of them who could hover 6" or more above the ground. If five of them could do it, he was prepared to part with £10,000. London Evening News 18 May 1977. They, in turn, said that when they got his challenge in writing, they'd try to get MMY's permission.

The story got a big spread in the Daily Mirror 14 July 1977 (Cr: Robert Forrest), in which reporter Michael

Hellicar spoke to MMY in person, and was refused a demonstration. 'We will not turn this into a circus,' one henchman said. However, having barred photographer Peter Stone from taking a picture, the guru's men gave him one taken only 2 days before, they said, (see Mirror), allegedly of disciples levitating, and Hellicar was allowed to interview those in the picture. But so far there's no sign they'll accept Berglas' challenge. I don't think they ever will.

LEVITATION TRICKS

Again, in my levitation article, I asked if it was possible for the levitating fakirs of the early 19th century (and probably before) to use a mechanical structure. Both Doc Shiels and Heathcote Williams wrote to say 'Yes!', enclosing xeroxes of different kinds of magician's apparatus to achieve different effects, including the balancing on swords effect, involving large baseplates, specially reinforced supports concealed in brooms, swords etc, harnesses and hidden assistants. OK...the next part of the question is, is it feasible that wandering fakirs had such sophisticated equipment at their disposal,bearing in mind their limited resources and lack of modern materials and manufacturing processes? And still, I ask, how was it possible for them to conceal inevitably heavy equipment about their persons - and how could they perform the trick - if it was a trick - out in the open (when all the props I've seen required a stationary audience and a prepared stage?

LEVITATION...AND INVISIBILITY TOO?

Our wandering correspondent, Ion Will, sent us a clipping from the 'Spectrum' column of the Malaysian New Sunday Times 3 July 1977, which relayed the claims of British author and poet, Richard Church, that: 'From the age of 10 I had this strange power to rise 6 or 7ft from the ground and fly through the air like an owl. It was always happening to me. Whenever I got excited or put out by anything I would rise above my difficulties and soar through the air.' Once, he says, he flew to Victoria Station. 'I must be invisible when I'm flying because even when I used to float down the stairs during my time in the Civil Service at Billingsgate, no one ever saw me.' Mr Church says he gave it up when he was 29. We wonder, from his choice of simile, 'like an owl', whether he lives in Cornwall, haunted by the Owlman (see FT16 & 17). Please yourselves on this one!

This piece by John Michell is not from
our book, Phenomena (see p12) but is in
the same mood, and meant as a foretaste.

Literary coincidences

by JOHN MICHELL

In the first volume of The Gulag Arch-
epelago, Solzhenitzin relates this anecdote about his fellow prisoner at the
Dmitrovsk Prison, the astronomer, Kozayev.
To keep sane in his solitary cell Kozayev
had been working out in his head a new
system of physics, but at a certain stage
technical information was required without which he could go no further. He was
wildly excited by his discoveries and
desperate at being frustrated. In his
situation there seemed no chance of getting the information. The prison library,
which contained only works like Red Army
novels and party texts, provided each
prisoner with a book, exchanged every
ten days. You took what you were given.
Kozayev prayed for help with the intensity of a lonely, obsessed man. Half an
hour later they came to change the books.
The volume they gave him was The Theory
of Astro-physics - the very book he needed. Somehow he knew that the miracle was
only a temporary one, and he threw himself on the book, memorizing all the relevant passages and tables. It took him
two days - and at the end of that time
an inspector visited his cell, noticed
the book and immediately confiscated it.

An odd story - almost incredible. Perhaps these foreigners are given to exag-
gerations. But here is Colin Wilson, a
straight forward native, claiming, in the
introduction to his book The Occult, to
have been helped substantially in researching for it by repeated interventions
of coincidences.

'On one occasion, when I was searching
for a piece of information, a book literally fell off the shelf and fell open
at the right page.'

This is really going a bit far; and
unlike Kozayev, Wilson did not even pray
to God for the information. There are
devout prayers and intense desires - and
somewhere, as Fort would say, there is a
merging between them - to the same effect.

As The Occult proceeds, it attracts
more and more coincidences of the same
sort - nothing quite so dramatic as the
poltergeist book, but just as beneficial.
Wilson begins to wonder what is happening.
He notes that 'items of required information have turned up with a promtitude
that makes me feel nervous.' However,
like a sensible fellow he decides to ride
his luck. Self-confidence returns...and
expands.

'After a while I got used to this, and
even began to feel a mild resentment when
some piece of information evaded me for
ten minutes or so.'

If there are people seriously engaged
in literary research who have not prof-
ited from the unreasonable coincidences
that Koestler attributes to 'library
angels', I have not yet met them. All
experienced writers recognize the phenomenon and will privately give examples
from their own experience. Heathcote
Williams , when asked about the effect,
immediately volunteered an experience of
the day before, when he was writing a
story in which - as I remember it - a
naked Jamaican Rastafarian roves London
inspired by a mad scheme to release Guy,
the Zoo gorilla, and overwhelm the city
with an orgiastic wave of liberation. It
seemed to Heathcote to be of stunning
relevance when, with the story going well

and the idea hot in his mind, he idly pulled a book from the shelf, opened it and read:

' His disciples said: "When wilt thou be revealed to us and when shall we see Thee?" Jesus said: "When you take off your clothing without being ashamed, and take your clothes and put them under your feet as the little children and tread on them, then shall you behold the Son of the Living One and you shall not fear."'

The book was Joseph Campbell's Masks of God, and the words came from the gnostic Gospel of Thomas. The passage was immediately incorporated into Heathcote's story, and throughout that evening similar coincidences kept turning up - words glanced at in books or newspapers seeming to echo or anticipate his train of thought.

Here is another example, recorded by that weird genius, August Strindberg, in his masterpiece, Inferno; a book which describes the abandonment of his marriage, his descent from fame and fortune into a life of poverty and solitude as an alchemist, and the dream-like coincidence-ridden state of mind to which it led. At that time the composition of sulfur was unknown. Strindberg had discovered that it contained carbon, and suspected that two other elements were involved. Walking down the Boulevade Saint-Michel, he picked up at random a book from a dealer's stall. It turned out to be a treatise on chemistry by the old Swedish chemist, Orfila. The sentence at which he opened it read: 'Sulfur has been classified among the elements. The ingenious experiments of H. Davy and the younger Berthollet tend to prove that it contains hydrogen, oxygen, and a certain base which it has proved impossible to isolate so far.'

By this miracle, as it appeared to him, Strindberg was thrown into ecstasy. The information that sulfur contains hydrogen and oxygen was the answer to the question that was then totally occupying his mind. He had already identified the third element, so at one stroke his work was completed (for his proof, see L'Hyperchemie, Paris 1897).

A remarkable sequence of events followed. Shortly after his revelation through the Orfila book, Strindberg was strolling in the Montparnasse cemetery when a fine tombstone, ornamented with the white marble features of an aged seer, caught his attention. It was the tomb of Orfila. Some days later he was attracted by a cloister-like building in the Rue d'Assas - the Hotel Orfila. With feelings of guidance, Strindberg

took a room in the Orfila. Its window looked out onto a wall in which were other little windows, reminding him of a monastery. They were, however, windows of water-closets, the sound of whose flushings destroyed his peace of mind and brought him to realize that he had fallen into the state described by Swedenborg as the 'excrementitious hell'.

The act of writing seems to attract whatever it is you are writing about. David Solomon , the writer and anthologist, was working on an anthology on the theme of shit* I was sorry, but not surprised, when he was arrested on a charge that the police consider so serious, that, at the time of writing, he is held in Bristol prison, no bail allowed. The excrementitious hell again! A happier illustration is the case of Kathleen Raine, the illuminated biographer of William Blake, who wrote a book on the English Platonist, Thomas Taylor. She became very intimate with Taylor and the society in which he moved at the very beginning of the 19th century. Like any conscientious writer, she became obsessed with her subject. Her son had recently married, and his wife was producing children. Judge, as they say, Kathleen Raine's astonished delight when she learned that her daughter-in-law was a direct descendant of the man who was then occupying her thoughts - and that her grandchildren were therefore of the lineage of the very same Thomas Taylor, the subject of her book!

To pile up anecdotes of literary coincidences - or any other sort - is easy enough. To comment helpfully is less so. The phenomenon is of intense desire spontaneously answered. If one becomes aware of the effect, and if, like Colin Wilson and many other writers, one experiences the possibility of invoking it, the normal sane reaction is to continue quietly taking advantage of it, rather than force it upon the attention of sceptics with their irritating, unpractical questions about whether one has counted the number of times a desire for information has not been answered. The effect is too subtle and personal, and the necessary state of mind too elusive to bear statistical analysis. For investigating the vast area of the irrational in human nature and in the world at large, Fort advised substituting observation for explanation. His books are full of records of desires, both in men and nature, answered spon-

* Extracted in The Fanatic 5 - A Paper of Passion - only £1.00, from the Open Head Press: BCM Open Head, London WC1.

taneously - and sometimes excessively or abortively: the prayers for rain followed by devastating floods, gluts of animals or insects after dearths, ponds newly dug which are soon found to have developed a fish population, and fish showering from the sky and missing all the ponds to fall on dry land.

To fit his observations, Fort suggested that the whole of nature is one organism and that, like any other live body, it acts unconsciously and automatically to satisfy its own needs. He referred to the universe as the great hermaphrodite with sterility as its ultimate principle. 'Perhaps that is why people see visions of blond hermaphrodites.'

A fascinating aspect of Fort's way of seeing things is the extent to which it repeats the views of ancient philosophers, such as the humorous Taoist sages and the mystical neo-Platonists. These schools reflected the magical science of their time and its dicta: 'As above, so below,' and 'Like attracts like.' Plotinus, in the 3rd century AD, stated the basic theory of magic: 'To attract anything in nature, make a recepticle designed to receive it.' On this principle the pond designed to receive fish will somehow attract them, and the scholar's desire for information will automatically produce the appropriate response. Magical invocation acts in the same way through the science of correspondences, based on the same idea as Fort's, that as nature acts spontaneously to satisfy her own needs, she will also act in response to needs artificially implanted in her. Thus rain-making magicians act out their desire for rain and perform other ceremonies to attract lightning, or to make the crops grow. Colin Wilson is stuck for a particular reference - the environment is charged with his desire for it - and the appropriate book springs open from the shelf.

Speaking about Wilson; in one of his novels, The Philosopher's Stone, he refers to the negative side of the creative coincidence effect - an opposite force which becomes active whenever a person starts to benefit from nature's revelations. John Keel, in Operation Trojan Horse, has a chapter on the same process, by which UFO prophets and contactees are first led on by true information to make inspired statements and predictions, and then disastrously let down by some grandiose but false message about an approaching millenium or whatever. History abounds in such cases, illustrating how a series of revelat-

ions may well lead one into the excrementitious hell experienced by Strindberg.

Some years ago, while keeping a coincidence diary, I noticed several examples of this process, in which an intense, successful period of work, punctuated by helpful coincidences, is suddenly brought to an end by a series of disagreeable, unexpected interruptions. On more than one occasion the same obsessed state of mind which attracts literary coincidences also attracted the same tiresome, frivolous visitor; a person who at other times might have been agreeable company, but who only manifested himself at the very moments when his presence was most disruptive. On one occasion I noted in the diary that I was then in the state of creative excitement to which he always responds - and the next day I had a card from him: 'I have been thinking about you lately, and will call...'

There is a name for this sort of thing - the 'Man from Porlock' effect, after the famous flow-breaker who interrupted Coleridge's Kubla Khan. No wonder the ancients regarded Hermes, god of revelation, as perfectly two-faced, and identified him with the will-o-the-wisp which leads its followers either to a treasure or into deep bogs.

Experience shows that all coincidences, intuitions, voices, angelic communications and so on should be treated with respect, but never to the point of becoming reliant upon them. There is a balance in nature whose effects may be like those of a cruel or infantile sense of humour which delights in deflating the earnestly credulous. Again, it may act in a most pleasing manner, as in the following literary coincidence recorded in Flammarion's The Unknown 1902.

Flammarion was sitting at his desk working on a chapter about the force of the wind for his book, The Atmosphere. All of a sudden the force he was writing about intruded upon him, and a 'minature whirlwind' carried his papers out of the window beyond hope of recovery. Yet this disaster attracted its compensation, immediately and delightfully. Some days later, Flammarion received from his publisher the proofs of his book, including the missing chapter set up in type. It turned out that the whirlwind which carried off the chapter on winds had deposited the sheets at the feet of the publisher's assistant, who gathered them up under the impression that he had dropped them, and delivered them to the office.

John Michell - July 1977.

■■■■■■■■■■■■■■■■■■■■■■■■■■■■■■■■■■■

UNIDENTIFIEDS

So far this year there have been a remarkable number of monster sightings on the coasts and in the lakes of the UK, and elsewhere. Here are a few of the most important recent ones, mainly photographic cases we are pleased to say - the others will be given in due course. There have been quite a few sightings in American and Canadian lakes, but lack of space forbids us doing more than referring you to the Fortean journals listed in our journal review section, for further details.

MORGAWR - THE DAVID CLARKE PHOTOS

Further to the sighting of Morgawr in the Helford estuary, near Falmouth, Cornwall, on 17 November 1976, by Doc Shiels and David Clarke, the editor of the Cornish Life magazine - see Doc's account in FT19, and David's account in FT 21), we have managed to obtain a copy of the photo (BELOW) by Mr Clarke. As those of you who have been following the story will know, David's camera malfunctioned at the critical moment. Here is his comment:

'After about 5 or 6 frames (of the Church at Mawnan Smith, etc), the film wind-on mechanism jammed and only wound on either one or two sprockets each time (though I didn't know this till later). The result was that frame 6 overlapped with most of frame 7 and part of frame 8, etc. I sent the full strip of negative to Tim Dinsdale, to see if he could 'lift' anything from it. I had previously done some enlargements myself, but was not happy with the results. However, I enclose one of the prints...so you have a 'scoop' for what it's worth!'

'The photo was taken with a telephoto lens and shows 'it' halfway across the river mouth, some 70ft away. Unfortunately, there are two sets of waves superimposed which gives the appearance that it was close by the bank. It also appears so 'seal-like'. In fact at this range it looked nothing like a seal, and this photograph was taken as the head turned away, the outline of its back visible breaking the surface. What you can see is the back of the head with

one of the two small 'buds', or rounded lumps, on the left. One of the other prints shows what appears to be an otter's head! So you can imagine my frustration. I had had a perfect close sighting and finished up with a spoiled film which apparently shows an otter and a seal.'

Nevertheless, we are pleased and grateful to be able to show you this still interesting and valuable photo. Compare it with those taken by Doc (see FT19 center pages).

MORGAWR - OTHER SIGHTINGS

From Doc Shiels' regular dispatches to FT, we have learned of other sightings, most of which never made the papers (and thus survived the scorn that passes for much of modern 'trendy' journalism). In Doc's village, Ponsanooth, Cornwall, a painter called Ray Hopley told Doc that he had seen Morgawr off Trefusis Point (Mary F country), on the 1st Feb, while he was out sketching. Apparently this also appeared on the BBC 'Spotlight SW', but treated as a great joke, simply, Doc says,'because he admitted that he knew me! As it happens, hundreds of people in Cornwall know me ...that's showbiz!' Two other undated items of gossip were: that MLA Andrews, exec. producer of BBC's 'The World About Us' told Doc his mother saw a Morgawr-like monster while sailing between Cornwall and Brittany; and Mike Truscott, of the West Briton, told Doc that he had spoken to a Falmouth policeman who had seen the monster but wished to remain anonymous. Hardly solid stuff, but a good indication of what's going on in the background down there.

Finally, Doc sent us a note, from the Falmouth Packet 27 May 1977 - that an unnamed Scotsman, on holiday at Falmouth, saw the monster on Gyllyngvase Beach. That's it! Annoyingly and typically brief! Doc points out the Fortean humour of it - that it must have happened on the 21st or 22nd May, about the same time as he was in Scotland clicking the shutter on Nessie (see below).

At the time of going to press, we hear of more Morgawrs near Plymouth - more details when we know them...

MORGAWR - GERRY BENNETT PHOTOS

Gerry Bennett, of Seworgan, Cornwall,

PHOTO on previous page:

An enlargement of the triple-exposed photo of Morgawr, taken by David Clarke, on Mawnan beach, 17 November 1976. Copyright: David Clarke.

was down on Mawnan beach, below Mawnan Old Church (the scene of the Owlman encounters - FT16 & 17 - and of several previous sightings including Doc's and Dave Clarke's photos) early in the morning of 31 January 1977. He had seen Morgawr before - around Christmas 1975 - and this time had a camera and colour film with him. He took three pictures, of which we have only seen the two we show here - which were rephotographed in B&W (for reproduction) from Gerry's positive transparencies. — See next page.

As you will notice from the photos, there is a large double-humped back breaking the surface in the center of each picture. We print these without having heard Mr Bennett's story for ourselves yet, though he has told it to Doc Shiels, and had them shown on the BBC regional programme 'Spotlight SW' on the evening of 9 Feb. So we make a few tentative guesses and hope to confirm (or correct) these later. Taking the direction of motion of the creature as suggested by the humps (the smaller in front, we think), and the hint of a wake (in photo 'B'), we think that they were taken in the order we show them, and that the beast was first heading up the estuary, turned and headed out to sea. It's clear that Gerry changed his camera position between these two shots, yet a consideration of the background headland, and the distractingly monster-like rock (center mid-foreground in A, and lower left in B) plainly shows the motion of the monster, even if it's change of profile hadn't. It is obviously not a rock!

Gerry describes the back as like that of a lobster or big crustacean, greenish black, with a 'kind of crusty parasitic growth' - though none of this is clear on the colour slide or the B&W enlargements. As Doc pointed out to me, the double-hump configuration, typical of Morgawr, seems to jibe with the idea of a 'hard-back', like a turtle. Gerry thinks it undulated, which, with the impression of a hard crustacean shell probably given by the parasitic growths, made him think of a segmented shell, like a lobster's tail. Again, Doc points out, if this is indeed what Gerry saw, then it is not the same type of creature that he and others have seen - Dave Clarke said of his sighting that it reminded him of a 'big black slug'! We'll give you more details when we know them. One last thought - a turtle-like hard-backed critter makes us think of the Barmouth Monster (see FT10 for references), often described in this way, and which may have moved south!

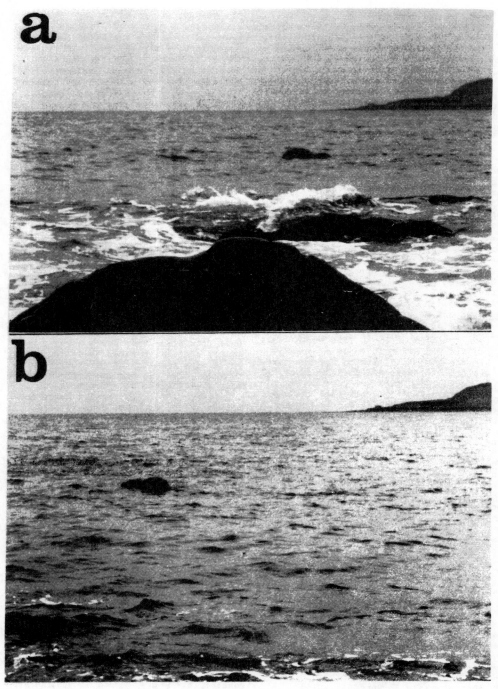

The Bennett photos of Morgawr - with backgrounds roughly matched to show
creature's change of direction and motion.

MORAG - HAZEL JACKSON'S PHOTO

Morag is Nessie's cousin in Loch Morar, and is annually pursued by the Loch Morar Survey (every bit as dedicated as their more famous colleagues at Loch Ness), lead by Mr Adrian Shine. By now they will be nearing the close of their programmed 1977 investigations using sonar. Undoubtedly they will be discussing two appearances of Morag that occurred (predictably) during their recent recess...

Hazel, and her husband Ray, of Wakefield, Yorks, stopped at Morar during their touring holiday (no date is given), and took a photo of their sheepdog with an Instamatic camera. Hazel says: 'We didn't see anything on the loch at the time, and it was only when we returned home and had (the film) developed that we saw what appeared to be a monster's head. It was just like one of those china monsters we bought as a souvenir. Ray and I had a good laugh and dismissed it. It was only when a customer (in their tailor shop) saw the photographs and referred to an article in the Yorkshire Post about the search for Morag. I've always been sceptical, but I believe more in them now than I did - though I would still have to see more before being convinced.' Ray Jackson said: 'I never believed in monsters. I thought it was a load of rubbish. But there is

obviously something there in the photographs. Two photographs were taken and there is some distance between what appears to be the monster's head on each frame, which indicates that it moved.'

The Jacksons' healthy scepticism is refreshing - but the question raised by the object has implications they have not considered. At the scene they could see nothing out in the loch that caught their eye - yet something behaving as if it were the head of a monster breaks the surface on the film. We are faced with several intriguing possibilities: that the Jacksons, concentrating on their dog, never noticed what was in range behind it; that we have an example of the effects associated with the 'phantom' monsters (favoured by FW Holiday, and some others) that can materialize and dematerialize, quickly and mysteriously; or that some kind of 'thoughtographic' effect has taken place, by which the Jacksons have unconsciously imprinted an image ('just like one of the china monsters we had bought as a souvenir') onto the film, before it was taken back and developed. We know very little about these pictures, drawing our details from the account in the Yorkshire Post 4 September 1976 (Cr: Jeremy Beadle, AJ Bell). Any of you so inclined to investigate and find out anything are asked to let us know.

The Jackson photo of Morag (center left in photo).

The Morag piece referred to above was in the <u>Yorkshire Post</u> 17 August 1976 (Cr: Anthony Bell).

MORAG - MISS M LINDSAY'S PHOTOS

We know very little about these, obtained by one of Doc's colleagues, Pat Scott-Innes, who is at present in the USA and uncontactable. Ms Scott-Innes had followed up several stories which emerged during the 'Monstermind' experiment (see FT21/27), and obtained statments and copies of the photos, some of which filtered through to Doc. These photos were allegedly taken on Monday, 31 January 1977, of a <u>40ft</u> monster in Loch Morar, by a Miss Lindsay, of Musselburgh. Doc says they have been shown on Grampian TV, and probably in the USA, and that some doubt has been cast on their authenticity. Ms Scott-Innes said in passing that 'negatives were not available', and we think it likely this means they were probably Polaroid originals re-photographed by Ms Scott-Innes (the scratches were already in the image of the prints we received, indicating a re-photographing at some stage).

Doc sent copies to David Shirt, the Scientific Officer of the Loch Morar Expedition, for examination, who thought they could have been taken from a <u>boat</u>, in a channel between two of the islands at the seaward end of the loch, but cannot identify the location more accurately. Mr Shirt also thought that for a 40ft monster there was very little evidence of water disturbance or a wake in the pictures, which, by the way, are of the creature's head - although in photo b there does seem to be the hint of a wake behind the head. We can understand any negative reaction to these pictures in view of the lack of additional details - and we hope that these will come to light in the near future.

Doc also told us he had the nagging feeling he had seen something like this suggested head before. My own impression was of a prominently muzzled head with bulges on either side of the front which may or may not be eyes - quite different from the small, almost spherical head in the recent Morgawr and Nessie pictures. Then Doc found what he was reminded of -

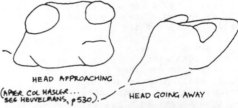

HEAD APPROACHING

(AFTER COL HASLER...
SEE HEUVELMANS, p530).   HEAD GOING AWAY

a

these sketches below are copied from the statement by Neil MacInnes of a monster he saw in the Sound of Jura, in the Hebrides, in 1964 (for full details see B Heuvelmans' In The Wake of the Sea-Serpents p529ff). In this latter case too there was no clear indication that the anterior-facing projection were in fact eyes.

We note two other points: the similarity with our first Morar photo (ie the pose of the head just above the surface), though of course they clearly differ in shape; and the involvement to various degrees in the latter story of two people with 'Innes' in their names!

NESSIE - DOC SHIELS' PHOTOS

Doc spent a few days in Scotland, and despite all the warnings he'd had, about tampering with the unknown and venturing near Urquhart Castle, the weather was good and Doc was startled by the ease and number of times he saw the monster. Doc's very aware of all the criticisms you could level at that but the fact is that he went up there, saw Nessie, and took two of the best photos yet of Nessie's head and neck.

The best day was Sat. 21 May - which

began with an 8am sighting of 3 black humps gliding through the mirror-surface of Borlum Bay towards Inverness, and in the company of other witnesses. Later Doc took photos of some long wakes on the opposite shore-line from below Castle Urquhart, and again outside Invermoriston. His best shots were of the head and neck which popped up suddenly below Castle Urquhart, at about 4pm that day.

Although Doc has sent us a lot of detail in his letters, I can't do better than to quote the more succinct report he gave to the Ness Information Service (see our journal reviews for details of NIS) printed in their Nessletter 22:

'The camera was a Zenith EM, 35mm SLR, with a 150mm telephoto lens. As I recall, I took the pictures at between f11 and f16 at 1/500/sec. The creature was rather less than 100yds away...the part of the neck showing above the water-line must have been around 4 or 5ft long. Don't take any notice of what appear to be eyes ((in photo A)) ...I could see no eyes as such in the original. The light patch above the mouth (if mouth it is...and I think it is) ((in A)) is merely a reflection off a kind of ridge. The colour of the animal was greenish brown, with a paler underside. Skin tex-

The Lindsay photos of a creature's head in Loch Morar - we have roughly aligned the backgrounds so its motion (from B to A) is readily apparent.

ture, smooth and glossy. The animal was visible for no more than 4 or 5 seconds. It held itself very upright, very still, except for a turning of the head and a straightening of the neck before it sank very smoothly, below the surface. It had powerful neck muscles. There is evidence, well possible evidence ((in B)) of parasitic growth at the back of the neck, on the dorsal ridge, as a pale yellow/green patch is visible near the water. Also in both pictures, a round pale object floats on the water close to the neck...I suggested to Bob Rickard this could be an empty McEwans beer can - so many of them are to be found along the lochside!!! On the other hand, it could be the same sort of round, pale, small object which appears in, for example, the Hugh Gray picture of Nessie (and several others).'

Doc's film was a high speed Ektachrome positive transparency film, and it's a real pity we can't afford to bring you these pictures in colour. We only have room to mention briefly some of the subsequent events. Doc handed the film over to David Clarke, editor of <u>Cornish Life</u> to develop - and rushed the best slide (A) to the Scottish <u>Daily Record</u>, who printed it <u>in colour</u>, and they wired a B&W version to the <u>Daily Mirror</u> - both gave it front page space on 9 June 1977. Alas, our attempts to get a copy of the <u>Record</u> item have proved fruitless - so if any Scottish reader has one to spare, we'd welcome it for our files.

Both of our pictures are enlargements from Doc's slides. After some heart-stopping delays, he finally received back the original from the <u>Record</u>; but the original of the second shot (B) was sent to Doc's colleague, Max Maven, in the USA, who immediately wrote back saying the letter arrived empty! Fortunately Doc had taken a B&W copy slide, from which our photo B was taken. This is the first time <u>both</u> photos have been printed together - by Charles! we've brought you some scoops lately!

Anyway - Doc and I both think there is a great similarity between these photos and the two taken by the surgeon, Wilson, in 1934 - however we disagree with the current opinion of Dr Roy Mackal (see his book <u>The Monsters of Loch Ness</u>, and the interview with him, by Jerome Clark, in <u>Fate</u> July 1977) that Wilson's photos represent a) a diving bird, and b) a partly submerged bird, distorted by tricks of the light - Doc's photos seem to show what could have happened <u>between</u> Wilson's two. In A, the water is fairly undisturbed, with the suggestion of a concentric ripple, but in B, the creature has turned and started to move forward

b

The Shiels photos of Nessie, and (left below) their candid Cornish cameraman.

and to sink. Here the water shows more evidence of being displaced. Doc's cannot be dismissed as 'diving birds' – there is too much detail, even in these relatively fuzzy enlargements. But Doc pessimistically expected them to be dismissed because of his madcap, showman image. Be that as it may, the response from the establishment to these, the most detailed pictures yet, has been one of deafening silence. But apparently Sir Peter Scott and Tim Dinsdale, who's opinions must count for something, are both favourably impressed. Tim wrote to us (7 July):

'Having corresponded with Doc extensively over the Mawgawr business ((see FT19)), having met him (once), and been aufait with the LN preambles and events leading up to the neck pictures, I am of the opinion they are genuine, and that they must represent, as a result, the most important stride forward in still photography that we have on record.'

'In Doc's experience the head and neck were manifestly <u>alive</u>, and its vertical submergence a noted characteristic of Monster behaviour, which demonstrates the fact that it can alter its displacement – perhaps as <u>P.dolichodeirus</u> did, a type of Plesiosaurus , which as Frank Buckland pointed out in the first half of last century, had such a peculiar rib structure it could probably compress the air in its lungs at will, and thus ascend or descend vertically.'

'I find these pictures of immense interest, and cannot wait to study them.'

We'll bring you more on the study of these important new photos as we hear of it.

Lastly - we'd like to pass on an announcement from Doc, that having seen and photographed both Morgawr and Nessie, and accomplishing to his satisfaction what he set out to do, he formally and ritually bowed out of the 'Monster-mind' experiment on 7th July (ie 7/7/77).

A PACIFIC PLESIOSAUR?

Once more events take an exciting turn as we near our deadline. This time it's the announcement that a Japanese trawler, off Christchurch, New Zealand, found an unidentified dead animal in its nets, 'at 9,000ft'*. The 2-ton corpse resembled a plesiosaur, with long neck and strong fore-flippers prominent in the photo. It stank so much that they threw it back after taking a few photos, sketches and measurements - or so the story went. Japanese scientists were said to be fairly convinced this was an important find of an animal hitherto unknown to science - and since the discovery, in April, joined the fishing company in urging Japanese trawlermen in the general area to keep their eyes open (and presumably, noses pegged) for more!   ((* another report says 900))

One later report we had said that the trawler men had after all kept a bit of one of the flippers. The photo appeared in the Daily Telegraph 21 July

1977, but was too poor for reproducing here - however we are attempting to learn more, and obtain better photos, copies of the sketches etc, and will let you have them as soon as we do. Meanwhile, the expected 'backlash' is on time. A letter from the Curator of the Royal Zoological Society of Scotland's aquarium, in Edinburgh, in the Telegraph for 26 July, says it's obvious immediately to any zoologist that the body is 'a decomposed sea-lion. The fore-limb is characteristic and the rather long, narrow skull suggests it was Hooker's Sea-lion (Neophoca hookeri) a species inhabiting the New Zealand area...' The writer, Mr Fraser-Brunner, goes on to suggest that the reported length of the Japanese object (variously as 30 and 180ft long, with a 6ft tail) must be regarded 'as an exaggeration' because sea-lions rarely exceed 15ft, and the elephant-seal, 24ft! Hmmm - he seems to be trying to make the witnesses' observations out to be errors because they don't fit his own theory! Another theory touted around, is that it is a large (possibly Basking) shark, which is frequently mistaken for a plesiosaur when its rotting remains are washed up on British shores. It's early days yet - but we'll cover the developments next issue. Other sources: Times & London Evening Standard 21 July (CR: Paul Devereux, Ian Thompson).

MYSTERY ATTACKS

The mysterious mutilations of cattle are continuing, unabated it seems, in the USA, as a heap of clippings from Thomas Adams recently informed us. The unfortunate animals are deprived of their lips, udders, eyes, ears, patches of flesh, blood, jaws, rectums and sexual organs (but not usually all at once). Now, according to our American correspondents, there are reports of other types of animals suffering the same ghastly fate. Some of these we'll give below, some we'll keep back because they'll be dealt with in more detail in

the USA Fortean mags (eg: the mystery animal that chews the ears of hogs in Mississippi is featured in the latest ARB - see our journal reviews). We also have an article from Loren Coleman on the strange sheep killings in Ohio, in a future issue. Meanwhile...

HORSES

Austrian authorities were faced with fears of a mystery disease - or sabotage, they couldn't decide which - when eleven horses were found in a critical condition on a stud farm at Marchfield, near

Vienna, in August 1973. The prize racers valued at about £11,000 were said to have suffered 'serious organic damage' - six died. We heard nothing later of any epidemic. Wolverhampton Express & Star 29 August 1973 (Cr: Anthony Smith.)

Johnny Mathews, 6, was in shock after finding his pet donkey foal hanging 5ft from the ground in an appletree, in a field ½mile from his home in Ash, near Farnham, Surrey. It's neck was broken. Police and members of the family were watching the field to protect the foal's mother. Johnny's father reckons that more than one 'maniac' must have been involved because of the weight of the animal, and the awkwardness of access in the tree, and that they must have done the cruel deed in the early hours of 6 Feb. We note that here is another case in 'Surrey Puma' country. Sunday Express 9 February 1975.

A 'sadist' struck twelve times in a fortnight, at the small village of Iver, Bucks, in the first half of April 1975, hacking the tails off ponies - seven times in one stable alone. The 'sadist' always seems to evade the special patrols and vigils mounted by villagers and police. It's not clear whether the whole tail, or just the hair, has been snipped, but the heartbreak among the village children is the same. In our own ghoulishness, we have snipped and collected data from many sources on 'mystery hair clippers' hoping someday to weave an article. This story is from Daily Mirror 15 April 1975.

The assailant that ripped the throats of at least two ponies, at Abington, Massachusetts, at 7am on 2 May 1976, was seen. Phillip Kane was woken by his daughter, and at her insistance, stumbled out into his backyard to check on her 2 ponies tethered there. He was startled to see them, their halters in a tangle, lying on their sides with their throats torn. Kane saw a dog hovering over one of the carcases, eating, and thinks it was a large black and brown German shepherd with some Doberman traits. It may have been fright, he says, but it seemed of huge and fearsome proportions - at least as big as the Shetland ponies themselves. Somehow he managed to chase the creature off, and it vanished into the woods and swamp that dominates the area. A week of police searches has failed to flush the beast out, & there are growing numbers of reports (most prove dead ends) from the frightened residents. Kane says in one week he was called 3 times to Weymouth, twice to Brockton and once to Whitman to identify dogs caught - but

none was the giant killer. Others see it crossing the street in daylight with blood dripping from its jaws! It seems very quickly to have become a living legend. Boston (Mass.) Globe 8 May 1976 (Cr: Loren Coleman).

A horse loved by many childen, kept in a field at Catherine Slack, near Halifax, Yorks, was found dead - a wooden stake had been driven through it. There were no clues to whoever perpetrated the horror. Daily Mirror 3 August 1976.

SHEEP

Hmmm - I missed the importance of this next note until I read it again just now. Towards the end of February 1975, a Bucks farmer, Peter Dutton, claimed that two Alsatian dogs killed two of his sheep and hurt 9 others so badly they had to be destroyed. It's not said that he saw them do this, but there's no doubt in local police minds that there were 2 Alsatians on the loose (whose owners they were trying to trace) - so they seem ripe for blaming. When 20 guinea pigs, 2 pet rabbits in one household, and a neighbour's cat and guinea pigs were found killed, the dogs were again blamed (again it's not said the dogs were seen at their savaging). I wonder...mainly because I note that the village concerned is Iver, which about a month later suffered the sadistical snipping of 12 pony tails (see 'Horses' above). The same fiend could be responsible!

EXOTICS

The beheaded carcase of a female bison, one of a herd belonging to the Duke of Bedford, was found on the Duke's estate at Woburn Abbey, Beds. The head, weighing about 30lb, is thought to have been cut off with a large knife and has not been found - nor were there any signs of a struggle, as there should have been because bison are fierce, strong and large. An estate official said: 'This is very much a mystery.' Daily Mirror 4 December 1968 (Cr: Ivan Bunn).

A tiger which mauled a woman at a zoo in Calcutta was saved from execution after being declared not a man-eater (if you'll forgive the chauvinism). However revenge has been had - shortly after it was taken to a tiger reserve it was found dead near its cage 'with body wounds'. London Evening News 5 Sept 1974.

Here's a weird one - the mutilated body of a 4ft porpoise was found at Burton, Lincs, more than 2 miles from the nearest river. RSPCA inspector William Russell said he would ask the police to remove it and investigate. He also appealed to any zoo or marineland to check if they had any missing - suggesting that someone stole and maimed the creature, a more likely possibility in his mind than that it swam up the rivers from the sea and came to grief, or that someone found it by the sea & took it inland. We heard nothing more on this case. Scunthorpe Star 16 May 1975 (Cr: Nigel Watson).

A red deer, kept at the pet's corner in Sherdley Park, St Helens, Lancs, was found 'brutally butchered' in a blood-stained compound - or rather what was left of him was found, for according to police it had been a thorough and professional job that left behind only the parts 'that could not be sold'. Police said: 'We're convinced the animal was slaughtered to be sold as venison.' Ten rabbits were also missing. Coincidentally a footnote to this report mentions that in the first 3 days of the deer season at Dordogne, France, 2,667 were killed -- and far away in England there is a faint echo of the deer-folk's agony. Daily Mirror 20 October 1976.

SKIN GAMES

The mention of a headless bison serves as an entrée for a collection of skinned animals in our files.

Following the mysterious slaughtering of a donkey at Crowthorne and a dog at Guildford, the Surrey and Berkshire RSPCA were warning pet-owners to keep their animals close at hand.They mention the latest incident in a series in the area in the 'past few months - that of a gypsy boy's pet sheep at Bray, Berks. Mrs Pam Peterson of Sandhurst, who found the animal, said it was stripped of skin and meat from the neck down. **Shades of Skippy (d.1967) who suffered the reverse of this fate - ie the missing parts were from her shoulders upwards.) The RSPCA spokesman said: 'The killer was obviously experienced in slaughtering animals.'** Sunday Mirror 3 November 1975.

Police were hunting 'rustlers' near Newcastle-upon-Tyne, who had shot and skinned 13 sheep. The Times 28 July 1976 (Cr: Ion Will.)

Any occult significance we could knowingly attach to the note - that in the past week 23 dogs, supposedly whippets, had been found skinned in Dorset, Avon and Somerset - is dispelled as 3 more were found in a field at Corfe, near Taunton, Somerset. Police and RSPCA investigators are not turning up much, and speculate that they were killed for their skins or used in black

magic rites. But who's ever heard of a whippet-skin coat - and handy though it is for authorities to blame such deeds on nebulous 'black magic rites' (in much the same way puzzled archeologists used to lable enigmatic artifacts as 'ritual objects') there is very little we can find to confirm either 'occult' practice. That was from the Daily Telegraph 11 January 1977 - and the next day the same paper reports a true magical practice - the transmutation of evidence (or at least statements about evidence) to conform with the most likely (that is the most acceptable) theory. It's said the whippets are now 'probably' foxes, and that they were 'probably' netted and clubbed. Just how they could tell that the skinned carcases had been 'netted' I don't know - I suppose it's a traditional poaching method! Whether it has any relevance as another stage in the ritual alteration of data, again I don't know, but I note that the same paper for 1 Feb 1977 recorded the reply of the Home Office Under Secretary, Dr Shirley Summerskill,to a Commons question on this or a similar matter. She said that police and RSPCA were investigating cases in which foxes were killed by strychnine for their pelts. (Cr: Mrs Valarie Martin; RTA Hill).

Three 'gentle family' dogs were maimed in the week prior to the account in the Oklahoma City Times 5 April 1977, in that city. One dog belonging to Kathy Hauton returned after a week's disappearance with the fur and skin cut away from a patch on its abdomen. Then her other two dogs vanished and returned in the same condition. Humane Society think there was an attempt to skin them alive and they escaped - a spokesman for the City's Animal Welfare Division thought they were victims of an acid attack -- but why confined to one woman's pets? Interestingly, he mentions that in the same 'general vicinity we had incidents several years ago, where animals were set on fire after being doused with a flammable liquid.' (Cr: Thomas Adams).

A little later, on our side of the great water...the remains of a black whippet was found partially skinned and beheaded, on wasteground at Mansfield Woodhouse, Notts. Police suspect 'Black Magic' (gasp!) and have frozen the carcase while they, umm 'make inquiries'. Newcastle-upon-Tyne Journal 15 April 1977. (Cr: Paul Screeton).

SOME WILD THEORIES

The USA cattle mutilations have been blamed on some exotic culprits, ranging from secret (possibly Mithraic-type) cults operating among the slaughterhouse men, or US Army, to a revival of Meso-American religion with its bizarre ritual slayings, to the more Western cults of both witchcraft and black magic; to UFOs. One story of the latter type, we find in the often dubious Midnight 8 November 1976:

Ted Nelson and his son, of Fairfax County, Virginia, were walking on the shore of Broke Lake, on 13 August 1976, when a 'hot red-orange' circular craft, with windows around the rim, silently landed on the opposite shore, about 800yds away. It seemed to spurt flame as it landed on an extended tripod - then took off after about 5 minutes. (There's a photo of him with a drawing of what they saw, below...)

Though Nelson and son suffered no subsequent ill effects, it seems the UFO left broken branches, scorched earth, burned and maimed squirrels and dead fish. A Virginia wildlife official confirmed the deaths, and said he too believed that a UFO was responsible. Indeed, Fairfax County police said they had received over 30 calls from spotters of a UFO at that time, and that radar operators at Dulles Airport had tracked the object. (Cr: Gary L Abbott).

Another factor is that undoubtedly there are some loonies on the loose. Consider the report in the Daily Mirror 14 May 1976 - that an anonymous phone-caller told the RSPCA at Mansfield, Notts, of a secret society calling themselves SASA, the Small Animals Stranglers' Association. He said they were sadists who stole animals, took them into the countryside and slowly strangled them, with side bets on how long each victim would take to die. He said they met in local pubs to plan their expeditions, and that among others they had taken dogs, rabbits and a goat. Well - you can imagine the dilemma of the RSPCA, wondering if the call itself

was a hoax. The Mansfield RSPCA Inspector said he was taking it seriously "in view of some of the things that twisted people are capable of doing." And well he might...for we have already noted the story of the skinned black whippet in that area (see bottom p28) this April, and note yet another evil doings, this time the drowning of 8 dogs in a stagnant pool on the Welbeck Park Estate, near Mansfield. Police suspected poachers getting rid of troublesome dogs - but an RSPCA spokesman, seemingly ignorant of the malignant SASA, commented only that they thought it unlikely. Daily Telegraph 2 June 1977 (Cr: Mrs V Martin).

Now we come into really bizarre territory - animal mutilations mixed with an outrageous SF strain that makes you wonder if there is more to the MIB-theory than meets the Third Eye, and makes assassination-mania look like mere paranoia. Ponder on this piece, from Dr Hunter Thompson's diary coverage of Jimmy Carter's presidential campaign in Florida:

'Last night, on this same radio station, I heard a warning about "a new outbreak of dog mutilations in Coconut Grove." The disc jockey reading the news sounded angry and agitated. "Three more mongrel dogs were found castrated and barely alive tonight," he said,"and investigating officers said there was no doubt that all three animals were the victims of the same bloodthirsty psychotic - a stocky middle-aged Cuban known as 'Castrato' - who has terrorized dog-owners in Coconut Grove for the past three months."

'"Today's mutilations, police said, were executed with the same sadistic precision as all the others. According to the owner of one victim, a half-breed Chow watchdog named Willie, the dog was 'minding his own business, just lying out there in the driveway, when all of a sudden I heard him yelping and I looked out of the door just in time to see this dirty little spic shoot him again with one of those electric flashlight guns. Then the sonofabitch grabbed Willie by the hind legs and threw him into the back of an old red pickup. I yelled at him, but by the time I got hold of my shotgun and ran out on to the porch, he was gone. It all happened so fast I didn't even get the license number.'"'

'The voice on the radio paused for a long moment, then dipped a few octaves and went on with the story: "Several hours later, police said, Willie and two other dogs - both mongrels - were found in a vacant lot near the Dinner Key yacht marina. All three had been expertly castrated..."'

'Another long pause, followed by a moaning sound as the radio voice seemed to crack and stutter momentarily...And then it continued, very slowly: "The nature of the wounds, police said, left no room for doubt that today's mutilations were the work of the same fiendish hand responsible for all but two of the 49 previous dog castrations in Coconut Grove this year."'

'"'This is definitely the work of Castrato,' said Senior Dog Warden Lionel Olay at a hastily called press conference late this afternoon. 'Look at the razor work on this mongrel chow,' Olay told reporters. 'These cuts are surgically perfect, and so is this cauterization. This man you call "Castrato" is no amateur, gentlemen. This is very artistic surgery - maybe 50 or 55 seconds from start to finish, assuming he works with a whip-steel straight razor and a 220-volt soldering iron.'"'

'"Olay ended the press conference on a humorous note, urging reporters to 'work like dogs' until this case is cracked. 'And if any of you people own mongrels,' he added,'either keep them out of Coconut Grove or have them put to sleep.'"'

'"Meanwhile," said the newscaster, "South Miami police have warned all dog owners in the area to be on the lookout for a red pickup truck cruising slowly in residential neighborhoods. The driver, a small but muscular Cuban between 40 and 50 years old, is known to be armed with an extremely dangerous high-voltage electric weapon called a 'Taser' and is criminally insane."'

Well Hunter Thompson is no mean artist himself, and I'd be interested to hear from any reader in Florida who can find us any further information on Jack the Castrato. The story (from Rolling Stone 3 June 1976) contains one paradox which is absurd enough to suggest that the story did not spontaneously generate in his head - which he admits was 'full of speed, booze and Percodan.' Simply - why would any sadist out to hurt mongrels bother to cauterize their wounds, and then dump them where they could die before they were found? And where the hell did he get a classic SF-type ray gun? (Cr: J Michell).

This brought to mind another couple of notes we had here, both from the Newport News, Virginia, Daily Press of November 1976 (Cr: Gary Abbott). The first dated 5th Nov, tells of a bar of radioactive material missing from a car that was stolen, stripped and abandoned in a wood at Milton, a suburb of Boston,

Massachusetts. The Cobalt 57 was in the toolbox of the car - we are not told why! The second story of snatched ominous implements was dated 13th Nov - that a nuclear testing tool, identified only as a 'Troxler Model 2401', said to be 'potentially dangerous to humans', was stolen from a Virginia Highway Department storage shed at Petersburg, Va.

With 'criminally insane' madmen armed with malignant technological weaponry the world is looking more like a Marvel Comic everyday. Stan Lee, you have much to answer for! ...but we'll stop here as we're slipping into other topics.

ANOTHER 'UFO' CASE?

As we go to press a story has come to light about a baffling death of 15 ponies on Dartmoor. Their bodies, described as 'mangled, torn and crushed' were found by Alan Hicks, a petshop owner, strolling with his family at the Cherry Brook Valley beautyspot, near Postbridge. They were all grouped within a hundred yard section. There were no cliffs or anything from which they could have fallen in the marshy grassland, and all appeared to have died at the same time. By the time the RSPCA investigated only 48 hours later, the bodies had decomposed enough to mask the cause of death. A spokesman for the Animal Defence Society and Dartmoor Livestock Protection Society, who made a joint investigation, said the ponies had broken bones and torn arteries. According to one paper one pony had a broken neck and their bodies had decomposed to skeletons with alarming speed (Mirror).

Theories of death by poisoning, disease, malnutrition and shooting were soon eliminated. The main theory - and we note the readiness of the papers to headline this tack - was that a UFO flew low over the area,'creating a vortex which hurled the ponies to their deaths.' - the words of John Wyse, of the Devon UFO Centre, who led his group over the area bristling with geiger counters, metal and UFO detectors. The last note we have to date proposes a theory by Ruth Murray, president of the Animal Defence Society. She thinks they were stampeded by rowdies in a Landrover-type vehicle which could have smashed into the sides of some ponies. But...no pony is going to stand still to be rammed, and then 15 of them crawl off together to die. Nor would this account for the apparently abnormally rapid decomposition. Mrs Murray bases her theory on her discovery of a 'skidmark' on the ground

CONT ON p 33...

FISH FALLS
AND WHIRLWINDS

by ROBERT SCHADEWALD

Fish-falls may not be the damnedest Fortean phenomena, but they are certainly an interesting study. There are so many cases on record that no one seriously denies that they happen. Rather, explainers are generally stuck to a single security blanket, the whirlwind. It's my intention to remove some of the fuzz from the blanket.

Before proceeding further, let it be said that many fish-falls have been caused by whirlwinds. For instance, on November 12th, 1913, a tornado cloud dropped fish at Quirindi, N.S.W., Australia (1). On June 11th, 1921, fishermen were drenched with seawater and pelted with fish by a waterspout near Avery Island, Louisiana (2). There are several other cases where a whirlwind is the obvious or probable explanation.

There are many more cases where the whirlwind explanation can't be effectively refuted. For instance, some of the herring falls upon the coastal regions of the British Isles could be due to waterspouts. Herring are found near the surface of the sea in very dense schools. Waterspouts are associated with violent squalls. If herring are found thinly and widely scattered over a coastal area after an extremely violent storm, most people would accept that they might have been picked up at sea by a waterspout and dropped on land.

But Fort raised several objections to the whirlwind theory as an explanation of all fish-falls. First of all, whirlwinds are seldom reported in association with fish-falls. Second, there is the apparent segregation whereby fish, and perhaps only one species of fish, fall unaccompanied by mud, lilypads or pond-debris. Third, whirlwinds scatter their acquisitions at random, whereas fish often fall into a very small area. Fourth, falls into small areas sometimes occupy a fairly long period of time, and occasionally cease temporarily and then begin again. Fifth, the strange absence of falls of tadpoles when there have been so many falls of fish and frogs(3).

It is worthwhile to return to the scattered herring for a moment. Only the first objection really applies, and that not very strongly. Generally a violent storm is accompanied by low clouds, and a waterspout could easily pick up its cargo of herring at sea, lift up, and then surreptitiously dump it from above the clouds.

But consider the famous Mountain Ash fish-fall of February 9th, 1859. At the time of the fall, it was pouring rain and a stiff breeze was blowing from the southwest. John Lewis, a sawyer, was preparing to cut a piece of timber when the fish began to fall on him. There were actually two falls, each about two minutes long, and with a ten-minute break between them. The fish were minnows and freshwater sticklebacks from somewhat over an inch up to five inches long. They fell in an extremely limited area, 80 yards by 12 yards, and very thickly. Lewis reported that he was hit by several, got one down his neck and several in his hatbrim (4). There must have been at least half a dozen per square yard, probably more.

The Mountain Ash fish-fall presents several enigmas. First of all, one might ask where sticklebacks can be found so densely. The male stickleback is a pugnacious little fellow who stakes out a patch of stream or pond bottom and, except for his mate, runs all other sticklebacks out. There is no such thing as a school of sticklebacks. Where would a whirlwind get so much ammunition?

Then there's the problem of concentration. Continuing with the ammunition metaphor, the following comparison is instructive. A full choke shotgun must be able to put at least 70% of its charge inside a 30" circle from a range of forty yards. A very skillful gunsmith might coax it up to 90% for a selected charge. So most of the charge of a tightly choked shotgun spreads in a cone with apex about 1° 12'. If the charge strikes at an angle, the pattern is elongated. By this standard, if the 80 yard by 12 yard pattern of fish at Mountain Ash came from a full choke whirlwind, said whirlwind was no more than a third of a mile away.

Finally, there's the time element. Picture a union whirlwind dropping fish in one place for two minutes, taking a ten minute coffee-break, and then resuming work. Not a very convincing picture.

I have long wondered about the aerodynamic properties of falling fish. On May 9th, 1977, I dragooned my friend Ned Dexter into assisting me with the following experiment. We bought several dozen suckers averaging $2\frac{1}{8}$" in length and 23 grains in weight (about 1/19th oz). These were dropped one by one from the rail of a bridge $114\frac{1}{2}$ feet above the Mississippi River. The falling fish were filmed with a Super-8 movie camera set at its highest frame rate, which was determined to be 29·14 frames per second.

Fall time <u>in vacuo</u> would have been 2·67 seconds. Actual fall time of fifteen fish were measured by counting frame, and they varied from 3·79 to 4·24 seconds, with a mean of 4·10 seconds. Terminal velocity can be calculated from fall time, and the average works out to about 34·1 feet per second, or 23·2 miles per hour. Timing uncertainties suggest an error of perhaps 5%.

Terminal velocity is the velocity at which aerodynamic drag exactly equals the force of gravity. Assuming all minnow-like fish have about the same aerodynamic properties, terminal velocity of a four-inch stickleback should be something like

$$23 \cdot 2 \sqrt{4/2 \cdot 125} = 31 \cdot 8 \text{ m.p.h.}$$

The updrafts in thunderstorms and whirlwinds often far exceed these velocities, so there's no problem lifting the fish once they're in the air. But the plot thickens. Suppose a whirlwind has an upward velocity component of 60 miles per hour (88 feet per second). Let us put a bucket of two and four inch fish into the bottom of the whirlwind and let it discharge them at a height of 5,000 feet. The terminal velocities of two and four inch fish are 33·1 and 46·8 feet per second. So the two inch fish will rise at (88 − 33·1) = 54·9 f.p.s., and the four inch fish at (88 − 46·8) = 41·2 f.p.s. When the two inch fish are discharged at the top after about 91 seconds the four inch fish will have risen to only about 3,750 feet. The four inch fish will reach the top about 30 seconds later (5). As the whole system is spinning, one would expect a whirlwind to rather efficiently sort fish by size, with each size discharged in a different direction, depending upon the time it arrived at the top.

If fish raised by a whirlwind then fall through a varying horizontal wind, there will be further sorting by size. And horizontal wind velocity always varies with altitude, slowing substantially near the ground.

One further point: Great Britain and my native Minnesota are very nearly the same size. Tornadoes are extremely rare in the British Isles, but Minnesota averages seventeen tornado touchdowns per year, with perhaps another twenty reports of funnel clouds (6). The "Land of 10,000 Lakes" has 4·8% of its surface covered with lakes, thousands of miles of rivers and streams, and a couple of hundred miles of Lake Superior shoreline. I have many reports of fish-falls from Great Britain, but none whatever from Minnesota.

Robert J Schadewald - June 77

CONT/

References

1. INFO *Journal* ¡10, p23.¡ "Falls: Fishes, Ice and straw."
2. EW Gudger, "More Rains of Fishes", <u>Annals and Magazine of Natural History</u>, 10th series, No 13, Jan. 1929, p22
3. C Fort, <u>Books</u>, p85f, p91f, p545f.
4. C Fort, <u>Books</u>, p83f gives an account drawn from most available references.
5. Figures are approximate; the situation is actually much more complex.
6. Tornado statistics from U.S. Weather Bureau. Just a week ago (on May 21st) a tornado touched down about 30 miles away, doing little damage and causing no injuries. ¡A few minutes later, there was an un-Fortean report of a "fall" of tree branches a few miles away.

■■■

PONY DEATHS cont from p30...

where the ponies grazed. If anything, the single 'skidmark' - surely her idea of a careening Landrover demands a whole tangle of tracks? - is more consistent with the so-called UFO 'landing trace'. We await further revelations, and the results of other UFO researchers. Story compiled from: Sheffield, Yorks, <u>Star</u> 14 July (Cr: Tim Jones); <u>Daily Telegraph</u> (cr: Judith Gee), <u>Daily Mirror</u> (Cr: Bob Forrest), <u>Daily Mail</u> (Cr: Lionel Beer, Judith Gee) all 15 July; <u>Daily Mirror</u> 16 July (Cr: R Forrest); <u>Sunday Express</u> 17 July 1977. Our guess is that they died sometime around 12/13 July.

■■■■■■■■■■■■■■■■■■■■■■■■■■■■■■■■■■■■■■■

LETTERS cont from p5...

I would not agree with John Keel's view that we should 'seriously question' <u>all</u> the airship incidents merely because the Hamilton case turned out to be a joke (I think 'hoax' is somewhat inappropriate). Obviously we should question all accounts, historical or modern, but I do not think it is proper to suggest that because Case A is a hoax, then Cases B through Z are hoaxes also. Undoubtedly there <u>are</u> hoaxes in the airship accounts which have been located and publicized, but a 'blanket condemnation' would be as undesirable as a 'blanket endorsement'.

Also one point about Vallee's role in the Hamilton case: You mentioned (Ref 1) that Vallee had quoted the entire account which originally appeared in the Yates Center <u>Farmer's Advocate</u> of 23 April 1897. Actually, Vallee omitted portions of the original 'affidavit' and changed some words in the portions which he did quote. One omission on his part has always intrigued me. He quotes Hamilton's remark that the airship 'was occupied by six of the strangest beings I ever saw,' but omits the following sentence: 'There were two men, a woman and three children.' I often wondered if this was done deliberately, so as to heighten the impression of 'hideous' beings. After all, to have been recognizable as men, women and children they could not have been <u>too</u> 'hideous' or strange-looking. Of course, the recent events render such a discussion academic, but I mention it for whatever it may be worth.

GIANT 'TADPOLE'

From James Colman, Lowestoft:
Recently, an aerial survey of the Hebrides was made by the Seals Research Unit, which used to be based at Lowestoft. On the island of Stockay, a large object has been found. It was photo'd amongst the seals and caused a lot of interest. The unidentified object is shaped like a tadpole and is twice the size of common seals. It may be a Nessiteras type animal, but all information is now being withheld. That is all I know.

It is probably covered by the Official Secrets Act, as the Seals Research Unit is a government organization and isn't likely to publish the information.

((Mr Colman did not elaborate further or include his address. If anyone can shed light on this interesting tad-bit please let us know - meanwhile we'll be trying to contact the SRU. - Ed))

'ALIENS AMONG US'

From Derek Longhurst, London:
A few notes to add to Peter Roberts' article 'Aliens Among Us' (<u>FT19</u>).

The Monarch butterfly has been reported about 200 times in Britain since the first capture reported in 1876. It is a native of America (nearly all British specimens resemble the North American sub-species), but only 3 specimens have ever been recorded from the West coast of Ireland, and only 6 from mainland Europe.

Another interesting oddity is the case of the Chequered Skipper. Never a common butterfly, it was only known by collectors from a few midland counties, until, in 1941, an astonished entomological world learned of its existence in a thriving colony in West Inverness, some 400 miles from the nearest known locality.

The experience of AW Bennett will be familiar to Forteans. Out walking in August 1911, near Tintagel, he noticed several large brown butterflies flying around loosestrife. Recognizing that they were not Silver-Washed Fritillaries (A. paphia.) he managed to capture one in his hat, which specimen he eventually forwarded to an entomological celebrity for identification. The specimen was finally returned, damaged, with 'A. paphia scribbled on the side. Subsequent examination showed the insect to be 'A. pandora', an exotic fritillary from Central Europe. Surely a unique migration would not be expected to bring several butter-flies to the same grassy bank?

1872 and 1945 were legendary years for bug-hunters. These were exceptional for the appearance of unusual butter-flies and the presence in large numbers of rarer species. Thus 50 Queen of Spain Fritillaries and 35 Bath Whites in 1872, 36 Queen of Spain Fritillaries and 650 Bath Whites in 1945, along with 31 Long Tailed and 3 Short Tailed Blues.

Our rarest native butterfly, the Black Hairstreak, is found in a few midland counties, particularly the old area of Huntingdonshire. However in 1919, larvae were found by AA Tullett near Haslemere, Surrey (Puma fans will know the area well), and six adult insects were bred.

I would refer interested readers to EB Ford's work Butterflies (Collins, 1945), where he refers to many similar occurences. (Other information from A Butterfly Book by Sanders - OUP, 1955).

HARDBACKS

The Jersey Devil by JF McCloy & Ray Miller Jr. (Middle Atlantic Press, Box 263, Wallingford, PA 19086, USA; 1976; $8.00.) -- For 240 years countless stories have circulated throughout southern New Jersey about a creature, part-legend part-fact, that emerges from the desolate region of the coastal Pine Barrens and periodically, for a few hours or days, terrorizes local communities. The earliest reports of the 18th & 19th centuries are of a legendary nature and give a variety of fanciful explanations for the origin of the monster. It was not until 1909 that really useful reports for today's Fortean researcher appeared in the local press. In January of that year the 'phenomenon' appeared in 30 different towns and left numerous footprints to substantiate eye-witness reports. Naturally the descriptions vary to some extent, but the consensus suggests an amalgam of features that would tax the imagination of Hieronymus Bosch. That it is zoologically improbable, if not impossible, is reason enough to explain why it has received scant attention from the authorities.

Varying 18 inches to 20 feet in size, the Jersey Devil is said to have a kangaroo's body, dog's head with the face of a horse, bat's wings, pig's feet, and a forked tail. He is impervious to cannonballs, flapping imperturbably away on leathery wings after receiving a direct hit from a Commodore who happened to be playing with a big gun when the Devil came into range. By the end of a week of appearances, in the flap of 1909, the inhabitants of the Delaware Valley were in complete terror, many refusing to leave their homes even in broad daylight. Workers stayed away from jobs, and factories and theatres closed. Since then there have been at least two claims that the Devil has been shot. Fort notes one of these in LO!(ch 9) from 1925. The only other report he has is of the showman who attatched tin wings and green whiskers to a kangaroo and exhibited it as the Jersey Devil. Fort wrote to the farmer who claimed to have shot it, but reported wryly: 'I have had an extensive, though one-sided, correspondence, with people who may not be, about things that probably aren't.'

In 1951, the JD was on the rampage again, leaving tracks in deserted areas and being associated with reports of dismembered poultry, cats and dogs. There is no doubt the JD is another of the weird beasts that inhabit the hinterland where our 3 dimensions merge into...what?

McCloy & Miller have done some valuable research looking through the early newspapers to compile this collection of reports, though, as they say in their introduction, many accounts were omitted to avoid repetition. Though the sources of individual cases are not cited, there is a list of books and papers consulted, also an index, maps and other illustrations. The book is a useful addition to the monster-hunter's library. Colin Bord.

Alternate Realities by Lawrence LeShan (Sheldon Press 1976; £3.95; pp232; notes) -- Quietly and surely there is begining to emerge a new school of phenomenology (the study of appearances). After the work of Husserl (d.1938) fell into obscurity, the hiatus was bridged by the modern awareness of the transience, ephemerality and paradoxical nature of phenomena and their existence. This awareness arises from two main sources: the discoveries of modern high-energy physics which are themselves bridging the old 'Cartesian Division' of the universe into objective & subjective (see F Capra's admirable Tao of Physics for many demonstrations of his theme, that the pronouncements of physicists today are often indistinguishable from the teachings of the mystics);and secondly, from the growing reservoir of general experience of altered states of consciousness, whether they be induced by disease, drugs or discipline.

LeShan was thinking about these areas on the frontier of human knowledge long before Capra, but his efforts were aimed towards deriving a general theory of the paranormal. The new phenomenology begins with   the postulate that the only consistent criterion for 'Reality' is that which is experienced, whether this be a relationship, pain, vision, thought, dream or hallucination   etc. If you can experience it, it is real; and the more of you who can experience the same thing to the same degree, the more real it is, or becomes (for there is no doubt that 'experiencing' is more than mere sensory perception, but an act of creation involving a reflexive relationship between individual and the rest of the universe.) In LeShan's first book, The Medium, The Mystic & The Physicist, he came to the realization that all attempts to study 'anomalous phenomena' based on the view that our generally accepted idea of reality is the only reality, are doomed to error, frustration and paradox. In the first place 'the generally accepted idea of reality' is a myth, varying widely from individual to individual, and from discipline to discipline (eg scientific orthodoxy compared to, say, consistent ESP, or psychic healing.)

Now 'anomaly' can only be defined in a purely arbitrary way, after you have decided what you will accept as normal. In his first book, LeShan found that there could be many different kinds of 'normal reality', all of them valid as long as they fulfilled their function. It matters little that they are often mutually exclusive from the phenomenological point of view, as long as they function in their role of providing a pattern through which the 2-way creative process of experiencing can work for that particular individual. Fort was coming to similar conclusions from his own studies of phenomena.

In Alternate Realities, LeShan extends his thinking, comparing two main patterns of reality; the physical one of today's scientific and teaching orthodoxy (what he calls the 'sensory' mode)in which phenomena are separated by time and space into unique events; and the view of a universe in which all things and events are interconnected (Fort's 'Continuity') and indivisible (LeShan's 'Clairvoyant' mode). He also identifies two others: the 'Transpsychic' mode, in which events and objects are neither separate nor contiguous, but in transition flowing from multiplicity towards a One; and the 'Mythic' mode in which correspondences, symbols and rituals form the basis of magic, myth and dreams. LeShan admits that he has not explored the structures of the last two in any detail yet and is largely speculating.

This is an important book - a stepping stone on the path to a radical new philosophy (alongside the works of JC Pearce, Langer, Fort, Bradley, Husserl, and even the Trickster Castaneda, and LeShan's own mentors, Henry Margenau & MR Cohen) - and attempts to demonstrate that psychic phenomena, despite being considered 'impossible' in the sensory mode, are logical manifestations in the Clairvoyant universe. The ideas are complex and far-reaching, and LeShan has taken great pains to spell out simply, if a little pedantically, the thinking step by step. RJM Rickard.

The Uses of Enchantment by Bruno Bettelheim (Thames & Hudson 1976; £6.50; pp328; notes, bib, index) --

The uses of the title are fundamentally practical ones. The child is introduced to fairytales about the time he is learning to read, and, argues Prof Bettelheim, the story has to function on a number of levels at the same time if the child's interest is to be held. It is the teaching dimension that receives the main analysis here - how the child is brought to accomodate notions of selfhood, moral obligation, justice, fidelity, courage, love and so on - for Bettelheim sees the the fairytale as a dramatization of an existential crisis, and, more importantly, provides a formula for its resolution.

Prof Bettelheim achieves a fine balance between Freudian and Jungian interpretations, admirably refereed by his own observations. Despite the fact that fairytales are dealt with more extensively in Jungian writings, the Freudian psychoanalytic approach is the more dominant here, since of the two main dramas characterized by these two approaches the crises of puberty are the more immediate and apparent to the child who forcibly identifies with the hero or heroine. In this case, Bettelheim presents discussion and examples of tales that deal with alienation, guilt, identity problems, masturbation, menstruation and Oedipal conflicts. The other main drama, extensively discussed in Jungian literature, is the role of the personal and unconscious forces and archetypes in the voyage to selfhood and psychic unity, and the various relationships between the elements of these forces and symbols precipitated in the child's psyche as he responds to or withdraws from his external environment.

Perhaps it is only through studies, ably represented by this book, of our own complexities that we can begin to understand the nature of the external world and its phenomena. Here, the key issues are clearly and simply set out for psychologist and layman alike.
RJM Rickard.

The Paradise Papers by Merlin Stone (Virago/Quartet Books 1976; paper, £2.50; pp275; charts, bib, index, photos). The Virgin by Geoffrey Ashe (RKP 1976; £5.25; pp262; notes bib, index, photos) -- In the Beginning God was a Woman... One of the most fascinating, important and far-reaching periods in the history of mankind must have been the time during which patriarchy, as an ideal for man and God, emerged to triumph and eventually suppress the ideal of matriarchy. Ms Stone set out to discover what could be known about those old matriarchal religions, and why they declined before the rising sun of a male God.(She notes that some of the oldest religions had a female Sun God!) concentrating her study on the Middle East and the emergence of the misogynistic Mosaic laws. Despite Ms Stone's clear bias (the book is subtitled 'The Suppression of Women's Rites') the book is perhaps the best (and most readable) study since Graves' The White Goddess.

Ms Stone points out that the early Goddesses were not just worshipped for their beauty, sexuality or fertility. The Great Mother was, in a way, beyond mere sexuality, being the source of all things, especially knowledge, wisdom and the law. It was only in the transition period, and to some extent in reaction to the more materialistic patriarchal ideas, that the attributes of the Great Mother were fragmented into whole pantheons of gods - a device that reinforced the male dominated religion (eg the randyness of Zeus before an increasingly ineffective Hera). It is this early personification of Wisdom that Ashe sees as the possible origin of the readiness with which Christians accepted the cult of the Virgin Mary. Once there was little place for Mary in the Christian cosmology beside a few brief mentions in the Gospels, and the natural esteem of her role as Mother of Jesus. But, as Ashe points out, traditions are usually retroactive, and it hardly seems credible that the cult of Mary was only recently formalized, historically speaking.

Ashe weaves around the central theme of a biography of the Virgin Mary (from all known sources, including inspired ones), the arguments about whether or not the Marian cultus was an intrusion into Christianity "from the dark realms of natural religion." The book's style makes for a hard reading slog, but if you are interested in such problems, you'll find the effort worthwhile. Ashe's own brave conclusion is also very interesting: "Far from treating Mary-worship in Protestant style as a disease of Christianity, we should confess that in at least one crisis it actually saved Christianity, which would have dwindled to nullity for the lack of what it supplied." This supports Ms Stone's assertion that a male-religion devoid of female attributes in its God is functionally incomplete, if not useless spiritually. If both writers are right, then the Marian cultus looks like growing even more, as in parts of the world it rivals even the worship of Christ. This growth will naturally restore and depend upon the long neglected attributes of the Great

Mother, echoing the days of the Goddesses with their (dependent) male consorts (eg Cybele & Attis, Isis & Osiris, Aphrodite & Adonis, Anath & Baal, etc). RJM Rickard.

We regret that because of a review backlog and shortage of space, some books received will be held over to the next issue. These include Berlitz's Without a Trace, Space Time Transients (Persinger & Lafreniere), & Handbook of Unusual Natural Phenomena (Corliss),etc.

PAPERBACKS

Rhythms of Vision by Lawrence Blair (Paladin 1976; £1.95; pp255; index illos). Unfinished Animal by Theodore Roszak (Faber 1976; £2.95; pp 271; index of names) -- It must by now be obvious to anyone with an interest in any of the diverse fields of paranormal phenomena that the last decade or so has seen the emergence of a new wave, or second stage, approach to the investigation of these enigmas. A small number of researchers, notably John Keel & John Michell with their significant contributions to UFOlogy and its adjacent mysteries, have sought to demonstrate that all extraordinary manifestations that cannot be explained by conventional means are very likely linked; that they are, moreover, attributable to a single all-pervading origin; in fact, different facets of the same controlling force. This book is a further application of the approach exemplified by Keel's contention that we should seek to dissolve the 'frames of reference' which seriously hinder our ability to assess as a whole aspects of the supernatural and psychical previously considered unconnected. It should be said, however, that Lawrence Blair's approach has obviously been arrived at independently, and is spiritual in nature.

His scope and conclusions go much further than simply suggesting a psychic solution to the 'damned' facts science ignores or yet hopes to explain. His underlying concern is to convey an impression of the amazing and intricate uniformity of order and pattern permeating all levels of being. He shows that Man himself, his natural and artificial environment, his social, spiritual and perceptive attitudes, and the non-material forces that surround and influence him, all conform to a fluid yet essentially unchanging symmetry, awe-inspiring in its beautiful efficiency.

Many thoughtfully chosen illustrations here must be worth volumes of explanation.

Blair, and Lyall Watson's foreward, refer to the collective pool of unconsciousness, the reservoir of inspiration held partially responsible for the modern acceleration of ideas, in contrast to the previously held notion that most major innovations originate with an individual or small group whose work did not gain general acceptance in their lifetimes (Charles Fort is an obvious relevant example). Worth considering also is Blair's opinion that our spiritual (and possibly even physical) evolution is in the process of developing to a higher stage of perception, almost entirely despite ourselves, and that we are being inexorably drawn toward a totally unique 'overview' of our existence and purpose by forces beyond our control and understanding.

The book has its faults of course: the end is a little perfunctory (forgiveable considering its scope and the nature of the subject hardly lend themselves to pat conclusions); it falls victim to an automatic reeling-off of anecdotal globs of information in the last few pages when mopping up the 'fringe-fringe' groups and beliefs not covered in the main text; there were even a few factual errors (eg twice listing the publishing date of Adamski's Flying Saucers have Landed as being "in the mid-twenties", and the re-discoverer of leys rendered as Charles Watkins). Despite this, it is well-written, and at times quite eloquent, and can be recommended with very few reservations as an important contribution to Forteanism. Stan Nicholls.

The book by Roszak covers much the same ground (what he calls the 'Aquarian Frontier'), but the style, approach and depth makes an interesting contrast to Blair's book.

Roszak identifies 12 major 'points of entry' into the Aquarian frontier: Judeo-Christian revivals (charismatic movements like the Jesus Freaks, etc); Eastern religions and their new followings; esoteric studies (occult philosophies, etc); eupsychian therapies (Primal, Transpersonal, Arica, Gestalt, Jungian, EST, Silva Mind Control, etc); body therapies (bioenergetics, orgonomy, T'ai chi chuan, martial arts, etc); etherealized healing (psychic surgery, acupuncture, aura, yoga, reflexology & other therapies); neo-primitivism & paganism (shamanism, wicca, primitive lifestyles, etc); organicism (whole & marcobiotic foods, biorhythms, etc); wild science (biofeedback, Kirlian, visionary physics, thanatology, ESP & dream research, drugs, etc); psychic & occult groups (Cayce, Geller, Eckankar,

The Process, etc); psychotronics (neural cybernetics, media mysticism, etc) and pop culture (SF, acid rock and dope, etc).

Blair has a doctorate in contemporary mystical studies; Roszak is a professor of history and sees the many movements of modern enlightenment, not as expressions of a mystical urge toward a unifying vision of nature as Blair does, but in terms of an evolving sociology of human consciousness - ie we are in transition to a new type of society, with new information demands and new ways of communicating. Roszak's study is the tighter of the two, and in my view, the more rewarding in terms of the picture it paints of today's individual, barely able to vocalize his urgent quest, and bewildered by the range of paths to salvation before him. Nor does Roszak ignore the warts of these paths, their dark, slippery and ephemeral nature often lurking behind a slick glossy contemporary image of fashionable commercialism. But this is what Roszak is interested in - the phenomena of human society and aspirations - whereas I found Blair eager to rush through his survey to get to what he was really interested in, the formulation of his ideas about the ordered complexity of universal phenomena. RJM Rickard.

Psychic discoveries behind the Iron Curtain (Abacus 1973; £1.95; pp446; bib/notes, index, photos). Handbook of Psi discoveries (Abacus 1977; £1.95; pp342; bib/notes, index, photos). The ESP papers (Bantam 1976; 65p/$1.95; pp236; small bib, index, photos). All by Sheila Ostrander & Lynn Schroeder. -- The authors have performed a valuable & Herculean feat of reading yards of Soviet literature on paraphysical and parapsychological research, and have distilled from it the most useful essence. The result is an invaluable set of reference material on paranormal data - a veritable mine of new and relevant information that we cannot do full justice to in this limited space. Suffice it to say that most if not all areas you could think of, and some you are bound not to have, are here. The Handbook also contains instructions for building your own equipment and experiments. Essential for Forteans in its fascinating glimpses of Soviet thought on Fortean problems. RJM Rickard.

Mysteries of Time & Space by Brad Steiger (Sphere 1977; 95p; pp283; bib, index, photos) -- the best of Steiger's books released in UK for a long time. He uses Fortean data (anomalous & impossible fossils, apparent time travel & teleportation, and MIB

phenomena) to support his notion that 'Reality' is plastic, and that we are unthinking pawns in some sinister 'Reality game'. It ends optimistically, suggesting that we are quite capable of learning the rules and usurping the puppet-masters.

Flying Saucers have landed by D Leslie & George Adamski (Futura 1977; 95p; pp281; bib) -- Desmond Leslie has revised this major classic of UFOlogy for its first UK paperback edition. It chronicles Adamski's contact with the saucer-folk and many speculations on UFOs in Celtic, Indian and Egyptian folk-myth, doubly interesting in the light of the current enthusiasm for the 'Ancient astronaut' concept. This too was the first serious linking of UFOlogy with spiritual and occult teachings, remarkable for its time, and still controversial. Worth getting.

My contact with UFOs by Dino Kraspedon (Sphere 1977; 75p; pp205) -- Again, a welcome paper edition of one of the classics of the field, worth getting if only for its historical value. Kraspedon changed his name to Aladino Felix, and became a bank robber and guerilla in Brazil, threatening to bring in his Venusian allies to defeat the then government. In 1971 he was imprisoned for his crimes and his 5yr sentence commuted to months if he underwent treatment for his mentally disturbed state. This book recounts his contact with a UFO in late 1952, and the teachings (pseudo-mystical and pseudo-scientific) he received from its captain. You must judge their value yourself.

The Humanoids edited by Charles Bowen (Futura 1974; 80p; pp256; refs) -- a reprinting of the modern classic reference on humanoids - the beings associated with UFOs. Expanded from articles in FSR, the leading writers & events (up to 1969) are represented in this valuable research volume. If you don't have it; buy it!

JOURNALS

We welcome journals on exchange, and give a review/listing upon receipt. Readers applying to mags might like to say they saw the mention in Fortean Times. It helps!

INFO Journal 23 (May 77) - Rocky Mountain Medicine Wheels; reevaluation of Tungus pyrotechnics; UFO news; Ancient sailors; Bigfoot & Manglers; Wisconsin lake monster. 24 (Jly/Aug 77) - Coloured rains; Bigfoot; UFO abductions; The Pelee eruption, 1902; Medicine Wheels pt2. 6 issues/yr/ $10.00. INFO: 7317 Baltimore Ave, College Park, MD 20740, USA...or joint sub with FT - see p40.

Pursuit 38 (Spring 77) - Dynamic biology of Little Green Men; 2 tiny footprints; Relativity; 'The Invisible Star' by Carlos Miguel Allende; Fluidice; Extant dinosaurs; Dinosaur graffiti. 39 (Summer 77) - Incorruptible corpses; Sunken aircraft; Pyramids as communications network; Combustible corpses; Demoniality; Faust and the student; Chinese designs in Mexican & Norse ornament. 4 issues/yr/$10.00. Published by SITU: Columbia, NJ 07832, USA.

Nessletter; published by Ness Information Service: Huntshieldford, St Johns Chapel, Bishop Aukland, Co Durham, DL13 1RQ. Keeps you up to date on monsternews from other lakes, lochs and loughs too, for $7.00/£1.25.

ARB 6 (June 77) - Profile of Curt Sutherly; religious apparition in Texas; anomalous Texan coin; the Mississippi 'Ear-eater'; phantom cat in Kentucky; freak quake in Indiana (don't worry! it was in 1897!). Anomaly Research Bulletin (ARB) edited by David Fideler: 7098 Edinburgh Drive, Lambertville, MI48144, USA. $3.00/£1.50/6 issues.

Lantern Summer 77 - Kids' invisible playmates; pt1 of a valuable Black Dog study by Ivan Bunn; historical Forteana; UFOs and other gleanings of East Anglian curiosa. 84p/4 issues - write for overseas rates. BSIG: 3 Dunwich Way, Oulton Broad, Lowestoft, Suffolk NR32 4RZ.

Vestigia Newsletter 2 (Spring 77) - Results of a field study of the 'Spooklights at Washington Township, New Jersey. Vestigia is a recently formed Fortean study group based in New Jersey; write for details: Box 1183, Perth Amboy, NJ 08861, USA.

NEARA Journal - chronicles the work and concerns of the New England Antiquities Research Association - a pioneering group in the study of pre-Columbian artifacts. Annual sub: $5.00. NEARA: 4 Smith St, Milford, NH 03055, USA.

KRONOS - a journal of interdisciplinary studies - perhaps the most important continuation of Velikovsky's studies today. Recent issues (vol 2, nos 3&4) have contained: Electrical charge of rotating Earth; measurements of orbits; dating the great Mahabharata War; ancient knowledge of Jupiter's bands; Leonardo, rocks & fossils; reactions to Velikovsky's new book Peoples of the Sea; the Sothic chronology of Egypt; and articles by Velikovsky himself. $10.00/ 4 issues. KRONOS: Warner Sizemore, Glassboro State College, Glassboro, NJ 08028, USA.

The Ley Hunter 77 - images in stone; Herefordshire ley; who was the 'Man of Straw'; magic mounds & fairies; 2 articles on leys & dowsing; the Celtic head mystery; Jubilee beacons. TLH merits our congratulations for surviving its first year in the new format, and for establishing a new professional image. $9.00(airmail)/£2.70/6 issues - or joint sub with FT (see panel p40. TLH: Box 152, London N10 1EP.

MUFOB ns7 (Summer 77) - the voice of New UFOlogy. An important article by Peter Rogerson serves as an effective summary of contemporary radical thought on ufology; Jenny Randles on recent UK contact reports; letters, reviews and PR's labour of love, the continuing catalogue of Type 1 records. $3.00(airmail)/£1.25/4 issues. MUFOB:John Rimmer, 11 Beverley Rd, New Malden, Surrey.

Christian Parapsychologist Dec 1976- St Augustine on psychical research; conference reports; journal & book reviews. March 77 - psychical research & religion; Mrs Piper & survival; a medium 'rescued' by Pentecostalists; discussion of Spiritism vs Spiritualism. $3.00(airmail)/£1.50/4 issues. CP: 284 Earls Court Rd, London SW5 9AS.

Flying Saucer Review 22:6 - landing in Co Durham; UFO causes tidal wave; UFOs and Puerto Rico animal deaths; Australian flap 1909/1910; 50 little green 'frogmen'; UFO photos, landings & sightings. 23:1 - reports on the recent Welsh flap; humanoids in N Staffs & Epping Forest, Venezuela, California, and a sex-encounter in Colombia; a 'solid light' feeler probes room; and more. Now $9.00/£4.20/6 issues. FSR: West Malling, Maidstone, Kent.

BUFORA Journal (Mar/Apr 77) - Lionel Beer's investigations of the Winchester encounters. BUFORA annual sub $10.00/ £5.00/ 6 issues BJ: 95 Taunton Rd, London SE12 8PA.

SOBEPS News - English summary of the Belgian Inforespace. Jan 77 - Bermuda Triangle; more about the Dean 'antigrav' drive; humanity's cosmic adventure; analysis of Las Grutas, Argentina, photo (1975); the Borinage flyover. March 77 - UFO dynamics; luminous cylinder & beams, June 1968, Epinois; landing at Peruwelz; analysis of Lake Chauvet, France, photo (1952). Inquiries: SOBEPS: Blvd Aristide Briand 26, 1070 Brussels, Belgium.

Clypeus - Italian UFO & Fortean mag, currently reviewing the airship flaps of late 19th & early 20th centuries.

Clypeus: Postale 604, 10100 Torino
Centro, Italy.

Fate May 77 - towers of Aksum; WW2
radar mystery; Ojibwa vision quest;
Celonese scrying; psychic surgery update; madonna catches thief; plus many
notes & fillers. June 77 - UFO hitch-
hiker; Newport mystery tower; automatic
writing; meditation; leaves dance; mystical experiences. July 77 - Clark interviews Mackal on Nessie; ESP; rescuing
kids from cults; dowsing rescue; UFO
hitchhiker pt 2; psychic healer; sat-
anic accidents?; many small notes.
August 77 - Clark/Mackal/Nessie pt2;
America's unknown ancestors; haunting;
Bermuda triangle; obsession; psychic
hunt for child; biomagnetism; exorcism;
many notes. Also Curtis Fuller's excellent informative column.

Journal of Meteorology - worthwhile
for Forteans interested in weather and
other met. freaks. June/July 77 - recent climate changes, recent thunders &
lightnings; unusual rainbow; tornadoes.
$16.00/£6.50/12 issues. J.Met: Cockhill
House, Trowbridge, Wiltshire BA14 9BG.

Undercurrents 23 - mainly an AT mag,
but   a consistent forum for alternative ideas on anything - sports 2 good
relevant articles -   One by
your editor on Fort & Forteanism; and
pt2 of a study of millenial movements in
history (& present) founded on 'Paranoia
& Conspiracy' by John Fletcher. If not
on your newsstands, send 45p to UC: 6
South St, Uley, Dursley, Gloucestershire.

*** NEXT ISSUE -- is our number 23rd!
which deserves some kind of celebration.
We hope to have a 'Fortean Funnies' by
Hunt Emerson & Steve Moore; Doc Shiels;
Loren Coleman; Larry Arnold with pt2 of
his mammoth SHC study; mystery illnesses;
and encounters with weird beings; and a
whole lot more good stuff ***

FORTEAN TIMES
strange phenomena - curiosities - prodigies - portents - mysteries

STRANGE
ENCOUNTERS
p6

FORTEAN
FUNNIES
P·23

75p : $1·50

UK ISSN 0308-5899

FORTEAN TIMES

A Contemporary Record
of Strange Phenomena

BOX 152, LONDON N10 1EP, ENGLAND.

FORTEAN TIMES is a non profitmaking quarterly miscellany
of news, notes and references on current and historical strange
phenomena, related subjects and philosophies. Formerly 'The
News'. Affiliated to the International Fortean Organisation
(INFO), and the Society for the Investigation of The Unknown
(SITU), and other Fortean journals in continuing the work of
Charles Fort (1874-1932).

Edited and published by Robert JM Rickard.
Contributing editors: Phil Ledger, Steve Moore, Stan Nichols,
Paul J Willis. Heading art by Hunt Emerson.

SUBSCRIPTION information and details of other deals can be
found on the back page.

CONTRIBUTIONS of articles, artwork, notes and letters-of-
comment on related subjects are always welcome. **YOU CAN
HELP** by sending us a copy or clipping of any item you think
will interest FT readers — just add a note of the DATE, the
SOURCE and your NAME (for the credit). All clippings go on
file to be published in due course. Please don't assume we
must know about it already — there are surprisingly few
duplications.
The editor regrets that it is not always possible to reply to all
correspondence. Acknowledgements of money received will
be sent via the following issue of FT.

RIGHTS: All articles and artwork in FORTEAN TIMES are
the copyright of the authors and artists. The views of contributors are not necessarily those of FT, and vice versa.
Uncredited material is by the editors.

AUTUMN 1977

FT REVIEW SUPPLEMENT

The number of books of interest to us
seems to increase yearly, and because of
the 40 page limitation (with our present
printing budget) we have regretted not
being able to give more room and greater
attention to reviews, as the books and
readers deserve. We feel we may have the
answer by issuing a Review Supplement
with the main journal. We hope costs can
be reduced by taking ads from book companies etc - and it will be limited to
subscribers only (to give yet another
incentive for subscribing; like the
index for 1975 (The News 8-13), ready
at long last.) We'll run the FT Review
Supplement as an experiment until the
end of 1978. Please let us know what
you think about this step.

FORTEAN PICTURE LIBRARY

Another plan we have on the boil is
the establishment of a library of Fortean illustrative material, primarily for
posterity and the writer/researcher. We
will build up its 'stock' from our own
files and act as its main aquisition
facility. Naturally we cannot compete
with the commercial ventures who can buy
material for fabulous sums, but we do
hope that copyright-owners and researchers (who come across likely stuff) will

be more sympathetic to us, because we
care about the material's preservation,
study and use. Clearly such a picture
library of strange phenomenal illustrations has some commercial value too, and
just as FT has been approached for use
of some of its photos, we expect the
Fortean Picture Library (FPL), as we'll
call it, to license the use of its materials and charge fees. These will be
used to cover costs and pay the retaining
copyright-owner on a percentage arrangement, unless they have donated the copyright to FPL. We are at present drawing
up information sheets for copyright-owners, and potential users. Ultimately
this will become a useful resource to
which writers and publishers will have
recourse - but we are fully aware that
most Fortean researchers are quite penni-
less, so non-commercial use (including
small Fortean journals etc) will be cat-
ered for as a Special Case. We are beginning to accumulate material right now,
though commercial operation per se may
be some time away. Janet & Colin Bord,
who run their own picture library on
ancient sites and stones, will be handling the administration, processing and
filing. Stay tuned for more details.

cont on p5/

MYSTERY ATTACKS

THE DARTMOOR PONY DEATHS

Last issue, p30, we told all we knew of the mysterious deaths of 15 ponies on a lonely part of Dartmoor. Their death still remains a mystery, but we thought you'd be interested to hear of yet another theory. The Dartmoor Livestock Protection Society have no faith in UFOs, exotic diseases, natural causes, or rowdies in a jeep - they believe the animals ate bog asphodel (Narthecium ossifragum), which can cause brittle bones. Someone else has suggested lightning - certainly there are cases where groups of animals have been struck, and have decomposed faster than usual - but we have no idea yet whether there was a local electrical storm. Perhaps someone could follow this tack up. **Western Morning News** (Devon edn) 19 July 1977 (Cr: David Sutton). Notes on two other mass deaths have come to light...

HORSES DIE AT DUGWAY

An AP report from Utah said that in the first week of July 1976, wild horses were dropping dead in great numbers on a hot, mile-high mountain range in the western Utah salt desert. At least 40 had died, and an 'unknown number' were near death, on the western slopes of the Cedar Mountain range. The report says that nearby is the Dugway chemical-warfare proving ground, and Skull Valley, where about 4,500 sheep died mysteriously in 1968. It is still denied to this day by Dugway officials that nerve-gas was responsible for the sheep-slaughter. Military officials are also strongly denying that any operation at the base could or has caused the horse deaths. Meanwhile the Bureau of Land Management (BLM) and the Utah Agriculture Dept are testing 'every element in the wild horse herd's environment' in the search for a cause. The BLM are especially peeved, having just completed a water project for the large herd, and are looking at the possibility that land disturbance contaminated water at Orr Springs, where many of the horses were found in a dusty gully. Kansas City Star 8 July 1976 (Cr: William Grimstad). The BLM reported in August, and the Utah Ag.Dept. gave their judgement in September - the horses suffered heat exhaustion and dehydration followed by water intoxication as they drank greedily when they came to water. The Dugway officials agree with both reports. However I have a note from the Des Moines, Iowa, Sunday Register 25 July 1976, that the BLM was at that early date, blaming their death on shock - whatever they meant by that! (Cr: John Michell). The official verdict does not satisfy the naturalists. Ron Hall, 'a government wild horse expert' who discovered the mass deaths, and who plainly said he'd never seen anything like it before, is finally quoted insisting that a pond was built as early as May 13th and was used by the herd frequently. 'When I arrived July 5 there was plenty of water, and there were plenty of tracks around the pond.' He is convinced something happened there, and finds it difficult to believe that the young and strongest horses would have died like this from dehydration. Arizona Daily Star 21 Aug; Washington Post 3 Sept 1976 - and X's Res Bureaux Bulletins 5-7. Readers will be quick to note that the allegation of military experiments with chemical warware substances was lodged during the American Legion sickness that same July (see FT20/10-13). The Arizona paper (above) also reported the belief of the Humane Society of Utah, and the American Horse Protection Association, that a rare African horse disease could produce the same syndrome, including the blood-froth found on the dead horses' nostrils. We learn that no tests were made by the BLM as they saw 'no reason to believe it was a cause of death'. (!!!)

MASS ELK DEATH

About the same time as the tragedy at Dugway, a herd of 61 elk, including 10 bulls, died in a way which suggested they

all fell to the foot of a cliff in mountains near Telluride, Colorado. About a
year later a hunter, Jack Pera, found
scattered heaps of bodies at the base of
a 60ft cliff. After examining their injuries, Colorado Wildlife officials think
they fell to their death, but they are
puzzled. One said: 'Occasionally a deer
or elk might slip and fall to its death.
But 61? It's just unheard of.' Well he's
heard of it now. The officers said there
was only one elk path up the ridge which
could easily be cut off. One said that
'elk rarely stampede when faced by bears,
mountain lions or coyotes, because they
usually know a way out.' The only theory
which hasn't been knocked out is that
perhaps they simply could not see where
they were going - and perhaps lightning
panicked them. It was believed they died
around July or August 1976; Pera found
them early July 1977. Alamosa, Colorado,
Valley Courier 6 July; Dallas, Texas,
Morning News, 10 July 1977 (Cr: TR Adams)

MORE UK HORSE ATTACKS

Last issue, p27, we told of a boy's
donkey foal found hanged in a tree at
Ash, Surrey. We are sad to report another
mindless act of foal-hanging, this time
at Cefn, Hengoed, near Swansea. The foal,
belonging to a girl who lived in Lans-
bury Avenue, was found in a nearby tree
with its legs bound. Police and villagers
mounted a search - we don't know if the
culprit/s were found. London Evening
Standard 12 August 1977.

After three stables were broken into
in 10 days, and several horses injured,
police in the Isle of Wight were said to
be hunting a 'sadist'. No further details
Daily Mail 5 September 1977.

In the night of 21 September, a savage
attack was made on three pedigree foals
in their field at Blackwood, Gwent, South
Wales. Out of 12 foals in the field,
owned by breeder Peter English, only
the 3 best were hacked. They were young
and, luckily, will survive. One theory,
based on this detail of selection, is
that some rival breeder may have made a
grudge attack with an axe. Police were
looking into the matter but apparently
had little to go on. No further details.
Daily Mirror 22 September 1977. (Cr:
Nigel Pennick.)

A mystery knifeman slashed the throats
of three horses grazing in a field at
Dagenham, Essex. Police, fearing 'his'
next victim may be human, 'hunted' -
we guess, inconclusively. Sunday Express
2 October 1977.

Did you notice the series of 3s in
these stories?

RABBITS

Police in Coventry were already
investigating the savage killing of
rabbits from 15 homes in the Radford
area, when on Monday 7 Feb this year,
Mrs Olena Konopacka, a rabbit breeder,
of Catesby Road, found 30 of her animals mutilated and dumped in a heap.
It is thought that one or more people
tore open the hutches and set their
dogs on the rabbits - but (there's
always a but) Mrs Konopacka says she
and her 2 dogs were inside the house
all the time. The dogs had not barked,
and neither she nor her neighbour had
heard anything in the night. Police say
that the killings were in homes along
Villa, Foster and Middlemarch roads,
and that in some places the rabbits
have been heard squealing between 11am
and 6pm. (Either the police have their
am/pms mixed up, or the killer, and
possibly his dog, or possibly bands of
killers and their dogs, have been roaming Radford in broad daylight, with
nobody noticing a thing!) Coventry Evening Telegraph 10 Feb 1977. The same
paper for 22 Feb reported more killings
- 2 that day in Burnaby Rd; 1 in Cap-
martin Rd on the 19th, and its mate in
the same cage the next night; and again
nearby that same night, the 20th. Police
said that in all more than 60 had died
- 'some seem to have been thrown or
crushed, others look as though they have
been killed by a dog!'. The Stephens of
Three Spires Avenue put their rabbits
to bed and retired themselves about
11pm, on the night of the 24th. Their
dog barked about 11.30pm but they heard
nothing suspicious and went to bed. In
the morning they found bits of 15 of
their New Zealand whites all over the
lawn. The doors seem to have been ripped from the hutches, the wire-net pens
torn open - the bigger bunnies had been
battered and strangled. No one heard
much noise! On the night of the 25th
more pets were killed and injured in
Sunningdale Ave. Coventry Eve.Telegraph
26 Feb. These latest attacks were more
bizarre - skin had been partly stripped
from one body and there were teeth marks
on its neck. The tail of the other
rabbit had been cut off. The paper for
11 March 1977 carried a police confession of their bafflement in the case
which had occurred sporadically since
Christmas 1976, and covered the Radford,
Holbrooks and Coundon suburbs of Coventry with dead rabbits. All the killings
took place at night (ah!) without alert-
ing the households. There were no forensic leads (no mention of things like
foot or paw prints); and no consistancy

in the manner of death, except cruelty. The paper alludes to a similar series of attacks on rabbits in the city in 1973 (in the Bell Green, Walsgrave and Wyken areas) but we have no data on that. (See back to The News 4/15f for a sadist who slew 288 pets in Jan 1970, including many rabbits; and the 'Welsh Rabbit Killer' of Nov 1970 - both never caught!)

After a hiatus of nearly 2 months the killings renewed. Seven were taken from their cages, in the Radford area, and killed, on the night of 2 May. One man, of Owenford Rd, said he had seen a large black dog with his 3 rabbits on his lawn. He rushed out to find the rabbits dead but not savaged. He trapped the dog in his garden shed but it escaped via a second door - which had been forced like the hutches! Curious and nagging detail that! The same modus operandi recurred 9-10 days later, at Stretton-on-Dunsmore, a village between Coventry and Rugby. In two separate attacks, hutches were ripped apart. The rabbits were found dead but not mauled. Police suspect a dog! These events in Coventry Evening Telegraph 3 and 14 May 1977, respectively (Cr: David Tame).

Police were hunting for the killer of 12 rabbits and 2 guinea pigs, killed over 12 days in Chelmsley Wood, Birmingham. No other details. Sunday Express 30 May 1976.

On the 5th Aug 1976, Mr Ken Marsden, of St John's Rd, Pembroke Dock, near Haverfordwest, South Wales, checked the hutch of his children's rabbits before going to work. He found it forced open, with 2 adults and one baby cowering inside with fright. On the lawn were 3 others, their heads and legs cut off. The police made a search of the garden and surrounds but found no sign of the heads and legs. Mr Marsden rules out an animal - the hutch had a bolted sliding door that only a human could open. Two mornings later the Calvers, neighbours, found their rabbit dead, its eyes gouged out and one leg cut off. He had been so worried by the Marsden's loss that he had moved his own hutch nearer the kitchen door and had sat up to 2am that night. When he got up at 5.30am he discovered the tragedy. He said he had heard of other killings on the estate but they had never been reported to the police. Interestingly this case is complicated by a fairly explicit sighting on the 15th Aug. Mrs Christine Lavender, of Arthur St, was wakened about 5am by the squealing of her rabbit. From the bedroom window she saw a large black labrador-type dog running off with it

in its mouth. Their own dog began barking and the intruder dropped the rabbit and ran. It had apparently torn some wire-netting to get at the rabbit. But the police said they could not discount links between this and the earlier cases - by which they mean we'd rather believe in dogs, even dogs that cut off heads, limbs and gouge out eyes, than believe we have a dangerous maniac loose in peaceful Pembroke Dock, or worse! In time they'll convince themselves that it was all the work of a dog - or better yet, forget about it completely! Until someone or something out there feels the urge to rip, slash and hurt again. The Western Telegraph, 19 August 1976 (Cr: FW Holiday.)

■■■■■■■■■■■■■■■■■■■■■■■■■■■■■■■■■■■■

Editorial stuff cont...

DOC SHIELS...

Firstly, despite our announcement last issue of the play 'Distant Humps', written by Ken Campbell and Doc, due to open at the Bush Theatre, London, it never made the journey. I'm told it had several successful nights in Falmouth (during which Doc flashed FT22 at the stunned audience), but he and Ken felt they wanted to develop it more before airing it in London. Let's hope we see DH mkII soon, the other side of Xmas.

Secondly, there have been some developments in reaction to Doc's astonishing photos of Nessie (FT 22/24,25). An American UFO group,who specialized in photo-analysis, have examined them and suggest that they do not conform with Doc's testimony. The group, Ground Saucer Watch (GSW), have virtually accused Doc of fakery! We have seen their report and are not convinced by their arguments. Nor is veteran monster-hunter Tim Dinsdale, who has sent us a letter saying so. Consequently Doc and Tim have sent the photos to the Joint Air Reconnaissance Intelligence Center (JARIC) for a more professional study - not the action of a faker! In the last few weeks different people have brought to our attention major differences of opinion with GSW from within the ranks of ufology, and serious criticism of their work. Naturally Doc is a bit taken aback, and is wondering why the hell he should go to a lot of trouble just to convince some cynical upstarts - but we are glad he is, and we support him all the way. Tread boldly, Doc! We'll have full reports on all this next issue.

SOME EDITORIAL MATTERS

Truss Fund - thanks for finacial support to RTA Hill, Chris Holtzhausen & John N Peldyak.   cont on p40/

FAIRLY CLOSE ENCOUNTERS

In Phenomena John Michell and I deal
with several aspects of teleportation
mysteries. Perhaps one of the most
interesting, and enduring, motifs is
that people who seem to have vanished
from one place to reappear in another
often blame the involuntary transit on
mysterious entities, described according to various times and traditions as
demons, fairies, spirits, witches, and
today, UFO-beings. We have to say once
more that this notion of abduction by
mysterious beings is no superstition
from the Dark Ages; it is the form of a
psychodrama that is very much alive
today to judge from the following tales.
Our own feeling is that these tales
contain two important data ; the mystery of teleportation (sometimes with
a weird timelapse), and the more var-
iable element (possibly due to cultural
conditionings) of the nature of the
abducting entities. Our first story is

FIVE DAY'S BEARD IN 15 MINUTES

On 17th May 1977, the story broke in
Santiago, Chile, that a Chilean army
corporal, on patrol duty on the remote
northern desert border with Bolivia,
vanished in front of his six men, and
reappeared in their midst 15 minutes
later, disorientated and incoherent.
This was said to have happened at about
4.15am on 25 April, when the patrol
noticed two bright lights descending on
them from the sky. According to later
testimony, they saw one drop behind some
foothills, its glow remaining visible.
The other came down within 500 yards of
their camp, putting out a violet light
with two points of intense red. Corporal Armando Valdes ordered his men to
pick up their weapons, then advanced
toward the light a little way, and disappeared. Then the light vanished too.

Later the patrol told their story to
a schoolteacher in Arica, the largest
town in the area, who taped them and
contacted a local newspaper. (Some
reports say the man was Pedro Araneda,
a university professor.) Araneda was
greatly impressed by the men's sincerity
in believing what they had seen. They
said they had called out for the corporal for several minutes, then, suddenly
15 minutes later, at 4.30pm, he was
among them as mysteriously as he had
disappeared. He gasped "Muchachos," and
fainted. His comrades noticed that he
had about five days' growth of beard,
and that the date on his calendar watch
had advanced five days. The watch itself
stopped about the time he reappeared.
As he regained consciousness Valdes
said: 'You do not know who we are, nor
where we come from. But I tell you that
we will soon return.' Valdes, apparently,
has no recollection of his abduction or
utterances. That's the last we heard.
Compiled from: Age (Australia) 19 May
1977 (Cr: B Ratcliffe); AP reports in
23 May 1977 newspapers (Cr: Larry Arnold & Ion Will); Sunday Express 29 May
1977 (Cr: AJ Bell, Don Robbins).

MALAYSIAN FOREST ELVES

A slightly more sinister version of
a similar scenario developed in Johore
state, Malaysia,in May this year, where
in two separate cases a mother of three
and a schoolboy have disappeared. The
woman, Saoma binti Bujang, has not been
seen since 5th May, in her village of
Kuala Paya, near Segamat. Curiously,
her husband, Mohamed Akhir, said that
he himself had been 'carried away' by
the forest elves in 1960, and found by
relatives a week later in a debilitated
condition that lasted five years. On
5 May 1977, however, he arrived home to
find all the doors and windows locked

from the inside and his wife missing. Villagers were said to believe that the 'invisible people' had come looking for Mohamed again, and failing to find him took his wife instead. Bomohs, Malayan shamans, said his wife was still there - but a search failed to discover her - she was as effectively invisible as her abductors.

In the second case, Azmi Othman, 9, and who had not been seen since he set out on a short familiar journey to visit his grandparents at Teluk Rimba, near Muar on Sunday, is still missing despite extensive searches. His mother consulted bomohs who said he was still alive but as a captive of the forest elves. These notes are from New Straits Times (Malaysia) 27 May 1977 (Cr: Ion A Will).

The same paper for 22 August 1977 shows us another side to the forest elves which will be more familiar to modern saucer buffs. Here we learn that villages in the Batu Pahat area of Johore have been pestered by a forest elf (Orang Bunian) in the guise of a woman in black (WIB?), who obstructs doorways and vanishes like a ghost. WW Skeat's work on Malay Magic (1965) says nothing much is known about the 'Orang Bunian', but he classes them with the fairies and elves, adding that, if anything, they are begnign and a little stupid!

A DWARF & SOME LITTLE MEN...
FSR 23:2 (Aug 1977) mentions the appearance of an 'extraterrestrial dwarf' in Italy, in its 'World Round-up' section. Quoting from the ABC (Seville) 11 Sept 1976, it mentions that this black-dressed, 1m20cm high creature, with two fissures in (or for) its face, has caused considerable alarm among the inhabitants of the La Spezia region in a mountainous part of NW Italy. In the grand tradition of ghosts, it glided rather than walked, and there are tantalizing references to witnesses suffering 'magnetic distortions' (whatever those may be) by the things presence. We merely note (again) that elements from the experience of UFOs are echoes of earlier traditions, and still manifesting today.

The same goes for the following case brought to light by John Michell, in which an 8-yr-old boy, NP (name & address known to us) and his friend share a vision, which according to NP's mother 'left him quite confused and frightened.' She adds that he is not in the habit of making things up and is fairly certain that they did see something. Here, in his own words, is his account:

'On June the 18th, 1977, I was out with my friend, when we went to Crick-lade ((Wilts)) water cress beds. Suddenly my friend called to me, "Come here! There's a red thing in the bush the same size as me," but I didn't see it. So we walked on to the old hut and had a look around and walked along the side of the cress beds. Then we saw some people in red and yellow one-piece suits with air tanks on their backs running about the hut. We were scared because they had red eyes and they were wearing helmets. They ran very quickly with their knees up high. We were so scared we climbed up a fallen-down tree which led to the road and ran home.' NP's mother tried to get him to draw them but it was difficult and she felt that it might agitate him to press him.

REVELERS IN A FOG PATCH
At about 1.30am on (probably) 9 August 1977, Pc David Swift decided to investigate a peculiar bank of fog on playing fields near Stonebridge Avenue, East Hull - he thought it might be smoke. As he walked across the field towards it he could make out three figures which seemed to be dancing, each with an arm raised as though around a non-existent Maypole. 'One figure was a man in a sleeveless jerkin and tightfitting trousers...the other two were women wearing bonnets, shawls and white coloured dresses.' Pc Swift said: 'I thought they were a lot of drunks playing around, so I walked out into the field. But when I got about 50ft away from them everything went. No one was there.' The sudden vanishing took the former Army man by surprise. He ran for his car and dazedly drove up and down a nearby road until the shock wore off, then reported it to his sergeant. He told the reporter that he'd be back there again on duty that night (10th), but we've heard nothing more. Hull Daily Mail 10 August 1977 (Cr: Derick Shelton & Nigel Watson)

MUFOB editor John Rimmer rightly places this story in relationship to the tales of fairy-rings. Not only do fairies vanish away when interrupted at their revels, but to step into the ring was to risk becoming trapped forever in dance, invisible to everyone. The Welsh fairy tradition provides a good number of stories of people foolish enough to venture into fairy circles. We give one story in Phenomena, in 'Taken Away & Brought Back'; others can be found in chapter 4 of Wirt Sikes' British Goblins (1880, rep 1973). One of these is even encountered in an unexpected mist! But usually the victim can be rescued on the anniversary of his disappearance unaware that outside the circle a whole year, not mere seconds, had passed. Like the Malayan cases, the victims were still on the spot, but invisible, or inaccessible to everyday reality. Another thread in these cases is the eerie motion of the entities - the irresistable gyrations of the fairies, the high-stepping folk in spacesuit-like attire seen by young NP, Pc Swift's misty revellers, and one of the Malayan WIBs who was seen standing board-stiff (like Nosferatu rising from his coffin!) outside a house after poltergeist-like rappings awoke the occupant - a motion, or lack of it, that puts the witness's hair on end. We have often met the same reaction to the motions of sea monsters and poltergeists! A third theme is the time-lapse (or time-acceleration) during the abduction.

Interestingly, in reviewing Rogo's Haunted Universe (see the Review Supplement) we find he revives the case of 'Manila's Disappearing Boy' from Fate August 1965. In the 1950s, the boy, Cornelio Closa, caused a sensation by repeatedly vanishing from locked rooms or out on the street, often before many witnesses. These mysterious transport-

ations, he said, happened when his childhood companion, a phantom girl dressed in white, would touch his hand. He knew nothing more, except dream-like sensations, until he came to himself at a different location.

This touches on the many amnesia cases where whole chunks of people's lives go missing, often leaving them confused and frightened. We have a heap of these, as they seem to overlap with the phenomena of 'Appearances' and 'Disappearances', and will give them another day.

TOUT ENCORE!
Finally, a throwaway! According to the News of the World 25 September 1977, a farmer at Tout, France, couldn't believe his eyes when a UFO landed in his field in broad daylight (or should that be broad delight?). He said that a man and woman, both naked, leapt from the UFO and made love three times before clambering back and zipping off into the sky. He tried to get nearer but was hurled back by the 'blast'. Gendarmes were said to be grinning as they 'filed' the report. Make of that what you will!

It's some time since we had a section on ice chunks dropping from our skies, and 1977 seems to have developed an unusual number. But first we'll give a few notes that have not been mentioned in our previous excursions into the subject (see The News 3/8f; 6/10,11,14.)

SHIRLEY, SURREY - 1972.
Although we had a note of this fall, on 23 January (News 6/10) previously, Janet Bord has handed to us some correspondence on the incident that she had with various officials. The ice block was said to have been about 4ft square, and made a 2ft deep dent in the garden of Peter Wakeford, in Lime Tree Grove, Shirley, just missing his house. This additional information is from Daily Telegraph 24 January 1972.

Janet wrote to the Air Registration Board (who had previously stated the official view on icefalls said to come

from airplanes - that because of modern de-icing equipment the problem should be insignificant; that waste-tank discharges over populated areas is prohibited generally; and that it is virtually impossible (mainly on economic and organizational grounds at present) to identify which aircraft were over certain areas at certain times) - who passed her query onto an official of the Department of Trade & Industry. He replied that his department's interest was confined to the problem as it affects the safety of air traffic. They collected a sample of the Shirley ice and had it analysed in the labs of the Royal Aircraft Establishment at Farnborough. They said it had the characteristics of ice which forms on the external surfaces of aircraft - but the implication is that this origin could not be definitely proved. Nor, with all the resources of
cont on p17/

Part 2 of an article, specially extracted for us, by Larry Arnold, from his forthcoming book <u>ABLAZE! The Case for, and cases of</u>, Spontaneous Human Combustion.

HUNT EMERSON

FIRE LEYNES

by LARRY E ARNOLD

Leaving Birmingham to cope alone for the moment with its burning mystery of twice-yearly fires, we travel southeast to Britain's capital city. The destination awaits our arrival, as it had for half a decade awaited an arrival far less welcomed by those who hosted the sinister visitor.

"Each year, around Easter", writes Frank Edwards (28,p196), "fire keeps an appointment with the family of Graham Stringer, who lives in a modest home in the Peckham district of London".

The uninvited guest arrived about 3 weeks before Easter in 1958 when the baby's rocking chair and toy basket were found smoking, leaving the Fire Brigade with a mystery. Good Friday of that year left the Stringers with a less-than-spiritual memory, for again fire erupted spontaneously - this time the flames ate a hole in a pile of infant clothing.

In 1959 the phantom flames came out of hiding to strike at Mr Stringer's shoes - and just as he was putting his feet into them. He <u>literally</u> had a hot foot that morning - two of 'em!

As the last week of Lent was being observed in 1960, the String-ers were confronted with another form of rebirth: the Peckham fire arose again, erupting in a pile of laundry that Mrs Stringer had just sorted. In less than a minute the combustion was complete, the garments purged of dirt - but as ashes they were unwearable. Soon afterwards "luminous smoke" swirled through Stringer's darkroom. The firemen came and "went away baffled". A priest came and performed an exorcism, then simply left...

1961 was quiet, fire-wise; but 1962 heralded combusting furniture in the living room. Scotland Yard suspected the obvious, until learning the Stringers had no fire insurance - and couldn't get any either!

Is there any truth after all in the ancient belief that the fires of Hades raged in subterranean recesses of the underworld, where sinister forces quite apart from magma were unleashed to haunt and destroy the lives of men above? In Kentucky a few years back, the ground was said to be afire and no one could explain why.

Might it be the Stringer house sat on a telleyne whose fiery vengeance was released or withheld not by religious observations but by a peculiar combination of terrestrial and/or cosmic lines of force which had to mix just right - like salt-petre, sulphur and charcoal must be, to yield an explosion - before combustion would manifest?

Had Stringer known as much about energies as the ancients, he would have insured his property heavily against fire; in fact, he probably wouldn't have lived in that house at all. Conversely, if insuring agents knew about fiery points of power, no sum of money would have purchased protection for this fire-prone piece of property.

Edwards also mentions the death on 4 Jan 1939 of Peter Seaton's 11-month-old child in Peckham Rye (28,p185). Quoting the London Daily Telegraph he states that a "fire of unknown type and origin killed the baby and seared the wall...but did no damage at all outside that one room". Though Edwards saw the similarity between this event and many he (and we) have chronicled under the description of SHC, he saw no connection between this episode and the one which began 19 years later in Stringer's Peckham home. It would be interesting to discover the proximity with which the Seatons and Stringers lived, wouldn't it?

Speaking of the nearness with which unusual combustions strike, we note the auto incineration of Messrs Beattie and Turner in their trucks outside Upton-by-Chester. Only 3 days separated their near-duplicate demises by inexplicable flames. Or how about the poor chap burned beyond recognition, whose charred body was pulled from an auto near Hessle, Yorkshire, in early 1949 - at a spot said "to be very near" the location where motorist G A Shepherdson burned to death "with startling suddenness" 11 years earlier?

Localisations...

Elsewhere, something equally frightening and far more sinister than drunken drivers and mechanical malfunctions stalks the motoring trackways. Police can find no culprit, only the evidence for his - or its - presence. Windshields are shattered along "Britain's Mystery Mile" in March 1951, southwest of London; on 16 June 1952 the phantom marauder finally leaves the highway, to attack shop windows in the nearby town of Esher (18, p129-31).

We sense a migrating power point, leaving the transience of a pastoral roadway for the concrete-and-glass of immobile shrines; an aerleyne whose energy pattern rivalled the celebrated glass-breaking voice of Enrico Caruso.

In the U.S., Indiana and Illinois also hosted a 'phantom sniper' in June 1952. Phenomenological proximities in time...

An aerleyne is created to balance its counterpart in Britain. They both move on, their mystery lying forgotten in a newspaper's archival tombs. In the middle of some farmer's field there is no glass to be broken. But near Muncie, Indiana, there is talk of constructing a jughandle to skirt the accident-prone zone. Imagine: half a roundabout nestled in the midst of an otherwise straight and level road!(29). An environmental design, made necessary to avoid an apparently stationary ley centre whose power warps human judgment and causes crashes. Explain that to a civil engineer!

Oh what the heck, no highway department in the world would believe such nonsense. That unseen forces should govern the design of roads is absurd! That outside Hessle and Upton-by-Chester, smack in the middle of some roads, are invisible power points which affect human or automobile combustibility - adversely.

HAUNTING FLAMES IN THE HACKLER HOUSEHOLD.

Firemen are like policemen in that they generally tend to deny the unusual, both in fact and in theory. This is not to castigate those who help safeguard our properties and our lives, but merely shows them to be human. As Fort would point out on occasion, Physics, Astronomy, Biology and Medicine (to be sure!) all have established boundaries beyond which it is respectable never to tread. Let us not digress too far, however...

The Earth Spirit, telleynes and aerleynes, power points and zone phenomena. Stories of strange fires - or fires that would be strange, if stories of similar fires weren't so embarrassingly common.

Indiana, again; near Odon, this time. Pre-1941. A full-page ad in Collier's Magazine (19 April 1941) is bought by the Traveller's Insurance Company to extol the benefits of purchasing fire protection coverage (You never know where you can find a lead, do you!).

At 8:00am fire erupted near an upstairs window. The Odon Fire Dept. answered the alarm and since the Hackler farmhouse had never been wired for electricity and no fire was in the kitchen range, the "cause was a mystery". Left with an enigma, the firemen themselves left - but not for long.

They soon responded to a second alarm, this time to extinguish a burning mattress. This time they lingered around, just in case. The 'case' came; then again, and again. By 11:00am nine fires had blazed forth: "Some were so strange as to tax the belief of the most credulous persons who visited the place". Overalls hanging on the wall ignited; a wall calendar went up "in a quick puff of smoke"; a bedspread inflamed before the eyes of several neighbours; a book was found, burning on the inside (its covers undamaged). Fifteen hours after the first alarm, 28 fires had broken out. Sounds much like some cases Fort catalogued, yes?

"Various explanations have been advanced", the ad stated, "some as weird as the happenings themselves. Some people believe the Hackler farm was the centre of a strong magnetic field where static electricity prevailed. Others have suggested that gases from an old well had permeated the building, finally bursting into flame by spontaneous combustion. These and other solutions appear none too plausible", said the Travellers. Yet we note the insurance investigators failed, as did the firemen, to find the cause.

Static electricity is discountable, yes; but not so easily discounted is a strong localised field of energy vitalised by subterranean or cosmic forces whose combining vibrational-frequencies struck the 'chord' of fire outside Odon, Indiana one day in the early 1940s. Whatever, the insurance company concluded its example this way: "The story remains even to fire officials a most baffling mystery".

FROM THE HIGHLANDS TO SUSSEX:
"BEWARE THE LEYNE OF FIRE!"

More mysteries follow - and maybe a solution as well.

Having reviewed this material before sending the mss. to our editor, we are struck anew with the fantastic voyage that lies before you. We insert this paragraph to

forewarn, for undoubtedly charges of "Impossible!" and "Absurd!" will be leveled at what will now be developed. There is one consolation: the same has been said about SHC. Well, what has been shown wrong once...

The phrase 'line of fire' is usually associated with the battlefield. Its re-ordered form, 'fireline', evokes a demarcation to prevent the advance of a crackling holocaust of lands aflame. We now propose a third meaning to these words, which captures both the combustion and destruction aspects and relates them linearly. Using our Fortean lexicon, a fire-leyne is a specific type of telleyne or aerleyne whose energy flow is conducive to generating combustion in objects sited upon its pathway.

Until now we have merely hinted at a relationship between lines of force and spontaneous combustions. It has been an exercise on paper only. Would the theory hold under the rigours of practical scrutiny?

To the drawing board, and more paper. Cartography, this time.

Since more ley work has transpired in Great Britain than anywhere else to date, we reach for maps of the British Isles. What secrets lie among the town names that greet our glance?

"The index of SHC cases, dear Watson, and a pen!" Three charts, a good gazeteer, and several hours of intense concentration produce a cartographic countryside filled with dots designating the places where strange fires baffled the townsfolk in their day.

"Now the straight-edge, quickly!" We begin in a maze of dots. Any 2 points establish a line. We look for a line with more than 2 dots. Are there any? Yes! Many lines connect 3 sites. Are we locating a new ley system, one marked not by churches and tumuli and monoliths but by enigmatic fires which in turn are caused by their superimposition on this particular energy pattern? But Alfred Watkins wanted "'four-point' evidence, below which number coincidence might creep in". (6, p 25)

The parameters tighten. Would our hours before the charts now be reduced to an exercise in futility? "Wait a moment...let's check this again". Yes! A four-point fire-leyne is found! And another! Why, some lines might have 5, 6 or more mysterious fires sited upon them!

Once again we think we know how Watkins felt that day in June 1921...

We pause to reflect a moment. Events so similar yet so incredibly bizarre and uncommon that Science says they don't - can't - exist, do exist. Furthermore, many are found in alignment to one another over scores, maybe hundreds of miles. If one were to calculate the odds against exceedingly rare events happening over centuries while occurring in a linear arrangement...

Enough of this unsubstantiated wonderment! The evidence, please.

The evidence appears in Fig 1, scaled from the original 1:1250000 BTA map produced by a leading British cartographic firm. Dots, however, mean little. On the other hand, to discuss here each case associated with a dot would be both laborious and impractical (The reader must await our book, or do his own research).

We shall compromise this nothingness versus totalness by focusing on one major alignment: Proposed Fire-leyne 1. Some incidents are quite involved, so the reader is asked to forgive our sketchy details while remembering that through all that follows appears to run a common thread, arrow-straight and scorchingly hot.

POINT 1: John Anderson, 50-year-old drunkard, suffered divine retribution for succumbing to "the demon of Intemperance by flaming up as does the vile liquor which permeated his body" (30, p54-6). His fiery fate came one half mile east of Nairn, on the Moray Firth in Scotland when, on 29 May 1852, his body was suddenly "so blackened and burned by the fire, that it was doubtful if it could be lifted without falling pieces". Anderson forms the northern terminus of the fire-leyne in question - or, as Watkins' jargon would phrase it, "the beacon point" of a south-southeast trackway.

A beacon point, shining with the spontaneous light of a blazing corpse...

POINT 2: The trackway crosses the Firth of Forth, passes through Blyth and Whitley Bay, and intersects dead-centre with Kingston upon Hull, Humberside.

Kingston has 4 projected fire-leynes through it. A fire-leyne centre, one might say. Elizabeth

Clark could not say, however. "She was unable to give an articulate account of the manner in which she received her dreadful injuries", stated the Hull Daily Mail (6 Jan 1905) in reference to the severe burns that covered her body (31).

Investigators were baffled, so they proposed this scenario: "it is surmised she got out of bed, and in striking a match, set her nightdress on fire. This must have burned away, and then the unfortunate woman must have got into bed again. How long she had been in this state it is impossible to say". Striking how Conventionalism rationalises, isn't it? Her stoicism must put the Spartan warriors and the Greek sect to shame! Hm...perhaps Clark could not explain her situation because it baffled her as much as her fellow pensioners! We suspect no-one in Hull knew that humans, and their clothing, could spontaneously combust; that this victim appears linked to a similar event in Scotland 489kms away and 52 years in the past (One is reminded that at Hull, 7 April 1938, G A Shepherdson died in his mysteriously burning truck).

POINT 3: Louth, in the midst of the Lincolnshire Wolds, received a bevy of oddly burned patients at its hospital in early 1905. Ashton Clodd, 75, was struck down at the end of January. Fort (1, p122) quotes a source saying the deceased fell into a grate, though no-one can testify to seeing hot coals therein. Ashton - a name of esoteric significance? - is certainly not the only person to burn up in a fireplace that held no embers!

The fire-leyne goes right past Louth. Actually, on our map it tracks 1·6km west of Louth; then too, Clodd's home might have been 1·6km west of Louth proper, and directly atop the fiery trackway in question. We just don't know for sure. We do know that initially we had misplaced this case elsewhere in England, and it wasn't until we followed the ruler and saw Louth sitting in Lincolnshire that we realised our error. Watkins and others have experienced similar 'confirmations' (7, p46 & 184).

What could be more convincing? "Another case - if you can find one", replies the die-hard skeptic. Done!

POINT 4: The coastal town of Blyth in southeastern Northumberland harbours more than boats: it

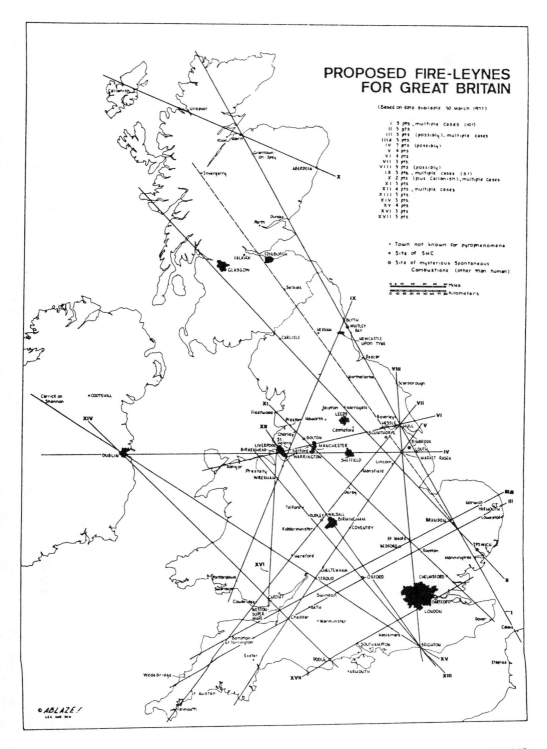

PROPOSED FIRE-LEYNES
FOR GREAT BRITAIN

(Based on data available 30 March 1977)

I   5 pts., multiple cases (10+)
II   5 pts.
III   3 pts. (possibly), multiple cases
IIIa   3 pts.
IV   7 pts. (possibly)
V   4 pts.
VI   4 pts.
VII   3 pts.
VIII   5 pts. (possibly)
IX   5 pts., multiple cases (5+)
X   2 pts. (plus Callanish), multiple cases
XI   3 pts.
XII   4 pts., multiple cases
XIII   3 pts.
XIV   3 pts.
XV   4 pts.
XVI   3 pts.
XVII   3 pts.

· Town not known for pyrophenomena

● Site of SHC

○ Site of mysterious Spontaneous
  Combustions (other than human)

Miles
Kilometers

© ABLAZE!

hosts baffling blazes. And Blyth is anchored upon the fire-leyne that extends from Nairn, 314kms to the north-northwest.

Barbara Bell, first. On 23 Feb 1905 smoke was seen issuing from beneath the 77-year-old widow's door. Her daughter rushed across the street to find "the place full of smoke". Creeping on her hands and knees, she groped across the floor until she bumped into her mother who was "quite dead then"(this instance is incredibly like a recent case of SHC, or perhaps Spontaneous Disruption, in America). The deputy coroner pronounced the body as "fearfully charred".

How?, the inquest jury wanted to know. After superficial examination of the disconcerting facts, they ruled "Accidental Death" because "it was quite clear that the poor woman had accidentally come in contact with the (grate) fire". (32)

When Conventionalism says anything is "quite clear", we suspect there's glare on the glass. Like the myopic glare that precluded them from remembering how the first witness on the scene saw no fire in the grate, or how medical theory could not explain the nature of her burns. Nevertheless, a conclusion which opposes every one of the reported facts is accepted, unquestioningly. SHC would have fitted all the facts, but SHC is unacceptable, unquestionably...

With one affront to Conventionality appeased, the citizens of Blyth found themselves facing another bizarre blaze. This time it's Charles Scholl, whose case we have never seen mentioned by other authors on SHC (including Fort). A German seaman in his mid-50s, he had just returned home from a voyage on 30 March 1908. Only on a ghost ship could he ever sail again...

Bunked at his Park Road lodging, he was to be awakened next morning by the landlady. To her shock, she discovered his "bed was in flames", recorded the Blyth News & Wansbeck Telegraph (33), "whilst upon the burning bed still lay Scholl". The doctor could only confirm the deceased was "badly scorched about the hands, feet and body". The fire brigade had no worries, except to explain the origin of the fatal blaze. "How the fire originated is unknown", said the newspaper in an effort at promoting truth in journalism.

Perhaps more surprising than these perplexing combustions themselves is that, rare as they are, two of them occured so close together in the same small town. One expects to find a mass of bizarre incidents in large metropolitan areas over the centuries, yes. But in Blyth, England, within 38 months two deaths by spontaneous combustion? Incredible! Yet there's more...

POINT 5: If one stood where Anderson burned in Scotland and fired towards Hull a magic flaming arrow that ignored all influences save the curvature of the terrain, it would pass (as noted) over Blyth and then, some 10·5km further on, zing over Whitley Bay and maybe shower a few mythical sparks upon this coastal town. The fire that struck the Dewar sisters in this community, however, was all too mystifyingly real.

Just a few days before tragedy would strike Scholl in neighbouring Blyth, an event of similar yet different nature came between these two spinster sisters. On 22 March 1908 Wilhelmina Dewar was, like so many others who live along this unseen line-of-combustion, struck down by mysterious flames; her charred body was found lying upon a bed which showed no trace of fire!

The case is extremely complex, and is pursued with general accuracy by Fort (34, p90-2). Suffice here to mention the inquest's verdict: "The Coroner, in summing up, said they were in the same position as at the opening of the inquest. They could not tell how the accident happened" (35). The verdict was death from shock and accidental burns.

This solves nothing. How were the burns generated? What was the accident? We're tired of reading "Accidental Death". Everything is an accident if you don't know what forces are involved. Accidental Death is a confession of ignorance, purely and simply. We think the nature of the "accident" involved an encounter - quite possibly twice in the same day - between Wilhelmina and a fiery line of force through Whitley Bay.

And like its sister city to the north, Whitley Bay's involvement with enigmatic fires doesn't end with one incident...

Joan and Mary Hart, says Allen Eckert in his popular 1964 article on SHC, were also involved in strange flames "at Whitley Bay, Blythe, England". He dates the case 31 March 1908(36,p105). Mary, an invalid, was found burning as she sat in a parlor rocking chair; she was taken upstairs to bed, where Joan later found her "reduced to ashes" on an unscorched bedsheet.

Now that sounds extraordinary, but there are documentable cases which parallel it. However, in this instance, only 9 days after the Dewar combustion, when one would be inclined to yell "Proof!" of the fire-leyne theory, we hesitate. There are problems, you see. First, there is no shire in England called Blythe; secondly, Whitley Bay is not a suburb of Blyth but a separately incorporated community; thirdly, the parallels to the Dewar case are just too similar for comfort without documentation - which Eckert doesn't provide; fourthly, there's the disturbing train of developments that entrenches the Hart case into the SHC literature: Eric Norman mentions it briefly in 1969, with embellishment (37,p108), Brad Steiger picks it up in 1971 (38,p22), then Ivan Sanderson quotes it in 1972(39,p275) by using Eckert as his source. We can find no mention predating Eckert's article, including a scan of the British Museum's holdings of The Blyth News & Wansbeck Telegraph for the period in question. Lastly, as our intrepid editor pointed out, Fort himself didn't mention it. Now Fort's seemingly omnipresent eyes missed a few Fortean clips (which we're sure just simply delights him), but in this instance we suspect, though not guaranteeing, that Eckert got wind of some sketchy details related to the Dewar case and changed some names - to protect the innocent, as policemen say, or an author's lack of scholarship? As Fort said once, until someone supplies us with clips of the incident, "all I can say...is that it is possible-impossible"(1,p70).

Thus while relegating the Hart case to indeterminacy, we aren't done with Whitley Bay. Another occurrence is found; we have handled the original clipping. We like this one. It's a bit different; gives us a change of pace.

In that mysterious year of 1938, when things and humans were combusting all around Great Britain (it's too bad Fort transitioned before this, or he could have written 4 more books just on these 12 months),

a man was walking through Whitley Bay when a lady shouted "You are on fire". Lo! The hat on his head was smoking. "Presumably some boys" were letting off firecrackers and one landed on the Trilby hat, says The Newcastle Journal (40). Or, maybe a fiery meteor struck his chapeau, which saved its owner from a nasty scorching...

Presumably careless lads are to blame, but there's no mention of exploding firecrackers seen or heard. Neither are irresponsible boys arrested - police can't capture what isn't seen or heard. "Accidentally" the hat ignites - from what? Maybe boys were playing with fireworks, in London or Anchorage, and one got away!

In Whitley Bay a hat smoulders. Different, yes. Yet not all that different. If clothing upon Rose Howes can ignite in Barre, Massachusetts on 16 July 1960 and transform her into a living torch (37,109) then why can't a hat attempt the same feat somewhere else in time and space? A letter from Adolph Heuer Jr, in the files of SITU, remarks on the time a wet chore coat burst into flames before his eyes. "It has always puzzled me as to how wet cloth can 'burn'. After all," he notes, "you can use wet cloth to put some fires out!"(41).

The threads of evidence we call clues to SHC are now found in fabrics, too! Coats and clothing that flame spontaneously. In Whitley Bay a hat ignites, spontaneously? Through Whitley Bay passes, undetected except by its results, a fire-leyne.

Michael Harrison, in his Fire From Heaven, makes a cogent observation when speaking of the Fire: "The fact that it should have killed both Wilhelmina Dewar and Barbara Bell within seven miles and three years of each other is a matter for remark and for possible future investigation".(42,p113).

The "fact" is all the more tantalising when one realises that at least five other cases of unusual, enigmatic fires occurred in towns along a 547km (339 miles) straight line from Nairn to Louth! Watkins would surely have viewed such a discovery with excitement. Furthermore, 3 cases happen within the first two months of 1905, and 2 more (possibly 3, maybe 4) are compressed into the one month of March 1908.

Now a ley purist might point

out that drawing lines upon a
1:1,250,000 map is too imprecise to
claim such astounding alignments.
Please note, if one is dealing with
megalith-associated ley-lines we
will promptly agree (to a point at
least). Conversely, as we have
shown to be the case with high-voltage electrical lines, the energy
pathway involved in our proposed
fire-leynes may not be pencil-thin,
so that much demanding accuracy is
not prerequisite. We hope the reader
is a bit lenient, and patient, with
us at this stage because, as incredible as it may seem, the Nairn-Blyth
-Whitley Bay-Hull-Louth alignment
might include still more...

POSSIBLE POINT 6: Paging through
The Blyth News & Wansbeck Telegraph
for 6 March 1908, an event that took
place 3 days earlier catches our
eye. Elizabeth Nicholson, 40, of
Whitfield, Northumberland, was found
wrapped in flames in a shed. It may
be suicide; it may be spontaneous
combustion; it may be carelessness.
You'll have to get the reference
(43) and decide yourself.

POSSIBLE POINT 7: Another fire
in Northumberland, perhaps along
its coast, that baffles two fire
experts. It occurred in "a working
men's club...in an industrial town".
The blaze is thought to have 2
seats (that is, separate points of
origin): the investigators find
this "rare enough" to write about
in detail (44).

Fires broke out simultaneously
in two areas near the floor of the
club, and there was no physical way
to connect the 2 fire seats. A disconcerting situation, especially
when suspicions of arson were quickly ruled out. An elaborate hypothesis is then constructed. In essence,
smouldering cigarettes in one room
inflamed, whereupon a column of hot
air rose up a partition and caused
paint on the other side to "flashover", whereupon flaming gases and
burning particles were convected
along the other room's ceiling,
down the far wall and into the window curtains which subsequently
ignited and, in turn, burned through
a duct cover allowing the fire to
spread to the upper floor and roof.
Whew!

There's only one problem, which
the investigators note with apparent
embarassment: "a rather surprising"
circumstance is that the ceiling and
the exposed insulation in the second

room show "no signs of intense heating" (44,p196). In other words, the
surprising fact is that what was
observed doesn't fit what is proposed. Fort would not find this so
surprising...

We think of when we yell across
a chasm: our voice is real, the
echo is heard, but what connects
them is ethereal and cannot be seen.
Two fires and nothing to connect
them. Is one the echoing or mimicking of the other? Great heat, isolated seats of fire, initial damage
is localised, the combustion of
fire-retarded materials, a "rare"
situation, and perplexed authorities: the very circumstances associated with the type of pyrophenomena
heretofore discussed.

With due respect to these gentlemen, we humbly propose 2 alternatives: both will deal with paranormal combustions, of course.

Alternative 1: The unidentified
club sits upon the previously described fire-leyne, whose activation
one night singled out 2 objects on
the floor of the establishment through which it passed and over-ener-
gised their atomic structures, causing great thermal activity which
culminated in spontaneous combustion. Or, if this is found too improbable, we're willing to let one
fire be caused by smouldering cigarettes...

Alternative 2: The tavern hosted a very short-lived poltergeist
attack. Perhaps an angry imbiber
left behind his wish that the place
would burn down; a disgruntled patron sought revenge for a short-shot
whiskey by creating physical flames
out of his fiery anger; a discarnate
drunk, seeking but unable to make
his presence known to the club's
clientele, tried a more visible method of attracting attention. Again,
there is support for each suggestion
in our files on spontaneous combustion...

Then there are the curtain burning episodes of weird fires, in
which only curtains are consumed
(45,p182;46,p324-5). Hmm...burning
curtains in a Northumberland tavern.

Uncanny blazes that baffle the
investigators, and are largely ignored by every category of special-
isation within today's Dogma. If
these fires lie outside the limits
imposed by Science upon itself, then
it is reasonable to expect the explanations to be alien from those same

restrictions. Ley lines and fire-
leynes certainly qualify as worthy
solutions then, don't they?

But there's another discovery
we'd like to mention before wrapping
up this examination. The reader is
surely aware of the purported Bermuda Triangle, which is said to produce apports and disappearances of
men and machines. We have found a
different kind of Triangle: it's in
England, and it burns things. We
call it, not without consideration
for its distant cousin, the Binbrook
Triangle...

Larry E Arnold, 1977.

(Continued next issue)

References
(Continued: see also part one)

28 Edwards, Frank. Strange World,
    Ace Bks, NY, nd.
29 Blazier, Sheldon & Millie; per-
    sonal interchange, 24 Aug 1975.
30 "A Drunkard's End". The Abstai-
    ner's Journal.
31 Hull Daily Mail. 6 Jan 1905.
32 Blyth News & Wansbeck Telegraph
    No 2148, 28 Feb 1905, p 3.
33 Blyth News & WT. No 2468, 3 Apr
    1908. p 3.
34 Fort,Charles. Wild Talents. Ace
    Bks, NY, nd.
35 Blyth News & WT. No 2468, 3 Apr
    1908, p 3.
36 Eckert, Allen W. "The Baffling
    Burning Death". True, May 1964.
    Fawcett Pubs, NY.
37 Norman, Eric. Weird Unsolved
    Mysteries. Award Bks, NY,1969.
38 Steiger, Brad. "Incredible Phe-
    nomena of Human Combustion".
    Occult, vol 2, no 2. June 1971.
39 Sanderson, Ivan T. Investigat-
    ing the Unexplained. Prentice
    -Hall, NJ, 1972.
40 Newcastle Journal. No 28869. 24
    Oct 1938, p 14.
41 Heuer, Adolph, Jr. Personal co-
    mmunication to Ivan Sanderson;
    14 July 1970.
42 Harrison, Michael. Fire From
    Heaven. Sidgwick & Jackson, Ldn
    1976.
43 Blyth News & WT, No 2460, 6 Mar
    1908, p 3.
44 Anderson, J, & Walls, HJ. "Two
    seats - One fire". Medicine,
    Science & The Law (Ed: F E
    Camps) Maxwell, Ldn, Vol 2,
    1961-2, p 189-196.
45 Gaddis, Vincent. Mysterious
    Fires & Lights. David McKay, NY,
    1967.
46 Price, Harry. Poltergeist Over
    England. Country Life Ltd, Ldn,
    1945.

■■■

Icefalls cont...

the RAE and DTI, could they establish
'positive identification' of an aircraft
in the area - which gives you some idea
of the problem, and why insurance companies won't touch ice-bomb clauses. The DTI
letter also confirmed that the crater
was about 4ft square in soft ground, and
that the ice had broken up enough to
prevent reconstruction of its thickness.

We have said before, and probably not
for the last time, that the plane-icefall
is an unsatisfactory and largely illusory
explanation. It takes no account at all
of the many falls of ice (and indeed
many other objects and substances) from
the sky before the advent of planes.
And furthermore, the only authoritative
study of the subject that we know of -
'The Ice-fall Problem' by James E McDonald (Inst.Atmos.Physics, Arizona U), in
Weatherwise June 1960, pp110-114,132 -
which correlated icefall data with air
traffic movements and meteorological
data (for 30 incidents in the 1950s in
the USA), found no significant correlation between these elements (eg that
a plane might be in the area but the
meteorological conditions made ice ac-

cumulation quite improbable). McDonald
could only plead for more research into
the subject.

ADDLESTONE, SURREY - 1972.

We have the briefest note from a CP
wire, that presumably a few days before
the story's date, 28 September, lumps
of ice were found in a garden in Addle-
stone. They were green! It was assumed
that they had fallen from an aircraft,
probably from a toilet discharge. See
Fort's Books for details of pre-aero-age
falls of coloured ice! (Cr: W Ritchie
Benedict.)

FULHAM, LONDON - 1975.

On 24 January, shoppers in the Fulham
Road heard a loud crash, then had to
run for cover as bricks and rubble
rained down on them. Police found the
roof of Mrs McKnight's home, in Fulham
Court, smashed by a block of ice, the
debris being hurled into the street
below. No one was hurt but at least one
car was damaged. Fulham Chronicle 31
January 1975 (Cr: Dave Baldock.)

cont over/

THORPE CONSTANTINE, STAFFS - 1975.

Eric Cooper, 58, was walking his dog on a private road at Lonkill Farm, near Thorpe Constantine, when a 61b chunk of ice whizzed from the sky to embed itself in the ground within yards of him. We presume this happened the day before our clipping, ie on 19 December. Eric said first he heard 'a terrible whizzing noise' and saw a white object flashing by at high speed. It was about 6ft in <u>diameter</u> and almost circular. As it came down at an angle, he saw three pieces break off, the largest landing near him making a hole a foot deep, the others landing about 50 yards away. The paper comments on the site being below the London-Manchester air corridor, but Eric doesn't mention seeing anything like a plane in the sky. (That doesn't mean there wasn't, of course!). The Civil Aviation Authority investigating the incident suggested that from the description of the size of the chunk, it might be 'a weather phenomenon' rather than a fall from a plane. Birmingham <u>Evening Mail</u> 20 December 1975 (Cr: David Sutton.)

TIMBERVILLE, VIRGINIA - 1976.

Most of our notes on icefalls are of single chunks, single ones that break up, or several lumps that come down at the same time - occasionally we hear of lumps that come down in the same place but at different times, the sort of item that had Fort back on his stationary-lands-above-the-earth tack. This happened when two blocks came down in the Virginian town of Timberville in the clear night of 7th March, with temperature in the mid-30s - later a third block was found about a mile away and assumed to have fallen with the first two.

That Sunday night, Wilbert Cullers and 2 others were watching TV, when at 8.45pm they were startled by a crash which shook the house. A lump of ice, 'about the size of a basketball', tore through a 2ft square thin metal roofing tile, and sheared a 4x2" roof strut, making two large holes in the plasterboard ceiling. Deputies from the Rockingham County Sheriff's Department arrived about 1 hour later and collected a 3 gallon bucketful of pieces of the murky ice. Sgt CR Hottinger described it as 'milky white, cold, and compressable in the hand.' A neighbour had been standing in his drive for about 3 minutes when he heard the impact ('like a muffled shotgun'). Then about 20 seconds later, he saw an object hit the roadway about 50yds away. He looked up and neither heard nor saw any plane. Hottinger described the object as broken pieces of ice 'like clear powder'.

A young girl living opposite had rushed out on hearing the first impact ('like a car crashed') and then heard a second noise. She said:'I looked up and heard this whizzing sound come flying,' and saw the chunk of ice hit the edge of the road. The first neighbour is sure he heard no sound. The third block was found by a farmer about a mile away as he fed his chickens early the next day (Monday 8 March). He went back, read of the previous day's falls in his paper at breakfast, and became interested enough to go back and retrieve the 'fist-sized'

Wilbert Cullers examins part of the ice which came through his roof (Timberville)

chunk. It was just lying on the ground, curiously, with no fragments or dent below it. If it fell, it fell slowly or only a small distance!

I'll skip the analyses of the retrieved fragments. Sgt Hottinger's 'Offence' Report, and a letter from Dr RC Lehman, of the Physics Dept, East Mennonite College, Harrisonburg (which detailed tests and results) can be found in an article on the 'Timberville Ice Fall' by Paul Willis, in INFO Journal 19, p14ff. We collected our details from the Harrisonburg, Va, Daily News Record 8-10 March 1976 (Cr: Mark A Hall.)

It may be worth noting that the other main alternative theory by which icefalls are explained-away, is the notion that the stuff is debris from a passing comet's head. In the Timberville case it was touted equally with the plane-theory, but one person seems to have taken it seriously enough. In the Daily News Record 9 March, Dr Charles Tolbert, of University of Virginia, said cryptically: 'The comet on Monday morning could not have caused the ice. There's absolutely no way that any material from that comet could get anywhere near the earth.' Well apart from noting his belief in absolutes we hadn't heard of a comet ourselves, but it seems one was there. We can't say with any of the absolute certainty of Dr Tolbert whether the comet and the icefall were linked or not - it's enough to note the fact of their synchronous existence.

READING, BERKS - 1976
A lump of ice the 'size of a football' and many smaller pieces smashed through the roof of a house in Hartland Road, Reading, punching a hole through the bedroom ceiling below. At the same time another smashed on the roof of a nearby house in Exwick Square, hurling tiles and guttering into the garden. The time was between 8.30 and 9am 15 May. In both houses the families escaped without injuries, being shocked more by the sudden impact. At Exwick Sq, the Leanage family collected some of the pieces of cloudy ice and stored them in their freezer - there was enough to suggest a football-sized mass. At Hartland Rd, the Peppiatt family were all out at the time - neighbours, who put the incident nearer 8.30am, called Mr Peppiatt back from work. He reckons the damage to his roof and bedroom carpet (on which the mass melted with plaster and rubble to form a fine mess) would cost about £50. He found another piece of ice, about 6" diameter, in the garden and was keeping it in his fridge. Both families said they would wait until it was possible to establish the responsibility, then press

charges. It's our guess they'll wait a long time! Reading Evening Post 15 May 1976.

BELGIUM - 1976.
Henri Prémont sent us a clipping of the following letter, from a Mlle JJ Waterloos, from La Libre Belgique of 6 August 1976. The lady was playing tennis with a friend (unfortunately she doesn't say where) at 10.15am on 2nd August, when a mass of blue ice plummeted from the sky to shatter on the court. They guessed from the amount of ice that its original size must have been about that of a football. Apparently the meteorological office she contacted showed little interest, suggesting it fell from a plane. If any of our French or Belgian readers know more about this incident (or others) we'd be glad to hear from them.

ENFIELD, MIDDLESEX - 1977.
James Pluck, 77, suffering from chronic bronchitis, was just about to go back upstairs to bed after watching TV, at about 8.20pm on 2nd January. Suddenly a large piece of ice hit the roof of the house, at 402 High St, Ponders End, Enfield, smashing through the ceiling above his sickbed, hurling plaster, slates and rubble with jagged fragments of ice all over the front bedroom. Had he been in bed he would certainly have suffered injury, or worse! Mrs Clara Pluck, 75, who had a stroke only six months previously, thought there had been a gas-explosion. She stopped her husband, who was deaf (he heard nothing but must have felt the impact, as did the neighbours), and opened the bedroom door first to find the room wrecked. The ice-block was said to have measured (appx) 3ft long by 6-8" thick. Pieces could still be seen melting on their lawn two days later.

A spokesman for Heathrow airport said incidents are rare, and that he'd not heard of any since January 1976 (which is not on our files - details anyone?). A spokesman for the Civil Aviation Authority curtly pointed out the 'impossibility' of proving the ice came from a particular plane, and - get this! - said it was 'up to the householder to get in touch with the airline concerned.' Since the CAA can't, or won't (the effect is the same) identify the airline, no one has a hope in hell of collecting any compensation. But this is academic as we don't think the phenomenon has much to do with planes anyway. I'm just amazed to see the spectacle of public authorities scrambling to clear themselves of hypothetical

culpability, while no one gives a damn
for the confused victims of an accident
of nature. Wolverhampton, Staffs, <u>Express & Star</u> 3 January 1977 (Cr: Frank
Adey); <u>Enfield Gazette</u> 6 January 1977
(Cr: Eric Charge).

Mrs Pluck's reference to gas-explosions sounded familiar - so we back-
checked, and sure enough, this incident
comes at the peak of the series of
mystery explosions that were blamed on
natural gas leakage, at the turn of the
year (see <u>FT</u>20/3-5). One other observation we have is more hypothetical. We
remember that Fort established a second
focus for poltergeist phenomena (after
the main adolescent link), around the
sick or dying...and that there is a
major overlap area between falls of
material and poltergeist phenomena (see
likely sections of <u>Phenomena</u>).

<u>NORRKOPING, SWEDEN - 1977.</u>
Having taken a risk and used one of
Frank Edwards' innumerable stories which
lack enough references to check on, in
the 'Missles from the Upper Regions'
section of <u>Phenomena</u>, I'm somewhat encouraged by a more modern and similar ▶

WORDS FROM THE WIZARD

by DOC SHIELS

During the past 23 months,
involved as I have been...with the
Loch Ness Monster, sea-serpents,
UFOs, telepathy, telekinesis, the
Owlman of Mawnan, the little people,
wizardry, witchcraft, ownership of
the Entire Universe, Mr Punch and
Ken Campbell...I have learned a
thing or two about...er...phenomena.
Take note, friendly Forteans, while
I spill a few beans, state facts
and ask some questions. Remember
I'm a wizard, but you don't have to
believe everything I say. Let's
concentrate on Nessie for now.

Right...here goes...straight in
the deep end of the loch. Monster
hunting by means of wizardry is far
more genuinely scientific than, say,
the Academy of Applied Science approach to the game. Wizards have
always been pretty good with drag-
ons; and dragons really do guard
hoards of treasure.

From that little group of facts
I'll jump to another. Did you know
that telekinesis, in various forms,
plays a very important part in monster spotting, raising, hunting,
filming and so on? Cameras often get
fouled up because of this...and camera fouling is closely related to
psychic metal-bending. Think about
it. Cameras are magical devices, so
are tape recorders.

The famous Loch Ness Hoodoo is
a mixture of telekinesis, cosmic
jokery, and psychic backlash. Most
successful monster spotters are
natural psychics, and those few who
manage to obtain photographs of
Nessie usually find themselves, or
their cameras, on the receiving end
of the backlash. Take a couple of
the better known examples. Only one
of Hugh Gray's 1933 photographs of
Nessie came out. He actually snapped

incident. In <u>Strangest of All</u> (Ace, 1962) p150, Edwards tells of the West German carpenter, skewered while on a roof, by a 6ft spear of ice from the sky! Well...

it seems that on 22 January 1977, a woman in Norrkoping was leaving a block of flats as the roof was being cleared of ice and snow. She was hit by the falling icicle and died instantly. Not really an icefall of great mystery, but I thought you connoeseurs of the bizarre would appreciate that! <u>Daily Telegraph</u> 22 January 1977. (Cr: Mrs V Martin).

John Barker, of 50 Albert Rd, Epsom, was just leaving for work on the morning of 29 July, when a block of ice crashed through his garage roof and damaged the back of his car. Its mass was estimated at 4 cubic feet - the largest piece, 1ft long and 2" thick, was found in a large pool of water. <u>The Sun</u> 1 July 1977; and the coincidentally named <u>Surrey Comet</u> 2 July 1977 (Cr: John Rimmer.)

*** We have accumulated quite a few notes on falls of frogs and other animals and hope to give you these next issue.

---

five, but four were blank. R K Wilson's classic 1934 portrait of the monster was snapped on All Fool's Day...and two of the surgeon's four shots were blank. Why? It's that old blank backlash!

An air of mystery surrounds so many of the Loch Ness photographs and films. Why should Nick Witchell think that the F C Adams 1934 photograph of Nessie was, in fact, taken by Dr James Lee? Why...in spite of all the details he gave to Ted Holiday...should Alastair Dallas now insist that the McRae film of the monster never existed? Why will not Dr Maurice Burton allow the Nessie film, shot by G E Taylor in 1938, to be shown?

You know, it's funny that Dr Burton's daughter, Jane, should have provided the cine camera with which Tim Dinsdale shot his amazing film of the beastie, in 1960... while Dr Burton was completing his book, <u>The Elusive Monster</u>, which attacks Nessie and her supporters quite heavily. Here's a nice little Fortean fact or two concerning Jane Burton and her camera...a Bolex H.16...I almost borrowed that very same camera a couple of years before Tim shot his film. I used to know Jane Burton quite well, I was at college with her for a while, and I actually handled the camera. In 1958 I visited Loch Ness for the first time (without a movie camera as it happens!), after reading Constance Whyte's <u>More Than a Legend</u>. I didn't see Nessie, but a sighting was reported, by Mr and Mrs Hugh Rowland, while I was there. The only camera I had with me, on that trip, was an old Rollei...the same one I used to capture Morgawr on film, in

1976. The last time I saw Jane was in 1959, in Cornwall, when she stayed at a cottage near Trencrom Hill ...a part of Penwith famous for its witches. Well, it could all add up to something, I'm not sure what, exactly, but its amusing to consider that I may, just possibly, have had some kind of influence on Jane Burton's camera!

Sky-clad witches make excellent monster bait...they attract newspaper men too. Luckily, I know a few witches.

But let's jump back to the backlash problem. Monster raising can cause illness. This happened to several members of my 'Monstermind' team, and I know it happened to such stalwart hunters as Tim Dinsdale and Ted Holiday. Why? The simple answer is that, in all things magical, you pay for what you get. The very best protection against this disturbing type of psychic backlash is <u>humour</u>. The protection, in turn, has to be paid for. So, although my humorous wizardry is successful, it is not taken too seriously by the monster hunting establishment. Imagine anyone refusing to take humour or magic seriously!

My 1977 photographs of Nessie have had some adventures, all part of the cosmic trickster's game. My original No. 1 colour slide went astray for days on end at the 'Daily Record' offices in Glasgow. Other photographs, from the same strip of film, vanished entirely after being inspected by the picture editor, Martin Gilfeather. My original No. 2 slide somehow escaped from its carefully sealed envelope somewhere between Cornwall and

Boston, Mass., USA. The only direct, negative, monochrome, glass copy-plate made from that slide (by David Benchley of Cornish Photonews) was accidentally dropped and broken (by me!) just a few days ago. It's a disturbing fact that hardly any of the original negatives of the better known Loch Ness Monster photographs, taken since 1933, have survived. Nessie pix are supernaturally accident-prone!

I wonder if the same sort of psychic jinx is responsible for the rapid sinking of that full-scale model of the monster in 'The Private Life of Sherlock Holmes'...the film, I mean. Then there's the expensive bad luck which has dogged the making of David Frost's multi-million dollar epic 'Nessie'. And did I tell you about Distant Humps?

Let me give you a few personal opinions concerning the nature of Nessie. First of all, I think she is closely related to sea-serpents of the Morgawr type; and, if she is truly organic, she is not an amphibian, nor is she a mammal. She could be a fish...or some kind of invertebrate...or a plesiosaur. She certainly looks like a plesiosaur; and, if we accept paleontologist Adrian Desmond's ideas concerning the hot-blooded dinosaurs, many of the arguments against a family of plesiosaurian monsters in Loch Ness can be dismissed. I think Nessie is a dragon...a dragon that looks something like a plesiosaur...but what is a dragon?

The Irish 'horse eel' is a kind of dragon, so is the Highland Scottish 'water horse'. Is the dragon, then, a sort of horse? It all depends what you mean by 'horse'. Look at the Uffington White Horse...370 feet long, cut in the chalk of the hillside. A small, beaked head with horns...a long neck, body and tail ...and what about those rear flippers? Yes, I think Nessie is a dragon. I also think it's quite possible that she may not, after all, be an organic entity, a solid, flesh and blood creature. There's nothing original about these thoughts, I know, but that doesn't matter. What does matter is the fact that dragons can be seen and photographed in Loch Ness.

Don't forget that the word 'monster' is derived from the Latin monstrum, a marvel or omen. How montrously, marvellously ominous!

There's something very weird in that there loch.

The man who has probably come closest, without prejudice, to solving the great mystery of Loch Ness and its dragons is Ted Holiday. He hasn't arrived at any firm conclusions, as yet, but he has probed the enigma more deeply than any other researcher. Holiday's intelligent and stylish writings on the subject have been treated with scorn by some of the self-styled Nessie 'experts'. A typical example of this pompous, blinkered criticism is to be found in Peter Costello's 'In Search of Lake Monsters'. Costello seems irritated by the fact that Holiday's book on the Great Orm received excellent reviews...and not just from the 'Milwaukee Journal'! Because he has dared to suggest that Nessie could be, somehow, 'supernatural', Ted Holiday has had to put up with quite a lot of that very prejudiced style of criticism. It's just another form of backlash. Don't let it bother you, Ted!

Another man who has come close to cracking the Loch Ness puzzle is, of course, Tim Dinsdale. Personally, I think Tim is a wee bit too easily impressed by the respectable scientists involved in the monster hunt. "Respectable" is, perhaps, the key word here...Tim seems so very keen that Nessie should become respectable. Although he knows that weird, unexplainable, paranormal things happen at Loch Ness, Tim is careful not to say much about them in his books. Eventually, I'd like to see an account of Tim Dinsdale's more supernatural adventures. I'm sure Professor Challenger would approve. Stay psychic, Tim!

I think I'll round off these ramblings with a few predictions: important new movie film of the Loch Ness Monster will be shown to the public within the next twelve months. Nessie will be seen and possibly photographed by a well-known showbiz personality. A previously unpublished photograph of the beastie, taken years ago, will be released in 1978. A direct connection between the monster and psychic phenomena will be demonstrated.

I really wanted to say a lot more about those naked witches. Perhaps some other time...keep watching the waters!

Doc Shiels, Sept '77.

FIRE FROM HEAVEN - A Critique

Recently Pan reprinted Michael Harrison's study of spontaneous combustion, **Fire From Heaven**, in paperback*. Flicking through it to see what was new (it says 'revised edition'), I was somewhat surprised to see my name in the index. I turned to the pages referred to wondering if I had spontaneously combusted without knowing it, and had been wandering for some time as a shade - but no! It was an incorporation into the new edition of Harrison's reaction to my critique of the first edition (see FT16/24-26). Ignoring most of my comments for and against his data, ideas and style, he chose to pick up on my criticism of his theory that the three sites of Russell's famous 3-in-1 burning were linked by the initial letter and sound 'U' (Upton-by-Chester, SS Ulrich, and Ubbergen), and that (according to Harrison) at the times of their ignitions each man (in turn, George Turner, John Greeley, and Willem ten Bruik) formed apexes of a giant triangle, the last two being 'exactly' (Harrison states) 340 miles from Turner at Upton. Harrison shrugs off my doubts that the 'U' sound in each case was pronounced pre-cisely the same (necessary for his vibration theory), and calls my suggestion of several other name/sound similarities (ie names of SHC victims & authorities, but not people **involved** one way or the other in the SHC controversy) 'sarcastic'. Fair enough - he even gets his own back by including one of my spelling mistakes in the quote he uses. But I'm sorry that my suggestion that a more substantial connexion could have been made with each victim being at the control of a vehicle at the fatal time (Turner in his lorry, ten Bruik in his Volkswagen, and Greeley at the helm of the Ulrich) has been ignored entirely. Nevermind; the whole triple case does not exist in fact, and our arguments are quite academic.

Some time ago I tried to locate the SS Ulrich in the Lloyds Register for 1938. It was not there; nor in the year before or after; nor was there any ship of that name in that period. I was about to check out the other two stories of this triplet, when friend and colleague Robert Schadewald told me that it had been done, by Philip Klass in his book UFOs: Explained, ch 14 'UFOs as Brutal Killers' (pp134-7). Now the story as it is told in the later accounts insists that Greeley burnt at 1.14pm on 7 April 1938, Turner at 2.14pm, and ten Bruik at 3.15pm; and that adjusting for timezone differences showed that in fact they all occured exactly at the same time! This is a glaring error - there are no time zone differences between the sea south of Ireland and the coast of Holland. Klass also could not find any record of the SS Ulrich, even enlisting the aid of the public information office at the US Maritime Administration HQ in Washington. He wrote to the police at Nijmegan, and was informed by a Mr F Perrick that the records for 1938 were lost in the war - in any case the foundation for the first Volkswagen factory was not laid by Hitler until May 1938, one month after ten Bruik is alleged to have been crisped in a Volkswagen. (VWs, Perrick said; were not on the roads publicly until 1947, 9 years later!) Klass also wrote to the police at Upton-by-Chester, who in turn enlisted the help of the Cheshire Observer back-files. There was no record of a lorry fire in which George Turner died - the nearest they could find was at 5pm on 4 April when an Edgar Beattie's truck burst into flames as it hit a bridge. A named witness tried to rescue him, but the flames in the cab made it impossible. (So much for the detail of the unignited petrol beside the cindered Turner!) If the triple fire-death was an invention, whose?

The story has always been credited to Eric Frank Russell, but in his first book Great World Mysteries (Dobson 1957) he gives the Dutch story (with ten Bruik unnamed), and the Turner case, quite unconnected. Curiously, in an article Russell did for _Fate_ (March 1955) on all the fire-deaths he found for the year 1938, these two cases are next to each other, though he admits that the ten Bruik case came to him as a translation from an unnamed Dutch paper. (In _GW Mysteries_, he dates this source as 1941.) I can only imagine that he did not think a mere month and year link between the two cases strong enough to mention in his book! By the time his close friend and colleague Vincent Gaddis brought out his celebrated pioneering study, _Mysterious Fires and Lights_ (1967), the triple-fire death story was fully fledged. The finger of blame for this invention hovers around the years just prior to Gaddis's book, and the only candidate to emerge so far is an article on SHC by   Michael McDougall in the Newark, New Jersey, _Sunday Star-Ledger_ 13 March 1966, the author of the 'three fingers of fire' quote.

I've dwelt on this case because it is an important one in the case of many modern writers trying to make a sensational case for SHC, and it shows the importance and necessity for any Fortean researcher to make the effort to get back to the original testimony. This is the only way that the many erroneous and invented incidents in circulation today can be discovered. Go to the primary sources and the deadwood, redherrings and confusing cross-arguments just vanish away. It is unfortunate that Harrison has fallen into error by relying on secondary sources (by taking cases at face value from Gaddis, say). This is the risk that faces us all if we don't check. Readers have to trust their authors, but an author should be careful whom he trusts blindly. In correspondence with some other first-class Fortean researchers, numerous errors have come to light in the works of Frank Edwards, John Macklin, EF Russell, Vincent Gaddis and some other more commercial writers. Now these authors did have some genuine interest in the subjects, and most of their material is soundly based. I prefer to believe that any errors or distortions arose because their own trust was betrayed under conditions which did not always allow them to check. Much of the errors which had sensational implications for the UFO field, say, were picked up and popularized by writers like Brad Steiger; the same goes for the Bermuda Triangle and Ancient Astronaut fields.

Harrison presents a different (and difficult) case. His book contains a wealth of serious and original material, in fact so much so that I can't under-

stand why he had to use sensational cases that he hadn't checked.(All the sources for the triple fire case could be found in the British Library, at Bloomsbury and Colindale, and in some books still available.) But there is another cause for concern. As I pointed out in my first critique, Harrison must have had a copy of the original source of the Phyllis Newcombe story in front of him to write most of the details he put in (in the first edition as 'note to p103' on p223, incorporated into (coincidentally) p103 in the paperback) yet here he is still insisting that the poor girl 'glowed with blue flames' as she danced, and was 'within minutes a blackened mass of ash', and that her boyfriend was 'fatally' burned trying to extinguish her with his hands. I tried to draw attention to the fact that according to the only testimony we have (the _Daily Telegraph_ 20 Sept 1938, which Harrison uses) the girl survived to die in hospital about an hour later, _not_ on the ballroom floor instantly. Nor is there any mention of the boyfriend attempts to help or hypothetical injuries. Harrison saw my criticism and saw fit not to correct his error. That disturbs me.

I have nothing against Harrison, nor indeed his arguments (and I was absorbed by the book, _despite_ his verbose style), nor against the other authors I've mentioned (as their works served to attract me and many others to these studies). But here we are not necessarily concerned with earning respectability, but with the furtherance of serious and useful Fortean studies, so it is imperative to locate false cases upon which much valuable time has been wasted (as many researchers could tell you. Larry E Arnold, author of our current series of SHC articles, has devoted considerable library hours to these very problems, and apart from independently confirming my own findings (and those of Klass, in the triple fire case) points out a few more errors in _Fire from Heaven_. We give them here, not in a spirit of vendetta, but to help save some benighted researcher wasting half his life in vain pursuit up blind alleys. (Page numbers in brackets are from the current Pan paperback; others are from the hardback which has the same pagination for the USA edition).

17(15) In all his researches Larry has not c'ome across the term 'Auto-Oxidation' that Harrison says is in current use in the USA in place of 'SHC'.
28(35) SHC and 'Preternatural Combustibility are _not_ the same! Dr Lester Adelson, a Cleveland pathologist who doesn't

believe in SHC, nevertheless defines it as: 'that phenomenon wherein the body takes fire without an outside source of heat and is rapidly reduced to a handful of greasy ashes...inanimate objects nearby escape relatively unharmed.' PC is similar 'but differing in that a spark or minute flame is necessary to ignite the body which then undergoes incineration.' Several of Harrison's 18 & 19th C sources also make this distinction.

46f(45) Fort was not the only researcher to say 'anything original'! Ivan Sanderson, in Investigating the Unexplained (1972) spends a chapter on 'inositol' as a possible cause of SHC.

51f(49f) Harrison doesn't seem to have checked the original accounts of the Kileys' deaths; his scenario follows that of later writers more closely.

93(92) It was Dr Floyd Clendenen (not Clemens) who was the LaSalle County coroner who reported on the Rooney case (see his 'A Case of Spontaneous Combustion in Man', The Theraputic Gazette, H Wood & RM Smith, eds, Detroit 15 June 1889, 3rd series v5 n6, pp387-8. There! That'll save some 'professional journalist' the heartache of paying one of us library ferrets!

101(101) Wihelmina Dewar was indeed a 'chronic alcoholic'.

104(107) Mrs Dulin (at 30yrs) can hardly be called 'one of the youngest victims' which Harrison maintains still in the 2nd edition, despite adding (p20) that he was wrong in assuming young children were exempt from the fire (giving a case of an 11-yr-old boy). Larry has a coroner's report on the fate of Ricky Pruitt, aged 4. If Harrison had asked us, we could have pointed him at our partial listing of child cases in The News 6!

123(134) To state that Mrs Reeser was 'mildly depressed' contradicts the firsthand evidence. Larry has interviewed her brother and the landlady's sister.

138(149) Countess von Gorlitz met her fate on 13 June 1847.

167(182) In misreading the notes of Rev. Custance, Harrison places the early part of the poltergeist activity in the Rev's home, Binbrook Rectory. It all occurred at Binbrook Farm. His quotes from the Louth/Lincs News are inaccurate.

169,171(184,186) The burning of Mrs Satlow's corpse was at Hoquiam, Washington not Oregon, as Harrison judged from the origin of his clipping.

218(244) Ruling out a 'nuclear type' of energy for SHC is bizarre and unjustified at this stage of investigation - especially in view of his (2nd edition, p126) comments, that: 'the value of the facts will be assessed only from their totality - we cannot know which are essential to an understanding...' etc.

8,225f(14,159f) Harrison gives several different dates for the Krogman interview. The correct ref is The Inquirer, Philadelphia, 15 June 1975.

Despite the absence of these corrections the Pan edition does incorporate some new material, and some notes have been moved to places in the text. I was glad to see that most of the SHC and allied cases we gave in FT16 (the issue containing the first review) have been used in the 2nd edition (some of the order and paraphrasing is distinctly familiar!), but I was sad to see that Harrison was piqued enough not to credit this. Similarly, FT16 carried the last part of Steve Moore's article on Greenwich phenomena in which he suggests the possible connexion between sites of Fortean events and nearby water. Interestingly, the publicity sheets that accompanied the review copy of the Pan edition told of Harrison's continuing research into the connexion between SHC sites and nearby water. I hope that the inclusion on his map of some of the dud cases we have talked about is only an oversight on his part, because the avenue of inquiry is worth pursuing seriously, and we look forward to his conclusions.

Our desire has been to establish some standards in our field (it deserves it) of rigorous research and cooperation between researchers. It's slow, but I like to think that FT has established good working relationships with a good many Fortean researchers, based on mutual aid. If Harrison had come to us we would have gladly helped. It can get awfully lonely out there ferreting at the fringes of a forgotten or unknown subject where no human hand has set foot. I hope Harrison will take this in the right spirit, too.

* Fire from Heaven was published by Pan Books; 1977; 80p; pp287; photos, bib & index. New material & chapter. 2nd edn.

RJM Rickard - October 1977.

■■

NEXT ISSUE
Next time we'll have the conclusion of Larry Arnold's study of linear fire phenomena, with a look at the 'Binbrook Triangle'; Robert Forrest on maths & numerology; JB Delair on strange clouds; a review of the Shiels Nessie-photo ruckus; with notes on holes, mystery illnesses, frogfalls, & electromagnetic oddities.

BOOM TIME

From the Press point of view, the controversy late last year over the mystery aerial booms heard all over southern England, is a dead duck. In one of the most brilliant displays we have seen for several years, of the public authorities and assorted scientists thinking aloud in public, the strange double-thump was finally pinned on the late evening flight of Concorde as it passed over the English Channel on its way out over the Atlantic to Washington. The reports from the period between August and December 1976 were summarized in FT19/21f.

MEANWHILE...

Back in England the Concorde controversy continued. The Parliamentary Under-Secretary of State concerned with aviation acknowledged in a letter to John Pardoe, MP for North Cornwall (published in Cornish & Devon Post 8 January 1977; Cr: Nigel Watson) that some of the mystery booms were indeed coincident with some British & French Concorde flights (they both use the same route from the Channel out); he also pointed out that their flight plan called for sub-sonic speeds over land, and that according to tests and calculations only the faintest of rumbles should reach listeners on the coast as the plane went supersonic over the Channel. Then the Bristol University 'Boomwatch' team, who had been on the problem now for about 5 months, pinned most of the blame for the 9pm series of noises on the incoming Air France flight. Daily Mail 25 January 1977 (Cr: Peter Hope-Evans) Sensing disaster, the Under Secretary of State (for evasion of responsibility?) says that now the aircraft is in service liability for damages lies with the airlines. Daily Mail 31 January 1977. Sure enough, within a month we begin to get a whiff of some claims - Torbay Towns Herald Express 25 February

1977 (Cr: Ian Lawes): that damage to 2 North Cornwall cottages is blamed on the 9pm booms...Dept of Environment investigating.

The booms have been heard as far West as Hastings, and as far North as Oxford and Reading. Two of our readers wrote saying that they heard them even further afield. John Hitchens, of Petworth, Sussex, has been hearing the noises since the Autumn of 1976, and friends in the area say they have heard them about 6 and 7pm, besides the main one at between 9.12-9.14pm (often through the 2ft stone walls of his house and the noise of his recordplayer. He mentions that, like the man from Porlock who has been hearing booms for the last 20 years (FT19/22f), he too was brought up to hear the 'Big Guns' booming 'for the last 20-30 years'. John believes that this noise comes from the military ranges on the Portsmouth downs, about 30 miles to the SW. The 'Concorde' shudder is similar, but stronger.

Alan Price, on the other hand, has a house in Cardiff with good views towards Weston-super-Mare and the Somerset hills. He says that 'Three times in the last ten days I have heard a bump followed by the rattling of windows (at) 8.55pm.' He says this is quite distinguishable from blasting in the nearby quarries, which is usually early afternoon, though the effects on the windows are similar.

ALL CLEAR...

The Bristol 'Boomwatch' finally announced their findings after sifting nearly 600 reports from witnesses. It was, they say, the refraction of sound waves caused by wind and temperature gradients in the upper stratosphere. The same effect, they boldly pronounce, allowed Samuel Pepys in London, in 1666, to hear an English vs Dutch battle in the Channel, whilst the residents of Dover and Deal heard nothing. Similarly, they say it explains why shelling in France in the WW1 could be heard in Kent, while soldiers nearer the action heard nothing. Ingenious! We'll accept that it is <u>one</u> solution, but not conclusively <u>the</u> solution. That's being scientific!

Ingenious! What about the 10am, 6.30, 7 and 8pm booms; and the places where the noise was only heard about once a week; or why there should be such timing discrepancies (assuming witnesses had an accurate timecheck) so that it could be heard in Cardiff, say, up to 20 minutes before Devon and Cornwall? And what about the times the booms were heard when no Concorde was airbourne? And why did not similar effects occur on the European leg of the other Concorde route, to Bahrain? And what (perhaps the biggest what of all) about the great mystery booms of pre-aviation (eg the 'Barisal Guns', the Mackimoodus of East Haddam in Connecticut, and many other aerial sounds recorded by Fort?

And what about this - mystery booms in the USA at the height of the series in England? One was particularly noted at 2pm, 27 December 1976, when a loud boom rattled windows in the Grand Rapids area of Michigan. Dick Wheaton, control tower chief at Kent County Airport, expressed the general opinion that it was not a ground explosion, but like a sonic boom in the air. Attempts to locate the offending aircraft failed, and being America, the usual mutterings about secret military projects could be heard. Grand Rapids <u>Press</u> 28 December 1976 (Cr: Dave Fideler.)

The Bristol report appeared in the national papers on 5 Feb 1977 (Cr: Mrs V Martin, P Hope-Evans), and that, you would have thought, was that...unless you're a Fortean.

<u>Cambridge Evening News</u> 19 March 1977: that near the famous Cambridgeshire site at Wandlebury, 'a rumbling sound like distant thunder' can be heard regularly each evening at 9.20pm, according to at least one man living nearby. He says pheasants start up seconds before the 'rippling thud' hits his house and rattles the windows. He thinks it's Concorde. A member of the Bristol team cautiously agrees, expressing surprise that it could be heard in Cambridgeshire. We express our surprise at the lack of reports from elsewhere, especially those boom-ridden places - or is it that the reporting has largely stopped because news-editors are bored with the story, now that the scientists have spoken? Curiously, the warden at Wandlebury, Mr Bill Clarke, says he's never heard the noise! (Cr: JP Kain.)

<u>Scunthorpe Evening Telegraph</u> 9 June 1977: that bangs, loud enough to shake houses in Messingham Rd, Scunthorpe, have been reported occurring at irregular intervals. Cause unknown. (Cr: Nigel Watson.)

The phenomenon continues!

SOME OBSERVATIONS

If not Concorde, then what? We don't know, but as connoisseurs of explanations we could mention a few situations in which a rolling thunder or boom or aerial detonation has occurred with other phenomena (which may or may not be connected, naturally!).

On FT19/22, we observed (Steve Moore did, actually) that the Winchester and environs series of Close Encounters was happening in the area of the booms and during its main build-up. These events featured several ambushes of Mrs Joyce Bowles by pink-eyed silver-suited entities (see FT21/32). This period also saw many reports of aerial lights (some call them UFOs) in Southern England and in South Wales (where schoolchildren saw a flying machine and occupant - see FSR 23:1/5). Now we don't wish to flog a UFO hypothesis for the Boom's origins, but to stir memories of the many cases where aerial lights coincided with aerial detonations, <u>and</u> tremors. Odd aerial sounds, or rather booms that shake houses etc, have been reported in the mystery quake area of Stoke-on-Trent (see FT16/6f). We remember the weird event at Llandrillo on 23 January 1974, when there were mysterious aerial booms and rumblings that shook houses in North Wales. The evidence for a tremor was slight - and some reports of aerial lights supported a meteor hypothesis. What boggled everybody was the odds-on coincidence of a quake and a meteor at the same site and time. There's no connexion according to current scientific notions. (see The News 4/4; & 5/10f).

And while following up some of Fort's references for the 'revised Fort' planned by X and your editor, another example presents itself - the great Hereford quake of 17 December 1896, which according to much reliable testimony, was preceeded firstly by a strange red glow in the sky like a flash of red flame, and secondly by a peculiar double concussion felt by witnesses to be in the air (as distinct from the quake shock which came through the ground). Whether the flash was a meteor or not (as many thought it was), authorities like Charles Davison were firm on there being no possible connexion between it and the quake - the timing was a monumental coincidence! Now here's the interesting bit: according to authoritative records all evidence of the quake was minimal. Birmingham was shaken, yet nothing was recorded at the Observatory on their seismometers; no traces on the magnetograph at Stonyhurst; and nothing on the Greenwich reflecting (earth current) galvanometer. The next day, the Astronomer Royal said only two tiny marks could be found for that time, 5.30am. GP Yeats (author of Observations on the Earthquake of December 17,1896), concluded the quake happened in the air not in the ground! Similar aerial effects happened during the great quake of 1884 in Essex, he said. Fort gives others: cannonading in the air during the quakes at Comrie, Scotland (Books p404) for example. But, and most damning, many accounts of artillery-like sounds in the skies of England, Wales, New Zealand, America in the 19th century - see New Lands ch15 (Books p403ff). There's more too, but we'll call it quits.

MYSTERY BOOMS - 1974

Hmmm, just discovered an unpublished boom-flap from 1974, in the files. It seems that shortly before 3.15am on 20 March 1974, a loud booming was heard in the air in the area surrounding San Francisco, California. Civil and military authorities said no planes of theirs could have caused it and there was no recorded seismological activity. San Francisco Examiner 20 March; San Francisco Chronicle 21 March 1974 (Cr: Loren Coleman.)

Then just 3 months later a series of phantom-tremors, house-rattlings and aerial booms jounced a 70 mile area around Los Angeles, from Camarillo to Whittier and the coast. Civil and military aircraft were once more cleared. Nor was there any evidence of quakes. A spokesman for the Caltech Seismological Laboratory said a similar phenomenon occurred in the same area in January 1930. This latter incident prompted the seismologist Charles Richter (the same), to postulate the notion of 'pseudoseisms', caused by distant sounds refracted from the stratosphere through air layers of different speeds and temperatures. (Look to your laurels, 'Boomwatch'). However, the theory presents the same difficulty as its modern counterpart, 'Concorde': the armed forces say there was no gunfire anywhere to refract! Par for the course! San Francisco Examiner 22 June 1974 (Cr: Loren Coleman.) These sounds were heard several times through 20 & 21 June 1974.

Four months later, on 23 October, a wide area around Grimsby, Cleethorpes, and surrounding villages in Lincolnshire, were severely shaken by a 'heavy bang'. The local police switchboard was so jammed with callers trying to find out what had happened, that, they said, had there been 'a real emergency' the essential rescue services would have been badly hampered. Inquiries eliminated explosions on the ground & sonic booms from aircraft. It remains a mystery. One clue, for what it's worth, is that the boom was heard as far away as Binbrook, the site of several of Fort's more horrifying poltergeist/fires/SHC/ animal-ripping stories. Curiously, the third part of Larry Arnold's 'Fire Leynes' will be concentrating on this very area next issue. In our case, the RAF station at Binbrook denied that any of their planes caused the noise. Story from Scunthorpe Evening Telegraph 25 October 1974 (Cr: Nigel Watson.)

And lastly, in our 1974 series, we learn that the Bedfordshire village of Caddington was rocked by noises 'like cannonfire or muffled thuds' which rattled windows and frightened children. They began about 6pm and sometimes continued until midnight - but we have no information about when this started or when it ceased that year. Certainly no one recalled it (in the press) during the 1977 'Concorde' boomflap. Perhaps one of our readers could check on this for us? Anyway it seems that inquiries into the sound's origin failed, and as there seemed no danger or damage, even the police inquiry dropped after a while. The Sun 4 November 1974 (Cr: Phil Ledger)

A PLANETARY POLTERGEIST?

Here's another hypothesis. We are struck by the similarity of outdoor aerial sounds with those heard in the air, walls and even furniture during so-called poltergeist infestations. Some day we must tell you about Calvados Castle (if you don't already know) which suffered such severe shakings and impacts against its walls that the terrified occupants could only imagine something the size of a battleship was out there invisibly battering. And yet there is an anomaly, typical of poltergeist cases, which occurs similarly in our mystery booms cases linked to supposed quakes - that despite the real shakings of houses etc, there is very little seismological evidence. An air-quake (or pseudoseism, if you will) could achieve this effect by transmitting some of its shock through buildings etc into the ground, faintly. We know of one case in the far East (can't find the reference right now) in which the terrified occupant fled his house which, by the severity of the blows upon

cont on p35/

...and now, on p32 (which is 23 backwards, of course, we are pleased to have Bob Wilson's account of his interest in the '23 phenomenon' he incorporated into the Illuminatus! trilogy. By way of introduction, we'd just like to throw in a couple of data that came our way recently. One mentions a devastating fire that wiped out the 23rd floor of the Red Road tower block, Glasgow, in which one boy died. It was said to be Europe's tallest block of flats. Daily Express 30 August 1977. Secondly, a story believed by many Indians to have been an omen of the downfall of Mrs Indira Gandhi. On 20th February 1977, her grandson, Rahul, hugged her as she was about to set out on her most critical election tour. Her

favorite necklace snapped spilling beads on the floor - it was a 'rudraksha mala', given to her and consecrated by the modern saint Anandamayi Ma. Mrs Gandhi, says the Amrita Bazar Patrika 21 Sept 1977, 'knew it was not an accident'. She searched franticly, retrieved all but 4, and restrung them - but the mala was now reduced to 23 beads. Its power as a charm seems to have ended, or Mrs Gandhi's belief in its protection ended; same effect! She wore it, but finally put it away on 2nd March, since when her fortunes (& those of her powerful family) steadily declined, until losing the election ended her dreams of founding a dynasty. (Cr: Ion A Will.)

THE 23 PHENOMENON

by ROBERT A WILSON

I first heard of the 23 enigma from William S Burroughs, the distinguished author of Naked Lunch, Nova Express, etc. According to Burroughs, he had known a certain Captain Clark, around 1960 in Tangier, who once bragged that he had been sailing 23 years without an accident. That very day, Clark's ship had an accident which killed him and everybody else aboard. Furthermore, while Burroughs was thinking about this crude example of the irony of the gods that evening, a bulletin on the radio announced the crash of an airliner in Florida, USA. The pilot was another Captain Clark and the flight was Flight 23.

Burroughs began collecting odd 23s after this gruesome synchronicity, and after 1965 I began collecting them also. Many of my weird 23s were incorporated into the trilogy, Illuminatus!, which I wrote

in collaboration with Robert J Shea in 1969-1971, and I will mention only a few of them here, to give the flavour of the thing to those benighted souls who haven't read Illuminatus yet:

In conception, Mom and Dad each contribute 23 chromosomes to the fœtus. DNA, the carrier of the genetic information, has bonding irregularities every 23rd Angstrom. Aleister Crowley, in his Cabalistic Dictionary, defines 23 as the number of "life" or "a thread", hauntingly suggestive of the DNA life-script. On the other hand, 23 has many links with termination: in telegraphers' code, 23 means "bust" or "break the line", and Hexagram 23 in I Ching means "breaking apart". Sidney Carton is the 23rd man guillotined in the old stage productions of A Tale of Two Cities (A few lexicographers believe this is the origin of the mysterious slang expression "23 Skiddoo!"). *

Some people are clusters of bloody synchronicities in 23. Burroughs discovered that the bootlegger "Dutch Schultz" (real name: Arthur Flegenheimer) had Vincent "Mad Dog" Coll assassinated on 23rd Street in New York when Coll was 23 years old. Schultz himself was assassinated on October 23rd. Looking further into the Dutch Schultz case, I found that Charlie Workman, the man convicted of shooting Schultz, served 23 years of a life sentence and was then paroled.

Prof. Hans Seisel of the University of Chicago passed the following along to Arthur Koestler, who published it in The Challenge of Chance. Seisel's grandparents had a 23 in their address, his mother had 23 both as street number and apartment number, Seisel himself once had 23 as both his home address and his law office address, etc. While visiting Monte Carlo, Seisel's mother read a novel, Die Liebe der Jeannie Ney, in which the heroine wins a great deal by betting on 23 at roulette. Mother tried betting on 23 and it came up on the second try.

Adolph Hitler was initiated into the Vril Society (which many consider a front for the Illuminati) in 1923. The Morgan Bank (which is regarded as the financial backer of the Illuminati by the John Birch Society) is at 23 Wall Street in Manhattan. When Illuminatus was turned into a play, it premiered in Liverpool on November 23rd (which is also Harpo Marx's birthday). Ken Campbell, producer of Illuminatus, later found, on page 223 of Jung's Memories, Dreams, Reflections, a weird dream about Liverpool, which Campbell says describes the street intersection of the theatre where Illuminatus opened (Jung, of course, was the first psychologist to study weird coincidences of this sort and to name them synchronicities). Campbell also claims Hitler lived briefly in Liverpool when he was 23 years old, but I haven't seen the reference for that personally.

---

* Eric Partridge's Dictionary of Catch Phrases (RKP 1977, p228) dates this theory back to Henry Miller's dramatization of 'Tale of Two Cities', in 1899. He also gives some other interesting theories. Cr: Peter Hope-Evans). - Ed.

Recently, I was invited to join an expedition to the Bermuda Triangle. I declined because of other commitments, but "the crew that never rests" (Sir Walter Scott's name for the Intelligence - or idiocies - who keep pestering us with this kind of phenomena) refused to let me off the hook that easily. A few days after the expedition left, I turned on the television and caught an advertisement for the new film, Airport 77. The advertisement began with an actor playing a control tower operator, shouting "Flight 23 is down in the Bermuda Triangle!"

A week later, Charles Berlitz, author of The Bermuda Triangle, claimed he had found a submerged pyramid "twice the size of the pyramid of Cheops" in the waters down there. You will find that monstrous edifice described in Illuminatus, and it is specifically said to be "twice the size of the pyramid of Cheops" - but Shea and I thought we were writing fiction when we composed that passage in 1971. In 1977, Berlitz claims it is real.

I now have almost as many weird 23s in my files as Fort once had records of rains of fish, and people are always sending me new ones.

Euclid's Geometry begins with 23 axioms.

As soon as I became seriously intrigued by collecting weird 23s, one of my best friends died, on December 23rd.

My two oldest daughters were born on August 23rd and February 23rd respectively.

According to Omar Garrison's Tantra: The Yoga of Sex, in addition to the well-known 28-day female sex cycle, there is also a male sex cycle of 23 days.

Burroughs, who tends to look at the dark side of things, sees 23 chiefly as the death number. In this connection, it is interesting that the 23rd Psalm is standard reading at funerals.

Heathcote Williams, editor of The Fanatic, met Burroughs when he (Williams) was 23 years old and living at an address with a 23 in it. When Burroughs told him, gloomily, "23 is the death number", Williams was impressed; but he was more impressed when he discovered for the first time that the building across the street from his house was a morgue.

Bonnie and Clyde, the most popular bank-robbers of the 1930s, lived out most American underground myths quite consciously, and were shot to death by the Texas Rangers on May 23rd, 1934. Their initials, B and C, have the Cabalistic values of 2-3.

W, the 23rd letter of the English alphabet, pops up continually in these matters. The physicist who collaborated with Carl Jung on the theory of synchronicity was Wolfgang Pauli. William Burroughs first called the 23 mystery to my attention. Dutch Schultz's assassin was Charlie Workman. Adam Weishaupt and /or George Washington, the two (or one) chief sources of 18th century Illuminism, also come to mind. Will Shakespeare was born and died on April 23rd.

(I have found some interesting 46s - 46 is 2 x 23 - but mostly regard them as irrelevant. Nonetheless, the 46th Psalm has a most peculiar structure. The 46th word from the beginning is shake and the 46th word from the end, counting back, is spear.)

Through various leads, I have become increasingly interested in Sir Francis Bacon as a possible ring-leader of the 17th Century Illuminati (Some evidence for this can be found in Francis Yates' excellent The Rosicrucian Enlightenment). Bacon, in accord with custom, was allowed to pick the day for his own elevation to knighthood by Elizabeth I. He picked July 23rd.

Dr John Lilly refers to "the crew that never rests" as Cosmic Coincidence Control Center and warns that they pay special attention to those who pay attention to them. I conclude this account with the most mind-boggling 23s to have intersected my own life.

On July 23rd, 1973, I had the impression that I was being contacted by some sort of advanced intellect from the system of the double-star Sirius. I have had odd psychic experiences of that sort for many years, and I always record them carefully, but refuse to take any of them literally, until or unless supporting evidence of an objective nature turns up. This particular experience, however, was especially staggering, both intellectually and emotionally, so I spent the rest of the day at the nearest large library researching Sirius. I found, among other things, that July 23rd is very closely associated with that star.

On July 23rd, ancient Egyptian priests began a series of rituals to Sirius, which continued until September 8th. Since Sirius is known as the "Dog Star", being in the constellation Canis Major, the period July 23-September 8 became known as "the dog days".

My psychic "Contact" experience continued, off and on, for nearly two years, until October 1974, after which I forcibly terminated it by sheer stubborn willpower (I was getting tired of wondering whether I was specially selected for a Great Mission of interstellar import, or was just going crazy).

After two years of philosophic mulling on the subject (late 1974 - early 1976), I finally decided to tune in one more time to the Sirius-Earth transmissions, and try to produce something objective. On July 23rd, 1976, using a battery of yogic and shamanic techniques, I opened myself to another blast of Cosmic Wisdom and told the Transmitters that I wanted something objective this time around.

The next week, Time magazine published a full-page review of Robert KG Temple's The Sirius Mystery, which claims that contact between Earth and Sirius occured around 4500BC in the Near East. The July 23rd festivals in Egypt were part of Temple's evidence, but I was more amused and impressed by his middle initials, K.G., since Kallisti Gold is the brand of very expensive marijuana smoked by the hero of Illuminatus.

The same week as that issue of Time, ie. still one week after my July 23rd experiment, Rolling Stone, a popular American Rock magazine, published a full-page advertisement for a German Rock group called Rameses. One of the group was named Winifred, which is the name of one of the four German Rock musicians who control the Illuminati in Illuminatus, and the advertisement included a large pyramid with an eye atop it, the symbol of the Illuminati.

Coincidence? Synchronicity? Higher Intelligence? Higher Idiocy?

Of course, the eye on the pyramid was a favourite symbol of Aleister Crowley, who called himself Epopt of the Illuminati, and subtitled his magazine, The Equinox, "A Review of Scientific Illuminism". And 2/3 equals ·66666666 etc. - Crowley's magick number repeated endlessly. Readers of this piece might find it amusing to skim through The Magical Revival and Aleister Crowley and the Hidden God, two books by Kenneth Grant, a former student of Crowley's (and note the initials K.G. again). You will find numerous references, cloudy and occult, linking Crowley in some unspecified way with Sirius.

The actor who played Padre Pederastia in the National Theatre production of Illuminatus informed me that he once met Crowley on a train. "Mere coincidence", of course; or "sheer coincidence" if you prefer. But the second night of the National Theatre run, the actors cajoled me into doing a walk-on as an extra in the Black Mass scene. And, dear brothers and sisters, that is how I found myself, stark naked, on the stage of the National Theatre, bawling Crowley's slogan "Do what thou wilt shall be the whole of the law", under the patronage of Her Majesty the Queen.

As a Fortean, I am, of course, an ontological agnostic and I never believe anything literally. But I will never cease to wonder how much of this was programmed by Uncle Aleister before I was ever born, and I'm sure that last bit, my one moment on the stage of the National Theatre, was entirely Crowley's work.

If you look up Crowley's Confessions, you'll find that he began the study of magick in 1898, at the age of 23.

Robert Anton Wilson, 1977.

■■■

Mystery sounds cont...

it, he was convinced was on the point of collapse. Once outside, all was quiet; not even his neighbours had heard the slightest sound! Anyway, consider the following cases, and judge for yourself whether what happens in one household could not happen on a larger scale in the countryside.

Each night for five weeks, beginning sometime in September 1975, Danielle Jankowiak, aged 10, was racked by weird choking coughs and sobs. At exactly 10.30pm she would begin to cough in her sleep; and the coughs and sobs would rise in pitch and intensity then suddenly stop. Almost immediately loud hammer-like knocking could be heard throughout the apartment block, in the Central French town of Stiring Wendel. The other 16 families were often kept awake by the noises, which made the whole block vibrate, until they ceased about 00.30am. The family's doctor could find no medical explanation for her symptoms; and the police, who watched in (and outside) the Jankowiak apartment for 15 nights, were equally baffled about the knockings. Soon crowds gathered around the building each night. They saw the phenomenon as witchcraft and called it 'The Devil Who Knocks'. On several occasions as Danielle and her mother, Monique, walked in the town, they were spat upon and stoned. This is modern France, folks! That was when the clergy stepped in. After the first exorcism, Danielle's coughing stopped; but when the family moved in with relatives to escape the hostility of their neighbours, the knocking followed them. We hear that it continued until the priest, Canon Armand Blanchebarbe, worked another exorcism in nearby Metz Cathedral. Then, as far as we know, the phenomenon ceased. Reveille 23 July 1976. Please see the 'Electric People' section of Phenomena for cases of mysterious knockings linked to some diseases and to seance and poltergeist phenomena.

Similarly, a young girl was the focus of a 'pounding, knocking noise', in Blendon Township, Franklin County, Ohio, in February this year. Everywhere in the house that Beth Hunsinger, 14, went, the noise would follow, according to Blendon police chief, Tom Heichel. He and Sgt Sonny Yinger preferred to think in terms of 'kids playing pranks' rather than in spirits, despite their admission that their watches and checks failed to turn up any mundane cause. Several people have said that we, in FT, seem to favour the 'supernatural' hypothesis, by our scorning of mundane explanations, even though these latter are quite inadequate. Well, we can see how the impression can arise, because people insist on seeing things in 'either/or' terms - like our good policemen of Blendon they think that if things cannot be accounted for in everyday terms they must, ipso fatso, be 'supernatural' (automatically equating the known with 'natural', and the unknown with 'supernatural'); and the natural human reaction is to cringe from the horror of an Unknown element in everyday life. They leave themselves no choice but to accept a more comforting solution in everyday terms, knowing it to be irrational. But if our studies of the phenomenal have taught us anything it is that rationality and rationalizing are two very different animals (the chronic schizophrenic can rationalize according to the strictest logic, for example.) By pointing out the inadequacies of conventional attempts to explain-away, it is not our intention to strengthen the spirit (or any other) hypothesis, as we feel that in the absence of conclusive data one way or the other, or any way, the most practical, the most scientific position is the sceptical one - ie not necessarily doubting per se, but having no allegiences to any theory prematurely. But back to our story: it is said that

these mysterious hammerings had been going on for several weeks, and at times were so violent as to be heard several houses away. Houston, Texas, Chronicle 26 February 1977 (Cr: Mark A Hall.) Note that this is concurrent with the end of the 'Concorde' booms!

*** We have many notes on the mystery hums, whirrs and clicks, over the same 'Concorde' period, which surprisingly were not blamed on the plane!, and we'll give these in this column soon. Also overlapping this period were the jamming radio signals of great power reported from many parts of the world as originating in Russia, and on which some blamed the USA's devastating winter of 1976/7 - we'll give these notes in the next issue under 'Electro-magnetic weirdiestuff!'***

RUNAWAY TRAINS
In 1965, one of the last steam locos, a 'Black Five', had a last defiant fling on track around Morecombe Bay, as new deisel locos were being introduced. Somehow it started up on its own and ran from the depot at Carnforth almost to Grange, without a driver. The poor man was chasing desperately in his car. The Yorkshire Post 21 October 1974 (Cr: Paul Screeton) says the incident was celebrated by a folk song.
This clipping came our way recently, and put us in mind of the runaway train story in News 5/5, which raced 9 miles through suburban London, early on 29 March 1974. Here are some others:
The London to Glasgow express began to slow down to 30mph between Carlisle and Lockerbie. The guard, Tom MacCondechie, wondered if the driver was ill, investigated and found the cab empty. Quickly, applied the emergency brakes. With the help of the Lockerbie staff, they found the driver further back along the track, staggering about. Six months later, a small note said that the driver had been found guilty of being drunk and endangering the lives of the passengers, none of whom was aware of the drama. The unresolved mystery seems to be where he got

out after boarding at Carlisle, and why the deadman's handle failed to operate. Daily Mail 25 January 1977; Daily Mirror 13 July 1977.
According to the News of the World 19 July 1977 (which places the incident about the time of the driver's trial, above) a train coasted at 18mph for 25 minutes towards Munich on its own, passing 12 level crossings, some of them unmanned. It was shunted to a siding where it crashed into a barrier.

DRIVERLESS CARS etc
According to clippings sent by Nigel Watson, the Cornish & Devon Post has quite an interest in runaway vehicles, in its reminiscence columns. In the 12 Oct 1974 edition, it said that on 10 Oct 1914 a car in Holsworthy had started up on its own, driven into town and smashed into a lamp-standard. In the edition for 27 Nov 1976, a curious coincidence occurs. They remember that on 21 Nov 1936, a car in Bude ran away with itself, crashing later. A separate, modern incident, involving a cake delivery lorry happened on 22 Nov 1976, also in Bude (1 day over 40 yrs apart). It careened off a van and went through railings coming to rest in gar-

dens. It was braked and left in gear and
police said they still could not account
for it.

The end of 1976 and early 1977 saw a
nice little run of runaways. A taxi, owned by a man in Grimethorpe, near Barnsley
Yorks, burst into life, gave its driver
a run for his money, then burst into
flames. <u>Daily Mirror</u> 3 Dec 1976.

In a scene recalling Ted Sturgeon's
'Killdozer', a digger on the back of a
transporter, negotiating a low railway
bridge, began to chug forward, falling
off the lorry and tipping nearly 1cwt of
rubble into the High St, at Staines. From
Slough <u>Evening Mail</u> 7 Jan 1977 (Cr: Peter
Hope-Evans.)

Finally, an amusing story from Palfrey,
near Walsall, Staffs. It seems that a car
moving slowly down a street without a
driver was stopped by a milkman who stepped in front of it, dug his heels in and
shoved. His name...Steve Austin! True!
<u>News of the World</u> (letters) 13 March 1977;
<u>Weekly News</u> 26 March 77 (Cr: P Hope-Evans)

SOME EXOTIC SELF-MOVERS

Apparently since 11 Jan 1976, a 500lb
tree stump has been migrating around
Ridgway, Illinois. It turns up suddenly,
and vanishes several nights later - so
far residents have found it inside a van,
a garage, and outside several houses. It
has people baffled. <u>Lebanon Daily News</u>
9 Feb 1976 (Cr: Curt Sutherly; <u>ARB</u> 4).

Physicists, explaining 'Maxwell's Demon'
to you, usually give the example that the
random motion of molecules makes it highly improbable that soup, say, will suddenly lurch out of your plate on its own.
Tell that to Esther Yungling, of Ventura,
California! It seems that she was peace-
fully sleeping on her waterbed, and the
next minute she was on the floor pinned
down by the bed. Firemen had to
rescue 68-yr-old Esther, and they confessed their bafflement at the incident. All
they could suggest was that 'The water
shifted for some reason, bouncing her on
the floor, and the mattress followed.'
<u>Evening Press</u>, Dublin, Eire, 9 Oct 1976.
(Cr: Leslie Shepard.)

<u>Films</u> -- 'Close Encounters of the Third
Kind' seems set to be released in the USA
in time for Xmas...but if 'Star Wars' is
anything to go by, we won't be seeing it
until next summer. 'Star Wars' will open
in at least 2 London central cinemas just
after Xmas. We learn from <u>PRL Newsletter</u>
20, that another UFO movie is being filmed. Tentatively called 'Skywatch' it is
intended to dramatize US government cover-up operations over the last 30 years
around 'a reenactment of actual cases,
using actual names'. Sounds great if they
can survive the injunctions. Former Air
Force, CIA and NSA personnel are said to
be advising the production to ensure max-
imum authenticity.

Then there is an Italian
production called 'The Yetti', said to
be filming in Canada with a giant model
of the creature 29ft tall, weighing 1.6
tons. The newsphoto shows their inter-

pretation of the Yeti to be very much
like an idealized Bigfoot (or hominoid,
I believe the academic term now is). <u>The</u>
<u>Advocate</u>, Stamford, Conn, 20 July 1977.
(Cr: Doc Shiels).

While we're on the subject of films,
have you noticed how many seem to have
Fortean overtones? Apart from the plagues
of bugs, frogs and squirming things, there
was 'King Kong'(which is to Bigfoot what
'Hound of the Baskervilles' is to the
Black Dog!); 'Picnic at Hanging Rock'
involving a mysterious quadruple disappearance; the revenge of a nature red in
tooth and claw in 'Night of the Animals';
a foreshadowing of the Big Bird saga in
the USA, in 'Food of the Gods' in which
a giant chicken stars (! a sort of cosmic
Col.Saunders?); 'Demon Car' in which said
vehicle develops a mind of its own (see
back to p36 this issue. Shades of 'Killdozer'!), and another film, 'Demon Seed'
portrays the allied theme of a breakaway

computer; not to mention the past or imminent films about psychic powers, reincarnation, possession and sorcery. Lastly I'd like to mention 'Carrie' (which was quite sensitive in parts), about psychic trauma, adolescence and TK: there was a scene in the film where carving knives rise up, fly through the air and transfix the body of Carrie's monomanic mother in a gruesome reenactment of the martyrdom of St Sebastian. Last issue (FT22/13) we told the story of Sister Rosa, tormented by poltergeist phenomena, but we had no room to mention the similarity between the roughly contemporary 'Carrie' and the way airbourne knives would hurtle towards Sister Rosa's chest. Stranger than fiction!

Speaking of fictional Bigfeet reminds us that another allegedly factual film of Bigfoot has come to light. Frank White took it while on holiday near Bellingham in the area of Mt Baker, Washington, on 7 October 1977. The ape-like beast was walking along a trail, and stopped twice to look back at the Whites. Palm Beach Post 18 October 1977 (Cr: J&C Bord).

The BBC 'Horizon' team, who produced the Bermuda Triangle debunking TV documentary based on Lawrence Kusche's book, are working on another TV special which will critically examine von Daniken's claims. Some of the footage was filmed during a 5yr study by 30 British archeologists among the ancient ruins of South America. No details of when it will be released. Daily Mail 25 May 1977.

In a maddeningly vague notice , in the Sunday Standard, Bombay, India, 16 October 1977, we learn that an (unnamed) group of scientists have located a previously undetected chamber in the Chefren pyramid, the second largest at Giza. The only other known chamber in the pyramid proved to be empty. The clipping also revealed that a Japanese university will be funding a project to build a smaller replica of the Cheops pyramid nearby. It has the backing of the Egyptian government, will employ 8,000 locals, and will study the problems and methods of raising such structures. (Cr: Ion Will.)

A lecture on 'The Welsh UFO Wave' will be given by local researcher Randall Pugh Jones (whose reports have appeared in FSR), at Kensington Central Library, London W8, 7pm, 3 December 1977. A BUFORA lecture but open to non-members. Paul Devereux, editor of the Ley Hunter, will talk on leys and UFOs, at the same venue, 7pm, 4 Feb 1978.

***We hope to have settled down a little more by next issue, to have more news, and to reintroduce our listings of interesting relevant material in the professional mags.

letters-letters-letters-letters

PHENOMENA

from Bob Rickard, London.
With our book now finally published, John Michell and I would like to make known a few corrections that have come to light, and which cannot be incorporated into the book until a second edition is printed. 1) In the caption to the Aberdare fishfall picture (bottom right) the correct date should be 11 February 1859. However it seems that there is some doubt about this date too as many of the major sources give different dates. Bob Schadewald and I are investigating these sources and will report on the problem in a future FT. 2) In the celebrated SHC case of J Temple Thurston (1919), the victim's name should be J Temple Johnson. This error came to light when I was checking the source given by Fort (Books 912f); I had a photostat of this source but didn't look at it properly. Mea culpa! 3) On page 81, the pamphlet, Wonderful Phenomena, cited in the middle column, is by Eli Curtis, not Curtis Eli.

BODIES

from William Grimstad, Illinois.
A collector of weirdiana wants me to tell you that the death of Geoffrey Hubbard ((son of the Scientology founder - see FT21/11)) was but the latest in a series of mysterious murders/'suicides' in the vicinity of Las Vegas International airport. Most of the rest have involved assailants described as looking like 'Mexicans', which is certainly a possibility around there, but might on the other hand be MIB types.
As for the Dennis Graham disappearance near West Point, Virginia in July 1976 ((see FT21/12))., you should know that this area is just across the York river from the Central Intelligence Agency's Camp Peary. Ironically, this supposed US Army base is actually one of 'the Company's' most sensitive installations, where training in assassination, demolitions and other highly illegal matters are allegedly carried

out. What it means I don't exactly know, but Camp Peary is known inside the CIA as 'The Farm' and as 'West Point' (a reference to the US Military Academy, in New York, I presume). So, mysterious disappearances around there probably aren't so mysterious as they'd be in, say, Possum Trot, Arkansas.

((Famous last words! In Bill's next letter to us was a brief note from the Washington Post 10 Aug 1977, that the previous day yet another body was fished from the James River, Virginia. An autopsy was to determine whether it was the body of a man drowned in a boating mishap about 2 days before...or that of someone else! Bill comments)) The James River site here is within 10 miles of the York River site ('West Point')... By my Fortean Synchronicity yardstick that's close enough for a 'Hmmmm' rating (one cut above a shrug!).

((We'll be having an article from Bill in a forthcoming issue, on Fortean happenings in US towns with Masonic name-links!))

LEVITATION

from Dr C Louis Wiedemann, New Jersey.
John Keel told me about a levitation which he witnessed in the far east (he might have written of it in his book Jadoo), which he was convinced was real levitation. I do not recall whether the levitee (if that's the correct term) used a cane or other contact with the ground, or whether he seemed to float totally suspended in the air. One might opine that this latter fact (would) mark the difference between a true levitee and a phoney. If there has to be contact with the ground or another object, however frail it might appear to be, one might easily construe that it is not a true levitation.

((Firstly, many thanks to the several readers who wrote in response to your editor's piece on fakir-type levitations - see FT21 - pointing out the many tricks and devices used by and available to the stage-magicians of today. I regret that we don't have the room for that avenue of the discussion and would like to confine it to the apparently genuine feats. Secondly, thanks, Lou, for reminding me of Keel's Jadoo (pub'd by Tower (USA) as Mysteries of the Orient: Jadoo). I had forgotten this case (given in the book on p186)...and yes, Keel's guru did keep his hand on his stick as he rose cross-legged into the air! I note your distinction between this mode of levitation and that of the free flyers who need no props of any kind, but I can't really accept that

one form should be less 'true' than another. Granted the mode of employing the forces involved differs, just as, say, some firewalkers need no purification rituals prior to venturing on the coals, and others cannot do it without them. If, as many sages have hinted, we can learn to do these things, then it's possible that the manner of the lessons sets the form for the practice - hence variations according to culture, religion, etc.))

FISHFALLS, etc.

from Steve Ogden, Kentucky.
There are a couple of points I'd like to make about Bob Schadewald's 'Fish Falls & Whirlwinds' (FT22/31f). He forgot to consider the acceleration of gravity - 32ft per sec. per sec. Any object falling from 5000ft or 3750ft elevations should have accelerated to a far greater velocity than that he shows. The other point is   the reason for the absence of reported falls in the Minnesota area. When you report unusual happenings in the USA, you may be sent to a psychiatric ward (at least the witnesses are afraid this might happen!).

((The points you raise are interesting. But firstly I urge you to reread Bob's article. Our fish are not falling through an ideal vacuum, but through a viscous medium (the air) which prevents acceleration at the ideal rate. Then there are two unknowns: we don't know the velocity the fish started with, nor the air currents that may additionally slow-down or speed-up their descent. Secondly, the velocities Bob is discussing are the 'terminal velocities' (ie the velocity at which drag, caused by the resistance to the smooth passage through the air of the surface of the fish, cancels the acceleration of gravity.) Thirdly, Bob was making a point regarding the whirlwind explanation of fishfalls; that in an area like Minnesota, with its high proportion of tornadoes, and large numbers of lakes and ponds, etc, you'd expect the whirlwind theory to hold water (forgive me!) and produce a higher number of fishfalls than are actually reported - another nail in the whirlwind explanation's coffin!

However, it is true that we cannot judge the actual number of happenings by the number of reports, though we can give educated guesses. Keel and others have commented on the various 'filters' a report has to negotiate - first a person must report it, then it is screened in turn by editors and others, before

appearing in the media. The proportion
that drops out each stage could be high.
Of course many people with experiences
of Fortean phenomena never tell anyway,
partly because of fear of ridicule
(though I've found that to be a fairly
low factor from my own encounters with
witnesses), but mainly because they
never knew who to tell it too. We hope
that the publication of Phenomena will
begin to encourage people, and establish
the Fortean journals as the people to
contact - to this end we printed an
appeal and a shortlist of journals at
the book's back.))

HOLLOW EARTH

from Frank Brownley, New York.
I would like to hear from FT readers
who are interested in and collect 'Hollow Earth' theory books. Are there any
clubs in England?
((As far as I know, there are no
clubs specifically for hollow-earthers
in England. We do know of the 'Hollow
Earth Society': GPO Box 563, Sydney
2001, Australia...secretary is KH Snell.
Tell 'em FT sent you! Others interested
in corresponding with or through Frank
should write to him at: 29 McCall Rd,
Rochester, NY 14615.))

Your editor regrets that he cannot
answer all correspondence, or immediately. But please write on topics of interest, and we'll consider them for
these pages. Our aim is to stimulate
discussion, and even contact if that's
your wish (like Frank Brownley above).

Editorial stuff cont...
Errata - thanks to the vigilance of
Robert Schadewald, we correct the date
of Harry Kellar's levitation article
cited in ref 12, FT21/23. It should be
1893, not 1897.
Can anyone knowing the address of
Robert F Landro (USA) let us know too,
please. He wrote forgetting his address!
Anyone comtemplating throwing out old
UFO and Fortean mags (including copies of
early The News) please donate them to us
instead, for our files. Write with list,
and we'll pay for postage etc. Thanks.

Joint Subscriptions: IMPORTANT!
Though useful to some of you, FT's joint
subscription plan failed to become widely
used, and thus could not absorb our loss
on the discount given. Besides, it proved
a real pain in the ass to administer, especially with the parties (FT, TLH & INFO)
having to frequently adjust their prices.
We have decided to offer these reduced
rates no longer - but for the convenience
of readers of these mags, each will still
act as agent for the other, passing your
sub on to the others. The full rates for
FT & INFO, and FT & TLH can be worked out
from our back page, and can still be paid
with one cheque, if you want. Subscribers
who have taken advantage of joint rates
(up 'til now) will be honoured.

Blanket apologies are hereby given to
publishers of books and journals not mentioned herein. Even with our latest page-
expansion, space is tight, and some items
have to take a lower priority. We promise
to fit it all in sooner or later.

FORTEAN TIMES

strange phenomena - curiosities - prodigies - portents - mysteries

Review Supplement

Published as a supplement to Fortean Times 23 (Autumn 1977) ISSN 0308-5899.

Inquiries for advertizing rates to Fortean Times: Box 152, London N10 1EP.

HARDBACKS

Phenomena: A Book of Wonders by John Michell & Robert Rickard (Thames & Hudson 1977; Hb £3.95, Pb £1.95; pp 128; 219 illus) -- It is an uneasy task for me, as a member of the FT staff, to review the work of our editor and his co-author without being accused of bias...but then this is an uneasy book, surveying a multitude of 'damned' events hardly conducive to the mental well-being of most scientists, rationalists and advocates of plain common sense. It is, in short, a genuine Fortean book; a great rarity (as it ever was) in these days of hackwork and superficial probing by exploitationalists.

The authors begin with a brief introductory essay, putting forward the admirable point-of-view that the best point-of-view is no point-of-view...a piece of contradictoriness which might at first seem like a passive acceptance that 'these things happen'; capitulation in the face of the unknown. Considering the great diversity and quantity of the phenomena presented, this would seem like a very reasonable attitude. However, there is more; for if it is our conceptual framework that labels these events 'unknown' or inadequately explained 'chance' occurrences, it is our concepts themselves that are inadequate...for the events keep occurring with damning regularity, defying both explainers and non-believers. So our authors pursue their way with admirable indifference to all explanations. If current concepts are to be put to the question, they must first be indicted; Michell & Rickard content themselves (apart from the occasional dry comment on the inanities of the defendents) with compiling evidence for the prosecution.

The explanation that all explanations are absurd is in itself absurd - so where does that leave us? We are left with the data, of which there is a great deal, most of which is totally absurd. In 57 chapters, the authors survey a broad spectrum of Fortean phenomena; dazzling, as much for their diversity as for their individuality. Here are old friends like showers of frogs, lake monsters, teleportations and mysterious lights, as well as many less well-known categories. Some of these, while obvious musts for such a Fortean survey, will be familiar to readers of FT, so it is a relief to find that much of the material in the book is previously uncollected, a considerable amount of it drawn from periods prior to 1800 (Fort's starting point for collection) and subsequent to 1932 (Fort's death).

Unfortunately, Forteans must also speak of the unspeakable - so here are also cattle-rippers, invisible assailants, strange deaths and spontaneous human combustions - the details of which are precise and unpleasant. It is easy to see why man has a horror of the unknown, for the unknown is frequently horrible.

At first, two pages per topic might appear inadequate for sufficient depth... until one discovers just how long it takes to read each section, for these are large format pages and the data is densely packed. This concise format ensures the book's quick acceptance as an essential reference work, besides being a highly recommendable primer on the main Fortean mysteries, for oldtimer and newcomer alike. Its data sources are referenced (which is pleasant), and a mass of cross-referencing (in situ) to other sections builds up a web of continuity showing the inter-relatedness of the categories. This cross-referencing also largely excuses the authors for not undertaking the nigh-on impossible task of indexing the book.

Some will doubtless be surprised at this seeming change of direction by John Michell after his previous works on 'Earth Mysteries'; and his unsought image as a 'hippy guru' may even perturb others. They can relax, because Michell proves himself just as much a Fortean as Rickard. Indeed, their approaches mesh together so well that it is virtually impossible to distinguish who worked on which section— an occurrance perhaps as remarkable as any in the book itself!

Lastly, the illustrations are as important in their way as the text, and equally diverse. Each section has a minimum of two illustrations, many of which are photographs (and many of these I have not seen before) collected together for the first time in an expansive visual conglomerate.

In order to prove my lack of bias, I have striven mightily to find some fault with the book...I must profess myself inadequate to the task, except to plaintively wish there were more. It seems superfluous to recommend the book; persons of taste and discretion will already have purchased a copy... Steve Moore.

((For further information on Phenomena please see the letter from Bob Rickard in the letters section in the main mag p38 . Until we settle the question whether FT can deal in the book, unsolicited orders should be sent to Dark They Were & Golden Eyed, 9-12 St Annes Court, London W1. Prices for the paperback plus post & packing: UK: £2.40; World (surface rate): £2.30/$5.00; USA,HK,Africa, Tibet (Air rate): £3.80/$8.00; Japan, Australia,NZ,Mongolia: £4.30/$9.00.))

Space-Time Transients and Unusual Events by Michael A Persinger & Gyslaine F Lafreniere (Nelson-Hall, Chicago, 1977;

$9.95; pp267; index, refs, graphs, maps) With the aid of an IBM 360-40 computer (to which the book is dedicated!), Persinger & Lafreniere made a study of 6,060 unusual events, covering just about every area of Fortean interest (with the exception of parapsychology, which they regard as a justifiable omission). Their sources were the books of Fort, 'known scientific journals', press clippings and Fate magazine. There academic qualifications (listed on the dust-jacket) are impressive.

Their method is based on a major theory concerning the origin and nature of human 'belief structures', and although I'm sure it will be familiar to most Forteans, this view should be outlined to gain a perspective on their approach. Fundamentally, there is the self-evident assertion that modern science has evolved from the systematic observation of recurring natural phenomena. Certain phenomena, being persistent and generally uniform, come to be regarded as 'data points', and when enough of these have established their reliability, someone postulates a systems theory that seems to logically link them together. In this way, science eventually provides a series of frameworks, which in their turn calcify into rigid 'Laws of Nature'. Unfortunately the whole process is based on the selection of those data points which suit the theory, and the rejection of those which do not.

The events we find acceptable, and which form the components of the current concensus or description of the world around us, are largely determined by the way in which our brains, and to some extent our nervous systems, function. We have conditioned ourselves to perceive the environment as three-dimensional - our notion of time, for example, as being like a straight line, is derived from the faculty of memory. We know that belief structures have existed in the past that are different from those in dominance today, but the only real divergence in most cases was the quality and quantity of the data points chosen to support them. In the context of recorded history, it has been common practice to ignore inexplicable events; which leaves a residue of data points which do not lend themselves to inclusion in the contemporary belief structure. Space-Time Transients is the record of a methodical attempt to discover any meaningful correlations between these 'leftovers'.

Using the United States as a primary yardstick, and comparing events worldwide to it, they employed their computer to sift through thousands of well documented cases, which had been grouped into classes (UFOs, mystery animals, falls etc) and plot out any patterns. This was irrespective of the seeming relevance of the similarities which showed themselves. They let the data points dictate the view structure.

One of the most interesting consistencies to emerge concerns the periodic frequency of phenomena. Thus, instances of animal falls are highest in July, while rock falls peak in June and July; ice falls, however show a strong summer preference outside the USA, but little monthly variation inside. UFOs, both aloft and grounded, show a peak in April, but the majority appear, again, in summer. Poltergeist and related disturbances favour no particular month; but you are more likely to spontaneously combust, or disappear while flying or at sea, during December and January. (You have been warned!)

It's early days yet to claim any really meaningful sets of coherent linkages between these events, but the importance of this approach is that it advocates a much looser interpretation of causative possibilities. A truly Fortean enterprise; and hopefully the forerunner of further pushes in this direction. Recommended.
Stan Nicholls.

Visitors From Outer Space by Roy Stemman (Aldus/Jupiter 1976; £3.25; pp144, illus) -- 'This book,' says the publisher, 'provides a balanced history of the whole UFO business.' As it is only 144 pages and contains over 150 illustrations, it is of necessity a very brief history; and considering the bizarre nature of the material he has to handle, Roy Stemman has produced a relatively sober and factual text. This book is one of a series on paranormal and occult subjects aimed at the general reading public, and as UFOs are usually associated in the public mind with the more sensational aspects of SF space opera, this new addition to UFO writings with its emphasis on the extraterrestrial hypothesis and its brightly coloured paintings depicting alien spaceships in action are unlikely to cause people to change their misconceptions. None of the material is likely to be new to the knowledgeable reader, though some of the photos of personalities involved in ufology are of interest.

The book is grouped into eight sections thus (our comments in brackets): 'The Coming of the Saucers' (early reports of 1940s & 1950s); 'The Conspiracy of Silence' (Blue Book, Robertson & Condon); 'Chariots of the Gods' (von Däniken rides again); 'Spacecraft in Early Times' (pre-1940s back to Biblical & Indian texts);

'The Aliens are Among Us!'(contactees Menger, Bender & MIBs); 'UFOs today' (the present state of ufology, Hynek, APRO & Pascagoula & other prominent entity cases) ; 'The inhabited Universe' (basic astronomy, spacetravel, Ozma & Sagan).

In a book dealing with this complex subject matter it would be almost impossible to completely avoid errors. Some of the picture captions are imprecise; eg a photo of Adamski's (p7) is said to be '.. a "scoutship" observing Earth from Venus', when the author probably meant '..a "scoutship" from Venus observing Earth'. But an error of greater magnitude relates to the double-spread colour illustration and caption on pages 69-71. In 1906 the crew of a British steamer in the Persian Gulf observed bands of luminescence travelling underwater from the horizon, passing beneath the ship and continuing unimpeded. This and similar events are not strictly ufological, though they have been used by Fort and Sanderson etc in a ufological connexion. In this book, however, this phenomenon has become a vast wheel of light in the sky whose vivid shafts of light passed right through the steamer - and to prove it there is a large colour painting of the dramatic incident. Thus are legends born!

If the names and comments in the brackets above are familiar to you, then you have probably nothing new to learn from this book. If our references are new to you, then this could serve as a broad introduction to the subject. But, as it has no index, references or bibliography, it won't enable you to go much further.
Janet & Colin Bord.

The Ancient Wisdom by Geoffrey Ashe (Macmillan 1977; £4.95; pp232; notes, bib, index, drawings, photos) -- Quite simply, this 'quest for the source of mystic knowledge' is Ashe's best and most readable book to date, and typical of the literary detective work we have come to associate with him. He begins by outlining the familiar notion of the explosion of interest in occultism today, and that its appeal is directly to some part of ourselves that scientific materialism fails utterly to touch, let alone satisfy. Then he isolates the fundamental teaching common to all schools of thought on the subject: that there is a body of inherited knowledge which has come down to us through ritual, myth, folklore, folk-memory, and traditional teachings (both esoteric and exoteric) which is connected to the very origins of culture, language, sciences, laws and religions. It is a structure of knowledge, a way of looking at the universe that claims unbroken transmission from the gods themselves in the Golden Age; the 'Ancient Wisdom'.

The first few chapters deal with Ashe's search for some basic set of knowledge which, when reconstructed from its fragmented forms in all the cultures down a major migration route, could point to *the* home ground of the Ancient Wisdom. Naturally this entails some brief but illuminating looks at the major mystery schools and origins of their teachings. Step by step, Ashe isolates the teachings and lore of the number seven and its links with the stars of the Great Bear. Allied to this is a belief in the 'axis mundi', the pivot of the heavens (about which the 7 revolve most plainly to all observers in the Northern hemisphere), and its (mainly mythical) terrestrial counterpart, the mountain of the gods and sages (Mt Meru/Sumeru/Zion etc) which was the mystical model for pillars, standing stones, pyramids, ziggurats and towers all over the world. By tracing these ideas, mainly through the migrations of shamanistic practices (Ashe is very convincing on linking the Mediterranean oracles with Altaic shamans, via the Apollo-Artemis cult) we come to the central idea of the book: that the origin of the Ancient Wisdom can be found in the land between the Altai and Himalayan mountains.

This theme is interwoven with several others to make a fascinating (one might even say irresistable) alternative to the ideas epitomized by von Däniken. They concern the belief, in this remote region, in a place called Shambhala, the refuge

A Short Life at the Land's End

John Michell has written and privately published a life and appreciation of JT Blight, the 19th C artist and scholar whose interest in, and illustrations of, the old stones, sites and antiquities of Cornwall, have long deserved recognition. He died hopelessly insane after failing to make it in the competitative world of metropolitan fame, despite (or perhaps because of) the patronage of two remarkable charactors, RS Hawker, vicar of Morwenstow, an eccentric Cornish poet-mystic, and JO Halliwell, the great Shakespearian scholar, adventurer and antiquarian.

Copies of the limited edition, signed and numbered by the author, and illustrated with 8 ½tones & 100 line drawings, are still available at £6.60/$12.00 each. Write to West Country editions: 11 Miles Buildings, Bath, Somerset.

from which the sages, messiahs, hidden masters, 'Great White Chiefs' (whatever) sally forth to lighten a benighted world. Ashe examines Madame Blavatsky's theosophy (and several other dubious occult teachings) and discovers that despite charlatinism, crankiness and doubtful scholarship, one is left with an impression that the heart of the teaching is based on sound principles, though their alleged origins are called in question. The Ancient Wisdom (and Ashe cites an impressive list of curators from Newton and Blake back through John Dee, Copernicus, Paracelcus etc) and its home are living symbols which have adapted to an acceptable form in each age: thus Ashe can say (without flippancy) that the theories of visiting aliens and UFOs are similar to Madame Blavatsky's 'in science fiction garb'. Correlated with the ideas of sky-people/secret Masters (whom Charroux calls 'Initiators') is the belief that the 'King of the World' will ride out from Shambhala and bring about the Apocalypse. Although Ashe does not explore the Millenial aspects of the salvation-from-space type of ufology, he does see the modern interest as a living form of the Ancient Wisdom, and to reinforce that view he cites from the diaries of Nicholas Roerich, the explorer who encountered a UFO on 5 August 1927. The account is very interesting indeed: preceeded by a form of a giant bird, a huge shiny spheroid moved at incredible speed overhead, as Roerich and guides move on from dedicating a stupa-like structure to Shambhala, high in the Humboldt mountains between Tibet and Mongolia. Interestingly the lamas suggest it was a thought-projection from that secret domain, a sign from the Masters to men. Ashe does not seem aware of the current discussions of psychic, psychological and paraphysical phenomena in the 'new ufology', but seems to have arrived at similar conclusions by a very roundabout route.

Another theme is the perenial rumour of magical warfare between good and bad adepts. Shambhala (which had direct communication with heaven still) had a dark counterpart in subterranean Agharti - and Ashe suggests in closing the book that Celtic Britain provides a duplicate structure. Not only did the term 'Hyperborea' refer to the North-Central Asian wanderings of the shamanistic Apollo, but also (on good authorities) to the British Isles with its shamanistic Druids. Here too we find the abodes of light and dark (in the Celtic Avalon and Annwn); and the sleeping King awaiting the day of his return. Indeed the Celtic migrations out of central Asia make a link with Altaic shamanism reasonable. But there Ashe leaves us. Hopefully he will continue to explore this theme, as his previous works on Arthur, the cults of Mary and the Virgin goddess, allow him to comment intelligently and creatively on the links between occultism, mysticism, ufology and 'von Dänikenism'. We have badly needed such a guide — the book is well worth your attention.   RJM Rickard.

Someone Else Is On Our Moon by George H Leonard (WH Allen 1977; £4.95) —— The index in Fort's collected works has, under 'Moon' and 'Lunar', over 60 entries recording anomalous sightings, ranging from moving patterns of lights to vast dark shadows moving purposively across its surface. The first satellite pictures were expected to produce answers to some of these enigmas; but it seems the more evidence available, the greater is the mystery. Leonard has been an avid amateur astronomer for 25 years and when he started to study NASA's moon photos he found shapes within the craters and on their rims which he interpreted as giant structures intelligently formed. These include 'mining rigs' several miles long, and 'A motor as big as the Bronx', to quote one chapter heading. He also concludes that 'More than one space race occupies the Moon', and that although they are largely self-sufficient they come to Earth for their fresh water (hence the reports of UFOs with hoses hovering over lakes and rivers). Fortean skyfalls of fish and blood are, he suggests, the dumping of wastes 'over the friendly skies of Earth, where animals and bacteria and vegetation take care of them'.

How is it then that the artifacts Leonard claims to see in the NASA photographs have not been noticed before? He is himself undecided: early in the book he states that the ostensible reasons for the space program did not add up.'We do not spend billions to reach something merely because it is there', which suggests governmental secrecy. But he also says that 'NASA has taken more than 100,-000 photographs of the Moon'; too much visual data for any two people to cover the same ground. Scientists are deeply involved in their own disciplines and largely unable to communicate with those in other studies, and very few can step back and see the whole when confronted with fragments. 'NASA drowns in a sea of data,' he says, which is another explanation of why no notice is taken of the anomalies so apparent. ((This portrayal of modern sophisticated technology seems overly simplistic to me - eg a lunar geographer has to know the surface like the back of his hand, and computerized mapp-

ing facilities linked to image analyzers and enhancers make sure that surface anomalies are quickly spotted - Ed.))

This popularly written account of these inexplicable shapes, markings and lights on the lunar surface is reasonably convincing, and with the extensive history of observed lunar anomalies (on which he includes a chapter) suggests that indeed something strange has been occurring on the Moon for centuries. It is his interpretations that are more open to criticism. Also, it is unfortunate that the publisher's small reproductions of the original 10x8" photos render invisible much of the detail the author describes.(However he has provided sketches which help a little.) But don't let this inadequacy dissuade you from reading what is probably one of the most original and thought-provoking books published in Britain this year. (It also includes an index, bibliography, and details of where to write to get copies of the original photos.)
                                    Colin Bord.

Canada's Monsters by Betty Sanders Garner (Potlatch Publications, 35 Dalewood Cres, Hamilton, Ontario, Canada L8S 4B5, 1976; bib, illus) —— Nessie seems in imminent danger of losing her place as No1 lake monster, as publicity is increasingly given to monsters of equal interest in lakes at all corners of the earth. Here Ms Garner makes strong claims for Canada's lake monsters: Ogopogo, Manipogo, Igopogo, and others less frequently reported from a further 12 lakes; not to mention the sea-serpents sighted off both east and west coasts, especially the monster nicknamed 'Cadborosaurus. She also gives coverage to the Sasquatch, quoting the nowfamiliar cases of Jacko (a possible young Sasquatch captured in 1884 in British Columbia), Albert Ostman (reputedly kidnapped and held captive by a family of Sasquatches in 1924), and William Roe (who in 1957 watched a female Sasquatch from close quarters as she took a meal of leaves).

This book was in fact intended as a children's book, but will serve as a useful introduction to the monsters of Canada. It is most attractively produced as a large format paperback, and is well illustrated in black & white, and colour (British publishers take note!), with engravings, photos and artist's impressions (some of which make the monsters look soulful and endearing). The 3-page bibliography is to be praised, but sadly there is no index. Another strange omission is the lack of page numbers in the table of contents.   Janet Bord.

Without a Trace by Charles Berlitz. (Souvenir Press 1977; £3.95; pp180; bib, photos) -- This much awaited sequel to **The Bermuda Triangle** does more to emphasize the critics views about the Triangle and supports the 'Establishment' opinion about Fortean research than any book I've seen in a long time! Critics of the Triangle, notably Lawrence David Kusche, have shown that few, if any, of the incidents happened as Berlitz (and other Triangle writers) have described them. Berlitz makes no attempt to reply to his critics. Even worse, he hasn't even the regard for his readers to correct the mistakes of his earlier book. Flight 19, **Raifuku Maru**, **Witchcraft**, **Star-Tiger** and **Ariel**; all the (ho hum) old favourites are here, along with such (ho hum) standbys as the British regiment which vanished (but didn't*) at Gallipoli in 1915.

I will find it difficult to believe anything Berlitz writes in the future. But **Without a Trace** and **The Bermuda Triangle** have done much more than destroy Berlitz' credibility. They have done a lot to destroy the credibility of Fortean studies in general. For years we've been on at the establishment to take an interest in Forteana, and when 'They' do - the interest being in the Triangle - they get false facts and Mr Berlitz.

Paul Begg.

((* Paul is preparing a short article for our 'Forteana Corrigenda' section on this notorious, much-quoted and quite erroneous case. Ed.))

The Undiscovered Country: Adventures into Other Dimensions by Stephen Jenkins (Neville Spearman 1977; £3.95; pp 240) -- It is becoming increasingly clear to all perceptive readers of UFO 'close encounter' and 'contact' reports that the theory of interplanetary visitors does not satisfactorily explain the phenomenon. A favoured alternative theory is that of another dimension of existence, interpenetrating our own but normally undetectable. However, as we know even less about other dimensions than we do about outer space, the problem of the nature and purpose of the mysterious UFO visitors comes no nearer to solution. Jenkins has jumped feet first into the fray, and in doing so has made a thoughtful and thought-provoking contribution. He asks the questions which ufologists should be continually asking themselves: What are they? Who are they? Where are they?, and the book is divided into three parts under these headings. It is a moot point whether his discussions further our knowledge of 'them'; we did not find any revolutionary ideas here - but then we, and many others, have for years pondered over similar evidence to that which Mr Jenkins presents. However, comparative newcomers to ufology *are* likely to have their horizons widened.

Where Mr Jenkins makes his real contribution is his work on leys and their possible link to UFOs and other strange phenomena. Such a link has already been suggested, especially in the recent Winchester encounters with UFO occupants of Mrs Bowles and Mr Pratt, which seem to have taken place on leys (see studies by Paul Devereux in **The Ley Hunter** 75; and by Frank J Woods, **PSR** 22:5). Jenkins' own strange experiences at points where leys cross (which he terms 'nodes') give a lead toward further important ley/UFO research. And what happened to him in 1975 at Saltwood, Kent, where a weird entity was seen in 1963, is particularly interesting...(Read the book to find out!)

Such personal experiences give the book an immediacy otherwise lacking, because the author is inclined to be repetitive. We get the impression of woolliness, which is not helped by the author's apparent inability to organize his material properly - parts 1 and 2 are followed by postscripts, and part 3 by an 'Additional Note' *and* a postscript. The footnotes often consist of material better incorporated into the text; and the four appendices read suspiciously like additional notes. Two further quibbles: 'radiesthesia' is consistently misspelled 'radiethesia'; and contrary to Jenkins' comment (p148) that 'ancient monuments (are) not very plentiful', the Orkney Islands are in fact covered with them.

This book should be read by all serious ufologists and Forteans, for despite our pernickety quibbles, the author has succeeded in highlighting some aspects of ufology which have, until recently, received less attention than they merit.

Janet & Colin Bord.

Handbook of Unusual Natural Phenomena (£14.95; pp542; subject & source indexes, drawings); Strange Universe vol A2 (£8.95; pp280; subject,date & source indexes, drawings, photos) both compiled by William R Corliss (Sourcebook Project, Glen Arm, MD 21057, USA; 1977) -- Strange Universe is the latest volume in the growing series of reference works from the Sourcebook Project, being the second one on the general topic of astronomy (A2). Others deal with biology (B series), earth sciences (E series), physical sciences (G series), ancient man & his artifacts (M series), and the mental sciences (P series). The format of loose sheets in a PVC-covered ringbinder allows you to collate the subsections as the series accumulates, as each entry is coded in sequence, and the indexes are cumulative. Each Sourcebook consists of a selection of quotations and summaries (often complete texts) of key and rare Fortean sources - many rescued from virtual extinction and in a useable form (as anyone who has strained eyes and patience at a microfilm reader will truly appreciate). A2 has notes on cosmic rays; myths of astronomical bodies, meteorite biology, and ET matter; notes on many aspects of optical astronomy from Bode's Law to Planet X and zodiacal light radio astronomy; and experiments relating to gravity, relativity, etc.

The loose-leaf format has not been received well universally; Corliss acknowledges that libraries in particular are reluctant to have it, though many do. So he has produced the Handbook, a hefty volume of essentially meteorological notes culled from the Sourcebooks, and which forms an excellent reference book in the subject. Here are superb collections of eye-witness accounts and discussions of all kinds of strange luminous phenomena (auroras, glows, flashes, lightnings & spook lights); optical & radio anomalies (sunset phenomena, mock suns, halo and rainbow phenomena, mirages, and radio & radar anomalies); unusual weather (from cloudbursts, darkdays & whirlwinds to strange fogs and clouds); mystery sounds (booms, hums, bells etc); earthquake phenomena; hydrosphere phenomena; falling material and objects; and finally, magnetic phenomena.

No researcher can afford to be without these books in some form; libraries will go for the Handbook because it's casebound, but the Sourcebooks themselves are more complete, flexible and useful.

RJM Rickard.

The Irish Giant by G Frankcom & JH Musgrave (Duckworth 1976; £3.95; pp128, index, bib, photos)-- If I were 8ft tall, my inclination would be to live as a recluse; but even if Patrick Cotter had wished to do the same, a lack of money forced him into the life of a showman-exhibitor. Born in Ireland in 1760, he exhibited himself under the name 'Patrick O'Brien, spending most of his time in England, and finally dying a rich but sick man, at 46. His life has been pieced together by Frankcom and makes fascinating reading for the general reader; for the specialist, Musgrave has contributed a detailed medical history of Cotter. Fortunately Cotter's bones were rediscovered at the beginning of this century, and it was possible to determine that he was a 'pituitary giant'. Besides this hormone imbalance, he suffered from osteoarthritis and a few other ailments. The whole book is greatly enhanced by many pertinent illustrations, including photos of objects he used, articles of clothing and even X-rays.

Janet Bord

PAPERBACKS

Fire from Heaven by Michael Harrison (Pan 1977) -- a lengthy critique appears in the 'Forteana Corrigenda' section in the main magazine, because we wished to take the opportunity to correct a few of the books major errors of fact.

The Tungus Event by Rupert Furneaux (Panther 1977; 60p; pp128, bib, photos) -- Perhaps the soundest of the new books on the subject as Furneaux does not seem to be foisting one theory on us at the expence of others or of objectivity. In a postscript he summarizes: 'There is no elegant answer. Each investigator pursues his own course of inquiry and every theory has been contradicted. Belief in the meteorite has been abandoned. The crashing nuclear-propelled spacecraft and the tiny black hole are highly improbable.' Furneaux hints at a novel possibility. The problem is that the 1908 explosion over Siberia has the characteristics of both a comet and the anti-matter hypotheses. Is it possible, he asks, that the two became combined somehow? 'But for that to have happened would require the almost inconceivable coincidence that two rare events...combined to cause the catastrophe.' No answers here, but a good bibliography and summary of the work of the primary investigators and theorists.

RJMR

The Fire Came By by John Baxter & Thomas Atkins (Futura 1977; 75p; pp162, bib, photos) -- Yet another contribution to the current stream of books on Tunguska (although, unlike its predecessors, any mention of that name is strangely absent from the cover blurbs). It really offers nothing new - the explanations offered, however, mostly swing between the unconvincing and the spurious - finally coming down on the side of the alien spacecraft hypothesis. SN

UFO Exist! by Paris Flammonde (Ballantine Books/Futura 1977; 90p; pp480, index, bib, glossary, photos) -- Interesting that we seem to have got to the point where a book advocating the idea of UFOs being the product of technologically advanced off-planet civilizations can be regarded as conventional, if not downright reactionary! Flammonde, author of The Age of Flying Saucers, has set out to write a reasonably comprehensive history of ufology, and also to expose, as he see it, a plot by the authorities to 'keep the truth from us'. With so many, other, better books available the value of this book is doubtful - more so with its heavy bias towards the 'solid spaceships' view, with only a few passing references to the activities of the 'new ufologists'. But it's his obsession with supposed government sponsored conspiracies that puts the level of debate back to the 50s and early 60s. I should admit to a prejudice against books that have titles both (seemingly) ungrammatical and complete with exclamation marks. SN

The Great Lakes Triangle by Jay Gourley (Fontana 1977; 75p; pp192, index, bib) -- An attempt to justify the theory that strange forces, at work over the Great Lakes of America and Canada, are causing disappearances similar to those which allegedly happen inside the Bermuda Triangle. A statistically high proportion of aircraft and shipping losses have occured, according to Gourley, in this area between longitudes 76°W and 92°W, and latitudes 41°N and 49°N; a region which has densely populated centers, but is on the whole sparsely peopled. Several of the cases cited do indeed seem inexplicable; and examples of possibly related phenomena (chiefly UFO-type objects capable of enormous rates of acceleration) add to the puzzle.
The notion that these incidents must be attributed to (the malevolence?) of a specific geographical location is rather over-determinedly pursued. There do seem to be places around the world which dem-

onstrate a high level of unexplained activity...however it seems unwise to allow this increasingly fashionable idea to develop into a standard prerequisite for research (or to sell a manuscript). SN

Pendulum: The Psi Connection by Francis Hitching (Fontana 1977; 85p; pp254, index, bib & notes, charts, tables) -- A noted dowser outlines the extent and practical application of psychometric and related powers, and attempts to widen the limited view held by most people about the nature of these gifts. Covers surprisingly broad range in an engaging, if dry, manner. SN

Your Life in Your Hands by Beryl Hutchinson (Sphere 1977; 85p; pp254, illus) -- A good basic guide to palmistry written in a straightforward and unpatronizing style. Should make clear the fundamentals of this form of divination to even the most uninformed student. SN

Jack the Ripper: The Final Solution by Stephen Knight (Panther 1977; £1.25; pp288, index, bib, illus) -- We boggle at the monumental smugness displayed in the choice of title, for this is a very silly and unconvincing book. Its contents reveal the usual modus operandi: a quick recap and body count; a shuffle through (and gentlemanly dismissal of) everybody else's theories, and an anxious sprint along the convolutions of the author's own beloved 'explanation'. Knight says the name 'Jack the Ripper' should be used collectively, because there were three Jacks out ripping on instructions from high places, to divert suspicion from the nocturnal pleasures of the Duke of Clarence, a favourite in the looney stakes. Rather you should believe the suicide theory! SN

The Fairies in Tradition & Literature (RKP 1977; paperback £2.95; pp261, index, bibs, illus); British Folktales & Legends: A Sampler (Paladin 1977; paperback £1.50; pp315) both by Katharine M Briggs -- Ms Briggs is the first lady of folklore (a past president of the English Folklore Society) and the high standard of scholarship in all her works has made them classic references - so it is a great pleasure to be able to afford them now that these two are in paperback. Fairies, first published 10 years ago, has not been superseded as a modern key sourcebook on the fairy traditions (and traditional fairies) since, except perhaps by her own later works. Pt 3 deals with the use of fairies and fairy-lore by writers and poets; pt 1 being one of the best summaries of knowledge of 'The Fairy People', and pt 2 concentrating with 'Traffic with the Fairies'.

The <u>Sampler</u> is a selection from her mammoth 4 volume <u>Dictionary of British Folktales</u> (totals 2558 pages!) under the following headings: Fables; Fairy Tales; Jocular Tales; Nouvelles; Nursery Tales; Black Dogs; Bogies; Devils; Dragons; Fairies; Ghosts; Giants; Historical Traditions; Local Legends; Saints; The Supernatural; Witches; Miscellaneous Legends. The scope is breathtaking, and it's simply amazing just how much can be crammed in. But that does not make for heavy going - for once the blurb is right, these are good tales well told, and each one a delight. Many of them are of interest to the Fortean (as are the fairy studies in the other book) since they hint at the kind of inexplicable powers or events that most interest us, like Black Dogs, etc. But this is more than a mere collection. A true folklorist like Ms Briggs has an eye and ear for the way motifs are picked up and changed perpetually, forming a continuous tradition and usage. Here, and in most entries in the book, Ms Briggs also provides a genealogy and other illuminating notes. Another hint to the sort of rich mine of interest and entertainment in this book is that random openings assume a meditational quality (like an <u>I Ching</u>, almost!) Fort would have been tickled to read the section on talking dogs. Both books highly recommended.
RJMR

<u>The Great Pyramid</u> by Tom Valentine (Panther 1977; 60p; pp144, illus) -- The author's thesis is that the GP was built in 4699BC by the mysterious Hyksos, who were actually survivors from Atlantis. Cheops, whose name has become linked with the GP, merely usurped the monument some 2000yrs later. All other and later pyramids are merely poor imitations of the GP.

The GP, according to Valentine, is <u>not</u> a tomb; it is a 'Monument to Man' erected in a time of prosperity and harmony. Its scientific message (pi, astronomical properties, etc) were incorporated into it to attract the attention of later generations, and to direct those attentions to the Spiritual Message of its interior system of passages. The passage system, Valentine claims, symbolizes the struggle of Man, individually and collectively, from beasthood to godhood.

The book is not really new in its approaches to the GP; much of it is derived from the older works of Smyth and Davidson. Its symbolism is derived from Marsham Adams' translation of the Egyptian <u>Book of the Dead</u>, and its first appendix deals with Flanagan's pyramid energy, and Kunkel's strange water pump theory. A second appendix is a miniature debunk of some of the Pyramid Games people play. 'It gets a bit far fetched at times,' Valentine remarks. On the whole, worth a read but not a startling one!
RF

<u>Cows, Pigs, Wars & Witches</u> by Marvin Harris (Fontana 1977; 80p; pp192, refs) -- The chapters are essays on various 'Riddles of Culture', from Hindu taboos on cattle-slaughter, and the Jewish and Moslem taboos against pork-eating, to ritual warfare and male-chauvinism among 'primitive' tribes. Perhaps the sections of immediate interest to Forteans are those dealing with cargo-cults and the great witch-crazes of Europe; and in many examples we see that Millenialism, especially a belief in a messiah or in salvation from outside the system, is a universal trait, usually when apathy, despair and desperation have set in. Harris writes entertainingly and informatively, but ends the book with some baffled head-shaking over the occult-explosion of recent years. Worth getting for its perspectives on the bizarre doings of the peoples of this planet, and how they justify them.
RJMR

<u>Levitation for Terrestrials</u> ed Robert K Morison (Ascent: 34 Elm Grove, London N8 - 1977; £1.25; pp104; illus) -- It would be unfair to dismiss the book as crank literature on the strength of its title. This modest private publication is mainly a condensation by Morison of CE Last's <u>Man in the Universe</u> (1954) and is worth investigation for those interested in the problems of motion, energy and relativity. The author amplifies with ideas and expositions of his own. Basically he believes that any object can be levitated if its constituent particles could be uniformly energized to reach escape velocity.
SN/RJMR

<u>The Haunted Universe</u> by D Scott Rogo (Signet 1977; $1.50; pp168, bib) -- One of the most intelligent books on the overlap areas between UFOs, Forteana and parapsychology yet. Rogo avoids many of the usual traps of sensationalizing his material (its already bizarre enough) and settles down to a serious (if erratic) discussion of teleportation phenomena, the Fortean events in so-called miracles, and the psychic aspects of UFO cases, much of it illustrated with relatively unexposed material. There is one glaring paradox at the book's close. Rogo notes that 'From years of investigation and laboratory work, we know that ESP is a very inaccurate information channel. In fact it is so bad as to be useless...' Yet he finds no alternative but to fall back on the notion of these unknown powers of the mind to account for the amaz-

ing complexity of apparently telepathic-
ally shared events such as the Pascagoula
abduction and the mass visions of the BVM
at Zeitoun and Fatima. He concludes: 'The
mind that releases the poltergeist is
also the mind that causes rocks to fall
from the sky, people to vanish, and UFOs
to appear...' But we are given no obvious
clues here (if indeed there are any at
all!) Worth getting.   RJMR

The Sirius Mystery by Robert KG Temple
(Futura 1977; 95p; pp304, index, bib,
photos) -- Temple's first book, now in
paperback, is a commendable piece of
writing. How, it asks, could an obscure
African tribe (the Dogons) possess a detailed knowledge of the white dwarf star
that orbits the Dog Star, Sirius, unsuspected and undiscovered until relatively
recently by the scientific community? Temple presents a plausible argument that
they heard it from intelligent visitors
from a planet in Sirius' solar system.
     However, as the dreaded von Däniken
school has shown, plausibility is no
yardstick when documentation and interpretation flow from the same pen. There
is undoubtedly a case for extraterrestrial
visitations, but to contend that the
original impetus for art, science, philosophy etc, is solely due to manipulative
aliens is giving far too little credit to
the creative abilities of Homo sapiens.
Likewise, the theory that life on this
planet was 'seeded' by outsiders, becomes
in the hands of these theorists the ultimate copout response on the crucial questions of man's origins, avoiding the
real issue by pushing it further, light-
years away, among other star-systems.
     In his argument and data, both keeping
to the point (unlike vonD's scattergun
approach) Temple's book is far superior
to the usual excesses of the 'ancient
astronaut' proponents.   RJMR/SN

UFOs: The Psychic Solution by Jacques
Vallee (Panther 1977; 85p; pp221, index, bib) -- Here's that word 'solution'
again, though this retitle of The Invisible College can at least justify some
claim to it. In advocating the theory that
UFOs might not be the material products
of alien supercivilizations, but perhaps
some kind of projected manifestation of a
non-physical force able to simulate appearances, Vallee votes for the ultraterrestrial lobby. He seems largely in agreement with John Keel; they both accept that
the experiences of witnesses and contactees, though real enough to them, may not
have objective reality in the generally
understood sense; they both speculate on
the selectivity of the phemomena, to certain types of people at certain times and
places; and they both place importance on

the post-contact ordeals of many observers, and the apparent mischievousness of
these encounters. But they part company
on their idea of purpose or function. Keel
(at least up to Mothman Prophecies) concerns himself with reinforcing the non-
material principle, preferring not to define a reason for these activities; while
Vallee sees the machinations of a 'control
system' (here likened to the thermostat on
domestic heating.) UFOs and other psychic
events, he suggests, are indoctrinating us
into an altered perception of our environment, presumably as a preliminary to a
forthcoming step up the evolutionary scale.
Vallee's theory (implying perhaps some
confirmation of Fort's unsettling idea
that this earth and its inhabitants might
be somebody's property) could well be
wrong, but at least he has broadened the
horizons of discussion beyond the usual
approaches to the UFO problem.   SN

Messengers from the Stars (Sphere 85p);
Gods & Spacemen in the Ancient East (Sphere 75p) both by 'ancient astronaut' pioneer, W Raymond Drake.
     The Sacred Mushroom & The Cross by JM
Allegro (Abacus 60p) - the controversial,
bold, original hypothesis about the ori-
gen of Christian mysticism.
     The Virgin by Geoffrey Ashe (Paladin
£2.50) - interesting scholarly study of
myths & cults of Virgin Mary in particular, and Virgin Goddesses in general.

*** We still have many books for review
next time. These include: Peoples of the
Sea, Velikovsky; The Twelfth Planet, Sit-
chin; The Book of Lists, Wallechinsky &
Wallaces; Lost Gods, Allegro; Perpetual
Motion, Ord-Hume; The Secret Discovery of
Australia, MacIntyre; The Wild Boy of
Aveyron, Lane; False Messiahs, Grattus;
Life after Life, Moody; Androgyny, Singer;
Child's conception of the World, Piaget;
The Mind Possessed, Sargant; Hallucinat-
ions, Seigel & West,eds; More Lives than
One, Iverson. And many others. ***

JOURNALS

We welcome copies of journals on related subjects on an exchange basis; and
review/list those received in return for
a similar note. No mag: no listing. Readers who respond to these notes might like
to tell where they saw the information -
it really does help us know what's useful.

INFO Journal 25 (Oct 77) - a Nazca hypothesis; a philosophical   psychological
look at UFOs; the Golden Section 'phi';
report on Fortfest 77; pt2 of the Mont
Pelee volcanic eruption, 1902; notes on
the NZ 'plesiosaur'; notes on the Illinois 'Big Bird'; Canadian Nessies. INFO:

7317 Baltimore Ave, College Park, MD 20740 USA. 6 issues/yr/$10.00...or via FT at £5.00.

Nessletter - a newsletter from Rip Hepple: Huntshieldford, St Johns Chapel, Bishop Aukland, Co Durham DL13 1RQ, on events and personalities associated with monster hunting in UK. Monthly: £1.25/ $7.00.

Lantern 19 (Autumn 77) - stones of E. Anglia; pt2 of Black Dog study; Fortean & UFO news from E Anglia, etc. Journal of Borderline Science Investigation Group (BSIG): 3 Dunwich Way, Lowestoft, Suffolk. 4 issues: 84p - write for foreign rates.

Forteana 2 - one of the most interesting and brightest developments on the Fortean scene this year is the founding of this quarterly Fortean'newspaper'; but unfortunately for some of us, it's all in Danish. Our Scandinavian readers are urged to support it, if they don't already. They even have their own bookshop in Copenhagen, specializing in Fortean publications. Published by the Scandinavian Fortean Organization (Scanfo) Classensgade 8, DK-2100 Copenhagen Ø, Denmark. Membership kr10; **Forteana** kr15.

The Seeker 1:11 (Oct 77) - a small, informal and largely personal Fortean journal, in which the editor, Ms Floyd-Kresse, gives her opinion on current Forteana, engagingly and intelligently. Also includes some news and book reviews; haunted houses; & the city-mirage over Alaska. Tri-weekly from R Floyd-Kresse: Box 422, Asotin, WA 99402, USA. $9.00 gets you 18.

Fate Sept 77 - rept on the disastrous Acapulco conference; report on New Jersey monsters; reincarnation; pulsing eggs; body of demon sealed in coffin in Mexico City cathedral?; locating America's first settlers by psychometry etc...; Oct 77 - your editor on a history of Morgawr; Christian holy places in Israel; Black Arts in India; an exorcism; guide to kinds of Yoga; phone calls from the dead; hiking ghosts; a dream of the next life?...many notes and fillers.

MUFOB 8 (Autumn 77) - a statistical look at vehicle-stoppages; vehicle-stoppages in folklore; aerial phenomena as portents of civil unrest etc; catalogue of Type 1 incidents pt13; notes & reviews. Good stuff! MUFOB: 11 Beverley Rd, New Malden, Surrey KT3 4AW. Quarterly: £1.25/$3.00 (inc airmail).

BUFORA Journal 6:2 (Aug 77) - scientific method applied to UFOs; news and sighting listing; variety of recent UFO-shapes; etc. BUFORA: queries to 6 Cairn Ave, London W5.

Page Research Library deal in new and used UFO books, mags, journals and related stuff. $4.50 will get you 6 issues of the **PRL Newsletter** (an up-to-date forum of UFO news and letters) and copies of their latest **UFO Collectors Catalog** (which lists their current stock). Their holdings of UFO mags virtually unobtainable in the UK, will interest many of you. Lots of Fortean interest too. PRL have also compiled one of the best studies of the BVM apparitions, at Zeitoun, Egypt; **Apparition Phenomena Manifest at Zeitun** with 32 photos ($2.75 inc post.) Write to PRL: 6708 Colgate Ave, Cleveland, OH 44102 USA.

Flying Saucer Review 23:2 (Aug 77) - car-stop in Lancs; the Little Haven humanoids; Hainault, Essex, landing; other sightings and encounters; talks with Betty Hill; etc etc. FSR: West Malling, Maidstone, Kent.

Awareness 6:3 (Autumn 77) - report on UFOIN; UFO camoflage; news notes & data. Journal of Contact UK: 59d Windmill Rd, Headington, Oxford.

WATSUP Journal 7 - Hollow Earth; Gosport airship; Folklore connexion; Winchester case soil samples; Bermuda Triangle; UFO notes, news & data from Wessex WATSUP: 180 Locksway Rd Milton, Portsmouth, Hants. £1.50/yr.

EUFOSG Journal 1:5 (Sept 77) - news, notes, data & studies on UFOs, from Essex & surrounds. Good on local investigations. EUFOSG: 16 Raydons Rd, Dagenham Essex RM9 5JR. £2.50/yr.

NEARA Journal 12:1 (Summer 77) - Excavations, studies, paintings, histories of ancient sites and artifacts from/in New England - much interesting incidental information. NEARA:4 Smith St, Milford, NH 03055, USA. $5.00/yr.

The Ley Hunter 78 - some notes on megaliths in India; comments on the OS maps; a magnetic mystery on the Yorks moors; A preview of the TLH editors' field guide to leys, with observations on working in the field; number geometry; Welsh quartz geodes; news, letters & reviews. TLH is essential for keeping up-to-date on the Earth Mystery scene in the UK. £2.70/ $8.00 (inc airmail). TLH: Box 152, London N10 1EP.

Ancient Skills & Wisdom Review; and **Terrestrial Zodiacs Newsletter** -- the first being mainly a book/journal review mag on Earth Mysteries etc; and the second is self-explanatory; both edited by Paul Screeton (keeping his foot in the door): 5 Egton Drive, Seaton Carew, Hartlepool, Cleveland TS25 2AT.

Journal of Geomancy 2:1 -- proceedings of 1st Cambridge symposium; the Lamanche 'linear' zodiac; zodiac research; numerology; 'the Sprig of Ely'; dragon legends; boundaries & metrology; etc. From Institute of Geomantic Research (IGR): 142 Pheasant Rise, Bar Hill, Cambridge CB38SD. IGR produce many pamphlets on geomantic studies; the most recent we hold back for review next issue.

The Christian Parapsychologist 1:8 (June 77) psychic research; witchcraft in 16 & 17 Cs; autoscopis & ecsomatic experiences pt1. 1:9(Sept 77) - a critique of recent books on charismatic prophecy; pt2 of ecsomatic experiences; children as psychic subjects, etc; both with news & reviews on parapsychology & religion. Quarterly: £2.00/$4.00. CP: write to Leslie Price, CFPSS, St Mary Abchurch, Abchurch Lane, London EC4N 7BA.

Journal of Occult Studies 1:1 - a fat new interdisciplinary journal on paranormal phenomena, under the aegis of the University of Rhode Island & the Occult Studies Foundation, edited by Howard Smukler. Contents of 1st issue are impressive: mass TK experiment with Uri Geller as agent; critical analysis of biorhythm theory in accidents & psychics; handwriting analysis of some UFO contactees; synchronicity of New England oil spills; antagonism between SF readers & those who have psychic experiences; effects of pyramid on tomato aging. Quarterly: $7.50. Really interesting stuff; eg the cluster of coincidences in the last 16 days of 1976 & oil tanker accidents; and a survey that shows psychic experiences to be minimal among SF readers, and conversely, minimal SF reading among psychics. Weird!

New Horizons 2:3 (June 77) - human typology & mental autonomy; Philip is 4; voice production by PK; recording PK sounds; the pyramid-power cult; biorhythms; are more babies born at full moon?; Kirlian variations; patterns of authorship. A worthwhile journal of discussion & experiments from the New Horizon Research Foundation & Toronto's SPR. Quarterly: write for details to: Box 427, Station F, Toronto, Canada M4Y 2L8.

Journal of Meteorology 2:22 (Sept 77) - a 1681 aerial mirage; mystery noise; triple tornado; lightnings. 2:23 (Oct 77) - sulphur rains; storms & lightnings; frog & grass showers, etc. An essential for Fortean meteorologists. Monthly: £6.50/$16.00. J.Met: Cockhill House, Trowbridge, Wilts BA14 9BG.

FORTEAN TIMES

strange phenomena - curiosities - prodigies - portents - mysteries

recent plagues & scourges p17

75p:$1·50

UK ISSN 0308-5899

FORTEAN TIMES

A Contemporary Record of Strange Phenomena

BOX 152, LONDON N10 1EP, ENGLAND.

FORTEAN TIMES is a non profitmaking quarterly miscellany of news, notes and references on current and historical strange phenomena, related subjects and philosophies. Formerly 'The News'. Affiliated to the International Fortean Organisation (INFO), and the Society for the Investigation of The Unknown (SITU), and other Fortean journals in continuing the work of Charles Fort (1874-1932).

Edited and published by Robert JM Rickard.
Contributing editors: Phil Ledger, Steve Moore, Stan Nicholls, Paul J Willis. Heading art by Hunt Emerson.

SUBSCRIPTION information and details of other deals can be found on the back page.

CONTRIBUTIONS of articles, artwork, notes and letters-of-comment on related subjects are always welcome. **YOU CAN HELP** by sending us a copy or clipping of any item you think will interest FT readers — just add a note of the DATE, the SOURCE and your NAME (for the credit). All clippings go on file to be published in due course. Please don't assume we must know about it already — there are surprisingly few duplications.
The editor regrets that it is not always possible to reply to all correspondence. Acknowledgements of money received will be sent via the following issue of FT.

RIGHTS: All articles and artwork in FORTEAN TIMES are the copyright of the authors and artists. The views of contributors are not necessarily those of FT, and vice versa. Uncredited material is by the editors.

FORTEAN PICTURE LIBRARY — We are laying the foundations for a long-needed pictorial archive to satisfy both research and commercial needs for the preservation and supply of visual material on Fortean subjects. Interested parties (users or those with material) can contact us via FT's editorial address.

Printed by Windhorse Press
at Sukhavati, 51 Roman Road, London E2.

FT24, WINTER 1977.

Status report
As we begin another year your editor is about to embark on yet another round of personal upheaval - it is hoped that the only effect this will have on FT will be unavoidable delays on correspondence. There is a possibility too of a regrouping or restructuring which may mean a new address by the end of the year. We'll give you plenty of warning, if so.

This issue finds us with a new printer whose facilities allow us to process photos easier and to get over the 40 page thickness barrier that forced the Review Supplement to be bound separately last issue. We hope you'll take to our present format...the 'yellow pages' idea, pioneered by MUFOB, seemed a good solution. We hope to carry more advertising in the RS, though the response from publishing companies has been dismally low so far. Sooner or later they'll wake up to the fact that here is a platform to reach a hardcore of interested book-buyers in a specialist range of subjects that has limited advertising outlets elsewhere!

Truss Fund
...in which we gratefully acknowledge donations from Janet & Colin Bord; R Cotton; EW Crew; Richard Crowe; CS Kershore; CR Mather; Bob Pegg; Paul Pinn; Leslie Shepard and Mike Wuchitech. It all helps and is put to good use.

Fortean Picture Library (FPL)
The response to our announcement of our plans to set up a pictorial archive of pictorial Fortean material has been very encouraging indeed. It will perform a valuable function in preserving and furthering this long neglected aspect of our studies. We hope to send an information sheet out with the next issue. Meanwhile we express grateful thanks to Thames and Hudson Ltd for an unexpected donation to get us started.

FT - Value for money
FT continues to survive - but only just! Income just balances costs. Naturally we are grateful to be alive, but our position is quite insecure. We have no room for the growth we desperately need, and rely on donations. This is pathetic - we ought to be doing so much better. We have kept our subscription stable since 1975, when other prices have gone through the roof (especially the punitive postal rates). We have added more pages, more material, more book reviews - and published some great scoops (like the Nessie photos in FT22). We give you more than many other Fortean

cont on p12/

FROGS

Recent accounts

As part of the publicity for Phenomena, John Michell and your editor were guests on a morning phone-in on London Broadcasting (LBC) on 12 October last year. As the topic turned to falls of animals from the sky, a listener called 'Bill' rang with a singular story. He had experienced two rains of frogs in his life, one at Brisbane, Australia in 1922, and one at a lake at Rickmansworth, Herts, in 1945. Alas time did not permit us to question him at length, and the conversation moved on before it occurred to me to get his address - too late! He did have time to tell us that in neither case did he notice strong winds or whirlwinds dropping the animals around him, as the orthodox explanation demands. I have two other observations of dubious merit: firstly that the Rickmansworth fall was into a lake (looks like the mysterious teleportative forces were on target for once); and secondly, a quick glance at my atlas shows several large lakes just to the south of Rickmansworth at a place called Frogmoor. Hmmm! If any reader knows, or can investigate, further details of these two incidents, we'd be obliged if you'd let us know - we have nothing more on them here.

There were two frogfalls towards the end of last year. On 29 August, thousands of "baby" frogs, "no bigger than a pea", showered upon the French village of Carnet Plage, near Perpignan, late that night. They were bouncing off cars and causing consternation generally. One local council employee said: 'Those falling on the grass survived. Those falling on roads were killed either by passing cars or by the impact.' Predictably the 'tornado' theory was trotted out - but we do note that there was heavy rain, and that there was heavy quake activity elsewhere in the world the days before and after (ie 29 & 30 Aug). Times, & Guardian 30 Aug 1977 (Cr: Sue Wagstaff, of T&H; Mrs Sylvia Mowday; Peter Rogerson.)

A brief note in the Sunday Times 18 December 1977, declared that sometime in the preceding week frogs had rained in the Moroccan Sahara. It ended tersely: 'Freak whirlwinds blamed.' One doesn't normally imagine pools bursting with frogs just lying around waiting for passing whirlwinds to cream off their excesses. We hold out a hope that one day a Fleet St editor will surprise us by including more details in such stories. 'Earlier' would place the incident provocatively near to more quake activity. I guess we will have to have another installment of 'Diary of a Mad Planet' sometime soon.

Some personal accounts

Since we had our last torrent of frog fall notes in these pages (The News 13/8-9) we have accumulated several personal accounts.

Firstly, a letter from Grace M Wright of Martindale Rd, Hounslow, Middx, which appeared in TV Times 12 February 1960: "More than 50 years ago, I was walking along a street in Hounslow with my husband and small son when a heavy storm broke. We first thought they were hailstones until we saw they were all tiny frogs and were jumping about. My son filled a sweet box to take home. The brim of my husband's hat was full of them while the storm lasted. They were everywhere." (Cr: Harold SW Chibbett.)

Secondly, in the woman's page column under the byline 'Veronica Papworth', a regular feature of the Sunday Express (in this case for 29 June 1975), is a discussion of bizarre excuses for turning up late at cocktail parties. Among enclounters with circus elephants in a traffic jam, and a cloud of flying ants, the columnist says that she herself was once delayed by a rain of frogs. Curious, I enquired and received back a letter dated 7 September 1976. 'Ms Papworth' had been living on top of a high ridge in Penn, Bucks, at the time "seven years ago". "It had been a hot stormy summer evening with rain in the air and very dark clouds. Suddenly there was a tremendous rain storm and when I looked out on the wide paving around the house there were hundreds of little black frogs the size of a thumbnail, jumping in the rain. The downpour continued for several minutes as the frogs fell on the paving and along the lawn. I was in a hurry and had to rush away so I do not know what happened to the frogs - by morning there was no sight of them. There is a long dyke running by the side of the house and I like to think this is where they vanished to. My husband saw them too."

In our third account the witnesses did see where the frogs went, but it is interesting for another aspect also. The fall described was mentioned by Fort (Books p545). It's not often that we can present an actual witness to one of Fort's data, and the credit must go to Colin Bord who noticed a reference to this event during his correspondence with the lady, Mrs JM Battell. She was with her parents and sister at the time and must have been six years old. They lived in Tottenham, north London, and were on a day's outing to Southgate, then in the country, but today built-up. On 17 August 1921, "We were walking along a country road, with hedges on either side and a ditch on the left. It began to rain very heavily and we took shelter under a tree standing beside a farm gate up a little farm track on the left of the road. When the shower stopped we emerged to find the road literally swarming with tiny frogs. The size of the body was about half an inch long with 4 little legs in proportion to the body size. They were crawling, not hopping, all over the road, and we couldn't walk about without treading on some of them. My father picked up a couple and we examined them closely. They appeared to be just ordinary tiny frogs. We stood and watched while they slowly made their way to the sides of the road, disappearing into the hedges and ditch until there was nothing to be seen of this extraordinary occurrence." (Letter dated 8 December 1977.)

More East Anglian frogfalls

In News 13 we presented some correspondence in an East Anglian newspaper on frogfalls, recovered for us by Nigel Watson and Ron Hill. This time reader Peter Christie has extracted letters from the East Anglian Magazine for 1958. Briefly, the later ones were responses to the first...

"About 60 years ago on a farm at Wetheringsett there was a shower of small frogs. The people called them 'Freshers'

or 'Threshers', I am not sure which. They were yellow or dull green and almost 1½ inches long. A local theory was that frog spawn was drawn up by the sun. When it hatched out it was heavy and fell to the earth. However, this could not have been so because the tadpole period had not been accounted for." Mrs A Blundell, Appletreewick, Yorks. (EAM January p167)

"I witnessed an incident of the self-same nature whilst serving on a farm at Stockton some 46 years ago...and like Mrs Blundell can assure readers that it was not a figment of the imagination. My friends and I were stack-making when a rain shower descended unawares, accompanied - much to our surprise - by a shower of tiny frogs. We called them 'Freshers'. Myriads of them swarmed over the top of the unfinished haystack. Incidentally, our visitors' disappearance was even more mysterious...I can offer no explanation." CE Riches, Heckingham, Norfolk. (EAM March p298.)

"My father was out cycling one dark night when he felt what he at first thought were large drops of rain hitting his face. Not being satisfied as to the real nature of this shower, he dismounted and examined the ground with the aid of his cycle lamp and found it covered with tiny frogs. The district was undoubtedly Suffolk and the time about 60 years ago." BG Palmer, Barkingside, Essex. (EAM March p298.)

"The letter in the January issue took me back to something I overheard in a conversation 25 years ago. An old farm hand was telling a group of workers that at West Row and Isleham, on the Cambridge /Suffolk border, when he was a young man, a waterspout was seen over the river Lark. Some hours afterwards there was a heavy thunderstorm and it rained frogs. They could be seen everywhere after the storm." H Bye, Burnt Fen, Cambs. (EAM April p310.) NB: It is suggested that the waterspout, in itself a rare and striking phenomenon in England, picked up the frogs and dumped them later. Apart from our usual objections to no other debris of the size or weight of the frogs, the point fall, and the curious selection of only frogs of a similar species and stage of development usual in these cases, we observe that the spout preceded the fall by 'hours'.

FISH

Also in News 13 we gave some letters about frogfalls from the world syndicated column 'Dear Abby'. There were a couple of fish falls too...

"I lived on a farm 3 miles from Ashland, Wis. A storm broke suddenly and afterwards I saw little tiny fish in the cowtracks around our barn. I am 80 years old." Richard Hagstrom, Zig Zag, Ore.

"A friend of mine named Ed Brady heard something strike the roof of his home during a severe rainstorm, and the next day he found a big eel in his rainbarrel. He lives at Ouaquaga, NY...and can verify it." HD Johnson, Walton, NY.

These notes appeared in the Camden, Ark, News 1 January 1973.

More recently, a letter appeared in the Daily Express 13 August 1977, unfortunately with no clue as to the date of the event. "Once when I was in Wales I left a white enamel bowl in the garden just before a very heavy storm. When it ended I found a dozen ½ inch long fish swimming happily in the bowl." CF Nash, High Wycombe, Bucks.

MISCELLANEOUS EXOTICS

Birds
On 3 June 1968, William Holmberg was in the garden of his Calgary, Alberta, home when Canada geese fell out of the sky around him. He had heard them honking as they flew overhead when suddenly 8 fell over a small area into gardens and the street. One crashed through the roof of his house. Officials, apparently puzzled, were making noises about poisoned grain. We have noted a fall of Canada geese before - in News 8/3. This one is from the Times 4 June 1968 (Cr: Janet Bord).

Ermin Bennes and his 2 sons, were out hunting on 9 November 1975 near their farm at Valparaiso, Nebraska, when a storm forced them to take shelter in an old machine shed. Moments later 13 mallards thumped to the ground outside. As they were all slightly burned we are asked to believe that they were killed by lightning. In my ignorance I've always believed that it was necessary to be grounded first! This is from the Harrisburg, Penn, Patriot 13 November 1975 (Cr: Larry Arnold, who will no doubt convince us soon that the ducks were spontaneously combusted in mid-flap!).

Insects
Peter Roberts has rescued this old note, whilst going through the backfile of the Exeter-Flying Post, Devon, dated 27 August 1789: "London and its environs were on Thursday evening covered with a black insect, in an astonishing manner. They seem to have been engendered in the atmosphere, at a considerable distance from the earth, as they could scarcely rise their wings, and had little more than the signs of existence, when they had accomplished their terrestrial visit."

According to Le Progrès (France) 27 April 1977, a huge cloud of unidentified insects suddenly appeared near Luçon, Vendée, on 24 Aug. The dearth of details, both over the identity of the insect (said to be a little larger than the local black ant), and to the manner of its arrival, makes things difficult for us. We put it here, though it could be a swarming, of course. (Cr & translation: Margie Ledger.)

Crabs
Ron Dobbins sent us the following datum which is not in Fort: Morton St, San Francisco, was the scene of a rain of tiny crustaceans which came down with a light shower a day or two before the clipping date. The "infant crabs", ranging in size from that of a dime up to that of a good-sized Californian oyster, were alive, covering the sidewalk and gutter for 20ft - some filled the spitoons being washed by a man on the sidewalk. Although "hundreds" came down on Morton St, a separate shower of the same animals happened between Sansome and Battery, at the same time, only involving a few. Lima, Ohio, Daily Republican 21 February 1890.

Worms
Another note that has come our way is likewise not in Fort, and although quoted in TB Henry's The Strangest Things in The World (Ace; NY 1958; p160) it is worth mentioning briefly as it will be new to many (as it was to us). According to the Levant Times 6 August 1872 (an English newspaper published in Constantinople) the 25th July 1972 was a cloudless stiflingly hot day in Bucharest. "Toward 9 o'clock a small cloud appeared on the horizon and a quarter of an hour afterwards rain began to fall which, to the horror of everybody, was found to consist of black worms the size of ordinary flies. All the streets of Bucharest were strewn with these curious animals."

*** Next time we run this column we will have a sprinkling of dust and soot falls; and a resumé of some recent cases of money falling from the skies. Providence indeed! ***

RJMR

```
NEWS CLIPPINGS
**************
If you see anything of interest to FT
readers, please cut it out, add a note
of the source, date, and your name...
then send it in to us. It all helps
and surprisingly there are very few
dulpications.
```

Part 3 of an article, specially extracted for us, by Larry Arnold, from his forthcoming book ABLAZE! The Case for, and cases of, Spontaneous Human Combustion.

FIRE LEYNES

by LARRY E ARNOLD

HUNT EMERSON

The Binbrook Triangle — towards a solution

Recalling that the fire-leyne under consideration runs a straight line route from Hull to Louth, one finds upon entering Lincolnshire the small town of Binbrook 7 km to the west.

Binbrook was not shown on the chart we first used to locate the fire-leyne; we discovered the proximity afterwards. Another example of Watkins' principle that lay plotting guides one to unanticipated revelations?

It may be that the distance involved is too great to associate Binbrook with this telleyne, but we don't know for sure. We'll mention the episode at Binbrook anyway —

Early 1905 again: a 'lonely farmhouse in the Lincolnshire Wolds', the Yarn Walk near Binbrook, belonging to Mr White. Uncanny events. Things are flying about; other things, like plates, disappear — for a while. A pan of milk is overflowing in the pantry; in the pan is found one of the missing plates! Rev. Custance writes to the SPR that things are bursting into flames.

There is a young girl. Aha, the culprit! This time one must reconsider such an 'obvious' perpetrator. 'A story that greatly dismays the unsophisticated people is that of the servant girl who, whilst sweeping the kitchen, was badly burnt on the back'. According to Mr. White, she was not near any visible fire and was not even aware her back was ablaze until he yelled out to her; nevertheless, she was 'badly burned' and 'in terrible pain' at the Louth hospital [47].

It is not so easy to blame the ubiquitous 'young girl' this time. Something, someone else, is afoot at Binbrook.

The newspapers have a field day with the event. The esteemed *Liverpool Echo* chastizes the peasantry for a 'firm belief in the resuscitation of witchcraft' and accepting the accounts of 'extraordinary terpschichorean [sic] performance' by objects that are supposed to lie where they are placed [48]. Quite naturally though, when a reporter makes the effort to check on these wild rumours, he finds them true [47].

A blanket catches fire in a room having no fireplace! So says a schoolteacher writing to the *Liverpool Echo* on 25 January, or so Fort says [1, 120], as do Price [46, 323] and Harrison [42, 167]. We have been unable to find this alleged letter in the holdings of the British Museum. Fort, amid his voluminous notes, is known to have made mistakes [49]; others perpetuate error.

Yet weird fires did break out. So too other things, like twisted and broken chickens. A vampire, or vampire-like force, is on the loose in the farmer's chicken coop; out of 250 fowls only 24 are left, the rest having their skin pulled off and their windpipes drawn out and snapped [47].

More curiosities. At Market Rasen, a few kilometres to the west (and sited on another proposed fire-leyne), the regional newspaper [50] notes that on January 16 a chicken coop fire consumed 57 fowls. Unnoteworthy, you think. We note that no-one discovered how the fowl-house caught alight, and that within 2 weeks Mr. White lost 90% of his chickens in a 'weird way'.

We see another link, unnoticed by anyone else. Fowls afire at Market Rasen; fowls attacked, but not burned, at Binbrook. Was the force involved trying not to ignite the hens the second time? We note a curious and equally unexplained 'rush of water' that flooded the kitchen of the Whites' house, the liquid coming from a tub that could hold less than half the volume that spewed forth from it [47].

Mysterious fires; a flood of water. Nature balances by overcompensating with one phenomenon the excess of another one. This event happened before the servant girl was burned. Was Nature or some *thing* so frustrated with a deluge of water intended for the chicken coop ending up on the kitchen floor that all further compensatory measures were dropped, after which a fury of pent-up fires was unleashed on whatever or whoever was unfortunate enough to be their targets?

This admittedly smacks of superstition, or, more sinisterly, black magic. The 'unsophisticated' at Binbrook, says the

Liverpool Echo (26 Jan), believe it's the latter. Yet only 3 days earlier this same paper admitted 'some curiosity as to the force which made the pots and pans jig about the kitchen, and we should certainly like to know the truth about the servant's burnt shoulders'.

So would the doctors at Louth Hospital, who in a little more than a week would be treating Ashton Clodd for burns of a similar and equally mysterious nature!

Every author who writes on this case, except Fort who, he would say, non-writes about it, has lumped the Binbrook-Market Rasen episodes into the very broad category of poltergeist (discarnate) activity. Even Fort postulates 'a *being* was there' [1, 122].

This may well be the correct explanation; we admit the tendency to embrace it also. But can't something else be considered? Lines of force, telleynes, fire-leynes, leys which channel poltergeist-like powers?

Nature seemed to have gone beserk in 1905, as waves of SHC and other paranormalities washes over the shores of this reality. Did the ley grid of the Earth, over-charged that year, discharge (corona-like) at power points or through zones of weakness along the lines of telleyne transmission? We believe so. As our editor notes: 'Evidence is slowly building up that there is indeed a correspondence between types of Fortean phenomena and proximity to Leys'. [2, 8].

We may be over-extending ourself now but since we've come this far, one more step, made together, won't matter —

We note Binbrook sits in the midst of a triangle formed by three proposed fire-leynes; on the east by the line presently being discussed, on the west by a 4-point line through Market Rasen and Stroud, and on the south by what may be a 6-point line from Louth westward through Liverpool (Fig 1 — see FT2; FT23/13).

The significance of this observation is found in material received by the writer from a higher level of consciousness, in which we learned that areas of turbulence in the Earth Spirit are to be expected at points opposite an intersection of 2 lines of force [51, 2]. Now, looking at the map, we find Binbrook is almost *precisely opposite each angle* of this triangle which, with sides of about 22 km, appears almost to be *equilateral!* (One can find the same arrangements in megalithic-formed leys.) In fact, the geometry is so striking that we can't help but feel we fudged something to make the neat fit (Fig. 2). Yet no matter what the detractors will say, we give assurance there was no manipulation — unless it was by some fiendishly clever fellow in the employ of the cartography firm who arranged the location of a score of towns so that we could 'stumble' onto a pseudo-discovery several years later.

The energies producing the documented pyrophenomena at 2 of the triangle's apexes (Market Rasen and Louth) would, according to our information, focus disturbing forces across from those angles — smack into the vicinity of Binbrook!

We now suspect the calamities on the White farm were not associated *directly* with the Nairn-to-Louth fire-leyne, but resulted from the concentration of 2 fire-leynes discharging their power simultaneously into a *center of fire* (Binbrook).

We point out that power generated within an angle is nothing new to the esoterist. Seth talks about all-pervasive energy flows that form 'certain invisible angles' where forces are channelled [20, 77]. Ross Nichols notes the connection between triangles and a witch's 'cone of power'. [52]. A cone is simply an angle rotated about its bisector. The white-witch Sybil Leek draws on her heritage to describe how 'cones of spiritual power . . . always retain high vibrations of mystical power', and how during WW II the Horsa coven of 13 English witches banded together to utilize a cone of power to thwart a German invasion of their homeland. So much energy was

involved that 2 of the witches died, but so too did a small German invasion corps found in the waters of the English Channel [53, 9 & 20].

We point out here what may be a crucial factor differentiating the ley lines as discerned by Watkins et al, from lines of force possessing other vibrational-frequency natures. Whereas ley points seem (or only have been noticed) to lie upon ley alignments, telluric currents such as fire-leynes can focus their power not only along the lines per se but into zones formed from the intersection of several (maybe always three) telleynes and activated when each component's energization exceeds a critical threshold.

If so, one begins to grasp the complexities of the 'lines of the world'. But at the same time progress in understanding the omnipresent but largely unseen forces that mould the environment is achieved through scrutiny of each type's specialized nature.

Now, as every occultist knows, under certain conditions the etheric realm will merge with (that is, bleed through) the human-perceived world. Have we been exploring one of these 'certain' conditions when discussing the Binbrook Triangle?

Let's hypothesize . . .

Late-December 1904, the fire-leynes are becoming active, as energy begins flaring off. A pan jumps off the shelf in Mrs White's kitchen. Mid January 1905; the leynes are crackling with power, as huge energy potentials begin breaking through the boundary between the etheric and the physical. A chicken coop and 57 hens at Market Rasen spontaneously combust. Late January 1905; their capacities exceeded, the fire-leynes can no longer contain the tremendous forces flowing through them; the angles of intersection arc and incredible power is unleashed in violent bursts upon the point opposite each angle. The fabric of space is rent asunder at Binbrook's Yarn Walk, as Mr. White's farm tries to weather the brunt of a *multidimensional* storm. Pots terpsichorate; plates teleport; etheric flames sear objects of wood and flesh; floods of water condense out of the ethers; vortices of frightful strength attack chickens and turn them inside-out.

Then the fury abates; balance is being restored. The southeast corner of the Binbrook Triangle flinches as its flow normalizes. Ashton Clodd's frail old body happens to be in the inauspicious spot; his bio-energies are over-energized as the re-ordering process continues. He dies in Louth Hospital, probably never realizing another patient there was struck down by the same malady.

The fire-leyenes dissipate the concentration of power away from the Binbrook Triangle's centre now, along a network that stretches for hundreds of kilometres. There may be other tottering, fragile souls living along the pathways, whose fiery fates remain undiscovered. Late-February 1905: the energy dispersal reaches Blyth, Northumberland, and aged Barbara Bell ignites on her kitchen floor.

Then, as normalcy is restored, the inflammatory holocaust ends — for the moment.

The plot thickens

Along the reasoning of the micro-to-macrocosm or 'As above so below' principles, an extension of the Binbrook Triangle concept can provide a solution to the global horde of paranormal phenomena in the period 1904-5 that Fort, Livingston Gearhart [22] and others have noted. That as there are 'lines of the world' invisible to geophysicists, so too there are 'lines of the Cosmos' undetected by astronomers but nevertheless vital to the maintenance and performance of the universe. Their angles of intersection also form zones of interstellar — or intergalactic or interdimensional — disturbance, through which   can pass and be affected a planet or a star

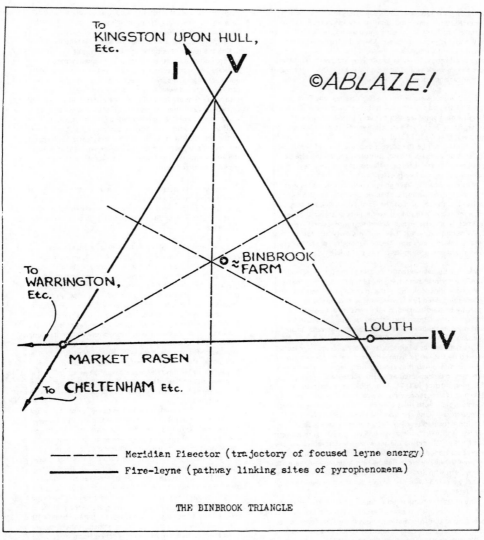

To KINGSTON UPON HULL, Etc.

I V

©ABLAZE!

BINBROOK FARM

To WARRINGTON, Etc.

LOUTH

IV

MARKET RASEN

To CHELTENHAM Etc.

——— — ——— Meridian Bisector (trajectory of focused leyne energy)

————————— Fire-leyne (pathway linking sites of pyrophenomena)

THE BINBROOK TRIANGLE

or a galaxy, depending on the size and power of the cosmic leynes encountered.

Thus, whereas Binbrook became the focus for energies requiring one month to peak and another month to dissipate (approx. 31 Dec 1904-28 Feb 1905), the Earth needed 2 *years* to pass into and out of an interstellar (or whichever) area of tortured space-and-time.

One who wishes to pursue this suggestion will be amazed at the ease in which this theory finds confirmation, for the author believes that herein lies the clue, a key, to resolving so many of the perplexities that make a wreckage of Science. Out of the ashes arose a phoenix . . .

But we digress a bit . . .

There are other Triangles of Fire revealed on the fire-leynes map of Great Britain. It is not realistic to attempt a detailed analysis here (You'll just have to buy our book). But we draw

attention to Fig. 1 again and fire-leynes I and II. We already know about alignment I.

Alignment II had three points: Ipswich [54], Brandon and Carlisle. Was this a significant fire-leyne, though? Then, inspiration. 'Quick, Watson, the dividers!' Marking off the bisector between these lines, we found it cut right through Market Rasen! It also passed close to Scunthorpe (another pyrophenomenon site) and very near Hexham.

'Quick, Watson, the files!' Ah, here it is. *The Newcastle Journal* [55] notes that Albert Purvie found his wife, Isabella, in flames on (presumably) 25 Oct 1938. Along with the charred body was 'a mystery which haunted her survivors', for which the inquest jury could find no solution. The Coroner rendered the official verdict: 'Death from shock as a result of burns accidentally received'. About as illuminating as a candle under a basket. . .

On the basis that the meridian bisector of fire-leynes I and II parallels the performance of the bisectors of the Binbrook Triangle, we conclude that alignment II is valid. But this raises an interesting question: just where does this second Triangle, isosceles this time, stop? Its sides are 423 km long, if one places its base through Carlisle; or, if the 1852 SHC at Nairn establishes the base, then the Triangle engulfs nearly all southern Scotland in a *huge* geometric outline that began in Suffolk, England, and contains approx. 54,000 square kms (21,000 square miles)! Maybe it even goes farther north, into the Arctic Ocean, where the scarcity of human beings fails to provide more plotting points for pyrophenomena —

Then, too, what of the *inverse* Triangle (the one that proceeds south from the apex near Brandon)? The extended bisector enters France just to the east of Gravelines, then skirts Arras, Pas-de-Calais, and continues into the Marne . . . We check our files. No case having pertinence, or revealing such, is found. Our collection of French pyrophenomena is limited. Maybe someone will look into the matter . . .

But maps and newspaper files are available to any scholar who wishes to avail himself of the secrets they hold; a few hours of honest research can avoid decades of dishonorable slander. (Reflect on the abhorrent treatment accorded Dr. Immanuel Velikovsky!).

Meanwhile we'll take solace in the words of Descartes — 'There is nothing so far removed from us as to be beyond our reach or so hidden that we cannot discover it' — and go on to discuss something else.

A Crescendo of combustion in Cincinnati

The Earth Spirit remains alive. Power points pulsate as the alchemical fusion between celestial and terrestrial forces revitalizes the planet. While mankind begins to worry about the limitations of petroleum and fossil fuels he walks obliviously through an infinite reservoir of energy. Sometimes *too* much energy . . .

Due to unseen disturbance, Power Point 39°7.5'N 84°30'W is activated 16-17 Nov 1976. The Fairmount section of Cincinatti, Ohio, just happens to lie upon these coordinates.

16 Nov 1976, 8:00 am, 1711 Harrison Avenue, Fairmount. Engine Company 21 arrives at the basement residence of Mrs May Caplinger, aged 59. They find the woman lying on the floor, her clothing and the rug beneath her still burning. 'Nothing else in the apartment was burning', a firefighter told *The Cincinnati Post* [56]. She was covered with 2nd-and 3-rd degree burns over 70 to 80% of her body. Firemen, however, could not locate the cause for the fatal fire. Next day we learn from a doctor at the hospital who couldn't save the victim's life that 'She was apparently cooking breakfast. . when her clothing caught fire' [57].

Firemen spend hours at the scene and find nothing rational; a physician pronounces the cause precisely — 'apparently'. It's amazing the advances that have been made in modern medicine! Shame on the fire department for overlooking a hot kitchen stove . . .

17 Nov 1976, 12:15 am, 2534 Liddell Street, Fairmount: A subterranean inferno rises from the basement of the Preston Sandlin family, routing all 8 members into the frigid night air. Fire Marshal James Eversole arrives with his men, and is mystified. 'I'm going to check today to see if we can come up with a reasonable explanation', he promises [58].

The reasonable inquiry begins with the children. Fort would have suspected as much, for after all children are notoriously clever with fires. Remember Rhoda and the Colwell fires in Brooklyn, NY, in 1895? Before scores of witnesses, her 'wild talents' enabled her to toss matches onto and through walls to ignite seemingly incombustible objects [34, 82-3]. But in the Sandlin case, the children are apparently absolved of guilt — unless a 'confession' was forced out of them. Twelve hours after the fire's outbreak,

the fire marshal still has found no explanation . . .

Two weird fires: originating below ground level, within a 16-hour period, in Cincinnati's Fairmount district. Two homes burnt, one inhabited by the Sandlin family, the other by the soul-entity named Mrs Caplinger. The power point beneath Fairmount has fulfilled its purpose for the moment; discharged, it returns to quiescence. There are no more weird fires.

Absurd? We think not. We know the Earth Spirit still functions, and remember a comment given psychically to the author on the nature of fire: 'Fire-heat is the product of combustion (chemical). Heat can be created also when the energy comes in a certain *predescribed, predetermined pattern* . . . Energy itself has no heat; energy creates heat *only* as it reacts and interacts with other energy patterns'. [59].

Rapid and intense heating can produce 2nd-and 3rd-degree burns, like Caplinger suffered; high temperature leads to dehydration (as occurs in many SHC cases). Likewise, a superheated area will produce a flashover if a fire seat is established.

We propose the fires discussed in amazement by Cincinatti's firefighters resulted when telluric currents manifested similar energy patterns in spaces bounded by the walls of the Sandlin and Caplinger basements, patterns which climaxed in a crescendo of combustion and flash of flames.

What do you think?

The fire department sounds mystified. Then too, they haven't been trained to consider telleynes and aerleynes and power points when investigating fires. In fact, they generally aren't even aware of the weird blazes that we've been detailing. Fire experts . . .

The corollary to fires associated with sites is that certain *shapes* could equally well create energy patterns capable of igniting fires within a body or a house. But to develop the evidence for this aspect of 'pyro-architecture' would require another three-part article in *FT*. Maybe another time . . .

Perhaps it's best to close with a quote from the avatar himself: 'I don't know whether these data are enough to jolt our whole existence into a new epoch, or not. From what I know of the velocity of thought, I should say not'. [1, 235].

Hopefully, the velocity of thought has increased since Fort's day, just as evidence accumulates that the velocity of light can increase beyond its assigned boundary. That fire-leynes and points of combustible power exist, looks pretty conclusive to us. Maybe fire officials will begin investigations with a broader understanding of the forces that affect their work, and affect all our lives. On the other hand some may think that our *personal* 'velocity of thought' has retrograded. Maybe — but with massive changes in the global/solar system energy patterns intensifying daily as we enter a New Age, we suspect that weird combustions will be on the increase as the fire-leynes become increasingly charged.

And so far the statistics are supporting us . . .

LARRY E. ARNOLD. 1977.

REFERENCES

47 'Bewitched Binbrook Farm'. *Louth & North Lincolnshire News*, no 1596, 28 Jan 1905, p.5

48 'Village Witchcraft', *Liverpool Echo*, no 7850, 26 Jan 1905, p3.

49 X, address to Fortfest 76, Arlington Va., personal interchange; 8 Aug 1976.

cont on p16/

BIRDS

BIG BIRD 1977

Late July 1977 saw another Big Bird flap in USA that lasted into August - this time in Illinois which has a strong indigenous tradition of giant birds (see the Piasa booklet in our review section).

It burst upon the world about 8.30pm on Monday evening 25 July, when two giant birds swooped down on 10yr-old Marlin Lowe, playing in the yard of his home in Lawndale, Logan County, Illinois. One gripped the 65lb boy by his shirt and carried him 25-30 feet about 3ft in the air. When it released the screaming struggling boy, he ran indoors. His parents and two neighbours, working in the yard, all looked up at the screams and saw the birds clearly. They described them at first "like overgrown vultures", dark and with white rings around their long necks, curled beaks and a wingspan of around 8ft. Mrs Ruth Lowe, the mother, thought they might have been condors, but when Logan County game warden AA Mervar showed her pictures of large birds, neither she nor the other witnesses could identify any with the pair they had seen.

The official responses were as dire as usual. Firstly, based on the description, they pronounced the birds to be "immature turkey vultures". Then, after advice from "experts", State Conservation knowalls said "there is no known bird on earth that could lift Marlon's weight." (They sound pretty confident don't they?) This statement, by people who weren't there, virtually accuses the witnesses of lying or misaprehension...it also brought in the nasty crank calls. A disillusioned Mrs Lowe said later: "I know what I saw and I'm not exaggerating - all four of us stood and saw it. I tried to be a good citizen and report it, but I'll never do it again. It doesn't pay off. It brings only heartache and misery."

Later still, Mrs Lowe was again convinced it was a condor - the game warden apparently had only shown her pictures of turkey vultures. A condor specialist, from the National Audubon Society in California, said that the only known condors, perhaps 40-45, were in California, and not known elsewhere. Besides, swooping on people is not in their nature he added, suggesting instead that the attacking birds might have been trained hawks or even a Great Horned Owl.

Mervar, in a longer interview, still claimed that the adults only thought they saw the boy in the air, when he must have been running with the bird on his back. Discrediting the witnesses is the only way officials in tight spots can cling to their pathetically unimaginative theories. Apparently, unaware of exactly what he is saying, Mervar, sticking to his turkey vulture belief, added: "We have turkey and king vultures here, but they are considerably smaller than the birds described by Mrs Lowe." !!!

And there the mystery lay, deadlocked by intractable witnesses and pigheaded experts, until the end of the week when Stan & Doris Thompson and some friends saw a giant bird - a 6ft body with a 9-10ft wingspan - flying over their farm at Lincoln, Illinois, heading for Bloomington. They swear it looked like a condor. The next day, another witness in Lincoln, Mrs Norma Knollenberg, said a giant bird had landed in their yard "a week ago", which puts it just before the attempted snatch of Marlin Lowe. Mrs Knollenberg described it as "the size of a turkey with a 4ft wingspan, long neck and small beak. It made a loud trumpeting sound." The paper said it looked like an African crowned crane! It's quite possible that the witnesses really are describing different birds, lumped together as one kind by the media.

Dr William Beecher, Chicago Academy of Science, jumps in by insisting that it can't be a condor because they are a type of vulture and quite ill-equipped for swooping and lifting. Again: "There has never been in the history of the world, living or extinct, a bird big enough to lift a person." He thinks it might be an immature bald eagle and that someone might shoot it. He likens the rash of reports to UFO sightings and urges people not to take the threat of skyward abduction seriously. Meanwhile, young Marlin and his mother have to drug themselves to sleep without nightmares.

On Saturday, 30 July, a 6ft wingspanned bird is seen on a telephone pole at Downs at 2 am. That same morning 'Texas John' Huffer, an experienced fisherman and naturalist writer sees two birds while fishing at Lake Shelbyville, and manages to shoot some blurred film.
He describes the larger of the two as

about 260lb with a 12ft wingspan. Experts could not identify the bird from the film but it certainly wasn't turkey vulture. Also that same afternoon a Waynesville resident saw an 8ft wingspanned black bird hovering around, at 2pm.

At 4pm the next day, Sunday 31st July, Mrs Albert Dunham saw a giant bird for 30 mins and also managed to film it, outside her home in Bloomington. As it circled 20ft over her head she noticed its long straight bill, black body with white marks on its neck and fan-like tail. Her husband and son also saw the creature.

By the 7th August, the story arrived in a horribly garbled version in the Sunday Express, here in England. The boy was said to be "Rodney Galton", playing in a field near Tuscola, and actually fought the bird in the air forcing it to release him, as it clacked like a Hollywood pterodactyl. This report bears so little relationship to the real events that SE reporter Dudley Freeman

---

The learned men, quoted above, denying that birds have ever been large enough to carry off people, don't seem to be aware of historical cases. I found the following in FA Pouchet's encyclopedia of natural history, The Universe (Blackie, London 1870). Pouchet writes:

"The last known fact of this kind took place in the Valais (French Alps) in 1838. A little girl, 5 yrs-old, called Marie Delex, was playing with one of her companions on a mossy slope of the mountain, when all at once an eagle swooped down upon her and carried her away in spite of the cries & presence of her young friend. Some peasants, hearing screams, hastened to the spot but sought in vain for the child, for they found nothing but one of her shoes on the edge of a precipice. The child was not carried to the eagle's nest, where only two eaglets were seen, surrounded by heaps of goat and sheep bones. It was not until 2 months later that a shepherd discovered the corpse of Marie Delex, frightfully mutilated, and lying upon a rock half a league from where she had been borne off."

In my English edition (above) Pouchet's translator has added a note of a case that occured in the USA in the year after Pouchet completed his work. It took place at "county Tippah, Missouri, United States of North America" in the autumn of 1868, and was related by an unnamed teacher from an unfortunately unnamed source (perhaps US researchers might like to track this down?):

"A sad casualty occurred at my school a few days ago. The eagles have been very troublesome in the neighbourhood for some time past, carrying off pigs, lambs etc. No one thought they would prey on the children; but on Thursday, at recess, the little boys were out some distance from the house...when their sport was interrupted by a large eagle sweeping down and picking up little Jemmie Kenney, 8yrs-old, and flying away with him. The children cried out, and when I got out of the house, the eagle was so high that I could just hear the child screaming. The alarm was given, and from screaming and shouting in the air, etc, the eagle was induced to drop his victim; but his talons had been buried in him so deeply and the fall so great, that he was killed - or either would have been fatal."

Eagle makes off with Marie Delex, 1838. (Fortean Picture Library.)

should be reprimanded. Tuscola was the
home town of John Huffer - at least
Freeman got the boy's age right (10)...
that's all.

We learn that 2 days after the Lowe
boy was attacked, Frank Jackson, a Lincoln farmer, claimed that a huge bird
carried off 2 piglets weighing about
20lbs each "one in each claw." Interestingly, we had on file a note that at
Rabbit Hash, Kentucky, a 5lb puppy was
wafted aloft for 600yds and dropped in
a pond by a large bird. The only witness
to this incident, probably 16 May 1977,
was a 7yr-old boy, and no identification
of the bird could be made. Lima News,
Ohio, 18 May 1977 (Cr: Mark Hall, Loren
Coleman.) We have a file a-building of
similar animal abductions, but we'll
keep that til later.

The last report we have of the Illinois
Big Bird was that it was seen heading
southwest toward Centralia. At 7am on
Thursday 11 August, John Chappell, of
Odin, noticed a huge grey-black bird
circling his pond. "It was so big it had
a hard time finding a tree-limb big
enough to land on." He said he was quite
familiar with turkey buzzards and this
was not one - he described it having a
6ft body with a 10-12ft wingspan, and
about 8 inches from beak-tip to the back
of its head...which sounds reasonably
consistent with previous accounts. Some
might think that suspicious!

Our sources include the following
Illinois papers: Lincoln Courier 26 July;
Decatur Daily Review 28 July; Chicago
Daily News 27, 30/31 July; Bloomington
Daily Pantagraph 27 July, 1 August; the
Champaign-Urbana Courier 31 July, 1 Aug.
Also: Billings Gazette, Montana, 29 July;
St Louis Post-Dispatch, Mo, 30 July; San
Antonio Sunday Sight, Texas, 31 July;
Alamosa Valley Courier, Co, 1 Aug; The
Star, Tx, 23 August. (Cr: Thomas R Adams,
Mark A Hall, W Ritchie Benedict, John
Peldyak & NJ Kautzman, Valerie Martin.)

Getting the bird...
Several times during this flap we
detected the sure hand of the Joke God.

Firstly: on the afternoon of 4 July,
six men wrestled with a tired ostrich
found wandering in the road in Wichita
Falls, Texas. No one knew where it came
from, and there were no reported escapes.
The next morning it was found dead in the
pound in which it was being kept temporarily, with its head in a bucket of
water (true!). Jim Goodner, of the Animal Control Center said: "It looks like
it went down to get a drink and just
stayed down." Wichita Falls Record News
5 & 6 July 1977 (Cr: TR Adams; RBB21/4.)

Secondly: on 30 July an African Mari-
bou stork escaped from Brookfield zoo,
in Illinois, to add to the giant bird
confusion. This bird with a 6½ft wing
span was one of six imported from Kenya
just 2 weeks before, and was the only
one whose wings had not been clipped to
prevent flight. It was captured the next
day at Lake Geneva, Wisconsin, shot by
a tranquilizing dart, and is said to be
doing well. Bloomington Pantagraph, Il,
31 July; Springfield State Journal-Reg-
ister, Il, 31 July; Bryan-College Station Eagle, Tx, 1 August 1977. (Cr:
Thomas R Adams.)

Thirdly: a spotted rail, a notoriously
poor flyer, was found in a driveway in
Brownwood, Texas, several thousands of
miles from its usual haunts in Cuba,
Central and South America. This little
creature has a green bead, red legs and
silver spots on its dark plumage. It
only survived a few days, dying on 9
Aug, leaving yet another bird mystery
on science's doorstep. Paris News, Tx,
11 August 1977 (Cr: Thomas R Adams.)

Lastly (and I'm sure you noticed it
really) the last sighting of the Illinois Big Bird was at Odin - a fitting
deity for cryptozoologists. Odin was
master of the Wild Hunt; god of magic
and inspiration; boss of the Valkyries;
owner of a 6 (some say 8) legged horse
and 2 large black ravens, Hugin & Mugin,
who flew to the 4 corners of the world
reporting back to their master;
associated with wily wolves, and whose
totem (probably after Roman influence)
was a giant Golden Eagle.

Food for Thor...eh?

RJMR

———————————————————

Editorial Stuff cont from p2...
and UFO mags in terms of value for money
and we'd like to give you more. The only
practical alternative to cutbacks and
price increases is to get more readers.
As we have no budget for advertising this
is where you come in. A personal recom-
endation is the best advert. Write to
your friends; mention FT; give a gift sub
to FT for birthdays or Christmas, or just
because it's the best damned Fortean mag
in the world. We'll extend your sub by a
free issue for each new sub (including
gifts) you bring in. Remember to claim
it!). INFO and SITU claim a combined
membership of 3000-4000...it's a crying
shame that we have only 10% of that and
yet are extolled as the brightest, most
data-filled, dynamic journal by established Forteans who regard us as really essential reading. Help us grow! Act now!

As we have frequently said before in these pages, the repetition of events seems more curious than the events themselves. Sometimes the 'Great scriptwriter in the sky' appears to be running out of ideas; so he serves up the same old plot over and over...only the names and locations have been changed. And so the time has come to pick up some more hitch-hiking ghosts...

We have covered the subject before (NEWS 10/4 & 5, FT 21/32). However, clearing out our back-files, we come across an archetypal case that we'd previously missed:

CHICAGO, ILLINOIS.

Every year, on the anniversary of her death, so the story goes, the ghost known as "Resurrection Mary" appears. An 18-year-old girl who died in the 1930s, and was buried in Resurrection Cemetery, she hitches a lift from a young man to her home on Archer Ave, and arranges a date with him for the following weekend. When the unfortunate driver turns up on the following Friday, he's informed that Mary is dead: having had an argument with her boyfriend, she decided to hitch a lift home, was hit by a car and killed. Every year, she is supposed to give a repeat performance.

(Chicago Sun-Times 9 Aug 1975) ((This story appeared in this paper as part of a write-up of the 1975 Fortfest held in Chicago; the reporter was given the story of 'Resurrection Mary' by Chicago Fortean Richard T Crowe. Rich also points out that the route of 'Mary's' haunting is one of the longest straight roads in the city and from the earliest settled times was built upon a sacred Indian trail. Rich runs one of the most successful of America's 'ghost tours', in Chicago, which includes this haunted route. For details write to him at: Box 29054, Chicago, IL 60629, USA - Ed.))

From a somewhat folkloric case, we move on to some recent news-clips:

NUNNEY, SOMERSET.

This tale, which received a surprisingly large amount of coverage between the 4th and 30th August 77, gives a good example of how these stories build up. In essence, the story is this: in the previous year, 'several' drivers stopped to pick up a hitch-hiker on the road leading from Nunney to Frome, 3 miles away. The 'Ghost of Nunney Lane', a man of between 30 and 40, wearing a check jacket, climbs into the car and then disappears. Examining all the clippings available to us reveals only two actual encounters, however, both by Mr Gerald O'Connor. On the first occasion, apparently taking place earlier in the year, the hitch-hiker climbed into the back seat, and Mr O'Connor locked the door for him. The stranger remarked how cold it was. Mr O'Connor asked him a question, received no reply, looked round, and saw that his passenger had vanished.

On the second occasion, also undated, Mr O'Connor saw the 'man' standing in the middle of the road, swerved to avoid him, and hit a lamp-post. Both encounters were reported to the police, who found nothing.

Alas, the only other reported encounter is rather of the third-rate kind. Mrs Valerie McPherson, 46, of Frome, dropped off a friend in the Lane, but had a strange feeling that someone was still in the car...but she dared not look round to see.

Regrettably, all else seems to be rumour and hysteria. There are 'stories' of the phantom appearing suddenly in the back seats of cars. Allusions are made to the Bloody Assizes of Judge Jeffreys, who hanged his victims along Nunney Lane; and it is said that some nights the creaking of the gibbets can still be heard... though it seems unlikely to me that any of the judge's victims would have been wearing a check jacket! Then the phantom was accused of spoiling Nunney's Silver Jubilee celebrations: an unpardonable crime which resulted in 24 men combing the lane with tape-recorders, light meters and a net (the logic of the latter escapes me).

The story hit the national papers on the 14th. A week later brought a letter claiming that 30 years ago one or two truck drivers met what could have been the same ghost at the same place: the story being that a man knocked off his cycle cursed all motorists with his dying breath.

Before the month was out, hoaxers were at work: an arrangement of strings between two high walls and a white sheet with a grin on it scaring motorists on two occasions. The 'real' phantom ceased to appear, as always seems to be the pattern, and we have heard nothing since. (Bath Evening Chronicle, 4 Aug 77; Sunday Express, S. People, 14 Aug 77; S.Express, 21 Aug 77; Bath Chronicle 30 Aug 77. Cr: AJ Bell, J Michell, GTM Meaden, P Screeton, N Watson).

CHATHAM, KENT.

The London Evening News, 12 Sept 77, carried a story of another phantom encounter, presumably occurring within the previous couple of days. Insurance broker Barry Collings and his friend Stephen Pope were driving up Bluebell Hill Chatham, when they saw a girl standing by the side of the road. She had long blonde hair and wore a white evening dress, which was in disarray, carrying a handbag. There was a strong wind blowing, yet the girl's hair did not move, and she was perfectly still. At first they thought she was in trouble; then they decided she was a ghost and drove off.

It seems that in 1965 a bride-to-be and her 3 attendants were killed in a crash on the hill, since when there have been at least 6 accounts of the girl being given a lift. Once in the car, she vanished. Churchmen have exorcised the hill, but the reports keep coming in.

SEAFORD, SUSSEX.

A road with a history of car crashes produced, not a phantom hitchhiker, but a phantom car. Gordon Spooner and his wife saw the car in their headlights: then it swerved toward a 3 foot high sea wall, and vanished. There was no trace of wreckage, damage to the wall, or sound. (Daily Mirror, 22 Oct 76).

BRADFORD-ON-AVON, WILTS.

A final snippet: an unnamed road, again with a history of cars plunging off the road for mysterious reasons. A television engineer and his girl-friend were driving along when the girl saw a woman crossing in front of them. She screamed. He saw nothing, and drove on. (Reveille, 13 Jan 78).

SM.

UNIDENTIFIEDS

GSW examines Doc's Nessie photos

The photos of Nessie, taken by our confidante, colleague and friend, Doc Shiels, at Urquhart Castle, at 4pm on 21 May 1977, have provoked quite opposing reactions. Some have vehemently den-ied the photos are proof of anything at all, and in the other corner some of the world's top monster hunters (eg Tim Dinsdale, Sir Peter Scott, etc) judge the photos truly show a living creature as yet uncatalogued by science (no one is quite sure if it is a Nessiteras rhombopteryx) lurking in the Loch. There seems to be somekind of law operating here - that vehemence of opposition is in direct proportion to the degree of detail in the challenging evidence - and there is no doubt these photos (see FT22/pp24-5) are the most detailed yet.

To forestall anticipated criticism, and because Doc - a long-time monster-hunter himself; see his article FT23/20-22 - is keenly interested in the question of proof of Nessie and other aquatic monsters, Doc agreed to have his films professionally examined. Through Jerry Clark, Associate editor of Fate magazine, a copy of the main colour-slide (photo A on FT22/24 - now designated 'ANS 1') was forwarded to Ground Saucer Watch (GSW), a Phoenix, Arizona, based 'civilian' UFO group who have made a name for their efforts to analyse UFO photos with modern computer programmes. Through Tim Dinsdale, a copy of the same slide was sent to the Joint Air Reconnaissance Intelligence Center (JARIC), the RAF team that studied Dinsdale's movie-film of Nessie taken in April 1960 (see Dinsdale's Loch Ness Monster, RKP, revised 1976).

GSW verdict

Doc forwarded to me a copy of the GSW report on ANS 1 in early Oct 1977. Following a summary of the techniques they used, they list 10 points, which I'll abbreviate.

1) analysis reveals an "alarming" feature - the wave ripples can be seen through the creature's neck and head, suggesting the creature is transparent or translucent "in construction".

2) the image was "relatively flat".

3) lack of "natural shadows".

4) an absence of water displacement.

5) analysis of wave-size and reflection suggest a 300mm lens was used, not 150mm as Doc states.

6) bright areas on creature's neck and mouth appear "unnatural, as if painted on".

7) indications that image is "smaller" than apparent size...possibly further away than Doc estimated.

8) time and camera direction were confirmed, agreeing with Doc's statement.

9) photo shows "patternized similarity" with others taken in the area.

10) wave-ripples seen through image - repeat of item 1 conclusion.

The report was signed by William Spaulding, Fred Adrian and Gene Price and they express their opinion that Doc's slide does not "represent a bonafide creature of large proportions."

In effect they imply that Doc has given wrong information about his lens (thus making the image look bigger); that it could easily have been double-exposed (ie creating the wave overlap effect - though GSW admit this could only be resolved by examination of the original slide); and they make a reference to fakery for profit which, because of its context, can only impute such a motive to Doc.

Comments and reactions...

Naturally Doc was dismayed by this verdict, but he was also angry enough to pass the data back to myself, Dinsdale and Jerry Clark (and others). In a letter to Jerry Clark and myself (dated 8 Oct 1977) Tim points out some of the "absurdities" in the GSW report. Firstly, that their analysis is based on a copy slide, and an enlarged one at that. Secondly, the transparency effect "is certainly novel, but one should remember that this phenomenon is sometimes apparent on one's TV screen...and although I don't know the reason for it, the one thing common to both a projected TV picture and a computer study readout picture is the electronic scanner used to scan both the studio subject and the photo under analysis. I would suggest therefore that this is an electronic aberration rather than a photographic one. I don't doubt the GSW 'report' was intended to be a serious contribution - and in the instance of the 'double exposure' prediction, it seems hardly likely that Shiels would submit a crudely faked double exposure for so-called 'computer analysis.'"

It is also clear from the GSW report that their analysis was jury-rigged. They admit that they have never ventured into Fortean evidence before, confining their activities to UFO photos; that they borrowed their 'software' programmes from at least two other separate studies (UFOs, and "nucular medical" sic) and was therefore untried on monster photos. Being aware of their lack of comparative material on water monsters..."Our Research Staff quickly acquired as many photo - graphs of the alleged Nessie and began to systematically digitize them for any patterns." This raises so many questions for me that their analysis becomes quite meaningless unless it can be independently confirmed. On what basis did they select other monster photos; and to what extent did they authenticate them, as there are many dubious ones in print, even in standard sources? On what basis did they select 'patterns'? How much of that selection relies on subjective action? And where is the study that justifies comparison of such arbitarily-selected 'patterns'? And when all this dubious data is put through a hastily-assembled and untried programme by people who admit it was very much an experiment and that they had nothing with which to compare the results, just how magnified are the margins of error?

In the UFO field itself, there is considerable criticism of GSW's methods, conclusions, and especially their offhanded way of branding someone a hoaxer when many respected and thorough researchers, who have known and personally investigated such witnesses, have vouched for their honesty and obvious sincerity - see MUFON UFO Journal, (Aug 1976) p1; no 108 (Nov 1976) pp3-5; no 112 (March 1977). APRO Bulletin 25:12 (June 1977) pp1,4-6. Letters in Fate Jan 1978 p113. And for discussion of GSW negative verdict on the Cottingley fairy photos see Page Research Library Newsletter no 20 p3f; and no 21 pp9-12.

Regarding their verdict on Doc's photo we make the following observations. Of course the image looks closer than Doc's statement implies; GSW are analysing an enlargement. There would naturally be some double-grain effect suggestive of double-exposure, as the grain of the original is superimposed on the reversal (slide) film stock, with its own grain, during the re-photographing of the original to make copies. GSW drew some significance from the 'lack' of water displacement in ANS 1, as though this was

---

Fire Leynes   cont from p9...

50   'Incredible Stories of Witchery at Binbrook', *Louth & North Lincolnshire News*, no 1595, 21 Jan 1905, p5.

51   'The Amal Sessions', Carlisle, Pa., no 60, 8 Jan 1974, 6pp.

52   Nicholas, Ross, 'Man's Monuments and the Leys', *The Ley Hunter*, no 11, 1970.

53   Leek, Sybil & Stephen, *A Ring of Magic Islands*. Amphoto, Garden City, NY, 1976.

54   'Fiery Meteor Injures 9', *Reynold's News*, no 4578, 29 May 1938, p1.

55   'Found His Wife In Flames', *The Newcastle Journal*, no 28873, 28 Oct 1938, p13.

56   'Firemen find woman ablaze in her apartment', *The Cincinnati Post*, 17 Nov 1976, p21.

57   'Woman, 69, dies of burns', *The Cincinnati Post*, 17 Nov 1976, p21.

58   'Family of eight homeless after fire destroys house', *The Cincinnati Post*, 17 Nov 1976, p21.

59   'The Amal Sessions', Carlisle, Pa., no 96, 13 Aug 1974.

CREDITS: The following deserve recognition for their contributions and co-operation: Messrs. Cousins & Goossmas, of the Colindale Branch of the British Museum, for some favourable rule-bending; J. A. Whitfield, editor of *Hull Daily Mail*; R.G. Roberts and Miss J. Crowther, of Leisure Services, Humberside County Council; Robert Warth of SITU; Vincent Gaddis; Sandra K. Nevius; and RJM Rickard, whose enthusiasm, ideas and immensely generous assistance has been a source of delight and enlightenment.

strong evidence for the picture being hoaxed. They take no account of the second picture (see FT22/25 - photo B, now designated ANS 2, the original of which has unfortunately been lost, leaving only a good, but monochrome, negative) which does show considerable water displacement.

The apparent transparency of the creature's image is indeed interesting. From our aquaintance with Doc, we believe that the photo is everything it appears to be, taken how and when Doc said it was done. We can understand the suspicions aroused by the number of monster photos taken by Doc, successfully, and that apparently by following his hunches (psychic sense, or whatever) he came to be in the right place at the right time with a camera. But it was done, and we believe Doc's photos to be authentic. That said, we are faced with the exciting and baffling paradox - central also to the fields of UFO and apparition phenomena - that an apparently insubstantial object, or image of an object, causes or is coincident with tangible physical effects; in this case a see-through monster is really rippling and displacing water. This appears to be confirmation of the paraphysical hypothesis: either we have evidence of creatures which can materialize and dematerialize; or we are faced with an equally earth-shattering notion that thought-forms can be created and imprinted onto what we call 'reality', that images could simultaneously be excited on Doc's retinas and film to coincide with real or psychokinetically produced effects in the 'real' world to substantiate the image. We are now right at the edge of the latest thinking about the nature of reality...and I hope to present an important article on current ideas next issue.

Those, to whom such things matter, may like to know that Doc has made a sworn statement before a Falmouth solicitor, that his account and slides are true and accurate records of the events that befell him. We have a copy on file here.

There is little more to add at this point - except that much more important and hard work needs to be done. Doc has sent his original of ANS 1 to JARIC, and of course we'll bring you word as soon as we learn of the results. In the meantime, whether you agree with GSW or not, it is only practical, only scientific, to suspend judgement on Doc's photos until we learn more. I do not believe they are fakes - Doc would have nothing to gain, and many friends to lose if he did - but important evidence of a rare kind. Perhaps revolutionary enough to baffle even JARIC's prowess.   RJMR

BUGS FROM SPACE

We have always found the ideas of Fred Hoyle and his colleague Chandra Wickramasinghe exciting, and perhaps none more so than their discussion of the possibility that flus and plagues could be being seeded on this earth from cometary and meteoric debris - New Scientist 17 Nov 1977. Of course the idea is not new, as the idea of panspermia played quite a part in the early evolution of scientific cosmology prior to the Renaissance, and more anciently in the general belief in comets etc as portents of great calamities here on earth. Hoyle and Wickramasinghe have written on this theme before (Nature 266:p241; 267:p133; 268:p610) and despite good corroboration of each stage in their theory, the present article brought disbelieving protests from "several quarters", who found it hard to accept that primary molecules had been found on meteoric material, that this extraterrestrial matter originated in comets, and that alien biological material could interact with terrestrial cells. Hoyle and Wickramasinghe reply in N.Sci 5 Jan 1978 (Cr: Ion Will) that their idea is essentially simple: as more complex lifeforms evolved on earth, they acquired new genes at high speed ("perhaps one per 1000 years"). Viruses have the ability to add new genetic material to the invaded cell - as witness the present concern over viruses with penicillin-resistance now incorporating this ability into a new strain of gonorrhea (see below to our VD section for references.) This process of accumulating genes led to the rapid development of complex biological structures and thence lifeforms. Now if extraterrestrial viruses interacted with the early molecular forms far in our past then their patterns are still being inherited today. They conclude: "If the cells of our respiratory tracts thus have a genetic connection with cometary viruses extending over billions of years, the possibility of such viruses affecting us ((today)) cannot be lightly dismissed." (Additional sources were news coverage of the Nov N.Sci article, Cr: Tom Adams, Ion Will.)

What is more interesting is the hint here of a more fundamental influence on the development of life on this earth than slow Darwinian mutations and adaptions. If this stuff is raining all around us from space, constantly barraging us with long-lost genetic relations, then one might expect any damned thing to develop! Waiter, there's an alien in my primeval soup!

We have assembled below a summary of some of the plagues of the last 2½ years. There seems to be a seething war raging between man and bug for their ecological niche - those unable to adapt get zapped. The more astute among you will notice that many of them are concurrent...but unfortunately, because of time limitations we were unable to correlate the data with terrestrial and celestial portents...perhaps one day we'll get the computer and finance we desperately need.

SMALLPOX

In April 1977, the World Health Organization (WHO) confidently announced the eradication of smallpox from India, "leaving only 48 known cases in the world." Jacksonville, Florida, Times-Union & Journal 24 April 1977 (Cr: Gary Abbott) Just three years before, in India an epidemic afflicted 188,000 Indians, killing 31,000 of them. The last known case, after a massive vaccination programme, was on 24 May 1975, since which India seems to have been free of the disease which ravaged it constantly for centuries. All 48 of the remaining cases are in Somalia, said WHO officials, and these could be contained and cured. In 10yrs, they say confidently, the disease could be wiped from the face of this planet. Such an appeal to certainty attracted our attention -- in our experience banishings have an embarassing way of backfiring.

Sure enough! The next month WHO said the cases had jumped to 173 in Somalia, and the disease was "spreading rapidly." Guardian 28 May 1977 (Cr: P Hope-Evans.)

The Sunday Times 5 June 1977, gave the end of May total for Somalia as 192 cases.

On 10th Sept, the WHO felt that as the African cases were now "clinically inactive", and there had been no new cases "anywhere" for the prior month, they felt the end of the smallpox scourge was near. Newport News, Virginia, News 12 Sept 1977 (Cr: Gary Abbott).

DIPHTHERIA

Within a short while there were two, apparently unconnected, diphtheria scares in England last summer.

After a baby was hospitalized in Manchester in August, doctors admitted to the Monsall Isolation Hospital there, 11 children all identified as carriers. One can only boggle that with so many carriers in one city there should be only one casualty. D.Telegraph 27 Sept 1977.

A 13yr-old boy in Wolverhampton came down with diphtheria, causing officials to warn parents of 2,000 children at his school, and a further 300 at a primary school attended by a sibling. D.Telegraph 14 Sept 1977 (Cr: P Hope-Evans.)

'BLACK DEATH'

In late July 1976 there was a resurgence of this medieval terror in the USA. Up to the end of that month 13 cases of bubonic plague had been diagnosed, with one death - a 45yr-old man in Bakersfield, California, who tried to sweat it out on his own, but who only succeeded in turning it into its more virulent form, pneumonic plague. In 2 weeks the infected areas nearly doubled, involving 17 counties in California, Arizona and New Mexico. Infected animals were also found in Wyoming and Nevada. Dr Bernard Nelson, California Health Dept, said bubonic plague had never really been eradicated from North America, and that the problem could worsen as the 'plague season' among carrier wildlife usually lasted into September. This was said to be the worst outbreak in the US for 25 years." Sunday Times 1 Aug 1976.

There was another outbreak this year, though medical officials said it was not an epidemic. Following the death, in July, of a 3yr-old girl in San Diego, of bubonic plague, a 55yr-old veterinary surgeon in San Jose contracted pneumonic plague and died on 17 Aug. Harrisburg, Penn, Patriot 19 Aug 1977 (Cr: Larry Arnold); Times, D.Telegraph 19 Aug 1977 (Cr: Valerie Martin, Peter Hope-Evans.)

Earlier the same year, in May, bubonic plague was reported breaking out in

Hanoi, Vietnam. Guardian, D.Telegraph 21 May 1977 (Cr: V Martin, P Hope-Evans.)

CHOLERA

Cholera raged over a good part of the planet since June last year. Our first notes are that at 18 June there were 50 cases in the port of Arida, Japan, and another in Tokyo. Sunday Times 19 June.

Early in September the biggest epidemic was underway in the Middle East, involving Jordan, Lebanon, Saudi Arabia and the United Arab Emirates; the worst hit was Syria, with 2000 ill and 68 dead. By 17 Sept, the WHO were speaking of the "encouraging" signs that the epidemic was on the decline. Two days later the casualty figures begin increasing again, levelling off (for Syria) at 3100 ill and 70 dead by the 20th. This levelling off is spoken of as "a waning". By now the disease has been reported in Turkey (where officials deny it, calling it merely "an intestinal infection "), Iran, Kuwait, Iraq and Israel. Many other countries, including England, had several alerts as travellors from these stricken areas came down with the sickness in the host country. As the time drew near for the 'Hajj', the pilgrimage to Mecca, health officials throughout the Islamic world expressed their concern. The expected disaster did not materialize, it seems, and we find very little in our papers on cholera after this date (2 October). D.Telegraph 7,13,14,17,21,26 Sept & 1, 12 Oct 1977; London Evening Standard 19 Sept 1977; Guardian 21 Sept 1977; Times 30 Sept 1977; Sunday People, Sunday Times 2 Oct 1977 (Cr: Peter Hope-Evans, Valerie Martin, Sam.)

While all this was going on there was an apparently unconnected outbreak of cholera in the Gilbert Islands. Before a medical team from New Zealand brought it under control, there were 183 ill and 17 dead. D.Telegraph 17 & 27 Sept 1977 (Cr: Peter Hope-Evans.)

An outbreak in Bangladesh was made worse by the terrible conditions after severe flooding with people drinking polluted water. Our last report mentions 522 dead before it was checked by an emergency vaccination programme. D.Express 20 Sept 1977; D.Telegraph 22 & 28 Sept 1977 (Cr: P Hope-Evans, V Martin.)

In Katmandu, Nepal, 8 died of cholera. Sunday Times 18 Sept 1977.

During the present civil war in Ethiopia, cholera had broken out in an over-crowded prisoner-of-war camp run by the Eritrean Liberation Front. War conditions will prevent quick diagnosis, treatment and prevention - official view is one of foreboding. D.Telegraph 20 Sept 1977. We've not really kept a track of this particular epidemic, but we believe it still thrives as the country is torn apart.

Lastly: During the great Middle Eastern epidemic, one Arab made his way down to Tanzania, and seeded the outbreak of cholera there that has raged for the last three months. At datum the toll is 3347 ill and 246 dead. Observer 22 Jan 1978.

VD

Following an epidemic of gonorrhoea, in Oct 1976, in USA and Liverpool, the CDC warned of a new strain - Beta/gonorrhea - resistant to penicillin, but amenable to another antibiotic, spectinomycin. The original penicillin-resistant strain was first identified in 1976 as originating in the Philippines, and since spread to nearly every country in the Far East, Europe, North America and parts of Africa and Australia. The average toll of gonorrhea is about 50,000 in England & Wales, and 2½-3 million in USA, so doctors are concerned that the new strain, which possesses a radical talent for "primitive sex" with other bacteria, may pass on their antibiotic resistance to, say, a meningitis strain, to produce a terrifying new scourge. Newport News, Va, Daily Press 3 Oct 1976; Sunday Times 15 May 1977; NY Times 29 June 1977 (Cr: Gary Abbott, P Hope-Evans)

POLIO

In 1976 there were 8 cases of paralytic polio in the UK, and by April 1977 there were nearly as many again - clearly the expected epidemic looked likely, and immunisation programmes took place in Surrey, London, South Wales, Cambridgeshire and the North. In the midst of health service spending cuts, one London hospital was appealing for second hand 'iron lungs' in anticipation. In June a case was found in Essex; and two in Stockport. In August there was another suspected case in Essex, and one in Belfast, where a huge vaccination alert followed the discovery of a woman carrier. Weekly News 16 April 1977; Times 7 & 16 April 1977; D.Mirror 4 March 1977; Guardian 10 June, 17 Aug 1977; Sun 22 June 1977; D.Telegraph 18 Aug 1977 (Cr: P Hope-Evans.)

TYPHOID etc

There was a steady stream of typhoid cases, and several of paratyphoid and typhus from Dec 1976 until Dec 1977 - most in people recently arrived or returning from abroad to England. We note only 2 deaths. Sunday People 19 Dec 1976; Sun 15 March 1977; Balham & Tooting, London, News 1 April 1977; D.Telegraph 2,14 Sept, 12,29 Nov 1977; D.Express 2 Dec 1977; D.Mail 26 March 1977 (Cr: P Rogerson, Sam, P Hope-Evans.)

The worst outbreak in Victoria, Australia, for 20yrs was traced to a 60yr-old woman immigrant from England, working in a Melbourne shop. Officials say she had been a carrier for 28 years - but we wonder why they only notice it now! Also Victoria is the original home of the flu-strain plaguing Britain at the time of this typhoid outbreak...they send us flu, we send them typhoid! D.Telegraph, Guardian both 10 May 1977 (Cr; Valerie Martin, P Hope-Evans.)

In Late August a huge typhus scare swept through Sicily and Southern Italy - 70 ill, 63,000 vaccinated. Sunday Telegraph 4 Sept 1977 (Cr: P Hope-Evans.)

WHOOPING COUGH

Following a long and bitter public debate about the relationship between the whooping cough vaccination and brain damage in some children, and the way it can aggravate certain diseases, Health officials expressed their concern over the large drop in immunisation. This, coupled with the fact that whooping cough epidemics follow a 3-4 year cycle - the last serious outbreak in the UK was in 1974/75 - focused this concern on the epidemic predicted for late 1977. According to Prof Gordon Stewart, Glasgow University, a rush for immunisation could do great harm, exposing more children to the possible risks of the vaccine side-effects. Ironically, he added that "No epidemic has ever been prevented in the past by vaccination, and we have records going back many years to show this." Other experts were confident that the brain damage risk of vaccine containing 'pertussis' (whooping cough) was very small - and a report on the problem (Whooping Cough Vaccination by Joint Committee on Vaccination & Immunisation, HMSO, 85p) quotes a recent study of 80,000 vaccinations on Prof Stewart's own doorstep, Glasgow, as having "no evidence of permanent brain damage", though that could be construed as having some transient damage. The report said there has been no case of a direct link in the 1961-1975 period. London Evening Standard 24 June 1977; Guardian 19 Dec 1977 (Cr: Ion Will.)

The epidemic came as predicted. Between 1 July and 14 October, 4500 cases had been reported...doctors expect figures to rise to 30,000 before winter is out. By late December there were 11,000 cases - increasing by about 1000 a week. We have heard nothing more since our last datum, from which we imagine that the epidemic is over or in decline. <u>Daily Telegraph</u> 4 Nov 1977; London <u>Evening News</u> undated (late Dec 1977/early Jan 1978?)

MEASLES

The Whooping cough vaccine/brain damage scare lowered the figures for all kinds of immunisation, and early in 1977 doctors were also predicting epidemics of polio and measles for late 1977. <u>Sunday Telegraph</u> 27 Feb 1977; <u>Weekly News</u> 16 April 1977 (Cr: P Hope-Evans.) As far as we know there was no epidemic announced in England, but in USA and Indonesia.

The Los Angeles health authorities announced their epidemic on 25 Jan - a potentially fatal strain of 10-day measles, known as rubella. At 3000 cases, it was already double previous known outbreaks and was yet to reach its peak. That same month outbreaks were reported in Georgia and Chicago. By mid-Feb cases also appeared in Indiana, Wisconsin, Pennsylvania, California, Iowa, Kansas and Minnesota. Experts said they expected measles and German measles cases to run into 40,000 - current figures were running at 2½ times the figures for the same period in 1976 - and they unanimously blamed the government's concentration on 'Swine Flu' (see below) which distracted attention and enthusiasm for other real immunisation programmes. We have no figures for the actual peak of the USA measles epidemics. <u>Daily Telegraph</u> 26 Jan 1977; Jacksonville, Florida, <u>Times-Union</u> 31 Jan, 3 Feb 1977; <u>National Enquirer</u> 15 Feb 1977 (Cr: Valerie Martin, Gary Abbott.)

In Indonesia, 60 children on the quake-stricken island of Lombok, east of Bali, had died of measles since April 1977. Because of lack of prompt attention from health authorities, children either die or develop immunity. <u>Bangkok Post</u> 31 Aug 1977; <u>Sunday Express</u> 25 Sept 1977 (Cr: Ion Will, P Hope-Evans.)

RABIES

In 1970 rabies was rampant in Europe, from Poland to West Germany, Netherlands, Switzerland and Austria. In 1975 it had spread to Belgium, France and Spain, where 4 died in Malaga. In that year there were 30,000 innoculations and suspected cases in the USA, but only 2 deaths. <u>D.Mirror</u> 24 Sept 1975.

Despite several scares, shootings of frothing animals, and idiots smuggling their drugged pets past customs officials, the UK has remained relatively rabies-free compared to the Continent.

Rabies is supposed to have been eradicated in Britain in 1922, since when there have only been, officially, 2

cases in the wild, the rest developing in quarantine. Scandinavia is the only other "clean" country in Europe.

By Sept 1977 rabies was said to have encircled Paris, bringing forward from 1980 this landmark of the disease's spread, as predicted in 1975. From Jan to April 1977 there were 718 cases of rabid animals in France. <u>Sun</u> 4 Aug, 10 Sept 1977; <u>Sunday Mirror</u> 7 Aug 1977; <u>Weekly News</u> 24 Sept 1977; <u>D.Telegraph</u> 2 & 24 Sept 1977; <u>Guardian</u> 28 Sept 1977 (Cr: P Hope-Evans.)

Outside England the problem rages. In the mountains of Alto Adige, northern Italy, 2500 wolves have been destroyed in an attempt to contain rabies there, brought from Austria. <u>D.Telegraph</u> 14 Oct 1977 (Cr: P Hope-Evans.)

INFLUENZAS

There have been quite a few fatal flu outbreaks in many countries involving new, unfamiliar and unidentified strains and even resurgences of strains not seen for some time.

Britain

A 'mystery flu' virus arrived suddenly in northern England and Scotland early in March 1977, and spread rapidly wherever it took hold, until it petered out in April. Many of these outbreaks remained unidentified until press coverage of widespread cases made it clear that a relatively unknown virus was responsible. In fact it turned out to be a flu virus that had caused hundreds of deaths only the year before - just why British doctors were caught napping is not clear... unless it was over-belief in medical theory. The flu was slow developing, but fever and other symptoms would appear suddenly and severely, aggravating heart and lung conditions almost universally among elderly patients. A spokesman for the Central Public Health Labs, at Colindale, London, said there was little expectation of epidemic. Flus usually start before February, they pontificated, so one starting up in March was "unlikely to come to anything." Besides, figures were still low for that time of year, they said. Little comfort to those who died. <u>Sunday Times</u> 27 March 1977.

The first deaths we noticed were early in March - in one week 7 old-folk died at a home near Bolton, Lancs. Mid-March: 11 old women die within 6 days at Bo'ness in West Lothian. 25 March: 27 die in 2 separate cases at Whitley Bay and North Shields, Northumberland. More deaths at these locations followed, as health inspectors were hampered by unseemly feuding between the Northumberland local

cont on p33/

Review Supplement

HARDBACKS

Peoples of the Sea by Immanuel Velikovsky (Sidgwick & Jackson 1977; £5.95;
pp261; index, illos) -- For all those
captivated, anything up to 25yrs ago, by
the revolutionary reconstruction of ancient history presented in Ages in Chaos
(vol.1),the news that the sequel volumes
promised by Velikovsky are finally being
published will be more than welcome. The
third volume in the series, Rameses II
and his Time, will appear this March,
while the fourth and final volume, Peoples of the Sea was published in Feb
1977. (Publication date for the second
volume has not yet been set.)

In his introduction to Peoples, Velikovsky explains to his patient readers
the reason for the long delay in publication of these sequels. He reminds us
of the sheer enormity of the task he had
set himself, and how the continuation of
his reconstruction, originally planned
as one volume, rapidly expanded into
three. His involvement in the heated dispute over the theories he had put forward
in Worlds in Collision (note 1) has also
seriously delayed the completion of what
Velikovsky considers to be his magnum
opus. He had hoped, largely in vain, that
his persistent attempts to secure radiocarbon tests on artifacts from the Egyptian New Kingdom in order to check his
'revised chronology' would have borne
some fruit. The tests have still to be
performed, though of the few that have
been carried out he is happy to report
that several support his view rather than
the conventional history of Egypt (note
2).

Peoples covers the period of Egyptian
history from the Persian Conquest of
Egypt in 525 BC to its liberation by
Alexander and the time of the Ptolemaic
(Greek) Dynasty of the 3rd century BC.

During the long Persian occupation Egyptian civilisation briefly reflowered
under the independent kings of the 28th
to 30th Dynasties, best known to us from
the accounts of Greek historians. Egyptologists have, for many years now, been
quite confident that these kings have
been correctly identified from the native
Egyptian monuments - they have also been
confident that the 20th Dynasty, followed
by the pendant 21st, ruled in the 12th
and 11th centuries BC. The 20th Dynasty
is probably best known for its Pharaoh
Rameses III, and his struggle with the
mysterious 'Sea Peoples' whom he drove
back from the borders of Egypt. The so-
called 'Sea Peoples' invasion' is supposed to have been part of a mass migration of barbarian tribes in the Near East
around 1200 BC, and this concept had been
used as a 'catch-all' by historians for
decades. The invasion (mentioned only by
Rameses III) is used as an 'explanation'
of the near simultaneous destruction of
practically all the Late Bronze civilisations of Greece, Anatolia, Syria and
Palestine.   It is also held responsible
for initiating an archeological 'Dark
Age' in which civilisations disappeared
from these areas for anything up to 500
years.

Velikovsky presents the startling hypothesis that the kings of the 28th to
30th Dynasties are really none other than
those of the 20th Dynasty, and that the
repulse of the 'Sea Peoples' is an Egyptian account of the abortive attempt of
the Persians to reconquer Egypt in 374
BC. The leading 'Sea Peoples' are called
Prst by Rameses III, and are usually identified with the Biblical Philistines.
Yet, as Velikovsky points out, Prst is
actually attested as an Egyptian rendering of the name 'Persians'. The 'Dark Age'
he argues, is a complete chimera - the
evidence of civilisation disappears from
many sites 'during this period' simply

because the 500 years did not exist.

He presents his reconstruction of the last dynasties of Egypt with a wealth of persuasive argument, and confronts the accepted scheme of history with an embarrassing series of archeological anomalies. For example, the tiles of Rameses III, now in the British Museum, show quite clearly on the reverse side letters of the Greek alphabet incised during their manufacture. (Photos of the tiles are given in the book.) Yet the Greek alphabet most certainly did not originate until the 8th century BC, some 4 hundred years after the supposed time of Rameses III. All orthodox attempts to explain the letters (which even appear to be of classical 4th century form) as, for instance, 'degenerate' hieroglyphics, have failed miserably, and the riddle has, in Velikovsky's words, been 'handled very much as though it were a parapsychological phenomenon.'

As a supplement, Velikovsky includes 'Astronomy and Chronology' - previously included in the Summer 1973 issue of the now defunct Pensee - a devastating attack on the theory that the Egyptians regulated their calendar by the rising of the star Sothis (Sirius), the cornerstone of the accepted astronomical dating scheme used by Egyptologists.

Revolutionary as all this is, Velikovsky's claims should come as less of a shock to archeologists than they would have done 25 years ago. Four years ago the evidence for the 'Sothic dating scheme' was rigorously examined by Ronald Long (see Orientalia vol.43 Nova series, 1974, pp261-274) who showed conclusively that far from being a 'scientific' and infallible method of dating, this much valued scheme was little more than an unsubstantiated dream of early 20th century Egyptology that had outstayed its welcome. Adopted for reasons of convenience and never proven, the theory had become dogma. The concept of the 'Sea Peoples' too has taken some hard knocks in the last decade - the eminent French archeologist, Claude Schaeffer, has questioned it, while the Egyptologist, Alessandra Nibbi (The Sea Peoples and Egypt, Noyes Press 1975) has shown that none of the current ideas of the 'Sea Peoples' are justified...the very name is a misnomer.

One hopes that the climate of scientific enquiry in Egyptological circles has improved sufficiently to afford Peoples of the Sea the open-minded reception it deserves.

Note 1: On 25 Feb 1974 the American Association for the Advancement of Science held a symposium on Worlds in Collision, which purported to be a definitive rebuttal of Velikovsky's astrophysical theories. The papers read appear (much amplified) in Scientists confront Velikovsky, just published by Cornell University Press. A special issue of the American journal Kronos has been published as a response by Velikovsky's supporters, arguing effectively that far from scientific examination, the symposium was more an exercise in ridicule.

Note 2: Some reeds and palm kernels from the tomb of Tutankhamun were tested by the British Museum and gave dates of 846 (BM 642) and 899 BC (BM 642a). Even within the margins of error of the radiocarbon dating method, these results are clearly in conflict with the conventional date of Tutankhamun, supposed to have died around 1350 BC, and in good accord with Velikovsky's date of around 835 BC. The British Museum apparently considers the samples to have been 'contaminated' and has refused to publish the dates as promised.

Peter James

According to the Evidence by Erich von Daniken (Souvenir Press 1977; £4.50; pp348; refs, many photos & illos) -- I looked forward with some anticipation to reading VD's latest...I hoped that this time he'd bounce back and nail the critics snapping ever more loudly and closer at his heels (see comments on the TV critique of VD on p50). The hopes were dashed against the brick wall of his own intractable position set out in his previous books: contradictions, bad choice of evidence, weird logic, sheer audacity and all. Obviously tiring of the scurrilous attacks on his 'ancient astronauts' industry, VD has here presented a summary of the other books but dressed-up like a submission to a Supreme Court, with the reader as jury. Unfortunately the 'proofs' and patter are by now so familiar, the fiery arguments so turned to a monotonous complaint that he risks the jury sleeping through the trial.

Some of VD's tactics, though, would have had the jury on their feet, and the prosecution shouting 'Objection!' He seems to have learned nothing from his critics: for example, in discussing the idea of 'directed panspermia' he quotes an article by the biologists Crick and Orgel which contains an amusing speculation on a robot spacecraft roaming the galaxy inseminating fertile planets with micro-organism cultures. VD immediately seizes this to triumphantly proclaim that our learned doctors say "in black and white that the creation took place according to a plan." And again, referring to the highly dubious Cabrera rocks, which purport to show dinosaurs coexistant with man and that the ancients had modern heart-surgery techniques etc, he quotes a geologist's report describing the Mesozoic origin of the rocks, hoping that you'll accept from that that they must have been carved then too! Here he clearly acknowledges that now the local craftsmen have started manufacturing 'ancient artifacts' at many of the old sites, because of media and tourist interest...but that he was lucky enough to have got there first and seen the genuine stuff. Naturally!

VD's thesis rests on four points (and this jury returns his verdict in the brackets: 1) that in earliest times this Earth was visited by beings from elsewhere (undoubtedly an exciting possibility but still in the realm of conjecture or there would be little objection of any substance); 2) that these beings deliberately created humans (extraterrestrial influence on the development of life is a serious consideration (see p/7) but that it was so, and was deliberate, is unproven); 3) that these beings created us in their likeness, hence anthropomorphic gods in ancient iconography etc (unproven; based on child-like logic, eg a neighbour's kid said to me: "Our cat is called Ginger. That's why he's ginger all over!"); 4) that these beings left traces upon our landscapes and mythologies (a distinct possibility contingent upon the truth of item 1, thus still conjecture.) In terms of rigorous logic, the evidences VD gives, far from narrowing down the possible solutions to the inescapable conclusion of ET intervention on Earth, actually open up such a baffling array of possibilities that we must in all honesty say his thesis is only one possibility. Personally, I found his discussions on space-colonies, the chemical origins of life and several anti-Darwinism swipes both interesting and amusing in places, but as soon as he gets back to his main theme his crankiness shows - by which I mean you can see his obsession reading things into innocuous data before your very eyes; that and his chief ideological error of seeing every facet of the alien 'gods' in terms of 20th century technology (eg pagoda architecture becomes reminiscent of ceramic electrical insulators, tail-feathers on a stylised bird become the flame-exhaust of a rocket, etc). His picture of the alien culture is pure Star Wars/Dan Dare! Some basic questions go unanswered: if they were so all-pervasive during a huge chunk of our development, why aren't they

still with us? are they anything to do with UFOs? if not, why not? and why the obsession to attribute the slightest detail of an enigma, or triumph of human art and engineering, to the damned ETs? There is much a Freudian analyst could make of such things. I'd say baby Erich was abandoned for long periods and is still psychologically waiting for an omnipotent Mummy/Daddy to appear from outside the confines of his cot/world to make things all right again. Aren't we all to some degree, but few of us have elevated it to a cosmic drama worth 6 books. After today's court hearing I'm reminded of an old stand-up comic's gag: "I move around a lot. With my act, I have to!" The end papers of Evidence show VD's travels on a world-map. There are still places he hasn't visited - and my advice to him is to keep moving. He has two qualities that will keep him ahead (only just) of the pack, his undoubted imagination and sense of humour, but sooner or later his persecution complex will betray him fatally - in the opening pages he likens himself to those on the shamefully long list of men (including Velikovsky, here as 'Velikowsky') who have been ridiculed or worse by the scientific establishment. Since VD fails to convince us of his rightful place on this list, his claim comes over as a conceit.

RJM Rickard

The Wolf Children by Charles Maclean (Allen Lane 1977; £4.95; pp324; index, bib, notes, glossary, photos) - The Wild Boy of Aveyron by Harlan Lane (George Allen & Unwin 1977; £6.95; pp 351; index, notes, bib, chronology, illos) -- When the Aveyron 'wildboy' was found living in woods in central France in 1799 (he had been seen several times before his capture) he soon became the wonder of France and the stimulus to a whole new wave of thought about the nature of man - Was this boy a living contradiction of Rousseau's concept of 'the Noble Savage', was he retarded, could he be reclaimed into the human society, and if not then just how much of our natures are conditioned by human contact since birth, and again, if so, then what is our residual archaic basic nature? Lane has painstakingly pieced together one of the least known but important turning-points in human self-understanding. The boy was turned over to a young physician, Jean-Marc Itard, whose attempted education of the boy pioneered the methods used today in the education of mentally-handicapped children. Lane has also found the three key papers by Itard, and one by the pioneer of psychiatry, Phillippe Pin-el, who also examined the boy, which have been lost since early in the 19th century. Victor, the boy, has been the object of plays, novels, poems and the film L'Enfant Sauvage by Truffaut, but for the first time the full story and the issues it raised have been thoroughly documented.

Although not much was known about the origin of Victor, he was not alone. Throughout recorded history there have been many accounts of wild men and women, boys and girls found wherever there have been wilds for them to roam. They were known well enough for the great systematizer, Linnaeus, in the 18th C, to devise the category of homo ferus in his classification of living creatures. Also, unlike Victor, many of these feral humans seem to have been adopted into the society of local animals - bears, wolves, gazelles and monkeys etc. The most famous of these are the wolf-girls of Midnapore, India, who form the kernel of Maclean's book. Maclean, also, has made an important contribution to the subject, for by following his hunches he managed to rediscover a box of papers by Robert Zingg (who studied the Midnapore children in 1920), lying forgotten in the attic of the Gesell Institute at Yale. Around the story of Kamala and Amala, the wolf-girls, Maclean weaves many references to contemporary thought on the subject, from child psychology to anthropology and mythology. Excellent as both these books are, they only scrape at the surface of the great mystery of the 'wildman' archetype, and both will undoubtedly earn their places as key reference works. I note, sadly, that the work and valuable observations of Fort, Heuvelmans and even Sanderson are not listed in either bibliographies.

RJM Rickard.

Prelude to the Landing on Planet Earth by Stuart Holroyd (WH Allen 1977; £6.95; pp338) -- In 1974 Andrija Puharich published his book Uri which told of his experiences investigating the psychic talents of Uri Geller. He wrote

Many of the books reviewed in these pages can be had from the following specialists in Fortean, occult, UFO magical, health, comic and alternative publications. Mail order or requests.

Compendium Books:
234/240 High St, Camden, London NW1.
Tel: 01 485 8944...&...01 267 1525.

Dark They Were & Golden Eyed:
9-12 St Annes Court, London W1.
Tel: 01 734 4260.

that while Geller was under hypnosis, an unknown voice was heard in the room giving a message foretelling that Israel was about to be attacked by the Arab states. Subsequently during their sessions with Geller, Puharich and his colleagues received many hours of messages from these communicators who claimed to be extraterrestrial intelligences whose intention was to guide mankind on this planet into certain courses of action. But Puharich had little success in convincing the world at large of the reality of his experiences, eminent scientist though he is. His cause was not helped by the fact that all the cassettes of recording tape and cine film on which the voices and the images of UFOs were recorded sooner or later dematerialized, allegedly by these same intelligences. Since then the situation has continued to develop - Geller, perhaps unwilling to be, and unnerved at being, the tool of the ETs, has dropped out, while Puharich has continued the contact with the ETs with a small group of mediums.

Stuart Holroyd, an established writer on psychic matters, was led by apparent chance to visit Puharich's house in New York state in January 1975. There he learnt that since March 1974 Puharich had been in constant touch with the ETs and that there were over 100hrs of taped communications, this time preserved intact. Holroyd returned to England, forgetting about the visit as he immersed himself in various writing projects, until, in September 1975, Puharich rang to tell him that the ETs thought the time right for a book on the subject, and would he write it? His initial reaction was that of the knowledgeable sceptic. Being aware of such pitfalls as fraudulent mediums, secondary personalities and unconscious telepathy, Holroyd was extremely cautious in accepting the material at face value. He finally decided that it could be authentic, and this volume is the result.

Some critics may think that Holroyd is extremely gullible, but no one should judge prematurely until they have read the book. Viewing it as a unique situation, many readers will find their credulity strained to the limit - but in the light of the overall UFO scene it is but the culmination of a continuing saga that stretches back beyond recorded history. In recent years hundreds, perhaps thousands, of small groups were established to receive communications from intelligences purporting to be outside the physical confines of this earth. Modestly priced booklets containing their messages circulate throughout the globe and many of these groups are in contact with one another - their messages are essentially similar though differ in detail, referring to the errors, potential and possible salvation of mankind. The activities of Puharich's group are one small part of this worldwide movement, and their results should be seen within this context.

Though Holroyd is versed in the pitfalls of psychic practices, and examines his material critically, he is, I suspect, less conversant with matters spiritual which have their own pitfalls. He feels that the most likely explanation is that the material originates from some exterior intelligences, and that the choice therefore lies between the ETs or spirits of the dead from the traditional seance-room. As the material is quite unlike the conventional trivial ramblings of the latter, the answer must lie, he says, with the former. Perhaps a wider knowledge of the reports of mediums and mystics from past ages would have alerted him to the multifarious levels of incorporeal intelligence that these esotericists have described, and to the deceptions that these 'spirit intelligences' can practise upon men for their own unknown purposes. The answer to the enigma this book poses must surely lie somewhere between these non-human intelligences and ETs. In short, here is another fascinating aspect of the psychic turmoil with which we have to contend at the start of this Aquarian Age. Clearly and intelligently written, this book makes compelling reading for all students of UFO and psychic manifestations.

Colin Bord.

The Crack in the Universe by Jean-Claude Bourret (Neville Spearman 1977; £4.25; pp264) - Early in 1974 an important series of radio broadcasts in France presented to a large audience a balanced and wide-ranging picture of the UFO scene. In this book are transcriptions of the 39 broadcasts, including an interview with the then Minister of Defence, Robert Galley. There are firsthand accounts of sightings old and new, including some close encounters; and a discussion with scientists and others presenting different points of view, including Jacques Vallee, Claude Poher, Prof JA Hynek, Gordon Creighton and Aimé Michel.

The content of these talks most likely had quite an effect on listners who knew nothing about UFOs. I can imagine the impact of such a series in the UK - but somehow such a series seems unlikely

here. Readers of this, Gordon Creighton's translation, are also likely to find much of value and interest, especially if the subject is new to them. Long-time readers of UFO literature might feel however, as I did, that much of the material merely repeats well-worn ideas, with too much emphasis on 'how' and not on the vital question 'why'. Creighton's contribution is one of the few to tackle this latter aspect, and his thoughts on angels and demons are so briefly given as to be almost unnoticeable. My conclusions: the book is ideal for the newcomer and anyone else who likes to keep his ufological feet on the ground. There are 12 pages of illustrations (photos of UFOs and personalities, and impressions of UFO encounters), an 8 page 'partial bibliography' by Creighton - but no index.   Janet Bord.

((Editor's note - Many readers have written asking why we have ignored some Spearman books in the past. This has not been our intention. We have written many times to Spearman asking for catalogues and specific review copies over the past 2-3 years, but they have chosen to ignore us completely - not even acknowledging my letters asking for correction or clarification of the situation. As we cannot afford to buy books for review, many of the reviews that appear in these pages are unsolicited and gratefully received. I have told Spearman that we can reach a strong core of book-buying interested readers...if they can't be bothered to keep us informed, or feel complacent enough to ignore such a group of potential buyers, so be it!))

Situation Red: The UFO Siege by Leonard H Stringfield (Doubleday, NY, 1977; $8.95; pp224) - If you could spend a few hours on a winter's evening sitting snugly by your fireside with a seasoned UFO buff yarning away about his investigations over the years, the frantic calls he's sometimes received from hysterical witnesses, his clashes and cooperation with authority (from local cops to the USAF), and the 'sworn to secrecy' tip-offs he's been given by those with 'inside info', the conversation might sound very much as this book reads.

Len Stringfield has been interested in UFOs since he was buzzed by a 'foo fighter' in WWII, and in the early '50s he published Orbit, one of the first UFO newsletters. Since 1969 he has been an investigator for the MUFON network, and his home area of SW Ohio has shown high UFO activity for many years. Other types of Forteana such as hairy bipeds have also been evident, and he features reports which show their possible connexions with UFOs. Stringfield takes his reports from 1973, an especially active year, starting with some close sightings of solid craft and continuing through cases of low-level car harassment and physical attack, quickening the pace with some of the weirder cases of paraphysical and entity encounters. He also relates some of those infuriatingly unsubstantiated stories of crashed UFOs and little dead humanoids seen in the desert surrounded by armed guards and with all participants sworn to secrecy. As a grand finale, the book ends with a detailed account of the abduction of 3 women from Liberty, Kentucky, investigated by Stringfield.

There is no in-depth theorizing on the paraphysical or psychological aspects of the subjects, but a readable and fascinating account of ufology as one very active American investigator has found it. There are several UFO photos (before and after computer enhancement) and of landing traces. There is a foreword by Major Donald Keyhoe...but no index.   Colin Bord.

The Book of Lists by David Wallechinsky, Irving & Amy Wallace (Cassell 1977; £4.75; pp304) -- The book is precisely what it claims to be, crammed with lists of the greatest, longest, shortest, worst etc (most superlatives that you can think of). As the editors have definite Fortean leanings there is much in here of interest to us. Quite apart from its obvious value as a reference for obscure facts, the book informs as well as entertains by direct stimulation of curiosity, and once picked up is damned hard to put down...Jack the Ripper suspects & victims, Gen.Patton's 6 past lives, 15 living fossils, 37 books on the Catholic Index of Forbidden Books, medical breakthroughs by nondoctors, anatomical relics, 3 people who died during sex, famous drug-takers, famous dinner guests (Irving Wallace adds Charles Fort to his list), 8 cases of spon.combustion, stigmatics, unsolved mysteries, best known embalmings, levitations etc etc. The perfect gift for curious people. RJMR

Victorian Grotesque by Martin Howard (Jupiter 1977; £5.95; pp154; illos) - Curious Myths of the Middle Ages by Sabine Baring-Gould (Jupiter 1977; £5.95; pp159; illos) -- Some months ago I managed to locate a remaindered copy of the Bell reprint of Anomalies and Curiosities of Medicine by Drs George Gould (no relation to Sabine) and Walter

Pyle, 1896; an acclaimed classic compendium of extraordinary medical cases, quite unobtainable generally. Howard's book, largely extracted from Gould & Pyle's tome offers us a selection of bizarre Victoriana from dwarfs and giants to two-headed, hairy or horned people. He claims to have added material from 720 other contemporary sources - a search which has thrown up additional illustrations too. Victorian Grotesque has been designed for the general reader, being more literary and less technical than Gould & Pyle.

Similarly, Curious Myths is a representation of Baring-Gould's long out-of-print classic. Its editor, Edward Hardy, however, confines himself to a brief introduction and the addition of some beautifully relevant Dürer woodcuts. The chapters are models of short scholarly essays on such subjects as the Wandering Jew, Prester John, the Divining Rod, Tailed Men, AntiChrist & Pope Joan, the Terrestrial Paradise, the Legend of the Cross, the Pied Piper, the Fortunate Isles, the Sangreal, and many others equally fascinating.

Both books are recommended for their Fortean relevance, and are finely printed editions.   RJM Rickard

The Avebury Cycle by Michael Dames (Thames & Hudson 1977; £6.50; pp240) - Those who read Dames' earlier book The Silbury Treasure will know what to expect from this new companion volume in which he considers the significance of those important prehistoric sites close by Silbury Hill - West Kennet long barrow, the Sanctuary, the West Kennet and Beckhampton Avenues, and the Avebury henge. Where earlier researchers have tiptoed round the fringes, Dames plunges in without hesitation, and the result is a bold, controversial and, to me, convincing assessment of the original function of these impressive monuments. He brings together information scattered throughout a number of disciplines, from archeology to folklore, and the skilful way in which he does so shows the breadth of his reading (a necessary qualification if we are to solve the long-standing mysteries; and anyone who has tried to keep abreast of the literature in just one field will know how daunting the task is.)

I will not spoil your own discovery of this book by attempting to summarise its contents. My only regret is that Dames did not take his research even further, to include information on the reactions of experienced dowsers at Avebury. If, as some suspect, the standing stones erected by ancient man were part of a power system, this surely had a part to play in the rituals Dames surmises were performed at such sites as Avebury. But even without mentioning this aspect he gives us plenty to think about, and his text is fully illustrated with relevant photos and diagrams. The book would have been even more attractive if some of the site photos were more evocative and atmospheric. There are very full references (11 pages) plus a bibliography (2 pages) and index (4 pages).

Janet Bord.

Ogopogo by Mary Moon (JJ Douglas Ltd, 1875 Welch St, N Vancouver, V7P 1B7, Canada, 1977; pp195; photos; price unknown) - Ogopogo is the monster believed to be living in Okanagan Lake, British Columbia, Canada, and this thorough book documents the sightings of him/her/it/them, from Indian legends up to the present. There have been many sightings, especially in the 1920s, and eyewitness descriptions are often completely incompatible with the favourite explanatory theories: sturgeon-in-a-line, oarfish, manatee etc. As for the other possibility, a prehistoric reptile...who knows? No remains of an Ogopogo have been found, though footprints have been seen and inconclusive photos taken (2 included here). The Ogopogo story follows the pattern of other much-investigated lake monsters - after years of sightings we are no nearer a solution to the mystery.

Mary Moon also gives us details of other mysteries in the Okanagan valley (including Stenwyken, the hairy giant and possible Sasquatch), and there is a chapter on other lake and sea monsters of British Columbia, plus a chronological record of sightings of Ogopogo. It adds up to a readable, informative, well designed, attractively produced large-format paperback. Recommended reading for monster hunters.

Janet Bord.

UFO RESEARCH SERVICE -- Page Research Library Newsletter covers Fortean news and UFO events. Send $2.00, or international postal coupons, for samples. Includes a 24page catalog detailing 100s of RARE and current books and magazines on UFO and Fortean topics. Try us, you'll like us! Page Reasearch (Dept FT), 30525 Center Ridge Rd, Westlake, Ohio 44145, USA.

An Anthology of I Ching by W A Sherrill & W K Chu (RKP, 1978; Hb, £7.95; pp 245; illos, tables, apps, index) Occasionally, a true gem of a book may escape the Fortean's attention simply because it falls outside his immediate field of interest. This work, apparently appealing only to those concerned with divination and Chinese philosophy, could well suffer the same fate. I hope not.

On the broadest level, this book appeals for its relevance to Fort's notion of 'Dominants': in pre-Reformation Europe the dominant mode of thought was astrologically based; since the reformation, materialistically scientific. In traditional China the Dominant was different again, being largely a combination of the I Ching with the Five Elements and the Sexagenary Cycle. Working from manuscripts largely neglected by other translators, Sherrill and Chu have given us the opportunity to study that Dominant and its widespread application; a contextual background against which all studies of Chinese Forteana (lamentably few as they are) should be seen.

For the most part, the book concerns itself with advanced forms of divination and cyclical change. It is definitely not a book for beginners, however, and a good text and a working knowledge of the I Ching (especially its mechanics) would seem essential, even though the authors provide an extremely compact guide to basic I Ching divination in the first chapter. From there, they move on to discuss advanced divination, five different systems of Horary Astrology (cycles of change based on time of birth, using I Ching hexagrams rather than planetary movements), the heretical T'ai Hsuan Ching, a theory of history based on I Ching cycles, and the I Ching's relation to meditation, geomancy and directionology.

Some may recoil from the idea of divination, although it seems to me to be a perfectly legitimate area of Fortean study, if only for the fact that it enables one to produce synchronicity on demand. For those who disagree, there is still the fascinating interplay of mathematics and symbolism and the widespread applicability of a mode of thought very different from our own.

The book is well supplied with tables, figures, instructions and some charming illustrative stories, many concerning the 11th century genius Shao Yung, a pioneer in the study of cycles, responsible for much that is in this book and, indirectly perhaps, for modern computer technology. But there is one slight niggle: RKP have published a series of excellent works on the I Ching over the years, including the authors' previous Astrology of I Ching; all with the Chinese names and words transliterated into Mandarin forms. Why then is this book using Cantonese forms (eg: Sau Yung)? The whole area is complex enough already without adding linguistic confusions.

Apart from that, very highly recommended.   Steve Moore

PAPERBACKS

The Fairy-faith in Celtic Countries by WY Evans Wentz (Colin Smythe 1977; £4.50; pp524; index) -- For too long a time this classic work on the fairy tradition was out of print or obtainable only in hard-to-find expensive foreign editions; but now Colin Smythe are to be congratulated in at last putting a reasonably priced edition within reach of the poorest scholar. The basic text looks like a facsimile of the original (1911) with a new introduction by the poet and scholar, Dr Kathleen Raine.

Those who have studied fairy accounts and traditions today realise their relationship to the witch and ghost traditions and to the new field of UFO narratives. It comes as an eyeopening pleasant surprise to discover that Evans Wentz was not only relating fairy events to shamanism but exploring the basic similarity with many types of psychical phenomena, including poltergeist phenomena. Here is one of the great sourceworks for the living belief in fairies as it survives in the written and oral traditions of Celtic countries, and for primary materials on related phenomena from 'fairy battles' and 'straight paths' to psychology of perception and belief, and into occult and mystical cosmology.   RJMR

WARK, a small mag that reviews other small and alternative mags (mainly comic and fantasy), is looking for a volunteer to write a column (twice a year?) on Fortean publications. Interested? Contact Rosemary Pardoe, Flat 2, 38 Sandown lane, Liverpool 15. (Wark sample: 30p.)

Flying Saucers by CG Jung (Routledge & Kegan Paul 1977; £2.75; pp184; index plates) -- As with Evans Wentz's classic, another key work of fundamental relevance to our studies today, long out-of-print in Britain, has been most welcomely reprinted. On rereading it I can only marvel at the statements Jung made, in 1958, which are only now being fully appreciated by the most liberal of UFO researchers. The UFO 'establishment' has shamefully neglected this important contribution to the debate because it does not primarily consider the question of whether UFOs are vehicles piloted by beings from other planets. Jung is far more concerned about the appearance of the UFO as a symbol in dreams, art and hallucinations. His idea of the UFO as the visual equivalent of a rumour is difficult to understand, but he patiently explains the process by which the UFO appears to be a sign of a change in the pattern of archetypes of our age, and as a symbol of the quest for psychic integrity (light, circle, sphere, vessica-shaped 'saucers', heavenly mandalas etc). Although he drew back at suggesting here the mechanism whereby this personal and collective unconscious material became seem 'objectively', there is ample evidence in Jung's other writings that he saw the UFO as part of a whole spectrum of 'synchronistic' phenomena. I believe he regretted not having taken the matter further, as he regretted ever abandoning his synchrony research, partly because he felt there was every chance of his work being misinterpreted and partly because he went on to other areas of major contribution. It is a pity Jung did not live to see the awakening of the modern interest in the UFO as a non-ordinary phenomenon that transcends the boundaries of dream, myth and reality. Lets hope that some of the 'new ufologists' can pick up and be worthy of the mantle that has fallen to them. One regret, and in this I concur with my colleague, MUFOB editor John Rimmer, is that RKP missed the opportunity to include an additional introduction placing this essential work in the context of the modern UFO research which owes to Jung a great debt.   RJMR

Messengers from the Stars by W Raymond Drake (Sphere 1977; 85p; pp238; index, bib) -- Raymond Drake, perhaps more than any other single person, laid the groundwork for the 'ancient astronaut' school, and yet like many English pioneers in other fields, seems to have got more recognition abroad than at home. His 'Gods & Spacemen' series grew out of

a series of articles on historical and
mythological references to what seem like
ET visitations, appearing in FSR as far
back as 1958. Although UK publication of
his books has been sporadic (to say the
least) they have been in print abroad
almost continuously. Several of his manuscripts for books written before VD's
Chariots (1969) - eg G&S/Ancient West and
G&S/Greece & Rome - were deliberately
ignored by British publishers who had had
them for a year before the VD bandwagon
broke into UK bookshelves. Neither VD
nor Robert Temple give any tip of the hat
to Drake for writing about the 'Sirius
Mystery' in G&S/Ancient East written in
1964-6 and first published in 1968, nine
years before Temple's book. Messengers
from the Stars is another case in point.
It was first published in the USA, by
Ray Palmer in 1964, but even there it was
never really publicised. Originally called Gods or Spacemen?, it appears now in
paperback and for the first time in Britain, nearly 14 years later.
   Like its successors, Messengers is jam-
packed with reference material gleaned
from classical sources and commentaries
from all over the world. Unlike VD, Drake
believes in giving sound references, and
even relates his material to the UFO enigma, and various occult and parapsychological traditions. This book stands up
well to the test of time, and joins his
other valuable works on the reference
shelf.   RJMR

Shambhala: Oasis of Light by
Andrew Tomas (Sphere, 1977; 85p;
pp 175; Photos; Bib) Tomas's
thesis is that the mysterious kingdom of Shambhala, mentioned in Tibetan legends as lying to the far
north (though Tomas places it with
equal facility to the east & south)
is an extant centre of superior
civilisation, unreachable for normal men, where the Great Ones of the
human race watch over mankind's
destiny. So long as he restricts
himself to collecting references
suggestive of Shambhala's existence
he does a fairly good, if somewhat
embroidered job. Alas, halfway through, the book degenerates into just
another version of the Ancient Astronauts theory. It comes as no surprise to learn that Shambhala was set
up by superior intelligences from
the stars, nor that if we don't stop
killing each other and thinking bad
thoughts the end of the world is
nigh. In the end, only the names
and places have been changed to tempt the innocent.   SM

The Universe by Lloyd Motz (Abacus 1977;
£1.95; pp343; index, bib, plates) - Prof
Motz traces the history of the universe
from hypothetical begining to hypothetical end; basic astrophysics make the
book a good primer for beginers of any
age. It's fairly straight, so don't expect to find Velikovsky et al here...

Yesterday, Today and Tomorrow by
Jeane Dixon (Bantam/Corgi 1977;
95p; pp504) You may not agree
with her political views, but this
is really quite a good astrology
book - best thing I've read by her
anyway - and mostly lacking the
doubtful political prophecies evident in the earlier books. Based on
the concept that the 12 disciples
each embodied a sign of the Zodiac;
divides each house into time-strips
for more accurate type assessment.
                                SN

More Lives than One? by Jeffrey
Iverson (Pan 1977; 75p; pp156;
4pp photos; bibl.) "The evidence
of the remarkable Bloxham Tapes" is
the loose sub-title. Concerns hypnotic regression of a bunch of people convinced of previous lives.
Was an interesting TV documentary
last year.   SN

Our Changing Universe: The New
Astronomy by John Gribbin (Futura
1977; 70p; pp142; 8pp photos; ind;
bibl.) By half of the team that
brought you 'The Jupiter Effect'.
This one is exactly what the title
implies: a general updating of recent astronomical discoveries and
new thinking. Competent: must be, I
understood it...   SN

The Secret Forces of the Pyramids
by Warren Smith (Sphere 1977; 85p;
pp220) This bunch of aliens, see,
came down and taught all us savages
how to build pyramids - oh, and
Atlantis was one of their bases,
and, yes, they'll be back one day
to sort us out if we don't progress
from the current primitive state
we're in, and all the answers to
all the cosmic questions are right
there in the pyramids if only we
could see them, and...   SN

Parallel Universes by Adi-Kent
Thomas Jeffrey (Warner 1977; $1.95c;
pp174; photos) First edition- and
hopefully the last. A piece of unconvincing junk (only lacks the inevitable '?' after the title)   SN

cont on p31/

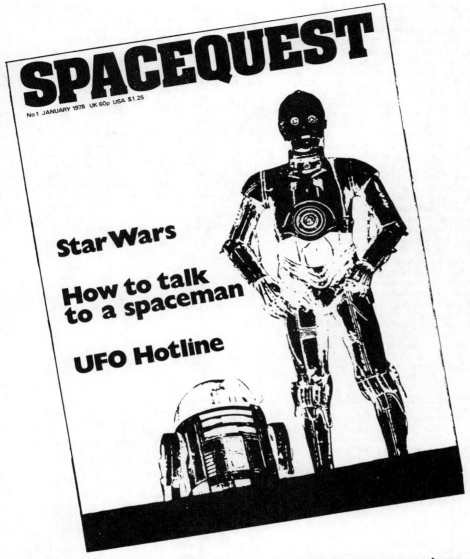

FEATURING IN THE FIRST ISSUE, NOW ON SALE, ARTICLES ON UFO SIGHTINGS, THE CENTER
FOR UFO STUDIES, THE BERMUDA TRIANGLE, THE EVOLUTION OF THE STARS, AND HOT TO
COMMUNICATE WITH EXTRA-TERRESTIAL INTELLIGENCE. ALSO A FEATURE ON THE FILM
'STAR WARS', THE LATEST NEWS FROM NASA AND TASS ON THE SPACE RACE, AN
ASTRONOMER'S SKY DIARY, AND THE UFO HOTLINE.

SPACE QUEST IS PUBLISHED BI₂MONTHLY BY SPACE CENTERPRISES. FOR A SAMPLE COPY
SEND UK £0.75/USA $2.00 (INCLUDING P&P), OR FOR AN ANNUAL SUBSCRIPTION
UK £4.50/USA $13.50, BY CHEQUE/POSTAL ORDER/INTERNATIONAL MONEY ORDER TO:

SPACE CENTERPRISES (FT), PO BOX 400, KINGS LANGLEY, HERTS.

cont from p29...

The Ancient Sun Kingdoms of The Americas by VW von Hagen (Paladin 1977; £1.50; pp351; index, bib, chronology, many photos) - reprinting of a useful reference work on native American cultures.

The Changing Face of Britain by Edward Hyams (Paladin 1977; £1.50; pp256; index, bib, photos)- a guide to the influences on our landscape from the megalith to motorway eras. Sound background for mystery hunters.

Magic and Mystery in Tibet by Alexandra David-Neel (Abacus 1977; £1.75; pp224) - Welcome reprint of this classic of magic, anthropology and parapsychology, first published in 1932, and still essential reading; written by a French scholar who became an initiated Tibetan lama, and surely one of the most remarkable women of this century. Splendid introduction by Aaron Sussman, which incidentally mentions Fort. Thoroughly recommended.

Body Time by Gay Gaer Luce (Paladin 1977; £1.25; pp330; 63page bibliography) reprint of a key reference on biorhythms.

Haunted London by Peter Underwood (Fontana; 60p; pp224; index, bib, photos) - A good gazeteer for ghost hunters.

You and Your Hand by Cheiro (Sphere 1977; 85p; pp187; photos;illos) Revised edition (by Louise Owen). A standard work, with lots of useful examples.

The Tao of Physics by Fritjof Capra (Bantam 1977; $2.95; pp332; index, notes, bib). Fills the gap between physics and metaphysics.

Mysterious Visitors: The UFO story by Brinsley le Poer Trench (Pan 1977; 70p; pp174; index, refs)- reprinting of The Eternal Subject, dealing with Biblical and psychic phenomena aspects of UFOs.

Beyond the Time Barrier 85p; On the Shores of Endless Worlds 85p; both by Andrew Tomas:rereleases from Sphere.

The Riddle of the Pyramids by Kurt Mendelssohn (Sphere 1977; £1.75p; pp208; 16pp photos;illos; index; bib) A re-issue of the Sphere-Cardinal edition of 1976.

The Bible and Flying Saucers by Barry H Downing (Sphere 1977; 85p; pp175; notes; bib) Reissue.

In Search of Myths and Monsters by Alan Landsburg (Corgi 1977; 85p; pp208; photos, bib).

Healing by Father Francis MacNutt (Bantam/Corgi 1977; 85p; pp308)

Focus on Fact No 3 - The Psychic World by Neville Randall & Gary Keane (Star 1977; 75p; pp128) Newspaper strip reprints.

A Soul's Journey by Peter Richelieu (Sphere 1977; 85p; pp208)

UFO Trek by Warren Smith (Sphere 1977; 85p; pp189).

THREE BOOKLETS OF NOTE:

The Piasa by Ruth Means (privately published by the Alton-Godfrey Rotary Club, Illinois) is a history of the legends among the Illinois Indians of the terrible Piasa, a monstrous dragon-like creature. Upon the bluffs of the Illinois River, at Alton, Indians painted a huge image of the Piasa , firing their bows at it whenever they passed down the river - later they used guns and the cliffface icon became obliterated by bulletholes. Since its discovery by pioneers in 1673, the image has been repainted several times - lately by Alton residents concerned with preserving a priceless heritage. Appended to this brief history of the legend and image, are two early accounts of the chief Ouatoga who rid his people of this scourge, and who must surely rank among the great dragon-slayers of this world.

Did WD Custead fly first? by Nick Pocock (index, bib) being a dissertation in support of WD Custead's claim for the flight of a winged ornithopter about six years before the Wright brothers did in 1903. Custead even formed an Air Ship company. This interesting little history of a forgotten pioneer is interestingly written with good references, contemporary material and many illustrations. Can be obtained for $2.00 from Nick Pocock: Box 672, Hillsboro, TX 76645, USA; or for £2.00 from DG Pocock: 15 Sheridan Rd, Merton Park, London SW19 3HW.

Bigfoot edited and published by Page Research Library: Box 5012, Rome, Ohio 44085, USA; price $3.25. -- This special report by Page Research follows their valuable booklet on the BVM apparition at Cairo in 1968. Essentially it is a collection of highly interesting papers by leading Bigfoot researchers. There are reports on Ohio and Montana Bigfeet; two reports on Australia's Yowie, which present valuable new data; and several papers on the paranormal dimensions of the Bigfoot phenomenon, eg their UFO link, and an encounter during astral projection. There's also one article on investigating procedure for would-be Bigfoot hunters; and another more general overview of Bigfoot phenomena, which includes many other types of humanoid sightings. The whole is fleshed out with many drawings and photos, and a list of Bigfoot material, much of which is available from Page Research. Recommended to all serious Forteans.

JOURNALS

We would be obliged if readers writing
to addresses or answering advertisements found in our pages say where
they saw the information. This helps
us and others judge the effectiveness
of these notices.

INFO Journal 26 (Dec 77): phantom snipers in Sweden; sci-phi; mystery booms;
Quetzalcoatl & the BT; brief notes &
reports. INFO: 7317 Baltimore Ave, College Park, MD 20740, USA. 6 issues/$10.00/
£5.00. FT readers can pay thru' FT (see
p52, panel.)

Pursuit Fall 77: report on Fate's UFO
congress; psychological problems of UFO
research; New York & New Jersey Bigfeet;
inter-galactic language; UFO propulsion
hypothesis; & Fortean notes & comments.
Pursuit is published by SITU who have
a new address. Write for details: SITU,
RFD #5, Gales Ferry, Conn 06335, USA.

Res Bureaux Bulletin conducted by Mr
X. One of the best Fortean newsletters
around. X is not after mass circulation
but will exchange for journals, info or
clippings. Dedicated Forteans only need
apply: RBB, Box 1598, Kingston, Ontario,
Canada K7L 5C8.

Stigmata - no-schedule (yet) newsletter
of Project Stigma (under editorship of
Tom Adams), investigating animal mutil-
ation and death phenomena (mainly USA).
Send SAE to Stigmata: Box 1094, Paris,
Texas 75460, USA.

Vestigia Newsletter 3 (Fall 77): Fortean investigation group (NewJersey base)
probe Bigfoot, the Lizard-man, the Monk-
ey-bird; plus notes on field photography.
Write: Vestigia, Box 1183, Perth Amboy,
NJ 08861, USA.

Nessletter: recommended newsletter of
Ness Information Service: Rip Hepple,
Huntshieldford, St Johns Chapel, Bishop
Aukland, Co Durham DL13 1RQ. £1.25/$7.00
gets you 12. Essential for monsterlovers.

Anomaly Research Bulletin 7 (Sept 77):
phantom kangaroo catalogue (get one
cheap, eh?), Big Birds; mutilations; report on Acapulco UFO congress. etc. ARB:
Dave Fideler, 7098 Edinburgh Drive, Lambertville, MI 48144, USA. £1.50/$3.00.

Journal of Occult Studies (mentioned
p12 FTRS last issue) - we forgot to give
the address. JOS: Box 32, Kingston,
Rhode Island 02881, USA. Quarterly:
$7.50 (Students: $6.00.)

SIS Review 2:1 (Autumn 77): Senmut's
Ceiling; Senmut & Phaeton; Birth of Mon-
otheism; 'Peoples of the Sea' in art;
Electricity in astronomy; more. SIS are
a study group exploring and promoting
Velikovsky's theories of catastrophic
geology and astronomy, and errors in
ancient chronologies. (See review on p21).
SIS: 6 Jersey House, Cotton Lane, Manchester 20. Write for details.

Lantern 20 (Winter 77): Victorian ghost;
Suffolk stones & lore; pt3 of Black Dog
study; notes. A quarterly journal of
East Anglian oddities, from BSIG: 3 Dun-
wich Way, Lowestoft, Suffolk. 1yr/85p.
Write for foreign rates.

Neurolog: journal of Network, Box 317,
Berkeley, CA 94701, USA. A product of the
teachings of Robert Wilson, Timothy Leary
and John Lilly, the 3 pillars of Network
are Space migration, Increased intelligence, and Life Extension (SMI^2LE), and
is an intelligent, aware, info exchange
on these and related subjects. Sample:
$1.00. Write for details.

MUFOB 9 (Winter 77): Danish airship of
1908; 'Facts, frauds & fairytales';
'Fairies & fireballs'; more. Brain jolt-
ing stuff as usual. MUFOB: 11 Beverley
Rd, New Maldon, Surrey KT3 4AW. 4 issues
£1.25/$3.00.

Journal of Meteorology: recent issues
have reports on whirlwinds, cyclones,
floods, weather freaks and extremes, hail,
lightnings, 'Atmospheric music', dark
bands on clouds, thunders. Essential for
all interested in Fortean meteorology.
J.Met, Cockhill House, Trowbridge, Wilts
BA14 9BG. Monthly: £6.50/$16.00.

Page Research Newsletter 21: letters,
'Close Encounters' photos; an 1958 report on humanoid/close encounters in the
1950s, with drawings, See their ad elsewhere in this issue.

The Ley Hunter 79: ghost lights & leys;
did Henry James crack-up on a Windsor
ley?; rings of festival sites?; ley in
suburban Sudbury, Middx; John Michell &
Bob Forrest at Land's End; a new 'Outline
of geomantic engineering'. TLH details
in panel on back page.

Christian Parapsychologist Dec 77:
gnostic and Egyptian concepts of immortality; 'Possession and the paranormal';
news, etc. Quarterly: £2.00/$4.00. CP:
St Mary Abchurch, Abchurch Lane, London EC4

*** We very much regret that space has
run out again, when we still have books
and journals to review. Senders of review
material are assured that sooner or later
all items received will be listed. ***

Flu cont from p20...

councils responsible for the homes. 29
March: 1 dead and many ill at Colchester.
2 April: 10 die at Dewsbury, Yorks. 18
April: 18 ill at Gateshead, saved only
by a panic innoculation after the earlier
Tyneside outbreak. Late-April: figures
said to be running treble the seasonal
average, exceeding the official 'alert
threshold'. 20 April: 30 deaths in 3
weeks in a geriatric hospital at Aylsham
Norfolk. 22 April: many ill at Evesham,
Worcs; and more deaths in Northumberland.
29 April: 10 dead, 40 ill at Corby,
Northants.

The peak for A/Victoria/75 (ie first
identified in Victoria, Australia in 1975)
seems to be over. I tried to tot up the
death toll from figures announced in our
clippings: over 100, maybe 200. According to the Daily Mail 29 June 1977, the
actual toll was about 1000 - a disconcerting discrepancy.

Sources: Daily Mail 8,23,25,26,28,30
March, 2,20,22 April 1977; D.Telegraph
26 March, 19,29 April 1977; D.Express
25,26 March 1977; Guardian 25,28,29 Mar
1977; Sunderland Echo 26 March, 18,21,
23 April 1977; Sunday Times 27 March 1977
Newcastle-upon-Tyne Journal 20,22,28
April, 2 May 1977; Hartlepool Mail 20,
22,25 April 1977 (Cr: Peter Rogerson,
Paul Screeton, Valerie Martin, P Hope-
Evans, Roger Sandell, Nigel Watson.)

Hmmm - immediately after typing the
above I go downstairs to see what's in
the second mail today...a heap of clippings from Ion Will, FT's roving clipster, on 'Red flu' in the UK. The present outbreak began at a USAF base at
Upper Heyford, Oxfordshire - it is a
version of the A1 virus resembling the
Russian epidemics of 1946-7, mild and
highly infectious, now officially designated A/USSR/77. The outbreak hits children and young people (a compensation
for the havoc among old folks earlier?)
who have no immunity - ie those not innoculated since 1958, its last appearance
in the UK. The USAF base began in mid-
Jan, hitting 300 children there. Soon
cases were reported in Oxford and Bath.
A TV news report on 25 Jan said that 700
pupils were affected at Oundle, near
Peterborough; nearly 1000 pupils at a
college in Norfolk; and several hundreds
in Somerset - and there's no sign of a
peak yet. Sunday Times 22 Jan 1977; D.
Mirror & D.Telegraph 24 Jan 1977; Guardian 26 Jan 1977 (Cr: Ion Will.)

More on A/influenza

Apart from a brief reference in FT18
we never recorded an outbreak of flu in
west New Guinea, killing 55 people, in
the aftermath of a quake there. NY Herald Tribune 25 Aug 1976 (Cr: Ion Will).

Early in 1977, Dr H Fukushima, head of
the Japanese National Health Institute,
warned the world of several new types of
influenza. From a study of captured migrating birds he found they carried 40
types of A/influenza virus, nine of
which were completely new. Animal-car-
ried viruses, he warned, can mutate into
forms which affect humans. Taiwan, China
Post 3 March 1977 (Cr: Ion Will.)

That same month, flu was raging in
Hungary with 860,000 people affected,
and 35,000 new cases just in the week
prior to the report. D.Telegraph 25
March 1977. According to other sources
it was the prototype of the present
A/USSR/77 strain. Read on...

The first we heard of the huge epidemic of 'Russian flu' was in late December
1977, when Russian doctors announced
controls to prevent the spread, and asked the World Influenza Center, in London,
to help identify it and develop a vaccine.
British doctors said "millions" in Russia
were affected and that it could hit Britain before a vaccine could be ready.

They were right. It appeared at the
USAF base, Upper Heyford, sometime in
mid-Jan (see above).

The papers for 30 Dec 1977 carried
confirmation of the Russian epidemic,
raging since the end of Nov 77; the
NYHT said that the flu had come from the
Soviet Far East, and was sweeping through all the major cities. The Guardian
5 Jan said optimistically that 26 millions were affected but they should be
better by the end of the week.

The flu seemed to spread rapidly - in
a few days it was reported taking hold
in Finland and Taiwan. At 22 Jan it was
firmly planted in Britain and the Philippines. At 24 Jan it was reported from
Israel, Switzerland and North America
(for which see below). D.Mirror 20 Dec
1977; D.Telegraph 30 Dec 1977, 5 & 24
Jan 1978; NY Herald Tribune 30 Dec 1977,
7 & 23 Jan 1978; Guardian 5 Jan 1978.
(Cr: Valerie Martin, Ion Will.)

FLU IN THE USA

Swine Flu

Early in 1976, about 500 soldiers at
Fort Dix, New Jersey, showed evidence of
contracting a variation of swine flu; 12
cases proved positive and 1 man died. It
awoke memories of a devastating influenza
epidemic in the USA that killed 450,000

Americans in 1918-19, related to a type of Spanish flu that killed millions worldwide in the same period. Dr David Spencer, director of the US Center for Disease Control (CDC), drafted a plan for a massive innoculation campaign based on a projection of ½million deaths - this we now know to be completely wrong. By the end of March 76, President Ford and Congress had been hoodwinked (in the opinion of many) into allocating $135 million for a vaccine programme. The virus grew too slowly by conventional methods so "to meet production deadlines" a civilian scientist undertook the lab. development of a man-made 'super-virus'.

By Oct 1976 it was clear something had gone horribly wrong - not only were there protests about the constitutional violations in rushing through a secret and hastily conceived plan to inject drugs into millions of people, and thus opening the way to possible future 'mind-control' methods, but there were serious doubts about the vaccine itself. According to the National Enquirer, which led a long campaign against the programme (see NE 12 Oct, 2 Nov 1976; 11 Jan, 22 Feb, 8 March 1977) the vaccine was given in doses so low as to be immunologically useless, and caused side-effects ranging from fainting, fever, hives, hypertension through to asthma and skin reactions. Worse still; it directly caused over 100 deaths and a rare form of paralysis called Guillain-Barre Syndrome, and some doctors were saying that it could trigger multiple sclerosis, Parkinson's disease, tendonitis and encephalitis. The programme was finally stopped on 16 Dec after 40 million people were innoculated. Top medical scientists were openly accusing the government of deceit to cover-up a grim hoax. The NE 22 Feb 77 reports at least 70 suits against the government for nearly $4 million, and 4 cases already in court for $13 million, plus up to 1200 cases in preparation, all claiming for damages. (We have so many sources of clippings on this subject that we haven't room for them all - they are on file here. Cr: Gary Abbott, Tom Adams, Ion Will.)

A classic irony came with the realization that in their panic the government scientists had overlooked a perfectly safe, tested and efficacious vaccine already on their shelves. NE 26 April 77.

Flu 1976/7

The real tragedy of the 1976/7 swine flu fiasco is that in spite of the CDC panic there had been just 1 death attributable to swine flu since Oct 1975, and its effect was to distract official att-

ention from the real killer, an A/Victoria strain, which claimed 7300 Americans over the same period. NE 2 Nov 1976.

Since early 1977 several strains of flu were pandemic in the US, but mainly A/Victoria and A/Texas (which is related to the former), A/Hongkong & B/Hongkong. The B/type hit the east coast from New England to the Gulf states and inland to Iowa & Michigan; the A/type mainly hit the southern states. This pattern soon dissolved as cases turned up everywhere.

Cynicism and resistance to flu innoculation was high in the wake of the swine flu blunder, and the only A/Victoria vaccine had been mixed with the swine flu vaccine which nobody now wanted. I have no figures for the tolls of these viruses in this period, but 11,000 died from A/Victoria alone the previous winter. NE 18 Jan 1977; Jacksonville, Florida, Times-Union 6,7,12,25 Feb, 26,30 March, 25 April 1977; Newsweek 21 Feb 1977 (Cr: Gary Abbott.)

The deaths and illnesses formed the background to yet another dramatic turn of events. Between 1 Jan and mid-March about 150 children across the afflicted states fell victims to the Reye Syndrome - a rare encephalitis-like complication of the central nervous system that usually attacks children after B/type flu or chicken pox, which causes their brains and livers to swell. We have reports of some Florida papers on the progress of six Jacksonville children - 4 died - and one boy in Kansas City, whose skull was opened to relieve the pressure on the brain; but we know nothing about the

I know it isn't really known where the PANDEMIC strains of the VIRUS originate....

...but you CAN't judge Edmund's condition by looking at TEA LEAVES....

Mind you, there always has been an element of MAGIC attached to INFLUENZA... the word comes from the Italian, meaning the 'influence' of the stars..

Actually, I'm not feeling very well, MYSELF...

Strange that this should appear in the Guardian (23 Jan 1978, Cr: Ion Will) so soon after Hoyle's star-plagues article (see back to p17)...or maybe not! The fact is that we can pinpoint the area of origin of a plague, but we have no idea at all of where the virus came from in the first place. Interestingly, we remember the cranky allegations that Legion Fever was caused by UFOs - FT20/13.

national figures. Florida Times-Union 15 Feb, 1,3,4,8,12,14,19 March, 27 April 1977; Carlisle, Penn, Evening Sentinel 26 Feb 1977 (Cr: Gary Abbott, L Arnold.)

Lastly, at the present time, as the Russian A/type flu begins to grip across the USA - amid ghastly winter conditions, we notice - "experts" were calling for a vaccine programme to get under way in case the fairly predictable epidemic comes between Feb and April. Forgive our doubletake, but isn't this where we came in...? NY Herald Tribune 14 Jan 1978; D.Telegraph 24 Jan 1978 (Cr: Ion Will.)

LEGIONNAIRE'S DISEASE
There have been a few developments since our write-up (in FT20/10-13) of the original outbreak in Philadelphia, in July/Aug 1976, which cost the lives of 29 people visiting a convention.

Bug Identified
The CDC continued its search for the agents of the disease. There were several attempts to link it to a metal-toxin - nickel carbonyl - but these remained fairly inconclusive. There was a good deal of cynicism, in view of the swine flu debacle, and the CDC were accused of trying to grab some good press by trying to nail the LF cause. NE 8 March 1977; Guardian 30 May 1977; Spotlight, USA, 5 Sept 1977 (Cr: P Rogerson, P Hope-Evans, Tom Adams.)

The metal-toxin theory was eclipsed by another anouncement (which also drew the same criticism) that a long, thin bacterium had been isolated by Dr JE McDade of the CDC, who decided to have a second look at some old path-specimens before discarding them. Cross checking in CDC records showed the same bacterium was responsible for 2 previously unidentified outbreaks in 1968, in Washington and Pontiac, MI, in which hundreds were ill and 16 died.

About the same time the bacterium was caught, an LF case in St Mary's, Penn, was successfully treated with two anti-biotics, gentamicin and erythromycin. By July 77, the CDC were confident that at last they had the bug and the treatment ...and just in time, because from June new cases came thick and fast... Time 31 Jan 1977; Jacksonville, Florida, Times-Union 16,26 March, 17 July 1977; Newsweek 31 Jan 1977; Family Weekly, USA, 7 Aug 1977; New Scientist 15 Sept 1977; Springfield, Mo, Sunday News & Leader 16 Oct 1977 (Cr: Tom Adams, Gary Abbott)

New Cases
Between the Philadelphia outbreak and the end of October 1977 there were 66 cases of Legion Fever (LF) in 19 US states, with 24 dead - the worst hit was Vermont in Aug 77 with 13 dead - these are positive identifications only. For cases, see Big Spring, Tx, Herald 19 June 1977; Daily Oklahoman 17 June 1977; Corpus Christi, Tx, Caller & Miami, Florida, Herald both 9 July 1977; Alamosa, Col, Valley Courier 10 Aug 1977; Bangkok Post 6 Sept 1977; D.Telegraph 7 Sept 1977; Daily News, & Evening Bulletin both of Philadelphia, Penn, 10 Sept 1977; Dallas, Tx, Morning News 20 Sept 1977; San Angelo Tx, Standard 23 Sept 1977; Time, Asia ed, 17 Oct 1977; The Star, Tx, 25 Oct 1977 (Cr: Thomas R Adams, Ion Will, Gary Abbott, R White). NB: these figures are up to late Oct 77 only and take no account of any cases or deaths since then; or deaths suspected, but not proved to be Legion Fever.

LF in Spain & UK
From June 1977 there were several cases of LF in England - but as the precise sequence of events is hard to determine at this distance, we'll give them in context. It seems that a Glasgow doctor, puzzling over the mystery death of a patient after a holiday at the Hotel Rio Park, Benidorm, Spain, thought the symptoms were similar to a case in 1973 when 3 tourists returned to Glasgow gravely ill after staying at the very same hotel. Samples and details of all four cases were sent to the CDC, who confirmed Legion Fever. Since then 11 cases (4 deaths) have been reported in Nottingham, and others in Manchester - These have no connexion with Benidorm. In a TV documentary ('Tonight', BBC1 13 Dec 1977) doctors confessed that although they can now identify and treat the disease they still don't know where it comes from or why it is so sporadic. South China Morning Post 10 Oct 1977; D.Mail & Sun both 11 Nov 1977; D.Telegraph 12 Nov 1977; Sunday Times 13 Nov 1977 (Colin Johnson, Valerie Martim.)

Sometime in November an alcoholic Scotsman died of LF in a London hospital after failing to respond to Erythromycin and other antibiotics. Doctors put the incubation period of LF at about a week and the man had been in London during that time and so "must" have caught LF somewhere in London. Panic fears of an epidemic quickly evaporated, and the doctors were left with the mystery of why no other cases were being reported anywhere in England. London Evening Standard 23 Dec 1977; Times, D.Express, & Guardian all 24 Dec 1977 (Cr: Ion Will, CR Mather.)

MISCELLANEOUS EXOTICS

Burkitt's lymphoma - this form of cancer, known in Africa and New Guinea but rare in N America, killed a boy in 1976, at Winchester, Virginia. In 1971 2 boys similarly died in the same area. How they contracted the disease is a mystery. _Modern People_, USA, 12 Sept 1976 (Cr: Ron Dobbins/cf _RBB_ 6.)

Anthrax - on quake-torn Sumbawa Island, 8 farmers die after eating infected meat. The measles is plaguing Lombok at the same time. _Bangkok Post_ 31 Aug 1977 (IW)

Rocky Mountain spotted fever - on 22 Feb, 2 men who worked for the CDC - one delivered, the other a maintenance man - came down almost simultaneously with an unidentified flu-like fever. They died on 28 Feb. It's ironic that this should happen on the CDC's doorstep while the swine flu fiasco was peaking. The illness was not identified until later in March. Florida, _Times-Union_ 2,3,11 March 1977; Taiwan, _China Post_ 3 March 1977; _Newsweek_ 7 March 1977 (Cr: G Abbott, I Will

Thalassaemia - a blood disease, rare in the UK, but becoming more common among immigrant groups. Questions asked in the Commons. _D.Telegraph_ 29 March '77.

Crohn's disease - an intestine affliction that remains "one of medicine's unsolved mysteries" is on the increase, say doctors. _Times_ 9 April 1977 (P H-E).

Meningoencephalitis - 2 cases of very rare primary amoebic meningoencephalitis found in USA (North Carolina & Texas). Harrisburg, Penn, _Evening News_ 18 Oct 1977 (Cr: Larry Arnold.)

Malaria and other tropical diseases have increased "20-fold" in the UK over the last decade, top scientist tells annual meeting of Pharmaceutical Society. _D.Telegraph_ 13 Sept 1977 (Cr: V Martin.)

Pneumonia - a new strain of antibiotic resistant pneumonia has emerged in South Africa. Bangkok, _Nation Review_ 4 Sept 1977 (Cr: Ion Will.)

Weil's disease, carried by rats, has killed a farmer at Rockbourne, Hants. Between 1966-1973 there were only 220 cases (37 deaths) of this rare disease. _D.Telegraph_ 6 Jan 1978 (Cr: V Martin.)

'Lyme disease' - 60 people at Old Lyme and East Haddam, Connecticut, have been crippled by a baffling form of severe rheumatoid arthritis that has defied attempts to trace its origin. _The Star_ USA, 25 Jan 1977 (Cr: Larry Arnold.)

'Balaqbala! the local name for an unidentified disease causing blood clots, which has killed 26 people in the north Moluccas island district of Gane. _South China Morning Post_ 1 Nov 1977; _Rising Nepal_ 2 Nov 1977 (Cr: Colin Johnson, Ion Will.)

Lassa Fever & Marburg Disease

Lassa fever, one of the world's deadliest infectious diseases, and endemic in Africa, caused several scares in the UK, Australia and Canada, mainly among people returning from Africa, in 1976. For local UK scares, which lasted well into 1977, see Wolverhampton _Express & Star_ 5 Aug 1976; _D.Mail_ 23,25 April 1977; _S.Times_, & _S.Mirror_ both 24 April 1977; _D.Mirror_ 10 June 1977; _D.Telegraph_ 3 Sept 1977 (Cr: P Hope-Evans,) Fortunately there were no positive cases, but the spotlight had been focussed on the possibility of a European lassa fever epidemic by another deadly African scourge, the Marburg disease.

The epidemic covered southern Sudan & northern Zaire, killing over 300 with possibly thousands ill. There is no vaccine. There seems to be some difference of opinion as to whether it is the Marburg virus or a related one (_Arizona Republic_ 15 Oct 1976; _New Scientist_ 28 Oct 1976; Cr Ron Dobbins/ _RBB_ 8), but either could be carried by the green monkey (Aethiops cerecopithecus), It was green monkey organs, imported from Uganda, that caused 30 cases (3 deaths) among laboratory staff in West Germany in 1967. The virus was quickly identified and named after the lab at Marburg. Prior to the 1976 epidemic, the only other known cases were 2 (1 died) in Johannesburg in March 1975 - but doctors believe that a number of East Africa's unidentified epidemics may have been Marburg disease. Before the current epidemic was identified, Belgian officials thought it might have been its close relation, Lassa fever, and from early October 1976 stringent controls were imposed on all planes from Africa, including spraying. England too clamped down and individuals who had been in the plague-area found themselves in 3 weeks isolation. _Times_ 15 Oct 1976; _S.Times_ 10 Oct 1976; Newport News, Va, _D.Press_ 7 Oct 1976; _South China Morning Post_ 30 Oct 1976 (Cr: Ion Will, Gary Abbott.)

Samples of the Marburg virus had been sent to the 3 top disease reserch centers, CDC, one in Belgium, and Porton Down in Wiltshire. A _BBC2_ TV documentary on the work of Porton Down, which mentioned Lassa and Marburg fever, was aired on the night of 11 Nov 1976. By a shocking coincidence the news the next morning said that Geoffrey Platt, working at the research center on the Marburg virus, had slipped with his hypodermic full of the germs and punctured his rubber glove. Incredibly he was merely sent home...but later on put in isolation with 44 of his contacts and a 26-strong medical team in a hastily evacuated London hospital. He seems to have been cured with the aid of 'interferon' an experimental extract of human cells also being studied at Porton Down. <u>D.Mirror</u> 16,20 Nov 1976; <u>New Scientist</u> 18 Nov 1976; <u>S.Times</u>, & <u>Observer</u> both 21 Nov 1976.

Our latest note is that a new Marburg epidemic was in progress in the Western province of Kenya, near Lake Victoria. <u>Bangkok World</u> 11 March 1977 (Cr: I Will.)

*** This extensive list of modern scourges is far from complete - we have as many again mystery illnesses of various kinds, including the "mass hysteria" kind...but I think we'd better leave that til next time. ***   RJMR

Having taken potshots at the errors of a few other authors, it would quite hypocritical for me to ignore my own - so this is an opportunity to correct a few mistakes in <u>Phenomena</u> (T&H, London 1977; Pantheon, NY 1977). John Michell and I agree that the book should stand as a record of our thought at that time - thought which continues to develop - so I will confine myself to errors of fact.

Firstly: the three corrections given in <u>FT23</u>/38 have been incorporated into the second printing of the UK large format paperback (available through FT - see panel on p52).

Polaroid 'Ghost Image'

Secondly: we wish to thank the photographer, DJ Girling, of Maidstone, Kent, who took the trouble to correct our impression that Polaroid films could not be exposed more than once. In <u>Phenomena</u> (p57 c3) we quote a case from Peter Haining's <u>Ghosts: The Illustrated History</u> (Sidgwick & Jackson, London 1975, p118-9) where 3 different images of Bill Watkins appeared on a Polaroid snap taken by his older brother Sam - later, according to Haining, Bill was killed standing in the same spot & in the same pose figured in the snap. Haining says firmly: "It is impossible to triple expose a polaroid film..." Although Haining gave no source for this case, nor any other clue to its authenticity, we decided to use it in <u>Phenomena</u>. We ought to have qualified it, but didn't. Mr Girling sent us several examples of, not double or triple exposure but, <u>quadruple exposure</u>, pointing out that cameras can indeed appear to lie. Lacking the information about the origin of the Sam Watkins photo we can take the matter no further; but we decide to keep the case in any future edition, but alter the text to allow for the new data, and emphasising the other point of interest, that the photo, hoax or not, appeared to prefigure a genuine tragedy.

The 'Bristol Mirage'

Thirdly: we have the problem of the alleged photo of a mirage of Bristol taken in Alaska, in 1887, by the pioneer Willoughby (see <u>Phenomena</u> p62 c3 & p63). Again we took a source on reasonable trust and seem to have stumbled into an intriguing mystery. The <u>Western Daily Press</u>, published in Bristol, thought the story of Willoughby's picture would make a good feature - which was duly written by their Deputy Features Editor, Chris Mosey, in the 7 Dec 1977 edition. Mosey went to see the well-known Bristol historian, Reece Winstone, and showed him the Bristol-mirage photo from our book. This photo, incidentally, is the one from Miner Bruce's <u>Alaska</u> (1900); Bruce having it straight from Willoughby.

Mr Reece Winstone immediately recognised the distinctive architecture of Bristol of the late 19th century - he even took Mosey to the top of Brandon Hill and identified nearly every feature in the photo and its corresponding reality. (You'll have to read the <u>WDP</u> article for the complete listing of features and buildings.) Judging by the present and missing features in the photo, Winstone dates the photo as between 1886-1897...and suggests that there was time for Willoughby, or Miner Bruce, to have got a contemporary photo of Bristol and touted it as a photo of the mirage of Bristol. He further points out that Miner Bruce's photo shows Bristol from Brandon Hill all right, but it is reversed.

Indeed Fort (Books p492) refers to Alexander Badlam's Wonders of Alaska, pointing out that he also prints a copy of Willoughby's photo, but that it is reversed compared to Bruce's. Whose was supposed to be the correct version we shall never know, and the question remains academic in the light of the greater question of whether they were in fact photos of a mirage. That mirages can be photographed is not in doubt - see Scientific American Jan 1976 pp102-111 for some good examples...and under extremely rare conditions one could imagine some degree of inversion or transposition occurring. Basically the dilemma is this: if the photos are of a genuine mirage, then the mirage city is remarkably like Bristol, and we have a major optical /meteorological problem to solve. The corollary is that if the mirage is truly one of Bristol, then, transposed or not, it would have been possible to photograph it, and the photo would have been not unlike the one before us.

Now because of the unlikelyhood or rarity of Bristol being seen in the skies of Alaska, according to modern theory, people would rather believe that Willoughby, or Bruce, concocted the picture... and this plunges into an argument about the nature of proof or evidence. Fort, and the sources he cites, give ample evidence of a tradition of exotic alien cityscapes seen in the sky over Alaska. Only with the arrival of those who had known Bristol could the comparison and identification be made. Willoughby thought it was a mirage of Bristol. One of Fort's sources (Books p491) quotes others as thinking it could have been Toronto, Montreal, or Peking - and this was in 1897, a full 10 years after Willoughby claimed it was Bristol. It seems reasonable that Willoughby's belief was genuine enough, and he was far too busy to perpetrate a fairly pointless hoax. Fort, citing Badlam and others, suggests that someone could have sold Willoughby some dry photographic plates pre-exposed to a Bristol scene. May I suggest another possibility based on Willoughby's honesty - that he had indeed several times seen the mirage he was convinced was Bristol, so convinced in fact that he could show round a genuine scene of the city to point out its similarities. If this was done enough he could easily slip into believing the photo was of the mirage itself; equally it is possible that Bruce made the error

Willoughby's 'Bristol' (below) compared with its contemporary original (right. Copyright: R Winstone), one of 26 period photos in Reece Winstone's Bristol in the 1880s, and reproduced by kind permission. Readers are invited to send for his prospectus of privately printed books on Bristol history, to: 23 Hyland Grove, Henbury Hill, Bristol 9.

of linking the photo with the mirage.
Here is a first class project for some
enterprizing researcher to disentangle.
And until it is settled beyond question
we're reasonably happy about presenting
Willoughby's opinion and photo.

Maximilian's Meteorite

Fourthly: at the end of the first para,
column 1, p16, Phenomena, the place and
date of Maximilian's "meteorite" should
be corrected to Ensisheim, in Alsace,
7 November 1492 (according to Greg's
catalogue, Rept BA 1860, p52.)

The Oliver Thomas 'Vanishing'

Lastly: several people have expressed
their surprise that we should include
one of the more notorious disappearance
stories, that of the boy Oliver Thomas
in 1909, on the authority of Brad
Steiger - especially as we had helped
expose the equally notorious vanishing
of David Lang (see FT18/6 and Robert
Schadewald's follow-up in Fate Dec 1977).
Our interest in the Oliver Thomas story
was in the way it contained all the
elements of 'phenomenal reality' that
make a story meaningful in a mythological and psychological sense - and
it is for this reason we wish to keep it
in the book. We point out that we did
indeed qualify this inclusion by saying
that there are no references to original
sources.

We knew that, as fact, the Oliver Thomas
story was suspect, but until recently we
didn't know just how much. Informally
we've heard that Steiger probably got
the story from one of John Macklin's
books - which gives it the kiss of death
as Macklin is notorious for fictional-
ising events and rarely giving sources.
Kevin Randle, writing in the APRO Bulletin 25:3, Sept 1976, identifies the
story as a rewritten version of the
disappearance of Oliver Lerch mentioned
by John Keel, Otto Binder and Morris
Jessup, who in turn got the story from
FATE Sept 1950. Loren Gross (APRO Bulletin Nov 1976) shows that Harold T Wilkins tried to investigate the story in
1932 but could discover nothing to substantiate it. Randle summarizes the
story elements (most of them contradictory) like this: "Oliver Lerch/Larch/-
Thomas, aged either 11 or 20, disappeared from either South Bend, Indiana,
or Rhayader, Wales, on either Christmas
Eve 1889, Christmas Day 1889, Christmas
Eve 1890 or 1909. He got either 50ft,
75ft or 225ft before 'They got him.'"
Wilkins dates the South Bend incident as
Christmas Eve 1900. I can only add that
I have searched the Brecon County Times
which covers the Rhyader valley area for
December 1909 and January 1910 and
found no mention of an Oliver Thomas
vanishing mysteriously at all. Our

cont on p46/

Geophysical Curiosities

SUBSIDENCES.

The causes of subsidences are usually
easily explainable (or surmiseable
after the event)...however, when we
find a sudden rash of subsidences,
as in the summer of 77, we start to
become interested. And so, a brief
round up from our 'holes in the
ground' file...

Toledo, Ohio: 1976. A letter to
The Blade (Toledo) 28 Sept 76, from
an anonymous woman, complains of a
hole in her backyard which had been
growing deeper for almost a year.
A city inspector surmised the cause
as being a spring, an underground
branch of the Delaware Creek or an
ancient home-made sewer; although
the city charts apparently contain
no evidence of anything. It was on
private property, so it wasn't his
problem. End of story. (Cr: Dave
Fideler).

Welwyn Garden City, Herts: 4 Apr
77. The (London) Evening News (Same
date) reports a hole big enough to
swallow a car appearing in a road
on a housing estate. The hole, 20
feet deep and said to be caused by
underground streams, stretched nearly the whole width of the road.

Aston, Birmingham: 2 May 77. 30yr
old housewife Vivian Flynn was hanging out her washing when the gro-
und gave way beneath her and she
fell into a 12-foot-deep hole. She
managed to cling to the edge until
a neighbour pulled her clear, and
she was taken to hospital with cuts,
bruises and shock. The hole was
caused by council engineers building a sewer tunnel under the garden.
(Daily Mirror, 3 May 77)

Munich, Germany: 1 July 77. Rain
water getting into a drilling for a
subway was blamed for a subsidence
in the road beneath a parked car.

The car had to be winched out of
the hole by firemen. (Daily Telegraph, 2 July 77)

Grays, Essex: 24 July 77. A large
hole appeared in the back garden of
Mr David Brightman's house in Lodge
Lane. It started being 6ft wide,
20ft deep, but then grew in the
following couple of days to, by
some accounts, 12ft wide, 30-40ft
deep, and a horizontal tunnel appeared at the bottom. The area is
known as the Daneholes (ie: deneholes) because of a series of tunnels
and holes cut in the chalk, believed
to be ancient mine-workings...and
there have been earlier subsidences
in the area. A council official
said the subsidence had been caused
by the washing away of a chalk und-
erlayer by heavy rain. (D.Mirror,
Sun, Evening News, 25 July 77. D.
Telegraph, 26 July 77. Cr: J Michell)

Pontardulais, W. Glamorgan: 25
July 77: A section of the M4 motorway began to subside, 12 weeks
after the road opened. Cause: underground working on a new coal seam.
Effect: the subsidence was expected
to spread over a 300yd stretch in
the following 2 months. One wonders
if motorway planners check anything
before they start work...(D. Teleg.
26 July 77)

Dudley Zoo, W. Midlands: 16 Nov 77
We have only the briefest details:
a 20ft wide, 50ft deep hole appeared
in the zoo. We suspect that the
animals were tunneling out, but
there are no records of any escapes!
(D. Telegraph, 17 Nov 77).

Tividale, W Midlands: 21 Nov 77.
John Stone was driving his van along the New Birmingham Road when the
road began to give way beneath him.
He managed to accelerate clear, and

the hole grew to be 30ft wide and 450ft deep. Council officials believe it to be the airshaft of a mine closed many years ago. (Sun, 22 Nov 77. Cr: Paul Hudson, IAN H. LAWES.)

ICE-HOLES.

Some may feel that this material belongs more properly in the 'falls' section, as that is the assumed cause for most appearances of holes in ice. However, as rarely is anything found that might have fallen, we prefer to reserve judgement, and classify merely by the event itself.

Lake Uppramen, central Sweden: 1968. Nearby villagers saw, heard and felt nothing; but suddenly a huge hole appeared in the 3ft thick ice on the lake. Triangular in shape, 60ft by 90ft, there seemed to be no explanation: a plane crash was discounted on the grounds that there were no traces round the hole, only thrown-up blocks of ice, an indication, according to Colonel Curt Hermansson who led the investigation, that something incredibly powerful had gone into the lake. A meteorite was discounted on the grounds that the hole was too big. A frogman found nothing. We wish we had more details of this tantalising case, but at the moment we can only find an undated clipping from the D. Mirror, 1968 (Cr: I Bunn). Anyone help?

Upper Scott Lake, Allegan Co., Michigan: 1st Jan 1970. 15 minutes after the New Year began, a mystery explosion shook the YMCA Camp Sears on the shores of the lake. There was damage to the health centre and the dining lodge, several hundred yards apart: both picture windows and storm windows destroyed, light fittings damaged, and three wooden shutters looked as if they had been cut to ribbons with an axe. The shockwaves were felt up to 4 miles away.

Next morning a large hole was discovered in the lake ice, 200yds from shore. The ice was 6-8 inches thick, the hole was 40ft across, and chunks of ice had been blown 100ft from the hole. Another oddity was the 3ft hole found 35ft from shore, through which mud and 'seaweed' had oozed to form a mound 2ft high. By afternoon, only muddy water remained. The blast was likened to a 1000lb bomb, and there were reports of an airplane being heard overhead. Deputies were working on the idea that the Lake had been dynam-ited, but a local said the explosion would have required at least 25 sticks. It seems no one went down to have a look in the Lake. (Grand Rapids (Mich) Press, 4 Jan 1970. Cr: Dave Fideler, who will be discussing the case further in Anomaly Research Bulletin).

Wakefield, New Hampshire: 10 Jan 77. The case of "McCarthy's Pond" has already been covered in INFO Journal 22 (p14) and Res Bureaux Bulletin 12 (p6), so we give only a brief outline here for the sake of completeness, referring the interested to the above periodicals for more information.

William McCarthy found that part of the ice on his pond had melted, leaving a hole 3ft square in ice variously reported as 15-36in thick. It was still snowing when McCarthy discovered this, and poking the hole with a stick he saw a flat black object, 2ft square, with a bubble-like protuberance. There was also a second hole in the 50ft diameter pond, linked to the first by a crack. In a few hours, all the ice melted.

McCarthy reported the event, and his farm was soon aswarm with police, officials, experts, reporters and sightseers. Then reports conflict: the pond was said to have an abnormally high radiation reading, which had disappeared 12 hours later. Something was reported to have been taken out of the pond: later a statement was issued saying that the object was not a space ship. When that didn't quell the curiosity, the whole thing was flatly denied, and spokesmen admitted to being under a 'gag' order. Last we heard, McCarthy was going to defiantly dig up the whole pond when the spring thaw came, and find the object he'd been told wasn't there. As we've heard nothing since, we assume that this is one hole that nobody got to the bottom of... (Grand Rapids (Mich) Press, 13, 14 Jan 77, San Antonio Sight, 13 Jan, San Antonio Express, Hong Kong Standard, 14 Jan, D.Mail, 15 Jan, S China Morning Post, Dallas Morning Post, 16 Jan 77. Cr: T R Adams, D Fideler, P Hope-Evans, Ion Will).

SM

Cover: 'Vision of the Valley of Dry Bones' by Gustave Dore. (FPL)

UFOs, CLOUDS & PSEUDO-PLANES

by J. B. Delair.

Although a few writers, such as Jessup [1] and the Lorenzens [2], have briefly discussed those clouds which, though externally resembling natural clouds, behave quite unlike ordinary clouds, and others — notably Valee [3] — have reviewed these cases involving cigar-shaped clouds associated with or created by cigar-shaped ufos, almost all other ufologists have paid scant attention to them. Nevertheless, if we are ever to perceive the true magnitude of the ufo phenomenon and the degree to which it sometimes manifests itself in almost undetectable guises, these aberrant 'clouds' cannot be ignored and actually reveal the extent of the great ufo problem in several specific but as yet little-studied areas. This paper concentrates on selected reports featuring aberrant 'clouds' and their various demonstrable connections with the ufo phenomenon.

The following twenty-five cases, arranged chronologically, are typical of the many known events in this category.

1. In 1794, a strangely *luminous* cloud passed over Sienna, in Italy, and jettisoned a number of stones. All the stones were seen to fall from this one cloud [4].

2. During the afternoon of April 26th, 1812, a rapidly moving fiery globe of great brilliancy passed over the neighbourhood of L'Aigle, in Normandy, France, and was followed in a few seconds by a violent explosion that *lasted five or six minutes*, and which was heard for 30 leagues in all directions. Three or four loud reports like those of cannons were heard and then succeeded by noises resembling musketry fire (i.e. a crackling sound), after which a dreadful rumbling occurred like the beating of a drum.

   These noises emanated from a small *rectangular* cloud, of which the longest side lay along an east-to-west alignment. The cloud remained motionless throughout the period of these detonations and noises, and was at so great an altitude that the inhabitants of two hamlets a league apart saw it directly overhead. At the time the air was calm and the sky serene except for a few scattered clouds. A multitude of stones then fell, amidst a hissing sound, from the rectangular cloud at the time of the explosions, some of them being afterwards collected and identified as 'aerolites' or 'meteorites' [5].

3. At 11.00 am on September 5th, 1814, when a stiff breeze was blowing despite a clear sky, there suddenly appeared at a great height to the NW of Agen, France, a slow moving sombre white cloud having a greyish centre and apparently only a few feet in diameter. It was

perfectly round in shape. After a short while it became completely stationary (despite the breeze) and remained so until a few minutes before mid-day, when it suddenly sped off to the south, revolving on its own axis as it did so, and began emitting rumbling sounds and thunderous noises culminating in an explosion. At the moment of detonation, the cloud discharged a shower of stones — some of considerable size — from two elongated chord-like features that formed simultaneously. After this, the cloud stopped again and slowly faded away.

   The explosion was heard loudly at Montpezat, Temple, Castel-moron, and Montclar, and more distantly at Mezin, Basas, Condon, and St. Macaire. The event understandably terrified many of the local populace [6; 7; and 8].

4. Interestingly, little more than a year elapsed before a markedly similar event occurred, this time at 8.30 am on October 3rd, 1815, at Chassigny, SE. of Langres, also in France. There, in the NE. quadrant of the sky, musketry-like sounds proceeded from a strange grey cloud that had *appeared* in an otherwise clear and serene sky. Shortly afterwards, a stone, later identified as a meteorite, fell from the cloud to Earth. An account of this event was communicated by a M. Pistollet to M. Virey, who published it the following year [9; 10].

   This event should also be compared with some previous falls of stones from unusual clouds as discussed by Marcel de Serres in 1814 [11], and also with the next event.

5. On August 7th, 1823, at approximately 5.00 pm, a stone fell at Noblesville, Indiana, USA, from a small whitish cloud, apparently some 40 feet *square*. This also had appeared near the zenith in a perfectly serene and calm day. Again, a crackling noise like that of musketry came from the cloud, which performed a curious *spiralling motion* downwards just before the stone was discharged from it [12].

6. At 4.55 am. on December 17th, 1852, a *triangular* cloud with a long tail and a dull *red* nucleus, in size about half the apparent diameter of the Moon, appeared during a storm near Dover, Kent. It remained visible for 13 minutes, during which time it increased in size, until an explosion occurred within it causing its dissipation [13].

7. In 1881, the Astronomer Royal of Scotland vacationed at Funchal, in the Madeira Islands. One afternoon he saw a strange isolated cloud forming at a great altitude over the bay by which Funchal stands. This cloud remained awesomely motionless, in the same place, for hours.

Under it a similar but large cloud materialized, then a third, a fourth, and a fifth — all stationary and on the *same vertical axis*. All the clouds maintained their position until sunset until, with the onset of darkness, disappeared in the *reverse order* of their formation. The highest cloud remained visible in striking colours until long after sunset, until 10.00 pm in fact, testimony of its very great height. This singular formation was also observed from ships almost 150 miles distant from Funchal, again confirming the immense altitude and size of the clouds [14].

8   At 6.05 pm on Friday, November 17th, 1882, many persons watched a well-defined, brilliantly white *spindle-shaped* cloudy body move across the sky from E. to SSW. in less than one minute. One observer, Thomas G. Elger, estimated the passage as being *only 6 seconds* in duration. The same body was also seen by Stephen H. Saxby at Clevedon, and was described by another, John L. Dobson, as resembling a cloudy *fish-torpedo* having a mottled appearance. Elger, on the other hand, reported it having a lenticular shape and being of a bright greenish-white hue [15].

9   Almost a year later, on October 16th, 1882, at Montussan, Gironde, in France, a thick cloud accompanied by rain and a violent wind, *appeared* and was seemingly composed of a white *woolly substance* in lumps. Each lump was about the size of a man's fist. Many of these fell to earth, were collected, and subsequently examined. The substance was found to be fibrous and had been *burnt;* it could not, however, be identified [16].

10   On August 9th, 1892, a very peculiar fast-moving yellow cloud appeared over Paderborn, in Germany, and discharged not only torrential rain but hundreds of living pond mussels of the species *Anodonta anatina* as well [17].

11   Closer to our own era we find equally perplexing reports about unusual cloudy bodies, as, for example, that seen on August 7th, 1961, when a cigar-shaped cloud was seen to release 20 or more small objects as it passed over Heaton Moor, Stockport, Greater Manchester [18].

12   At 5.30 pm October 14th, 1961, Mr and Mrs Burson, of Sunset, Utah, USA, watched,with two other residents, two weird objects they described as 'puffy daubs of cotton' pass over that locality in an easterly direction. These bodies were joined together by 'long stringy stuff', and were followed at a short interval by a pair of smooth disc-shaped objects.

The following day two more 'puffy' objects passed over the same locality at high speed in the same direction [19].

13   Mr F. Burrows of Manchester, together with another witness, saw an unusual cloud formation one night in November 1961, positioned to the left of the Moon as seen from his vantage point. A sword-like object was visible in the middle of this cloud, and a moving silvery object resembling a submarine — about 3 inches long at arm's length — emerged from the sword's hilt. After approximately 35 minutes, this object and the cloud formation disappeared into the darkness. Later on, a similar though otherwise smaller submarine-shaped object was seen travelling across the sky on another course [20].

14   On or about November 10th, 1961, a strange dark-grey cloud passed over Vukovar, in Croatia, Yugoslavia, and caused not only the local radio-station to black-out, but some sodium lamps stored on a shelf to mysteriously start glowing [21].

15   Shortly before May 1965, a lady holidaying at a cliff-top house near Sydney, New South Wales, watched a beautiful stationary pink cloud from 5.30 to 6.00 pm one evening. At 7.00 pm, when she looked again, the witness was astounded to see the cloud begin to move

from its position towards the rocks at the base of the cliff. As the cloud came nearer and descended below the witness's eye-level, she was able to look down into it and was amazed to see that it contained a round snow-white object having a base tapering to a point about 3 feet wide. It was emitting grey-coloured steam from vents round its outer edge, and this, thoroughly enveloping all but the uppermost portion of the object, soon turned pink and was in fact the substance of the 'cloud'.

A noise like that of a high-powered, well-cared-for-engine was heard, and, as the object descended still further, a shining ladder was lowered from a hatchway on its underside. A manlike occupant then climbed down the ladder and sat on one of its rungs, from which position he shone a strong beam of light into the sea below — as if looking for something. Shortly after this, a brilliant pink flare went up farther out at sea, and almost immediately the ladder, with the occupant still on it, was retracted into the object which then sped off in the direction of the flare. The witness also discerned a long shape in the water approximately where the flare had been released. When the ufo reached this object, both it and the elongated shape disappeared in a 'vivid pink flash' *beneath* the sea [22].

16   One evening in April 1966, Miss Susan Everett saw several white 'fluffy balls' pass across the sky near Battlesbury, Wiltshire, at no great height above the ground. They have never been satisfactorily explained, but bear comparison with the essentially similar objects observed five years earlier over Sunset, Utah (see case 13) [23].

17   Strangely manoeuvring pink clouds suggest a discernible pattern within these many extraordinary events, for another was seen about 11.00 pm on September 12th, 1967, over Meir, Stoke-on-Trent, Staffordshire. As with the aforecited 'clouds', this, too, was never adequately identified [24].

18   Numerous people reported watching a markedly circular cloud exhibiting very odd behaviour from many places in the Republic of South Africa — including Vryburg, Bloemfontein, Heilbron, Stilfontein, near Jagersfontein, Thabazimbi, Bethlehem, Brandfort, and Abrahamskraal — on July 6th, 1968. That this cloud was visible from so many widely sundered localities (Vryburg, Bethlehem, Jagersfontein, and Stilfontein are all over 100 miles apart) means that it was of gigantic size and its manoeuvres correspondingly enormous at a great altitude [25].

19   On February 3rd, 1969, unusual noises emanated from two odd-looking clouds over Jacksonville, Florida, USA, Among the hundreds of persons who reported the clouds to chief-of-police James Alford, one described the sounds as like someone rattling a hug sheet of sellophone, while another compared them to a 'giant walking on pebbles'. Police-captain Harold Ryan was instructed to follow the first cloud, but, although he did so for a short while, the cloud then abruptly vanished. Shortly afterwards a second crackling cloud appeared, but, when chased by Ryan in his car, it too suddenly disappeared. The noises proceeding from these clouds compare favourably with those described in cases 2 and 5) [26].

20   A distinctly strange formation of eight orange clouds was watched at 5.25 am. on August 15th, 1969, by military personnel at Kolka, some 60 miles S. of Myllykoski, in Finland. The clouds maintained regimental precision as they moved steadily across the sky, and were still proceeding in unison as they disappeared over the horizon [27].

21   Finland again hosted the next case, which occurred on January 7th, 1970, when, at 3.45 pm that day, ski-

enthusiasts Aarno Heinonen and Esko Viljo saw, near Imjarvi, a very bright *luminous* grey-red cloud in an otherwise cloudless sky. There was also no wind. Soundlessly, the cloud changed course towards the two startled men and began to lose altitude. After a short while, a humming noise was heard, the cloud began to pulsate, and it descended to about 50 feet above ground-level. At that point, a shiny grey metallic-looking round object with a flat base could be seen inside the cloud, which continued to descend until it stopped about 10 feet above the ground.

The object then tilted towards the witnesses, and disgorged a very slender man-like entity approximately 3 feet tall. This being pointed a black box at the two men, from which luminous sparks or short rods of light floated outwards. These were coloured red, violet, and geeen, but although some of them struck Heinonen they did him no harm. Finally, the object and the entity became enveloped in thick mist or fog that, upon subsequent dissipation, revealed no trace of the object or its strange occupant. Understandably, both eyewitnesses were greatly shocked by their experience and later required medical treatment [28].

22   Mr and Mrs W. Hamilton's farmhouse in McLain, Mississippi, USA, was severely damaged by a ball of 'smoke' that *suddenly* appeared out of a cloudless sky at 2.30 pm. on April 12th, 1971. It was accompanied by a strange noise and caused pots and pans in a kitchen to rattle, three two-by-four planks to fall out of a wall, the total demolition of another wall, and the porch roof to be blown some 500 feet away. A small outside wash-house was also torn up and part of an adjacent barn was destroyed. The 'smoke' was also seen by nearby mill workers, one of whom reported that a closely similar incident had occurred at her home the week previously. Investigators declared that sonic booms and tornadoes were not responsible since they did not fit the facts [29].

23   1971 seems to have been a good year for 'flying smoke', for during the afternoon of October 13th, two educational officers watched an amazing aerial phenomenon over Bosanka Posavina, Bosnia, in Yugoslavia. It resembled dense smoke — apparently one kilometre long and one metre wide — that passed in a wave-like or undulatory manner across the sky. This phenomenon was also watched by several other local inhabitants, and seems to have been virtually identical to 'flying smoke', seen by farmers at Kladar, also in Bosnia, where it was visible for 15 minutes before passing northwards out of sight. While over this area it was noticed that sheep, cattle, hens, and other animals, were greatly disturbed by it, one farmer stating that they 'scared to death' [30].

25   Finally, as an illustration of the fact that aberrant clouds exhibiting unnaturally controlled movements are still being observed at the time of writing, we cite a letter from G. Sloane of Bideford, Devon,   that was published in February 1977 by the *Daily Mirror* in response to that newspaper's centrespread on ufos of a few days previously. The letter reads:

'I was watching a football match on a bright Sunday morning. A few woolly clouds were scattered in the sky. My attention was caught by a procession of clouds in line coming swiftly over the horizon. They were white, roughly *cube shaped* (my italics) and travelling against the wind. In about a minute they crossed the sky and disappeared over the horizon. The speed was incredible'. [31].

The speed of these clouds should be compared to that reported in case 8.

These cases, so typical of dozens more, show that cloudy bodies generally resembling, but acting very differently from, normal clouds — or of oddly symmetrical configurations but behaving like ordinary clouds — have not only been observed

over many years but occur on a global basis and are often indisputably associated with ufos proper (e.g., cases 13, 14, 16, and 21). Moreover, those cases featuring definite ufos also often include descriptions of so-called 'carrier ufos' (cases 12 and 14), are strongly reminiscent of the 'cloud-cigars' discussed by Vallee [32] and even link up with those observations of submersible objects of unknown origin, but evidently associated with ufos, reviewed by Sanderson [33].

A direct connection between these clouds and alien entities (e.g. cases 16 and 21), and between electro-magnetic and animal reaction effects (cases 15 and 23), now also seems to be beyond dispute. An intriguing additional example of associating entities and clouds occurred at 9.15 pm on October 18th, 1973, when W. Hines and a companion watched a hazy *green* cloud rise up from behind trees just after they had ineffectually chased a shimmering 3 to 4 foot tall humanoid creature that moved sideways at White Oak Mountain, near Danville, Virginia, USA [34].

The unnaturally symmetrical appearance of several of these clouds (cases 2, 3, 5, 6, 8, 18, and 24) strongly suggests artificial origins, and therefore, intelligent creation. This suspicion is supported by those accounts describing speeds, regimented arrangements, and/or manoeuvres impossible for conventional clouds (cases 5, 7, 8, 11, 18 and 20), or, conversely, complete immobility during windy or breezy conditions (cases 3, 6, 7 and 11).

The expectoration by some of these clouds of hard objects like stones and mussels, and especially by those clouds that had previously been stationary for appreciable periods (cases 1-5, and 10) — in one instance for almost an hour — suggests that the stones (commonly identified as meteorites) were either not conventional meteorites at all or, if they were, they had, like the mussels, been suspended aloft by forces capable of nullifying gravity. Certainly the mussels, before their fall, should not have been aloft in the first place. But mussels held aloft by intelligent agencies may well have been collected initially by agencies able to negate gravitational effects.

Surely, the collective testimony of substantial objects apparently suspended where they should not have been, of the aberrant clouds associated with them, and of the singular behaviour of all these things, indicates decidedly unnatural origins — in other words, artificial origins, Reviewed in combination, all factors like those just discussed lead to the conclusion that these cloudy bodies — far from being unusual specimens of otherwise natural clouds — are not clouds at all but ufos that either deliberately disguise themselves as clouds (as suggested in cases 11 and 16), or that, due to particular operational methods, generate enveloping vapours and cloudy effects. 'Cloud-Ufos', as they may henceforth be conveniently termed, possibly occur much more often than is generally realized, but pass unnoticed for what they actually are in Earth's frequently cloudy skies. This is indeed a sobering thought.

Surprisingly, the possibility that some ufos *deliberately* camouflage themselves as clouds, or hide within natural clouds, is rather strong, for numerous cases are known in which ufos have been observed to enter clouds from which they have *not* emerged. Even terrestrial devices (some with human occupants) have similarly vanished. In some instances these clouds were isolated and quite small, and sometimes abruptly vanished.

Below is a chronologically arranged selection of reports representative of such events, and of others in which ufos emerged from aberrant clouds, or came out of and then re-entered the same cloud.

A   Ten or twelve discoidal objects came out of a revolving golden-coloured cloud seen during November 1947 from Albany Avenue, Toronto, in Ontario, Canada [35].

B   Whilst on a meteorological reconnaissance mission

over Korea during March 1952, wing-commander J. Baldwin, with the jet aeroplane he was flying, disappeared into a cloud from which he did not emerge. Neither he nor his aeroplane were seen again [36].

C   At approximately 5.50 pm, on March 9th, 1955, a silver bell-shaped object was seen by observers at Paris, Illinois, USA, to 'swallow' an aeroplane [37].

The two cases immediately above should be compared with the event which occurred on November 23rd, 1953, when an F-89 jet from Kinross US Airforce base, Michigan, was dispatched to intercept a ufo. The jet was crewed by Lt. Felix Moncla Jr and Lt. R.R. Wilson, who closed the distance between them and the ufo at a speed in excess of 500 mph. Ground radar, monitoring the event, observed that the jet blip suddenly merged with the much larger ufo blip, which they moved off at high velocity. Jet and crew were never seen again [38].

D   During daylight hours on February 2nd, 1959, two witnesses saw three white disc-like objects pass into a cloud over Warsop, Nottinghamshire, from which they never reappeared [39].

E   When east of Somerton, South Australia, at 6.15 pm on November 21st, 1961, Mr. G. Page watched 6 to 8 crescent-shaped objects enter an isolated cloud within which they apparently remained [40].

F   At 8.30 pm on July 22nd, 1963, three people observed a low-flying bell-shaped object pass into a cloud over Parr, Merseyside. It failed to reappear [41].

G   At 6.45 pm, on October 2nd, 1963, a black oval object was seen to come out of and then re-enter a lone cloud over Audenshaw, Greater Manchester [42].

H   A large discoidal object was seen by observers at St. Helen's, Lancashire, to move slowly into a cloud, from which it failed to emerge, at 2.00 pm on an undetermined date in June 1966 [43].

I   During the evening of July 15th, 1967, an object resembling a domed disc came out of and then re-entered an isolated cloud over an area approximately one mile south of Sedalia, Missouri, USA [44].

J   On September 6th, 1967 — just six days before a pink cloud was observed (see case 18) — three people at Meir, Stoke-on-Trent, watched, at approximately 9.50 pm, an oval object come out of a remarkable sausage-shaped cloud [45].

K   Around 1.00 pm on an unnoted date in April 1968, a wingless rocket-like object was seen to enter a cloud over Woodford, Essex, wherein it then apparently remained stationary, for it was not seen again [46].

L   Late in August 1969, two witnesses at Masbro, near Birmingham, saw, at 1.30 pm, a spherical object enter and remain inside a cloud motionless over that locality. Very interestingly, this cloud was subsequently 'inspected' by a jet aeroplane [47]. Also see later comments on pseudo-planes.

M   Late in the afternoon of May 24th, 1971, two MIG jet fighters were sent up by the Hungarian Air Force to investigate an unknown object, also being monitored on radar from Zagreb, in Yugoslavia. The Zagreb radar operators watched all three blips for about ten minutes, after which the blips suddenly merged into a single blip, which then disappeared from the radar-screen. Enquiries made by Zagreb of the Hungarian flight-controllers revealed that no further information was forthcoming 'because the fighter planes had not returned to base'. Upon being pressed further, this statement was truncated to 'No comment'. So far as is known, the Hungarian planes were never seen again [48].

This incident, so much like cases B and C above, is also somewhat reminiscent of the loss of instruments from

a weather balloon that passed through a cloud, and from which later emerged a silvery domed object that changed course as it moved, watched by meteorological station personnel at Trindale Island, off Brazil, only a few weeks before the celebrated Trindale Island ufo photographs were taken [49]. The instruments were never seen again.

N   On August 13th, 1972, A. Acosta saw 20 lights emerge from an oval cloud over Yauco, Puerto Rico, and enter a closely similar one nearby, in which they remained [50].

There can be little doubt remaining that ufos frequently employ clouds, or created artificial clouds, to camouflage their activities and thus make them less easy to detect. These traits should now be considered in relation to the following information about objects that, although often described by eyewitnesses as various kinds of terrestrial aircraft, may in fact not always be. If, as suspected, ufos disguise themselves as clouds on occasion, then the duplication of man-made aeroplanes follows almost naturally as an extension of this camouflage syndrome.

In case L, the inspecting jet aeroplane may well have been dispatched by local air authorities monitoring the cloud and sphere involved, particularly the latter's mode of disappearance; yet we should consider it alongside the jet aeroplane observed on June 19th, 1959, over Clitheroe, Lancashire, by Rosemary Miller and Norma Stephenson, *hovering* over a saucer-shaped object stationary in the sky [51]. It needs hardly be stressed that, in 1959, no jet aeroplanes capable of hovering had been built.

Before we dismiss the Clitheroe 'jet' as some unidentified type of helicopter, it should be compared with the essentially similar cases below, and in particular, with the 'helicopter' that appeared near a low-level oval-shaped ufo seen at 9.30 am on March 14th, 1975, from Enfield, Connecticutt, USA [52]. On September 3rd, 1975, two 'helicopters' *appeared* near a mysterious object that changed shape from round to diamond, to chevron, to domed-saucer according to several eyewitnesses who had it under observation from Trijunga, a spot about 15 miles NE of Los Angeles, California [53].

All the foregoing 'jet' and 'helicopter' incidents should be assessed in relation to the amazing event that occurred in broad daylight on October 1st, 1975, when an amoeba-like cloudy object appeared in the sky over King's Lynn, Norfolk, before *turning into* something closely akin to a jet aeroplane. Shortly after this transformation, the 'jet' suddenly vanished [54].

The King's Lynn 'jet' evidently falls into that category of objects that can be best referred to as 'Pseudo-Planes'. These objects — frequently long-fuselaged, stubby winged objects lacking identification marks, and sometimes unnervingly silent — have been repeatedly reported down the years, both as isolated objects and in groups. A rather famous case dates from July 22nd, 1968, when a very low flying and extraordinarily elongated pseudo-plane visited San Carlos de Bariloche airport, near Bahia Blanca, Argentina, where it was observed by mystified airport staff [55]. Another interesting case involved objects, described as 'jets' by eyewitnesses, seen pursuing a mushroom-shaped ufo over Winchester, Hampshire, on October 27th, 1967 [56]. Significantly, enquiries made at the time of local Air Force authorities disclosed that no jets had been scrambled to intercept the ufo.

Virtually the same denial was made by American police and air authorities respecting a group of nine extremely low flying black domed objects with silvery tails, superficially resembling helicopters, seen by girl scouts near East Derry, New Hampshire, USA, about 6.40 pm on August 28th, 1965 [57]. These objects were never identified. Certainly, if these and the two Winchester 'jets' were not terrestrial aircraft at all, one begins to understand why the relevant authorities denied owning or dispatching them, and why many then contemporary ufologists concluded that those same authorities were being less than honest in their disclaimers. The true interpretation may involve *very* different things.

Almost certainly falling into the same category are the helicopter-like objects — often unmarked and silent —reported in recent years from the English Midlands and from many American states. In Colorado, Oklahoma, Texas, and other states, these mystery craft have been repeatedly seen in areas and at times close to animal mutilations. These have caused widespread concern and have so far not been satisfactorily explained [58]. In Montana, where the problem has been especially acute, the cases have been partially published in a fascinating tome by Donovan and Wolverton [59], in which the association with ufo activity seems to be reasonably well established.

Many additional cases could be cited, although the above probably more than suffice to demonstrate the fact that aberrant clouds and their associations, direct or inferred, with ufos form an important facet of the ufo enigma. It is this writer's contention that the material discussed in this paper forms a much neglected aspect of the overall ufo problem, and that properly studied it will yield valuable data. The demonstrable links between these 'clouds' and ufos, on the other hand, and the abduction, animal mutilations, and alien entities on the other, and of all with objects here termed pseudo-planes, represent ufo behaviour trends as yet largely unrecognised. In view of their implications it is high time that in-depth studies were conducted on these pieces of the ufo jigsaw on an international basis and a system developed for detecting 'Cloud-Ufos'.

J.B. DELAIR.   1977.

References

1   Jessup, M.K. 1955, *The Case for the UFO*, pp.105-111.
2   Lorenzen, C., and J. Lorenzen, 1969. *UFOs: The Whole Story*, pp. 232-233.
3   Vallee, J. 1965. *Anatomy of a Phenomenon*. (Tandem edn.), pp. 151f.
4   *BerlinMonatschrift*, August 1796.
5   *Philos. Mag. & Journ.*, vol. 44, 1814, p.316.
6   *Annales de Chimie et de Physique*, tome xcii, Oct., 1814, p.25.
7   *Philos. Mag. & Journ.*, vol. 44, 1814, p.316.
8   *Ibid*, vol. 45, 1815, pp. 23-6.
9   *Annales de Chimie et de Physique*, tome 1, Jan., 1816, p.45.
10 *Philos. Mag. & Journ.*, vol. 47, 1816, pp.349-353.
11 *Ibid*, vol. 44, 1814, pp. 253-260.
12 Jessup, M.K. 1957. *The Expanding Case for the UFO*, p.36.
13 *Proc. Roy. Soc. London*, vol. 6 (1850-4), pp. 276-277.
14 Jessup, M.K. 1957. *Op. cit.*, pp. 34-35.
15 *Nature, 27*, Nov. 23rd,, 1882, pp. 82-87.
16 *La Nature*, 1883, p.342.
17 *Nature, 47*, Jan. 19th, 1893, p.278.
18 Vallee, J. 1965. *Op. cit.*, pp.152, 155.
19 Lorenzen, C., and J. Lorenzen, 1969. *Op. cit.*, pp. 232-233.
20 *Orbit*, (Tyneside UFO Soc. Journ.), vol. 3, no. 4, 1961, p.19.
21 Vallee, J. 1965. *Op. cit.*, pp.152, 155.
22 *Australian Flying Saucer Review*, no. 3, 1965, p.17.
23 Shuttlewood, A. 1967. *The Warminster Mystery*, p.151.
24 Stanway, R. and Pace, A. 1968. *Flying Saucers — Report on Ufos, Unidentified, Undeniable*, p.15.
25 *Flying Saucer Review*, vol. 15, no. 1, 1969, p.iii.
26 Hervey, M. 1976. *UFOs: The American Scene*, p.149.
27 *Argosy*, Oct. 1976. *Op. cit.*, p.172.
28 Lorenzen, C., and J. Lorenzen, 1976. *Encounters with UFO Occupants*, pp. 129-131.
29 Hervey, M. 1976. *Op. cit.*, pp. 151f.
30 *The UFO Register*, vol. 3, pt. 1, 1972 (pp 21-2.
31 *Daily Mirror*, Feb. 7th, 1977 (reader's letter).
32 Vallee, J. 1965. *Op. cit.*, pp. 151f.
33 I.T. Sanderson, 1974. *Invisible Residents* (Tandem edn).
34 *Danville Bee* (Va), 19th Oct., 1973.
35 *Canadian Flying Saucers*, 1957, p.12.
36 Wilkins, H.T. 1954. *Flying Saucers from the Moon*, p.282.
37 *Telonic Research Bulletin*, vol. 2, No. 3, 1956, p.15.
38 Hervey, M. 1976. *Op. cit.*, p.51.
39 *Mansfield and North Nottinghamshire Chronicle*, 19th Feb., 1959.
40 Hervey, M. 1975. *UFOs Over the Southern Hemisphere*, p.171.
41 *Flying Saucer Review*, vol. 10, no. 3, 1964, pp. 24-25.
42 *Orbit* (Tyneside UFO Soc. Journ.), vol. 5, no. 3, 1963, p. 24.
43 *Northern UFO Network News* (Manchester) no. 15, August 1975, p.12.
44 *UFOLOG*, no. 80, 1971, p.5.
45 Stanway, R. and Pace, A. 1968. *Op. cit.*, pp.14-15.
46 *Interplanetary News*, vol. 7, no. 3, p.14a, 1969.
47 Unpublished case in Contact (UK)'s archives.
48 *The UFO Register*, vol. 3, pt. 1, 1972, pp. 6-7.
49 Kettlecamp, L. 1972. *Investigating UFOs*, pp.31-2.
50 Unpublished letter from eyewitness in Contact (UK)'s archives.
51 *Ibid*.
52 *Skylook*, no. 99, 1976, p.9.
53 *Ibid*, pp.8-9.
54 *Northern UFO Network News* (Manchester), no. 25, 1976, p.5.
55 *Flying Saucer Review*, vol. 14, no. 6, 1968, p.iii.
56 *Awareness*, 1967/68, p.25.
57 Fowler, R. 1974. *UFOs: Interplanetary Visitors*, pp.7-74.
58 *Ufology*, vol. 2, no.1, Spring 1976, p.25.
59 Donovan, R., and K. Wolverton, 1976. *Mystery Stalks The Prairie*, pp.44-45, 47-59, 61-63.

Oliver Thomas cont from p39...

conclusion is that factually the story is as bogus as the David Lang non-event, and its only value is its mythical content which seems to involve the basic elements seen in, for example, the kidnappings in the fairy tradition.

I hope there are no more than these - but no matter how much care we seem to take (and we took our time over 2 years) checking back to sources, a few errors crept in. Short of eye-witness testimony, you are only as good as your sources, and a certain amount has to be taken on trust (as I've said before). I'm pleased at least that this list is as short as it is.

RJMR

SOUNDS AND ECHOES

We expressed, in our review of mystery booms, airquakes or pseudoseisms last issue (FT23/29-32,35,36) that these puzzling aerial noises are one of the most perennial of Fortean phenomena. Well, it seems you can't get rid of them merely by listing them, for no sooner was FT23 mailed out than reports were coming in on new series in the US and SW England.

Blasts Rattle Eastern States
2 Dec - a blast strong enough to shake houses, break windows and items thrown from shelves was heard and felt in the Charleston area of the South Carolina coast, at about 10am EST. Later, at 3.45 pm EST, another blast rocked the coast from Cape May, New Jersey, to Long Island and Connecticut (Cape May is about 500 miles north of Charleston). Dr William Donn, chief atmospheric scientist of Columbia University, NY, estimated their equivalence to 50-100 tons of TNT exploded above the sea , perhaps 50 miles offshore. Los Angeles Times, Dallas,Tx, Times Herald both 17 Dec 1977; San Antonio News 19 Dec 1977; Trenton,NJ, Times 20 Dec 1977 (Cr: Dr EC Krupp, Tom Adams, Loren Coleman.)

15 Dec - 5 more booms - descriptions vary from muffled rumbles, double booms, loud claps to quake-like tremors - felt in Charleston area only, between 8.30-10.30am EST, seeming to come from 2-3 separate locations.

20 Dec - 2 booms off South Carolina. Further north another boom was felt at New Jersey, which may or may not have been one of the 3 loud booms "closely spaced" heard at New Canaan, Connnecticut at 11.43pm EST, during which (or just before or after - reports not specific) the sky to the east of the town was lit brightly by a red glare.

21 Dec - 2 booms heard at Charleston. In New Jersey, a resident of Toms River felt an "explosion" seconds before his fire-alarm went off at 2am EST. He said he saw "an intense globular-shaped light outside his window before it disappeared. There were further booms at 7pm EST.(X's RBB28 puts this incident on 20 Dec.)

22 Dec - a series of 5 booms at Charleston at 8.15am EST. One paper (Boston Globe) claimed that 4 booms were heard off South Carolina between 8.48-10.15am EST (which contradicts or supplements the earlier report?), and others heard at Westport, Conn.

This was the main series, drawn from: Manchester,Conn, Journal Inquirer, Huntsville,Alab, Times both 22 Dec 1977; Los Angeles Times, Manchester,Conn, Journal Inquirer, Nashville,Tenn, Tennessean, Boston,Mass, Globe, Atlanta,Ga, Constitution all 23 Dec 1977 (Cr: Tom Bearden, Loren Coleman, Dr EC Krupp, John Gore.) There was of course, among these reports, several mentions of the great quake at Charleston in 1886 - but initially the 'experts' seemed quite sceptical about any connexion between the sounds and geophysical activity.

During this series the public was treated to a barrage of fatuous explanations from 'experts' put on the spot by media demands for official opinions. Boggle at: sonic booms from Concorde, 'secret' US or foreign supersonic planes; undersea explosions from oilrigs, foreign powers, offshore garbage dumps, or natural gas; thunder or meteor showers; weather balloons with TNT payloads; and re-entering satellite junk (interesting in view of what was to happen scarcely a month later in Canada - next FT). At first experts thought that the public was over-reacting to some fairly explicable natural phenomenon, but as the damned things kept on coming they were forced to be more critical. Only Dr Donn seemed to take the events seriously from the start, and in successive reports he claims ignorance or disinterest from top establishments including the Pentagon and NORAD, and many scientists. One of the troubles was the ambiguous nature of the evidence. On the one hand you had the testimony of many hundreds of residents of these areas and on the other there were quite insignificant seismic or barometric traces of the events - at least not enough to cause concern about quakes or terrestrial explosions.

Gradually some light glimmered in the brains of a few...and it was soon being pointed out (with all the wisdom of after thought) the similarity to our well loved Fortean data on the Barisal Guns, the Guns of the Seneca, the Moodus sounds, the 'mist pouffers' of Belgium etc etc. See discussions in last FT; Los Angeles Times, & Manchester,Conn, Journal Inquirer both 24 Dec 1977; International Herald Tribune 20 Jan 1978; INFO Journal 26 (Dec 1977); and X's RBB 28 which lists (for the first time) the 50 or so cases in Fort's Books over the period 1808-1922

Is there a Quake Connexion?
With the mention of the aerial lights accompanying some of the booms (omitted in the earliest reports) thoughts inevitably turned to yet another correlation pioneered by Fort and only now gaining scientific credance - the aerial lights often seen during quakes. In fact, in mid-1977, the US Geological Survey published an important study of quake/light phenomena and we are awaiting a copy to prepare an article for FT on the subject of Fortean quake phenomena. (Our thanks to Ron Dobbins, Tom Adams, Ion Will, Gary Abbott, Loren Coleman and others for data & clippings on this long delayed subject.)

On 23rd Dec, Richard Golob, Center for Short-lived Phenomena, Cambridge,Mass, said: "Between 1-20 Dec there were numerous reports of earth tremors in the Toms River, NJ, area, although none were recorded. But on 15 Dec, when 5 booms were heard in S Carolina, two earth tremors were recorded in Charleston." (Boston Globe 23 Dec 1977. Cr L Coleman). We underlined part of the above because it is not clear whether the tremors were mistaken for the booms and not reported, or too weak to affect the seismographs. Another possibility is the hint (in the Observer 1 Jan 1978. Cr: John Michell, Ion Will, Douglas Watson) that a curious coincidence disabled Donn's seismic event recording equipment at the Columbia University's observatory at Pallisades,NY.

Other correlations came thick and fast. Prof Edward Chibouris, of the Weston Observatory of Boston College, Mass., said there had been a 3.1 Richter tremor at Wareham, south-eastern Massachusetts, at 12.44pm EST on 20 Dec - that is just about 1 hour after the noises and lights at New Canaan, about 60 or so miles away in Connecticut. Chibouris added that there have been many tremors in New England over the years, but "just too small to be heard or felt." He mentions faint tremors just noticeable in Spring 1976, 1 near New Bedford,Mass., and 2. in Rhode Island; and another in SE Connecticut in Dec 1976. (Boston Herald American 21 Dec 1977. Cr: Loren Coleman.) New Jersey state geologist Kemble Widmer claimed a similar series of mystery noises was reported from the NJ coast in 1975, "but scientific investigation failed to yield any conclusions." (Can anyone tell us more about this?)(Trenton,NJ, Times 20 Dec 1977. Cr: Loren Coleman.)

The Observer 1 & 8 Jan 1978 (Cr: John Michell, Ion Will, Douglas Watson,) gave another date for mystery bangs - 24 Dec - though we have no US data on this one. We can report, though, that residents of Hopkinton, New Hampshire, and surrounding towns got an unexpected Christmas present the next day - a 3.4 Richter tremor at 10.36am EST, 25 Dec. Chibouris pops up again, as though it had just reminded him ...ah yes, there was a similar quake at Portsmouth, NH, in March 1976. (Boston Globe 26 Dec 1977. Cr: Loren Coleman.)

We can add a few correlations of our own. On the same day as the 2 Dec noise, there was a 5.5 Richter quake in Iran, at 1.13am. Hours later there was a strong tremor on the Kamchatka peninsula,Russia. On the same day as the 20 Dec noises another severe quake (6.2 Richter) hit Iran at 3am.(We'll give the refs in a future quake listing.) We also note that 1 of the mystery booms in Cornwall (see below) coincide with the 21 Dec noises in the US. According to the International Herald Tribune 20 Jan 1978 (Cr: Ion Will) there were further aerial noises heard at Charleston on 5 and 12 Jan 1978...the former approximating in time to another Russian quake - details of the latter can be found in NY Herald Tribune 14 Jan 1978 (Cr: Ion Will.) Someday we'll have a computer to correlate all this stuff!

Earlier Cases
A strange series of noises baffled Dr Walter Arabasz, seismologist at Utah University...his records showed "a confusing signal" on 1 Sept 1977, when a heavy booming repeated in the local sky of North Ogden, Utah, at 1.06, 1.11 and 1.22 pm (local time). The first 2 events rattled windows and shook houses; the last one seemed to be more seismic - "The ground rolled," said one witness - and subsonic frequencies caused "queasy stomachs." Arabasz's equipment showed a "flurry of erratic air waves...superimposed on a local earthquake." If it was

a quake, he said, it was about 1 Richter. Similar aerial detonations, heard only in the small area of North Ogden, were reported at 1pm 29 Aug, and 8-8.10am 30 Aug. On these occasions Arabasz found "airwaves" but no seismic activity. Locals admit they get many sonic booms from aircraft in the area, but claim justifiably that they are familiar with these, the new sounds being "entirely different." Ogden Standard-Examiner 30 Aug, 2 Sept 1977 (Cr: Thomas R Adams.) The physical effects of these sounds seem similar to those recorded just 4 months later for the eastern seaboard.

A little bit nearer to the December coastal blasts was the loud explosion and flash of light that rocked buildings in Texarcana, Texas. Although several hundreds phoned the police, others including 2 policemen near the area saw and heard nothing. There were no physical traces of an explosion...police baffled. Interestingly, one man said he saw something falling from space before exploding. Texarkana Gazette 14 Nov 1977 (Cr: Tom Adams.) This event was on 12 Nov evening.

Loren Coleman sent us a report from the Boston Globe 8 Sept 1976: that fishermen in Massachusetts report "loud, recurring explosions about 100-125 miles south of Cape Cod, since that July. Military, Navy, geological and oil sources all denied culpability, and no cause was ever identified.

Further Correlations

A theory discussed by Fort, long ago, based on his own studies, suggested some correlation with the Martian cycle, particularly the opposition of Mars. X's excellent re-opening of this fascinating facet (RBB 28) points out that the recent series of booms coincides with Mars' closest approach in 2 years (ie 18 Jan 1978), or at least its approach...but the mechanism this would imply remains obscure.

In the references to the historical precedents to aerial cannonading in NE America, much mention was made of records of such noises in the Finger Lakes region of northern NY state, among the Cayuga, Seneca, Onondaga, Mohawk and Oneida Indians "dating back to the Owasco Indians who left the area during a drought in 1220," said the Cayuga Museum director Walter Long. Interestingly, a myth associated with the noises said they were caused by the tail-thrashings of a giant serpent that lived in Canandaigua Lake. This prompted me to wonder if any other noise areas also had dragon, serpent or monster associations, and the two that sprang quickly to mind are Cape May and other New England monster-spots, and the equally sea-serpent-haunted Cornish coast (see back to FT 15,16,17,19 & 22, for the Cornish monster, Morgawr. New England monsters can be found in Heuvelmans' In the Wake of the Sea Serpents and other sources, including Fort.) I'm sure others will occur to you.

Lastly, we also note, historically, the 'Moodus Sounds' heard by Indians and white-folk alike in the East Haddam area of Connecticut, since at least 1729. Is there anything to the fact that in our plagues summary (p36) East Haddam figures, so ill-favoured, almost a year before the current booms series?

More Booms in SE England

Mr X intriguingly ends his RBB 28 with a promise of coverage of a series of aerial detonations at Cornwall, Ontario, in his next issue. If this is not an error in refering to similar events in Cornwall, England, then we have yet another stimulating coincidence in this amazing,truly Fortean affair.

The major reported booms were on 21 Dec (the day of a US series), and 1 Jan 1978, though from the reports it seems that booming noises, sometimes "distant thunder" or "sharp explosions", sounding both in the air and "subterranean" have been heard intermittantly on other days. On 21 Dec the most powerful blast came at 2pm, heard by the coast guards at remote stations on the Cornish coast. One of them, Peter Baker, said: "I have heard these bangs while on duty at ((the extreme-west lookout)) Gwennap Head and St Just, and once the explosion was powerful enough to rock the lookout. The noise was also heard by others. Auxilliary coastguards have frequently rung up to find out if we had fired a maroon." The 1 Jan blast was heard at 7pm...it was "a series of explosions...rather like a rumble of thunder. The birds shot into the air,"said another coastguard." They checked and found there was no military gunfire at these times, nor seismic blasting at sea...and all the coastguards now claim expertise in distinguishing these noises from the now familiar sonic booms from Concorde. Besides,they do not fit into the Concorde schedule.

At St Ives the bangs sound like underground explosions just after 6pm, and louder between 8-8.15pm, shaking houses. Single and quadruple cracks and bangs have rattled windows in the Penzance area. At Redruth "crescendo" sequences of triple bangs are preceded by a quieter doublebang. They have also been heard at St Mawgan. The mystery continues.

Peter Baker, echoing similar sentiments among the New England witnesses, said: "There is something going on out there that defies explanation." D.Mail 3 Jan

1978; **West Briton** 5 Jan 1978 (Cr: Ivan Bunn, John Michell, Doc Shiels.) *** We have had to keep back reports of

booms, hums, clicks, tones, throbs and other mystery noises until we have more room - hopefully soon. *** RJMR

Another TV documentary worth comment is the BBC 'Horizon' team's attempted demolition of Von Daniken, screened a few weeks after we mentioned it in FT23 (p38). They tried to repeat their previous success on the Bermuda Triangle, but succeeded only in making themselves look petty and peevish. In concentrating on several of VD's more important evidences, they juxtaposed interviews with him and an 'authority' . Apart from Thor Heyerdahl and Maria Reich who showed practical proof of terrestrial rather than extraterrestrial accomplishment, and one lady archæologist who showed how giant stone blocks could be fitted together perfectly, the rest of the proof consisted of asking us to believe in an orthodox opinion against VD's opinion. I take the side of the underdog. One archæologist protested weakly that the design on the sarcophagus lid could not be an astronaut because it was a coffin lid! Then the programme used complicated computer graphics to show how details of Mayan glyphs can be stylized and rotated to form separate elements of the Palenque design. Not even VD goes to these lengths to make his data fit.

OK, VD needs rapping on the knuckles, but it should be done properly. This effort was wrongly motivated, branding by implication all unsolved enigmas as the product of gullibility or deceit. With enemies like these, VD doesn't need friends!

Mention must be made here of an event that startled several thousands of TV watchers in Southern England. At 5.06pm, just as the news was being read on Saturday evening, 26 Nov 1977, a deep voice, accompanied by an eerie booming sound likened to a "hollow drumming", drowned out the newscaster's voice and delivered a short message: ...

... "This is the voice of Asteron. I am an authorized representative of the Intergalactic Mission, and I have a message for the planet Earth. We are begining to enter the period of Aquarius and there are many corrections which have to be made by Earth people. All your weapons of evil must be destroyed. You only have a short time to learn to live together in peace. You must live in peace...or leave the galaxy." Some how the originators of the message had jammed the sound-signals from Southern TV's transmitter at Hannington, Wilts, so viewers from Newbury and Reading to Winchester and Andover heard the weird voice superimposed over the ITN news bulletin. It caused sufficient panic for Southern TV to put out half-hourly announcements insisting that it had been a hoax and that the planet was not being invaded. Predictably the IBA and Post Office took a rigid humourless stand vowing prosecution of the culprits... and if the planet had been invaded we'd like to have seen them try! Whoever did the deed knew their stuff, for the "android" (as one PO representative persisted in calling the mystery voice) needed sophisticated equipment or techniques to break into and dominate a TV transmission. One perceptive letter in the Times pointed out that if this was the first time this had ever happened in Britain, as the IBA claimed, then how could they be sure it was a hoax? Indeed! Inexplicably the News of the World and D.Mail call the owner of the voice 'Gillon, of the Ashdown Galactic Command' and that he said: "Unless the weapons of Earth are laid down, destruction from outer space invasion will quickly follow.' I hope their regular news reportage is more accurate than that, for the indication is that they've simply invented a more shocking message. The Sunday Times claimed to have tracked down a student group who invented a new kind of transmitter (for £80) which can 'hitch a ride' on conventional transmissions...but again how can they be sure that this claim isn't also a bandwaggon hoax? Incidentally, we're sure you noticed that the 'entity' and message closely conform to the messages given to UFO prophets, psychic sitting groups and contactees (eg: see Keel's UFOs:Operation Trojan Horse, and Clark & Coleman's The Unidentified for discussions of names and messages from UFOs.) Who ever perpetrated the incident had done his homework; especially if he was a terrestrial. Of course the massive TV publicity of the imminent Star Wars about that time must have reinforced its effect among those ripe for the salvation-from-the-stars belief. People have their own standards about what is or isn't credible. One professor (quoted in the Carlisle,Penn, Evening Sentinel 3 Dec 1977 Cr: Larry Arnold) said the reference to Aquarius proved the message was a hoax...he reasoned that as the most intelligent body on earth, the scientists, do not believe in astrology, then ipso fatso intelligent life elsewhere would not believe in it either. (For other 'intelligent' responses by 'scientists' see the next item.) item). News of the World (Cr: Ian Lawes) S.Express, San Francisco Examiner & Chronicle, Oklahoma City Oklahoman all 27 Nov 1977; D.Mail, Delhi Statesman, Torrance,Calif Daily Breeze, the Sun all 28 Nov 1977; the Times 28,29 Nov 1977; Times of India 30 Nov 1977; S.Times 4 Dec 1977 (Cr: Thomas R Adams, John Michell Ion Will, J&C Bord, John Hitchens, Paul Screeton, & MUFOB ns9.)

The Committee for the Scientific Investigation of the Claims of the Paranormal (CSICP) are rapidly becoming tiresome Cassandras. Formed to combat the disgraceful backsliding of the public into "the abandonment of reason and logic", they are taking every opportunity to trumpet their pugnacious opinions throughout the land. They have loudly attacked astrology from its serious aspects down to the popular newspaper horoscopes. They have published a journal, The Zetetic, in which they appear unhealthily obsessed with proving Geller a fraud, and all other 'unknown' subjects from UFOs to psychic phenomena to be abberations of gullible minds. These zealous arbiters have even brought a suit against NBC and Readers Digest, alleging that their series of documentaries on mysteries "In Search of..." (soon to be screened in the UK) were presenting paranormal subjects "as if they were scientifically credible" and that their treatment of

the BTriangle, Noah's Ark and UFOs was nothing less than a "scientific scandal". DR Paul Kurtz, co-chairman of CSICP,has said that the group are concerned about the degree of "irrationality" in today's society, pointing, for example, to an (alleged) 200 suicides because of unfavourable horoscopes. He also complained about the lack of books debunking paranormal topics on campus bookshop shelves. (One good answer is that so few have been written!) His answer seems as extreme as the extremist sects he fears - if in doubt, throw it out. They also promote the myth that magicians (especially the alleged "Amazing" Randi) can detect hoaxes and trickery better than us ordinary folks, and especially better than scientists. Randi's logic is that since he can reproduce Geller's effects Geller must be using the same tricks, or as near as dammit - and from there it's a small step to damning everything with a question-mark over it.

Already there have been schisms in their ranks, and those who have pleaded for a more open-ended view of the meaning of "scientific investigation" have wisely chosen to leave this distinguished but deluded group. For a lengthier critique of their posturings read Dr J Gordon Melton's guest editorial in Fate Dec 1977.

No sooner had President Carter been accused of going back on his word to release government data on UFOs by Dr Hynek, Dr Leo Sprinkle & nuclear physicist Stanton Friedman (The Star, Texas, 27 Sept 1977. Cr: TR Adams), than the White House announced that NASA was to be asked by the Science & Technology Policy Office to study the UFO question, after considerable public pressure on the White House in the ten years since the Condon Report. In fact, we are told, the approach to NASA had been made back in July. Even earlier than that, about the time of the disastrous Acapulco UFO congress in April, it was reported that the Prime Minister of Grenada, Eric Gairy, was taking an interest in the subject. In September he put a resolution to the UN General Assembly, and opened the debate on 29 Nov with a 1½ hour speech. The press gleefully reported widespread yawning and joking - sad to say, little seems to have come from it. Gairy claimed that the UN was in the unique position of promoting an international agency for UFO investigation, a move, rumours said, that would be blocked by the USA (according to their own leaked info) - see national papers 29 & 30 November 1977. Since then we have heard nothing... Meanwhile, there was a violent disagreement between NASA and the White House, and the study project was turned down as "wasteful and probably unproductive." (<u>Sun</u> 29 Dec 1977). Dave Williamson, NASA's spokesman for special projects,goes on record with this quote of the year: "A photograph is not a measurement. Give me one little green man - not a theory or a memory of one - and we can have a multimillion dollar program. It's a scientific dilemma. How do you prove something that doesn't exist?" God's teeth! The true scientific dilemma is that clods like Williamson are in positions of authority when he reacts in a naive superstitious fashion. How can he know something doesn't exist until it is studied? He wants the results before he starts - damned typical of the total lack of imagination of a "science" that is nothing less than a branch of the civil service. Pah! There is a little glimmer of hope, however -- According to the <u>Sun</u> 2 Dec 1977, Henry Rothblatt, who defended the Watergate burglars, has begun suing the CIA on behalf of Ground Saucer Watch, under the Freedom of Information Act, claiming that they have been withholding vital data from accredited investigators, since their files began in 1952. The fuse has been lit... Facts culled from papers of many dates and origins (Cr: Paul Screeton, TR Adams, Ion Will, Valerie Martin, R Cotton, W Ritchie Benedict, Ian Lawes.)

<u>BUFORA Conference</u> - 15-16 April 1978. Talks on: Dyfed humanoid cases; Hill star map; ET life; vehicle interference cases; radio noise monitoring; detection equipment, etc. Write for fees and info to Conf.Organiser: 5 The Ridgeway, Farnsfield, Newark, Notts NG22 8DG.

Peter James, assistant editor of the Journal of the <u>Society for Interdisciplinary Studies</u> (SIS), the UK Velikovsky study group, tells us that there will be a major UK conference on Velikovskyan topics at Glasgow University, this April. He says: "The weekend conference on the 'revised chronology', open to the public, at which the pros and cons of <u>Ages in Chaos</u> will be debated, will include talks by Dr Euan Mackie (on radiocarbon evidence), Dr Archie Roy, Prof of Astronomy,Glasgow, (on 'Sothic dating and the feasibility of Velikovsky's <u>Worlds in Collision</u> thesis), and Dr John Bimson, Cambridge (on Biblical archeology). Health permitting, the 'great heretic', Velikovsky himself will be there." See Peter's review of the latest Velikovsky book (review section) for additonal context. For further details, write to: Ralph Amelan, Secretary SIS: 6 Jersey House, Cotton Lane, Manchester 20.

*** We would like to see more letters of discussion - it's up to you. But if you send us your opinion on Fortean matters please include the <u>sources</u> of material you criticise, quote, praise or refer to. We can't always answer your letters immediately, sometimes not at all - so please be patient. We really appreciate your responses though. Feedback is important.

FORTEAN TIMES

Fortean Times

attacks by animals 14
phantom cats on the prowl 33

75p·$1·50

UK ISSN 0308-5899

FORTEAN TIMES

A Contemporary Record of Strange Phenomena

FORTEAN TIMES ℅ Dark They Were & Golden Eyed,
9-12 St Annes Court, London, W1, England

FORTEAN TIMES is a non profitmaking quarterly miscellany of news, notes and references on current and historical strange phenomena, related subjects and philosophies. Formerly 'The News'. Affiliated to the International Fortean Organisation (INFO), and the Society for the Investigation of The Unknown (SITU), and other Fortean journals in continuing the work of Charles Fort (1874-1932).

Edited and published by Robert JM Rickard.
Contributing editors: Phil Ledger, Steve Moore, Stan Nicholls, Paul J Willis. Heading art by Hunt Emerson.

SUBSCRIPTION information and details of other deals can be found on the back page.

CONTRIBUTIONS of articles, artwork, notes and letters-of-comment on related subjects are always welcome. **YOU CAN HELP** by sending us a copy or clipping of any item you think will interest FT readers — just add a note of the DATE, the SOURCE and your NAME (for the credit). All clippings go on file to be published in due course. Please don't assume we must know about it already — there are surprisingly few duplications.
The editor regrets that it is not always possible to reply to all correspondence. Acknowledgements of money received will be sent via the following issue of FT.

RIGHTS: All articles and artwork in FORTEAN TIMES are the copyright of the authors and artists. The views of contributors are not necessarily those of FT, and vice versa. Uncredited material is by the editors.

FORTEAN PICTURE LIBRARY — We are laying the foundations for a long-needed pictorial archive to satisfy both research and commercial needs for the preservation and supply of visual material on Fortean subjects. Interested parties (users or those with material) can contact us via FT's editorial address.

Printed by Windhorse Press at Sukhavati,
51 Roman Rd, London E2

FT25, SPRING 1978.

CHANGES

You will already have noticed several changes in this issue. We have a new, and more legible logo, which we hope carries some flavour of our bibliographic efforts - the old logo was chosen for its similarity to the gothic heads of some newspapers and the whole post-Caxton era; the new one suggests that our roots go even further back into the manuscript millenia. Hope you like it!

The opportunity for the logo change came up with our change of address. Our long-time friends at the central London SF and comic bookshop, Dark They Were & Golden Eyed, suggested using their premises as a base (for which our thanks go to Derek Stokes). This made further good sense by the fact that Stan Nicholls, who is taking over the job of looking after our sub and mailing affairs, also works there. I'd like to express publicly my sincere appreciation to Paul Devereux and the Ley Hunter staff (especially Kay Thompson) who allowed FT to share their PO Box, and who collected the mail for us for the last year and a half, often putting themselves out for us out of pure friendship and kindness.

However, travel and time restrictions on both of us made meeting Paul more than once a week very difficult, and I was begining to find that a week's delay (sometimes more) on the mail was creating problems I didn't need. Paul and I will continue to meet once a week though to talk over matters of mutual interest to FT and TLH.

So we ask you all to update your address books with FT's new address, but please note that the full address must be used (part of the conditions) and ask you to include "c/o Dark They Were & Golden Eyed", which may be abbreviated to "c/o DTWAGE".

TRUSS FUND

in which we gratefully acknowledge the donations of the following: David Dunthorn, Bill Figorski, SN Morgan, Steve Ogden, JW Scaife, Mike Ward, Douglas K Watson, Ms AF Wood, & Geoffrey Chibbett (in memory of Harold SW Chibbett).

From the small heap of notes we have on things zipping around us in Earth-local space, and appearing in our skies if not our telescopes, we have had or are having a hazardous time lately.

NEW PLANETS etc

There seems something portentious about the number of new 'planets' being spotted. Progres Soir (Lyon, France) 6 Jan 1977, opened the year with the announcement of a Mexican mathematician, Jacinto Amor de la Pena, that after years of calculations he had finally pinpointed the 10th planet, which he called 'Jano'. He is not dismayed by the fact that no observatory has yet seen the planet he claims is 8,790,000,000km from the sun, completing its orbit every 450yrs, resting on the ancient tradition in astronomy of prediction before discovery. Forteans know that the actual history of such wonders of 'scientific prediction' are murky to say the least - see Fort's New Lands and Lo! for insights. (Cr: Phil Ledger.)

On the evening of 3 Nov 1977, Chinese astronomers, at Tzuchinshan, near Nanking, spotted a fast-moving, blurred celestial body which they considered a new comet. Los Angeles Times, South China Morning Post both 8 Nov 1977 (Cr: Colin Johnson, Ron Dobbins.) About a month previously, the Bangkok World announced, incredibly, that Soviet "astrologers" (sic) had found a "new constellation" (sic), meaning Russian astronomers had located a new comet against the constellation of Pisces. Whether this relates to the Chinese discovery we know not, but two in a month...gee! Bangkok World 6 Sept 1977 (Cr: I Will.)

Early in Nov 1977, Charles Kowal, of Mt Palomar Observatory, announced the discovery of a new body in the Solar system - it could be a new class of asteroid, or the 10th and smallest planet. Between 100-400 miles in diameter, it is smaller than the largest asteroid between Mars and Jupiter, and its orbit is way out beyond the usual asteroid belt, taking it across the orbit of Uranus,

whose own previously undetected rings were telescopically revealed earlier that March. Kowal later named the object 'Chiron', though there is some uncertainty as to its proper classification; not properly an asteroid or planet, Kowal suggests 'planetoid'. But Dr Brian Marsden of the Central Bureau for Astronomical Telegrams says computer tracking studies of its orbit indicate the elliptical characteristics of cometary objects. A closer look will have to wait until the 1990s. Kowal found the object during analysis of photographic plates taken on the nights of 18 & 19 Oct. For confirmation Kowal asked Dr Tom Gehrels to examine plates of the same portion of sky Gehrels had exposed at the University of Arizona on the nights of 11 & 12 Oct. A graduate at CalTech found the same object on plates exposed on the nights of 3 & 4 Nov. Los Angeles Times 8 Nov; Indianapolis Star 9 Nov & 11 Dec; Daily Mirror 11 Nov & 3 Dec; Sunday Statesman (Delhi) 27 Nov; General News (Cedar Rapids, Iowa) 11 Dec; South China Morning Post 21 Dec; Daily Telegraph 21 Dec 1977 (Cr: Kurt Lothmann, Ron Dobbins, Lucius Farish, Sam, Ion Will, Colin Johnson, Ian Lawes.)

SOME CLOSE SHAVES...

No sooner was Chiron labled than more asteroids headed our way. One, estimated to be nearly a mile in diameter, zipped by within 8 million miles of us on 15 March. A slightly larger one came within 12 million miles on 8 March. Both had been discovered by Dr Hans-Emil Schuster of the observatory at La Silla, Chile, earlier in Feb. It was said the closest known pass of a similar object was in 1937 when the asteroid Hermes squeaked by only ½ million miles away. Evening News (Harrisburg, Pa) 14 March; New Straits Times (KL, Malaysia) 17 Mar; Sun (Sydney, Aust) 21 March 1978. (Cr: Larry Arnold, Ion Will.)

LIGHTS IN THE SKY

Of the many kinds and reports of luminous phenomena seen in our skies, we just have room for two astronomical ones.

From midnight to dawn on 11-13 Aug, the public was told in advance, sky-watchers would be able to see many fiery 'shooting stars' throughout the world, as lumps of rock and ice from the close passage of Comet Temple-Swift burn up in the atmosphere. Daily Telegraph 3 Aug 1977 (Cr: Mrs V Martin). We don't remember whether this prediction came true or not, so we consulted our crude but right trusty day-log card-file. Nothing much for 11th except a 5.5 Richter tremor in Japan. 12 Aug saw a 4.4 Richter tremor in California; a mystery light off Bognor Regis, Sussex, believed at the time to be a plane crashing into the sea or a shooting star; and several witnesses to UFOs at Russ Green, Essex. (Full stories and sources will be given in future citations.) 13 Aug saw a late night rain of yellow "dust" on Springwell Estate, Sunderland. There were other events in this period - polt, accidents, attacks on animals, 'Son of Sam' caught, and the loony on the crane in France scattering his money to the wind (see 'Falls' this issue) - quite a Fortean period in fact; but it's also possible that those lights seen on the 12th were cometary debris.

A similar situation to the phantom plane crash at Bognor Regis (above) was caused on a larger scale by a meteor "as big as a house" (according to one witness) that trailed across the southern USA on the night of 18 Oct. At about 8pm CDT, the bright object was seen by witnesses in Texas, Arkansas, Oklahoma, Missouri, and Louisiana, causing phone lines to all authorities and media to be jammed with calls ranging from fears of a Martian invasion, to the object landing on a relative's house. Two plane crashes were reported as witnesses saw fiery material plummet earthwards, and many callers claimed the meteor had come down in their yards. SAC radar, in Nebraska, tracked the object as it "fell apart" in the air - confirmed by an Air Force pilot, in a jet at 16,000ft, who saw the object "light up my cockpit and split up into bits and pieces" at an estimated altitude of near 55,000ft. Texarkana Gazette, Northwest Arkansas Times (printed in Fayetteville, folks - see Grimstad article this issue), Log Cabin Democrat (Ark), Marshall News Messenger (Tx) all 19 Oct 1977 (Cr: Lou Farish, Tom Adams.)

Our card-file revealed another synchronicity here: 18 Oct was also the first night Kowal photographed Chiron unawares. Also...the night the CalTech graduate photographed Chiron unawares, 3 Nov,

astronomers in China were spotting their new comet. These are Fortean times!

DUCK THE JUNK

One of the theories put forward to account for the series of mystery booms on the East coast of N America - more in desperation than good sense - was the explosion of re-entering space junk. Within a few weeks that's what really did happen. We had to smirk at that one! Apparently Russia's Cosmos 954 satellite was punctured by a meteorite and its orbit decayed sufficiently for it to threaten to come down in North America. Most of it burned up on re-entry - hardly a comforting prospect as it had on board about 100lbs of Uranium 235. As it happened the debris eventually located east of the Great Slave Lake in Canada had far less radioactivity than originally feared. It was a remote area - it could have been much worse! The crash and search for debris was covered in most of the world's papers between 24 Jan and 2 Feb 1978. (Thanks to our regular clipsters for material.)

As an aside, we might mention that one paper told of two tiny townships in the initial estimated danger zone, called Fort Radium and Uranium City!

Other notes of space-junk on file: A UFO widely sighted over northern Japan on 26 Oct 1977 was said by Japanese government sources to be the remains of a satellite shot down by a Soviet 'killer satellite'. A US Defence Dept spokesman said this looked like the third such test of a Soviet 'killer' satellite. South China Morning Post 12 Nov 1977. Similarly, a UFO that "crashed" near Tlaxcala, Mexico, on 16 Jan 1978, was said to be the cremation of a dead US satellite. South China Morning Post 18 Jan 1978 (Cr: both, Colin Johnson.)

Not really a space-junk story, but related in a way... No sooner had the hoohar over the Canadian spy satellite crash died away than a Rolling Stone journalist, Howard Kohn, claimed that the CIA had hired mountaineers to plant a spying device powered by 10lbs of Plutonium 238 on the high slopes of Nanda Devi on the Indian border, to monitor China's atomic experiments in Sinkiang Province. However, the device was swept away in an avalanc and Mr Kohn alleges the outer casing will rust away in 10yrs to raise the serious possibility of nuclear pollution of the headwaters of the Ganges, India's holy river. Official investigation was demanded of President Carter...but we've heard no more on this. London Evening Standard 13 April 1978.

SEE LAST MINUTE NOTE ON p8, COL 1...   RJMR

FATEFUL FAYETTE

by BILL GRIMSTAD

'What's in a name?' — that handy phrase condensed from Shakespeare — has been forcibly retired by many American editors these days. Perhaps rightly: it does tend to find its way with frequency into stories and headings. The saying obviously fills some need. But I will avoid using it here, mainly because the answer to its question, usually left dangling, is the subject of this little disquisition. That is, I will assume for the moment that there is an answer . . . somewhere.

The American writer John Keel was, so far as I know, the first to notice name-frequency correlations in paranormal events. In his deceased magazine, *Anomaly*, Keel observed that the name McDaniel has recurred at far greater than random rate. A man named McDaniel was confronted by a three-legged 'creature' at his farm near Enfield, Illinois, in 1973. Another family of that name was the centre of the 1966-67 'Mothman' episode in West Virginia; and a man named McDaniel was involved in an encounter with 'the Devil' in the Catskill Mountains of New York in the 1870s. [1]

My candidate for this peculiar nomenclature is the name Fayette and its variants Lafayette and Fayetteville, which appear in a number of localities scattered across America. In the course of cataloguing all sorts of weirdities, I soon noted the frequency with which 'Things', as Ivan Sanderson used to call them, arise in conjunction with this name.

The historically minded might think first of the prestigious Marie Joseph Paul Roch Motier de Lafayette, the French revolutionary general and statesman who played such a role in the early years of the United States. Lafayette travelled widely in this country and doubtless must have been the inspiration for many or most of the 18-odd counties and 28 towns and cities across the land that I have been able to find with some form of his name.

But not all of them, apparently. In New England, the name first appears on a divergent site in 1759, when Elder Paul Coffin noted in his diary that 'There is Magic and Witchcraft in Fayette' (state of Maine). He referred particuarly to the 'Moving Arm Ghost', said to rise up from the spring near Jolly Hollow with a copper dipper for thirsty passersby, while at least accommodating times, something irritably splashes water on those visiting the spring. 1759 is but two years after Marquis de Lafayette was born, in France, so there must have been some earlier naming antecedent. [2]

In a moment, I would like to come back to what some regard as the darker side of Marquis de Lafayette, together with some of the more sinister manifestations connected today with his name. But first, let me take a quick skim through my Fayette case file.

In Fayette County, Alabama, is the Musgrove Methodist Cemetery. The tombstone of one Robert L. Musgrove there bears a discoloration, not specially realistic, that is locally believed to be the bridal-veiled figure of Musgrove's fiancée. Apparently he was killed just before the wedding, and the sorrowing girl decal'd her outline onto the marble by her many visits to the grave.

The enigma-laden state of Arkansas has two sites. The city of Fayette-ville, in the northwest corner, has long been legendary for oddities. UFO and aerial lightshows, water monsters in the nearby White River and Springheel Jack-type window peepers are among the manifestations. In the southwest angle of Arkansas is a Bigfoot hotspot that has been immortalised, in America at least, by the movie *Legend of Boggy Creek*. The critters have been known hereabouts since 1856, centring their activities lately upon the town of Fouke in Miller County and ranging eastward into adjacent Lafayette County.

In the scenic Bluegrass area of Kentucky, the university city of Lexington sits atop one of America's more dramatic lost cave stories. Historian G.W. Ranck recorded in 1872 that hunters in 1776 had found a tunnel behind a rock panel of 'peculiar workmanship' and covered with hieroglyphs. The descending portal widened to a sort of gallery running downward a few hundred feet to a huge underground room. Ranck cited the hunters' reports that this chamber contained idols, altars and about 2,000 human mummies. Although the entrance to the amazing cavern was (of course) lost, there still are cave true-believers who poke about looking for the weird mausoleum beneath this part of Fayette County.

In a famous travelling cat incident of a few years back. Chat Beau, a four-year-old male, successfully located his human family in Texarkana, Texas, after they had moved 300 miles from Fayette, Louisiana. [3]

Followers of ghost lore may have heard of the recent antics of a supposed phantom in Lilac Hill, a large old farmhouse at Fayette, Missouri. A number of psychically sensitive individuals have been trying to discern what is troubling the alleged spirits, of whom there are said to be at least two. [4]

In New York State, a farm near Cardiff, ten or so miles south of Syracuse, was the starting point in October 1869 for one of the more sensational fossil controversies. The 'Cardiff Giant' is still displayed at a museum near Cooperstown: although it has long since been dismissed as a total hoax, there are some puzzling aspects to the case that seem to make it a bit less than 'open and shut'. I cannot explore these now, but will merely note that many legitimate instances of petrification of animal and human remains have been reported from this area of Onondaga County south and east of Syracuse.

I must also note a certain historical confusion that I have not yet resolved: the modern city of Fayetteville, lying ten miles east of Syracuse, is some distance farther from Cardiff than was the 19th century town of La Fayette, which appears from contemporary accounts to have been only a short way from the 'Giant's' point of origin.

At this writing I am awaiting exact information from New York sources. I hope that this also will help elucidate an episode several decades earlier which, although little noted at the time, was to have great consequence in the history of religious movements. It was in April of 1830 that the Church of Jesus Christ of Latter Day Saints (Mormons) was founded by Joseph Smith and a few disciples — who claimed to have received more than a little help from certain 'angelic' friends in the neighbourhood. The place: Fayette, New York. Today, the Mormon Church is the fastest-growing Christian denomination in America, if not the world.

Another haunted house story takes us to an American state that perhaps rivals New York and Arkansas in the number and interest of its anomalies. It also brings us back across the trail of the peripatetic Marquis de Lafayette. This is the A.S. Slocumb mansion, located in the North Carolina city of Fayetteville. The Slocumb house is supposed to have a number of spectral occupants. It also has, or had, a secret vault in the basement and at least one tunnel leading to the Cape Fear River channel — which river has historically been the site of many Bigfoot reports.

Local records connect the Slocumb house with the affairs of the mysterious Bank of the United States (hence the vault), which was extirpated by the forces of President Andrew Jackson, amid charges of all sorts of hair-raising conspiracies. Whether Lafayette's own recorded visits to the house have any connexion with either the ghosts or the conspiracies is, unfortunately, not recorded.

Early this year, the United States experienced one of its most severe winters. Certain places were especially belaboured with extreme cold and repeated snowstorms. As of February 3, 1977, the National Weather Service announced that the 'hardest hit area' of the north-central states region was Fayette County, Ohio, about 44 miles southeast of Dayton. [5] In 1897, however, during the celebrated 'great phantom airship' excitement that swept across the country, Fayette County skies had been decorated with flurries of a different kind: mysterious paper balloons and kites, which are now usually described as the work of 'pranksters' inspired by the publicity growing from the cavortings of the 'airship'. [6]

As soon as spring arrived this year (1977), a farming area in north-western Ohio began experiencing a different sort of bedevilment. By early May, 140 sheep, five peacocks and possibly a dog were mysteriously killed by a something that tore out their throats. Footprints resembling those of a large felid were found. In mid-May, a motorcyclist was swept off the road by a mysterious force that he was at a loss to describe afterward. All of these untoward events occurred in the vicinity of Fayette, Ohio. [7]

Whether the hobby exists in other countries I do not know, but a very widespread diversion in America is the search for lost treasures. There are countless books and magazines on the subject, although if I were to do one I would focus on the obvious psychological factors at work. The 'treasures', real or imagined, seem to be more a pretext to go rambling off in search of the legendary lost than a quest of wealth per se.

Treasure stories time and again display Fortean aspects. One that suits the present purpose is the story of 'Braddock's gold', in which the British general of that name is said to have lost a wagon-load containing his own personal fortune and the crown revenues for his campaign. In 1755, Braddock's force was routed by a French and Indian attack not far from Fort Cumberland, on the Monongahela River. The gold wagon disappeared and has been fervidly sought by treasurologists ever since. Somewhere along the way, and presumably after the fact, the area became incorporated into Fayette County, Pennsylvania.[8]

Ordinarily, the Bigfoot phenomenon expresses only a fugitive interest in human situations, skulking in the shadows of lovers lanes, metal trailer houses (accidental Reichian 'orgone boxes'?) and women undergoing their menstrual periods. However, one of these hairy horrors became rather more aggressive on April 23, 1976, when it attempted to carry off a four-year-old boy from his backyard on a farm in Tennessee.

A sheriff's posse pursued the entity and seems to have shot

enough high-powered rifle fire into it to have felled King Kong* himself. However, as if tiring of the game, the creature finally leaped out of its cul-de-sac and simply vanished. These events occurred within a few miles of the hamlet of Fayetteville. [9].

In Fayette County, West Virginia, atop a low peak named Mt. Carbon, is one of the more curious ancient remains in North America. This is a series of semicircular and V-shaped stone 'windrows' strung out along the mountaintop. Archaeologists so far have been at a loss to explain such hilltop stone workings, which are also found in New England and in certain Western states.

Another Bigfoot-type creature was seen in Lafayette County, Wisconsin, in early September, 1970. It was seven feet tall with whitish fur and the usual shiny red eyes. More than 50 persons from the vicinity of Benton joined in a search for it, but were unable to find anything. [10] In 1936, an amateur aviator touched off a still hotly debated question around Rock Lake, which lies midway between Madison and Milwaukee in the southeast quarter of Wisconsin. A resident of the neighbouring town of Lake Mills, this pilot claimed that he had seen what looked like manmade rock structures beneath the shallow waters. The flyer's name: Fayette Morgan.

Recently, there has been a renewed Rock Lake controversy in underwater diving circles with amateurs claiming that they have rediscovered the 'pyramids', while professional underwater archaeologists sternly denounce such foolishness. [11]

Now I would like to consider some examples of more ominous character. We find the 'Lafayette factor' in the Abraham Lincoln assassination in the 1860s, although admittedly in comparatively trival ways. A slippery character named Lafayette had been brought in to head the Secret Service by the enigmatic Edwin Stanton, President Lincoln's arrogant secretary of war. Otto Eisenschiml, the pioneer revisionist historian of this amazingly crude murder conspiracy, delved into the story as far as the surviving evidence would allow.

His findings suggest that Lafayette Baker and Stanton had manoeuvred to facilitate the escape into the South of assassin John Wilkes Booth, and when that proved impossible (owing to his unexpected broken leg), to assure that the killer was *not* brought back alive and that his evidently incriminating diary did not survive intact. But the full story will have to be sought in the writings of Otto Eisenschiml. [12]

At the same time as the President was being shot in the theatre box, his secretary of state, William Seward, was attacked and savagely knifed by a deranged giant named Lewis Paine who had forced his way into the Seward home. This house fronted upon Lafayette Square, just across Pennsylvania Avenue from the White House. Washington's resident ghost expert, journalist John Alexander, has written of this square:

As you read these tales involving many of the residents of the square, you may find yourself in agreement with Washingtonians who refer to it as 'Tragedy Square'. No other section of Washington has had so much intrigue, mystery, murder and macabre happenings as has the area directly opposite 1600 Pennsylvania Avenue . . . [13]

Ironically, Secretary Seward had had a different brush with the Lafayette vector himself a few months before the assassination. A man named John Yates Beall had been convicted of spying for the Confederacy and was sentenced to die. Apparently this was another of those many cases in which there was much more than has met the official eye of history, for somebody or other galvanised a surprising number of Establishment bigwigs, who brought great pressure upon Lincoln to commute the death sentence.

However, it was Seward who reportedly encouraged the

*—KK, of course, had a crush on *Fay* Wray — Ed!

President to stand firm, and Beall was accordingly hanged at Fort Lafayette near New York City's 'Hell Gate' — on February 24, 1865. An insight into the bizarre affair emerged some years later when a close companion of Beall's at Fort Lafayette expressed his opinion that agent Beall may well have been involved in the planning of Lincoln's killing. Others were quick to infer that the attempt upon Seward may have been in retaliation for his insistence on executing Beall. [14]

Moving along almost a century, we find another grisly 'executive action' being carried out by conspirators unknown. According to New Orleans District Attorney James Garrison, one of the very few local authorities with the fortitude to carry out any kind of investigation of the John F. Kennedy killing, much of the actual planning of the 'hit' carried out in Dallas, Texas, was done in New Orleans.

The location: various sites centring on Lafayette Square and a decrepit office building just across Camp Street from it. In the *Warren Commission Report* on the assassination, the address of the building given is actually its side entrance: 531 Lafayette Street. [15]

On July 3, 1977, 23-year-old Gary Rock was charged on two counts of criminal homicide after two local volunteer firemen were killed by a sniper while responding to a fire alarm at Rock's isolated cabin, near Fayetteville, Pennsylvania [16]

On July 31, 1977, two young people sitting in a parked car along the Brooklyn, New York, seashore were shot several times by a mysterious assailant who had become known as the 'Son of Sam'. The girl, Stacy Moskowitz, died of her injuries; her companion, Robert Violante, suffered eye damage. Miss Moskowitz was an alumna of Lafayette High School. When she and Violante were shot, it was while they were sitting 'not far from Lafayette High School', according to the *New York Times*. [17]

I have other such instances in my files, but I think I have conveyed the general idea. What kind of interpretation can we make?

I suppose it might be argued that a similar case could be made by selecting any of a number of other names or places where 'Things' happen and then rummaging out enough incidents to suggest a pattern. If so, I haven't bothered to make the attempt. The Fayette factor was so obvious and so wisespread — an important aspect — that it required no forcing by me. Indeed, I have noted several other such names that seem to have a weird wont around the country: Bell (or Beall, as in the Lincoln conspiracy); Francis and St. Francis; Montpelier; Mount Vernon, and Parsons.

However, the number of instances I have found to date is far smaller than for Fayette. (There also is a very striking 'data cluster' pertaining to the mineral quartz, and it even has a tie-in of sorts with Fayette, but I must save that for consideration another time.)

So, what does it all mean? Merely a high order of 'coincidence' that for some reason happened to zero in on this name? It's possible, I suppose. I admit that I have nothing to fall back upon except my own intuition that there is more to the matter than this. But for those positivists inclined to dismiss possible anomalies too quickly on such semantic grrounds, let me recommend a quick review of Fort's remarks on coincidence (for example, pages 849-850 in the *Complete Books* — New York, 1974). Arthur Koestler's recent *Roots of Coincidence* takes up where Charles Fort left off.

An 'explanation', I grant, is out of the question. Besides, who wants one, anyway? My first impulse is simply to analyse the word. Literally, the meaning would be something like 'little enchantment' or 'little fairy' (from the Old French root *feer*, 'to enchant', plus the feminine diminutive *-ette)*. This much is easy. But of course I haven't the tiniest ghost (fayette?) of an idea how to parlay a word root into a mechanist scenario for the physical and psychical phenomena we have examined. Perhaps 'black arts' students of the technology of name magic

used in controlling supposed supernatural entities can shed some light here.

My second suggestion could lead off into vast, trackless wastes of arcane speculation, so I will try to be as concise as possible. We must go back once more to Marquis de Lafayette for a topic that may not be totally persuasive to all, but which will, I hope, prove stimulating to the Fortean imagination, pro or contra.

In addition to his political pursuits, Lafayette was busily involved in certain circles that should be of interest to contemporary Illuminati buffs. A subject of the utmost interest to the intellectual elite of Lafayette's day is one that gives signs of a comeback, in this day of Kirlian 'auras' and subatomic particles imbued with 'charm' and Buddhahood by sobersides Ph.D. physicist types.

The subject then was known under the general heading of 'magnetism', and referred to a supposed biophysical energy that was felt to be innate to all organic processes, and to possess other powers verging on the magical. Although the general idea is said to date from Rosicrucians and alchemists of the middle ages, and has been investigated by people ranging from chemist Karl von Reichenbach ('Odyle') to psychoanalyst Wilhelm Reich ('Orgone'), perhaps its most famous exponent was Anton Mesmer, the Viennese physician whose findings led to the modern study of hypnotism.

But Mesmer also seems to have been active in that vague twilight zone where esoteric matters merge into the crypto-political; more than one writer on the Bavarian Illuminati has identified him as a member of that group. Another suspected member was the colourful Cagliostro, the subject of much speculation by Charles Fort who seems to have regarded him as a virtual byword for the inherent trickiness and fraudulence of the visible universe. Although I do not have any evidence at hand, there seems little question that Cagliostro must have been *en rapport* with Mesmer when the former set up his 'Magnetic'Masonry' as an offshoot of the Egyptian Masonry by which he was cutting such a wide swath in French high society, and laying such fateful groundwork for the upheaval to come in 1789.

According to the contemporary American scholar Manly Palmer Hall, one of the more levelheaded writers on the extremely convoluted and controversial history of 'occult' matters, Lafayette was affiliated with both of these fateful men:

> . . . In 1785 the Marquis . . . joined the Egyptian Masonry of Cagliostro and proclaimed his absolute confidence in the Grand Cophte. When Anton Mesmer arrived from Vienna with his theories of animal magnetism, Lafayette was one of his first customers. [18]

But Lafayette also had the closest ties with Benjamin Franklin, the American revolutionary sage (and member of Dashwood's crypto-Satanist 'Hell-Fire Club' in Britain). As Hall puts it:

> Benjamin Franklin was a philosopher and a Freemason — possibly a Rosicrucian initiate. He and the Marquis de Lafayette — also a man of mystery — constitute two of the most important links in the chain of circumstance that culminated in the establishment of the original thirteen American colonies as a free and independent nation. [19]

Lafayette, Hall summarises, 'is a direct link between the political societies of France and the young American government. [20]

What I have to ask (perhaps never to learn the answer) is whether this 'man of mystery' was involved in anything other than the vague deism and 'rights of man' posited by the public face of the secret societies which worked behind the backdrop of the supposedly spontaneous American Revolution. Was this 'magnetism'-steeped gentilhomme whose celebrated

tours about America were virtual Masonic pilgrimages from
one prominent lodge to another actually an adept of sorts?

There is a very strong tradition in New Orleans that
Lafayette made a special point of meeting the powerful Voodoo queen, Marie Laveau, when he made his spectacular visit
there in April 1825. In fact, Laveau herself insisted that the
general had even kissed her on the forehead. As historian
Raymond Martinez points out, in his *Mysterious Marie
Laveau:*—

> In justice to those who think that Lafayette may have
> been interested in seeing Marie, it is fair to state that he
> had been at one time a patient of Franz Anton Mesmer,
> who introduced into general medicine magnetic therapy
> based on the laying on of hands. [21]

Voodoo, it would appear, is intensely magnetic.

Does all of this hint at the ever tantalising links between
Fortean phenomena and esoteric matters? Was the possible
Illuminist Lafayette a magician of such power that the mere
application of his name has been eough ever since to make a
given place 'act up'? Or was he himself a mere unwitting
function of che Fayette factor?

Bill Grimstad — 1977.

Notes of References

1 *Anomaly, a Journal of Forteana,* no. 10, Nov. 1973, p.189.

2 *Kennebec Journal,* Augusta, Maine, Oct. 30, 1976.

3 *Time.* July 18, 1972, p. 91.

4 *Fate,* July 1977, p.28.

5 'All Things Considered', National Public Radio, Feb. 3, 1977.

6 *Cyclone and Fayette Republican,* Washington Court House,
Ohio, April 22, 1897; cited by G.M. Eberhart, 'The Ohio
Airship Story', *Pursuit,* no. 37, Winter 1977, p.4.

7 *Lima,* Ohio, *News,* May 6, 1977; *Bluffton,* Ohio, *News*
May 5 & 19, 1977.

8 *Lost Treasure,* Sept. 1977, p.29.

9 *National Enquirer,* June 29, 1976.

10 *Bridgeport,* Connecticut, *Post,* Sept. 5, 1970.

11 *Skin Diver,* Jan. 1970, pp. 24ff.

12 Otto Eisenschiml, *Why was Lincoln Murdered?* Little,
Brown & Co., Boston, 1937, *passim.*

13 John Alexander, *Ghosts: Washington's Most Famous Ghost
Stories.* Washingtonian Books, Washington, D.C. 1975, p.33.

14 Eisenschiml, *op. cit.,* p.375.

15 Jim Garrison, *A Heritage of Stone.* New York 1970, pp.79,
94ff.

16 Associated Press dispatch. *Tampa,* Florida, *Tribune,* July 4,
1977.

17 *New York Times,* Aug. 1, 1977, p. 34C.

18 Manly Palmer Hall, *America's Assignment With Destiny,*
Philosophical Research Society, Los Angeles, 1951, pp. 88-
89. What could be more appropriate to this peculiar name
game than that Hall draws heavily upon the learned French
historian Bernard Fay for his account of this period?

19 M.P. Hall, *An Ecyclopedic Outline of Masonic, Hermetic,
Cabbalistic, and Rosicrucian Symbolical Philosophy.* Philos.
Research Soc. Los Angeles, 1962, 16th ed., p. cc.

20 M.P. Hall, *America's Assignment With Destiny, op. cit.,* p.94

21 R.J. Martinez, *Mysterious Marie Laveau,* Harmonson, New
Orleans, undated, pp. 32-33. Robert Tallant, *Voodoo in New
Orleans,* Collier, New York, 1962, p.41.

from p4 -- as we go to press the Sunday
Times 21 May 1978 reports a monumental
row in the Indian parliament, with former PM, Indira Gandhi, being accused of
concealing an authorisation for USA to
install a second device in 1967.

HUMAN CURIOSITIES

Last issue, in our review section, we
reviewed two very important books on
wolf children - important for their
insight and research as well as the
fact that any book on the subject of
feral children is a rare and welcome
event. Since then we have two incidents
- one a rescue, and one a feral child
report - giving us an opportunity to
herewith plop the contents of our
feral-children file before your gaze.
(These reports have accumulated since
we last dealt with the subject in FT3.)

LITTLE RED RIDINGHOOD...

One case we seem to have missed even
from FT3 was from 1970. Six year-old
Elmira Godayatova had travelled through a wood to visit her grandmother,
in Azerbaijan, USSR . Her grandmother,
(who does not appear to have had big
teeth, eyes and ears), told her to go
back home...but the girl never arrived
back. After desperate searches for 23
days, she was found exhausted, sitting
under a tree deep in the woods. When
she told her story, it became evident
she had been sheltered by wolves. She
said she had eaten berries and drank
water from springs, and played with
wonderful "doggies and puppies".
Times, Daily Mirror 4 July 1970 (Cr:
Janet Bord, Anthony Smith.)

The whole delightful episode parallels the story (on FT3/4) of a modern
'Goldilocks' - a 5yr-old, lost in woods
in Jugoslavia, who spent the night with
a bear and her cubs, in 1971.

One of the recent stories is about
another 'Little Red Ridinghood', this
time - a real surprise this - back in
Azerbaijan, USSR (given in one source
as Azerbeidjan), near the Caspian Sea,
involving a 3yr-old girl, Mekhriban
Ibragimov. She became lost overnight
in a snow-filled ravine, and was found
16hrs later sheltering in a cave with
a wolf and her three cubs. The girl
said: "A big wolf licked my face. I
snuggled up and she kept me warm. The

little puppies cried." The searchparty retrieved the human cuckoo and left the hospitable wolves in happy peace. Sunday Sun (Australia) 29 March 1978; & News of the World 9 April 1978 (Cr: Ion Will, Sam.) SOUTH CHINA MORNING POST 29 MAR (CR: COLIN JOHNSON)

MONKEY BOY

One big case, now old news, deserves a summary in FT - the monkey-boy of Burundi, in Central Africa. He was found by a party of missionaries, playing in a group of monkeys. In fact when he first scampered towards them on all fours, they thought he was a monkey. Other sources say hunters found him. Although some reports say he was found in 1975, it seems clear from later reports that the boy was actually found two years earlier, but had spent the time in a madhouse at Bujumbura, the Burundi capital. In 1975 there was an attempt to rehabilitate him. The boy was aged about six, had a slightly enlarged head, and without doubt the manners and behaviour of a monkey, most of the news stories claimed. Daily Mirror 22 Nov 1975, News of the World 23 Nov 1975, National Enquirer 24 Feb 1976, Weekend 3 March 1976, Observer (Magazine) 28 March 1976 (NB: this has good colour photo of the boy)(Cr: Sam, Anthony Smith, John Michell).

These reports must have attracted some professional attention because Dr Harlan Lane, who must have been putting the finishing touches to his brilliant study of The Wild Boy of Aveyron at the time, flew to Nairobi's Kenyatta National Hospital to examine the boy, with his colleague Dr Richard Pillard, both of Boston, Mass. After two weeks of "the most sophisticated analysis of the consequences of an extended period of living in the wild that has yet been possible," the doctors pronounced that the boy's condition was due to suffering "disastrous illness" at the age of two resulting in organic retardation. The NYT, reporting the press conference when the doctors returned to Boston, said they claimed to have accounted for every year in the boy's life. "He was never in the wild. For one thing there are no monkeys in that part of the country. It's densely populated. He was cared for at three orphanages, and spent three years in an adult psychiatric ward of a hospital," Dr Lane said. "His history had been lost because of inadequately kept records in a country with a strong oral tradition." So there you have it - we should have suspected something when different papers gave the kid different names, John, Charles, Francois, etc. Still...something niggles, that ole Fortean suspicion that rises when a mystery is easily and authoritatively dismissed or explained. Some of the earlier reports, particularly the Nat.Enq one (above), quote local people and officials who seemed convinced the boy had lived among monkeys; and according to an American anthropologist they interviewed, Diane Skelly, who had studied the child, the boy's body had been covered in a fine layer of hair when he was brought in,

which soon disappeared once he took to wearing clothes. Such details must be accounted for fully before we can accept or dismiss the case. Daily Mirror 15 May 1976, unidentified US clipping, apx May 1976; Daily Mirror, Daily Express, Newport News (Va) Daily Press all 4 June 1976; New York Times 9 June 1976. (Cr: Bob Forrest, Ion Will, P Hope-Evans, Gary L Abbott, Nigel Watson, Mike Rickard, Mark Hall.)

KANGEROO GIRL

About the time of the 'monkey-boy' of Burundi, came reports of a half naked white-skinned girl seen living wild, sporting with kangeroos, in the Australian outback. She was named 'The Nymph of Nullabor', after the desert of that name. Somewhere around this room, in the heaps of files and clippings, is a report on her from Newsweek, but a whole day's search for it proved as fruitless as the searches for the girl herself. So, with much deep-blushing we'll move on to stories with data to hand, pausing only to promise to give you the details on 'the Nymph' when they surface...

BUFFALO GIRL

Almost as improbable as a 'kangeroo-girl'...but why not when we've feasted on such delights as the 'gazelle-boy' (FT 4/14)...
Hunters in the jungles of Sri Lanka spotted a naked teenaged girl several times living with a herd of buffaloes. They claim that she was an illigitimate child who was abandoned in the jungle, then found and reared by some female buffaloes. The story is classic in its simplicity and interpretation and conforms to worldwide archaic traditions, both of disposing of 'embarassing' children, and of animal charity towards same...usually, though, in myth, such children grow to be heroes. Daily Mirror 8 Nov 1976.

Continued overleaf

BEAR BOY

About mid-April this year the story emerged of a boy, about 8yrs-old, found in a bear's cave in the jungles of Lucknow, India - fortunately, the hunters said, the 'parent' was out hunting for food. The story came to light because the boy was taken from the jungle village(where he was kept in a cage by villagers for at least a year) by nuns of Mother Teresa's famous Sisters of Charity order, in Lucknow. According to the scant details we have, the boy seems medically and psychologically capable of improving and learning. The Universe (India) 28 April 1978, The Herald (Australia) 19 Apr 1978 (Cr: Ion Will, H Thomas.)

RJMR

Forteans should never be amazed at the wonders of the universe, but I guess we're only human... The fact is that there has been an amazing accumulation of falling-material stories in recent years, as you may have noticed from our own coverage. Next issue we'll give you falling webs, hay and other veg matter, and some of the very recent ice-falls. But for now we'll deal with stones and artifacts...

BOLTS FROM THE BLUE etc

Firstly some notes on stuff falling, or apparently falling, from planes. W. Ritchie Benedict sent us an unfortunately undated Canada Press wire item from 1955 - that a piece of hot metal, about 9" long, plunged from the sky, embedding itself in a hole smashed in the wall of Mrs Agnes Joyce's home in Vancouver, BC. Mrs Joyce claimed it was still hot when she picked it up. It looked like part of a propeller, but there were no reports of aircraft in trouble over the city at that time.

Better authentification can be offered for the 7lb bolt that smashed through the roof of 80-yr-old Violet Collard's bedroom, at her home at Alma Rd, Windsor, Berks, rebounded off the floor and flew up to the ceiling again, finally coming to rest under her bed. Like ice-fall cases, it was blamed on a passing plane for which there seems to be no substantive evidence. Daily Express 12 Oct 1972.

When such identification is ever made it is quickly and obviously positive. Eg: part of a Rolls Royce engine on a TWA Jumbo jet fell off on a flight from Chicago to Los Angeles. Daily Express 12 Jan 1973.

A couple of interesting cases happened last year. On 25 April, a Lufthansa Boeing 737 landed safely at Heathrow after radioing that it had been "hit by something" in mid-flight. On landing it was clear the side had been hit a glancing blow by a hard falling object. Part of the flight was over a Belgian military zone, so they naturally assumed... London Evening News 25 April 1977.

On 16 Aug, RAF experts were called in to identify two "smoke-blackened pieces of alloy" that fell out of the sky over March, Cambridgeshire. No further reports appeared in the papers. Daily Express 17 Aug 1977. Interestingly, we had noted the very same day a light plane had taken off from a field in Berwickshire and apparently vanished - at least we saw no more reports. We send them planes, they send us blackened bits if they can be bothered! Daily Express 13 Aug 1977.

According to the Sunday Times 28 Aug 1977, that month had seen atleast three incidents of debris "falling from aircraft" to date, apparently unconnected. They mention one: a one-foot-square piece of metal fell "from 10,000ft", nearly hitting a mother and daughter in their garden at Crowborough, Sussex, on 20th Aug. Once again,the plane is implied rather than seen - after all,bits can only fall from planes. It would be too shocking to think of stuff waiting up there, or teleported there from cosmic junkheaps, waiting, then falling. The husband, Mr David Russell, thinking as anyone can be excused for thinking, that the chunk that nearly brained his wife and daughter had fallen from a plane, complained loudly to the Dept. of Trade - and they admitted the other similar reports. We don't know of the third incident ourselves. A predictable silence descended.

MODERN MANNA RAINS

In Phenomena John Michell and I gave some examples of coins and money falling from the sky, as welcome to the recipients below as was manna to the Israelites in the desert. (Phen.p19)

We remember hearing of a fall of silver coins in the Gorky region of Russia but were never able, til now, to get a literary fix on the datum. All credit to our wandering clipster, Ion Will, who saw it mentioned in the Sunday magazine of Calcutta. It seems that several thousand kopecks' worth fell on 17 June 1940, during a storm. It was surmised that a treasure had become uncovered in a landslide somewhere, and was picked up by a tornado and gifted to the people of Gorky. We note the novel use of a theory usually used to excuse falls of fishes, and that here, as there (if you follow me), no account is taken of the accompanying debris demanded by such a process. This time round, however, we have no smart data to back this up. Instead, it seems, easier ways have been found to work the miracle.

On 8 Oct 1976 a light plane 'bombed' Rome's Piazza Venezia with banknotes of 500, 1,000 and 10,000 denominations. Amazed police were said to be puzzled at being unable to find out who did it and why! Newport News (Va) Daily Press 10 Oct 1976, Reveille 7 Jan 1977 (Cr: GL Abbott, P Hope-Evans) In France, however, a businessman was nabbed for scattering more than £2000, in francs, from the top of a 150ft crane. He was taken by police to a mental clinic (they get no marks for imagination!) Reveille 12 Aug 1977... the incident happened at Nice!

In the quiet steel-town of Bethlehem, Pensylvania, police were called when a plumber had to fish out of a service-station toilet more than $3,000 in torn $100 bills, on 24 July 1977. On the 26th, a cleaning woman found another $1,000 in torn $100 bills clogging a restaurant toilet. Treasury officials say the money does not appear to be counterfeit; and the FBI said the bill-numbers do not match those of recent local robberies. Bafflement reigns!

Someone, or something was obviously feeling flush - or perhaps he was round the bend! Dallas (Tx) Times Herald 27 July, Dallas Morning News 29 July 1977 (Cr: Tom R Adams.)

Tom's Fortean eye noted another Pennsylvania windfall -- the day after the second lot of bills went down the tube in Bethlehem, on 27 July, a broken sack scattered about $250,000 in $20 bills out of the back unlocked door of an armored bank truck in the rush-hour in a Philadelphia street. Despite the hectic grabbing that ensued police proudly claim that at least $242,000 had been recovered. Dallas Morning News 28 July 1977 (Cr: Tom Adams.) A similar incident happened in Nottingham, England. nearly 2 months later. On 2 Sept, a security van drove along a street showering loose change from its back. The money was recovered - the men sacked. Daily Telegraph 3 Sept 1977 (Cr: Sam.)

STONE-FALLS

I know some of the above were not 'proper' falls, but the following notes might atone.

On Saturday afternoon, on 12 July 1975, a rain of small stones lasting several seconds, astonished people in the rue des Tongres, Etterbeek, Belgium. The stones were black and sticky, and harmed no one. Police issued a statement of their suppositions; that the stones were meteoric, or that they had been lodged in the landing gear of planes flying into or out of nearby Zaventem airport and shaken loose overhead. Le Soir (Belgium) 15 July 1975 (Cr: Henri Prémont.)

I have had a not-close-enough encounter with a sticky stone before. On the evening of 12 May 1969, Mr Joe Bloomer, of Sycamore Rd, Aston, Birmingham, was working in his garden when something fell out of the sky to thump the path infront of him. It looked like a rock - apx 1½lbs and about 4"x3" - but was "warm and sticky" to the touch. It did not appear to be damaged, and "seemed to expand as it cooled down." The report, in Birmingham Evening Mail 13 May 1969 (it only appeared in the night-final edition), said that the 'rock' had been sent to 'scientists' at Birmingham University. My attempts to locate it, or anyone who knew about it, at B'ham U proved fruitless. I was even palmed off with the suggestion that the witness must have been thinking of the famous Barwell meteorite, the sense of which completely escaped me, as that happened in Leicestershire on 24 Dec 1965!!! I wrote to Mr Bloomer many

Joe Bloomer with the stone that nearly brained him, 12 May 1969, Birmingham.

times - once even offering to take him
for a drink - but either I had got his
name embarassingly wrong, or he didn't
want to know. Unfortunately I could not
go to his address. But there the matter
lies for now. One bright aspect though:
I managed to rescue, from the paper, a
photo of the object held by Mr Bloomer
(see this page). It was not taken by
their staff photographer and they did
not have a neg - all efforts to trace
the photographer failed, so our apologies are proffered. We will keep this
photo in the Fortean Picture Library
(FPL) files, acting as agents until the
owner can be established.

A more sinister and poltergeist-like
case is said to have happened to Dr
Olavo Trindade, a Brazilian surgeon, as
he was driving with four friends, near
midnight on 18 Sept 1975 on a deserted
highway near Brazilia. The car began to
overheat mysteriously, and as the driver got out to investigate, the car was
bombarded "from every direction" by
rocks. "It was a windless moonlit night
with no one in sight. We sped away but
the stones kept smashing against the

car. We were racing toward a police
station 2 miles down the road when
something even more terrible happened.
Right before my eyes a stone materialized out of nowhere inside the car and
hit Mrs Queiroz on the head. Then it
leaped over to (her nephew's wife) and
hit her on the head. The women screamed.
The car was sealed tight - there was no
way the stone could have gotten inside.
Incredibly, the rock barrage didn't
stop until we reached the police station." Two policemen went back with them
to the spot where it had begun. Suddenly all hell broke out once more. Police
Sergeant Jorge Paos described his experience: "The moon was bright...and no
one in sight...suddenly the stones
began to crash against Dr Trindade's
car. Officer Rambero and I searched
both sides of the road, but there was
nothing. Then weird clouds of dust rose
up and swirled around the car, and to
my horror I saw enormous human shapes
inside the   dust cloud - giant forms
8 or 9 feet tall. I tried to fire at
them but my gun jammed." Rambero's gun
had jammed as well. Dr Trindade added:

"We drove furiously back to the station, and all the way our car was surrounded by these giant humanoid shapes and flying rocks." At one point the driver stopped the car and tried to fire his own gun at the frightening forms - but his gun jammed too. As they resumed their journey, the locked doors sprung open and only with the greatest application of their strength could the passengers pull the doors shut as they sped along. By now the men were shouting as the women screamed - but one, Manoel Queiroz, began praying "to God" and the racket and forms quickly vanished. They were convinced they had been attacked by "forces of evil". Any of you interested in the phenomena of alleged UFO abductions and Close Encounter experiences will have recognized several details here, suggesting to us that both UFO and Fortean phenomena do merge with religious phenomena. How and why is anyone's guess at the moment. National Enquirer 24 Feb 1976.

We have given examples of such overlaps before - but here's the taste of another. According to the Sunday Times 3 Oct 1976, a bizarre "spiritual coup d'etat", in which an impressive number of Indonesian religious leaders were tricked into signing documents designed to oust President Suharto, was exposed in late Sept 1976. It centered on an obscure former government official, Sawito Kartowi, who had managed to harness the moral indignation of various closet dissenters by playing on their sympathies. Over the years we have glimpsed briefly the doings of Sawito, and weird they are too. We hope to give you them in more detail one day. But for now, we give you the tantalizing words of one of Sawito's dupes in publicly denouncing Sawito: he said that Sawito was a "lunatic" who claimed to receive messages from God "to oust President Suharto", after stones had fallen from heaven into his hand, with a portrait of Jesus on one side and himself on the other. The Times correspondent adds that it is by no means certain that Sawito is a mere crank. For one thing Sawito was in the same weird cult as several of his dupes... but I must stop calling them dupes, as we only have the Indonesian government's word on this, and they have no small vested interest in discrediting Sawito. But fancy, if he really had shamanistic powers... One final comment ...Forteans will be reminded by the alleged images on the stones, of Fort's case of the figured hailstones of Rem-

irement (see Books p967f; if you don't have a copy, see p59 of Phenomena).

SOME EXOTIC FALLS

Beads -- One story that has fascinated me since I first heard of it, back in Fate Jan 1955 p9, impressed me so much I had to use it in Phenomena - it is about the periodic rains of small beads, at Bijori, India, of all sizes and colours, and holed ready for threading. Even in 1955 the phenomenon was acknowledged to happen after most rainstorms, "covering the fields" with beads. Once more to our magic clipster, Ion Will, goes credit for snipping another illuminating note, although he hadn't heard of it before himself. In New Thrills (Malaysia) 17 Aug 1977, the bead rains are said to be continuing today "in irridescent profusion". We ought to have the resources to investigate, but right now we don't. Let's hope they keep on raining till we do, and that the locals of Bijori, in Mandla district of Central Province keep on stringing the beads into the necklaces they call 'Sulaimandana'(King Solomon's Rosaries).

Bottles -- Our last datum merges into the 'phantom sniper' type of phenomena. A block of flats in Hamilton, New Zealand, was subject to a torrent of milk, beer, soft-drink and coffee bottles against its sides and roof for three consecutive days. After the first night, police and their dogs kept a vigil, but the onslaught, which began at 9.30pm, continued through to 1.30am. The same happened the next night, and the police confessed their inability to find any culprit/s. Maori elders, however, know precisely what has happened. The land was once forest, they say, and the spirits of the land in that area became offended. No firm dates can be offered for this story, but we'll be interested to hear from NZ readers who can look into it for us. Sunday Express 8 Dec 1974.

Finally...
a plea for some specialist help. Our reader, CW Murray, experienced a fall of strange hair-like filaments during a storm over Acton, London on a July evening, about 1964. He was quickwitted enough to gather some samples, which he has sent to us, and which we would like analysed or identified. Offers or suggestions would be most welcome as we have no contacts for this sort of expertise just yet. The other plea is to any London reader who may be able to remember such an event, or help us pinpoint the time.   RJMR

MYSTERY ATTACKS

THE WAR ON MAN...

It seems to us highly justifiable when animals occasionally fight back against their conquerors; but the bulging girth of our file seems to indicate full-scale war has broken out! Alas, space limits us to a few brief selections here, but we'll return to the subject later...

THE ARMED STRUGGLE...

Tales of hunters shot by their own dogs are neither new nor uncommon. Morton St. Philip, nr Bath: William Bull, 31, hunting moles, lay down to sleep and woke up with half his face blown away. His dog was alleged to have pawed the gun...with fatal results. Grimsby News, 27 Aug 1909. (Cr: N Watson).

Coburg, W. Germany. 7 Oct 74. Paul Jahn, 53, a millionaire, was shot to death when his dog jumped into the car and tangled his lead in the triggers. Times, 8 Oct 74, Weekly News, 11 Jan 75.(Cr: P Ledger, N Watson)

Erringden Moor, Yorks: Michael Kelly put his shotgun against a wall as he was climbing over, and his Setter puppy leapt against the trigger, shooting him in the shoulder. D. Mirror, Express, 28 Oct 78.

Luneville, France: A hunter leaned his gun against his hotel window. His dog jumped on it, and shot a passing soldier, again in the shoulder. Evening News, 8 Nov 76, D. Mirror, D. Express, 9 Nov 76, New Musical Express, 27 Nov 76. (Cr: P Hope-Evans).

And then everyone was doing it: Chartres, France: Vincent Caroggio had shot 6 rabbits when he put his gun down for a drink. Lucky rabbit No 7 stuck his head out of his burrow, bumped into a trigger... and shot Caroggio dead. News of the World, 25 Jan 76 (Cr: N Watson)

Queensland, Australia: Aborigine Charlie Banjo tied a wild piglet to a loaded rifle. In its successful struggle to escape, the piglet shot him in the foot. Birmingham Evening Mail, 21 June 74. (Cr: R Willey).

Vienna, Austria: A young boar charged a hunter, got entangled in the rifle sling, and fired it. Alas, he missed. D. Mirror, 26 Feb 77.

Nr Sarzana, N. Italy: Francesco Cortesi, his wife and two sons went rabbit-hunting on their farm. A hen went with them, making so much noise it scared the rabbits away for 2 hours. Cortesi lost his temper and rushed at the hen...which promptly stepped on the trigger of his gun, and shot all four of them. Super-chicken got away, too... D. Telegraph, 12 Mar 77, Reveille, 1 Apr 77. (Cr: P Hope-Evans).

And doing it in spades...

San Bernadino, California: Whenever a farmer caught a coyote on his land, he would tie a stick of dynamite to its tail, light the fuse and chase the animal away. Thankfully, natural justice prevailed (though the punishment hardly seems adequate): one of the coyotes ran under his car and blew it up... News of the World: 29 Jan 78.

FERRETS.

Skegness, Lincs: The case of 9-yr old Linda Wright has received such extensive coverage (Most national daily and evening papers, 27, 28 Jan 78, Cr: many) that we shall be brief: Linda woke at 2am when she was savaged by a wild ferret which had somehow got into the house, presumably when the cat was let out for the night. It bit her on both cheeks, and was still attached when she ran, screaming and bleeding, into her parents' room. Mr Brian Wright managed to pull the ferret from her face and shot it dead with an air rifle. Only suggested reason for the attack was that the ferret was hungry...which is a frightening thought...

High Wycombe, Bucks: In April 77, Darryl Pitchford and Richard Elliff where killed when their car ran into the back of a lorry. A dead ferret was found stuffed between the front seats. It was conjectured that the ferret could have got out of a box (which is not mentioned as being actually present in the car when found) and ran wild, causing the crash. Sun 7 June 77.

SNAKES:

Eating people...
North West Bangladesh: Villagers fought a tug-of-war with a 30-foot python which had half-swallowed a man. Both man and snake died. S. People, 3 July 77.

Central Sulawesi, Celebes, Indonesia: A 20-ft python was killed by villagers, who found the fully-clothed body of a 45-yr old man, with some broken ribs, inside. D. Telegraph, D Mirror 19 Nov 77, Observer 20 Nov 77.

Mount Tinombala, Indonesia: We know not whether this is the same story re-emerged, or a new case, but the Sunday Times, 7 May 78 reports a man attacked by a 6-yd python, which was killed the following day and cut open to reveal the fully-clothed body of the man.

And not eating people...
Nigeria: A bus company, complaining about rumours spread by their competitors, took an advertisement in the Nigerian Daily Times: "We wish to state categorically...that none of our numerous drivers was ever swallowed by a boa constrictor in a bush near Ore Town"! We're glad to hear it... Reveille, 10 Sept 76.

Crushing people...
Naples, Italy: 2 12-ft pythons strangled and crushed snake-charmer Janco Simba, 30, in the midst of his circus act. He was dead before performers could cut and axe the snakes from his body. Evening News, 11 Feb 77, D Mirror, D Telegraph, 12 Feb 77

Biting people...
Drayton Manor Park Zoo, Staffs: Zoo worker John Foden, trying to free another snake behind a rock,

was bitten by a diamond-back rattle snake. He was taken to hospital seriously ill, but recovered after police rushed serum to the hospital. D Mirror, Sun, 2 Apr 77.

Sandown Zoo, Isle of Wight: Keeper Douglas Corney was bitten while transferring a rattlesnake to a new enclosure. He had to be helicoptered to Southampton for serum. D Express, 19 Aug 77.

Vung Tau, Vietnam: Poisonous sea-snakes, 1-3 ft long, native to the central coast but having moved south in search of food, were blamed for dozens of deaths among swimmers and fishermen in the few weeks preceding our reports: S.F. Chronicle, Houston (Tx) Chronicle, 11 June 74. (Cr: L Coleman, MA Hall)

AMPHIBIANS...

Johannesburg, S Africa: Grandmother Nella Van Niewenhuisen, 60, was weeding the garden when she was savaged by a 2 lb 'shark-toothed' bullfrog, which bit a chunk from her hand. Her son-in-law beat the bullfrog to death when it attacked him too. Evening Standard, 8 Feb 77. D Mirror, 9 Feb 77.

And randy toads were blamed for the death of thousands of goldfish in Britain's ponds in spring, 77. There was, it seems, a shortage of female toads, an imbalance of up to 10 to 1, and the libidinous toads were making love to everything in sight...sticks, water-lilies, goldfish, clutching them in a strong grip for hours...a grip strong enough to crush the fish. D Mirror, 3 Mar 77, S. People, 6 Mar 77.

"SCIENTIST EATEN BY MONSTERS"

So declares the delightful headline in the South China Morning Post, 3 Oct 77. (Cr: C Johnson).

Kamodo, Indonesia: The varans, usually known as Kamodo Dragons, have turned savage due to shortage of food. And the 12-ft long lizards, of which there are only a 1000 pairs left, are blamed for the death of an unnamed scientist who went there to study them. He disappeared, and the only trace found was his camera, near where the varans live.

PRIMATES...

Southsea, Hants: A thief who broke into and set fire to a pet shop, was thought to have been bitten by a poisonous African monkey, the only survivor of nearly 200 pets. D. Sketch, 29 Dec 65

San Francisco: A monkey, using the Victorian scrollwork on housefronts as a trapeze, held a crowd in the street enthralled...until he descended and attacked a girl, biting her shoes. The monkey was captured and handed over to the SPCA. S.F. Chronicle, 22 Feb 74. (Cr: L Coleman)

Eelberdale, Hargesia, N. Somalia: On the 12th & 13th Dec 74, 25 villagers armed with heavy sticks fought a pitched battle with 5-600 Somali Monkeys (4ft 6ins, weighing 10 stone at maturity). The monkeys threw stones, bit and gashed, and threw people to the ground (one such throw resulting in a dislocated hip). Hunger resulting from drought was believed to be the motive. Casualty figures vary: 254 or 353 monkeys dead, 6 people injured. The remaining monkeys retreated to the hills at 4pm on the second day. S.F.Chronicle, 16 Dec 74, Reveille, 2 May 75. (Cr: L Coleman, N Watson)

Tarzana, California: We chuckle that the area surrounding the home of the late Edgar Rice Burroughs, creator of 'Tarzan', should be ravaged by chimpanzees. Mrs Debra Kessler heard a commotion among the eucalyptus trees at the back of her tennis-court and called the police. A sergeant arrived, stepped into the wood, and was pelted with broken branches. Mrs Kessler's son used the police car's radio: "Please send assistance. Officer surrounded by gorillas." A message that brought 23 armed men to the scene. Bravely stepping into the woods, they were pelted with bark, branches and cabbage stalks (the chimps were obviously waiting for them!), but they caught sight of at least 3 chimpanzees before beating a retreat. We have no further word of the chimps, but the sergeant who had to be rescued went into hiding... D Mail, 20 March 76.

Lamar County, Texas: 2 Orangutans escaped from their cage in a pasture and scratched two boys, 8 & 12 yrs old, as they walked through the field...for which crime they were duly hunted down and shot. Paris (Tx) News, 6 Jan 77 (Cr: TR Adams).

Kuwait: Seven crazed monkeys escaped from their zoo cage and killed two children, by biting and scratching. A zookeeper was seriously bitten too. Police shot one monkey and captured the others. S. Express 18 Sept 77 (Cr: P Roberts)

Bogota, Colombia: Marco Polo, a pigsty keeper and TV star, was reprieved from a death sentence for killing a 70-yr-old woman, on the grounds of provocation. Marco is a 5-yr old performing monkey. D. Express, & Indian Express 12 Oct 1978; & Calcutta Statesman 13 Oct (Cr:Ion Will)

Kenya: A baboon ran off with a 6-yr old child. D Express, 1 Nov 77.

Malaysia: Enraged at his master's insistence that he should take a daily swim, a pet monkey turned on the man and bit him to death. Neighbours killed the monkey with sticks. Evening Standard, 12 Jan 78. (Cr: I Laws).

FATAL ATTRACTIONS...

What fools we mortals be...sometimes we make it just too easy...

W Germany, place unknown: Berhard Griebner, 20, an animal lover, had to be identified from documents in his wallet. He broke into a zoo cage, and 16 lions promptly ate him, leaving only bones and scraps of clothing. D Express, 19 Jan 78.

Rome, Italy: On 23 Feb 78, Renato Fioreno, deaf and nearly mute, and also an animal lover, climbed into the Rome zoo, tried to open a cage, and was badly mauled by a 330-pound tiger. Herald Tribune, 25 Feb 78. (Cr: I Will).

Indonesia: According to the South China Morning Post, 20(?) Jan 78 (Cr: C Johnson) the bodies of two men, Sunarmin, 62, and Amarlack, 58 were found by a companion in the north Sumatran jungle. Both were experts in Silat, the local variety of martial arts, and both were badly clawed. Nearby lay a dead tiger, 'but there were no indications how it had died'. There's got to be a story behind that one..!   SM

Late News
As we assembled this issue two attacks appeared in the papers --North of Toronto, three youths were mauled to death by a 300lb black bear, which was found shot dead near them. Daily Telegraph 17 April 1978. -- At Heathrow airport, a small private passenger plane taxiing for takeoff was halted when a passenger's dog went berserk and bit him. Sunday Express 14 May 1978.

The Great
Fortean Computer
Project

Stay still·long enough and you foss-
ilise - that applies equally to physical
remains as it does to thought. Change
is forced upon us, and we adapt or go
under. FT, Fortean thought and Forteans
themselves are no exceptions. A small
but growing number of Forteans are begining to appreciate that our thought,
our organisational structures and the
relationships between the various Fortean bodies, our data handling methods
and our resources are all reaching their
limits. Indeed some of these factors
have already broken down or are simply
proving cumbersome or faulty in their
application or administration.

Perhaps the biggest and certainly most
pressing problem is the accumulation of
Fortean data. Fort estimated he had between 40-60,000 notes - not all were included in The Books; and Carl Pabst, of
SITU, has patiently deciphered and restored most, if not all, of CF's unpublished notes (Carl's project however is too
vast to include in a journal like FT &
needs a special publication, which must
come in due time.) And Fort only creamed
off the top of all the material he refers us to in the Books - a fact that
has prompted X to begin a periodical
archive of Fort's source material (see
note in our 'News' section this issue.)
Now Fort only covered the period 1800 -
1931 (with brief excursions), and the
rich veins of Fortean data outside, before and after that time, have yet to
be systematically plundered - although
some stalwarts have gone through, say,
the whole backfile of a local paper,
this hardly scratches the surface of
available records worldwide of historical material, periodical backfiles, personal research and anecdote collection
etc etc. Add to that the daily accumulation of notes from today's papers, and
I estimate we are talking about data in
the thousands of millions.

Already, on the small scale your edit-
or has to operate, the limit has been
reached. Files take up space; accessing
and coding takes time; both take a certain amount of financing - and there is
not enough of any of these things. And
out there, in the world, there are many
other Fortean researchers with their
own files, angles, problems and potentials. Forteans are a strange breed. The
nature of our material makes the quest
quite often a lonely pursuit, and most
Forteans of character or experience seem
to be fiercely individualistic, rogue
elephants and lone wolves suspicious of
the regimentation of thought in the pack
and the tendancy to institutionalise
knowledge and bureaucracy in the herd.
Consequently many Fortean researchers
tend to value communication with another
Fortean of similar calibre above much
else. FT was founded to serve this
kind of need, and so I feel it is a good
place to start the impetus for better
thought, tools and methods.

Basically the sort of problems generated by dealing with such huge volumes
of data are not unique to ourselves, and
there has evolved a large body of experience in the computer world, but mainly
applied to the academic, commercial and
scientific problems of this nature. Our
data, and the sorts of things we wish to
do with it are ideal for contemporary
computer applications. There were two
main obstacles for a tiny operation like
ours: cost and knowledge. Because of
recent rapid and truly amazing developments in microprocessing components, the
first, and originally greatest, obstacle
has now been completely removed. Fully
functional desk-top computers, with
enough memory and muscle, are now available for well under £1000 - and prices
will inevitably tumble lower because of
the explosion of interest in the use of

cont on p36/

Aert de Gelder's 'UFO' Painting

by PAUL SCREETON with CHRIS CASTLE

One of our regular clipsters, Valerie Martin, recently asked if we'd noticed the preponderence of some very Fortean looking artwork around these days on the covers of books and records etc. Indeed we had wondered about having some informed comment on Fortean themes in modern graphics and invite someone to offer us an illustrated article. Meanwhile we noticed this piece in a recent issue of the *Journal of Geomancy* (2.2.1978) the organ of the very active Cambridge based Institute of Geomantic Research (see our journal review section for details), and which we reproduce in an edited form, by kind permission of the parties involved.

A whispered 'Paul must see the flying saucer picture' whilst staying in Cambridge alerted me to the contents of the most extraordinary painting that I have ever seen. A hurried viewing of *The Baptism of Christ* at the Fitzwilliam Museum persuaded me that here was a picture of mystical content and that the strange object casting light upon a memorable religious occasion could well be placed in the UFO phenomenon context. It did not have to be an exact replica of the archetypal, supposedly extraterrestrial, vehicle photographed in dramatic circumstances by the late George Adamski; the similarity to countless reports of alleged interplanetary craft and the curious juxtaposition with a highlight of the Christian tale was sufficient.

But this was no psychedelic portrayal from the palette of the hip awareness of turned-on, tuned-in, dropped-out consciousness of the late 20th century visionary art. The brushes here were in the hands of Aert de Gelder who died in 1727!

Aert (or Aernt) de Gelder is hardly held in high esteem by the art world. His work, however, is widely dispersed and seemingly ignored as far as published studies are concerned (1). But what of the man? He cannot be discussed in isolation, for his art is welded into the flow of the Dutch School, and the mystical nature of the picture may have been inspired by a special religious outlook.

De Gelder was born on 26 October 1645, becoming a portrait painter who also depicted religious scenes and tableaux showing oriental influence. He was a pupil of Samuel van Hoogstraten, and between 1665 and 1667 studied under Rembrandt van Rijn, whose manner he followed closely. In Rembrandt's own later work his technique is free and bold, and suggests an obsession to express a vision. He had lost his former rapport with the public, who found themselves unable to follow him in his 'profound search for the spiritual essences of the biblical subjects which increasingly occupied him'. (2)

It is speculative link of religious brotherhood between Rembrandt, van Hoogstraten and de Gelder which concerns us primarily, hence it is reasonable to sketch a few details of the prevailing religious climate within which their work was produced. On breaking bonds early in the 17th century with Spain, Holland became a Calvinist nation, set apart from the Roman Catholic world. Consequently this rupture was decisive for artists. Previously the Church commissioned great numbers of new works covering large-scale treatments of religious motifs. Calvinism, however, deplored the Roman Catholic display of religious paintings in churches, hence such subjects were only commissioned by private individuals for their own homes. Religious art waned.

But for Rembrandt the Bible continued to be the main source of material for his compositions. And as for Calvinism, following his wife Saskia's death and the entry into an asylum of a woman he took into his service named Geertyhe Dirox, he fell foul of the Calvinist church of Amsterdam regarding his relationship with Hendrisje Stoffels. Their neighbours were upset by his liaison, but the couple failed to answer the summons. The charge was repeated in July 1654, citing only the woman and on a third summons she was admonished. Biographers deduced Rembrandt was not a member of the national church. Furthermore, Filippo Baldinucci related that the artist had joined the Mennonite sect, 'which is possible but not proven'. (3)

One of his pupils was Samuel van Hoogstraten (1627-1678), who had previously studied under his own father. The Rembrandt influence in his drawings and some of his paintings is obvious, but his lively mind stopped his being a copyist. A man who travelled widely, his art also covered several territories, such as landscapes, marines, animals and still-lifes. He caused a scandal in his native Dordrecht, when he was expelled in 1956 from the Mennonite community to which he belonged, for marrying without the community's approval and for wearing a sword.

A scientific theoretician, Hoogstraten had pupils at various periods, including Aert de Gelder, and in his old age composed for their benefit an elaborate treatise on painting, *Introduction to the High Art School,* illustrated with his own engravings. At one stage his study of optics led to his painting pictures producing uncanny visual effects. (4) Contemporary judgement places Rembrandt on a pinnacle, Hoogstraten as interesting only for his optical effects work and de Gelder as a minor painter. Indeed, market prices of de Gelder's work reflect this conspicuously.

A characteristic of at least two of Rembrandt's Biblical scenes is that 'aerial' personages occur in the top left hand corner: a winged angel in *The Sacrifice of Abraham* and a floating figure in the *Sacrifice of Manoah.* It may, of course, be pure coincidence that Aert de Gelder placed his aerial object left of centre at the top of his picture (5).

There would not seem likely to be a metaphysical link between Rembrandt and his pupil, de Gelder. In his major study of Rembrandt, Muller mentions several pupils of Rembrandt, but not de Gelder. There, however, is a postulated religious link between Rembrandt and van Hoogstraten through the Mennonites, but this Quaker-type sect seems unlikely to have induced a mystical-style view of religion. Consequently, we are left to examine the painting on its own merits. Physically the canvas is 19'' x 14-5/8'' and the Fitzwilliam Museum catalogue suggests its date as c1710. I asked a Cambridge artist, Chris Castle, for his opinion of the work, and this is his critical commentary:

'It is twilight, a hilltop, a landscape stretches away, the slightly glowing outlines of two towns, then mountains beyond.

'But on *this* hill top, a gathering of people in ancient dress gaze, motionless, entranced at the scene taking place before them. Two figures, the one kneedeep in water, head bowed, hands in attitude of prayer, stoops slightly toward the other who with outstretched arms sprinkles him with water.

'Something momentous indeed has caught the attention of the surrounding onlookers. The water and the two figures are bathed in a special kind of light, softly glowing. High in the sky above hovers a greenish disk at the centre of which is a tiny dove with outstretched wings. From that disk emanate four narrow rays which seem to travel down to earth penetrating the centre of the place/event below. The rays seem both to support the disk above and to come down as a blessing and completion of the baptism. But the rays themselves are painted in such a way as not to appear as light beams. Perhaps some other kind of 'light' is intended. The peculiar light quality of the scene is enhanced by the glow of the central event; indeed one feels the water to be charged with some spiritual energy.

'The overall harmony of the painting is maintained throughout by de Gelder's strict control of his palette. The rulebook of his master Rembrandt is in strong evidence in his coloration and his handling of the paint. The painting doesn't break through any revolutionary ground on the technical level. It is basically quite safely in the Rembrandt tradition. But the subject matter and overall atmosphere created is so unusual an interpretation of the Baptism of Christ that the shortcomings of the painting technique are overshadowed and soon forgotten. As Rembrandt's later works were those which influenced de Gelder, the surface of the painting is loose and almost impressionistic in soft smudgy brushmarks. No detail of importance emerges from either the figures looking on or the landscape beyond. Both landscape and people function only as setting for the cosmic fusion of sky and earth spirits.

'There is some doubt about the artist's intentions regarding the distribution of land masses in the painting. The Baptism seems to be taking place in water (the Jordan?) on a hilltop (a river on a hilltop?). Maybe a dewpond is intended or maybe this is not the Baptism of Christ at all.'

Assuming that there is a revelatory message in the scene as depicted by de Gelder we might consider a few aspects which appear to be relevant. Firstly the disk in the sky is so tantalizingly akin to reported UFOs that it could easily be utilized to substantiate the tiresomely tedious welter of paperbacks in the 'Was-God-an-Astronaut?' genre. Uncle Erich von Daniken and a horrendous host of bandwagoners have quarried this strata and their banalities have devalued the mercurial link between the UFO syndrome and mysticism. Central beneath the disc is a dove, and the Gnostics (regarded by Christian orthodoxy as heretics for their numerical interpretations) believed that 'the divine spirit, represented by the dove, entered into Jesus, the man, at his baptism, while the Church held that the spirit and the body of Jesus Christ were indivisible, and looked forward to bodily resurrection'. (6) This prophetic, rather than priestly, notion seems to be specifically pointed at in this painting. It can

be added that another dis object, the Holy Grail, is accompanied — as here — with beams of light and sometimes preceded by the flying in of a dove (7). Altogether hardly a Mennonite Brethren dogma.

In *UFOs from Behind the Iron Curtain* pictures are reproduced of 'astronauts' on the walls of mediaeval Jugoslavian monasteries, particularly in association with Christ's crucifixion. Also similar pictures have been identified in Russia and Rumania (8).

But our quest has been to delve into the inspiration of a Dutchman; the subject of the piece hanging in a corner of a sedate university city museum. This has been necessarily only a speculative account of one man and an isolated creation of his, but I regard the painting as being an astonishing depiction of the inexplicable.

Paul Screeton/Chris Castle — 1978.

Notes and References:

1) The only book devoted to him — *Arent de Gelder: Sein Leben und Sein Kunst* (published in Holland in 1914) by Karl Lilienfeld — does not appear to have been translated into English.

2) Sewter, AC., *Baroque and Rococo Art*, (Thames and Hudson, London.1972).

3) Muller, Joseph-Emile; *Rembrandt* (Thames & Hudson, London, 1968).

4) Wilenski, RH.; *An Introduction to Dutch Art* (Faber & Gwyer, 1924).

5) (A note by *J. Geomancy* editor, Nigel Pennick): In Hieronymus Bosch's painting *The Ascent into the Empyrean*, souls are seen being escorted by angels into a tube of light in the sky. The focus of this tube is on the top left of the panel. For further details see *The Complete Paintings of Bosch* by Gregory Martin and Mia Cinotti (Wiedenfeld & Nicolson, 1969).

6) Michell, John; *City of Revelation* (Garnstone, 1972/Abacus 1973).

7) Crow, Dr. WB; *A History of Magic, Witchcraft and Occultism* (Aquarian, 1968).

8) Hobana, Ion, and Weverbergh, Julien; *UFOs from behind the Iron Curtain* (Souvenir, 1974).

(Postscript: Readers interested in pursuing the psychological interpretations of the UFO, or glowing aerial disc, or numinous hole in the cosmic fabric, are referred to Dr CG Jung's *Flying Saucers* (recently reprinted by Routledge & Kegan Paul, London, 1977) which discusses generally the UFO as a symbol of psychic unity, and which has a chapter on the UFO-symbol in art — Ed.)

■■■

THE OBLIGATORY TOUT...
For every new subscriber you bring in we'll extend your sub by a free issue. We can send you leaflets if you want - stick them where people will notice! Give a gift sub for birthdays, Christmas, whatever, or just because you approve of our work and think a friend should know about it. Cajole your library into taking our a sub...it's good educational stuff! A larger circulation is the only way we can continue to maintain our standards and steady improvement. We are always interested in expanding our outlets, and shops interested in stocking FT are invited to apply.

ERRATA
Flu - the citations given at the foot of column 1, p33 last issue, credited to Ion Will, were wrongly dated by your editor as 1977 - they are all 1978.

ℜEVIEW ℨUPPLEMENT

We welcome books and journals for review or exchange on all topics of related interest. The details and
contents of journals are given in the next issue after
receipt, and the return favour in their pages would be
appreciated.

Natural and Supernatural: A History
of the Paranormal from Earliest Times
to 1914 by Brian Inglis (Hodder and
Stoughton, 1978; £9.95; pp   ; bib,
index) -- Brian Inglis's book is a
sad history of human credulity. It
shows how a religious belief or scientific theory can utterly blind even (or
particularly) educated people to all
the evidence of history, experimentat-
ion and their own senses. By the second
half of the nineteenth century, both
science and religion had become dominated by the doctrine of materialism,
"one of the most powerful faiths ever
to acquire a hold over man's mind". Yet
the same materialism-defying phenomena
- poltergeist outbreaks, shamanistic
powers and the like - which have always
and everywhere been inseperable from
human nature and history, continued as
actively as ever. Indeed, the more fer-
vently materialism was embraced, the
more extreme and insistent became its
reaction. The greatest of the 'spirit
mediums', DD Home, recreated the traditional feats of shamanism (necromancy,
apports, levitation etc) at the very
time when scepticism about such things
was at its height; and his integrity
survived every scientific test and under-
hand trick that his opponents could
devise. But since the powers he exer-
cised were those among whose existence
the religion of materialism denied, he
was loudly decried as a self-evident
charlatan. Respectable professors descended to publishing lies against his
reputation, and the few brave scientists, like Sir William Crookes, who
dared to subject him to honest inquiry,
were professionally victimised. Whether
they are persecuting witches in defence
of moral faith or mediums for the up-
holding of materialism, the inquisitors
of every generation are similarly motivated. Belief is more important than
evidence.

This is a big book - some 200,000
words - very informative and with a
good bibliography. The extent to which
the 'paranormal' has always pervaded
human existence is demonstrated with
examples from all ages, and for every
example, says Inglis, he could find
dozens of others. His purpose is to
show that the materialist paradigm of
science does not, and never did, adequately represent the full range of effects that make up our experience of the
world. Physics has long abandoned it,
but it continues to inhibit the development of other sciences, like anthropology, whose professors have consistently refused to investigate the methods
and achievements of tribal magic on the
grounds, first that it involved traffic
with the devil, and secondly that it was
an ineffectual superstition. Andrew Lang,
who suggested that the phenomena of
modern spiritualism might help to explain the origin of miracles and wonders
in religious history and folklore, was
violently attacked by other anthropologists for allowing that such things
could be anything else but conjuring
tricks or morbid delusions. Thus, as
Inglis points out, anthropologists over
the last 200 years have thrown away the
chance of investigating entire codes of
traditional magic in societies which no
longer exist.

Inglis's book, like so many others on
the 'paranormal', is directed, somewhat
defensively, at a liberal-academic readership, and he limits his sources to
those which seem most reputable and well
documented. We miss therefore the type
of material that Fort delighted in, the

spontaneous oddities which occur to un-
remarkable people outside any magical,
religious or spiritualistic context,
and which hint, through such trivial-
ities as falls of little fishes, at the
operations of cosmic forces never fully
comprehended by any magician.

Inglis believes that a revolution is
taking place in our way of thinking
which will require the re-writing of
science textbooks and history. His book
certainly shows that such a revolution
is overdue. Yet he must admit that the
spirit-rappers, card-guessers and spoon-
benders, their devoted investigators
and all their quasi-scientific talk of
magnetic fluids and universal plastic
media have actually achieved or proved
very little. There is a disembodied
sense of humour abroad in the world
which seems to delight in mocking the
efforts of earnest people to provide
definitive explanations for any of
life's recurrent mysteries. If the revolution in thought predicted by Brian
Inglis is to have any real value, it
will mean not just the replacing of
one belief-system by another, but the
development of an 'inclusionist' science
on the Fortean model, based pragmatic-
ally on effects as repeatedly observed
rather than on whatever set of prejud-
ices happen to be dominant.

                                John Michell.

The Secret Discovery of Australia by
Kenneth G McIntyre(Souvenir Press 1977;
£6.50; pp427; indexes, bib, notes,
maps & photos) -- Australia was discovered by Captain Cook in 1770, as
every schoolboy is taught - but as
McIntyre shows in a monumental piece of
historical detective work, this 'fact'
is a lie and skilful   propaganda; before Cook were the Dutch in 1606, and
before them were the Portuguese in about
1516. One of the great enigmas of marine history is why the Portuguese, possibly the most accomplished sailors of
their day, should have stopped their
explorations at the island of Timor,
and not gone on to colonize Australia
a mere 285 miles further on. By a pains-
taking analysis of ancient and forgotten Portuguese maps, and the clarification of some obscure details in the history and accounts of the early navigat-
ional explorations of the East Indies,
McIntyre has assembled an impressive
(in quality and quantity) body of proof
that the Portuguese discovery of Australia was deliberately suppressed by
the Portuguese themselves.

The main reason derives from the
staggering arbitrary action of Pope
Alexander VI in dividing the then unexplored parts of the world between the
Spanish and the Portuguese - the new
continent was substantially on Spain's
side of the Pacific 'demarcation line'
(long 129°E, which today forms the
boundary of Western Australia.) Spain
disputed the Pacific demarcation line
anyway and the militarily less-powerful
Portugal wished to avoid any confrontation, such as would inevitably proceed
from the announcement of the finding
of a new continent that straddled the
disputed area. Besides, Portugal was
damned if she was going to hand Spain
a free new continent to plunder. The
secret was so well kept that McIntyre's
discovery of it is a brilliant feat of
patient scholarship, all the more so
when we learn that he is a retired
lawer and ex-mayor, and Australian-
Portuguese history was only a hobby,
albeit a passionate one.

The burden of proof in a revision of
this kind necessarily lies in its chapters on the minutiae of cartography and
navigation. Personally I found the sup-
plementary evidence of more immediate
interest: the Portuguese cannon found
at Carronade Island; the ruined fort at
Bittangabee, NSW, that McIntyre argues
was a Portuguese base in 1524; the mysterious wreck of 'The Mahogony Ship' mentioned by early English sailors on the
Western Australia coast; the mystery of
the distinctly 'European head' carved
in profile on a sandstone rock among
Aborigine 'wandjina' paintings in the
Collier's Bay area, WA; the identity
of the curious kangaroo-like animals
decorating De Jode's map of 1593; and
the implications of Cook's apparant
"prior knowledge" of Australia's coasts
in making straight for the "best port".

The blurb accompanying my copy claimed
this book "will cause the history books
to be rewritten". That may be inevitable,
but if the orthodox inertia over Colum-
bus's precursors is anything to go by,
it will be a drawn-out and shameful
process.

                                RJMR.

A Guide to Ancient Sites in Britain
by Janet & Colin Bord (Latimer, 1978;
£5.95; pp183; indexes, bib, photos) --
Perhaps, like me, you don't have much
opportunity to travel around and spend
some time appreciating the ancient sites
that dot our land, and whose names I
know from daily reading (almost). If
you are interested in the questions of
prehistory, archæology and folklore you
have often wondered what these lore-
laden places looked like, if not act-

ually wanted to see them. Well this calm and collected guide was made for you and me. In their brief introduction the Bords make no pretence about their necessarily limited approach. They say that there exist something like "1000 megalithic tombs, 30,000-40,000 round barrows (in England alone), over 900 stone circles, around 3000 hillforts and countless thousands of standing stones...in various states of decay or preservation." To whittle this down to a description of 126 sites must have been a difficult and unenviable task, and inevitably purists will have their own ideas on what should have been included. But this guide is aimed at the armchair- and desk-bound as well as for the general reader and traveller who may not be aware of the current interest and controversies over the megalith builders, their methods and their artifacts. The Bords' criteria for selection are those which strike the ordinary man; the impressive visual qualities of the site, and certain details of historical and legendary merit. The entries are presented in the form of photos and maps with a brief text giving essential details, map references and access information, and a few hints on further reading. The austerity contrasts sharply with their previous book, The Secret Country (reviewed in FT18, and recently issued in paperback - see pb reviews) which dealt with the fabric of folklore woven around ancient site, and to which this book must be seen as a complement. Most of the photos in this splendidly illustrated book are from the Bords own collection, the result of many photographic tours...and a word of praise for Colin's photography will not be amiss here. His skilful and appreciative eye elevates many of the pictures from being merely technically good to superb evocations of the atmosphere of remote and timeless mystery surrounding these magical places. Aficionados can undoubtedly point to wider-ranging and more detailed surveys, but for the non-specialist here is a useful and visually stimulating begiñing. Archæological terms are explained, and a timechart gives an idea of temporal perspective - and for those interested in learning more there is a comprehensive reading list.

RJMR.

The False Messiahs by Jack Grattus (Gollancz 1975; £6.00; pp285; index, notes, bib) -- I know we're a bit late with this review but the subject matter is well worth mentioning. In recent years some of the UFO scholars (particularly the MUFOB group) have drawn our attention to the parallels between messianic cults and the belief in UFOs as physical vehicles of the Space Brothers who have come to rescue mankind from nuclear extinction. This 'deus ex machina' complex can be most dramatically seen in the various 'cargo' cults around the world, where modern technological man has overwhelmed a remote archaic society and shattered their way of life. Such a one in New Guinea makes its own crude runways in the jungle and waits for the great flying machines who will bestow wonderful cargo upon them made in distant magical factories. It never comes, of course - because they are too sinful, of course. But in every European society there have been great changes which isolate some group or another; a group that usually prefers a more ideal, if dogmatic, spiritual way of life. When events degrade their beliefs, when the messiah fails to turn up on time, and it's two minutes past the Millenium, then the ground is ready for a whole crop of 'false messiahs'. Grattus here presents an outline history of messianity (if I may call it that) concentrating on some of the more bizarre characters that left a mark on the history of Western Europe, including those of the various dissenting groups like Shakers, Ranters and Quakers. Gratus seems to have confined himself to Jewish and Christian religious history with only the briefest of illustrative skirmishes into the realms of other exotic beliefs. However, I venture that those of you interested in the sociology of UFO cults will find many parallels herein to the weirdness of today. RJMR

Perpetual Motion by Arthur WJG Ord-Hume (G Allen & Unwin, 1977; £5.50; pp235; index, bib, illos) -- a wise and witty book on the epitome of cranks ...and levers and weights and springs... This is the extremely well-told and well-illustrated story of man's obsession with finding the perfect motor, which like its relatives, anti-gravity, the elixir of life, squaring the circle, and the Philosopher's Stone, has motivated the famous, the rich and powerful, speculators and investors, crooks and believers, as well as the inventor - all get caught up in the pursuit and eventually caught out (many tragi-comic episodes are related). Mr Ord-Hume, an authority on early musical mechanisms, proves a knowlegeable guide taking us through all manner of odd ideas about how the universe operates mechanically, chemically, electrically, using weights, capillary action, evaporation/condensation action, expansion/contraction, rising/falling and so on. Forteans will relish the chapter on the Keely Motor Company, which was one of the last things Fort ever wrote about - and on why PM inventors are barred from the US patent office.

Useful as the book is as a reference, it is the sad story of failure even with human ingenuity stretched to incredible and credulous limits, for despite the many thousands (possibly more) of man-hours spent on the problem of perpetual motion over many centuries, it remains a dream, tantalisingly out of reach. However, Mr Ord-Hume becomes more equivocal about the paradoxical states of matter and energy discovered by modern physics. Curiously he acknowledges that the phenomenon known as 'Superconductivity' (in which the electrical resistance in say a coil can be reduced practically to zero, so that a current placed in the coil will continue undiminished for astonishing lengths of time), discovered in 1930s, seems to provide the electrical equivalent of a "perfect flywheel", but adds that "it is impossible to see any practical use"! Like the laser, the superconductor is being applied in research, today, to generate novel devices and processes, which previously were only, SF. Interestingly, despite the books emphasis on mechanical, chemical and electrical devices, the author does not conclude that science's 'laws' are immutable; only that, so far, all attempts to contravene them in practice have failed. The only perpetual thing Ord-Hume tips his hat to is that people keep on trying - and the subject has lost none of its fascination today.
RJMR.

Ghosts over Britain by Peter Moss (Elm Tree Books 1977; £3.95; pp173, photos, drawings) - The accounts in this book (60 in all) are told simply, so that the reality of the experience shines through. The author began his research by advertising in local newspapers and following up the most interesting letters - the result is a book of value both to the reader who just wants to be entertained, and to the researcher seeking hard facts. These are here aplenty, the cases covering a wide field: crisis apparitions, 'memory' ghosts, malevolent ghosts, poltergeists, talking ghosts etc., even a case of water issuing from walls, ceiling and floor. There are many illustrations, with some photos of witnesses and haunted locations, and a large number of full-page drawings, some of which are effective but rather wasteful of space. Altogether an entertaining and useful book, which helps to show that ghosts are very much an ever-present phenomenon.
Janet Bord.

Lost Gods by John Allegro (Michael Joseph, 1977; £4.95; pp191; index) -- Allegro, who outraged many with the thesis of his Sacred Mushroom & The Cross that Christianity originated in an Eastern Mediterranean cult of mushroom-eaters similar to the peyote-mystics of Mexico, must have appeared to have finally gone round the bend with this book. However there is little that is strictly original here, except that by assembling a few unorthodox approaches (sexuality, shamanism, witchcraft, psychology, evolution & anthropology, etc) to orthodox religion and rites he gives us the benefit of his own undoubted fresh originality. His enemies will not be disappointed; here he follows the powerful archaic forces of sexuality, the ritual control/appeasment of nature, and the quest for visionary experience in their transition from early religious movements into Christianity - a sort of sacred 'Roots'!
RJMR

*** Among the many books received for review, and which, in order to give them the space they deserve, will be kept for next issue, are: the giant 2 volume Encyclopedia of Occultism & Parapsychology (Gale; edited by Leslie Shepard); Hallucinations (Wiley; edited by Siegel & West); and In Search of Ancient Astronomies (Doubleday; edited by Dr EC Krupp).

paperbacks

Cosmic Trigger - Final Secret of the Illuminati by Robert Anton Wilson (And/Or Press 1977; $4.95c; pp269; refs, ind) Like 'Illuminatus!', the sheer range of this book makes it something of a reviewer's nightmare. On one hand, it is largely autobiographical; a record of Wilson's personal evolution, shaped by conspiracy theories, Forteana, drugs, magic, his friendship with Dr Timothy Leary, and an awful lot of weirdness. On the other hand, it is also an examination of several topics of interest to Forteans: the 23 phenomenon; telepathic communication from allegedly extra-terrestrial sources, specifically Sirius, and Wilson contributes more evidence from occult history to the work done by Temple in 'The Sirius Mystery'; the nature of physical reality; Immortalism; Leary's theory of the evolution of higher consciousness (which Wilson explains quite lucidly, in contrast to Leary's own bafflingly peculiar and inaccurate foreword to the book) and much more. Some of the flavour of the book may be gained from Wilson's article in FT23.

Wilson also discusses several theories to explain all this weirdness, and presents a triple-barrelled, Leary-ist view of the future: Space Migration + Increased Intelligence + Life Extension (SMI^{2}LE). Peculiarly, though, in a book that constantly appeals for the consideration of alternatives, Wilson sticks rigidly to a linear progressive view of evolution: that all physical and mental change must point continually upwards, and occur at a progressively accelerating rate... to the 'Omega Point' (apparently 2012AD) where changes are occurring at such progressively shorter intervals that the whole thing goes pop, and mankind evolves into an entirely new species.

Frankly, although the idea is extremely appealing, I just can't see the world in such optimistic fashion (us cynics'll probably be left behind when the galaxy goes pop). But Wilson obviously writes with a great deal of conviction, honesty, style and humour...and it is a damn good, thought-provoking read, well-referenced and with much interesting material, as well as some intriguing illustrations by John Thompson. Recommended.   SM

Abducted: Confrontations with Beings from Outer Space, by Coral and Jim Lorenzen (Berkeley Medallion, 1977; $1.75; pp230) -- The Lorenzen's latest compilation of material from the files of the Aerial Phenomena Research Organization (APRO) is obviously intended to catch the eye of those who have seen the film 'Close Encounters' and are eager to learn more. And it is a good book for them to turn to, as it will go some way to correcting the misleading impression conveyed by the film. They will soon discover that UFO occupants are not friendly, timid creatures but rather menacing, unemotional. Seven major US abduction cases from 1973-76 are described in detail: Patty 'Price', taken from her house with 3 of her children, who later said 'They treated me like a guinea-pig. They didn't care about people as people"; Carl Higdon, taken while elk-hunting in Wyoming; Sergeant Charles L Moody, abducted while watching for meteorites in the New Mexico desert; Sandra Lawson, taken from her car along with a friend in North Dakota; David Stephens and another young man, taken from their car in Maine; Travis Walton, zapped by a beam of light from a UFO in an Arizona pine forest went missing for 5 days; 3 Kentucky ladies taken from their car while returning home late one night. The chapter on Travis Walton is especially long because his case aroused controversy and acrimony in which APRO were much involved. The case is continued in Appendix 1, which gives in full the disputed Walton polygraph test and accompanying interview. The two other appendices are a paper on 'Hypnotic Time Regression Procedures in the Investigation of UFO Experiences' by Dr R Leo Sprinkle, and the text of Philip J Klass's '$10,000 UFO Agreement'.

All the material mentioned so far is first-rate valuable data, but when we read the Lorenzens' interpretation, as given in chapter 11, it becomes clear that the authors are living in the past, in those heady days when flying saucers equalled extraterrestrial visitors, no more no less. Talking about the aliens' interest in our minds, they state quite seriously that the aliens who abducted Betty and Barney Hill would have found out about the US postal system from Mr Hill, a postal worker. Eg: "...there would be considerable insight into some very human phenomena: the deluge of Christmas cards in December, the first-of-the-month bills, heavy mail promotions...direct-mail advertising as well as the mail-order business."(p153) And they analyse all the abductees in the same way, assessing what information on the US way of life could be obtained from each. It is as if they've never heard of, let alone read about, the other theories that have been put forward to explain the existence of UFOs. This parochial attitude to their data stresses the need for all UFO investigators to cast aside their natural preoccupations with 20th-century life and to realise that the UFO occupants see us in an entirely different way. Our inability to examine the problem without any pre-conceptions whatever is a major reason why we still do not know where UFOs come from or why.

Omitting their ETH hangups, the Lorenzens have produced another excellent book which all researchers should read. At the time of writing we have not heard if there is to be a UK edition, but I hope there will be, to help counteract some of the trash reprinted lately.

JB.

Life after Life (Corgi, 1976; 65p; pp187; bib.); Reflections on Life after Life (Corgi, 1978; 85p; pp149; bib.) both by Raymond A Moody -- One of the subjects hotly debated in the US currently is the notion that there is indeed a life after death, the revival of this ancient controversy centering on the claims made by people who despite being pronounced "clinically dead" spontaneously revived. According to the accounts collected by Dr Moody over five plus years, no two experiences are the same, but seem to have the same structure: patients hear themselves pronounced dead, then comes a floating sensation often accompanied by ringing or buzzing sounds, then moving fast down a dark tunnel, then looking down at his own body from a point in space - soon he sees figures, some he knows are people who have already died; a "being of light" appears; the patient flashes through a review of his whole life, and then experiences some kind of encouraging pastoral scene from which he strangely and inexorably pulls back to consciousness in his body. These kinds of 'post-mortem' experiences have since been noted by other doctors and researchers (eg Elizabeth Kubler-Ross, whose own book is a best-seller and who contributes a foreword here; Karlis Osis, etc) and recently we heard of a new book that also gives as many experiences of a "Hell" as of "Heaven". Emotive stuff; not only taken by the religious as proof of sorts, but taken by the equally religious of the opposing view that it is all the work of 'demons'! The doctors however are wisely cagey about drawing conclusions - briefly, there is not doubt about the body of experiential anecdote, only what it means, and how it happened. In the first book Dr Moody acknowledges that the book cannot be called a scientific study, and that he was not "broadly familiar with the vast literature on paranormal and occult phenomena." The statement has attracted some criticism, especially on the fact that Dr Moody thereby could not benefit from the rich comparisons with Astral Projection, where eg the prolific work of Dr Robert Crookall shows the AP or out-of-the-body experience to have a similar series of stages. The second book is more a collection of responses to the first, especially religious response, with new material on 'Cities of Light', a 'Realm of Bewildered Spirits' and the mystical feeling of universal knowledge. Dr Moody also adds a chapter on historical examples of the 'life after death' experience. The key questions are far from being resolved - are these experiences the results of delusions, or hallucinations, or supernatural intervention, or processes we have not yet accounted for in our material interpretation of the universe? - and Dr Moody can only give his own opinion. He, and other researchers in this field, are sure of one thing however, that man does have a life that extends beyond mere physical appearances. Recommended introductory reading on a difficult and emotive subject.

RJMR

Castaneda's Journey by Richard de Mille (Abacus 1978; £1.50; pp249; index, notes, bib); Don Juan, Mescalito and Modern Magic by Nevill Drury (Routledge & Kegan Paul 1978; £2.95; pp229; index, bib,notes) -- De Mille's masterful analysis of the works of Carlos Casteneda (reviewed in FT21) now in print in the UK in a popular edition, will make many readers aware of Castaneda's skill in adapting the latest theories and research of anthropologists and psychologists, dressing them up as the lectures of his fictional Yaqui Indian sorcerer, Don Juan. De Mille's own wit and wisdom ensures that this is not a 'sour grapes' expose of a literary fraud, but on the contrary turns into a celebration of Castaneda's special genius. After all, doubts about the authenticity of many books (including the Bible) have not dulled their spiritual and mystical messages. Essential reading. Drury's book was written before deMille went iconoclasting - but in a way that doesn't matter too much because his is a personal subjective interpretation of the teachings of Castaneda's Don Juan in the light of modern ritual-magical theory, and the whole tradition of visionary wisdom from the use of hallucinogens and other drugs. He reviews these three approaches to the problem of the magical reality very competently, and with many illustrations from personal experiences and those of friends. The latter part of the book, meditations on the major arcana of the Tarot, is wholly subjective – I much preferred the earlier discussions of shamanism – but as Drury is after a unification between theory and practice, preferences are meaningless, and the Work must be toward the whole man. All interested in Magick will find this modern defining of the magician's role of interest, but there is little here that will help those less convinced that the use of drug and Magick jargon holds any answer to the central problem of what reality means to each one of us. This is one man's view, well expressed but difficult to relate to.   RJMR

Close Encounters: The Strange Truth about UFOs, by Alan West & David Jefferis (Arrow, 1978; £1.75; pp96; illos, bib) -- a large format superficial review of UFO phenomena to catch the eye of the post- Star Wars & Close Encounters of the Third Kind (CE3K) film audiences. There is a competent journalistic review of types of UFO cases, and a perfunctory description of the major alternatives to "nuts and bolts" ufology. The whole project adds little new, except perhaps the first public airing of recent UK and USA cases by now well-known to the people who are really interested. It may channel a few young minds into the subject, which mollifies the fact of its blatant commerciality. Still - there were far worse books for an interested youngster in my young day, and this at least gives them a good read.   RJMR

The Lost Tribes From Space by Marc Dem (Corgi 1977; 75p; pp212; index); Our Mysterious Spaceship Moon by Don Wilson (Sphere 1976; 60p; pp172; notes, bib) -- two singular viewpoints on ancient-astronaut-type material. Wilson confines his argument to our Moon effectively, and establishes a case for lunar mysteries better than I had expected - includes the 'Blair Cuspids', lunar lights, alleged footprints, magnetic & gravitic anomalies, enigmatic landscape features, and the hollow-moon 'spaceship' theory (first applied to the moons of

Mars and rather unsuccessfully in my view transplanted here to Luna). Dem's book is, by comparison with Wilson's, more hysterical. Briefly it mixes the 'Lost Tribes of Israel' with the 'God was a spaceman' brand of inspired raving. Worth reading for its high baroque revision of the Old Testament, which starts to develop fatal flaws when it spills over into more modern and better documented history.   RJMR

The Book of the Strange by editors of The World Almanac (Signet, NY, 1977; £2.50; pp482) -- an encyclopedic listing and summary of contemporary mysteries under the major headings: Human Being, Animals & Plants, Astronomy, Strange Peoples, S.Groups, S.Places, S.Customs, S.Activities, Possession, S.Persons, S.Objects, S.Creatures, Psychics, Psychic Phenomena, Divination, UFOs, Legends & Myths, Hoaxes & Forgeries. The idea is to provide the reader with a reasonably unbiased assessment of several hundred topics of interest. Against the odds the editors have managed to produce a thoroughly sane stroll through the modern menagerie of mysteries and madness - a good sign is that their list of credits acknowledge the advice of a number of US Forteans. Worth buying and keeping handy.   RJMR

The Hynek UFO Report by Dr J Allen Hynek (Sphere 1978; 95p; pp299; bibl, 16pp photos) The publication of this book at the present time is obviously due to Hynek's recent elevation to superstar status via 'Close Encounters of the Third Kind'. Obviously so because, frankly, this personal analysis of the recently declassified Project Blue Book files is a very dry piece of investigation with little to add to the comments made last year by Brad Steiger in his equally tedious book on the same subject. The signs are we may be about to witness the widespread (ie, non-UFO logical-circle) acceptance of a semi-respectable cadre of old guard "experts" in the field. As most of its members are likely to subscribe to the ET argument, this in itself may be no bad thing from the point of view of those who favour the alternative, 'paranormal' argument; it being preferable to attack, rather than defend from, a position of entrenched commitment.   SN

The Cosmic Question by John A Keel (Panther 1978; 75p; pp224) Another title change for the British market: this was formerly 'The Eighth Tower'. I have a great respect for Keel, but I wonder where he is taking the line of speculation he began to develop in his earlier books, notably 'Operation Trojan Horse'. In that one he was nicely ambiguous in the way he presented his theory; reluctant to theorise in a specific sense and leaving a number of rough corners, both from obvious necessity and, one assumes, to leave room for fleshing out later. Since then he has started to cite specifics, and rather spoilt the original presentation. In Trojan Horse he put forward the idea that UFOs may be just one aspect of a 'force' that manifests in many ways, and was careful not to commit himself to any firm opinion regarding a possible controlling agency. Now he speculates that this 'control' is a frighteningly advanced computer at the far end of time, which has gone gaga and is responsible for our current closed cycle of unexplained phenomena and psychic harrassment. Perhaps he should be concentrating more on reinforcing his original theory and not be so anxious to construct an overall answer to his cosmic question. Let's hope he gets back to basics next time. SN

A Dictionary of British Folk Customs by Christina Hole (Paladin 1978; £2.50; pp349; bibl, ind.) A nationwide index of folk customs and practices, in alphabetical format, and including a useful calendar of the year's events. Nowhere near exhaustive of course, but I enjoyed it and it certainly has a function for reference purposes. SN

Glastonbury - Ancient Avalon, New Jerusalem. Ed by Anthony Roberts (Rider 1978 (Rev. ed.); £2.95; pp177; illoes) A fine anthology of 12 original articles pertinent to Glastonbury and the earth mysteries in general. Particularly good are Mary Caine on the Glastonbury Zodiac, Nigel Pennick on the Abbey, Kenneth Knight's Gematria in the Hebrew Cabala, and a too brief piece by John Michell; though none of the contributions is less than interesting and all display great knowledge of their subject. Many good illustrations, and each piece has its own bibliography. SN

The Space Gods Revealed by Ronald Story (NEL 1978; 80p; pp157; notes, ind, 16pp photos) Another from the lucrative anti-von Daniken industry, and by no means the best refutation of the hotelier's bestselling theories. God knows von Daniken has touted many ideas ripe for ridicule, but blanket condemnation as displayed by Ronald Story is not the way to go about it. Story seems to think that all contentious theories can be demolished simply by reference to an 'expert' in the relevant field. At no point is any attempt made to get to the origin of either myth (in the falsified sense) or scientific acceptance, making the book as suspect as that which it seeks to expose. SN

The Secret Country (More Mysterious Britain) by Janet & Colin Bord (Paladin 1978; £1.95; pp247; bibl,ind,illos) A very readable attempt to interpret the field of earth mysteries: ley lines, standing stones, henges, mounds, etc, in terms of folklore and 'race memory', now in p/b. With lots of well chosen and relevant pictures. SN

The Ley Hunter's Manual - A Guide to Early Tracks by Alfred Watkins (Pentacle Books, 6 Perry Road, Bristol 1; 1978; £2.25, pp 107; ind, illoes) Reprint of the 1927 edition.
Velikovsky Reconsidered by the Editors of Pensee (Abacus 1978; £1.50; pp274; ind) Now in p/b. Reviewed FT 19.
The Man in the Shroud by Peter M Rinaldi (Futura 1978; 90p; pp 127; bibl, notes, 14pp photos) Again in print: Turin Shroud.
Guide to PSI Periodicals 1978 - Newspapers, Magazines, Newsletters. Compiled by Inner-Space Interpreters, PO Box 1133, Magnolia Park Station, Burbank, Ca., 91507, USA; $3.00; pp100) Sixth edition. Elizabeth M Werner, editor. SN

*** <u>Ogopogo</u> - UK readers will be interested to know that the Canadian paperback <u>Ogopogo</u> by Mary Moon, reviewed last issue, can be obtained by Canonegate Publishing Ltd, 17 Jeffrey St, Edinburgh EH1 1OR.

*** We have many more paperbacks for review (including the Jim Brandon guide to <u>Weird America</u>) and an assessment of the 'Amityville Horror'. ***

journals

<u>Pursuit</u> Winter 78: articles on Nessie (mainly Searle's work), the Palenque remains, the biology of beings from low gravity planets, speculation on vibration energy & holograms. Articles meriting the attention of all serious Forteans are, John Ott on the role of artificial light and other radiations in influencing plant and animal growth (and even cancer!); Andrew Rothovius' analysis of the 'flap' effect from a comparison of the 1897 Ohio airship series and the spread of 'The Great Fear' in France in 1789 (note the numerical anagram there!); the text of the paper by R Martin Wolf before the Mexico City Conference on Paranormal Phenomena, a brilliant summary of new theories and how they might affect Fortean studies. For details write to <u>SITU</u>: Membership Services, RFD 5, Gales Ferry, CT 06335, USA.

<u>INFO Journal</u> 27 (Jan 78): East coast mystery booms; UFO 'triangles'; Swedish 'phantom snipers'; 'Sci-Phi'; notes old and new - 28 (Mar 78): Lake Champlain's monster; giant fish; 'Silbury Hill'; more notes on booms, Bigfeet, archived notes, etc. $10.00/£5.00/yr. <u>INFO</u>: 7317 Baltimore Ave, College Park, MD 20740, USA - or subscribe via FT (see p52). Also note that <u>Fortfest 78</u> will be held over 5-6 Aug, at the Americana University, Washington; with speakers on UFOs, Bigfoot and monster research, ET life, ancient astronauts & cultures. Write to <u>INFO</u> for further details and booking.

<u>ARB</u> 8: the Anomaly Research Bulletin bounces back just when we were begining to worry about its absence - fatter, meatier, good to sink Fortean fangs into. Articles on 'The Dover Demon'; odd goings on in cemetaries; 'parahumans'; notes on synchronicities, the LNM, and guidlines for field investigators; and editor Dave Fideler's chronology of 1977 mystery creatures, Bigfoot and phantom phelines (worth the entry price). <u>ARB</u> new price $5.00/£3.00/yr: 7098 Edinburgh, Lambertville, MI 48144, USA. This excellent Fortean journal deserves your support.

<u>SIS Review</u> 2:3 (Special issue 77/78): The whole issue, edited by Peter James, celebrates and re-examines the subject matter of Velikovsky's volume <u>Ages in Chaos</u> with some very thorough, stimulating and learned papers: 'Dating the "Admonitions" of Ipuwer'; 'A Chart to Illustrate the Conquest of Canaan'; 'The Hyksos & the Archeology of Palestine'; 'Did Thutmose III despoil the Temple in Jerusalem?'; 'Dating the El-Amarna Letters'; 'The Sulman Temple in Jerusalem'; 'The Two Jehorams'; 'A Chronology for the 18th Dynasty'; & 'Radiocarbon Dates for the 18th Dynasty'. The <u>SIS</u> also have ready a brief paper on 'A Revised Chronology for the Ancient Near East' which clearly sets out the matter at the heart of the controversy about Prof Velikovsky's work. All interested are recommended to write to the SIS Secretary, Ralph Amelan, 6 Jersey House, Cotton Lane, Manchester 20.

<u>Brain/Mind Bulletin</u> - a highly recommended fortnightly update on the <u>very</u> latest news, notes, discoveries and theories from the frontiers of psychology, learning, memory, biofeedback, perception, physics of consciousness, meditation, hypnosis, physics, parapsychology, creativity and related research programmes. $15/yr in US; outside US airmail $21.00/yr. Or write for details to <u>B/MB</u>: Box 42211, Los Angeles, CA 90042, USA.

<u>Page Research Newsletter</u> 22: chatty news, letters and often an article on UFO and Fortean subjects - good for keeping your finger on the pulse of what's happening in the USA. <u>PRL</u> also deal in rare and current books on Forteana and UFOs - send $2.00 or IPCs for a yrs supply of lists & newsletters, to <u>PRL</u> Box 5012, Rome, OH 44085, USA. Please note, this is a <u>new</u> address.

<u>Specula</u>, the Journal of the American Association of Metascience, edited by Tom Bearden, and dedicated to the unfettered scientific exploration of unexplained phenomena, ranging from healing to psychic photography. The group is conducted at a fairly lofty technical level, but all interested in the new theoretical developments out of the frontiers of the known and the unknown,

will be especially interested in the up-to-the-minute comments (eg in 1:1 - Jan 78) on Andrija Puharich's studies of Tesla's work, psychotronic weapons, astral projection, thoughtography experiments, Bigfoot, UFOs, the Geller effect, and the new paradigms of physics as well as the 'corrected physics'. Published quarterly: $15.00/yr. Specula: 1902 Willis Rd SE, Huntsville, AL 35801, USA.

Nessletter - a monthly newsletter for monsterhunters based on latest news from Loch Ness - $7.00/£1.75, from Rip Hepple: Huntshieldford, St Johns Chapel, Bishop Aukland, Co Durham.

Stigmata 2 - already established newsletter for those interested in and investigating mutilation mysteries, primarily in the USA, but also worldwide. It seems to be getting useful media publicity, and the cooperation of many local police departments. Edited by Thomas R Adams. For details write, Project Stigma: Box 1094, Paris, TX 75460, USA, enclosing an SAE (those outside US enclose an International Reply Coupon).

Christian Parapsychologist 2:1 (March 78): mainly reviews this time; but articles on Christian mysticism, and mediumship. For details write to CP: St Mary Abchurch, Abchurch Lane, London EC4N 7BA.

Journal of Meteorology - essential for the serious Fortean - recent issues have dealt with the freak snow in US; UK tornadoes, gales, blizzards, storms, the freak April rainfall, lightning strikes, ball lightning, magnifying mirages; drought in New Hebrides and heatwave in Australia. For details write: JMet: Cockhill House, Trowbridge BA14 9BG, UK.

Northern UFO News, the common communication journal between many UFO groups in northern Britain (and from other parts) acting as a clearing-house for the latest info. Really hot on UK CE3 events. Essential for latest UFO news. Write for details, NUFON: 23 Sunningdale Drive, Irlam, Lancs M30 6NJ. (Eg: the case that's about to break in FSR etc, about lights filmed for 50 minutes over Stonehenge, no less, was first told of here.) Jenny Randles, and NUFON, have received much press attention via the recent wave of CE3s and other UFO sightings, and to meet the PR head-on have produced a booklet, Close Encounters of the Northern Kind, summarizing some recent, with notes on UFO encounters, and what to do if you see one - price 30p from NUFOIS: 443 Meadow Lane, Nottingham NG2 3GB.

Awareness, journal of Contact UK, 6:4 (Winter 77): articles on UK wave of 77; sky mysteries; cloud UFOs; other notes new and historical. Excellent material. For details write, Contact UK: 28 Lodden Ave, Berinsfield, Oxfordshire.

EUFOSG Journal, regular news, data and often articles of interest (Winter 78, has the full text of the 'Alien' TV broadcast in UK's Southern Region last Nov), and sightings from Essex UFO Group. For details write, EUFOSG: 16 Raydons Rd, Dagenham, Essex RM9 5JR.

Flying Saucer Review 23:5 (Feb 78): Juicy details of close encounter cases in Spain (soldiers fire at entity); Chile (the soldier at Arica who vanished for 15 minutes & reappeared with 5 days advance on his calendar watch etc); Brazil (attempted abduction) and its parallel in France; MIB study by Dr Berthold Schwarz; humanoid at Epsom; car stop at Barnard Castle; solid light effect at Irlam; UFO oddities in Wales and Canada. Essential. FSR: West Malling Maidstone, Kent.

Pulsar 1:4 (Jan 78) articles on terrestrial zodiac symbols, UFOs, ancient maze designs, & general UFO interest. Pulsar - 30p/single copy - Pulse Publications: 29 Bairstow St, Preston, Lancs PR1 3TN.

Institute of Geomantic Research continue their onslaught against pamphlet paucity with the latest in their Occasional Paper series - 8: reprinting of an 1879 study of the group of 3 Cornish stone circles known as 'The Hurlers' 60p; 9:'The Ongar Zodiac' by Jim Kimmis, 85p; 10: reprint of 2 papers (1936 & 1940) on German 'Troytown' mazes, trans. from German. Two other publications, are the extensive IGR study of Cambridge Geomancy (£1.25); and a trans. of J Heinsch's classic 1938 'Principles of Prehistoric Sacred Geography' (50p), put out by Fenris-Wolf from the IGR address. Please add 10p or more for p&p to these prices. Joint the IGR (for £3.00/yr) and that year's papers free. You also get 4 issues of the Journal of Geomancy. J.Geo 2:3 had articles on metrology; proofs of ancient trax; history of metric system; metrology & chance; dragonslayers; a Bristol zodiac; Hebden Bridge zodiac; a Stonegate zodiac. IGR:142 Pheasent Rise, Bar Hill, Cambridge CB3 8SD.

Ancient Skills & Wisdom Review - a review journal on latest mags, books, pamphlets on nearly all fringe and 'new wave' overground publications. £2/qtrly from Paul Screeton: 5 Egton Drive, Seaton Carew, Hartlepool, Cleveland TS25 2AT. Paul also publishes Terrestrial Zodiacs Newsletter for those interested in the subject.

Stonehenge Viewpoint - newspaper format, long articles on stones, circles and related mysteries. Free copy can be had from SV: Box 30887, Santa Barbara, CA 93105, USA, or: 51 Charminster Ave, Bournemouth, Dorset BH9 1RS.

The Ley Hunter - mandatory reading for all interested in ancient sites and Earth Mysteries. TLH:Box 152, London N10 1EP. UK & Europe £2.70. Overseas $8.00/£4.00. May be ordered thru' FT.

NEARA Journal, news, notes, studies and articles on the antiquities of New England, and related topics. Single copy: $1.50; Sub: $5.00/yr. NEARA are also publishing the proceedings of their 'Ancient Vermont' conference, including a debate on the pre-Columbian discovery of North America, and the preceding talk by Prof.Barry Fell. For details and membership info, write NEARA: 4 Smith St, Milford, NH 03055, USA.

The following foreign journals, on exchange with FT, may be of interest:-

French -- L'Heure d'Etre, religious, spiritual & psychic phenomena & topics: Autricourt, 21570 Brion sur Ource, Frnce. - Ouranos, UFOs & related topics: BP 38, 02110 Bohain, France. - Les Extraterres-tres, UFOs & related topics: St-Denis-les-Rebais, 77510 Rebais, France. - La Revue des Soucoupes Volantes, UFOs and mysteries generally, some Forteana: 83630 Regusse, France. - Phenomenes Spatiaux, first class UFO research & reporting: GEPA, 7914.47 Paris, France.

Danish -- Forteana, newspaper format quarterly, excellent coverage of all Fortean topics, well illustrated: SCANFO, Classensgade 8, DK 2100 Kobenhaven Ø, Denmark. - Uforalia, a review journal of the Dansk UFO Center, books, mags etc: Postbox 7018, DK 9200 Aalborg SV, Denmark.

German -- Esotera, a glossy monthly on all aspects of the unknown, mysteries, parapsychology, some Forteana, & related subjects: Postfach 167, HvStephen-Str 20, 7800 Freiburg, Germany.

Dutch -- Tijdschrift voor Ufologie, quarterly review of UFO news, books etc: TVU, Lange Akker 28, 9982 HL Uithuizermeeden, Holland.

Swedish -- Arbetsgruppen för Ufologi, attempting to build up a specialist archive/library of UFO research documen-

tation, publish a review/newsletter, Nyhetsblad; AFU: Box 5046, 151.05 Söder-tälje, Sweden.

Italian -- Clypeus, the leading Italian research group produce 2 journals: UFO & Fortean Phenomena, which is just what it says, covering events worldwide but often reprinted from other journals for the benefit of Italian readers; and Piemonte Insolito, on folklore & antiquities of Northern Italy; Highly recommended to all who read Italian: Clypeus: Casella Postale 604, 10100 Torino Centro, Italy. - La Quarta Dimensione, quarterly journal on mysticism, philosophy and 'new age' thought: Bresci Editore, Via A Vespucci 41, Torino, Italy. - Spazio e Civilta', inner and outer space, exploration oriented: Via M Benincasa 11, 84013 Cava de'Tirreni, Salerno, Italy.- Vimana, UFOs, folklore, some Forteana: CSUI, Via delle Cave 14, 38100 Trento, Italy.

Belgian -- Inforespace, first rate UFO research & investigation; their English language supplement, SOBEPS News, has been conspicuous by its absence, but we hope they will continue with this laudable project when possible: SOBEPS, Ave P Janson 74, 1070 Bruxelles, Belgium.

Serbo-Croat -- the Yugoslavian UFO research group, NLP, publish a bimonthly newsletter, Odiseja, on latest events and researches; edited by Milos Krmelj: Milcinskega 6, 61000 Ljubljana, Slovenija, Yugoslavia. (Welcomes exchanges.)

others

Star Encounters of the Jaws Wars Kind (a review of 'Close Encounters of the Third Kind' film, directed by Stephen Spielberg, released by Columbia) -- Spielberg is accurate on two points at least - chaos and confusion. This is not conveyed by any subtle skill of the movie-makers art but by a blasting soundtrack in which most of the cast are yelling against incessant background noise, be it a sandstorm, domestic TV, the technical chatter of a radar control center, or a milling panicky crowd. Most of the time it is difficult to to be sure of what is happening, but as the storyline is slight and the treatment broad rather than detailed, it appears to be the director's intention. The film relies on a youthful audience familiar with the general concept of the UFO - an older audience

cont on p48...

obituaries: EFR & HSWC

We learn with regret of the death of two pioneers of British Forteanism within five days of each other: Eric Frank Russell and Harold SW Chibbett. Our sympathies are offered to their wives and families.

Eric Russell was born on 6 Jan 1905 at Sandhurst, Surrey, where his father was serving in the army. He spent his early years at military bases in Egypt and elsewhere, returning to England for an extensive technical and scientific education. For most of his life he lived and worked in the Liverpool area.

In the mid-1930s he began to write SF and joined the Fortean Society of New York. Following a visit to the US, he wrote his first major novel, Sinister Barrier, which combined his two interests. John W Campbell chose it to lead-off the first issue of his new fantasy magazine Unknown Worlds, and Eric's reputation was made. The novel has since been reprinted many times.

His writing was interrupted by WW2, but he continued to promote Forteanism throughout the war as the British representative of the Fortean Society. The first one-volume indexed editionof Fort's four books (Henry Holt, NY, 1941) owed more than a little to him, and with great effort he was able to import and distribute copies, which did much to popularise Fortean ideas. This was no small feat during the German U-boat attacks on Atlantic shipping when only priority cargo was shipped from the USA.

In 1941 he was conscripted into the RAF, and by 1945 he was in command of a mobile radio unit attatched to General Patton's army in Europe. His experiences when various concentration camps were freed made a profound impact and were reflected in his subsequent writing.

After the war he became the foremost British SF author; his stories and novels originally appearing in American SF magazines, mainly by his friend John Campbell. They have appeared in many languages and are still in print today. Most are influenced either by the Fortean philosophy of questioning dogma, or by the horror of military rule (which he saw as a consequence of not questioning dogma). To the end of his life he felt a bitterness towards Authority.

During his long creative period he continued to promote Forteanism, but the gradual decline of the Fortean Society of New York and the lack of popular interest reduced his enthusiasm. About 1960,

at the height of his reputation, he stopped writing and withdrew from both Forteanism and SF, partly due to ill-health. He died suddenly on 28 Feb 1978, aged 73, probably from heart-strain following influenza.

Harold Chibbett was born 19 Feb 1900. After army service in WW1, he worked in the Civil Service in London and became interested in psychic research. He founded 'The Probe', a group which investigated occult phenomena...and joined the first London SF club (ca.1937). As a result he met Eric Russell in 1942, when the latter attended an RAF radio course at the London Polytechnic. The two became lifelong friends and took part in several investigations before Eric's course ended.

After the war, Harold extended his interests to cover many other paranormal subjects. In contrast to Eric he was able to devote much of his spare time to meeting and following-up people who had attracted his attention, and in the course of about 50 years he met and often worked with nearly every one in the British occult field. Crowley, Harry Price, Kuda Bux the fire-walker, Sammy Soal, Mrs Goldney and many others were amongst his acquaintances, and his philosophy of asking "Why?" something happened, rather than "How?" became a byword.

His health deteriorated in the late-1960s. As a distressing side-effect of radiation treatment he suffered from haemorrhages which ultimately caused his death. In 1969, he revived a wartime idea that he had produced in 1944 to maintain contact with his friends: a postal chain-letter - and in the last ten years of his life he circulated more than 600 issues of this postal-exchange at great personal expense and labour. It became a medium of communication on esoteric subjects without equal. Its members included many famous scientists and occultists. He conducted it in the Fortean mode of temporary acceptance of practically anything, and encouraged everyone to think for themselves and not to reject any possibility until they had done so. All who knew him were never quite the same again.

Harold Chibbett died, aged 78, on 23 Feb 1978, from a heart-attack, five days before his friend Eric Frank Russell. Their joint work in promoting Forteanism should never be forgotten.

Sid L Birchby - 18 May 1978.

cont on p43...

OUT OF PLACE

Well we haven't had a round-up of reports of lions, pumas etc on the loose in Great Britain for a long time (since FT18 & the 'Nottingham Lion' episode). On the subject of mystery animals generally, 1977 saw a bewildering number of reports from the USA. In the latest ARB (see our reviews of journals) Dave Fideler has patiently compiled a chronology of MAs; while in Fate Nov 1977 Loren Coleman detailed the wave of phantom panthers in Ohio; and Dave teamed up with Loren to present an overview of US phantom kangaroo reports from recent years, in Fate April 1978. And here we are, once more with feline:

'PUMA' - SURREY/SUSSEX etc
What was described by one paper as 'the summer ritual of puma spotting' got under way with the sighting, on 18 July 1977, of a "large, grey and lean animal with a small head and 3ft tail," in the grounds of a nursing home at Patcham, near Brighton. It was seen by Douglas Brownjohn, a director of the home, from a mere 40ft away, before it ran off into woods. A police hunt failed to flush it out. Daily Mail, Daily Mirror, Daily Express all 19 July 1977 (Cr: Mollie Cairncross, Sam, Paul Hudson,) One paper (D.Exp.) said there had been two sightings that day.

The next sighting we have record of was on 14 Oct 1977, by building workers on a site near Reigate, Surrey. One of the workers claimed to see it several times in the days that followed, and even managed to photograph it. The LEN news report on the 17th Oct mentioned that as the police had at least six more witnesses they were taking the photo and a cast of a pawprint seriously. Searches with tracker dogs through nearby woods failed as usual to find anything that we know of. The man who took the photo (one source said there was more than one photo), Keith Livingston, said he had brought his camera to work after seeing it the previous day,

hoping it would show up again. He said it was definitely a large cat, the colour of a labrador, and looked like a lioness. Intrigued, I phoned Reigate police who referred me to the public relations dept of their Surrey HQ, where a very helpful officer gave me some not very helpful information. Yes, he said, they had examined Livingston's photos and in their opinion he had simply mistaken a "large housecat" on three seperate occasions. The image on the photos was too tiny to identify but they were certain it was a cat of some sort; and the conditions of the time the photos were taken, very misty morning, made the animal too indistinct. I was so disappointed by this I quite forgot to ask if they had actually enlarged the photos or not. Oh yes...the paw-print had been so poorly made that again identification was impossible. There was only one avenue left to persue - I asked them how I could contact Mr Livingston, and they could only suggest trying the building site at Gatton Close, near Gatton Point, Reigate. I wrote to him there, but the letter was soon returned unopened. If any reader in that area would like to help us locate Livingston and his photos, the only additional info we have is that he lives in Shere, between Guildford and Dorking - address unknown. Observer, News of the World both 16 Oct 1977; London Evening News 17 Oct 1977 (Cr: James Lake.)

Like all good mysteries the 'Surrey Puma' sometimes surpasses itself. Just to show that she is more than mere cat, she had the police out searching again on the 21st Oct, after two farmworkers swore they had seen a 'puma' at Send, between Guildford and Woking, not 16 miles from Reigate. Daily Mirror, Daily Express 22 Oct 1977 (Cr: Chris Hall.)
SEE LATE NEWS ITEM p47...

'PUMA/LION' - FURTHER NORTH
For good measure, we noted that dur-

ing the above 'flap', on the 15th Oct, there was a real lion scare when one escaped from a zoo in Sunderland, Northumberland. The incident was blamed on "vandals" - we suspect they might have been imaginary - and the lion was quickly caught. News of the World 16 Oct 1977.

Now if that time-coincidence alone wasn't a nod of the cosmic head towards us Forteans, I had to strain, while I was boggling, to sort the following out. The Sun, 15 Dec - just two months later - said armed police and farmers were out hunting on the 14th, at North Sunderland, for a sheep-killer, thought to be a puma. Wow! Sunderland linked in phenomenal punning through its recent lion-escape to Surrey 'Puma' sightings. Fortunately an eagle-eyed reader sent an additional clipping which helped clarify the situation. The Sun said the hunt was at a place called Bettyhill, but they had wrongly placed it in Sunderland - being a misprint for Sutherland, in Scotland! The misprint seems almost too good to be true - but the inclusion of the name Bettyhill adds another delicious layer to this saga - as UFO buffs will recognise the name of Mrs Betty Hill, the famous contactee now turned investigator of psychic phenomena! Anyway, back to the depredations at Bettyhill, Sutherland. On the morning of 14 Dec 1977, a gamekeeper, Donald Mackenzie, of Dunedin House, Bettyhill, and his son, found the carcases of six sheep out on the barren moorland. Then they saw what they believed to be "a lion or puma", shot at it, and believe they winged it. But it escaped. Only the day before, crofters out hunting foxes, started the cat-like beast from cover, and believe they too might have nicked it with their shots. The local report closes with the info that this same (or similar) animal was sighted back in the Spring, in Caithness. Aberdeen Evening Express 14 Dec 1977; Sun 15 Dec 1977 (Cr: Jake Williams, Paul Screeton)

For the period between the Spring and December sightings of a puma-like animal, above, on the northernmost edge of Scotland, we can only offer a series of 'lion' hunts, perhaps 70 miles further south across Scotland's least inhabited mountains, around Inverness. On 27 Sept a "lioness and two cubs" were seen in a field at Crask, near Farr, not 10 miles from Inverness, about 5.30pm... or so the report says - the only nearby Crask is in Strath Glass more like 20 miles away - and (hold onto your hats)

the only Farr on my map is less than 2 miles away from the Bettyhill of above fame. Passing strange! Anyway; John Jenkins of Inverness, his son and nephew, all got within 20ft of this 'lioness' and her cubs, and saw them clearly. Sometime in the next two days the animals were seen again - by a boy at Culduthel, near Inverness. The police hunted on 30 Sept - no luck! Daily Telegraph 29 Sept & 1 Oct 1977; Sunday Express 2 Oct 1977 (Cr: Valerie Martin, Anon.)

Our last and latest record is that a "lioness or puma" was seen by a housewife at Cononbridge, near Dingwall, just north of Inverness, sometime on the 4th or 5th Feb 1978. She described it as a "big, powerful-looking cat of some kind," and added that in the same area last year two men had seen a 'lioness'. Sun 7 Feb 1978 (Cr: Paul Screeton.)

Considering the number of reports we have of large exotic predators, we hear very little of the depredation we could reasonably expect. In fact it's quite a rare report that mentions animal-slayings in the same breath as a mystery animal sighting; like the Bettyhill case above. Curiously, Fort has one for this area in Jan 1927 (see Books p600f). - that after strange pawprints and carcases of sheep and goats were found, a farmer in the mountains above Inverness shot and killed a "large, fierce yellow animal of unknown species." The slaughter continued, and another farmer shot another similar animal. Then a third animal was caught in a trap. London Zoo identified it as a lynx (which is not indigenous). The London papers of 14 Jan 1927 proclaimed the mystery solved!

'TIGER/COUGAR/PUMA' - CENTRAL ENGLAND

According to the Liverpool Echo 24 Jan 1978, sightings of a "mystery Beast" in the Bickerton Hills, Cheshire, near the middle of the month, were "solved last week" when a knowall from Chester Zoo decided that the 4½" pawprints in the area were made by a "large dog."

Such certitude deserves any raspberries it gets - and one was not long in coming. Whether or not the prints were "large dog", and whether or not they had any connexion with the Beast of Bickerton Hills is one thing - a moonlight close encounter with a large cat is quite another. Two youths, Mark Richardson and David Roebuck, were out at 10 o'clock at night, the bright moonlight making visibility good, when out of bushes in front of them came "a young tiger or cougar...partly hidden ...but certainly some kind of big cat and its front legs appeared shorter than its back." A policeman added that there were no reports of missing animals and no livestock-killings in the area. (Cr: Ion Will.)

The last note we have to date on the subject 'at large' - is that a 'puma' was seen racing along Rectory Rd, Rochford, Essex. Police, with a logic almost idiotic in its simplicity, assumed someone's pet had escaped. London _Evening Standard_ 4 May 1978 (Cr: I Will.)

MA - HONGKONG

On the evening of 30 Oct 1976, villagers in the Hang Hau area of Sai Kung, in HK's New Territories, saw what they thought was a large "leopard". A representative for Yau Yue Wan and Pik Uk villages said: "We didn't think it was a dog...The beast had glistering eyes, black-greyish hair and a long tail." He also said that in the past two weeks more than 20 dogs, some of them large, had been bitten to death in Pik Uk and Junk Bay, both close to where the beast was spotted. At this point a police search found nothing, and civil administrators said they had had no complaints from villagers.

A few weeks later, early in Dec 76, a villager from Hang Chai told police that he had seen a "tiger" twice in the last ten days, describing the animal as "about 3ft high, 4ft long, and of a dark colour". A police search found some pug marks and the matter was referred to the Ag.&.Fish Dept, which seems to have effectively silenced the mystery as far as further information goes. _South China Morning Post_ 4 Nov & 9 Dec 1976 (Cr: our intrepid Far Eastern clipsters Guy Audebrand, Colin Johnson & Ion Will.)

MA - NEW ZEALAND

Sometime around 10 July 1977 a woman told incredulous police about a large tiger-like cat seen in her garden, in the Kaiapoi area of NZ, about 4am. A search turned up nothing. A few days later, about 21 July, the search renewed on a much larger scale after large paw-prints and droppings, positively identified as those of large cats like tigers or lions, were found on sandhills at Pines Beach. Although there were no reports of escaped animals, and no attacks on livestock, we are told there is enough wild game to keep a tiger alive. By the 25th there was still no sign of the 'Kaiapoi Tiger' and all the press and official signs that the unproductive mystery was soon to be dropped. The officer in charge of the hunt said he still thought the tracks were genuine, but that someone's private pet tiger had escaped and /been secretly recaptured. Just how this was accomplished when his own men were vigilantly combing this area north of Christchurch we are left to imagine. _Aukland Star_ (NZ) 22 & 23 July 1977; _Herald_ (NZ) 25 July 1977; _Sydney Morning Herald_ (Aust) 23 July 1977; _Sun-Herald_ (Australia) 24 July 1977 (Cr: Mrs PD Dixon, Bill Chalker.)

MA - VICTORIA, AUSTRALIA

Someone once called the Antipodes 'the attic of the world' as far as the crazy local zoology goes - well, cryptozoologically speaking, it seems just as full of forgotten things (like the Bunyip) and mixed-up things (like the regular press confusion between marsupial tigers and marsupial wolves). Recently we were delighted to receive (from Bill Chalker, via the Bords) a copy of Bruce L Owens' article on 'The Emmaville Panther' (from _Outdoors & Fishing_, Australia, April 1977), the first detailed account of this feline phantom we had seen. It includes a very interesting photo, taken by a Ms Rilla Martin (whom Owens has failed to locate after exhaustive searches) of a very tiger-like animal seen in Victoria in 1964, and Owens is convinced from years of study that the 'Queensland Tiger', 'Queensland marsupial cat', 'Emmaville Panther' and the 'Victoria Tiger' (which Ms Martin snapped) refer to the same animal. Naturally the mystery quietens and pops up again from time to time, and the press never tire of reminding us that at the end of World War 2, US airmen, stationed in Victoria's Grampian mountains, loosed six pumas. The observant among you will note that the beasts in the following recent notes don't all have the puma's sandy colouring.

At Horsham, 320km NW of Melbourne, 3 hunters using spotlights at night encountered a "puma-like" beast about 30yds distant. _Sun_ (Aust) 28 April 1977 (Cr: Bill Chalker.) Once more, the cosmic punster shows his hand - Horsham, back in England, is on the edge of the 'Surrey Puma' territory, and the Scottish Grampians, of course, range over the south of Invernesshire, on the other side of Loch Ness from the recent 'lioness & cubs' sightings mentioned above!

A report in the _Daily Mirror_ (Aust) 15 Nov 1977, claims that after years of sightings in the area of Cambewarra Mountain, near Nowra, on the NSW coast south of Sydney, a "killer puma" had at last been shot by a father and son out hunting. In the mist on the mountain, they saw the large puma-like cat, yellow eyes glaring, preparing to leap. They shot and skinned it. (Cr: Bill Chalker.)

Back in the Horsham area of the Wimmera Lands of Victoria, later that same month, two local department officials laying a poison trail in the bush encounter a very sleek "jet-black big, beautiful creature" about 50yds away "outlined clearly against a white sandhill...It was slender in the shoulders and rump, like a cat, with a very small nose and ears and a beautiful cat-like tail. It was about 60cm high and 1m long." It sat there sniffing the wind and then stalked off into the scrub, apparently unconcerned. The witnesses said they had heard of sightings of large black cats in the area during the last six years, but this was the first time they had ever seen one. Sun (Aust) 25 Nov 1977 (Cr: Bill Chalker.)

'TASMANIAN TIGERS' & 'WOLVES'

The Thylacine - a dog-like marsupial with dark hoop stripes on the hindparts of its slender body - is very rare in Tasmania and supposed to have been extinct on the Australian mainland for several thousands of years - the papers consistently confuse the issue by calling them both 'tigers' and 'wolves'.

The photo below appeared in the Sunday Telegraph (Aust) 27 March 1977,

labelled a female "mainland tiger", is clearly a Thylacine. A group of farmers had been observing a pack of them (in a deliberately unidentified area on the NSW/Victoria border) when they noticed tiny paws hanging from the pouch of one of the larger bitches. Conservationist Bruce Jacobs was alerted and they obtained several photos, including this one of a female believed to be carrying a baby in its pouch. (Cr: Bill Chalker.)

Another Thylacine was seen several times in the Wyong area, about 50mls north of Sydney, in the headlights of cars, in Aug 1977. Central Coast Express (Gosford, NSW) 26 Aug 1977 (Cr: Bill Chalker.)

1977 also saw several sightings on Tasmania itself, but although the witnesses say they are positive the animal was a 'Tasmanian Tiger', we cannot clearly make out whether they mean a marsupial wolf or a marsupial cat! In the second week of Feb one was seen by a woman in Black River, and there had been two other sightings in the area. Sunday Mirror (Aust) 13 Feb 1977 (Cr: B Chalker)

On the evening of 19 Aug, two policemen in a patrol car, driving between Gladstone and Derby on the NE tip of the island, about 11pm, almost hit a 'Tasmanian Tiger' as it sauntered slowly across the road in front of them. Sunday Telegraph (Aust), Sun-Herald (Aust) 21 Aug 1977; The Australian 23 Aug '77; Daily Telegraph 24 Aug 1977 (Cr: Bill Chalker, RTA Hill.)

■■■■■■■■■■■■■■■■■■■■■■■■■■■■■■■■■■■

Fortean Computer / cont from p17...

mini-computers among smaller users and hobbyists. The remaining obstacle is knowledge.

I take the inevitability of Fortean use of electronic data processing as understood. I would like to appeal to any FT reader, who has knowledge and experience of systems analysis, programming, computer sales, any relevant field, to make themselves known to me. We need to plan and get knowledgeable advice for developing a program using a computer to its full advantage in our studies. Beyond the data handling side, we see the construction of special research programs and other avenues opening up for a Fortean database. A computer would also affect the future of FT with a word-processing and editing program. A long-term plan for compiling and coding data would be necessary. Are we eligible for grants or aid etc? Can the new TV data-networks (CEFAX etc) help us? And how will this affect Forteans, at home and internationally?

I see a new era opening up for the serious researcher with his own terminal and access to an authoritative Fortean database. If the prospect excites you, let's get together and make it work. But it will be long and hard work, so the faint-hearted need not apply. The prospects could take many forms, from jobs for the boys to a dynamic decentralised personal datanet. I'm serious, and if you contact me, I'll expect you to be also. I look forward to hearing from one or two of you; write via FT.

Bob Rickard.

PHANTOM PLAYMATES.

A few cases in which children were the major percipients:

Quinton, Birmingham: The Dutton Road council house of the Dennis family was haunted by a little, fat, red-faced, elderly man with a walking stick, according to 8-yr-old Beverley Dennis, who saw him often enough to be able to draw him. He kept waking her up and standing by her bed, although all the family of 5 had seen him. Albert, or Alfred (sources differ) as he was known also had a disconcerting habit of stamping round the house in hobnail boots, moving ornaments, calling the names of the family, and resisting exorcism. The ghost was identified from the description as being Alfred Harvey, who had lived in the house 15 years previously, dying aged 70 after threatening to come back and haunt the house. The Dennis family were asking the local Council for a move. D.Express, 15 Jan 73, News of the World, 21 Jan 73

Clifton, Nottingham: Another Dennis family were also having trouble with a ghost. Mr and Mrs Keith Dennis, and their four children fled their home after the eldest child, Mandy, 9, screamed after waking to see a grunting black shape at the foot of her bed, as the room went icy cold. The phantom had first appeared to Mr Dennis, but he had been too frightened to tell his family about it. The story was featured on the local "Midlands Today" TV programme, in which psychic Simon Alexander claimed to have seen a face at the window when visiting the house. The house was to be exorcised by Rev Frank Crowther, who had carried out 6 other council house exorcisms in Clifton in the preceding few months. The ghost was thought to be that of a previous resident who was said to have appeared to his wife while she survived. Both were cremated and their ashes scattered in the front garden of the house. Nottingham Evening Post, 19,20 Aug 75 (Cr: DO Mayes).

Eastbourne, Sussex: another council house, the home of Albert Morgan and his family, was haunted by a grey-haired old lady with bandaged legs, likened to the first occupant of the house. She appears to be solid, and has been seen by the 2 Morgan children, aged 8 & 6, who asked their mother who the old lady was that was living with them. She has made frequent appearances, on the stairs, in the toilet, but most favours sitting on a pile of logs in a storeroom, vanishing instantly rather than fading away. Occasionally she makes her invisible presence felt too, moving through the house and opening doors. The Morgans apparently felt no fear of the apparition. Reveille, 9 Jan 76 (Cr: N Watson)

Paignton, Devon: The Prince Regent Hotel, managed by Don Mudge, was haunted by a ghost who switched on radios and lights, and tampered with beer in the cellar. But he especially appeared to 6-year-old Paul Mudge, as the shadowy figure of a man sitting on his bed. Paul was far from frightened...he was trying to find out the ghost's birthday so he could send a card (to where?) D. Mirror, 12 May 76.

Hyde, nr Manchester: The ghost of a woman in grey dress and bonnet appeared several times in 3 weeks to Peter Atherton, 12, of Sussex Place. She smiled at him, but he was frightened because he didn't know what she wanted. A couple of weeks later, he was looking through some old family photographs, and recognised one as the ghost: his great, great grandmother, who died in the 1880s. The family put flowers on her grave at Mobberley, Cheshire, in the hope of laying the ghost...but we have no word of the case since. News of the World, 11 Dec 77. (Cr: CR Mather).

A COUPLE OF FREAKS.

Elsewhere in this issue we deal with finds of incomplete bodies; now, an incomplete ghost:

Vanderbijlpark, S. Africa: Mr Lourens Killian and his family moved into No 1, C M van den Hee-ver St. on a Monday. On Tuesday, a legless ghost of an old man, covered in long hair and with glowing eyes, appeared first to the maid, Emma Mtimkula, and then to Mrs Koekie Killian. Drifting through the air accompanied by a cold wind, the ghost also appeared to a neighbour. Through that week, the ghost appeared several times to the whole family, and on the Friday the family moved again, to another house in the same town. Come Monday, in the new house, Mr Killian felt a cold wind pass through him, took 3 blankets, kissed the children, and disappeared. Mrs Killian returned to the first house, and was duly chased by the ghost again. The next day, after the case had received enough publicity to draw crowds of ghost watchers, an unidentified man living on a plot outside the town approached Mrs Killian and offered to rid her of the ghost. Digging under a willow tree in the garden, he found a wooden doll with hair, a face, and nails through it. He talked to the doll, 'made it harm-less' and reburied it. The ghost was not seen again. Mr Killian ret-urned the following day, and then the whole family disappeared, along with their furniture. It was thought they had returned to their first home in Port Elizabeth. Rand Daily Mail, 11,12,13,15(?) Nov 75. (Cr: CJ Holtzhausen).

And from a lack to a surfeit:
Oviedo, N. Spain: A white clad phantom had made several appear-ances in the town, forcing people to kneel down and pray. It was variously reported as having two heads, or two green lanterns on its head. Anyone know more about this? The Journal (Newcastle) 3 Dec 76 (Cr: P Screeton), Sun, D Mirror, 4 Dec 76.

FACTS ON FIGURES...

Having an hour to spare while compiling this column, I did a swift and not very thorough survey of the ghost-apparitions in the first 25 issues of FT, 90 in all, including the above, using only those cases where human faces or forms were actually seen (the rapid approach of the almighty deadline prevented me extending my research).

Percipients: the major percipient was Male in 34 cases, female in 26, multiple or unidentified in 30.

Apparitions: Male forms: 40, Female forms: 31, Unidentified: 19.

In slightly more detail...
Male percipients saw: 15 Male, 9 Female, 10 unidentified.

Female percipients saw: 17 Male, 7 Female, 2 unidentified.

Unknown or multiple percipients: 8 Male, 15 Female, 7 unidentified.

My original notion had been that females might see more male ghosts, (which they do), and males see more females (which they don't). So all the above figures seem to show is a preponderance of males both in percipients and apparitions. Can we perhaps tempt someone into a more thoroughly researched ghost-sexing survey?
                                    SM

■■■■■■■■■■■■■■■■■■■■■■■■■■■■■■■■■

BINDERS
Some readers have wondered what hap-pened to our plan to have binders made for their collections of FT. We had a quote for the smallest possible econom-ical number (200) of a very neat and handsome design, however to date the orders for binders have been very low indeed (apx 10%). We fully intend to go ahead with this plan but it must wait until we can afford to tie up a chunk of our funds in a large number of bind-ers which may or may not be sold event-ually. Those of you who are fed up waiting, and who have paid the £2/each we asked for as an initial figure, may ask for a refund, or have the credit set against a sub-renewal, back-issues etc. Just write in... As some consolat-ion to those who have ordered them so far, we promise they will not incur any extra charges, but will receive their binders (when available) at the £2 price. We must close the order books until we can next go ahead firmly, but by then, of course, they are bound to cost a bit more than £2. More news when known.

'THE PARADIGMS ARE SHIFTING'

an introduction
to new thought
on reality and
the brain/mind problem

by BOB RICKARD

Perhaps the single most exciting aspect of Charles Fort's work which attracted me was his realisation of the transience of all phenomena; that they don't just stop but transmute into other phenomena changing and merging in a continuous and infinite flux of shifting appearances. At this time of my life I was afire with Eastern mysticism and Fort's vision appeared to me to be a uniquely Western expression of a very ancient cosmology typified by this imperfectly remembered fragment of a Vedic hymn:

> 'Never the Spirit was born;
> Endings and beginnings are dreams.
> Never was time it was not;
> The Spirit shall cease to be never.
> Birthless, deathless and changeless,
> Remaineth the Spirit forever,
> Dead though the house of it seems.'

Fort called his vision 'Continuity'. We could never know absolute universal values, he argued, but what we experience are the graduations between extremes. For example; absolute heat, up, good, black etc become more hypothetical the more we chase them, and so do their extreme opposites, absolute cold, down, evil, white etc. They are concepts. But in the experimental universe, Fort said, everything contains everything else in varying degrees. Heat, up, good and black etc can only be defined in terms of their opposites, and vice versa.

The inescapable conclusion is that all forms of measurement, representation or partition of the universe into finite units, symbols and categories are quite arbitrary and can never guarantee any congruence with the hypothetical absolute values they are supposed to represent.

The immediate effect of this approach is apparently to divide the universe into complementary forms: the infinite and the finite, the numenal and the phenomenal, the universally latent and the particularly expressed, etc. The expediency of this has suited mens' purposes throughout history despite its limitations and the warnings of mystics, mediums (and today, even physicists) that it is not enough. The wedge between the forms was driven home around the 13th century by the speculations of Albertus Magnus, St Thomas Aquinas, Roger Bacon and William of Ockham who sought a distinction between science and theology, matter and mind, Man and God, etc — and upon this 'Cartesian split' later philosophers, like Francis Bacon, laid the foundations of the modern scientific method, upon which the modern world has built a shrine to all that is material, finite and transient.

Science has changed quite a lot from Fort's day but his observations are still valid because he was laying bare the processes by which we, as fallible humans, distort by carelessness and fear the very mirrors in which we have to see the universe reflected (we'll come back to this point). Fort's basic argument is straightforward and contained in the opening chapter of *Book of the Damned* (1); and the remainder of his works amplify and illustrate his points. The fabulous 'scientific experiment', Fort said, is in essence an attempt to define a part of the universe by excluding the rest of the universe. It ends up, like all other semantic creations, an arbitrary statement that only works within its own parameters. It may work, but only locally, finitely and when supported by circular reasoning (2) — there can be no confirmation in any absolute sense (as eg suggested by the word 'law') that the same experiment will work in the same way, anywhere in the universe, or for all time. Yet, extrapolating from the local and particular to the universal, the orthodoxy of Science behaves as if its 'laws' were universal. With many Scientists (3) this is an act of faith every bit as fundamental to their cosmology as a belief in God is to devout monotheists.

The popular image of Science is that it should be reasonable, reassuring, conservative, incontrovertible and authoritative. The trouble is that many Scientists believe this too. In terms of the human spirit there is no inexorable march toward a glorious extra-galactic sunset. True science is a warfare with Reality as its prize; the Known against the Unknown. The tiniest battles topple semantic universes and shape their replacements. Like Castaneda's sorcerer (4) the true scientist must be impeccable.

Science, then, is a semantic construction through which we filter the universe. It restricts our incoming data as effectively as the finite limits of our senses. So Fort decided to look outside Science at the data it excluded, rejected, ignored or suppressed. He surmised that in the realm of reported experience there were many reflections of strange aspects of the universe (or even of different universes) which an ignorant science could not recognise, and a fearful science would not. These fragments of a shattered universe he called 'the Damned' because by design or accident they had been excommunicated and banished to an outer darkness of neglect. From his huge data collection — his own estimates ranged from 40,000 to 60,000 notes at various times — he saw clearly that if the semantic straightjackets could be avoided, much of our experience of the world suggests characteristics the very opposite of those Science valued so fiercely.

This universe of 'Fort's had an 'underlying oneness' in which phenomena were like islands in a sea: separated above the surface but connected to each other through the bedrock, accounting for both individuality and difference in the same theory (5). Continuity emphasises contiguity over isolation. Strictly, a phenomenon is the result of the complex interaction of all the forces operating in the universe at that moment through that nexus . . . but more than that it has temporal extension too. Conventional physics tends to deal with moments in time, split off from the universal flux, frozen like a photograph while events continue on regardless. Time is as much a semantic construction, a tool of the mind, as space, or any other concept.

For me the notion of Continuity had the same sort of satisfying appeal I found in the metaphysics of Eastern mysticism, particularly in Ch'an or Zen Buddhism, or the older Taoism. It united opposites and transcended them, suggesting a unity greater than the sum of its parts. It defied definition, subdivision or categorizing showing these to be illusory, however much we depend on them in our affairs. The Taoists in particular voiced the folly of ignorant dependance on the artificially created reality in the face of the greater one. It was both beyond and the source of all appearances; if it could be heard, seen or spoken about it was not the source but a reflection. 'That which imparts form to forms is itself formless. Therefore Tao cannot have a name.' (6).

Continuity, manifesting in the world of human experience, takes two simultaneous and paradoxical forms: one implies a connecting principle linking every thing; and the other a state of connexion in which all things are both united or contiguous while maintaining any individuality they may have. These aspects apply to the Absolute Principle, whether conceived of in theistic terms (God, Allah, etc, beside whom there is no other . . .) or non-theistic terms ('the Aleph', or point that contains all other points, etc — or 'the Tao', the 'Uncarved Block', etc).

However, they also apply to the paradoxical states of existence currently being conceptualised in modern high energy physics, where matter is seen to be another form of energy (or vice-versa), and in which energy can function simultaneously as a wave and a particle. (7)

Recently, the psychologist Lawrence LeShan outlined a fresh approach to the mysteries of parapsychology based on his intelligent studies of psychic healing (8). In his first book he claims that the breakthrough came when he shifted approach to ask a new kind of question; as a scientist he had been asking: 'How does a sensitive gain information not known to her by normal channels?' or 'How does a psychic heal?' After getting nowhere for a long time, he tried asking: 'What goes on when it is done; what is the structure of the paranormal event when it happens?' Basically he found two complementary answers which must be considered together. Firstly, the medium or healer was in an altered state of consciousness; and secondly, felt that there was complete unity between themselves and the universe which transcended normal limitations, including space and time . . . and of course, the patient or source of information. LeShan concluded from a pioneering programme — in which he taught himself and others to heal effectively by shifting their awareness to this 'Clairvoyant' mode of being — that 'reality' is determined by our mode of consciousness; and that in the greater Reality of the universe many different modes of reality, each mutually exclusive and obeying their own sets of rules, can be operating simultaneously; and that a person can, and does, shift continuously between these different modes every day.

About the same time, another breakaway psychologist, Joseph Chilton Pearce, was also suggesting that 'reality' is not necessarily physically determined, but a mental phenomenon. Pearce's argument overlaps and illuminates LeShan's. He says that all our criteria for determining what is real are the products of social and cultural conditioning; that we are born with an instinct to form a semantic conception of the universe (through which to regulate our growth and adaption on which personal survival depends) and just as automatically we are initiated into the consensus of reality of our parents (9). This adult consensus of reality has evolved over millenia, like an organism, forced to change and adapt or perish, in a continuous non-material transmission (10). The consensus is a unifying pool of references, symbols and formulae, accumulating from practical use and tradition, which dominates our perceptions and conceptions, and provides the language through which we communicate with others and the universe (11) and on which our social survival depends. Circumstances ensure that we are imprinted with the adult consensus from the moment we are born. It surrounds us, and at the time of optimum imprinting overwhelms us — in our state of innocence we are unable to resist with a personal reality of our own (12).

The ability to form new or alternate realities is never lost, but in most of us lies buried under the weight of millions of people and centuries of their common acquiescence. Acquiescence, because part of our conditioning involves the subtle undermining of any hope of revolt against this semantic tyranny — by the age of seven, reckons Pearce, we are so completely in the grip that even rebellion is only in terms allowed by the consensus. The consensus colossus has to have some degree of flexibility to survive, but it is slow and delayed. Man still has the capacity for inventive and creative acts, and where these catch the imagination of more and more people, they form the nucleus of a smaller consensus. As they grow they get strong enough to challenge the prevailing consensus — the loser is soon forgotten outside the history books. Should I wish to levitate, I'll have to overcome my own conditioning to convince myself that such an idea is absurd and 'against science and nature', that levitation is not only possible but that I can do it, and then convince other people to believe in the same things. Any new perception or idea has to run the same gauntlet, and the more fundamental its threat against its older counterpart the harder it is resisted (13). When it comes down to it the inertia of the many must be overcome before any idea gets a foothold. There is strong evidence from LeShan, Pearce and others that new or alternative realities can be created and sustained by groups of people (14). But work on testing, applying and understanding these new approaches has barely begun. They are exciting breakthroughs because they offer a more inclusive view than the present scientific orthodoxy — a view which includes parapsychological and paraphysical phenomena for starters.

One of the more important insights these ideas give us is the degree to which the human mind actually creates a complex replica of the universe, and psychological and cultural processes to reinforce this artificial reality as the prime reference for personal and social behaviour. The model reality acts as a sophisticated buffer, a self-defence mechanism to protect man from the universe. Desperate for security and fearful of change, man accepts the limitations of a semantically structured universe as the lesser of two evils — it at least offers a refuge while resisting growth; whereas the other path leads to illumination or madness. So naturally language-orientated man feels threatened by that which defies or transcends expression in categories, labels or measurements. LeShan and Pearce both voice the deep fear with which many (especially those who consider themselves sincerely rational) face what Pearce calls 'the empty category' — a fear that should they recognise even for a split second that any of their cherished values (especially strong beliefs in dogmatic principles) may be in error then their entire world will 'collapse into chaos', for then truly would the universe seem a mad place and we would be powerless to keep its manic shouts from echoing within our own terrifying empty shells. We need language, symbol, the semantic consensus of reality to structure the formless void, to bring order out of chaos . . . at any price (15).

Fort's experiment was to observe relationships between things, not the things themselves . . . and it certainly yielded an exciting new approach to the world of phenomena. This view has since been independently supported by Capra, Pearce and LeShan, and I refer the reader to their important books for discussions, authorities, examples and further reading. Fort concluded that individual existences (including our own) bore the same relationship to the absolute totality, as, say, a cell to the whole body; and that this relationship (part to the whole and vice versa) was a primal organising force structuring all the expressions in both directions. Fort put his conception of the reflexive organic universe in these terms:

'. . . I can think of our existence as an Organism. If human thought is a growth, like all other growths, its logic is without foundation of its own, and is only the adjusting constructiveness of all other growing things. A tree cannot find out, as it were, how to blossom, until comes blossom-time. A social growth cannot find out the use of steam-engines, until comes steam-engine-time. . . . no part of a growing plant needs guidance of its own devising, nor special knowledge of its own as to how to become a leaf or a root.' (16)

Or as Fort expressed elsewhere: 'The whole is God to its parts.'

Recently, another piece of the puzzle emerged — perhaps because its time had come, for like the power of steam, the properties of laser-light had been known for some time before the invention of its applications. I'm referring here to the hologram which contains in every part of it the information to reconstruct the whole picture according to the special position of that part in relation to the scene pictured (17). Karl Pribram, a neuropsychologist at Stamford University, California, and David Bohm, a physicist at the University of London, postulate that 'primal reality would be an invisible, omnipresent matrix of energy frequencies encoding the sum total of information about the universe and its contents into every subdivision (however minute) of itself. Like the 'Uncarved Block' of the Taoists, infinite potential for form lies pregnant in every part of it, until an act of expression mutilates its completeness and imprisons it in finite form.

The brain, acting like 'a hologram interpreting a holographic universe' decodes according to its organic and semantic limitations. As we have seen, these limitations are largely set by ourselves from birth (barring of course congenital defects), and they come in 'sets' which in turn determine the various types of consciousness in which we need to function. It is well known that the universe contains far more information than that which trickles through our perceptual channels. Now we have a model for the way in which the brain is programmed to select and reject different sets of phenomena and their interactions in order to construct creatively the relevant 'concrete' model reality complete with its appropriate rules and phenomena.

The hologram model has so far proved so satisfying in its applications in offering a more simple and elegant solution to the diversity of phenomena, that in its short existence so far it has not met with any serious criticism — in fact it has proved so exciting to researchers in physics, psychology, biology, genetics and cybernetics that the *Brain/Mind Bulletin* (an excellent newsletter that serves these and other overlapping interests) brought out a special issue devoted to the discussion of the ideas of Pribram and Bohm on this subject (18). Pribram confidently believes that ' . . . we're in the middle of a paradigm shift that encompasses all of science'. One unexpected benefit has been to parapsychologists and paraphysicists who also see in the hologram model the foundation of new theories for many (if not all) the genuine phenomena in their specialties which apparently contradict the present known 'laws' of science — theories which will allow for scientific testing and prediction, and account for the phenomena in a way which will be more acceptible generally to their scientific colleagues. (19)

Indeed this approach is so new and startling, uniquely merging both science and mysticism, that its full impact and implications will not be known for some time. Pearce and LeShan laid the groundwork for the acceptance of this theory in parapsychology and the new studies of altered states of consciousness, and it provides a scientific illustration of what Fort meant by 'Continuity'.

RJM Rickard   April 1978.

Notes & References.

1) First published in 1919; collected and reprinted with his three other books in *The Complete Books of Charles Fort* (Holt, NY, 1941; Dover, NY, 1974).

2) For the full Fortean nuance, the reader must serve his apprenticeship and read through the *Books*, wherein lie many illustrations of the limitations of orthodox thought (eg. strata dated by the fossils found in them, and fossils dated by the strata in which they were found). This logic-paradox of the difficulty of absolute proof ensures, to quote Sir Karl Popper, that 'every scientific statement must remain tentative forever. It may indeed be corroborated, but every corroboration is relative to other statements which, again, are tentative'.

3) Science with a capital 'S' denotes the dogmatic orthodoxy, which these days owes more allegiance to the political and commercial sources of its funding than to the unbiased quest for truth and understanding — similarly Scientists (as opposed to scientists) tend to be 9-5 bureaucrats motivated more by the need for status, security and reward than the 'lust to know'. Hence such statements as: 'not all Scientists are scientifically minded'. (Bernard Heuvelmans), 'Science is not always what Scientists do', (J Allen Hynek), and 'Science has done its utmost to prevent whatever science has done', (Fort).

4) Despite the exposé of Carlos Castaneda by Richard deMille (see review of his *Castaneda's Journey* in FT 21/35) as a literary hoax, there is no denying that Castaneda's books contain genuine scholarship and insight. I have no hesitation in referring the reader to his *Tales of Power* for a brilliant evocation of the noumenal and phenomenal aspects of the world, which he calls the 'Nagual' and the 'Tonal'. DeMille shows that Castaneda was well aware of the work of Joseph Chilton Pearce (and perhaps LeShan for all we know; both of whose thought we summarise below) and lost no time in incorporating Pearce's views in some detail into the lessons of his (Castaneda's) Yaqui Indian sorcerer, Don Juan Mattus.

5) The caveat is that you must recognise that you are still thinking semantically. A model of the universe may be more complete than the scientific model, and may approximate more clearly to the universe itself, but will still remain a model.

6) *Chuang-tzu* ch.22.

7) See Fritjof Capra's *The Tao of Physics* (many editions) for a sensitive and intelligent study of the similar pronouncements of mystics (both East and West) and modern physicists.

8) Lawrence LeShan: *The Medium, The Mystic and The Physicist* (Ballantine Books, NY, 1975); and *Alternate Realities* (Sheldon Press, London, 1976).

9) Joseph Chilton Pearce; *The Crack in the Cosmic Egg* (Pocket Books, NY, 1973); and *Exploring the Crack in the Cosmic Egg* (Pocket Books, NY, 1975).

10) . . . similar to the genetic transmission of life, regardless of species or form. Truly it is said (by Heathcote Williams) 'Life doesn't give a rat's ass who lives it!'

11) The arbitrary nature of language as a model of the universe was illustrated by Martin Gardner, whose *Fads and Fallacies in the Name of Science* (Dover, NY, 1957) contains a profile of Fort and Forteanism. Gardner observed that a science that decided to accept red things and reject yellow would be in trouble over orange. The reflexive nature of language prompted the physicist Werner Heisenberg (quoted by Capra) to say that in much of science, 'What we observe is not nature itself, but nature exposed to our method of questioning'. Language   not only interrogates the universe but structures all the responses. I like the comment of the Duck in the adventures of Alice, who observed innocently: 'When I find a thing it's usually a frog or a worm'.

12) There are interesting implications in this about the essential nature of man; e.g. in the problem of feral children, it could be argued that at the time they were ready they were imprinted with an imperfectly expressed wolf's consensus reality, or some other, for barring mental debility and a quick rescue there have been little or no successful rehabilitations into human society.

13) Progress is never easy or overnight. See Thomas Kuhn's *The Structure of Scientific Revolutions* (University of Chicago Press; 2nd edn, 1970) for a superlative historical assessment of the resistance of the Old Dominant to the New (Fort's terms). Such resistance seems to be a grander form of the resistance to change within ourselves. The breakthroughs do not always come as smoothly as we like to suppose but often only after we have prepared the ground with a frustrating and fruitless long-drawn out wrestle with a problem, and suddenly, in a moment of illumination, we make the jump to a new way of looking at the matter which brings with it an exciting and often 'obvious' solution. Social and personal history is full of such discontinuities.

14) One exciting example is the work of the New Horizons Research Foundation, of Toronto, in scientifically creating a 'poltergeist' in their lab! -- see their reports in *Conjuring up Philip* by Iris M Owen (Fitzhenry & Whiteside, Toronto, 1976).

15) see back to Note 11, One drama of terror was briefly mirrored in the *Observer* 11 and 18 Dec 1977, & 1 Jan 1978. Dr Harold Hillman, of Surrey University, has claimed that at least five or the main structures of the cell, as revealed by the electron microscope, are in fact artifacts generated by the methods of preparing the sample. They have to be 'stained' by heavy metals or they cannot be seen by the electron beam. . but this seems to create illusions, e.g. the two-line appearance of the cell 'unit membrane'. It seems that once again man has come up against the barrier-fact that what he sees is a product of his own language or technique. In this case no-one knows what the detail of the natural unstained cell looks like. This suggests, says Hillman, that research programmes all over the world 'are using extensive resources and skilled personnel in a quest which can never give them meaningful results.'

It seems that publication of Dr Hillman's paper has been 'inexplicably' delayed, and has been emotionally resisted with inadequate arguments by the Royal Microscopical Society. Last I heard, Dr Hillman had challenged them to a debate before a scientific audience. Silence!

16) Fort, *Books,* p557.

17) Holography, or 3D photography, was first described in 1947 by the brilliant Prof. Dennis Gabor; but it had to wait until after 1969 before successful holograms were constructed with the newly invented laser. A laser beam is split, half to illuminate the hologram plate, the other half to illuminate the scene or object from which the reflected light is directed to the plate. This 'negative', made without lenses, is not like a photograph but consists of the interference patterns between the two beams of laser light, looking a lot like the intersecting ripples on a pond when stones are dropped in different places. When a laser beam is shone through the hologram plate, it projects a 3D image of the scene. The interesting thing is that this image is relative to the direction of viewing. If we had holographed a table, for instance, a beam shone downward through the top part of the plate would show the table seen from the angle (i.e. the top of the table); now, if you angle the beam to point upwards, the image of the table will tilt to show the underside as though you were actually looking from that angle. You can do this in every part of the plate because each part has all the information to reconstruct the whole image -- unlike a negative, you could get the whole picture from a tiny portion snipped off at random

18) *Brain/Mind Bulletin* (2:16) 4 July 1977. A complimentary copy of this issue may be had on request, from *Brain/Mind Bulletin,* Box 42211, Los Angeles, CA 90042, USA.

19) There have been several holistic ventures into Forteana to my knowledge. My colleague, R Martin Wolf, of SITU, read a paper at the First International Congress of Paranormal Phenomena (Mexico City, 19-27 Nov 1977) which superbly summarizes modern Fortean phenomena in the light of the new theories we have mentioned here; and I urge all interested readers to read this paper in the Winter 1978 issue of *Pursuit* (see our journal review section for SITU details). Coming next issue in FT is a paper by Tom Bearden, who seems to have come to similar conclusions about alternate realities and Fortean phenomena but from his own deliberations on the nature of a physics which transcends the limits of orthodox physics.

■■■■■■■■■■■■■■■■■■■■■■■■■■■■■■■■■■■■■■■

Obituaries cont from p32...

Obituaries cont from p32...

I would like to take this opportunity to express my own appreciation of the work of Eric Russell and Harold Chibbett. At the time I began The News (as FT was then called) EFR, with characteristic humour, declined my invitation to contribute material. It was 1973; he had been an active Fortean for nearly 40 difficult years, and felt he had earned his rest. I had long been a fan of his SF writings, and indeed it was mention of Fort in some of his stories (and in the editorials of John Campbell, in Astounding SF, as Analog was then called) which alerted me to Forteanism. The first Fortean book I ever read was EFR's Great World Mysteries, which changed my life. My contact with Harold Chibbett was more recent, and apart from one brief meeting, consisted of sporadic correspondence over the last three years. He always seemed to have the time for his correspondents; always witty, informative, and always encouraging. To judge from the rollcall of names on many of his newsletter-files, there are a goodly number of the famous, and the unknown, who owe him a huge debt of thanks, for almost single-handedly keeping Forteans in contact with each other. (His newsletter will be continued by Sid Birchby - see the ad on p 47). For my part this debt of appreciation and gratitude for the encouragement and influence these two pioneers had on my own endeavours will be better expressed in the pledge that FT will continue in their spirit of dedication and respect in the service of Forteans and Forteanism. Wherever they are now, I like to think that they are with Fort gossiping like long-lost friends newly-met in some celestial tavern.

RJMR

BITS AND PIECES...

Raking through a file of body-reports can be depressing at the best of times, so this issue we're turning to lighter matters: persons lighter by an arm, or a leg, or...

HEADS...

A pair of twos...

Wandsworth Common, London: on 11 Oct 75 a skull was found in a pond and sent to Scotland Yard for forensic tests. Another skull had been found in the same pond in July, but tests on it were not complete at the time of the second find. Sunday Express, 12 Oct 75.

Trinidad, Colorado: Around 18 Apr 77, the mummified heads of a man and woman aged about 60 were found in a sealed, waterfilled 5-gallon greasebucket, which had been standing in a junkyard (one report says a field) for 3 to 6 months. Police sent the heads to the Colorado Bureau of Investigation for identification, began searching for other remains, and checked local cemeteries,..but obviously none too well, for it was more than a week before the corresponding bodies were found in a mausoleum, variously reported as being only 50 or 300 yds away. Graveyard vandals were blamed, as other coffins in the same crypt had been disturbed. Valley Courier (Alamosa, Co) 19 Apr 77, Daily Courier Democrat (Russellville, Ark) 21,28 Apr 77, Sterling Journal-Advocate, 2 May 77. (Cr: TR Adams)

...AND TAILS.

The other side of the coin...

Brake Hill Farm, Cockley Cley, Norfolk: On 27 Aug 74 the headless body of a shapely young woman, 5ft 1in high and 23-30 years old, wearing a pink nightdress, was found in a trackway, tied up and wrapped in a plastic sheet. Four months later she was buried, still unidentified, the cause of death still unknown. News of the World, 5 Jan 75 (Cr: N Watson).

On the Birmingham to Worcester railway line, between Barnt Green and Blackwell stations, a headless body was found, on 3 Sept 74 (Birmingham Evening Mail, same date. Cr: D Driscoll) Police thought the man, in his 60s and believed to live locally, had been hit by a train in the night. No mention of what became of his head...

Wewoka, Oklahoma: Several weeks before our reports, Silas Narcomey, a Seminole Indian, had been decapitated in a hit-and-run accident. His head had not been recovered, and police said it may have fallen inside the car that struck him, and assumed that it would have been thrown out further down the road. Narcomey's relatives complained that weeks of searching had not found the head, but then reluctantly buried the body. According to Seminole belief, the body should be buried whole...otherwise the unfortunate Narcomey's ghost will spend eternity wandering in search of its head. Valley Courier (Alamosa, Co.) 17 Feb 78, Saturday Oklahoman, 18 Feb 78 (Cr: TR Adams)

ARMS, LEGS & FEET.

Falmouth, Cornwall: A decomposed human arm, hand and part of a rib-cage was found in an attic on 20 Dec 76, by builders who merely left it lying on the scaffolding with a note attached: "In case you need a hand". Builders taking the scaffolding down on 18 Jan 77 left the limb in Hull's Lane, where it was found 5 hours later and finally reported. The right arm of a female, nearly 2 ft long, it had been sawn off "very neatly" from the rest of the ribcage, and was partially mummified.

Estimates of its age (since severance) ranged from 5 to 100 years... yet its origin remains a mystery. The West Briton, 20 Jan 77. (Cr: P Roberts).

Strangles Beach, nr Crackington Haven, Cornwall. In August 73, a decomposed body of a man aged between 25 & 30 was found on the beach. A week later, a 'human leg joint', which we gather refers to part of the leg and the foot was found. No positive identification was made, and both finds were subsequently buried. However, Cornwall County pathologist F D M Hocking told the inquest he had been unable to establish any direct connection between the body and the limb. Post & Weekly News, 2 Mar 74. (Cr: N Watson).

Walberswick, Suffolk: a peculiarly similar case. On 17 Jan 77 a foot was found on the beach. The previous November, a head in a plastic bag was brought up in a fisherman's net off Great Yarmouth, and during the 2nd week of Jan, a headless body was washed up at Sizewell...but no mention as to whether it was footless as well. D. Telegraph, 18 Jan 77.

Television personality Dr Magnus Pyke, of the British Association for the Advancement of Science, received a toe in the post from Chicago. It came from a woman butchered to death in a double murder... but why it was sent to the voluble Dr Pyke remains a mystery. Sun, 30 Apr 77.

OTHER PARTS.

Fareham, Hampshire: Part of a body, believed to be a baby, was found near a railway line. A woman was helping police inquiries. Scunthorpe Evening Telegraph, 18 July 74. (Cr: N Watson).

The Thames, nr Shell Haven: On the weekend of 22-23 Oct 77, a man's armless, legless body was found. Police identified the remains as Simon Archer, 46, lost from his yacht off Canvey Island sometime previously, after sailing off to investigate the Bermuda Triangle. Fate seems to have caught up with him rather prematurely...D. Telegraph, 24 Oct 77. (Cr: J Gee)

AND A COUPLE OF STRANGE ONES...

Buenos Aires, Argentina: A woman jailed for killing a man, dismembering his body and boiling his head, was to be retried on a plea of self-defence! Wonder if she got off? D. Express, 12 July 77.

Sand Springs, Oklahoma: Digging in his backyard, CL Hufford discovered what appeared to be a hand, with 5 fingers, human-like nails, fur, webbing between the fingers. It was flesh-coloured and flexible. A doctor at the University of Tulsa said it was a duck's foot. (Wha..?) Dallas Morning News, 17 Jan 73. (Cr: TR Adams). SM.

We intended to deal with a variety of 'death ray' type material ranging from the microwave transmissions out of Russia in the last two years (allegedly based on the work of Tesla) to the rather hysterical speculations about the Cold War use of paranormal phenomena – but rather than cut the piece to fit the small space left to us, we'll give it fully next issue. Meanwhile we found a few other notes of interest which may or may not have something to do with unusual configurations of electro-magnetic energy.

SHOCKING STORIES
A new children's slide, erected in the village of Roffey, near Horsham, Sussex, is giving all its users a hefty belt. No obvious cause could be found except that

perhaps the children generated the static charge by their sliding. London *Evening Standard* 15 May 1974 (Cr: L Beer.)

A Stewarton, Lincs, man's new Triumph Dolomite car became so charged that apart from heavy shocks, he saw sparks flying between key and lock. It had never happened to him before with other cars. *Sunday Post* 27 April 1975 (Cr: Nigel Watson.)

Thousands of users of a multi-storey car-park in St Helens, Lancs, town center get the old frogs-legs treatment in their arms as they take tickets from the barrier machine. Despite £1000 worth of investigation, and statements from the manufacturer, council and Electricity Board officials that the machine is, as far as they can discover, technically safe and sound, the shocks continue. *Liverpool Daily Post* 23 Sept 1976 (Cr: Peter Rogerson.)

On 15 Jan 1977, a lady leading her young husky dog along a snow-covered pavement in Harlem, NY, stepped onto a section that was strangely wet and free of snow. Her dog howled, its hair stood on end and it collapsed and died. A vet said later death was caused by cardiac arrest and respiratory failure indicating electrocution. Other dogs were known to have yelped and run from that section. Con Ed troubleshooters found the sidewalk warm, and a test bulb glowed on contact. It was leaking between 20-40v; hardly enough to kill a dog, they said. To be safe, current was isolated from the cable in the vicinity and the story neatly ends. St Louis (Mo) *Post-Dispatch* 20 Jan, Atlanta (Ga) *Constitution* 21 Jan 1977 (Cr: Mark A Hall.)

ELECTRIC PEOPLE
Two old notes...for the record.

Vyvyan Jones, 12, of Henbury, Bristol, has been shocking people, making lights flicker, watches stop and the TV crackle since he broke his arm! For two days afterward his hair stood on end, he gave people huge jolts, and once had to be hauled quickly out of the bath because he was "tingling." Someone at Southmead Hospital, Bristol, where he was treated, said it was "a natural phenomenon" but not unique (see *Phenomena* for other cases), adding casually: "We've even had cases of people being able to lift iron bars because they are so magnetic." *Sunday People* 15 Feb 1976 (Cr: P Rogerson.)

The case of Mrs Grace Charlesworth is less straightforward. After living in their detached house in Congleton, Cheshire, for a trouble-free 38yrs, Mrs Charlesworth's trouble began in 1968. In the garden and the house electric shocks

torment her day and night: "Sometimes they have swung me round bodily and in the night my head has started to shake as though I was using a pneumatic drill. One day sparks ran up the walls. Our lights flicker from time to time and nearly go out. The electric wiring has been tested and nothing could be found wrong." She discounts the possibility that she is the main focus: "The shocks occur only in this house and garden. I do not get them when away on holiday, staying with my sister, or even in the house next door." Psychological explanations could be offered for this, of course, but some apparently incidental info adds other dimensions to the story, and the overlaps with other phenomena will not go unnoticed. Mr Charlesworth remembers that about the time the trouble started, they and other local residents had petitioned the council over " weird humming and whizzing noises" from a nearby factory."At first we connected the trouble with the factory (although) I heard the humming (but) never felt any shocks...The noise lessened. Now we hear it only occasionally." Chief health inspector Ronald Whiston said: " When we received the petition from 46 residents, I traced the noise to a compressor on the first floor of the factory. The firm moved the motor to the ground floor and it could not then be heard. But we were told that Mrs Charlesworth's experiences continued. I could find nothing to go on. It was like looking for something that didn't exist. It is a complete mystery." Cryptically, Mrs Charlesworth herself adds: "Our phone has been hit by lightning five times in the last few years. Whether it is the house or me that attracts electricity I don't know." *Sunday Express* 19 March 1967 (Cr: Peter Rogerson.)

FORCE FIELDS?
But we can't help wondering how little we really know about the invisible matrix of forces that surround us. Tesla's largely neglected work on the wire-less transmission of power (he lit 20 bulbs at about 25 miles) by using the earth itself as part of the circuit, opens staggering unanswered questions. Sadly the new interest has a sinister appeal to the paranoid and the power-hungry, as we'll see next issue with the claims that the Soviets are experimenting along this line to control weather and minds. The new science of MHD can generate electricity in clouds of hot (ionised) gas...but our bodies too contain ionised particles and in our daily peregrinations we cut across magnetic

'lines of force'; and our water-filled tissues are just right for trapping micro-waves - we simply don't know enough about the human body's energy fields, our 'ergosphere'. There have been startling claims made recently for 'psychotronic' devices which can be charged with 'mental energy'. When released near plants in short bursts there are astonishing improvements in growth. They can also deliver 'psychic whammies' and trigger post-hypnotic commands etc. We have finally technologised the Curse of the Pharaohs! Consider the following in the light of unknown fields of force and shorn of their background belief system:

Mrs Dilys Cant is emphatic - an unseen barrier resisted her car as she tried to park in a bay in a new multi-storey park in the center of Durham. "It was as if I had come up against a kerb...but there was nothing there. It was uncanny." She tried 3 times, revving her engine to force the car past, and failed. She returned later with her daughter-in-law and they watcher another motorist having the same problem in that spot. Then, whatever it was resisting incursion into that space, left. Council officials tried and succeeded in parking there - and Mrs Cant, demonstrating for a TV film crew, was herself surprised when she backed straight into the space. She adds: "But I know what happened before was real. It's the truth - even if it does make me look rather foolish." Good for her! Sunday Express 14 Dec, Newcastle Journal 8 Dec 1975 (Cr: Paul Screeton, Tony Roberts.)

In the Fijian capital, Suva, tribal leaders performed a traditional ceremony ('bulubulu') to placate two spirits angry at a powerhouse built on tribal land, after inexplicable power failures every day

for two weeks. Apparently it worked! Kansas City Times 25 June, Atlanta (Ga) Constitution 3 July 1977 (Cr: Richard Indin, Mark A Hall.)

Similarly, "mischief-making spirits" inhabiting a tree on Jalan Assam Lumbang, in Taiping, Malaysia, were blamed for "yet another" fatal road accident, after a car swerved off the road into another tree "without any apparent reason." Inter-tree rivalry or hatred? or mebbe they don't like cars! The Star (Penang) 11 March 1978 (Cr: Sam, I Will) And in the same country we learn of a mystery 30ft wooden 'pillar' in the heart of Rimba Mas Mas (Forest of Wealth on the Chuping sugar plantation about 16 miles from Kangar, north Malaysia. Sacrilege and attempts to demolish the 'pillar' have met with ill luck, even death. A plantation worker who cursed it was instantly dropped with a heart attack (when recovered he went back to beg forgiveness.) A 17yr-old Thai boy who urinated on it became 'hysterical'; so did his companion. Apparently possessed, they asked for candles and eggs to be placed at the foot of the structure, and when done they returned to normal. A tractor-driver who stole those eggs was later killed when his tractor overturned. Etc. There had been a local legend that in earlier times a king, Raja Bersiong, had built a beautiful palace deep in the jungle of the Thai-Malaysia border. Plantation workers, clearing a new field, came across the object, believed to be several centuries old. According to one, there were several 'pillars', which they thought might be the remains of Raja Bersiong's lost palace, but one was pulled down, since when bad luck has dogged the plantation. The Echo (Malaysia) 19 April 1978 (Cr: Ion Will.)

RJMR

■■■

Late Cats/cont from p33...

Officially cougars haven't been seen in Pennsylvania since 1894, but residents of Oakdale say they have seen one and found tracks in the "past 2 weeks". No reported escapes. Police nonchalant. Texarcana Gazette 4 March 1978 (Cr: Tom Adams).

The 'Surrey Puma' was seen "last week", about 7.30pm sitting and walking along the railway line at Blackwater, Surrey, by Mrs Janet Rutherford of Kings Way, who described it as "big, black and moved like a cat." The paper says the SP was last seen close-up at Star Hill, Hartley Wintney in July 1976. We don't think we have a note of this one, but 'Star Hill'; hmmmm! Fleet News (Surrey) 19 May 1978 (C.Hall)

Chicago Ghost Tour	* NEWSLETTER *
Fortean Richard T Crowe runs a regular guided coach tour around Chicago's many sites of 'supernatural' and Fortean interest. Charges are low, and the tour is twice weekly. Write for more information to Richard T Crowe: Box 29054, Chicago, Illinois 60629, USA.	...an informal postal exchange for studies in paraphysics and the esoteric arts, founded 1944, Non-sectarian, non-demanding. For an introductory leaflet, send a stamp to NL, 40 Parrs Wood Rd, Didsbury, Manchester M20 OND.

'Other' Reviews/cont from p31...

ience will find parts of the film difficult to comprehend.

Ufologists are unlikely to feel that the phenomenon they study has been accurately depicted. UFOs do appear to affect electrical equipment, but not to the extent of causing toys, vacuum-cleaners and cookers to operate on their own; poltergeist phenomena are sometimes connected with UFO events, but not to the extent of wrecking a house's contents; UFOs do hover over houses, but not to the accompaniment of thunderous roars, violent winds and rolling clouds. Probably the most blatant fact-twisting is in the final scenes when a vast intergalactic battlecruiser-type UFO (unknown in the records of ufology but quite familiar from the covers of SF paperbacks) comes in to land at a prepared rendezvous and landing pad made ready for the alien's first contact with earthmen. Here we see technological mankind in charge with his floodlights, cameras, recorders and computers awaiting the momentous touch-down. The truth is that it is not we who are in charge, or decide the when and where of close encounters, but they. Also, the alien visitor we meet on the screen appears to be childlike, wistful, timid and friendly, whereas the real CE witnesses, especially those who have been abducted, have described their aliens' attitudes at best one of indifference to humans and at worst one of menace and hostility. However, the scene where powerline repairman Roy Neary (played by Richard Dreyfuss) is immobilised and in a state of shock inside his truck while a UFO hovers above catches something of the strange terror that witnesses have been reporting for many a year. And Francois Truffaut, playing an international French UFO investigator, Claude Lacombe, presents us with a sympathetic character who is aware that there's a lot more afoot than goddarn aliens zooming around in spaceships.

Perhaps the scene where the technicians play the five-note 'space-theme' on their electronic synthesizer, is not without significance - the alien craft replies with blasts of what can only be described as 'galactic raspberries'! As a piece of light-hearted entertainment using the UFO theme, this overlong (2¼ hrs) insensitive movie will be enjoyed by SF buffs and the hard-of-hearing - but as a step forward in the task of informing the public about the full enigma of UFOs it is a non-starter.

J&CB

letters-letters-letters-letters

23/SIRIUS/NUMEROLOGY

from Tony Bond, Toronto:
Robert Wilson was wondering aloud (FT23/33) whether Hitler had in fact ever lived in Liverpool. On p151 of A Man Called Intrepid, by William Stephenson (paperback edition) there is a reference to his having lived there from November 1912 till April 1913.

from Peter James, London:
The Wilson article (FT23/32-35) was stimulating in a bizarre kind of way , and stirred up a mess of oddities that have been brewing in my head for some time now about the 'Sirius Mystery'. For what it's worth, Bob Temple seems to have missed out a lot of material, suggesting his spacefish-from-Sirius theory is a bit too simple, although it is rather neat. The Dogon might have had different reasons for associating Sirius with fish-beings if they shared the ancient tradition (quite widespread) that Sirius actually has an effect on Earth's bodies of water. For example; the 23rd July rising of Sirius in Egypt coincided with the Nile flood. Pliny (Natural History 9:58) wrote that: "The whole sea is conscious of the rise of that star Sirius, as is most clearly seen in the Dardanelles, for seaweed and fishes float on the surface, and everything is turned up from the bottom." The Babylonian goddess Ishtar (Sirius as well as Venus) was thought to stir up the waters under the earth. Etc, etc - see Hamlet's Mill, Santillana and von Dechend, pp215-6.

What's this got to do with Wilson's article? Well, the element of water in Hebrew Cabbalism is represented by the letter 'Mem', first letter of the Hebrew word for fish, which also happens to go on path 23 of the Cabbalistic tree. How's that for fragile evidence!

On the subject of Cabbalism, I can't fathom out why Wilson, who's a bit of a Cabbalist, didn't fathom out the following: he refers twice to the coincidences of the letters K and G in his 23 mysteries -- but he seems to have missed that, in both Greek and Hebrew gematria, K has a value of 20, and G of 3!

As a final red herring, the 23rd word of the 23rd Psalm, to which Wilson refers, is "waters" in the NEB translation; unfortunately it isn't in the KJ - I'll check the Hebrew sometime.

POTATOES & FLU: A THEORY

from Steve Ogden, Kentucky:
Since the middle of the 16th century when the white potato was introduced into Europe, the main cause of influenza has been poisonous potatoes. Potatoes and tomatoes both belong to the Deadly Nightshade family of plants, and develop concentrations of solanine, a poisonous narcotic alkaloid. New potatoes contain more solanine than mature tubers, and sprouting increases solanine. It also increases when the tubers turn green; or when the plants are grown during hot dry, or very wet weather. The growing season was too hot and dry in 1899, 1918, 1930, 1946, 1957, 1963, 1976 and 1977. ((Though Steve doesn't specifically say so, I assume he's arguing that flu was fairly rampant in these years - it certainly was in 1918, 1976 and 1977 - Ed))

I learnt recently that many people can't eat new potatoes because their systems will not digest them. This is exactly the result I suggest that solanine gives. Undigested starch paste, lodging in the system, allows the rapid growth of pathogenic bacteria. The toxins from this rapid growth quickly pervade the body bringing the onset of influenza. I have ample evidence to show that a 'virus' is merely the result of this toxic action. I have seen colds of all kinds, and flu, quickly stopped by flushing away bacteria.
((Comments, anyone? - Ed))

NESSIE PHOTOS & THE NEW PHYSICS

from Tom Bearden, Alabama:
As usual, your FT24 was simply superb - so much so that I wish to comment on the Doc Shiels photos of Nessie (FT22/24-5). The GSW analysis (FT24/14-6) in fact showed just what I would have expected if the photos were genuine! From where I'm at, water monsters, sasquatches etc are materialized projections from the collective unconscious, starting as archetypal forms, but kneaded and shaped by the progressively shallower layers between the entire-species-unconscious and the personal-unconscious of the observer. In fact, Doc's following of his "intuition" or hunches would be the proper way to actually try to "intercept" tulpoidal/archetypal materialization .

The reason for the "alarming feature" of transparency is quite simple: the mind-realm is a virtual-state realm existing as a concrete, real, physical universe three orthogonal spatial turns away from our 'normal' 3D frame, in infinite dimensional space. Ie: there is an infinity of such 'mind frames' three orthoflips away - each person's mind is one of these frames. Further, there is coherent crosstalk between a person's mind-universe (of thought objects/changes) and his physical body "channel tuner." The crosstalk is two-way; essentially, that is the definition of a living biological system, a finite set of phenomena (soma) in this common frame coherently cross-talking with a multiple orthorotated universe (mind frame). In his mind-world one is a god indeed, for his thought objects are actual physical creations in that realm. Finally, all the mindworlds crosstalk a wee bit; and this common crosstalk is the collective human unconscious, where we have selected the crosstalk common to the entire human species (all human minds). ((For a discussion of concensus 'reality', see my article elsewhere in this issue - Ed))

Pressure (stress) on large groupings of the human race exerts sufficient pressure on the collective unconscious to focus enough coherence in the greater crosstalk level to get materialization popouts in our common 3D physical frame. Much of Fortean phenomena seems to result from this; especially UFOs. In fact, one can do a direct 'dream analysis' on many of the UFO waves if one first understands that the Cold War has been the major stress, on the human species as a whole, for the last 30yrs or so, and that the Soviets have secretly developed psychotronic weapons of certain types.

At any rate, when a tulpoidal form is rotating into our 3D frame for materialization, it first passes through the frame that is one turn removed. This is the frame for ordinary electromagnetic field (eg. 'light' etc), and so when the kindling reaches a certain point, only a 'light-form' is present in this frame at the intersection. As kindling continues to increase, the form has partial materialization (3D) to us, while still having partial 'light-form'

(2D) constituency. As kindling continues, the tulpoid gets more and more
solidly physical and less and less
light-like. Finally the full materialization results. All of this is directly evidenced in thought-photography and
in UFO phenomena.

So, since GSW found exactly the
characteristic I would predict, then I
am strongly inclined to accept Doc's
photos as _genuine_, other things being
equal.

((Tom has developed a series of papers exploring the implications of the
'corrected physics' of the Everett/
Wheeler/Graham many-worlds interpretation (MWI) of quantum mechanics,
which among other things rewrites the
basic 'laws' of physics in some radical and startling ways and allows   the
accommodation of much Fortean phenomena. These will be contained in two
books to be published shortly, and to
be reviewed in FT, naturally. Tom also
edits a new journal, _Specula_, dealing
with these topics - see journals review section. Meanwhile, the above letter proves a good introduction to Tom's
article, next issue, in which he exp-
ounds and expands his ideas on UFOs,
cattle mutilations, the Cold War and
psychotronic weapons - Ed))

We also heard from:

David Tame - who pointed out that I
had wrongly dated the report of rabbit
mutilation at Three Spires, (FT23/4).
It should have been 1976, not 1977,
placing it almost exactly a year earlier than the 1977 killings in that
area - and the source was Coventry
Evening Telegraph 26 Feb 1976.

Valerie Martin - who answered our
query about the poet/levitator Richard
Church (FT23/14). She says:"...at the
time of his death (several years ago)
and for years previously, he lived in
a converted oast house somewhere in
the Kent weald."

Tom Adams - editor of the authoritative US mutilation investigation
newsletter, _Stigmata_, would like to
contact any Australian readers who
could keep him informed about the
state of mutie mysteries down under;
or indeed those interested in the
gruesome subject anywhere on this far-
flung globe. Contact him at: Box 1094,
Paris, Texas 75460, USA.

Kurt Lothmann - avid Fortean, who
would like to make contact with other
Forteans within his US zip-code prefix
area (ie Texas 770--). Write to him at:
4625 Creekbend, Houston, TX 77035.

Recently, Mr X of the Res Bureaux at
last made public his plans to publish
a review-serial on historical Fortean
sources, reference material and attendant discussion and analysis. Naturally
it will pay particular attention to
Fort's own notes and sources. This will
be a mammoth task that speaks volumes
for X's dedication to our field. However, he needs at least 250 subscribers
before the project can roll, and I urge
as many of you as possible to support
this priceless and long-needed project.
It will be called CHAOS: A Review of the
Damned and published 8 times a year. A

full sub will cost $15.00 for Canada,
$13.50 for USA, and £7.00 for UK, for
all other nations the Canadian rates
apply. Air mail rates for USA will cost
an additional $4., and for UK an addit-
ional £2.50., and for other nations an
extra Canada $2.50. Single copies will
cost: $2.00 (Canada), $2.00 (US), £1.00
(UK), and other nations Canada $2.00.
For additional info write to X: Box 1598,
Kingston, Ontario K7L 5C8, Canada.

On p40 of FT23, we gave an Australian
address for an outfit calling themselves
the Hollow Earth Society. We had a feeling that this was not the only one. Sure

enough - in Daily Mirror 11 Nov 1977 is a letter from Mr O Everson, claiming to be the founder of another society . He adds in his letter that far from raising the sea-level, a grand melting of all polar ice would actually lower the sea-level! Those of you who'd like to hear more can contact him at Drury Lane, Martin Hussingtree, Worcester, Worcs.

From Australia comes news of a very interesting film containing Fortean-type events. Called The Last Wave, it follows director Peter Weir's previous eerie masterpiece, Picnic at Hanging Rock which was a deliciously understated mystery of the disappearance of a group of school-girls around 1900 at an Australian Abo-riginal ritual site, with parapsychol-ogical and 'Close Encounter' overtones. In the Last Wave international star Richard Chamberlain plays a young law-yer drawn into the lives of two aborig-ines, the older of whom is the guardian of a secret underground chamber housing the relics of a long dead civilisation in Australia. Chamberlain is plagued by symbols (in his daily life) and dreams of the destruction of Sydney by a giant wave. The film continues the evocative mood of Picnic of impending doom and its signs and effects on the human psy-che. Among the omens featured are sud-den storms, heavy hailstorms in the Outback where none was seen before, odd-ly marked rocks, ESP, dreams, entrances to subterranean worlds, and death by bone-pointing. Sounds fascinating, but we may have to wait. I believe it was shown once at the NFT and has no nat-ional distribution signed yet...so keep an eye on the club and specialist film theaters. Our US readers may have an even longer wait, as I believe Picnic has not been shown yet in the States. When it is, I urge most strongly that every one who can should see the film at least once. It is a veritable master-piece of pure Fortean feelings.

Also keep an eye open for two of Doc Shiels' productions in the West Country, which may come to London soon (or some-time). One called Spooks is a 2-part drama of Count Dracula vs Sherlock Hol-mes, laced with Forteana, and starring most of the Shiels clan aided and abet-ted by a few others. The Shiels clan also appear in Gallavant which achieved instant notoriety when the Sun a few weeks ago gave a 'shock/horror' type coverage, bewailing that it dwelt unnec-essarily on sex, violence, nudity and swearing, especially as it was aimed at children, and starred Doc's own kids.

Quite rightly Doc said the kids are in-terested in these things and their int-erest cannot be ignored or suppressed. Besides the critics missed the real po-int that once the childrens' interest is caught it is steered toward a much more interesting health, holistic, even magical view of the complex universe around us. There are plans too for the reincarnation of Distant Humps (Doc's story of his own Fortean encounters) in London sometime. We'll keep you in-formed...if the Arts Council Police and Whitehouse's anti-anything-that-smacks-of-porn-in-disguise Stormtroopers don't get Doc first!

All those interested in Earth Myster-ies and ancient sites will be glad to learn that there is to be a repeat of last year's very successful meeting, the Moot, organised by The Ley Hunter. It will begin at 10.15am on 8 July, as last year at the Olde Gate House, at the top of North Rd, London N6. Speakers so far include Nigel Pennick, Don Robbins and John Barnat. Other events are planned for later the same day - hopefully the weather will hold for a repeat of last year's splendid ramble over Hampstead Heath. If you're thinking of going, you are asked to write to the Ley Hunter so they have an idea of numbers and refresh-ments to arrange for. TLH 'Moot': Box 152, London N10 1EP.

The 4th Northern UFO Network Confer-ence, to be held in Scunthorpe this year, is being hosted by the Scunthorpe UFO Research Society, at Scunthorpe Film Theatre, on Saturday 24 June. The theme will be 'UFO Close Encounters' with lectures and discussions, from 10am to 6pm (with a break for lunch). At 7,30, Philip Jenkinson, media film critic,will give an illustrated film and chat show on the UFO (etc) in SF films. Full ticket is £1.50 - half-day is 60p. For further info or booking write to Nigel Watson: 1 Angerstein Rd, Scunthorpe, S Humberside DN17 2LZ. NB: cheques, POs etc to be made out to Nigel Watson.

News comes of another conference - - the International Conference on Christ-ian Parapsychology, Wed 30 August 10am to Fri 1 Sept, at Digby Stuart College. It will be followed immediately by a weekend conference of the Churches' Fellowship for Psychical & Spiritual Studies (for which seperate application must be made). Registration for the Int.Conf.CP. is £25/$50.00 - rooms may be booked at extra cost. Programme de¢-

ails and other charges are not known yet. For further info etc write to the Conference Secretary: St Mary Abchurch, London EC4N 5BA.

A new bookshop has opened in Hove to cater for the growing interest in parapsychology. It will stock everything from Acupuncture to Zen, including UFOs, homeopathy, numerology, occult sciences, religious experience and spiritualism. Their main interest though is in those often hard-to-find specialist books on serious paraphysics and parapsychology, including imported books. They intend to publish special lists for mail order. Contact or visit: The Transpersonal Bookshop, 19 Sterling Place, Hove BN3 3YU (Tel: 0273 734132.)

We read, with great interest, in the D Telegraph 30 Dec 1977, that news agency teleprinters (noisy old tickertape machines) are to be installed in some American schools to make learing to read more attractive. The schools will receive the general wire-news for 40mins, with 20mins of related programme, for 12 hours a day. In addition the Center for Short-lived Phenomena will donate a special bulletin on quakes, meteorological events etc. This is something we really ought to have. Last year I wrote to all the big news agencies (AP, Reuters, UPI, etc) asking for details of their services, but they didn't want to know. If any reader knows about such services and can advise us, please write to FT. Ideally FT ought to subscribe to a wire-service teleprinter, but as we haven't the money, we'd settle for buying job lots of scrap bulletins from the printer wastebasket! But there'll come a day when we'll be in demand, providing a Fortean news service.

Finally, we note the arrest of Billy Dodson, in Jacksonville, Florida, in July 1977, for various incomprehensible acts. He had gone into a church scantily dressed, placed pamphlets on the pulpit and walked out; later he was seen ramming his car into the church doors, apparently annoyed at the building being closed. He was arrested after sitting in his car staring at the church for hours. After incriminating himself in conversation in his cell, he was also accused of a series of acts at city hall in which chairs were overturned in a conference hall and a chess king placed on the head table, on top of a religious pamphlet on which was written "He is risen" and "OB1-K". The baffling notation "OB1-K" was also found on scraps of paper left in the

mayor's desk on the 14th floor. Dodson told investigators that "OB1-K" stood for "Oh boy, one king" but declined to explain further...Police think it's a reference "to the game of chess or to the Deity." Lexilinkers will have a field day with this one. My own idea, for what it's worth, is a connexion with the film Star Wars, in which a mysterious old knight, played by Alec Guinness, is called 'Obiwan Kenobi'. If that's not the link, then it's a good coincidence. Jacksonville Journal 13 July 1977 (Cr: Gary Abbott). May the farce be with him!

Hoc vno arcana recludo.

F I N I S.